The System of

Freedom of Expression

Thomas I. Emerson

The System of Freedom of Expression

VINTAGE BOOKS
A Division of Random House
New York

Foreword

I began this book as a technical law book on the First Amendment. It has branched somewhat beyond that. I have retained, however, the detailed technical analysis of Supreme Court decisions with which I started. This may be of interest primarily to legal experts, but I hope others will find it useful as well. The main purpose of the book has been to formulate the legal foundations for an effective system of freedom of expression. This has necessarily entailed an abundance of abstract legal discourse characteristic of law books.

I realize that the construction of complex rational systems is not in particular favor in some quarters today. Generally speaking, the average person does have some reason to be skeptical. Such structures have a tendency, particularly as time passes, to become overextended on an abstract level and to lose touch with the earthly facts from which the general principles originally sprang. Such a fate has befallen many of our current institutions, and this is the root of many of our present troubles. But we cannot afford, for that reason, to reject all attempts to build a rational system, especially if it is one that might prove useful to the future as well as the present society. In any event I have tried to find the proper balance between abstraction and reality, and to test the proposed legal structure against the needs and hopes of the everyday world.

The book undertakes to elaborate and to apply in concrete cases the basic ideas set forth in my *Toward a General Theory of the First Amendment* (New York, Random House, 1966). As a result of working with the problems further, however, I have in a few instances changed my mind about propositions expressed in the earlier book. The most important of these revisions has occurred in my views on reconciling freedom of expression with other "individual interests," most notably in the area of libel and privacy.

I have also attempted to key the present volume into the collection of materials published in 1967 by David Haber, Norman Dorsen and myself under the title *Political and Civil Rights in the United States* (Boston, Little, Brown & Co., 3d ed. 1967). Rather than making extensive notation to background and other materials in the footnotes I have simply referred the reader to the appropriate pages of the *Politi-*

cal and Civil Rights book. I have, however, included references to some of the major material which has appeared subsequent to the publication of that work.

With respect to matters of form, I have tried to confine the footnotes, inevitable though they be in a legal study, to references only. Readers who are not interested in the reference may thus safely skip the footnotes. I have also attempted to reduce the burden on the reader by dropping footnotes only at the end of a paragraph. In quoting from Supreme Court decisions or other sources, footnotes in the original have been omitted without express notation to that effect.

The basic cut-off date of the material discussed is the end of the Supreme Court's term in June 1969. A few later developments of particular significance have been added. For all practical purposes, however, the book terminates with the passing of the Warren Court.

My principal debt in the preparation of this book is owed to my collaborator in earlier projects, Professor David Haber of Rutgers Law School. While I absolve him fully for any particular statement or conclusion, his ideas, and the discussions with him of the drafts of each chapter, have greatly shaped and immeasurably enriched the result. I am likewise indebted to colleagues on the Yale Law School faculty, to many students who have worked over these areas with me, and to a series of research assistants. Dean Robert Kramer of George Washington University Law School kindly made an office available to me during a sabbatical year in Washington, and I enjoyed and profited much from the association with him and his faculty. I also wish to express my appreciation for the pleasant and effective service rendered by the staff of the Yale Law Library and by my secretary, Mrs. Helen Minor. My wife, Ruth Calvin Emerson, assisted nobly at crucial points and put up with me at all times.

T. I. E.

NEW HAVEN, CONNECTICUT
SEPTEMBER, 1969

Contents

The System of

Freedom of Expression

I

The System
of Freedom
of Expression

A system of freedom of expression, operating in a modern democratic society, is a complex mechanism. At its core is a group of rights assured to individual members of the society. This set of rights, which makes up our present-day concept of free expression, includes the right to form and hold beliefs and opinions on any subject, and to communicate ideas, opinions, and information through any medium—in speech, writing, music, art, or in other ways. To some extent it involves the right to remain silent. From the obverse side it includes the right to hear the views of others and to listen to their version of the facts. It encompasses the right to inquire and, to a degree, the right of access to information. As a necessary corollary, it embraces the right to assemble and to form associations, that is, to combine with others in joint expression.

Any system of freedom of expression must also embody principles through which exercise of these rights by one person or group may be reconciled with equal opportunity for other persons or groups to enjoy them. At the same time, the rights of all in freedom of expression must be reconciled with other individual and social interests. It is this process of reconciliation that has given rise to most of the controversial issues in the past and continues to be the major focus of attention today.

Assurance of these rights to freedom of expression involves limitations upon the power of the state to interfere with or abridge them. But

3

ate also has a more affirmative role to play in the maintenance of ystem of free expression in modern society. It must protect persons and groups seeking to exercise their rights from private or nongovernmental interference either by way of force or to some extent by other methods. It must also undertake positively to promote and encourage freedom of expression, as by furnishing facilities, eliminating distortions in the media of communication, or making information available. Moreover, the increasing role of large organizations in our society now presents the question whether the government should take action to assure individuals in these private centers of power rights to freedom of expression similar to those guaranteed against the public power of government. In addition, the government itself participates extensively in the process of expression, through publication of official statements and reports, by its control over the educational system, and in other ways. Many of these problems are new to our time and are not readily answered on the basis of past theory or experience.

Finally, an effective system of freedom of expression requires a realistic administrative structure. It is not enough merely to formulate the broad principles or simply to incorporate them in general rules of law. It is necessary to develop a framework of doctrines, practices, and institutions which will take into account the actual forces at work and make possible the realistic achievement of the objectives sought. Although we have had long experience with these aspects of the problem we have done little to explore the dynamics of operating a system of free expression.

This interrelated set of rights, principles, practices, and institutions can be considered a system, at least in a rough way, because it has an overall unity of purpose and operation. To view it in this manner facilitates the development of the rules for its governance, for such rules must be derived from the basic functions and dynamics of the system. Furthermore, they must accommodate the system of freedom of expression to other features of our national life.

The main concern of this book is to examine the legal foundations upon which the system of freedom of expression rests in the United States. Such a concentration upon the legal framework should not be taken as an underestimation of other facets of the problem. Obviously, the success of any society in maintaining freedom of expression hinges upon many different considerations. Some degree of fundamental consensus—some minimum area of agreement or acquiescence—is essential for a community to operate on any basis other than one of sheer force or terror. Economic institutions and economic conditions, the degree of security or insecurity from external threats, political traditions and institutions, systems of education, methods and media for forming public opinion, public attitudes and philosophy, and many other factors play a vital part. Those who warn us not to rely too much on legal forms are entirely correct that excessive emphasis can easily be placed upon the role of law. Yet in the United States today we have come to depend upon legal institutions and legal doctrines as a major technique for maintaining our system of free expression. We have developed and refined this technique more than has any other country. These legal institutions and ideas in turn affect public attitudes and philosophies; both philosophers and protest movements argue in terms of constitutional rights. Hence, while the other factors should not be slighted, an analysis of the legal supports for freedom of expression is a first and fundamental step.

In recent years much uncertainty and controversy have marked the effort to formulate the legal doctrines pertaining to freedom of expression and to fix the role of legal institutions in maintaining them. This is due not only to the inherent complexities of the problem. It arises also out of the changes wrought in our society by shifting economic, political, and social forces. The basic theory underlying the legal framework has remained substantially unchanged since its development in the seventeenth and eighteenth centuries. But the conditions under which it must now be applied have greatly altered. There has been little effort to reappraise legal doctrines and institutions in light of the new situation. And even less consideration has been given to the extension of legal theory to new problems posed by modern conditions.

Any study of the legal doctrines and institutions necessary to maintain an effective system of freedom of expression must be based upon the functions performed by the system in our society, the dynamics of its operation, and the general role of law and legal institutions in supporting it. It must also formulate the fundamental concepts upon which legal support for the system can be predicated. An examination of these preliminary issues was undertaken in my *Toward a General Theory of the First Amendment* and the conclusions there reached will be briefly reviewed in the remainder of this chapter. The principal task of this book is to apply the basic principles which underlie the system of freedom of expression to the solution of concrete problems which arise in the operation of the system today.[1]

A. The Structure of the System

1. VALUES AND FUNCTIONS

The system of freedom of expression in a democratic society rests upon four main premises. These may be stated, in capsule form, as follows:

First, freedom of expression is essential as a means of assuring individual self-fulfillment. The proper end of man is the realization of his character and potentialities as a human being. For the achievement of this self-realization the mind must be free. Hence suppression of belief, opinion, or other expression is an affront to the dignity of man, a negation of man's essential nature. Moreover, man in his capacity as a member of society has a right to share in the common decisions that affect him. To cut off his search for truth, or his expression of it, is to elevate society and the state to a despotic command over him and to place him under the arbitrary control of others.

Second, freedom of expression is an essential process for advancing knowledge and discovering truth. An individual who seeks knowledge and truth must hear all sides of the question, consider all alternatives, test his judgment by exposing it to opposition, and make full use

1. See Thomas I. Emerson, *Toward a General Theory of the First Amendment* (New York, Random House, 1966). An extensive collection of materials and references on the system of freedom of expression may be found in Thomas I. Emerson, David Haber, and Norman Dorsen, *Political and Civil Rights in the United States* (Boston, Little, Brown & Co., 3d ed. 1967), Vol. I. Later writings include Milton R. Konvitz, *Expanding Liberties* (New York, Viking Press, 1966); Robert M. O'Neil, *Free Speech: Responsible Communication Under Law* (Indianapolis, Bobbs-Merrill Co., 1966); Harold L. Nelson (ed.), *Freedom of the Press from Hamilton to the Warren Court* (Indianapolis, Bobbs-Merrill Co., 1967); Peter P. Miller, "Freedom of Expression Under State Constitutions," *Stanford Law Review*, Vol. 20 (1968), p. 318; Hugo L. Black, *A Constitutional Faith* (New York, Alfred A. Knopf, 1968); Norman Dorsen, *Frontiers of Civil Liberties* (New York, Pantheon Books, 1968), Sec. II; Samuel Krislov, *The Supreme Court and Political Freedom* (New York, Free Press, 1968); Peter Brett, "Free Speech, Supreme-Court Style: A View From Overseas," *Texas Law Review*, Vol. 46 (1968), p. 668; Donald M. Gillmor and Jerome A. Barron (eds.), *Mass Communication Law* (St. Paul, West Publishing Co., 1969).

of different minds. Discussion must be kept open no matter how certainly true an accepted opinion may seem to be; many of the most widely acknowledged truths have turned out to be erroneous. Conversely, the same principle applies no matter how false or pernicious the new opinion appears to be; for the unaccepted opinion may be true or partially true and, even if wholly false, its presentation and open discussion compel a rethinking and retesting of the accepted opinion. The reasons which make open discussion essential for an intelligent individual judgment likewise make it imperative for rational social judgment.

Third, freedom of expression is essential to provide for participation in decision making by all members of society. This is particularly significant for political decisions. Once one accepts the premise of the Declaration of Independence—that governments "derive their just powers from the consent of the governed"—it follows that the governed must, in order to exercise their right of consent, have full freedom of expression both in forming individual judgments and in forming the common judgment. The principle also carries beyond the political realm. It embraces the right to participate in the building of the whole culture, and includes freedom of expression in religion, literature, art, science, and all areas of human learning and knowledge.

Finally, freedom of expression is a method of achieving a more adaptable and hence a more stable community, of maintaining the precarious balance between healthy cleavage and necessary consensus. This follows because suppression of discussion makes a rational judgment impossible, substituting force for reason; because suppression promotes inflexibility and stultification, preventing society from adjusting to changing circumstances or developing new ideas; and because suppression conceals the real problems confronting a society, diverting public attention from the critical issues. At the same time the process of open discussion promotes greater cohesion in a society because people are more ready to accept decisions that go against them if they have a part in the decision-making process. Moreover, the state at all times retains adequate powers to promote unity and to suppress resort to force. Freedom of expression thus provides a framework in which the conflict necessary to the progress of a society can take place without destroying the society. It is an essential mechanism for maintaining the balance between stability and change.

The validity of the foregoing premises has never been proved or disproved, and probably could not be. Nevertheless our society is based upon the faith that they hold true and, in maintaining a system of freedom of expression, we act upon that faith. The considerations just outlined thus represent the values we seek in a system of freedom of expression and the functions that system is intended to perform. It should be added that, while our current system of freedom of expression is a product of constitutional liberalism, the values and functions which underlie it are essential to any open society regardless of the particular form its political, economic and social institutions may take.

Two basic implications of the theory underlying our system of freedom of expression need to be emphasized. The first is that it is not a general measure of the individual's right to freedom of expression that any particular exercise of that right may be thought to promote or retard other goals of the society. The theory asserts that freedom of expression, while not the sole or sufficient end of society, is a good in itself, or at least an essential element in a good society. The society may seek to achieve other or more inclusive ends—such as virtue, justice, equality, or the maximum realization of the potentialities of its members. These are not necessarily gained by accepting the rules for freedom of expression. But, as a general proposition, the society may not seek them by suppressing the beliefs or opinions of individual members. To achieve these other goals it must rely upon other methods: the use of counter-expression and the regulation or control of conduct which is not expression. Hence the right to control individual expression, on the ground that it is judged to promote good or evil, justice or injustice, equality or inequality, is not, speaking generally, within the competence of the good society.

The second implication, in a sense a corollary of the first, is that the theory rests upon a fundamental distinction between belief, opinion, and communication of ideas on the one hand, and different forms of conduct on the other. For shorthand purposes we refer to this distinction hereafter as one between "expression" and "action." As just observed, in order to achieve its desired goals, a society or the state is entitled to exercise control over action—whether by prohibiting or compelling it—on an entirely different and vastly more extensive basis. But expression occupies an especially protected position. In this sector of human conduct, the social right of suppression or compulsion is at its lowest point, in most respects nonexistent. A majority of one has the right to control action, but a minority of one has the right to talk.

This marking off of the special status of expression is a crucial ingredient of the basic theory for several reasons. In the first place, thought and communication are the fountainhead of all expression of the individual personality. To cut off the flow at the source is to dry up the whole stream. Freedom at this point is essential to all other freedoms. Hence society must withhold its right of suppression until the stage of action is reached. Secondly, expression is normally conceived as doing less injury to other social goals than action. It generally has less immediate consequences, is less irremediable in its impact. Thirdly, the power of society and the state over the individual is so pervasive, and construction of doctrines, institutions, and administrative practices to limit this power so difficult, that only by drawing such a protective line between expression and action is it possible to strike a safe balance between authority and freedom.

2. THE DYNAMICS OF LIMITATION

In constructing and maintaining a system of freedom of expression the major controversies have arisen not over acceptance of the basic theory, but in attempting to fit its values and functions into a more comprehensive scheme of social goals. These issues have revolved around the question of what limitations, if any, ought to be imposed upon freedom of expression in order to reconcile that interest with other individual and social interests sought by the good society. Most of our efforts in the past to formulate rules for limiting freedom of expression have been seriously defective through failure to take into consideration the realistic context in which such limitations are administered. The crux of the problem is that the limitations, whatever they may be, must be applied by one group of human beings to other human beings.

First of all, it is necessary to recognize the powerful forces that impel men towards the elimination of unorthodox expression. Most men have a strong inclination, for rational or irrational reasons, to suppress opposition. On the other hand, persons who stand up against society and challenge the traditional view usually have similarly strong feelings about the issues they raise. Thus dissent often is not pitched in conventional terms, nor does it follow customary standards of polite expression. Moreover, the forces of inertia within a society ordinarily resist the expression of new ideas or the pressures of the underprivileged who seek a change. And the longer-run logic of the traditional theory may not be immediately apparent to untutored participants in the conflict. Suppression of opinion may thus seem an entirely plausible course of action; tolerance a weakness or a foolish risk.

Thus it is clear that the problem of maintaining a system of freedom of expression in a society is one of the most complex any society has to face. Self-restraint, self-discipline, and maturity are required. The theory is essentially a highly sophisticated one. The members of the society must be willing to sacrifice individual and short-term advantage for social and long-range goals. And the process must operate in a context that is charged with emotion and subject to powerful conflicting forces of self-interest.

These considerations must be weighed in attempting to construct a theory of limitations. A system of free expression can be successful only when it rests upon the strongest possible commitment to the positive right and the narrowest possible basis for exceptions. And any such exceptions must be clear-cut, precise, and readily controlled. Otherwise the forces that press toward restriction will break through the openings, and freedom of expression will become the exception and suppression the rule.

A second major consideration in imposing restrictions upon expression is the difficulty of framing precise limitations. The object of the limitation is usually not the expression itself but its feared consequences. Repression of expression is thus purely a preventive measure and, like all preventive measures, cuts far more widely and deeply than is necessary to control the ensuing conduct. Moreover, the infinite varieties and subtleties of language and other forms of communication make it impossible to construct a limitation upon expression in definite terms. Thus a wide area of expression is brought within reach of the limitation and enormous discretionary power placed in the hands of those who administer it.

Again, the apparatus of government required for enforcement of limitations on expression, by its very nature, tends towards administrative extremes. Officials charged with the duties of suppression already have or tend to develop excessive zeal in the performance of their task. The accompanying techniques of enforcement—the investigations, surveillance, searches and seizures, secret informers, voluminous files on the suspect—all tend to exert a repressive influence on freedom of expression. In addition, the restrictive measures are readily subject to distortion and to use for ulterior purposes.

Finally we must take into account the whole impact of restriction upon the healthy functioning of a free society. Limitations are seldom applied except in an atmosphere of public fear and hysteria. This may be deliberately aroused or may simply be the inevitable accompaniment of repression. Under such circumstances the doctrines and institutions for enforcing the limitations are subjected to intense pressures. Moreover, while some of the more hardy may be willing to defy the opposition and suffer the consequences, the more numerous are likely to be unwilling to run the risks. Similarly, persons whose cooperation is needed to permit the full flow of open discussion—those who own the means of publication or the facilities for communication—are likely to be frightened into withholding their patronage and assistance.

The lesson of experience, in short, is that the limitations imposed on discussion, as they operate in practice, tend readily and quickly to destroy the whole structure of free expression. They are very difficult to keep in hand; the exceptions are likely to swallow up the principle. Maintenance of a system of free expression, therefore, is not an easy task. This is especially true as we confront the conditions of today. We have tended over the years to refine and delineate more carefully the restrictions we seek to impose. But the new problems arising out of modern industrial society make the issues more delicate and troublesome than at any other time in our history.

3. THE ROLE OF LAW AND LEGAL INSTITUTIONS

The legal system is, of course, one of the most effective instruments available to a society for controlling the behavior of its members so as to realize the values and goals sought by that society. Because of certain characteristics of a system of free expression, the role of law is of peculiar significance in any social effort to maintain such a system.

First, a system of free expression is designed to encourage a necessary degree of conflict within a society. To be sure, it attempts to avoid resort to force or violence by channeling this conflict into the area of expression and persuasion. And it contemplates that a longer-range consensus will ultimately be achieved. Yet, because it recognizes the right of the citizen to disagree with, arouse, antagonize, and shock his fellow citizens and the government, such an arrangement of human affairs is hardly likely to be automatically achieved. In its short-term effects it may indeed be highly volatile. Hence the system needs the legitimizing and harmonizing influence of the legal process to keep it in successful equilibrium.

Other features of a system of free expression likewise demonstrate the need for buttressing it through law and legal institutions. The full benefits of the system can be realized only when the individual knows the extent of his rights and has some assurance of protection in exercising them. Thus the governing principles of such a system need to be articulated with some precision and clarity. Doubt or uncertainty negates the process. Furthermore, the theory rests upon subordination of immediate interests in favor of long-term benefits. This can be achieved only through the application of principle, not by ad hoc resolution of individual cases. And it requires procedures adequate to relieve immediate pressures and facilitate objective consideration. All these elements a legal system is equipped to supply.

Further, as already observed, the theory of freedom of expression is a sophisticated and even complex one. It does not come naturally to the ordinary citizen, but needs to be learned. It must be restated and reiterated not only for each generation but for each new situation. It leans heavily upon understanding and education, both for the individual and the community as a whole. The legal process is one of the most effective methods for providing the kind of social comprehension essential for the attainment of society's higher and more remote ideals.

Finally, the principles of the system must be constantly reshaped and expanded to meet new conditions and new threats to its existence. This requires the deliberate attention of an institution entrusted with that specific obligation and possessing the expertise to perform such a task.

The function of the legal process is not only to provide a means whereby a society shapes and controls the behavior of its individual members in the interests of the whole. It also supplies one of the principal methods by which a society controls itself, limiting its own powers in the interests of the individual. The role of law here is to mark and guard the line between the sphere of social power, organized in the form of the state, and the area of private right. Judicial institutions function as a mediator between the government and the people. The legal problems involved in maintaining a system of free expression fall largely into these realms. Indeed the use of law to achieve this kind of control has been one of the central concerns of freedom-seeking societies over the ages. Legal recognition of individual rights, enforced through the legal process, has become the core of free society.

The main legal institutions upon which we rely for implementing the principles of free expression are (1) a written constitution, embodying an express (if general) statement of the rights guaranteed to the individual; (2) an independent judiciary possessing the power of judicial review over legislative and executive action; and (3) an independent bar. Of these, the part played by the judiciary is our major concern here.

In considering the role of the judiciary in a system of freedom of expression it is essential to narrow the issues and establish a fundamental distinction. We are not dealing here with any general function of our judicial institutions to foster the whole range of freedoms in a democratic society. Nor are we dealing with any broad power to supervise or review all major actions of the legislative and executive branches. We are concerned with the specific function of the judiciary in supporting a system of freedom of expression. This involves the application of general principles of law to assure that the basic mechanisms of the democratic process will be respected. It does not involve supervision over the decisions reached or measures adopted as a consequence of employing democratic procedures. Responsibility for this is primarily that of the legislature. In other words, the judicial institutions are here dealing essentially with the methods of conducting the democratic process, not with the substantive results of that process. In this differentiation of function lies a generic distinction between the role of the judiciary and the role of the legislature.

Within this narrower context the courts must play a crucial part in maintaining and extending our system of freedom of expression. Their competence to do so rests upon their independence from the other branches of government, their relative immunity to immediate political and popular pressures, the training and quality of their personnel, their utilization of legal procedures, and their powers of judicial review. The need of the courts to perform this function has become more imperative as the nation has moved from nineteenth-century economic liberalism to twentieth-century mass democracy. In our society today it has become necessary to develop methods for maintaining the system of freedom of expression, not as a self-adjusting by-product of laissez-faire, but as a positive and deliberate function of the social process. What is required is a consciously formulated structure of protection, embracing legal doctrines that are operationally workable and utilizing legal institutions that are equipped to handle the problem.

Nor can it be said that the Supreme Court, and our other judicial institutions, lack the political power and prestige to perform an active role in protecting the system of freedom of expression. Certainly judicial institutions must reflect the traditions, ideals, and assumptions, and in the end must respond to the needs, claims, and expectations, of the social order in which they operate. They must not and ultimately cannot move too far ahead or lag too far behind. The problem for the Supreme Court is one of finding the proper degree of responsiveness and leadership, or perhaps better, of short-term and long-term responsiveness. Yet in seeking out this position the Court should not underestimate the authority and prestige it has achieved over the years. Representing the "conscience of the community," it has come to possess a very real power to keep alive and vital the higher values and goals toward which our society imperfectly strives. Our experience as a nation confirms the strength of the Court's role in this respect; with the possible exception of the Eleventh Amendment, the people have never changed our fundamental law to withdraw individual rights to which the Court has given sanction. In any event, the issue at stake is nothing less than the maintenance of the democratic process. Given its prestige, it would appear that the power of the Court to protect freedom of expression is unlikely to be substantially curtailed unless the whole structure of our democratic institutions is threatened. Even then, we cannot assume that the American people, if the issue were made clear to them, would choose to pursue this course of action. And surely the Court should not, in anticipation of such a turn of events or through a negative or timid attitude, abandon the leadership which history has thrust upon it.

B. The Formulation of Legal Principles

The major source of legal doctrine supporting the system of freedom of expression is the First Amendment. That constitutional guarantee is: "Congress shall make no law . . . abridging the freedom of speech, or of the press, or the right of the people peaceably to as-

semble, and to petition the Government for a redress of grievances."
The precise meaning of the First Amendment at the time of its adoption is a matter of some dispute. In the broadest terms, however, the
provision was plainly intended to assure the new nation the basic elements of a system of free expression as then conceived. As our constitutional law has developed over the years the First Amendment has
come to have the same broad significance for our present, more complex, society. The fundamental meaning of the First Amendment,
then, is to guarantee an effective system of freedom of expression suitable for the present times.[2]

Other constitutional provisions also have an important bearing
upon the system of freedom of expression. The Fourth Amendment's
protection against unreasonable searches and seizures, the Fifth
Amendment's privilege against self-incrimination, and the due process
rules against vagueness and overbreadth in legislation all play a significant role in maintaining the system. In fact, the courts have come to
give these constitutional guarantees a substantially different meaning
when invoked in behalf of First Amendment rights. Thus the First
Amendment has an umbrella effect, drawing within its shelter doctrines from many other areas of the law. Equally pertinent are various
procedural rules, such as those providing judicial relief by injunction;
other legal doctrines, such as those governing Federal control over
State action; the operation of various institutions, such as the prosecutor's office; and innumerable practices and policies, such as those of the
Federal, State, and local police. Extensive consideration of all these
elements would be required to give a complete picture of the operation
of the system. Nevertheless, while such matters are by no means ignored, the concentration here is on the First Amendment, which remains the legal heart of the system.

The outstanding fact about the First Amendment today is that the
Supreme Court has never developed any comprehensive theory of
what that constitutional guarantee means and how it should be applied
in concrete cases. At various times the Court has employed the bad
tendency test, the clear and present danger test, an incitement test, and
different forms of the ad hoc balancing test. Sometimes it has not

---

2. An extensive survey of the philo-
sophic and legal background of the First
Amendment may be found in Leonard
Levy, *Legacy of Suppression: Freedom of
Speech and Press in Early American His-*
tory (Cambridge, Harvard University
Press, 1960). For other materials see
Emerson, Haber, and Dorsen, *op. cit.*
supra note 1, pp. 29–35.

clearly enunciated the theory upon which it proceeds. Frequently it has avoided decision on basic First Amendment issues by invoking doctrines of vagueness, overbreadth, or the use of less drastic alternatives. Justice Black, at times supported by Justice Douglas, arrived at an "absolute" test, but subsequently reverted to the balancing test in certain types of cases. The Supreme Court has also utilized other doctrines, such as the preferred position of the First Amendment and prior restraint. Recently it has begun to address itself to problems of "symbolic speech" and the place in which First Amendment activities can be carried on. But it has totally failed to settle on any coherent approach or to bring together its various doctrines into a consistent whole. Moreover, it has done little to deal with some of the newer problems, where the issue is not pure restraint on government interference, but rather the use of governmental power to encourage freedom of expression or the actual participation by government itself in the system of expression.

It is not surprising that this chaotic state of First Amendment theory has produced some unhappy results. The major doctrines applied by the Supreme Court have proved inadequate, particularly in periods of tension, to support a vigorous system of freedom of expression. Thus the bad tendency test offers virtually no protection to freedom of expression. The clear and present danger test is not only inapplicable in many situations but permits the government to cut off expression as soon as it comes close to being effective. The incitement test is open to much the same objections. The ad hoc balancing test is so unstructured that it can hardly be described as a rule of law at all. All the tests are excessively vague, little more than exercises in semantics. Efforts of the courts to deal with the more complex theoretical problems, such as "symbolic speech," have only made the situation worse. All in all doctrinal support for the system of freedom of expression is in a sad state of disarray. And this has had a most unfortunate effect upon the work of the lower Federal and State courts, upon the performance of government officials, and upon the understanding of the public.

The details of these developments are traced in subsequent chapters. Our main effort, however, is to apply a comprehensive and effective theory of the First Amendment to the various problems that arise in the operation of the free expression system. That theory, previously set forth in *Toward a General Theory of the First Amendment*, needs to be outlined briefly at this point. It involves the following propositions:[3]

(1) The root purpose of the First Amendment is to assure an effective system of freedom of expression in a democratic society. This means that the implementing rules of law derived from the First Amendment must be based upon the functions performed by our system of freedom of expression, the dynamics of limiting free expression, and the role played by the courts in supporting the system.

(2) The central idea of a system of freedom of expression is that a fundamental distinction must be drawn between conduct which consists of "expression" and conduct which consists of "action." "Expression" must be freely allowed and encouraged. "Action" can be controlled, subject to other constitutional requirements, but not by controlling expression. A system of freedom of expression cannot exist effectively on any other foundation, and a decision to maintain such a system necessarily implies acceptance of this proposition.

(3) The character of the system is such that freedom of expression can flourish, and the goals of the system can be realized, only if expression receives full protection under the First Amendment. This is to say that expression must be protected against governmental curtailment at all points, even where the results of expression may appear to be in conflict with other social interests that the government is charged with safeguarding. The government may protect or advance other social interests through regulation of action, but not by suppressing expression. Full protection also means that regulations necessary to make the system work, or to improve the system, must be based upon principles which promote, rather than retard, the system in terms of its basic nature and functions.

(4) In constructing specific legal doctrines which, within the framework just outlined, will govern concrete issues, the main function of the courts is not to balance the interest in freedom of expression against other social interests but to define the key elements in the First Amendment: "expression," "abridge," and "law." These definitions must be functional in character, derived from the basic considerations underlying the system of freedom of expression.

(5) The definition of "expression" involves formulating in detail

---

3. The restatement here contains minor modifications of, and some additions to, the original statement in *Toward a* *General Theory*. These changes are a result of applying the theory in detail to concrete problems.

the distinction between "expression" and "action." The line in many situations is clear. But at some points it becomes obscure. All expression has some physical element. Moreover, a communication may take place in a context of action, as in the familiar example of the false cry of "fire" in a crowded theater. Or, a communication may be closely linked to action, as in the gang leader's command to his triggerman. Or, the communication may have the same immediate impact as action, as in instances of publicly uttered obscenities which may shock unforewarned listeners or viewers. In these cases it is necessary to decide, however artificial the distinction may appear to be, whether the conduct is to be classified as one or the other. This judgment must be guided by consideration of whether the conduct partakes of the essential qualities of expression or action, that is, whether expression or action is the dominant element. And the concept of expression must be related to the fundamental purposes of the system and the dynamics of its operation. In formulating the distinction there is a certain leeway in which the process of reconciling freedom of expression with other values and objectives can remain flexible. But the crucial point is that the focus of inquiry must be directed toward ascertaining what is expression, and therefore to be given the protection of expression, and what is action, and thus subject to regulation as such.

(6) The definition of "abridge" is not difficult in most situations in which the government seeks to limit expression in order to protect some other social interest. But it is likely to become more complex when the government controls undertake to regulate the internal operations of the system of freedom of expression itself, or when the status of an individual in an organization imposes obligations different from those of the ordinary citizen to the general community. In any case the decision as to whether there has been an "abridgment" turns on the actual impact of the regulation upon the system.

(7) The definition of "law" arises largely in cases, such as those involving the right of expression within private associations, in which the question is whether the First Amendment applies at all. The problem is thus usually the same as that of defining the scope of "state action."

(8) Different legal doctrines, derived from the definition of the foregoing terms, apply to different kinds of protection which legal institutions must provide for a system of freedom of expression. Most of the issues fall into three categories:

(a) First is the protection of the individual's right to freedom of expression against interference by the government in its efforts to achieve other social objectives or to advance its own interests. In the past this has been the chief area of legal controversy. The principal issue is one of distinguishing "expression" from "action" and giving full protection to expression. In some situations the government regulation affects both conduct consisting of action and conduct consisting of expression; then the rule of full protection requires that the regulation be drawn in such a way as to restrict only the action, leaving the expression uncurtailed.

(b) Second is the utilization and simultaneous restriction of government in regulating conflicts between individuals or groups within the system of free expression; in protecting individuals or groups from nongovernmental interference in the exercise of their right to expression; and in eliminating obstacles to, or affirmatively promoting, effective functioning of the system. These are all problems of fashioning controls within the system of freedom of expression itself, not of adjusting the system to other social interests or to other systems. The key concept in resolving such issues is "abridgment." Development of this concept involves formulating specific rules for mutual accommodation of participants in the system, fairness in allocation of scarce facilities, and assurance that the system will be expanded rather than contracted.

(c) Third is the restriction of the government insofar as the government itself participates in the system of expression. Here the applicable doctrines derive both from "abridgment" and from "law." The issues turn on the special character of government expression and the need for special protection to the system through rules such as requiring the government to make a balanced presentation of the issues.

(9) Other legal doctrines are necessary to solve particular problems. These pertain to the place where First Amendment rights may be exercised, the relationship of the system of freedom of expression to the system of privacy, and similar matters. Such issues likewise must be resolved on a functional basis, taking into account the objectives and operation of the system.

(10) Finally, it is necessary to define the "system" to which the foregoing principles are applicable. For reasons peculiar to each case, certain sectors of social conduct, though involving "expression" within the definition here used, must be deemed to fall outside the system with which we are now concerned. The areas which must be excluded embrace certain aspects of the operations of the military, of commercial

activities, of the activities of children, and of communication with foreign countries. This does not mean that the First Amendment has no application in these sectors. It simply recognizes that the functions of expression and the principles needed to protect expression in such areas are different from those in the main system, and that different legal rules may therefore be required.

The justification for these principles, and the manner in which they should be applied, are developed in the ensuing chapters.

II

Freedom of Belief

Freedom of belief is the right of an individual to form and hold ideas and opinions whether or not communicated to others. It lies at the heart of a democratic society. The effort to coerce belief—to employ the powers of the state to force public expression of beliefs or to punish beliefs—is the hallmark of a feudal or totalitarian society. Yet the techniques for coercing belief, inherited from feudalism or borrowed from totalitarianism, are not unknown in the American community. The most notorious is the test oath, the imposition of a declaration under oath affirming a belief. Other forms of governmental control which may involve infringement upon freedom of belief include the compulsory flag salute, the forced disclosure of beliefs by a legislative investigating committee, and the use of criminal penalties or other official sanction to punish those who hold certain beliefs or to deprive them of benefits or privileges otherwise available. New pressures to coerce belief tend to form in our society as government becomes more encompassing, and seeks to control the conduct of citizens through techniques of manipulation and preventive law. In mass society the right to explore ideas and form opinions freely and openly—freedom of the mind—is thus more hard pressed as it becomes the more crucial to a democratic form of existence.

Belief, in the sense used here, is not strictly "expression." Forming or holding a belief occurs prior to expression. But it is the first stage in the process of expression, and it tends to progress into expression. Hence safeguarding the right to form and hold beliefs is essential in maintaining a system of freedom of expression. Freedom of belief, therefore, must be held included within the protection of the First

21

Amendment. This proposition has indeed been accepted consistently and without hesitation by all courts and commentators.

It should be noted that we are not dealing here with the power of the government to influence belief through education, propaganda, or other methods of persuasion. The extent to which the First Amendment restricts governmental conduct of that nature is considered in a later chapter. We are concerned at this point with efforts by government to coerce belief. It is true that the line between persuasion and coercion may not always be easy to trace. But the distinction is fundamental. By its very nature a system of free expression involves—in fact is designed to achieve—persuasion. The government is entitled to participate in this system. But the introduction of coercion destroys the system as a free one. The same is true of belief.

Neither are we concerned here with the power of the government to deal with beliefs which are an integral part of past action that is a legitimate object of state control. Thus the intent with which an alleged criminal act was performed may constitute an element of the crime, and in attempting to establish the requisite intent the government may delve into areas of belief. There are constitutional limits to this power. A belief, being an inner state of mind, can never be proved by direct evidence; it can only be shown through evidence of overt conduct, either expression or action. The use of expression to establish a belief may, under some circumstances, impair freedom of communication. Similarly, where the state is prosecuting an inchoate crime—one in which the conduct has not actually reached the stage of final action—its probe into pre-action areas of belief and expression may infringe First Amendment rights. These matters are discussed in a later chapter. At this point it suffices to say generally that inquiry into beliefs that are closely linked to action which the state may prohibit does not by itself abridge freedom of expression.

Considering the problem within the confines here outlined, the right to freedom of belief falls readily within the coverage of the First Amendment. Coercion of belief plainly constitutes an "abridgment" of freedom of expression. The basic theory that governmental regulation must be directed specifically to action, and may not control action through control of expression, is fully applicable. Thus any alleged conflict between the interest in protecting the right to hold beliefs, and other individual or social interests, must be resolved in favor of freedom of belief. The legal doctrine, therefore, should be that the holding of a belief is afforded complete protection from state coercion.

In examining in detail the factors supporting this conclusion, we turn first to freedom of religious beliefs. Thereafter we take up the issues concerned with (1) compulsory affirmation of belief; (2) compulsory disclosure of belief; and (3) punishment for holding a belief.

A. Religious Belief

The right to freedom of belief was first asserted in connection with religious belief. Early struggles for freedom of the mind centered around religious freedom, and legal protection for freedom of belief has developed most explicitly and most extensively in this area. Thus freedom of religion is the subject of special guarantees in the First Amendment: "Congress shall make no law respecting an establishment of religion, or prohibiting the free exercise thereof . . ." [1]

As a general proposition the Supreme Court has interpreted the First Amendment to afford complete protection to religious belief, though only limited protection to religious action. In one of its earliest decisions on the subject, while rejecting the claim of the Mormon Church that the advocacy or the practice of polygamy was protected against government controls as an exercise of religious freedom, the Court said:

> [The First Amendment] was intended to allow every one under the jurisdiction of the United States to entertain such notions respecting his relations to his Maker and the duties they impose as may be approved by his judgment and conscience, and to exhibit his sentiments in such form of worship as he may think proper, not injurious to the equal rights of others, and to prohibit legislation for the support of any religious tenets, or the modes of worship of any sect.[2]

The point was made even more sharply in *Cantwell v. Connecticut,* upholding the claim of a Jehovah's Witness to protection of the First Amendment in presenting to passersby on the street a religious argument that was peaceful but obnoxious to them. Justice Roberts said:

1. See J. B. Bury, *A History of Freedom of Thought* (New York, Oxford University Press, 2d ed. 1952); J. M. Robertson, *A Short History of Free-thought* (New York, Russell & Russell, 1957).

2. *Davis v. Beason,* 133 U.S. 333, 342 (1890).

The constitutional inhibition of legislation on the subject of religion has a double aspect. On the one hand, it forestalls compulsion by law of the acceptance of any creed or the practice of any form of worship. Freedom of conscience and freedom to adhere to such religious organization or form of worship as the individual may choose cannot be restricted by law. On the other hand, it safeguards the free exercise of the chosen form of religion. Thus the Amendment embraces two concepts,—freedom to believe and freedom to act. The first is absolute but, in the nature of things, the second cannot be. Conduct remains subject to regulation for the protection of society.[3]

Other decisions of the Supreme Court have confirmed this position. In *West Virginia State Board of Education v. Barnette,* the Court invalidated a compulsory flag salute as violating freedom of expression, without relying upon the free exercise of religion clause; but at least four justices, all of those in the majority who expressed a view on the religious argument, would have included the religious ground as well, apparently giving absolute protection to religious belief. In *United States v. Ballard,* in which the leaders of the I AM movement were charged with conspiracy to defraud in obtaining money through false representations that they were divine messengers, the Court held that it would be improper to consider the truth or falsity of their religious beliefs; under the First Amendment, Justice Douglas declared, man "was granted the right to worship as he pleased and to answer to no man for the verity of his religious views." In *In re Anastaplo* all parties and all courts agreed that an applicant for admission to the bar could not be forced to disclose his religious beliefs, even though they might have some bearing upon his qualifications to take the oath required of new attorneys. And in *Torcaso v. Watkins* a unanimous Court held that a newly appointed notary public could not be denied his commission because he refused to take an oath, as required by the Maryland Constitution, declaring his "belief in the existence of God." Said Justice Black: ". . . neither a State nor the Federal Government can constitutionally force a person 'to profess a belief or disbelief in any religion.' "[4]

3. *Cantwell v. Connecticut,* 310 U.S. 296, 303–304 (1940).

4. *West Virginia State Board of Education v. Barnette,* 319 U.S. 624 (1943), discussed in more detail in the next section of this chapter. Justices Black, Douglas, and Murphy expressed their views in separate opinions in the *Barnette* case; Justice Stone's view appears from his dissent in *Minersville School District v. Gobitis,* 310 U.S. 586 (1940). *United States v. Ballard,* 322 U.S. 78, 87 (1944). *In re Anastaplo,* 366 U.S. 82 (1961). *Torcaso v. Watkins,* 367 U.S. 488, 495 (1961); the Court was quoting from *Everson v. Board of Education,* 330 U.S. 1, 15 (1947).

There is some authority to the contrary. In *United States v. Schwimmer* and *United States v. MacIntosh* a majority of the Supreme Court held that an alien applying for naturalization who on grounds of religious belief refused to agree to bear arms in case of war could under the applicable statutes be refused the right to become a citizen. Furthermore the Court, by a vote of five to four, followed these decisions in *In re Summers*. In that case it upheld Illinois in refusing an applicant admission to the bar on the ground that he could not in good faith take the attorney's oath to support the Illinois Constitution because of his conscientious scruples against participation in war. But the naturalization cases were expressly overruled in *Girouard v. United States,* in which the Court reinterpreted the naturalization statutes as not imposing a willingness to bear arms as a condition of citizenship. The *Girouard* decision would appear to have seriously undermined *Summers*. Furthermore, while these cases in one aspect raised issues of religious belief, the Court tended to treat them as involving an actual (rather than a hypothetical) refusal to serve in the armed forces, that is, as a case of religious action. Hence they can hardly be taken as overruling the *Cantwell-Torcaso* doctrine.[5]

Under certain circumstances an individual may voluntarily reveal his religious belief in order to take advantage of an exemption from laws which would otherwise interfere with his religious belief. Thus a person claiming exemption from the Selective Service Act as a conscientious objector must give proof of his religious views in order to qualify for that status. Likewise in *Sherbert v. Verner* a Seventh-Day Adventist asserted her religious position in order to avoid disqualification for unemployment compensation benefits because she refused to work on Saturday, the sabbath of her religion. These affirmations of religious belief are made necessary by the operation of general statutes which accidentally impinge upon a particular religious faith. They expand rather than contract the free exercise of religion, and are in no way incompatible with the guarantees of the First Amendment.[6]

In summary, then, it is a fair conclusion that today the Supreme Court would grant full protection to religious belief, whether the infringement came from an attempt to compel affirmation of a belief,

5. *United States v. Schwimmer,* 279 U.S. 644 (1929); *United States v. MacIntosh,* 283 U.S. 605 (1931). Accord is *United States v. Bland,* 283 U.S. 636 (1931). *Girouard v. United States,* 328 U.S. 61 (1946).

6. On conscientious objection, see *United States v. Seeger,* 380 U.S. 163 (1965). *Sherbert v. Verner,* 374 U.S. 398 (1963).

from an effort to force disclosure of a belief, or from any kind of sanction upon belief including disqualification from a benefit or privilege. The reasons for this constitutional protection afforded by the First Amendment were explained by Justice Field in *Davis v. Beason:*

> The oppressive measures adopted, and the cruelties and punishments inflicted by the governments of Europe for many ages, to compel parties to conform, in their religious beliefs and modes of worship, to the views of the most numerous sect, and the folly of attempting in that way to control the mental operations of persons, and enforce an outward conformity to a prescribed standard, led to the adoption of the amendment in question.[7]

In earlier times religious belief was the most precious form of belief, and the one most in need of protection. Today other forms of belief have assumed equal or greater importance in the lives of many people. Thus freedom of political belief has come to have larger significance as citizen participation in community affairs has expanded. The question is posed whether secular beliefs should not be entitled to the same degree of protection as religious beliefs. To that question we now turn.

B. Compulsory Affirmation of Belief

State intrusion upon freedom of belief occurs, in perhaps its most acute form, when the government demands that a person publicly subscribe to a particular belief. This invasion of freedom is especially grave when the individual does not himself hold the belief in question. But the objections to compulsory affirmation of belief apply with almost equal force when the individual does share the belief.

Efforts by official authority to compel affirmation of a belief have, at various times and places, taken the form of requiring an oath, the recitation of a creed, a salute, a genuflection, or some similar expression of conformity with the sovereign will. Fortunately in the United States the phenomenon has been rare. Test oaths are not infrequent in America, but they have been used as a basis for disqualification from privileges or benefits, and are discussed in that connection. The chief

7. 133 U.S. 333, 342 (1890).

American example of requiring affirmation of a belief has been the flag salute in schools.

It was the flag salute controversy which gave rise to the major statement of the Supreme Court upon the constitutionality of the state demanding of its citizens an affirmation of belief. In the period following World War I an increasing number of States and school districts enacted laws making the flag salute compulsory for all school children. The ceremony was found objectionable by several religious groups and in *Minersville School District v. Gobitis* the issue reached the Supreme Court.

In the *Gobitis* case the local Board of Education required teachers and pupils to participate daily in the flag salute ceremony. The pledge, recited in unison, was: "I pledge allegiance to my flag, and to the Republic for which it stands; one nation indivisible, with liberty and justice for all." The Gobitis family, members of the Jehovah's Witnesses, objected to engaging in the flag salute on the ground that it violated their religious beliefs, principally the command of the Bible not to "bow down" to any "graven image." The Gobitis children were expelled from school for refusing to participate in the ceremony, and suit was brought to enjoin the school authorities from requiring the flag salute as a condition of school attendance.

The Supreme Court, with only Justice Stone dissenting, upheld the Board of Education. The constitutional issue was treated throughout as primarily one of religious freedom. Justice Frankfurter, writing for the Court, took the view that, "Conscientious scruples have not, in the course of the long struggle for religious toleration, relieved the individual from obedience to a general law not aimed at the promotion or restriction of religious beliefs." Applying the balancing test, he found that the legislative judgment which had determined that the interest in national unity outweighed the interference with religious belief was a reasonable one and hence should not be set aside by a court. He added, as an aside: "Nor does the freedom of speech assured by Due Process move in a more absolute circle of immunity than that enjoyed by religious freedom." [8]

Justice Stone viewed the issues differently:

> The law which is thus sustained is unique in the history of Anglo-American legislation. It does more than suppress freedom of speech

8. *Minersville School District v. Gobitis,* 310 U.S. 586, 594, 595 (1940). For the background of the flag salute cases see David R. Manwaring, *Render Unto Caesar: The Flag Salute Controversy* (Chicago, University of Chicago Press, 1962).

and more than prohibit the free exercise of religion, which concededly are forbidden by the First Amendment and are violations of the liberty guaranteed by the Fourteenth. For by this law the state seeks to coerce these children to express a sentiment which, as they interpret it, they do not entertain, and which violates their deepest religious convictions.[9]

Justice Stone then went on to apply the rule of full protection for religious belief:

If these guaranties [freedom of speech and religion] are to have any meaning they must, I think, be deemed to withhold from the state any authority to compel belief or the expression of it where that expression violates religious convictions, whatever may be the legislative view of the desirability of such compulsion.[10]

Three years later the Supreme Court changed its mind. In *West Virginia State Board of Education v. Barnette* the Court overruled *Gobitis* and held that a resolution of the West Virginia Board establishing a compulsory flag salute violated the First Amendment guarantees of freedom of speech as applied to the State through incorporation in the Fourteenth Amendment. Justice Jackson wrote the prevailing opinion, in which Justices Stone and Rutledge joined. Though writing separate concurrences, Justice Murphy was in agreement and Justices Black and Douglas "substantially in agreement" with the Jackson opinion. Justices Roberts and Reed adhered to the *Gobitis* opinion and Justice Frankfurter, also dissenting, wrote a long separate opinion.[11]

The Jackson opinion, like the Stone opinion in *Gobitis,* viewed the issue as whether the state could require "affirmation of a belief and an attitude of mind." It was a question of "a right of self-determination in matters that touch individual opinion and personal attitude." Unlike the Stone opinion, however, the Jackson opinion relied exclusively on the free speech provisions of the First Amendment and did not invoke at all the religious provisions. "There is no doubt," Justice Jackson said, "that, in connection with the pledges, the flag salute is a form of utterance." And he concluded:

We think the action of the local authorities in compelling the flag salute and pledge transcends constitutional limitations on their power and invades the sphere of intellect and spirit which it is the purpose of

9. 310 U.S. at 601.
10. 310 U.S. at 604.

11. *West Virginia State Board of Education v. Barnette,* 319 U.S. 624 (1943).

the First Amendment to our Constitution to reserve from all official control.[12]

The precise doctrinal basis of Justice Jackson's opinion is not entirely clear. Twice he observes that the government can restrict expression only to prevent a clear and present danger to a legitimate interest. And Justice Frankfurter apparently viewed the majority position as resting on the clear and present danger doctrine. But the Jackson opinion plainly does not attempt to apply the clear and present danger test to the actual problem at hand. It also rejects any idea of balancing interests: "Hence validity of the asserted power to force an American citizen publicly to profess any statement of belief or to engage in any ceremony of assent to one, presents questions of power that must be considered independently of any idea we may have as to the utility of the ceremony in question." In the end the Jackson opinion extends the unqualified protection of the First Amendment. It would forbid any compulsion to affirmation of belief, under any circumstances. This can be the only meaning of Justice Jackson's famous concluding paragraph:

> If there is any fixed star in our constitutional constellation, it is that no official, high or petty, can prescribe what shall be orthodox in politics, nationalism, religion, or other matters of opinion or force citizens to confess by word or act to their faith therein. If there are any circumstances which permit an exception, they do not now occur to us.[13]

The issues at stake in the *Barnette* case have not again come before the Supreme Court. Nevertheless occasional instances may be found where oath requirements are imposed which demand affirmative expression of belief. Thus the National Defense Education Act and the National Science Foundation Act require that an applicant for fellowship aid must swear that "I bear true faith and allegiance to the United States of America." The State Department for a time demanded a like oath from applicants for a passport. Some State oaths are similar. All these oaths, like the pledge of allegiance to the flag, seek to compel a public avowal of belief and are subject to the same objections as those upheld by the Supreme Court in *Barnette*.[14]

12. 319 U.S. at 633, 631, 632, 642.
13. 319 U.S. at 634, 642.
14. A Federal District Court has followed *Barnette* in upholding the refusal of Jehovah's Witnesses' children to stand during the singing of the national anthem. *Sheldon v. Fannin*, 221 F. Supp. 766 (D. Ariz. 1963); see also *Lewis v. Allen*, 5 Misc. 2d 68, 159 N.Y.S.2d 807, 11 App. Div. 2d 447, 207 N.Y.S.2d 862, 14 N.Y.2d 867, 252 N.Y.S.2d 80, cert. denied 379 U.S. 923 (1964); 20 U.S.C. §581(f) (N.D.E.A. oath); 42 U.S.C. §1874(d) (N.S.F.A. oath).

The full protection extended to the right of belief in the *Barnette* case is essential to an effective system of freedom of expression. Forcing public expression of a belief is an affront to personal integrity. It can indeed be considered an invasion of the constitutional right to privacy, established in *Griswold v. Connecticut,* as well as an abridgment of freedom of expression. Beyond that it is designed to instill a disposition to conformity and to substitute the will of the state for the free expression of the citizen. It establishes the psychological tone of a closed society. And nothing of social value is gained. Whatever outward conformity is achieved is undoubtedly more than offset by the inward hostility engendered. As Justice Jackson remarked, "Compulsory unification of opinion achieves only the unanimity of the graveyard." [15]

C. Compulsory Disclosure of Belief

A second form of infringement on freedom of belief occurs when government attempts to compel disclosure of belief. The demand here is not for public affirmation of belief, but simply that the individual reveal his beliefs, held but not expressed, to official authority. Disclosure of belief may be demanded in any proceeding involving application of a sanction or deprivation of a benefit or privilege for holding a belief. In such a situation the disclosure is allegedly justified by, and is secondary to, the right to apply the sanction or impose the disqualification. These matters will be considered shortly. The focus at this point is on a narrower area where the government seeks disclosure for some other purpose, such as framing legislation, or sheerly for the sake of exposure. In present-day America the most likely source of a demand for such a disclosure is a legislative investigating committee.

It seems to be generally accepted at the present time that compulsory disclosure of belief under these circumstances is beyond the authority of the government. Even legislative investigating committees, whose powers of inquiry are the broadest and most ill-defined, have not asserted the right to probe into matters of mere belief. And there

15. *Griswold v. Connecticut,* 381 U.S. 479 (1965); the Jackson quotation is from 319 U.S. at 641.

appear to be no judicial decisions in which the issue of disclosure, in this isolated form, has been squarely raised.

The constitutional doctrine applicable to this situation is scarcely open to dispute. Any attempt by the government to compel disclosure of belief would fall within the scope of First Amendment protection. The impact of such action upon freedom of expression is immediate and harmful. Nor would there appear any reason not to apply the rule that the protection afforded by the First Amendment is complete; that under no circumstances could the state force such a disclosure of belief. Most of the factors discussed in connection with compulsory affirmation of belief are equally applicable here. Any official demand that an individual disclose his beliefs constitutes an unwarranted invasion of personal integrity and creates an atmosphere incompatible with freedom of thought.

Two further considerations require brief comment. The first is that constitutional acceptance of the right to compel disclosure of beliefs which are not part of some illegal action would give the government a powerful weapon for harassing unpopular persons and opinions. The obligation to testify about one's beliefs involves also the obligation to testify truthfully. And the truth of the testimony may be put to the test in a perjury or similar prosecution. In this elusive inquiry virtually any thought, opinion, or action of the accused over his entire past life might be relevant to the question whether he testified falsely in stating his beliefs. And the outcome would be in the hands of a jury that would probably be hostile. To the extent that the government found it worthwhile to invest time and resources in investigation and prosecution, almost any unpopular citizen would be at its mercy.

A partial illustration of the point is furnished by the example of Owen Lattimore. In 1952 Lattimore, Director of the Page School of International Relations at Johns Hopkins and a world authority on Far Eastern affairs, appeared before the Internal Security Subcommittee of the Senate Judiciary Committee, headed by Senator McCarran. The Subcommittee was investigating Communist influence in the Institute of Pacific Relations, with which Lattimore had been connected for some years. Back files of the Institute had been seized by the Subcommittee and combed over by its staff. For thirteen days Lattimore was subjected to a gruelling investigation based upon materials from the files not made available to him. Upon the basis of this testimony Lattimore was indicted on seven counts of perjury. One of the counts was that he had testified falsely when he said that "he had never been a sympathizer or any other kind of promoter of Communism or Communist interests." It is true that Lattimore had volunteered this particular statement. But his problem in meeting the perjury charge was the same as if he had been compelled to answer the question whether he believed in (was sympathetic to) Communism. Virtually his entire past career was open to scrutiny by government investigation and to interpretation by a jury hostile to Communism. Fortunately for him, Lattimore never went to trial; the main counts of the indictment were dismissed on grounds of vagueness. But the episode makes clear that any official power to inquire into beliefs puts the nonconformist citizen in a highly vulnerable position.[16]

The second point to be considered is the striking absence of any social advantage to be gained from compelling disclosure. We are not dealing with belief linked to action, or with belief as a qualification for obtaining a benefit or holding a position. Compulsion to reveal isolated beliefs may serve partisan or private political purposes. But it is hard to conceive of circumstances when it would be of any legitimate use to government. Compulsion of this kind would not even assist the goal of national unity, the claimed basis for requiring affirmation of belief. The rule of full protection is not open to serious challenge in this situation.

D. Punishment for Holding a Belief

The government may also interfere with freedom of belief by imposing sanctions upon persons who entertain unpopular beliefs. It seems fully accepted that the government cannot subject any person to direct criminal punishment because of his beliefs. Chief Justice Vinson made this clear in *American Communications Association v. Douds,* the leading Supreme Court treatment of the subject: "Of course we agree that one may not be imprisoned or executed because he holds particular beliefs." The Court did not stop to explain why this is so, or why the government may not punish belief by criminal sanction on the theory that holding the belief creates a clear and present danger of

16. *United States v. Lattimore,* 112 F. Supp. 507 (D.D.C. 1953), 215 F.2d 847 (D.C. Cir. 1954), 127 F. Supp. 405 (D.D.C. 1955), 232 F.2d 334 (D.C. Cir. 1955). For Lattimore's earlier experiences, see his account in *Ordeal by Slander* (Boston, Little, Brown & Co., 1950).

some evil the government has a right to prevent. We may assume, however, that the reasons are those outlined above for extending full protection of the First Amendment to freedom of belief.[17]

In any event no issue has been presented in terms of direct punishment, criminal or otherwise. Rather the problem has arisen when a person is disqualified from obtaining a benefit or privilege, or holding a position, because of his beliefs. That such disqualification is a sanction, or form of deprivation, which impinges upon First Amendment rights is not disputed. Justification is claimed on the ground that the government is seeking to achieve another objective, by eliminating in advance persons whose beliefs indicate they are likely to cause harm, and that other effects are purely incidental. The question is whether the First Amendment precludes such a preventive regulation where it constitutes an infringement of belief, and thereby of expression. In the only case in which the Supreme Court has squarely faced this issue—the *Douds* case—the result was a draw.

The *Douds* case involved the validity of the non-Communist affidavit provision of the Taft-Hartley Act. Under this provision each officer of a labor union, as a condition of his union's obtaining the benefits of the National Labor Relations Act, was required to file an affidavit "that he is not a member of the Communist Party or affiliated with such party, and that he does not believe in, and is not a member of or supports any organization that believes in or teaches, the overthrow of the United States Government by force or by any illegal or unconstitutional methods." The Supreme Court upheld the first part of the oath—disclaimer of membership in or affiliation with the Communist Party—by a vote of five to one. That aspect of the case is considered in Chapter VI. At this point we are concerned with the requirement that the union officer not "believe in" or be a member of an organization that "believes in" the doctrines enumerated. On this the Court divided three to three and, in a later case raising the same point, four to four.[18]

Chief Justice Vinson, author of the prevailing opinion in *Douds,* took the position that the oath requirement did not prevent any person from holding the belief in question but merely provided that such a person could not also be an officer of a union that sought to invoke the National Labor Relations Act. He considered this a very limited re-

17. *American Communications Association v. Douds,* 339 U.S. 382, 408 (1950).

18. The later case is *Osman v. Douds,* 339 U.S. 846 (1950).

striction on freedom of expression, both as to the number of persons affected and as to the actual degree of restriction. Further, he thought that the belief qualification was reasonably related to the purpose of the legislation in that a union officer believing in the overthrow of government would be more likely to instigate political strikes than one who did not. In his view any absolute prohibition against considering beliefs in determining qualifications for holding strategic positions would be absurd. "Suppose, for example," he said, "that a federal statute provides that no person may become a member of the Secret Service force assigned to protect the President unless he swears that he does not believe in assassination of the President. Is this beyond the power of Congress . . . ? An affirmative answer hardly commends itself to reason . . ." Applying the ad hoc balancing test Chief Justice Vinson concluded that the oath "does not unduly infringe freedoms protected by the First Amendment." [19]

The opposing views were stated in three separate opinions. Justice Frankfurter, dissenting only as to the belief provisions of the oath, thought that they were too uncertain and vague. Justice Jackson also objected only to the belief provisions, but his dissent proceeded upon much more fundamental grounds. In his view Congress had no power "to proscribe any opinion or belief which has not manifested itself in any overt act." He stressed two main considerations. One related to the problems of enforcing such a prohibition through perjury prosecutions:

> I know of no situation in which a citizen may incur civil or criminal liability or disability because a court infers an evil mental state where no act at all has occurred. Our trial processes are clumsy and unsatisfying for inferring cogitations which are incidental to actions, but they do not even pretend to ascertain the thought that has had no outward manifestation. Attempts of the courts to fathom modern political meditations of an accused would be as futile and mischievous as the efforts in the infamous heresy trials of old to fathom religious beliefs.[20]

Justice Jackson, reiterating the ideas he had expressed in the flag salute case, rested his other objection on the broad ground that any attempt by government to proscribe beliefs was inconsistent with intellectual freedom:

> While the Governments, State and Federal, have expansive powers to curtail action, and some small powers to curtail speech or writing, I

19. 339 U.S. at 408–409, 412.   20. 339 U.S. at 436, 437.

think neither has any power, on any pretext, directly or indirectly to attempt foreclosure of any line of thought. Our forefathers found the evils of free thinking more to be endured than the evils of inquest or suppression. They gave the status of almost absolute individual rights to the outward means of expressing belief. I cannot believe that they left open a way for legislation to embarrass or impede the mere intellectual processes by which those expressions of belief are examined and formulated. This is not only because individual thinking presents no danger to society, but because thoughtful, bold and independent minds are essential to wise and considered self-government.[21]

And he concluded, as he had in *Barnette,* that First Amendment protection to freedom of belief was absolute: "I think that under our system, it is time enough for the law to lay hold of the citizen when he acts illegally, or in some rare circumstances when his thoughts are given illegal utterance. I think we must let his mind alone." [22]

Justice Black thought that the non-Communist affidavit was invalid in all its parts. Once it is conceded, as Chief Justice Vinson did, that the proscription rests on "beliefs and political affiliations," these "inescapable facts should compel a holding that [the provision] conflicts with the First Amendment." Specifically as to the belief provisions he declared that the government could not "tamper in the realm of thought and penalize 'belief' on the ground it might lead to illegal conduct." He pointed to the history of test oaths—"implacable foes of free thought"—and argued that the Vinson position could not be narrowly confined but opened the door to widespread suppression of "political belief, speech, press, assembly, or party affiliation." The opinion represented Justice Black's first clear-cut expression of his "absolutist" position on the First Amendment.[23]

The Supreme Court has never again taken up the question left unresolved by *Douds*—whether a person can be disqualified from holding a position because of his beliefs. In enforcing the Taft-Hartley oath the government did not bring any prosecutions for false swearing based upon the belief clauses, and in 1959 the entire oath provision was repealed. Only in peripheral form has the issue been raised again.[24]

21. 339 U.S. at 442.
22. 339 U.S. at 444.
23. 339 U.S. at 446, 448, 452. In *Osman v. Douds* Justice Minton agreed with Chief Justice Vinson and Justice Douglas voted to hold the belief provision invalid.

24. 73 Stat. 519, 525 (1959). The substitute provision was held unconstitutional as a bill of attainder in *United States v. Brown,* 381 U.S. 437 (1965), discussed in Chapter VI. The enforcement cases under the original provision are collected in Thomas I. Emerson, David Haber, and

In *Killian v. United States,* a prosecution for perjury in filing an allegedly false non-Communist affidavit, Justices Black and Douglas returned to the fray. Justice Douglas took occasion to align himself with Justices Jackson and Black, saying: "Congress has no power to exact from people affirmations or affidavits of belief, apart from the accepted form of oath of office demanded of all officials." But the indictment in *Killian* was not founded on the belief provisions of the oath and the remainder of the Court refrained from consideration of the problem.[25]

The *Konigsberg* and *Anastaplo* cases also touched on the belief question. Both Konigsberg and Anastaplo, in response to questions by bar committees examining their fitness for admission to practice as attorneys, discussed their political beliefs at length. They raised no issue in this regard, however, and the cases turned on their refusal to answer questions concerning membership in the Communist Party. In the *Anastaplo* case Justice Harlan, writing for the majority, noted that the report of the Bar Committee observed that there was a serious question whether "Anastaplo's views on the right to resist judicial decrees would be compatible with his taking of the attorney's oath, and that 'certain' members of the Committee thought that such views affirmatively demonstrated his disqualification for admission to the bar." But Justice Harlan took care to emphasize that the Bar Committee as a whole and the Illinois courts had relied only on the refusal to answer questions concerning party membership, and thereby avoided any issue of belief.[26]

Finally, the issue again arose indirectly in *Schneider v. Smith,* decided in 1968. Schneider, a merchant seaman, was refused clearance by the Coast Guard under the port security program because he declined to answer various questions concerning his associations, opinions, and beliefs. Among other things, Schneider was asked to state his

Norman Dorsen, *Political and Civil Rights in the United States* (Boston, Little, Brown & Co., 3d ed., 1967), pp. 247–252 (cited hereafter in this chapter as *Political and Civil Rights in the United States*).

25. *Killian v. United States,* 368 U.S. 231, 260 (1961).

26. *Konigsberg v. State Bar of California,* 366 U.S. 36 (1961); *In re Anastaplo,* 366 U.S. 82, 95–96 (1961). Justice Black in dissent, however, argued that the re-

fusal to admit Anastaplo did in effect turn upon objection to his beliefs. The issue was again raised in the Supreme Court in *Baird v. Arizona,* unreported (Ariz. Sup. Ct. 1969), cert. granted 394 U.S. 957 (1969); *In re Stolar* (Ohio Sup. Ct.), cert. granted 396 U.S. 816 (1969); and *Law Students Civil Rights Research Council v. Wadmond,* 299 F. Supp. 117 (S.D.N.Y. 1969), cert. granted 396 U.S. — (1970).

"present attitude" toward "the principles and objectives of Communism" and "the form of government of the United States." Schneider brought an action seeking a declaratory judgment that the refusal of clearance violated his constitutional rights. A three-judge District Court dismissed his complaint, but the Supreme Court unanimously reversed. Justice Douglas, writing for the Court, held that the statute creating the port security program did not authorize inquiries of the kind undertaken. The Court made quite clear that this interpretation was decisively influenced by the desire to avoid holding the statute unconstitutional. "We are loath to conclude," said Justice Douglas, "that Congress . . . undertook to reach into the First Amendment area." It was therefore unnecessary to consider "whether government can probe the reading habits, political philosophy, beliefs, and attitudes on social and economic issues of prospective seamen on our merchant vessels." Justices Black, Stewart, and Fortas, concurring, would have stated explicitly that "the interrogatories which petitioner refused to answer offend the First Amendment." [27]

While the Supreme Court has thus never conclusively determined whether disqualification for holding a belief conforms to the requirements of the First Amendment, the problem remains alive. A number of State loyalty oaths, some employing the identical language of the Taft-Hartley oath, impose disclaimers of belief. The Federal loyalty-security programs do not expressly make eligibility for Federal employment turn on tests of belief. But there is no doubt that these programs, in practical application, delve at great depth into matters of belief. Likewise Federal laws pertaining to aliens, in some cases explicitly and in some implicitly, impose conditions for admission, deportation, and naturalization based on requirements of belief.[28]

27. *Schneider v. Smith,* 390 U.S. 17, 25, 24, 27 (1968). Justice Marshall did not participate.

28. With respect to State loyalty oaths see *Political and Civil Rights in the United States,* pp. 313, 319, 412. For examples of Federal loyalty investigations that probe into belief, see Adam Yarmolinsky, *Case Studies in Personnel Security* (Washington, Bureau of National Affairs, 1955); Rowland Watts, *The Draftee and Internal Security: A Study of the Army Military Personnel Security Program* (New York, Workers Defense League, 1955; Supp. 1956); Eleanor Bontecou, *The Federal Loyalty-Security Program* (Ithaca, Cornell University Press, 1953), pp. 85, 87, 109. Psychological tests administered by the government may also involve inquiries into belief. See William A. Creech, "Psychological Testing and Constitutional Rights," *Duke Law Journal,* Vol. 1966, p. 332; Lawrence H. Mirel, "The Limits of Governmental Inquiry into the Private Lives of Government Employees," *Boston University Law Review,* Vol. 46 (1966), p. 1. For a collection of laws pertaining to aliens, see *Political and Civil Rights in the United States,* pp. 320–330.

The prevalence of qualifying tests based upon belief, as compared with the rarity of compulsory affirmation or disclosure, indicates that this aspect of freedom of belief has raised the most troublesome questions. Considered in the light of the purpose and operation of a system of free expression, however, these questions must be resolved in favor of protecting belief.

The justification for imposing sanctions on the holding of a belief is not, of course, that the belief in itself causes any injury to a social interest or conflicts with the interest of another individual. It is that the government may try to prevent the occurrence of some unwanted action at a later point by eliminating in advance certain persons whose beliefs indicate they are predisposed to engage in the action. The justification rests, however, upon somewhat shaky assumptions.

In the first place, it is by no means certain that the beliefs entertained by an individual can in most instances be ascertained with accuracy by the cumbersome processes available to government. It is not easy to explore a man's mind through the administrative process. Concealment of beliefs not manifested in overt conduct is not inordinately difficult. The effort to ascertain belief therefore tends to punish the honest and favor the dishonest; or, if an attempt is made to catch the dishonest, the result is a heresy trial. The result may be to corrupt the entire political climate, to destroy the basis of public morality. Furthermore, as Justice Jackson demonstrated in his *Douds* opinion, proof of falsity in disclaiming a belief is equally conjectural and imports equal dangers.

Secondly, the value of using belief as a prophecy of future action is also dubious. People develop and change as they live. A belief hitherto unexpressed and unacted upon may not be a sure guide to action in the realities and responsibilities of a later concrete situation. Nor does the fact that a belief was once held mean that it is still entertained. Yet a government investigator would have no sure way of knowing this. The connection between thought and action, upon which the whole justification rests, is thus in actual practice remote and highly speculative.

Third, even if the belief can be ascertained and is deemed useful as prophecy, the net result is loss of intellectual freedom. Surely Justices Jackson and Black are correct in their judgment that penalizing belief is destructive of the whole process by which independent, imaginative, and innovative thought develops in a society. Their fears are even more persuasive today when the forces of conformity are more technically proficient. This form of suppression attempts to inject government restrictions into the very sources from which free expression should flow.

Moreover, the effort to shape action at this premature stage necessarily involves the development of administrative machinery and techniques that greatly magnify the repressive impact. This is true whether administration is based upon an investigatory program or relies upon the device of a test oath. In the former case the process of investigating beliefs brings almost every aspect of a person's life under government scrutiny. The process of decision leaves awesome and unreviewable discretion in the hands of a government official whose job it is to seek out objectionable beliefs. The process of enforcement subjects individuals to the hazards of a perjury trial in which the issues are ill-defined and hopelessly speculative.

The test oath operates differently but is equally destructive in its impact. This device requires that all applicants for the benefit, privilege, or position at stake swear that they do not hold the disqualifying beliefs. The test oath thus automatically eliminates all those who entertain the beliefs and are conscientious about taking an oath; all those who are uncertain about the meaning of the oath or whether it would be construed to embrace their beliefs; and all those who are opposed on principle to test oaths. Furthermore, all who take the oath thereby come under the power, to a greater or lesser degree, of the oath-giver. For they are subject to a kind of heresy trial for swearing falsely. While these trials are now rare, if the subsequent behavior of the oath-taker is objectionable enough (controversial enough) to warrant the expenditure of the time and resources, such a trial can be mounted. The test oath thus operates to weed out the nonconformist and to enchain more securely those who already believe.

It is necessary at this point to distinguish the traditional oath of office, taken by all officers and employees of government. Such an oath does not in its usual form raise any question of freedom of belief. Thus the oath prescribed for the President in Article II, Section 1 of the Constitution declares: "I do solemnly swear (or affirm) that I will faithfully execute the Office of President of the United States, and will to the best of my ability, preserve, protect and defend the Constitution of the United States." And Article VI requires that Federal and State officers "shall be bound by oath or affirmation, to support this Constitution." Other oaths of office are more elaborate. All include commitments or promises. But they do not, in this basic form, impose any test of belief or imply any risk of harassment. In *Bond v. Floyd* the Supreme Court took it for granted that such oaths do not violate the First Amendment. But it made clear that any effort to employ them as tests of belief would run afoul of that provision:

> [W]e do not quarrel with the State's contention that the oath provisions of the United States and Georgia Constitutions do not violate the First Amendment. But this requirement does not authorize a majority of state legislators to test the sincerity with which another duly elected legislator can swear to uphold the Constitution.[29]

Finally, the further justification given in the *Douds* case for disqualifications based upon belief—that only a few persons are affected in only a minor way—does not bear examination. The belief qualification has wide potential application. Granting its assumptions it could reasonably be invoked with respect to every profession and almost every occupation. The doctrinal limitation proposed by the Vinson opinion in *Douds*—the ad hoc balancing test—would not operate as a realistic restriction. As Justice Black pointed out in that case, there is no ready stopping place either in theory or in practice. In fact, the dynamics of the process lead to expansion, not contraction. The belief test generates its own pressures to apply to ever new areas and its use leads to competition between powerful forces to employ it more widely to suppress opponents. Even if the regulation starts out as a bona fide attempt at establishing a qualification it tends to end up a sanction pure and simple. Its extensive use would lead to the disintegration of democracy.

It follows that the only sound rule is one which affords full protection to belief. The most plausible area for admitting a test of belief might be thought to be government employment. Yet, even in the case of the Secret Service agent assigned to guard the President, reliance upon an oath, as Chief Justice Vinson himself acknowledged, would be absurd. Nor would an attempt to probe unexpressed beliefs yield more practical results. In some forms of government employment, where performance of duties demands particular attitudes or policies, inquiry can legitimately be made as to how the prospective employee

---

29. *Bond v. Floyd*, 385 U.S. 116, 132 (1966). The oath of office for Federal employees is set out in 5 U.S.C. §3331. Some States have required persons who are not government employees, such as teachers at private schools, to take the so-called positive oath to support the Constitution. A New York statute of this sort was upheld in *Knight v. Board of Regents*, 269 F. Supp. 339 (S.D.N.Y. 1967), aff'd 390 U.S. 36 (1968). While such an oath would not appear to raise any substantial issue of freedom of belief, there are objections to it on other grounds, considered in Chapter VII.

would deal with specified problems arising on the job. And this would involve disclosure, in some sense, of a belief structure or a system of values. But taking account of such factors is quite different, in purpose and results, from requiring a test oath or formally conditioning the job upon adherence to certain prescribed beliefs.[30]

E. Conclusion

Experience in America with attempted control of belief supports the conclusion that the government should stay out of this area. Certainly the Jehovah's Witnesses and others who shared their position were not made more disposed toward national unity as a result of their children's being forced to salute the flag. One can hardly doubt that Mrs. Schwimmer and Rev. MacIntosh would have made excellent citizens. Or that Summers, Konigsberg, and Anastaplo would have been valuable members of the bar. The belief provisions of the Taft-Hartley non-Communist affidavit were never enforced. The oath as a whole proved ineffective and was abandoned. There is, in short, little to show on the positive side to compensate for the damage that is wrought through efforts to control belief.

In a democratic society the government should not attempt to reach back into the realm of belief for purposes of controlling future action. When it tries to do so the First Amendment should afford complete protection.

30. The characteristics of government employment which permit some qualification of the rules protecting belief and expression, without "abridging" freedom of expression, are discussed in Chapters VII and XV.

III

Consensus, Efficiency, and Direction of Change

Where belief passes into the stage of an idea, opinion, or statement communicated to others, the possibility of conflict between freedom of expression and other values or goals of society becomes more acute. Most of the controversies involving the system of free expression have concerned the efforts of government to protect or advance such values or goals through restrictions on expression. It thus becomes necessary to examine the relations between freedom of expression and these other social interests, and to formulate in each instance the legal doctrines best fitted to effect an adjustment within the framework of the First Amendment.

There are certain areas in which the command of the First Amendment most clearly contemplates unqualified protection of the right to expression. In these cases, the social interest at issue is the promotion of national unity or consensus, the maintenance of general efficiency in government operations, or the direction of orderly change. The power to restrict freedom of expression in order to promote these social interests is not often explicitly asserted. Nevertheless, such a claim is frequently implicit in much popular, and even legal, thinking on the subject. Thus the House Un-American Activities Committee (now the House Internal Security Committee), the loyalty programs, and the Internal Security Act of 1950 are based in large part on such premises. It is important, therefore, to bring these issues fully into the open. This discussion will also serve as a statement of the general considerations that govern the approach to the more overtly controversial questions that follow.

A. Consensus and Efficiency

Any society must, in order to function and survive, maintain within itself a certain unity. It requires sufficient agreement among its members not only to settle differences according to the rules and without resort to force, but to make the formal rules work in practice. No mechanism for government can by its mere existence hold a society together. This is especially true of a modern industrial community, with the interdependence of its parts and the complexities of its operations. Hence any society must seek to promote consensus among its members, and in this the machinery of the government will necessarily play an important role.

In earlier centuries unity was sought through laws prohibiting heresy, blasphemy, treason, and seditious libel. But a modern democracy may not seek to promote its broad interest in consensus by means of restrictions on expression. In the first place, the very function of the system of freedom of expression is to permit and indeed encourage conflict within the society. Conflict is just as vital to a community as consensus. And the system of freedom of expression provides the structure in which the most useful, and the least destructive, form of conflict can take place. It would be anomalous to say, therefore, that freedom of expression can be cut off in the interest of promoting a greater consensus.

Furthermore, at a higher level of accommodation, there is no fundamental conflict between freedom of expression and national unity or consensus. It would contradict the basic tenets of a democratic society to say that the greater the freedom of expression, the less the area of agreement among its members. On the contrary, a healthy consensus is possible only where freedom of expression flourishes. Such freedom is essential to the whole process of legitimation of social decisions. Suppression not only is ineffective in promoting general agreement or stability, but hinders the process by engendering hostility, resentment, fear, and other divisive forces.

Finally, a principle of suppressing freedom of expression in any situation where that right is found to be outweighed by the general social interest in achieving consensus is administratively unworkable. The principle is not susceptible of any meaningful limitation. The difference between a society governed by such a principle and a totalitarian society becomes one of mere expediency.

The state may use its other powers to promote the social interest in consensus. It may control conduct other than expression. It may establish the economic, political, and social conditions in which the necessary agreement is possible. It may engage in programs of education or propaganda, or otherwise participate in the system of freedom of expression. Institutions apart from the state exist or may be devised to achieve the same ends. But if these measures are insufficient to maintain the necessary degree of national unity, the suppression of expression will not solve the problem except by destroying the democratic character of the society.

The principle that the government cannot restrict expression in order to coerce conformity to social norms means that freedom of expression must receive full protection in this context. No matter how deviant the expression may be—how obnoxious or intolerable it may seem—the expression cannot be suppressed. The First Amendment extends, as has been pointed out many times, not only to things that do not matter much but to fundamental challenges to the basic premises of the society. And the protection must be afforded even though the unwanted expression is injected into a sensitive situation where the need for unity may be, or may appear to be, urgent. In times of stress pressures to abandon the principle of full protection mount. It is argued that a small amount of repression will restore consensus and save the community. But such a course of action would probably be self-defeating. It would be more likely to bottle up the frustrations, hide the underlying grievances, and ultimately end in explosion. Of one thing we may be sure: it would not bring back the consensus.

There is also a social interest in the effective operation of government. This interest is of increasing importance as the functions of government expand and grow more intricate. Exercise of the right to expression may create dissatisfaction with governmental policies, institutions, or officials, tend to add difficulties to the formulation or administration of law, or otherwise appear to impede the smooth operation of government. But this general social interest cannot be the basis for limiting expression. Again the conflict is more apparent than real. In the long run, open criticism of the government's operations results in a more responsible, alert, and fair administration, and hence in more effective government. And again any criterion of limitation which attempted to balance these two interests could only result in nullifying all freedom of expression.

Claims for the restriction of freedom of expression in order to promote consensus or increase government efficiency have seldom been expressly made before the Supreme Court. The principal instance was in the flag salute cases, discussed in the previous chapter. Justice Jackson, rejecting the claim, stated the policy of the First Amendment:

> Struggles to coerce uniformity of sentiment in support of some end thought essential to their time and country have been waged by many good as well as by evil men. Nationalism is a relatively recent phenomenon but at other times and places the ends have been racial or territorial security, support of a dynasty or regime, and particular plans for saving souls. As first and moderate methods to attain unity have failed, those bent on its accomplishment must resort to ever-increasing severity. As government pressure towards unity becomes greater, so strife becomes more bitter as to whose unity it shall be. . . . Those who begin coercive elimination of dissent soon find themselves exterminating dissenters. . . .
>
> It seems trite but necessary to say that the First Amendment to our Constitution was designed to avoid these ends by avoiding these beginnings. There is no mysticism in the American concept of the State or of the nature or origin of its authority. We set up government by consent of the governed, and the Bill of Rights denies those in power any legal opportunity to coerce that consent. Authority here is to be controlled by public opinion, not public opinion by authority.[1]

B. The Direction of Change

Society must also concern itself with the dynamics of change. While endeavoring to maintain a proper balance between stability and change, a society must be prepared to accept constant and substantial adjustment to new conditions. If there is one certain aspect of modern

1. *West Virginia State Board of Education v. Barnette*, 319 U.S. 624, 640–641 (1943).

life, it is that no modern society can survive for long by merely preserving the status quo. A democratic society therefore has a vital interest in the process of orderly change, that is, in change which is accomplished by methods that are legitimate, at a rate of speed that allows satisfactory adjustment, and in a direction that advances the ultimate goals of the society.

This social interest, however, cannot justify restrictions upon expression. The principle is plain that there can be no interference with freedom of expression on the general ground that it will lead to social change, or change at the wrong rate, or in the wrong direction. Here again there is no real issue of reconciling conflicting interests because there is no basic conflict. On the contrary, freedom of expression is one of the chief instruments for achieving orderly change. No objection can be made that the use of expression is an improper method of influencing change, for adjustment through public discussion is the essence of the democratic process. As for the rate of social change, the problem of modern society is more likely to be that the pace is too slow than that it is too rapid; the forces of stability and conformity tend to outweigh the forces of movement. In any event, there is no known technique by which the rate of change can be regulated through restricting freedom of expression without destroying that freedom altogether. The same is true of the direction of change. Under democratic principles this must be determined by the sovereign people themselves, and that decision is possible only by the process of full and free discussion. There are risks in this procedure, as the theory of freedom of expression recognizes, but they are the risks which must be assumed by a democratic system.

These propositions have been seriously challenged at only one point. It has sometimes been asserted that freedom of expression should not be extended to "anti-democratic groups." Such groups, according to this position, consist of (1) those who believe in or advocate principles contrary to the democratic process; or (2) those who, if they attained power, would deny freedom of expression to others, or substitute a non-democratic for a democratic system. While the exclusion would apply to groups which advocate the use of force or violence, it would not be limited to them. Any group hostile to democratic principles, whether or not urging the use of illegal means to attain its ends, would be subject to suppression by the state, or to lesser restriction. Advocates of the theory concede that it might not always be expedient to prohibit the operation of such groups, but they assert the right of the government to do so if it appears wise policy under the circumstances.

The view that democratic rights should be denied to groups which repudiate democratic principles—that toleration is not owed to the intolerant—has always possessed considerable appeal. Thus Bury notes that the Roman Emperors, while following a general policy of tolerating all religions, felt impelled to limit or proscribe Judaism and Christianity because these religions were intolerant and exclusive. Nevertheless the prevailing view of modern theorists has been that freedom of expression should be afforded all groups, even those which seek to destroy it. The classic statement of this view is that of Justice Holmes: "If in the long run the beliefs expressed in proletarian dictatorship are destined to be accepted by the dominant forces of the community, the only meaning of free speech is that they should be given their chance and have their way." [2]

The same position has been expressed by most of the leading writers in the field of civil liberties, and is the accepted position of the Supreme Court.[3]

A minority view, however, has from time to time received support. This position, stated most elaborately by Professor Carl Auerbach, has also been advanced by Karl Popper, E. F. M. Durbin, E. H. Carr, Walter Lippmann, and others. The matter became of prime importance in the years following World War II because many of the restrictions imposed upon the Communist Party and its members were, covertly or openly, based upon this theory.[4]

2. J. B. Bury, *A History of Freedom of Thought* (New York, Oxford University Press, 1913), pp. 40–51. The Holmes quotation is from his dissent in *Gitlow v. United States,* 268 U.S. 652, 673 (1925).

3. Zechariah Chafee, Jr., *Free Speech in the United States* (Cambridge, Harvard University Press, 1941), pp. 431–435; David Riesman, "Civil Liberties in a Period of Transition," in *Public Policy,* Vol. 3, Carl J. Friedrich and Edward S. Mason, Editors (Cambridge, Harvard University Press, 1942), pp. 52–58; Alexander Meiklejohn, *Political Freedom* (New York, Harper and Row, 1960), pp. 42–43, 57, 76–77; William O. Douglas, *The Right of the People* (New York, Doubleday, 1958), pp. 91–94; *American Communications Association v. Douds,* 339 U.S. 382, 429, 439 (1950) (Jackson,

J.); *Dennis v. United States,* 341 U.S. 494 (1951). For less clear-cut statements, see Thomas Jefferson, "First Inaugural Address, March 4, 1801," in Saul K. Padover (ed.), *The Complete Jefferson* (New York, Duell, Sloan and Pearce, 1943), p. 385; John Stuart Mill, *On Liberty* (R. B. McCallum ed., Oxford, Basil Blackwell, 1948), Ch. II; Walter Bagehot, "The Metaphysical Basis of Toleration," in *Works of Walter Bagehot,* Vol. 2 (Hutton ed., 1889), pp. 339, 343; C. L. Becker, *Freedom and Responsibility in the American Way of Life* (New York, Alfred A. Knopf, 1945), pp. 35–36.

4. For expressions of this view, see Carl A. Auerbach, "The Communist Control Act of 1954: A Proposed Legal-Political Theory of Free Speech," *University of Chicago Law Review,* Vol. 23 (1956), p. 173; Evan F. M. Durbin,

One main argument urged in support of this minority view is a highly abstract one. It is asserted that under the principles of democracy the people, or a majority of them, cannot by vote or otherwise abolish democracy and substitute a totalitarian or other non-democratic form of government; and similarly a majority has no right to abolish the basic mechanism of democracy by voting to prohibit freedom of expression. An existing majority, it is argued, cannot commit the future to a system in which a later majority cannot exercise its will. There is in short no power in a majority to alienate its freedom; there is no freedom not to be free.

The argument is buttressed by the contention that the right of a majority to abolish democracy is inconsistent with another principle of democracy, namely the moral right of the people to revolt against a dictatorial and unjust government. "Certainly then," Professor Auerbach argues, "it is inconsistent to maintain that the Constitution protects a totalitarian movement on its road to power, so long as it employs constitutional means, but once it comes to power, it becomes the moral right and duty of the people 'to throw off such government.' " [5]

The argument is purely a semantic one. The "principles of democracy" can equally well be defined, as they normally are, to contemplate the possibility that the people may decide if they wish to abolish democracy, and to require that even the enemies of democracy have the right to freedom of expression. Under the usual concept of democracy the people have the ultimate control; there is no higher authority to which an appeal can be taken. A democratic system is not, of course, simple majority rule; it exists only where the structure permits general freedom of expression, the right to vote, and other democratic procedures. And the structure may be protected by tradition, constitution, or other institutions such as judicial review, which limit the majority and make change difficult. If the structure is altered in an essential way, there is no longer a system of democracy. But the initial determi-

---

The Politics of Democratic Socialism (London, G. Routledge, 1940), pp. 275–279; Karl R. Popper, *The Open Society and Its Enemies* (Princeton, Princeton University Press, 1950), Ch. 7, esp. fn. 4, pp. 265–266; Edward H. Carr, *The Soviet Impact on the Western World* (New York, The Macmillan Co., 1947), pp. 13–17; Walter Lippmann, *The Public Philosophy* (New York, New American Library, 1956), pp. 96–103. See also the material cited in Riesman, *op. cit. supra* note 3, pp. 33, 52–68; G. E. G. Catlin, "On Freedom," in *Aspects of Liberty*, Milton R. Konvitz and Clinton Rossiter, Editors (Ithaca, Cornell University Press, 1958), p. 49; W. F. Berns, *Freedom, Virtue and the First Amendment* (Chicago, Henry Regnery Co., 1957).

5. Auerbach, *op. cit. supra* note 4, pp. 192–193.

nation to form a democracy, and the continued agreement to maintain it from day to day and year to year, must rest in the agreement of the people who compose it, as expressed by the current majority. A theory that a people functioning in a democratic system cannot vote to end it necessarily assumes that a minority in the nation can decide for the majority what the structure of government shall be. One cannot say by abstract definition, therefore, that a system in which a majority possess the right to end the system is not a "democratic" system.

Nor is the right of the majority to abandon democracy inconsistent with the moral right of revolution. Obviously the majority, or the same persons, would not be acting simultaneously to end democracy and to revolt against the system they are at the same time installing. The right of revolt, if and when exercised, would be invoked by different individuals, or at a different time and under different circumstances.

The second main argument proceeds on a less abstract basis. It points out that the purpose of freedom of expression is to enable a society to make a common judgment, in accordance with the will of the people, through rational methods rather than by force. This process is essential to a democratic system. Hence, it is argued, the majority of the people, as represented by the government in power, has a right and indeed the duty to protect this fundamental process. And this requires the suppression of those groups which would destroy the process itself. Such suppression does not deny freedom but rather enlarges it.

This argument is sometimes stated in more concrete form. It asserts that the democratic process can function only if its members conform to its rules of rational debate. Otherwise the system will break down. All members therefore have a responsibility to conduct themselves according to these rules, and the government has the right and duty to suppress those groups that do not adhere to them.

This argument comes closer to the real issues at stake but it assumes rather than demonstrates the conclusion. It is true that a majority, or the government, has the right to protect the basic process of democracy, and that proper action by the government may enlarge rather than restrict the freedom of members of a democratic society. But the real question is whether suppression of anti-democratic groups is the best method of maintaining a democratic system. Proponents of suppression pass over this issue without really confronting it. Their view of the democratic process is an oversimplified one. They do not conceive that the actual functioning of a democratic society is a complex and delicate affair, not necessarily held in balance by suppression of nonconforming groups.[6]

If we examine the issue in light of the theory underlying freedom of expression, it would seem apparent that a democratic society should tolerate opinion which attacks the fundamental institutions of democracy for much the same reasons that it tolerates other opinion. By and large the same considerations are applicable. Without reviewing in detail all the elements making up the traditional theory, certain observations may serve to illustrate and clarify the point.

(1) Even if we consider freedom of expression an absolute value, forever true and unchangeable, nevertheless it is important that it remain open to challenge. Otherwise it becomes "a dead dogma," ill-understood, lacking in vitality, and vulnerable to erosion or full-scale attack. It is not enough, as Professor Auerbach suggests, that the "value of freedom of speech and opinion will constantly prove itself as it is practiced." It must be subject to the criticism of its enemies as well as its friends. As Alexander Meiklejohn said, "the citizens of the United States will be fit to govern themselves under their own institutions only if they have faced squarely and fearlessly everything that can be said in favor of those institutions, everything that can be said against them." If, on the other hand, we look upon freedom of expression as subject to modification, improvement, or even abandonment in whole or part, then of course we should remain ready to discuss it and the basis upon which it rests.[7]

(2) Groups which express views hostile to democracy, or which would abolish democratic institutions if they came to power, do not

6. Two other arguments in support of the minority view should be noted. One is that toleration of anti-democratic groups "deprives democracy of any absolute moral foundation." "On this thesis," E. H. Carr argues, "the function of democracy is, so to speak, to hold the ring for all opinions, to give equal opportunity to good and evil alike, and finally to award the palm to that opinion which secures a majority of votes." Carr, *op. cit. supra* note 4, p. 15. This is an objection not only to the toleration of anti-democratic groups but to the whole theory of freedom of expression which, as already noted, contemplates that any particular expression may be used for good or evil.

The other argument is that the tolera-

tion of anti-democratic groups implies doubt as to the value of democracy, and that, conversely, defense of the democratic process arouses support for an active cause. But, among other objections, this argument assumes the conclusion. If the democratic process is viewed as forbidding suppression of anti-democratic groups, then toleration evinces faith in the democratic process. And it can hardly be said that engaging in suppression of freedom of expression is likely to arouse enthusiasm for protecting freedom of expression.

7. Auerbach, *op. cit. supra* note 4, p. 188, fn. 49; Meiklejohn, *op. cit. supra* note 3, p. 77.

operate in a political vacuum. They advance other ideas that may be valid, or partially valid, or at least relevant within the democratic framework. Moreover, groups holding the prohibited views usually represent real grievances, which should be heard and heeded. This has been a characteristic of minority groups throughout our history; it is commonplace that the accepted laws and institutions of today were the subversive heresies of yesterday. Suppression of the group, however, would suppress all its activities, and would tend to divert public attention from the substantive issues which underlie the dissatisfactions and strivings that animate the protesting group.

(3) It is difficult or impossible to say when the anti-democratic opinions of a group go to the essence of the democratic process, and would destroy it, or when they are mere modifications of the process within the framework of basic democratic theory. Would the exponents of the restrictive view contend that the Jeffersonians on coming to power had the right to suppress the Federalists, who had enacted the Alien and Sedition Acts? A spokesman for the Roman Catholic Church has defined the right to freedom of speech and the press in the following terms: "Men have a right freely and prudently to propagate throughout the State what things soever are true and honorable, so that as many as possible may possess them; but lying opinions, than which no mental plague is greater, and vices which corrupt the heart and moral life, should be diligently repressed by public authority, lest they insidiously work the ruin of the State." Is this position so contrary to the principles of democracy that a group adhering to such views may be outlawed? Walter Lippmann has argued that orthodox principles of democracy are an inadequate basis for formulating and executing a modern foreign policy, and that decisions in this field should in effect be left to a group of trained experts. Should an organization advocating this position be proscribed? [8]

Lippmann has carried to its logical conclusion the theory that the government has the right to outlaw "counter-revolutionary movements threatening liberal democracy." He sums up his position by saying: "The borderline between sedition [which in his view can be suppressed] and radical reform [which cannot] is between the denial and

---

8. On the Federalists and the Alien and Sedition laws see James Morton Smith, *Freedom's Fetters* (Ithaca, Cornell University Press, 1956). The Catholic spokesman is Pope Leo XIII and the extract is quoted from his Encyclical Letter, *Libertas Praestantissimum* (1888), printed in John A. Ryan and Francis J. Boland, *Catholic Principles of Politics* (New York, The Macmillan Co., 1947), p. 174.

the acceptance of the sovereign principle of the public philosophy: that we live in a rational order in which by sincere inquiry and rational debate we can distinguish the true and the false, the right and the wrong." Clearly the application of such a test would give the government a right to suppress virtually every group currently operating on the political scene. Thus realistically the theory of restriction becomes hard to distinguish from totalitarian theory, in which groups are allowed to operate "within the framework of the system" but not in opposition to its "fundamental principles." [9]

(4) Resort to the suppression of anti-democratic groups imperils the process by which freedom of expression promotes unity and achieves consent throughout a society. It intensifies hostility, drives the opposition underground, and encourages the solution of problems by force rather than by reason. It does not remove doubts or differences, but rather eliminates the procedures by which doubts can be resolved and differences adjusted. It provokes recriminations and reprisals that tend to feed upon each other, until the entire basis for agreement and compromise has been rendered untenable. In short, it undermines the whole principle of political legitimization.

(5) Suppression of any group in a society destroys the atmosphere of freedom essential to the life and progress of a healthy community. It can be accomplished only at the price of fear, hatred, prejudice, and hysteria. It curtails the freedom not only of the groups suppressed but of others as well. It eliminates the possibility of winning over opponents to the ways of democracy and establishes motives and precedents for the destruction of all democratic procedures. It is not possible for a society to practice both freedom of expression and suppression of expression at the same time. The attempt to preserve freedom on this basis may well bring about the end of freedom.

The conclusion must be, therefore, that the state possesses no power under the First Amendment to restrict expression because government officials disagree with the direction in which the speaker seeks to go, or with the goals he seeks to attain. The rule of full protection for all expression applies without qualification.

9. Lippmann, *op. cit. supra* note 4, p. 102.

IV

External
Security

A major interest of any society is its national security. Indeed, the overriding need for security has traditionally constituted a chief incentive for the institution of government among men. One concern of national security is protection against external enemies. In a broad sense the interest in external security embraces all relations between the society and other societies or nations. The problem is to determine the manner in which the social interest in external security can be achieved consistently with an effective system of freedom of expression. Those aspects of the problem which relate to carrying on a war or maintaining an effective defense have been the subject of most controversy and will be dealt with first. Thereafter other aspects of our relations with foreign countries, insofar as they impinge on freedom of expression, are considered.

A. War and Defense

War and preparation for war impose serious strains on a system of freedom of expression. Emotions run high, lowering the degree of rationality which is required to make such a system viable. It becomes more difficult to hold the rough give-and-take of controlled controversy within constructive bounds. Immediate events assume greater importance; long-range considerations are pushed to the background. The need for consensus appears more urgent in the context of dealing with hostile outsiders. Cleavage seems to be more dangerous, and dis-

55

sent more difficult to distinguish from actual aid to the enemy. Lesser but similar stresses arise in connection with the nation's defense effort even in times of peace. Here, the constitutional guarantee of free and open discussion is put to its most severe test.

It is not surprising, therefore, that throughout our history periods of war tension have been marked by serious infringements on freedom of expression. The most violent attacks upon the right to free speech occurred in the years of the Alien and Sedition Acts, the approach to the Civil War, the Civil War itself, and World War I—all times of war or near-war. Yet it was not until the end of World War I that judicial application of the First Amendment played any significant role in these events. Up to this point there had been no major decision by the Supreme Court applying the guarantees of the First Amendment. Then, in 1919, the Court issued the first of a series of decisions dealing with federal and state legislation that had been enacted to restrict free expression during the war, and thus began the long development of First Amendment doctrine.[1]

During World War II, in contrast to prior wartime periods, freedom of speech to oppose the war or criticize its conduct was not seriously infringed. This unusual turn of events may have been due, in part, to the increasing judicial protection afforded free expression through the First Amendment, particularly by the liberal decisions which began in 1930 under the Hughes Court, and the ensuing education of public opinion that those decisions engendered. Some of these gains were lost during the McCarthy era in the early nineteen-fifties, which coincided with the hostilities in Korea. On the whole, however, the free speech issues of that period did not relate directly to the war itself, but rather to a more general fear of Communism within the United States.

By the time of the Vietnam war the controversy over freedom of speech in wartime had moved to another level. The general right to oppose the war by speech was fully recognized. New modes of opposition began to develop, however, and these raised different issues concerning the border between expression and action. Moreover, as always, there were serious problems of realizing in practice the acknowledged rights guaranteed in theory.

---

1. For a collection of materials dealing with these periods, see Thomas I. Emerson, David Haber, and Norman Dorsen, *Political and Civil Rights in the United* *States* (Boston, Little, Brown & Co., 3d ed. 1967), pp. 35–68 (cited hereafter in this chapter as *Political and Civil Rights in the United States*).

In considering freedom of expression connected with war or defense, there must be some delineation of the boundaries between the civilian and military sectors of our society. Generally speaking, the military sector embraces the conduct of military operations and the internal governance of the military establishment. The latter includes the military law governing the armed forces, martial law, and military government of occupied territory. This military system is outside the civilian system of freedom of expression and is subject to different rules.

The reasons for making this demarcation between the two systems are apparent. A military organization is not constructed along democratic lines and military activities cannot be governed by democratic procedures. Military institutions are necessarily far more authoritarian; military decisions cannot be made by vote of the interested participants. This is not to say that the military sector does not remain under the ultimate control of the civilian sector. In a democratic society it must. Our civilian courts have not only asserted the power to determine where the border lies but have been steadily increasing their supervision over the military sector. Nor does the existence of the two systems mean that constitutional safeguards, including the First Amendment, have no application at all within the military sphere. It only means that the rules must be somewhat different. Indeed, an attempt to apply the same First Amendment doctrine to both sectors could only result in watering down the protection afforded the civilian sector.[2]

The problem, then, is to determine when civilian expression enters the domain of the military, and when members of the military are under the protection of the civilian system. Some of the points of contact are clear. Certainly, general discussion of the organization, procedures, or operations of the military are well within the system of free expression, indeed are essential to maintaining the principle of civilian control. Similarly, expression dealing with all facets of the civilian economy that supplies the armed forces is part of the civilian sector.

2. Discussion of the military sector, and the extent of civilian judicial supervision over it, may be found in Joseph W. Bishop, Jr., "Civilian Judges and Military Justice: Collateral Review of Court-Martial Convictions," *Columbia Law Review*, Vol. 61 (1961), p. 40; Earl Warren, "The Bill of Rights and the Military," *New York University Law Review*, Vol. 37 (1962), p. 181; Note, "Constitutional Rights of Servicemen Before Courts-Martial," *Columbia Law Review*, Vol. 64 (1964), p. 127; Note, "The Court of Military Appeals and the Bill of Rights: A New Look," *George Washington Law Review*, Vol. 36 (1967), p. 435; Note, "Servicemen in Civilian Courts," *Yale Law Journal*, Vol. 76 (1966), p. 380.

On the other hand, communications dealing with military movements in wartime are plainly subject to military censorship. Likewise, dissemination of information classified as a military secret is subject to controls based on the requirements of the military system, although the issue of what constitutes a military secret may be subject to civilian judicial review. Access to military installations for purposes of exercising the right of free speech is also subject to different rules than is access to non-military public places. More difficult questions involve the extent to which civilian communication can be addressed across the border to members of the military, as in the insubordination cases, and the rights of a member of the military to enjoy the benefits of the free expression system when temporarily acting in a civilian capacity.

Another matter to which preliminary attention should be directed concerns the underlying body of law that protects the social interest in effective pursuit of war or defense by regulating conduct classified as "action." First among these is the law of treason. Others include the laws against rebellion or insurrection, against seditious conspiracy, and against espionage and sabotage. There are also numerous State and local laws directed against violence of all kinds and similar conduct. All this legislation, together with such additional laws as the Federal, State, or local governments may enact within the general limitations of the due process clause, protects the war and defense effort against interference by any form of "action." We are concerned here only with attempts to promote war and defense programs through restrictions on expression.[3]

Perhaps a word should be added concerning the classification of espionage as "action." It is true that espionage usually involves the communication of information, and this by itself would normally be considered "expression." But espionage does take place in a context of action; the espionage apparatus is engaged primarily in conduct that dwarfs any element of expression. Essentially, espionage is analogous to stealing. Moreover, espionage cannot be considered expression within the protection of the First Amendment for another reason. Most espionage consists of conveying information concerning military secrets and would fall within the system of military operations. And all espionage involves aiding a foreign country and would be subject to governmental control as part of the power to regulate relations with

3. 18 U.S.C. §2383 (rebellion and insurrection), §2384 (seditious conspiracy), §794 (espionage), §§2151–2157 (sabo-

tage). See generally *Political and Civil Rights in the United States,* pp. 73–77.

another sovereign, a matter discussed below. Hence even if espionage were considered "expression" it is not that form of domestic, civilian expression that is embraced within the system of freedom of expression.

The main problems concerning freedom of expression as it relates to war and defense include (1) the law of treason; (2) general criticism of the war or defense effort; (3) more specific communications which may lead to insubordination in the armed forces, obstruction of recruitment, or resistance to the draft; (4) other forms of protest; (5) practical problems of protecting wartime dissent against illegitimate harassment. Issues relating to marches and demonstrations, which do not differ greatly from those involved in the right of assembly generally, are dealt with in Chapter IX.

1. THE LAW OF TREASON

Historically, one of the major legal weapons employed by governments to protect themselves against external (and also internal) dangers has been prosecution for the crime of treason. In England before the nineteenth century, and to a lesser extent in the American colonies, treason was given a very broad definition. It was used to eliminate almost any form of political opposition, violent or peaceful, by action or by utterance. When the American revolutionaries came to draw up the Constitution they took particular care to give the crime of treason a limited meaning and to surround it with procedural safeguards. The provision they included in the Constitution, one of the few protections for individual rights embodied in the original document, reads as follows:

> Treason against the United States, shall consist only in levying War against them, or in adhering to their Enemies, giving them Aid and Comfort. No Person shall be convicted of Treason unless on the Testimony of two Witnesses to the same overt Act, or on Confession in open Court.[4]

Thus, the crime of treason is given an express constitutional definition which cannot be extended by any act of the legislature or judi-

---

4. U.S. Const., Art. III, §3. On the history of the law of treason and the adoption of the treason provision in the Constitution, see *Cramer v. United States*, 325 U.S. 1, 8–35 (1945); James Willard Hurst, "Treason in the United States," *Harvard Law Review*, Vol. 58 (1944–1945), pp. 226, 395, 806; and other materials collected in *Political and Civil Rights in the United States*, pp. 74–75.

ciary. The statute which officially establishes the offense follows the
constitutional provision, simply making it explicit that the crime can
be committed "within the United States or elsewhere." [5]

The treason provision of the Constitution has been uniformly interpreted to mean that the crime of treason cannot be committed solely
through expression, but only through some form of action. This interpretation is based in part upon the constitutional requirement of an
overt act. However, it is primarily an attempt to follow the intent of
the framers. In *Cramer v. United States,* the leading decision concerning the treason provision, the majority opinion of the Supreme Court
said: "Historical materials aid interpretation chiefly in that they show
two kinds of dangers against which the framers were concerned to
guard the treason offense: (1) perversion by established authority to
repress peaceful political opposition. . . ." It added: "The concern
uppermost in the framers' minds, that mere mental attitudes or expressions should not be treason, influenced both definition of the crime and
procedure for its trial." The dissenters, disagreeing with the majority
on the extent to which the required "overt act" must indicate the whole
crime, agreed that expression alone could not constitute treason:
"[T]he requirement of an overt act is designed to preclude punishment for treasonable plans or schemes or hopes which have never
moved out of the realm of thought or speech." [6]

Under the treason provision, therefore, the test is not whether the
expression has a tendency to aid and comfort the enemy, or presents a
clear and present danger of doing so. Nor is the interest in national
security balanced against the interest in freedom of expression.
Rather, the test is whether the conduct in question constitutes expression or action. In most of the decided cases the behavior alleged to be
treasonous has clearly come within the action category. A group of
cases arising out of World War II, however, present a closer issue. In
Gillars v. United States, it was charged that the defendant was guilty of
treason in making broadcasts from enemy territory under the sponsorship of the enemy government as part of the psychological warfare
directed against American soldiers and citizens. The argument that the
broadcasts constituted only expression and hence could not be treason
was rejected by Judge Charles Fahy in the following terms:

5. 18 U.S.C. §2381.
6. 325 U.S. 1, 27, 28, 61. For further
material in support of the proposition,

see Hurst, *op. cit. supra* note 4, pp. 806,
830–831.

While the crime [of treason] is not committed by mere expression of opinion or criticism, words spoken as part of a program of propaganda warfare, in the course of employment by the enemy in its conduct of war against the United States, to which the accused owes allegiance, may be an integral part of the crime. There is evidence in this case of a course of conduct on behalf of the enemy in the prosecution of its war against the United States. The use of speech to this end, as the evidence permitted the jury to believe, made acts of words.[7]

The court seems right on construing the conduct in the case as constituting "action" rather than "expression." The broadcaster was part of the enemy war apparatus and in effect engaged in military activities. In any event she was operating in the military sector and outside the protection of the civilian system of freedom of expression. The more fundamental point is that the court adhered to the rule that, under the law of treason, expression is fully protected and only action (even when the charge is treason) is subject to governmental sanctions.[8]

This interpretation of the treason clause is arrived at independently of the First Amendment. Indeed, at the time the treason provision was included in the Constitution the First Amendment was not yet a part of that document. But the same result should be reached by way of the First Amendment. It is clear that this guarantee applies to prosecutions for treason, as it does to the exercise of all other governmental powers. The basic test for the First Amendment's protection, that expression must be distinguished from action, is the same as that which is in fact used in interpreting the treason clause. The treason provision, both in theory and in practice, thus lends support to the position that the First Amendment affords full protection to all conduct classifiable as "expression."

7. *Gillars v. United States,* 182 F.2d 962, 971 (D.C. Cir. 1950).

8. In *Chandler v. United States,* 171 F.2d 921 (1st Cir. 1948), cert. denied 336 U.S. 918 (1949), a similar case, Judge Calvert Magruder appears to have proceeded upon the theory that the broadcasts occurred in the military sector. For other broadcasting cases, which did not find it necessary to discuss the expression-action problem, see *D'Aquino v. United States,* 192 F.2d 338 (9th Cir. 1951), cert. denied 343 U.S. 935 (1952); *Best v. United States,* 184 F.2d 131 (1st Cir. 1950), cert. denied 340 U.S. 939 (1951).

2. GENERAL CRITICISM OF WAR OR DEFENSE EFFORT

During the Civil War, opposition to the war that took the form of expression was controlled, to the extent that any control was attempted, by executive measures, primarily based on military power. The writ of habeas corpus was suspended and many persons accused of disloyal utterances were confined to military prisons. In some areas martial law was declared and the press shut down or subjected to censorship. The Post Office was closed to "treasonable correspondence" and passport controls were instituted. The degree of freedom to criticize the war or its conduct varied greatly in different places and at different times. But in general the problem was handled as a part of the military conduct of the war and safeguards against suppression of speech were ignored.[9]

During World War I, restrictions on antiwar expression, which were both widespread and intensive, were based primarily upon specific legislation enacted for that purpose. The Espionage Act of 1917, in addition to dealing with actual espionage and protection of military security, provided:

> Whoever, when the United States is at war, shall willfully make or convey false reports or false statements with intent to interfere with the operation or success of the military or naval forces of the United States or to promote the success of its enemies and whoever, when the United States is at war, shall willfully cause or attempt to cause insubordination, disloyalty, mutiny, or refusal of duty, in the military or naval forces of the United States, or shall willfully obstruct the recruiting or enlistment service of the United States, shall be punished by a fine of not more than $10,000 or imprisonment for not more than twenty years, or both.[10]

Another provision of the Act made punishable the mailing of any matter advocating treason, insurrection, or forcible resistance to any law of the United States, or violating any of the other provisions of the Act.[11]

9. See James G. Randall, *Constitutional Problems Under Lincoln* (Urbana, University of Illinois Press, rev. ed. 1951); Dean Sprague, *Freedom Under Lincoln* (Boston, Houghton, Mifflin, 1965); Harold L. Nelson (ed.), *Freedom of the Press from Hamilton to the Warren Court* (Indianapolis, Bobbs-Merrill Co., 1967), pp. 221–247; and materials collected in *Political and Civil Rights in the United States,* pp. 45–48.

10. Act of June 15, 1917, ch. 30, §3, 40 Stat. 217, 219, incorporated as amended in 18 U.S.C. §2388(a).

11. Act of June 15, 1917, ch. 30, Tit. XII, 40 Stat. 230, incorporated as amended in 18 U.S.C. §1717.

In 1918 the Espionage Act was amended to bring within its prohibitions a variety of other offenses, including saying or doing anything with intent to obstruct the sale of United States bonds, except by way of bona fide and not disloyal advice; uttering, printing, writing, or publishing any language intended to incite resistance to the United States or promote the cause of its enemies, or any disloyal, profane, scurrilous, or abusive language, or language intended to cause contempt, scorn, contumely, or disrepute regarding the form of government of the United States, the Constitution, the flag, or the uniform of the Army or Navy; urging any curtailment of production of any things necessary to the prosecution of the war with intent to hinder its prosecution; advocating, teaching, defending, or suggesting any of these acts; and speaking or acting in support or favor of the cause of any country at war with the United States. Many States enacted similar legislation, some of it even more broadly worded.[12]

These laws were vigorously enforced. Almost two thousand prosecutions were brought under the Federal statutes and many others under the State legislation. The resulting suppression has been described by Professor Chafee:

> It became criminal to advocate heavier taxation instead of bond issues, to state that conscription was unconstitutional though the Supreme Court had not yet held it valid, to say that the sinking of merchant ships was legal, to urge that a referendum should have preceded our declaration of war, to say that war was contrary to the teachings of Christ. Men have been punished for criticizing the Red Cross and the Y.M.C.A., while under the Minnesota Espionage Act it has been held a crime to discourage women from knitting by the remark, "No soldier ever sees those socks." [13]

As a result of these wartime prosecutions the attention of the courts was directed to the constitutional protection of free speech embodied in the First Amendment. Ultimately a number of cases reached the Supreme Court, although no decisions were rendered until after the war was over. It was in these cases that the Supreme Court began the remarkable development of First Amendment doctrine which has

---

12. Act of May 16, 1918, ch. 75, 40 Stat. 553, repealed, Act of March 3, 1921, ch. 136, 41 Stat. 1360. The summary is taken from Zechariah Chafee, Jr., *Free Speech in the United States* (Cambridge, Harvard University Press, 1941), pp. 40–41. See also Chafee, pp. 100–102, for a description of the State legislation.

13. Chafee, *op. cit. supra* note 12, pp. 51–52. For other material on the status of freedom of expression in World War I, see *Political and Civil Rights in the United States,* pp. 60–61; Note, "Legal Techniques for Protecting Free Discussion in Wartime," *Yale Law Journal,* Vol. 51 (1942), p. 798.

continued to the present day. At the outset, however, the development
was hesitant and faltering. In every case the Court, applying the clear
and present danger test, rejected First Amendment claims.

The first decision, *Schenck v. United States,* illustrates the Court's
attitude and approach. Schenck, who was general secretary of the Socialist Party, and others, were indicted under the Espionage Act of
1917 for conspiring to obstruct recruiting and cause insurbordination
in the armed forces. The charge was based upon the fact that Schenck
had distributed a leaflet opposing the war and the draft, some of the
copies of which had reached men who had been drafted. Justice
Holmes, speaking for the Court, described the leaflet as follows:

> The document in question upon its first printed side recited the first
> section of the Thirteenth Amendment, said that the idea embodied in
> it was violated by the conscription act and that a conscript is little bet-
> ter than a convict. In impassioned language it intimated that conscrip-
> tion was despotism in its worst form and a monstrous wrong against
> humanity in the interest of Wall Street's chosen few. It said "Do not
> submit to intimidation," but in form at least confined itself to peaceful
> measures such as a petition for repeal of the act. The other and later
> printed side of the sheet was headed "Assert Your Rights." It stated
> reasons for alleging that any one violated the Constitution when he re-
> fused to recognize "your right to assert your opposition to the draft,"
> and went on "If you do not assert and support your rights, you are help-
> ing to deny or disparage rights which it is the solemn duty of all citizens
> and residents of the United States to retain." It described the arguments
> on the other side as coming from cunning politicians and a mercenary
> capitalist press, and even silent consent to the conscription law as help-
> ing to support an infamous conspiracy. It denied the power to send our
> citizens away to foreign shores to shoot up the people of other lands, and
> added that words could not express the condemnation such cold-
> blooded ruthlessness deserves, etc., etc., winding up "You must do
> your share to maintain, support and uphold the rights of the people of
> this country." [14]

On the First Amendment issue Justice Holmes' opinion was abrupt
and begrudging. "It may well be," he said, "that the prohibition of
laws abridging the freedom of speech is not confined to previous restraints." But he made it clear that the First Amendment did not protect all speech: "The most stringent protection of free speech would

14. *Schenck v. United States,* 249 U.S.
47, 50–51 (1919).

not protect a man in falsely shouting fire in a theatre and causing a panic." He then went on to enunciate the clear and present danger test: "The question in every case is whether the words used are used in such circumstances and are of such a nature as to create a clear and present danger that they will bring about the substantive evils that Congress has a right to prevent." [15]

Without specifically finding that the leaflet created such a clear and present danger, the opinion concluded by affirming the convictions.

Other cases went even further in sanctioning curtailment of wartime expression under the Espionage Act of 1917. Eugene V. Debs, the Socialist leader, was prosecuted for creating insubordination in the armed forces on the basis of a speech in which he denounced the war as a capitalist plot and supported fellow socialists who had been convicted of resisting the draft. His most extreme statement was, "You need to know that you are fit for something better than slavery and cannon fodder." Debs was given a ten-year sentence and the Supreme Court unanimously upheld the conviction. The officers of a German-language newspaper were found guilty of violating the provision against false news reports by publishing articles slanted toward the German position. And Victor Berger's *Milwaukee Leader* was denied second-class mailing privileges for printing editorials, strongly pro-German in tone, attacking the war and the draft. The extreme provisions of the 1918 amendments to the Espionage Act were likewise upheld in *Abrams v. United States,* where the defendants had thrown out of a window and into the street militantly worded leaflets calling for a general strike.[16]

Starting with the *Abrams* case, Justices Holmes and Brandeis began to express dissenting views. But a majority of the Court held firmly to the position that any expression which showed a tendency to interfere with the war effort could validly be suppressed. The clear and present danger test, while accepted in theory, was not applied in practice to check this result.

15. 249 U.S. at 51, 52.

16. *Debs v. United States,* 249 U.S. 211, 214 (1919). Debs, aged sixty-three, served in prison from April 13, 1919, until Christmas Day 1921, when President Harding released him without restoration of citizenship. In 1920, while in prison, Debs ran for President on the Socialist ticket, receiving 919,799 votes. *Schaefer v. United States,* 251 U.S. 466 (1920). *United States ex rel. Milwaukee Social Democrat Publishing Co. v. Burleson,* 255 U.S. 407 (1921). For denial of second-class mailing privileges for even less outspoken material, see *Masses Publishing Co. v. Patten,* 246 F. 24 (2d Cir. 1917), reversing 244 F. 535 (S.D.N.Y. 1917) (L. Hand, J.). *Abrams v. United States,* 250 U.S. 616 (1919). For a collection of cases and materials, see *Political and Civil Rights in the United States,* pp. 77–83.

At the outbreak of World War II, statutes restricting wartime dissent were on the books, ready to be enforced. Although the 1918 amendments to the Espionage Act were repealed in 1921 and have never been revived, the original 1917 Act, applicable only in time of war, remained in force. The passage of the Smith Act in 1940, moreover, added a somewhat similar provision not limited to wartime. This provision made it unlawful

> for any person, with intent to interfere with, impair, or influence the loyalty, morale or discipline of the military or naval forces of the United States—
> (1) to advise, counsel, urge, or in any manner cause insubordination, disloyalty, mutiny, or refusal of duty by any member of the military or naval forces of the United States; or
> (2) to distribute any written or printed matter which advises, counsels, or urges insubordination, disloyalty, mutiny, or refusal of duty by any member of the military or naval forces of the United States.

In addition, the Selective Service and Training Act of 1940, the first draft law enacted after World War I, established criminal penalties for any person "who knowingly counsels, aids, or abets another to evade registration or service" or any of the requirements of the Act.[17]

Nevertheless, by this time both judicial and public attitudes toward general criticism of the war had moderated somewhat. There were a few prosecutions under the Espionage Act of 1917 but only one case reached the Supreme Court; there, a conviction was reversed for want of sufficient evidence, the Court not reaching the First Amendment issues. A prosecution was commenced in the District of Columbia against twenty-eight alleged pro-Nazis for conspiracy to violate the insubordination provisions of the Smith Act. But the trial judge died after seven months of trial and the prosecution was not reinstituted. A prosecution was also instituted against twenty-nine members of the Socialist Workers Party in Minneapolis under these and other provisions of the Smith Act. Here a conviction of eighteen of the defendants was obtained and affirmed by the Court of Appeals, the Supreme Court denying certiorari. The one conviction under the Selective Service Act

17. Act of March 3, 1921, ch. 136, 41 Stat. 1360 (repeal of 1918 amendments); Act of June 28, 1940, ch. 439, §§1–5, 54 Stat. 670, incorporated as amended in 18 U.S.C. §2387 (Smith Act); Act of September 16, 1940, ch. 720, 54 Stat. 885, incorporated as amended in 50 U.S.C. App. §462(a) (Selective Service and Training Act).

which came before the Supreme Court was reversed for want of sufficient evidence.[18]

The new attitude and changed position of the Supreme Court were clearly reflected in *Taylor v. Mississippi,* the only case it decided during World War II involving a state sedition law. Two members of the Jehovah's Witnesses had been convicted under a Mississippi statute prohibiting the teaching or dissemination of literature "designed and calculated to encourage violence, sabotage, or disloyalty to the government of the United States, or the state of Mississippi." They were charged with making statements such as "It was wrong for our President to send our boys across in uniform to fight our enemies," and "these boys were being shot down for no purpose at all." The Supreme Court unanimously reversed. Although the doctrinal basis of the decision is not precisely stated, the point of view is clear:

> The statute as construed in these cases makes it a criminal offense to communicate to others views and opinions respecting government policies, and prophecies concerning the future of our own and other nations. As applied to the appellants, it punishes them although what they communicated is not claimed or shown to have been done with an evil or sinister purpose, to have advocated or incited subversive action against the nation or state, or to have threatened any clear and present danger to our institutions or our Government. What these appellants communicated were their beliefs and opinions concerning domestic measures and trends in national and world affairs.
>
> Under our decisions criminal sanctions cannot be imposed for such communication.[19]

The right of dissent in wartime again became a major issue with the escalation of hostilities in Vietnam. The statutory base for imposing restrictions on antiwar protest (in the form of expression rather than action) remained essentially unchanged. The Espionage Act of 1917 continued in effect after World War II by virtue of a 1953 enactment which provided that it should remain in force "until six months

---

18. *Hartzel v. United States,* 322 U.S. 680 (1944) (Espionage Act of 1917); *United States v. McWilliams,* 54 F. Supp. 791 (D.D.C. 1944), 163 F.2d 695 (D.C. Cir. 1947) (prosecution of pro-Nazis); *Dunne v. United States,* 138 F.2d 137 (8th Cir. 1943), cert. denied, 320 U.S. 790 (1943) (Socialist Workers Party); *Keegan v. United States,* 325 U.S. 478 (1945) (Selective Service Act). See generally on the World War II cases *Political and Civil Rights in the United States,* pp. 83–84. See also Note, "The Effect of the First Amendment on Federal Control of Draft Protests," *Villanova Law Review,* Vol. 13 (1968), pp. 347, 350–354.

19. *Taylor v. Mississippi,* 319 U.S. 583, 589–590 (1943).

after the termination of the national emergency proclaimed by the President on December 16, 1950." The Smith Act provision was not changed. The Selective Service and Training Act of 1940 was modified by the Universal Military Training and Service Act of 1948 (also known as the Selective Service Act) to provide that anyone "who knowingly counsels, aids, or abets another to refuse or evade registration in the armed forces or any of the requirements of this title," or anyone "who shall knowingly hinder or interfere or attempt to do so in any way, by force or violence or otherwise, with the administration of this title . . . or the rules or regulations made pursuant thereto," is guilty of an offense punishable by five years in prison or a $10,000 fine, or both.[20]

Despite the language of these statutes, and their very early interpretations, it had become clear that general opposition to the war or defense effort, no matter how vigorously asserted, was constitutionally protected. The fact that such expression might reach members of the armed forces or have some detrimental effect on the operation of the draft was not sufficient reason for denying that protection. The case of *Bond v. Floyd,* decided in 1966, left no doubt about this proposition.

Julian Bond, a Negro, had been elected to the Georgia House of Representatives. He was refused his seat by the legislature because of statements by him opposing the draft and criticizing United States policies in Vietnam. Among the offending statements was one by the Student Nonviolent Coordinating Committee, which Bond, then S.N.C.C.'s Communications Director, had endorsed. It declared in part:

> Samuel Young [a Negro] was murdered because United States law is not being enforced. Vietnamese are murdered because the United States is pursuing an aggressive policy in violation of international law. The United States is no respecter of persons or law when such persons or laws run counter to its needs and desires.
>
> . . . We maintain that our country's cry of "preserve freedom in the world" is a hypocritical mask behind which it squashes liberation movements which are not bound, and refuse to be bound, by the expediencies of United States cold war policies.

20. Act of June 30, 1953, ch. 175, 67 Stat. 133, as amended 18 U.S.C. §2391; Proclamation No. 2914, 3 C.F.R. 99 (Supp. 1958), 50 U.S.C. App. at 9497. The Universal Military Training and Service Act amendment is incorporated in 50 U.S.C. App. §462(a). For some of the State laws in the area, see Note, "The States, the Federal Constitution, and the War Protestors," *Cornell Law Review,* Vol. 53 (1968), pp. 528, 535–536.

We are in sympathy with, and support, the men in this country who are unwilling to respond to a military draft which would compel them to contribute their lives to United States aggression in Viet Nam in the name of the "freedom" we find so false in this country. . . .

We therefore encourage those Americans who prefer to use their energy in building democratic forms within this country. We believe that work in the civil rights movement and with other human relations organizations is a valid alternative to the draft. We urge all Americans to seek this alternative, knowing full well it may cost their lives—as painfully as in Viet Nam.

The Supreme Court unanimously held that the refusal to seat Bond violated his First Amendment rights. As to the right of general opposition to the Vietnam war the Court said: "Certainly there can be no question but that the First Amendment protects expressions in opposition to national foreign policy in Vietnam and to the Selective Service system. The State does not contend otherwise." [21]

If one compares the statement upheld in the *Bond* case with those denied protection in *Schenck* and *Debs,* the distance traversed in First Amendment interpretation is quite apparent. The development had taken place in decisions relating to First Amendment protection of expression in circumstances not involving wartime dissent, but the *Bond* case confirmed the application of the broader meaning of the First Amendment to the war and defense situation.

In doctrinal terms, however, the *Bond* case is not very enlightening. The Court simply declared that the statement in question was protected by the First Amendment and found no need to elaborate. There was no talk of clear and present danger, or of balancing, and merely an oblique reference to incitement. The *Bond* case does suggest, however, that the doctrine demanding complete protection for expression has strong judicial support in this area. Free and open discussion of war and defense issues is essential to the life of a democracy. As the World War I experience demonstrates, restrictions on speech of this character, whereby "expression" as well as "action" is inhibited, can easily reach such proportions and have such a stifling effect as to bring the nation close to a police state.

Thus, by the mid-nineteen-sixties, the general right to express

21. *Bond v. Floyd,* 385 U.S. 116, 132 (1966). For a different view of the doctrinal basis of the *Bond* case see Alan H. Finegold, "Julian Bond and the First Amendment Balance," *University of Pittsburgh Law Review,* Vol. 29 (1967), p. 167.

strong dissent to war and defense policies had been broadly accepted, certainly in theory if not always in practice. Both government officials and public opinion had come, if not to appreciate the full value, at least to recognize the inevitability of such protest in a society that aspires to remain democratic. By this time, indeed, the legal issues had shifted and the question was no longer one involving the general right of open dissent. The controversial areas had become (1) the extent to which the First Amendment protects expression specifically urging resistance to the Selective Service laws; and (2) the constitutional line between "expression" and "action" employed in various forms of protest.

3. COMMUNICATIONS SPECIFICALLY URGING OR ADVISING INSUBORDINATION OR RESISTANCE TO THE DRAFT

As dissent concerning war or defense policy moves from the general to the particular, it presents more controversial questions. And as it is directed towards the armed forces and their system of recruiting it touches especially sensitive areas. By the mid-sixties opposition to the Vietnam war that took the form of urging or advising resistance to the draft began to raise these issues on a widespread scale.

Existing case law on the subject was sparse, mostly out of date, and generally unsatisfactory. Shortly after enactment of the 1948 Selective Service Act a number of prosecutions were brought under Section 462(a), several of which received the attention of the higher courts. One case involved Dr. Wirt A. Warren, a Kansas physician. Dr. Warren was a Unitarian and a pacifist, opposed to all wars on religious grounds. He "advised, counseled and urged" his stepson not to register for the draft and offered to provide funds for him to go to Canada or Mexico. The stepson rejected the advice and registered. Dr. Warren was convicted and sentenced to two years in prison; his conviction was upheld on appeal. The Supreme Court denied certiorari. On the First Amendment issue, the Court of Appeals view was:

> Freedom of religion and freedom of speech, guaranteed by the First Amendment, with respect to acts and utterances calculated to interfere with the power of Congress to provide for the common defense and to insure the survival of the nation are qualified freedoms. They may not

be construed so as to prevent legislation necessary for national security, indeed, that may be necessary for our survival as a nation.[22]

In another case, Larry Gara, Dean of Men at Bluffton College (a Mennonite institution), was prosecuted under the same provision. Dean Gara was a Quaker who had himself refused to register in World War I and considered it his religious duty to oppose all forms of cooperation with war. He had consistently advocated that men of draft age who opposed war on grounds of conscience should refuse to register. The particular incident for which Gara was indicted involved a student at the college who was arrested for failing to register. Gara, present at the arrest, said to the student, "Do not let them coerce you into registering." The District Court held that, since the student had a continuing duty to register, this counsel violated the Act. The Court of Appeals affirmed the conviction. On the First Amendment issue, the Court conceded that general expression of opinion opposed to the Selective Service Act "might well be protected." But it held that this protection did not extend to counseling others to violate the law, "the counseling being also expressly forbidden by statute":

> No decision has been handed down by the Supreme Court holding that violation of an express statute enacted by Congress in the exercise of its constitutional power to provide for the common defense is excused under the First Amendment because the acts of violation are consummated, as counseling always must be, through the medium of words.

The Supreme Court, dividing four to four, affirmed without opinion.[23]

While the *Warren* and *Gara* cases indicate the nature of the problem, neither opinion throws much light on the First Amendment issue. The courts simply failed to come to grips with the question, at least in terms that would now be required by First Amendment theory.

The later decision of the Supreme Court in *Bond v. Floyd* is not much more helpful. The Court there expressly held that "Bond could not have been constitutionally convicted under 50 U.S.C. App. §462(a)." His statements "were at worst unclear on the question of the means to be adopted to avoid the draft" and did "not demonstrate any incitement to violation of law." The Court was plainly moving

22. *Warren v. United States,* 177 F.2d 596, 599 (10th Cir. 1949), cert. denied, 338 U.S. 947 (1950).

23. *Gara v. United States,* 178 F.2d 38, 41 (6th Cir. 1949), aff'd 340 U.S. 857 (1950). See also *Baxley v. United States,* 134 F.2d 937 (4th Cir. 1943), and *Bagley v. United States,* 136 F.2d 567 (5th Cir. 1943), prosecutions under the 1940 Act.

away from the *Warren* and *Gara* cases. But it did not make clear how far it would go, nor did it elaborate the doctrinal basis of its holding. Further analysis of the problem is necessary.[24]

The actual forms of communication employed in opposition to the draft during the Vietnam war appear to fall into three categories, representing a progression. The first category comprises that expression which does not specifically advise or urge anyone to violate existing law. Many persons, of course, have urged others not to enlist voluntarily in the armed services. Many individuals and groups have offered advice about the rights of conscientious objectors and the most effective way to present a case for conscientious objector classification. Others have urged potential draftees to claim any possible exemption or seek any possible deferment, even though they may not be clearly qualified.

The second category comprises communication that advises or urges persons of draft age not to register, not to submit to induction, or not to cooperate with the Selective Service System in other ways. Such advice or exhortation may be limited to support of those who already have moral or religious scruples against service in the armed forces, or it may be addressed to a wider audience. In either case the action urged, if taken by the draftee, would constitute a violation of the Selective Service Act. The communication might vary widely in its impact, depending on such factors as whether it was in writing or in speech, addressed to a large group or to an individual, couched mildly as advice or intensely as urging, issued by an individual or by an organization, or uttered outside an induction center or at a dinner in the ballroom of a luxury hotel.

Communications urging or advising this form of resistance to the draft were widespread and open. In September of 1967, for example, a group of 320 ministers, professors, writers, and others, many of them well known in their several fields, signed a document entitled "A Call to Resist Illegitimate Authority." In it they recounted various methods of resistance to the war being used by different persons, noting that "some are refusing to be inducted." The signers approved these efforts, saying: "We believe that each of these forms of resistance against illegitimate authority is courageous and justified." They pledged themselves to raise funds to "aid resistance to the war in whatever ways may seem appropriate," called on "all men of good will to join us in this confrontation with immoral authority"; and concluded: "Now is the

24. *Bond v. Floyd*, 385 U.S. 116, 133,   *lissi*, 293 F. Supp. 1339 (D.N.J. 1968).
133–134 (1966). See also *Straut v. Ca-*

time to resist." Shortly afterwards, eighteen Protestant, Roman Catholic, and Jewish leaders, joined by fifty delegates to the United States Conference on Church and Society, issued a public statement in which they declared: "We hereby publicly counsel all who in conscience cannot today serve in the armed forces to refuse such service by nonviolent means." Similar statements were made by numerous organizations and individuals.[25]

The third category includes advice or instruction in various illegal methods of evading the draft—for example, how to feign insanity, drug addiction, homosexuality, chronic illness, or the like. Communications of this sort could be made under a variety of circumstances, ranging from a casual remark to a thorough training in the preferred technique of deception. In actuality, while such communications undoubtedly took place, they were not normally given publicity and an estimate of their frequency is not possible.[26]

Assuming that all these forms of communication in opposition to the draft are prohibited by a literal reading of the Espionage Act or the Selective Service Act, to what extent are they protected by the First Amendment? One can analyze the problem in terms of the ad hoc balancing test, the clear and present danger test, the "incitement" test, or the expression-action test.

The results under the ad hoc balancing test are highly uncertain. Balancing the interest in freedom of expression against the interest in national security or in maintaining the armed forces does not yield any clear or certain answer. The factors on each side of the scale are in no way comparable. There is no common ground, or unit of measurement, between the value to national security and the injury to the sys-

25. "A Call to Resist Illegitimate Authority" was printed in *The New Republic*, Oct. 7, 1967, p. 35, and *The New York Review of Books*, Oct. 12, 1967, p. 7. It is reprinted as an Appendix to the majority opinion in *United States v. Spock*, 416 F.2d 165, 192 (1st Cir. 1969). The statement of the religious leaders may be found in *The New York Times*, Oct. 26, 1967, p. 10. We are not concerned here with the question whether, if the counselor believes in good faith that the conduct urged by him is not a violation of law, he is nevertheless guilty of a breach of the Selective Service Act. See Note, "Counseling Draft Resistance: The Case for a Good Faith Belief Defense," *Yale Law Journal*, Vol. 78 (1969), p. 1008.

26. For more detailed accounts of the Vietnam war protests, see Ted Finman and Stewart Macaulay, "Freedom to Dissent: The Vietnam Protests and the Words of Public Officials," *Wisconsin Law Review*, Vol. 1966 (1966), pp. 632, 641–661; Note, "The States, the Federal Constitution and the War Protestors," *Cornell Law Review*, Vol. 53 (1968), pp. 528–529; Note, "The Effect of the First Amendment on Federal Control of Draft Protests," *Villanova Law Review*, Vol. 13 (1968), pp. 347, 362–363. See also "Symposium—The Draft, the War and Public Protest," *George Washington Law Review*, Vol. 37 (1969), p. 433.

tem of freedom of expression. Hence there is no standard of reference on which to base a reasoned, functional determination. The formula is so loose and open-ended, so lacking in judicial guidelines, that it becomes difficult for a court to do more than confirm (or, perhaps, reject) the judgment of the legislature.

It is possible that under the balancing test the line might fall between the first and second categories, the first being protected and the second and third not, on the theory that the action urged in the first category is not a violation of existing law. But this feature of the case would not by itself be decisive. The violation factor in the equation might still be outweighed by other factors favoring freedom of expression. Or the ensuing action, even though not a violation of law, might be deemed so detrimental to the state as to outweigh the interest in freedom of expression. There is no readily apparent point at which to strike the balance. In view of the abstract weight popularly given to national security in our society, however, it could even happen that the line would be drawn somewhere through the middle of the first category.

The clear and present danger test presents other difficulties. Unless one considers the clear and present danger test as identical with the balancing test, it is useful only as a supplement to that test. In those situations in which the balance (omitting elements of clear and present danger) is plainly against freedom of expression, the clear and present danger test can be employed to protect more expression than plain balancing otherwise would. This is true, for instance, in most situations in which the evil apprehended is a violation of law resulting from physical violence. If the balance (apart from clear and present danger) favors freedom of expression, the clear and present danger test is not useful; in fact, it becomes restrictive. Thus, if it is determined that freedom of speech outweighs the interest in keeping litter off the streets, the question whether distribution of leaflets would create a clear and present danger of littering the streets is irrelevant. In short, the clear and present danger test makes sense only in those situations in which, apart from the clear and present danger element, the balance of interests would be struck against the First Amendment right.

In the context of anti-draft expression, the clear and present danger test would operate to protect some speech in all three categories that would otherwise be outlawed by the balance-of-interests process. By its very nature, however, expression that did not create a clear and present danger of persuading the person to whom it was addressed would tend to be ineffective or innocuous. The clear and present danger test would be beneficial in limiting the scope of an enforcement campaign by cutting down the possibility of bringing prosecutions for "harmless" expression, but it scarcely seems to meet the needs of a system of freedom of expression.

The "incitement" test, which may be the test that the Court used in the *Bond* case, would operate something like the clear and present danger test, protecting some portion of expression in all three categories. The boundaries of protection are, however, even more vaguely delineated than under the clear and present danger test. Justice Holmes was correct when he said, "Every idea is an incitement." The concept of "incitement" thus affords no concrete frame of reference upon which to base a decision. It poses an exercise in semantics, not concretely related to the function and operations of a system of freedom of expression. No rational application of the concept is possible.[27]

The expression-action test would clearly protect all communication falling within the first and second categories. The dividing line, under this test, would be drawn somewhere in category three. Within that category, conduct that amounts to "advice" or "persuasion" would be protected; conduct that moves into the area of "instructions" or "preparations" would not. The essential task would be to distinguish between simply conveying an idea to another person, which idea he may later act upon, and actually participating with him in the performance of an illegal act. It is true that the distinction does not offer automatic solutions and that courts could easily disagree on any particular set of facts. But this process of decision making is related to the nature of "expression" and the functions and operations of a system of freedom of expression. It is therefore a rational method of approaching the problem.

These constitutional issues were dramatically raised in 1968 by the indictment of five leading opponents of the Vietnam war for conspiracy to "counsel, aid and abet diverse Selective Service registrants to . . . neglect, fail, refuse and evade service in the armed forces" and to refuse other obligations required by the Selective Service Act, in violation of Section 462(a) of that statute. In this test case, the individual defendants were the well-known pediatrician, Dr. Benjamin

27. The Holmes quotation is from *Gitlow v. New York,* 268 U.S. 652, 673 (1925).

Spock; Yale's chaplain, Rev. William Sloane Coffin, Jr.; Marcus
Raskin, co-director of the Institute for Policy Studies in Washington;
Mitchell Goodman, a New York writer and teacher; and Michael
Ferber, a Harvard graduate student. After a well-publicized trial
Raskin was acquitted by the jury and the four others found guilty.
Sentences of two years in prison were imposed. The Court of Appeals
for the First Circuit reversed the convictions. Rejecting claims that the
conduct of the defendants was protected by the First Amendment, the
majority nevertheless dismissed the case against Spock and Ferber on
the ground that there was insufficient evidence of their intent to participate in the illegal aspects of the conspiracy, and remanded Coffin and
Goodman to a new trial because the trial judge had erroneously asked
the jury to answer ten special questions in addition to returning a general verdict of guilty or not guilty. One member of the Court would
have dismissed the case as to all defendants on the ground that, in the
area of public discussion, the government could not cast its conspiracy
net as broadly as it had attempted to do.[28]

The Court's treatment of the basic First Amendment issues in the
case is obscure and unsatisfactory. Neither majority nor minority opinion even takes the trouble to state in detail just what the conduct was
that it found to be unprotected by the First Amendment. So far as can
be gleaned from the opinions as a whole the facts proved to constitute
the conspiracy consisted of the following: (1) drafting and signing "A
Call to Resist Illegitimate Authority," the document referred to above;
(2) signing a "cover letter" that requested additional signatures to the
Call, asked for contributions, and urged the formation of local groups
"to support young men directly resisting the war"; (3) participating in
a press conference to publicize the Call and announcing a demonstration to be held in Washington as an act of "direct creative resistance";
(4) conducting a meeting at the Arlington Street Church in Boston at
which draft cards were collected to be turned over to the Department
of Justice at the Washington demonstration; and (5) participating in
the Washington demonstration where draft cards that had been previously collected at the Arlington Street Church and elsewhere were deposited with the Department of Justice. The majority apparently con-

---

28. *United States v. Spock,* 416 F.2d
165 (1st Cir. 1969). Shortly after the decision the government announced that it
would not appeal the dismissal of the case
against Spock and Ferber. *The New York
Times,* Aug. 8, 1969. Coffin and Goodman also decided not to appeal, *The New
York Times,* Sept. 9, 1969.

ceded, in a footnote, that all this conduct, except "the surrender of draft cards," constituted mere "speech." [29]

The majority opinion, rejecting the clear and present danger and incitement tests, held that the First Amendment issue "calls for a weighing." It misconceived the balancing test, however, and viewed the issue as one of "comparing the present private and public interests." Even this one-sided formulation was not seriously applied. The Court found that "maintenance of an army in peacetime is a valid, in fact vital, governmental function," and went on to say: "If a registrant may be convicted for violation of the draft laws, surely '[a] man may be punished for encouraging the commission of [the] crime.' " It then noted that the "government's ability to deter and punish those who increase the likelihood of crime by concerted action has long been established"; argued that the expression here was more than the "sympathy and support" involved in the *Bond* case; declared that the defendants engaged in "a call for immediate action"; and, examining briefly "the circumstances," concluded that "[i]n this context the 'soft sell' may be the most telling." The essence of the Court's view was that "effective persuasion" is not protected by the First Amendment. The dissenting judge, agreeing on the application of the balancing test, apparently accepted fully the majority's disposition of these issues.[30]

The Court of Appeals decision in the *Spock* case illustrates the looseness of the balancing test and its ineffectiveness in protecting First Amendment rights. Under the Court's analysis any speech which had the result of "encouraging the commission" of a law violation, or constituted "effective persuasion," even though couched as a "soft sell," could be punished by five years' imprisonment. On this formulation of the rights of war protestors, much of the criticism of the Vietnam war could be eliminated. The expression-action theory, of course, would not lead to this kind of suppression. As far as appears from the evidence recited by the Court, all the conduct for which the defendants were convicted constituted expression rather than action. This was admitted by the Court, except concerning the surrender of draft cards. For reasons to be set forth at a later point the turning in of draft cards must also be classified as expression. Hence the entire conduct consti-

---

29. 416 F.2d at 177, fn. 28. Not all the defendants engaged in each one of the events recited.

30. 416 F.2d at 170, 171, 172. Questions concerning the application of conspiracy doctrine in the First Amendment area are discussed in Chapter XI.

tuted expression and would therefore be protected by the First Amendment.

It is fair to ask whether in the specific context of the military draft the application of the expression-action test is, from a realistic point of view, viable. There are strong reasons for thinking it is.

No one can doubt that communications expressing opposition to the draft during a war have been, and are likely to be, a highly significant feature of the process of formulating decisions made necessary by the crisis. Those communications perform the precise function that expression is intended to serve in a democratic society. This is true even if the communication advises or urges violation of the draft law. Indeed, such communication discloses, as no other form of expression could, the intensity of opposition to the war and the proximity of the nation to irreparable division and disaster.

Yet the question remains, can society afford to permit these utterances within the limits of the expression-action rule? This theory of the First Amendment gives to the government full power over the ensuing action, if any there be. There is no reason why that power cannot be effectively exercised. The government always has the authority to prosecute for refusal to submit to induction, or for any other violation of the Selective Service Act. If such prosecutions are inadequate to control the situation, it is not conceivable that prosecution of those expressing dissent or opposition would do so.

Punishment for expression and restrictions on free speech are subject to serious limitations in terms of both the requirements of due process and public expectations of democratic conduct. Repression might be effective against a small, unpopular minority. But if it is applied to a substantial and prominent portion of the population it is almost sure to fail. Moreover, sanctions would be particularly ineffective against the kind of offenses and offenders involved in draft protests, in which the issues are usually seen as religious and moral ones and the opinions fiercely held. The beliefs and convictions of most persons who counsel violation of the draft laws are not lightly tossed aside when opposition develops. It is difficult to believe that a campaign of prosecutions aimed at the restriction of expressions of opinion would have a deterrent effect. Nor would it be likely under such circumstances to reduce the underlying opposition to the draft.

At the same time, the danger to the system of freedom of expression and to society as a whole inherent in such a policy of repression would be enormous. Once under way, a campaign to restrict expression would not readily find a stopping place. It would arouse the most irrational and divisive forces in the community, and in the end it could stop encouragement to draft resistance only by curbing all expression opposing the war.

The problems with respect to communication tending to cause insubordination in the armed forces are likewise best dealt with through the expression-action principle. The clear and present danger test, as the World War I decisions demonstrate, could lead to suppression of all opposition to the war. So could the balancing test. In actual practice there would seem to be few occasions when communication reaching members of the armed forces could have any immediate effect. Civilians normally do not have access to military installations for purposes of direct address. Expression must be in the form of writing or, if oral, made to a mixed audience which includes some voluntary listeners from the armed forces. It is not surprising, therefore, that the Espionage Act and the Smith Act have never been applied in any situation involving "direct incitement" to mutiny. In any event the full protection rule would seem completely viable. Here again, if the sanctions available to punish any ensuing action taking the form of actual insubordination are not sufficient to safeguard the social interest, it is hardly likely that punishment of expression will make the difference. And any such attempt can only add to the social disruption or crush all public discussion of war issues.

4. OTHER FORMS OF PROTEST AGAINST WAR OR DEFENSE EFFORTS

Protest against war or defense efforts may take many forms in addition to those considered in the previous section. As the Vietnam war progressed, opposition was displayed by burning, turning in, and refusing to carry draft cards; physical obstruction of draft boards; lying down in front of troop trains; pouring blood over files in draft board offices; and in numerous similar ways. These methods of protest, which came to be called "symbolic speech," represented an important development in the system of freedom of expression. They were attempts to achieve new forms of communication that would reach a wider audience than was possible through ordinary procedures. Their justification rested on the proposition that the mass media of communication were not open to those lacking the necessary funds or established position, and hence such persons could convey their message effectively only by some kind of novel or dramatic conduct. It was noted, for example, that a war protestor who called a press conference to announce his opposition to the war received no coverage in the mass media; but one who burned his draft card obtained nationwide attention.

In constitutional terms these forms of protest raised squarely the issue whether the conduct involved was to be classified as "expression" or "action." Discussion of this problem requires that we jump ahead in the chronological story and consider later and more sophisticated forms of First Amendment doctrine.

Up to the draft card burning cases the courts had paid remarkably little attention to the fundamental question of defining "expression" and "action." In *Stromberg v. California*, decided in 1931, the Supreme Court had assumed that displaying a red flag as a symbol of opposition to organized government constituted expression, but had not elaborated upon that position. Later, the Court had touched on the problem in the labor picketing cases, but only in the most superficial manner. The civil-rights movement of the early sixties again presented issues of this kind, particularly in the sit-in and demonstration cases, but even at this late date the Court never fully came to grips with the problem. As a result there was no body of governing doctrine available when the question came to the fore in the Vietnam war protests.[31]

Before considering specific instances, certain general features of the problem should be kept in mind. To some extent expression and action are always mingled; most conduct includes elements of both. Even the clearest manifestations of expression involve some action, as in the case of holding a meeting, publishing a newspaper, or merely talking. At the other extreme, a political assassination includes a substantial mixture of expression. The guiding principle must be to determine which element is predominant in the conduct under consideration. Is expression the major element and the action only secondary? Or is the action the essence and the expression incidental? The answer, to a great extent, must be based on a common-sense reaction, made in light of the functions and operations of a system of freedom of expression.

Yet often there is something more to go on—some extrinsic points

31. *Stromberg v. California*, 283 U.S. 359 (1931). On the picketing and civil-rights cases, see Chapters IX and XII. A summary of the "symbolic speech" cases may be found in Note, "Symbolic Conduct," *Columbia Law Review*, Vol. 68 (1968), pp. 1091, 1093–1105.

of reference which provide useful guides. The conduct must, of course, be intended as a communication and capable of being understood by others as such. Moreover, the problem does not arise in the abstract, but in the context of whether specific governmental controls are valid or not. In order to determine whether the governmental control is directed against that element of the conduct which constitutes expression only, it is sometimes helpful to consider what comparable forms of action, divorced from expression or the particular kind of expression involved, are normally subject to governmental control. In the political assassination case, for example, murder is usually the object of official sanction regardless of what is intended to be expressed by the murderer. But opening and shutting the mouth, the action connected with making an address, is not commonly an object of governmental control. Likewise, other extrinsic factors, such as the objective of the legislature in framing the regulation, may indicate whether the government is actually seeking to curtail the expression element of mixed conduct. The type of sanction invoked is a useful guide as well; the penalty may be clearly excessive when tested against the usual sanction applied to comparable conduct when not combined with the particular expression. Thus the problem of separating governmental control of expression from governmental control of action is open to some degree of rational analysis.[32]

The issues came to a head in the draft card burning cases. In 1965 several well-publicized incidents occurred in which persons subject to the draft publicly burned their registration certificates or notices of classification. The Selective Service Act did not at the time contain any provision specifically prohibiting the intentional destruction of these cards. But the regulations issued by the Selective Service System required each person registered under the draft to have his card in his possession at all times, and violation of the regulations was punishable as

---

32. On the question of the intent of the communication and its impact on others, see Note, *op. cit. supra* note 31, pp. 1109–1117.

It should be observed that we are not at this point concerned with a situation involving two distinct sets of conduct, one constituting expression and the other action, in which the problem is one of separating government control of the action from government impairment of expression. Such an issue would arise, for example, if an association engaged at different times in political speech and political violence, and the government sought to punish the latter by outlawing the association altogether. These issues are discussed subsequently, particularly in connection with the membership provisions of the Smith Act (Chapter V) and legislative investigating committees (Chapter VII). Here we are considering a unitary course of conduct which must be dealt with as either expression or action.

a violation of the Act, by a fine of $10,000, or imprisonment for five years, or both. Hence a person burning his draft card would later be subject to prosecution under the regulation for failing to have the card in his possession. In 1965 Congress passed an amendment to the Selective Service Act to provide that anyone who "knowingly destroys" or "knowingly mutilates" his draft card is guilty of an offense under the Act and subject to its penalties. Following passage of the amendment the number of draft card burnings increased and several prosecutions were commenced.[33]

The handling of this rather novel First Amendment problem by the lower Federal courts illustrated the uncertainty and poverty of existing First Amendment doctrine. None of the courts gave adequate consideration to the issue of whether the conduct consisted of "expression" or "action." All of them concluded or assumed, however, that draft card burning includes some expression and, hence, came within the protective scope of the First Amendment. They then addressed themselves to the question whether the expression was protected or unprotected by that constitutional guarantee. None utilized the clear and present danger test, although in these situations the clear and present danger concept would have been relevant. Rather, all relied upon the balancing test, one balancing in favor of First Amendment rights and the others against.[34]

The issue reached the Supreme Court in *United States v. O'Brien* and, by a vote of seven to one, that Court upheld the statute. Chief Justice Warren, writing for the majority, rejected O'Brien's argument that the burning of his registration certificate was "symbolic speech" protected by the First Amendment. The essence of the Court's position is set forth in the following paragraph:

33. For an account of the draft card burnings and the background of the 1965 amendments, see Dean Alfange, Jr., "Free Speech and Symbolic Conduct: The Draft-Card Burning Case," *Supreme Court Review,* Vol. 1968 (1968), p. 1. The relevant provisions of the Selective Service Act are in 50 U.S.C. App. §462. The Selective Service regulations are in 32 C.F.R. §§1617.1, 1623.5.

34. *O'Brien v. United States,* 376 F.2d 538 (1st Cir. 1967) (balancing in favor), rev'd. 391 U.S. 367 (1968); *United States v. Miller,* 367 F.2d 72 (2d Cir. 1966) (balancing against), cert. denied, 386

U.S. 911 (1967); *United States v. Smith,* 249 F. Supp. 515 (S.D. Iowa), aff'd per curiam, 368 F.2d 529 (8th Cir. 1966) (balancing against); *United States v. Cooper,* 279 F. Supp. 253 (D. Colo. 1968) (balancing against).

All the courts balanced the general interest in national security against the interest in freedom of expression. But more precisely, the question under the balancing test would seem to be: Does the government's interest in preventing non-possession *by burning* (not non-possession in general) outweigh the interest in freedom of expression?

We cannot accept the view that an apparently limitless variety of conduct can be labeled "speech" whenever the person engaging in the conduct intends thereby to express an idea. However, even on the assumption that the alleged communicative element in O'Brien's conduct is sufficient to bring into play the First Amendment, it does not necessarily follow that the destruction of a registration certificate is constitutionally protected activity. This Court has held that when "speech" and "nonspeech" elements are combined in the same course of conduct, a sufficiently important governmental interest in regulating the nonspeech element can justify incidental limitations on First Amendment freedoms. To characterize the quality of the governmental interest which must appear, the Court has employed a variety of descriptive terms: compelling; substantial; subordinating; paramount; cogent; strong. Whatever imprecision inheres in these terms, we think it clear that a government regulation is sufficiently justified if it is within the constitutional power of the government; if it furthers an important or substantial governmental interest; if the governmental interest is unrelated to the suppression of free expression; and if the incidental restriction on alleged First Amendment freedom is no greater than is essential to the furtherance of that interest. We find that the 1965 amendment to §12(b)(3) of the Universal Military Training and Service Act meets all of these requirements, and consequently that O'Brien can be constitutionally convicted for violating it.[35]

The Court also rejected the contention that the purpose of the legislation was specifically to punish expression. It invoked the "familiar principle of constitutional law that this Court will not strike down an otherwise constitutional statute on the basis of an alleged illicit legislative motive." [36]

The Supreme Court's decision in *O'Brien* is a serious setback for First Amendment theory. The Court makes no attempt to determine whether the conduct of burning a draft card is to be classified as "expression" or "action." Instead of looking at the whole course of conduct, and its relation to the system of freedom of expression, the Court stops after noting that the conduct may involve a "communicative element." It then proceeds to hold that in such a situation, when "speech" and "nonspeech" elements are combined in conduct, regula-

---

35. *United States v. O'Brien*, 391 U.S. 367, 376–377 (1968).

36. 391 U.S. at 383. Justice Douglas dissented on the ground that the Court should have considered the question whether "conscription is permissible in the absence of a declaration of war," a point not raised before in the case. Id. at 389. Justice Marshall did not participate.

tion of the "nonspeech" element is permissible, no matter what the effect on the speech element, so long as it "furthers an important or substantial governmental interest." What this novel analysis does is relegate the "expression" protected by the First Amendment to a "communicative element" and allow all other aspects of the conduct to be restricted or suppressed regardless of the impact on freedom of expression. On this theory, so long as the governmental regulation does not *directly* deal with the "communicative element," it may prohibit or control all other aspects of holding a meeting, marching or demonstrating, distributing literature, exhibiting a motion picture, publishing a newspaper, forming an association, and many other forms of "expression." The formula would also seem to imply that any "indirect" regulation of expression, such as a loyalty program, a legislative committee investigation, a disclosure requirement, and the like, would be upheld so long as the governmental interest involved were "important or substantial." This degree of protection for expression falls far short of even that afforded by the balancing test. The Court's view embodies an artificial, sterile concept of the expression protected by the First Amendment, one wholly incapable of meeting the needs of a modern system of freedom of expression.

The burning of a draft card is, of course, conduct that involves both communication and physical acts. Yet it seems quite clear that the predominant element in such conduct is expression (opposition to the draft) rather than action (destruction of a piece of cardboard). The registrant is not concerned with secret or inadvertent burning of his draft card, involving no communication with other persons. The main feature, for him, is the public nature of the burning, through which he expresses to the community his ideas and feelings about the war and the draft.

Moreover, it is apparent that governmental control was directed at prohibiting the expression in draft card burning, not at punishing the action. The destruction of a small bit of paper, the action element involved, is not normally punished by five years in prison. A different problem is presented by the fact that the action results in a failure of the registrant to have a card in his possession and hence interferes with the operation of the draft system. This problem of insuring the "continuing availability of issued certificates" can be and is handled by a different form of legislation. As noted above, the Selective Service regulations already made it a criminal offense for a registrant not to have a draft card in his possession. Congress might have wished to incorporate that prohibition in a formal statute, but it did not do so. Certainly it would make no sense for Congress to prohibit loss of possession *by reason of burning,* rather than loss of possession generally. What Congress did, in short, was simply to punish a form of expressing opposition to the draft; the effect of the amendment in improving the operation of the draft system was trivial and superfluous.

This conclusion is confirmed by, though it need not rest upon, the legislative history of the 1965 amendment. The Supreme Court argued that legislative motive cannot be considered if the legislation is valid on its face. Yet the only consideration necessary is that ordinarily given to a problem of statutory interpretation. Moreover, the Court itself recognizes an exception to its rule where, as in determining whether a statute is designed to impose a penalty, "the very nature of the constitutional question requires an inquiry into legislative purpose." Surely the exception applies here. When a statute deals with conduct containing elements of both expression and action, the First Amendment issue turns in part upon the question whether the legislation is directed at the expression or the action sector of the conduct. If one examines the legislative history here it is difficult to avoid the conclusion that the obvious and indeed acknowledged purpose was, as the Senate Committee on Armed Services explained, to punish "the defiant destruction and mutilation of draft cards by dissident persons who disapprove of national policy." [37]

Once we come to the conclusion that O'Brien's conduct in burning his draft card must be classified as "expression," there remains the question as to what test of the First Amendment should be applied in determining whether that expression is protected by the First Amendment. The issue is roughly the same as if O'Brien had made a speech denouncing the Vietnam war and making plain that he did not intend to be inducted. The clear and present danger test, the incitement test, or the balancing test might be invoked, and either result could be reached under any of these formulas. The full protection theory, on

37. 391 U.S. at 383, 387. Extracts from the committee reports are printed as an appendix to the Court's opinion. For the debate, see 111 *Cong. Rec.* 19, 746, 19, 871, 20, 433 (1965). The Court's contention that Congress was also concerned with "the smooth functioning of the Selective Service System" appears, at least to this reader of the record, unsupportable. Moreover, it is interesting to compare the Court's refusal to examine legislative motive in *O'Brien* with its decision a few months later in *Epperson v. Arkansas* holding invalid the Arkansas anti-evolution law on the ground that "the motivation for the law" was "to suppress the teaching of a theory" because of religious objections. 393 U.S. 97, 109 (1968). For further discussion of the legislative motive issue, see Alfange, *op. cit. supra* note 33, pp. 27–38.

the other hand, could lead to only one conclusion—that O'Brien's expression was protected and the 1965 amendment invalid. This outcome is consistent with the Supreme Court's decision in the Julian Bond case. It is fully justified by all the considerations of theory, practice, and experience previously discussed.[38]

The same analysis applies to the conduct of turning in draft cards. This method of expressing opposition to the war came to be preferred to draft card burning, which receded into the background. Some thousands of registrants returned their draft cards to Selective Service boards, deposited them with the Department of Justice, or otherwise surrendered them to some government official. In making this gesture the quality of expression clearly prevails over the element of action. The conduct is hardly different from writing a letter of protest. Actually, the turning in of draft cards is not, as such, a violation of any express provision of any existing statute or regulation. It might, of course, be taken as offending the prohibition in Section 462(a) against hindering or interfering with the administration of the Selective Service Act. In addition, some draft boards might use it as the basis for ordering immediate induction of the registrant. But, the conduct being expression, such direct sanctions would plainly violate the First Amendment.

The turning in of a draft card does, however, give rise to collateral problems. The registrant is then in the position of not having a draft card in his possession, a violation of the Selective Service regulations. Some draft boards have applied the sanction of reclassifying the registrant or accelerating his induction on the ground that he was "delinquent" under the regulations. The separation of expression and action under these circumstances involves some difficulties, but they are not insuperable. The failure to keep a draft card in one's possession would seem to be conduct classifiable as action, not expression. Though the initial destruction or return of the card may have been expression protected by the First Amendment, the consequent failure to carry the draft card is conduct in which the action (or inaction) element predominates. The requirement of carrying identification is not an uncommon form of regulation. Refusal to comply with such a regulation on grounds of conscience or belief, although expression, is no different

38. For other discussion of the draft card burning problem, see Lawrence R. Velvel, "Freedom of Speech and the Draft Card Burning Cases," *Kansas Law Review*, Vol. 16 (1968), p. 149; Note, *op. cit. supra* note 31; Alfange, *op. cit. supra* note 33; Louis Henkin, "Foreword: On Drawing Lines, The Supreme Court 1967 Term," *Harvard Law Review*, Vol. 82 (1968), pp. 63, 76–82.

from refusal to conform to the laws requiring automobile drivers to carry licenses. The total context, particularly the nature of the government's interest in relation to the expressive qualities that have come to be attached to the conduct, differentiate the burning or turning in of draft cards from a refusal to have them in one's possession.

As action, the failure to have a draft card would not be protected by the First Amendment and would be subject to appropriate sanction. But such sanction would have to be directed to the action, not to any accompanying expression. Thus no person could be reclassified after turning in his draft card except insofar as other persons, willfully failing to have draft cards in their possession for other reasons, are treated in the same way. Likewise no criminal punishment could be inflicted greater or different from that customarily employed to maintain effective operation of the draft system through requiring registrants to carry draft cards. Thus, the element of expression in the conduct could not be penalized by the application of a sanction not otherwise invoked or by any aggravation of the punishment.[39]

Laws prohibiting the burning or other desecration of the flag involve similar issues. All States, as well as the District of Columbia, have had statutes of this type for some time, and in 1968 Congress enacted a Federal law. These statutes are obviously supported by strong emotions and have never been held to violate constitutional rights. But their validity under the First Amendment is questionable if the conduct is intended as a symbolic gesture of defiance or opposition.[40]

In 1969 the Supreme Court had an opportunity to pass on the validity of flag desecration statutes, but turned aside. *Street v. New York* involved a conviction under a New York statute which makes it a misdemeanor "publicly [to] mutilate, deface, defile, or defy, trample upon, or cast contempt upon either by words or act [any flag of the United States]." Sidney Street, a Negro bus driver, was sitting in his Brooklyn apartment on the afternoon of June 6, 1966, when he heard

39. This was the position of the Court of Appeals for the First Circuit in *O'Brien v. United States*, 376 F.2d at 541–542. But *cf. Wills v. United States*, 384 F.2d 943 (9th Cir. 1967), cert. denied 392 U.S. 908 (1968); *United States v. Gutknecht*, 406 F.2d 494 (8th Cir. 1969) reversed 396 U.S. — (1970). The discussion above does not attempt to consider any of the due process, privacy, or other con-stitutional questions involved in the possession requirement. Nor does it deal with the question whether "delinquency" under the Selective Service Act can, as a matter of statutory interpretation, be penalized by ordering induction. See the *Gutknecht* case, *supra* and the *Oestereich* and *Breen* cases, cited in footnote 47.

40. The Federal statute is 82 Stat. 291, 18 U.S.C. §700.

on the radio that civil rights leader James Meredith had been shot by a sniper in Mississippi. Street got his American flag from a drawer and took it down to the street. He placed a newspaper on the sidewalk, lit the flag with a match, and when he could hold it no longer he laid it on the newspaper, taking care it did not touch the sidewalk. A crowd gathered and a policeman arrived. Street admitted to the policeman he had burned the flag and said, "If they let that happen to Meredith, we don't need an American flag." The Supreme Court reversed the conviction, five to four.[41]

Justice Harlan, writing for the majority, held it unnecessary to decide whether punishment of Street for burning the flag would violate the First Amendment. He found that the conviction might have rested solely on the words spoken by Street to the policeman, which could have constituted a violation of the New York statute by themselves. Applying an elaborate balancing test, in which he weighed four possible State interests, Justice Harlan concluded that the words uttered were protected by the First Amendment. Hence the conviction must be overturned. Chief Justice Warren and Justices Black, White, and Fortas dissented, all urging that the conviction was actually for the burning. Only Justice Fortas discussed the First Amendment issue in detail, but all the dissenters took the position that the burning was not expression protected by the First Amendment.

Under the expression-action analysis here proposed it is hard to avoid the conclusion that the element of expression was the essential feature in Street's conduct, and the element at which punishment was directed. The action element—consisting of making the fire in the street—was incidental to the expression. It is possible to consider desecration of the flag as equivalent to "fighting words," likely to provoke an immediate breach of the peace, and therefore classifiable as action. But this seems something of a stretch. It is also possible to uphold the flag desecration statutes by applying the balancing test or the clear and present danger test. Yet ultimately it is difficult to avoid the conclusion that desecration of the flag, however obnoxious it may be to some of us, is realistically intended as expression and nothing else. It should therefore be treated as such. For those who may be shocked by this conclusion it is well to remember that loyalty to the flag, like loyalty to the country, cannot be coerced.[42]

41. *Street v. New York*, 394 U.S. 576 (1969). The statement of facts in the text is taken in part from the briefs.

42. For discussion of the flag desecration problem, written prior to the *Street* case, see Note, *op. cit. supra* note 31, pp. 1103–1105; Note, "Desecration of National Symbols as Protected Political Ex-

Certain other forms of protest against the war effort more clearly consist of conduct in which action predominates and which is therefore not protected by the First Amendment. Mass physical obstruction of draft boards, induction centers, military installations, or other places constitutes action, except insofar as the obstruction is an integral part of the right of assembly. Obstruction of troop movements by lying down in front of troop trains or blocking traffic on a city street falls within the same category. So also does the more unusual conduct of pouring blood over Selective Service files. To attempt to bring such forms of protest within the expression category would rob the distinction between expression and action of all meaning, and would make impossible any system of freedom of expression based upon full protection of expression.[43]

Action protest is often undertaken as a form of civil disobedience. This leads us to the question whether such civil disobedience is compatible with a system of freedom of expression. For present purposes civil disobedience may be defined as conduct which (1) is in violation of a valid (constitutional) law; (2) is undertaken on the basis of a moral principle held sufficient to overcome the normal obligation to comply with the law; (3) is nonviolent in nature; and (4) causes no direct injury to other persons. By definition, civil disobedience constitutes action, not protected expression.

On the face of it there is some conflict. Civil disobedience tends to undermine law and order, at least the law and order of the moment, which are necessary to the functioning of a system of freedom of expression. Civil disobedience attempts to achieve results through a kind of coercion or pressure, at a tense emotional level, whereas expression usually operates through more moderate means of persuasion. En-

pression," *Michigan Law Review,* Vol. 66 (1968), p. 1040. In *Tinker v. Des Moines Independent Community School District,* 393 U.S. 503 (1969), discussed in Chapter IX, the Supreme Court held that wearing black armbands in protest of the Vietnam war was "the type of symbolic act that is within the Free Speech Clause of the First Amendment." See also *United States v. Smith,* 414 F.2d 630 (5th Cir. 1969) cert. granted *sub nom. Schacht v. United States,* 396 U.S. 984 (1969).

43. On the extent to which physical obstruction is permissible as part of the right of assembly, see Chapter IX. For an account of a blood pouring incident see *The New York Times,* Oct. 28, 1967, at 5, col. 3. The participants were subsequently convicted of violating the Selective Service Act, two being sentenced to six years in prison and one to three years. *The New York Times,* May 25, 1968, at 1, col. 3. See *United States v. Berrigan,* 283 F. Supp. 336 (D. Md. 1968). A similar group of war protestors, who removed files from a Selective Service Board in Catonsville, Md., and burned them with napalm, were sentenced to two to three and a half years in prison. See *The New York Times,* Oct. 9–11, 1968, and Nov. 9, 1968.

forcement of the law against acts of civil disobedience may spill over into suppression of freedom of expression. In these and other ways there is a tension between these two means of political communication.

In the long run, however, there is no necessary incompatibility between a system of freedom of expression and a measured amount of civil disobedience. In some ways civil disobedience serves the same ends as freedom of expression. By calling attention to the problems that give rise to such drastic action, it forces reconsideration of the issues and promotes a better chance to reach consensus. By disclosing the intensity with which a position is held, it measures an important factor in the political process. By giving sharp warning of stress in society, it greatly increases the likelihood of achieving a satisfactory balance between stability and change. In short, acts of civil disobedience can supplement a system of free expression in rendering a democratic structure more responsive and more effective.

The principal difference is that civil disobedience is strong medicine. There is no such thing as too much freedom of expression in a free society. But there can be an excess of civil disobedience. An overdose may be fatal. Civil disobedience can be compatible with the First Amendment, as with other institutions of a democratic society, but its existence is always a signal of danger.

5. REMEDIES AGAINST HARASSMENT OF DISSENT IN WARTIME

It is apparent that, as a matter of constitutional theory, the First Amendment affords a substantial measure of protection to expression directed against a war effort. The problem remains, however, of realizing those rights in practice amid the stresses of an actual war. It is important to keep in mind, therefore, the nature of the harassment that can beset a system of freedom of expression in wartime and the possible role of the courts in affording legal remedies.

During the Vietnam conflict expression in opposition to the war was widespread, increasingly frequent, and on the whole accepted as a constitutional right. But various forms of harassment appeared at certain points throughout the system. Some of this came from high Federal officials. President Johnson on several occasions acknowledged the right of citizens to dissent on war issues, but he also let it be known that he "was dismayed by the demonstrations and has given his full endorsement to the Justice Department's investigation of possible Communist infiltration of the antidraft movement," and, on another occasion, that the Federal Bureau of Investigation "was keeping an eye on 'antiwar activity.' " Attorney General Katzenbach told a news conference that "the Justice Department [has] started a national investigation of groups behind the antidraft movement." He added, "There are some Communists involved in it. . . . We may very well have some prosecutions." Six months later the national secretary of the Students for a Democratic Society asserted that there "seems to be a national investigation" of his organization by the F.B.I. There was also evidence that opposition to the Vietnam war was being taken as unfavorable evidence in loyalty-security investigations.[44]

Similar attacks upon wartime dissent came also from the legislative branch. Many individual legislators, on and off the floor of Congress, denounced opposition to the war as disloyal conduct. In 1965 the Senate Internal Security Subcommittee made public a staff report which attacked a number of individuals as having "persistent records of Communist sympathies and/or of association with known Communists and known Communist movement and front organizations," and asserted that the antiwar demonstrations had "clearly passed . . . into the hands of Communists and extremist elements." No opportunity was given the named individuals to reply. In March 1967 the House Committee on Un-American Activities issued a report on a protest scheduled for April known as Vietnam Week, the theme of which was: "The real objective of Vietnam Week is not the expression of honest dissent to promote the best interest of the American people and their Government, but to do injury and damage to the United States and to give aid and comfort to its enemies." [45]

44. The statements by President Johnson appear in *The New York Times*, Oct. 19, 1965, p. 1, col. 8, and April 16, 1967, p. 1, col. 1; that of Attorney General Katzenbach in *The New York Times*, Oct. 18, 1965, p. 1, col. 6; and that of the S.D.S. secretary in *The New York Times*, April 19, 1966, p. 6, col. 1. On the loyalty-security investigations, see *American Civil Liberties Union Bulletin* No. 2259, Mar. 7, 1966.

45. See, e.g., *The New York Times*, May 6, 1967, p. 1, col. 6; *Hearings on H.R. 271 Before Subcommittee No. 4 of the House Committee on the Judiciary*, 90th Cong., 1st Sess. (1967); *Senate Committee on the Judiciary, Subcommittee to Investigate the Administration of the Internal Security Act and Other Internal Security Laws, the Anti-Vietnam Agitation and the Teach-In Movement: The Problem of Communist Infiltration and Exploitation*, S. Doc. No. 82, 89th Cong., 1st Sess. 45, XV (1965); House Committee on Un-American Activities, *Communist Origin and Manipulation of Vietnam Week* (April 8–15, 1967), H.R. Doc. No. 186, 90th Cong., 1st Sess. 2 (1967).

Other forms of harassment included police interference with the right of assembly and incidents of police brutality, as well as police photographing of persons participating in peaceful antiwar marches, vigils, and other demonstrations. Attempts by draft boards to accelerate the induction of antiwar demonstrators also occurred. Summarizing the situation in June 1967, the American Civil Liberties Union stated:

> The random collection of incidents attached to this statement . . . illustrate[s] the steadily accelerating strains on unpopular expression. . . . Such instances show that dissent is now the object of official and private intimidation and harassment. Unless these, and others, are vigorously and courageously opposed, unless the right and importance of dissent are re-affirmed and defended, the nation could slip back into a new era of McCarthyism with its dangers to a free society—fear, conformity and sterility.[46]

An effective system of freedom of expression ought to provide some remedy for these interferences and harassments. Unfortunately there is no ready solution. Judicial relief, at least at the present time, is often unavailable or inadequate. Thus, there are serious obstacles to imposing legal restraints on governmental expression; under most circumstances statements of public officials or warnings of investigation are not subject to judicial redress. Nor is it possible to obtain court review of most activities of legislative committees, apart from citations for contempt, or of many aspects of the loyalty-security program. In other situations the issues can be brought to the courts, as in the case of legislative contempts or draft board reclassifications, but only at a stage in the proceedings when much damage has already been done and when failure to prevail in court results in criminal punishment. In still other situations, such as interference with the right of assembly, judicial relief is theoretically possible, but often cumbersome, time-consuming, or ineffective.

There is a vital need to devise methods for improving judicial performance in these areas. Some progress is being made. When a New York draft board reclassified and sought to compel immediate induction of two students who had taken part in an antiwar demonstration, suit was brought to enjoin the draft board from proceeding. The complaint was dismissed by the District Court, which followed the stand-

46. American Civil Liberties Union, *The Vietnam War and the Status of Dissent*, June 4, 1967. See also Finman and Macaulay, *op. cit. supra* note 26, pp. 661–677.

ard rule that a draft board classification may be attacked only in a subsequent criminal prosecution for refusing induction. The Court of Appeals reversed, carving out an exception to the usual rule if "the threat to First Amendment rights is of such immediate and irreparable consequence not simply to these students but to others as to require prompt action by the courts to avoid an erosion of these precious constitutional rights." This is an example of the way in which the judicial system can be developed to provide more effective protection to the system of freedom of expression. But a major challenge remains. The issues are complex and largely unexplored.[47]

In the end it must be recognized, however, that the judicial structure is not capable, by itself, of fully protecting in practice the theoretical rights guaranteed under our system of freedom of expression. Full realization of those rights must depend ultimately upon attitudes ingrained in the public mind and support extended by the body politic as a whole.

B. Communication with Foreign Countries

The social interest in external security poses certain problems for a system of freedom of expression insofar as participants in that system engage in communication with foreign countries. Some new elements enter the picture at this point. Principally they are that the inhabitants of another nation are not part of our society; they are not subject to our laws, institutions, customs or loyalties; and they do not share the rights or obligations of our citizens. Similar considerations apply to foreign governments. Our own system of free expression may have to take these factors into account under some circumstances. The issues can arise either in connection with communication from a foreign so-

---

47. *Wolff v. Local Board No. 16*, 372 F.2d 817, 820 (2d Cir. 1967). See *Oestereich v. Selective Service System Local Board No. 11*, 393 U.S. 233 (1968), in which the Supreme Court allowed judicial review prior to prosecution in a case where the draft board deprived a registrant of an exemption prescribed by statute, for the reason that he had turned in his draft card. But compare *Clark v. Gabriel*, 393 U.S. 256 (1968). The *Oestereich* rule was extended to a student deferment case in *Breen v. Selective Service Board No. 16*, 396 U.S. — (1970). See also Robert M. O'Neil, "Review of Selective Service Reclassifications," *George Washington Law Review*, Vol. 37 (1969), p. 536; and *National Student Association v. Hershey*, 412 F.2d 1103 (D.C. Cir. 1969).

ciety to us, communication from us to a foreign society, or travel between the societies for purposes of communication.

With respect to communication addressed to us from foreign sources, the beginning proposition is that the First Amendment guarantees the right to hear as well as to speak. Hence all communication emanating from any quarter, domestic or foreign, must be given the protection of the First Amendment. This principle constitutes the basic premise of *Lamont v. Postmaster General* and indeed has not been questioned. It follows, also, that ideological influence from foreign sources is not a valid ground upon which to base regulation of expression in this country. The decision in *Communist Party v. Subversive Activities Control Board,* which seems to indicate otherwise, cannot be reconciled with the theory of the First Amendment. There may, however, be some small area in which government can properly control the relations between a foreign government and our system of expression. The factors mentioned above would, for instance, justify some control of monetary subsidies by a foreign government to influence public opinion in the United States. And disclosure regulations could be more widely applied to communication from foreign countries since they would not hamper freedom of expression within our system.[48]

Concerning communication from our system to a foreign country, the starting point again is that all such expression is protected by the First Amendment. There has indeed been little effort to control the flow in this direction. The only legislation that comes to mind is the Logan Act, enacted in 1799. This statute provides that "correspondence or intercourse with any foreign government or any officer or agent thereof, in relation to any disputes or controversies with the United States, or to defeat the measures of the United States," constitutes a criminal offense. The statute, enacted under the same influences as the Alien and Sedition Acts, would almost certainly be declared unconstitutional today. The government can prevent an American citizen from posing as a United States official or purporting to conduct official negotiations, but it cannot prevent him from expressing his views to agents of a foreign government. It is significant that, in spite of communication which occurs every day between private American citizens and foreign officials, no prosecution has ever

---

48. *Lamont v. Postmaster General,* 381 U.S. 301 (1965); *Communist Party v. Subversive Activities Control Board,* 367 U.S. 1 (1961); both are discussed in Chapter V.

been instituted under the Logan Act. The one area where governmental control is justified is that of espionage. For reasons mentioned earlier, however, espionage is not in any event part of a system of free expression.[49]

As to travel between countries, such conduct would probably have to be classified as "action" rather than "expression." It is true that foreign travel may be undertaken for purposes of communication, and it may affect expression by enlarging the traveler's understanding or sensibilities. Taken on the whole, however, foreign travel primarily consists of action-type conduct and would not seem entitled to the same kind of protection as is extended to "expression." Constitutional limitations upon governmental control over travel must therefore rest, as a primary matter, upon the fact that it is a "liberty" under the Fifth and Fourteenth Amendments rather than "expression" under the First.

This is not to say that the First Amendment has no relation whatever to the regulation of foreign travel. There are clearly First Amendment overtones to foreign travel that would influence the manner in which the courts apply doctrines of vagueness or overbreadth. More significantly, a restriction upon the foreign travel of persons who had engaged in certain forms of expression would, of course, at once raise crucial First Amendment questions. As a matter of fact most of the constitutional issues involving foreign travel have arisen in this form. They are discussed in Chapter VI.

The area where our system of freedom of expression impinges upon foreign systems has not thus far given rise to much controversy. The situation could change and unexpected problems develop. But they are not presently foreseeable.

49. The Logan Act is now codified in 18 U.S.C. §953.

V

Internal Security: Sedition Laws

The social interest in national security extends not only to matters of external security but to equally vital issues of internal security. Before we examine the relations between a system of freedom of expression and the various methods of fulfilling that social interest in internal security certain general observations should be made.

The social interest in internal security may be described as the interest in maintaining national law and order. It is to be differentiated, for present purposes, from the social interest in maintaining local law and order. Questions of the latter type arise if the threat to order is geographically restricted and relatively isolated. So far as freedom of expression is involved, such questions come up in connection with maintaining order at meetings, parades, demonstrations, and the like, or in securing adherence by individuals to the ordinary laws of the community. Problems of internal security, again as they relate to freedom of expression, involve anticipated dangers that affect the country on a broader scale, usually arise out of organizational activities, and may involve a whole political or social movement. These two aspects of securing law and order in a society cannot, of course, be kept fully apart. But the problems relating to freedom of expression are somewhat different and hence the two areas are dealt with separately.

Confining our attention to internal security, then, it is imperative to keep firmly in mind exactly what, in the context of a democratic society, that social interest comprises. Essentially it is protection of the structure of government or the major institutions of society against change by force or violence, that is to say, by undemocratic methods. No problem for internal security is presented in a change of the form of government or of other social institutions through lawful, democratic methods. The threat to internal security may arise from differing forms of force or violence, including armed conflict, wide-scale rioting, sabotage, or guerrilla warfare. It may occur in time of war, taking the form of fifth column activities, or in times of peace or economic crisis. The dividing line between undemocratic and democratic methods may at times be obscure or controverted; thus whether a general strike or other form of pressure falls within or without the category of "force" may be uncertain. It is not necessary to draw that line with precision at this point. The crucial factor is that the interest in internal security is concerned with protecting the mechanisms of the democratic process against alteration by methods that can loosely be called "force or violence," not with forestalling decisions that emanate from the democratic process, including decisions respecting the basic form of government or other social institutions.

Our concern is to what extent, if any, this interest in internal security can be effectuated, within the framework of the First Amendment, through restrictions upon expression. The major kinds of control over expression usually justified in the name of internal security are (1) direct prohibition of expression through laws such as the Smith Act, the Internal Security Act, and the Communist Control Act; (2) indirect restrictions in the form of imposing qualifications upon the obtaining of benefits or holding of positions; (3) the loyalty-security program; and (4) the operation of legislative investigating committees. The first category, loosely called sedition laws, is considered in this chapter, the remaining categories in the following chapters.

A. Background of the Sedition Laws

Our sedition laws come from an English background in which the concept of internal security and the role of free expression were totally unlike those prevailing in our society today. In sixteenth-century England all opposition to the government in power was sternly suppressed through treason and various types of sedition laws. Throughout the seventeenth and eighteenth centuries a gradual expansion of popular participation in the political process and a corresponding increase in the protection afforded to freedom of expression took place. Yet even toward the end of the eighteenth century, just before and during the writing of our Constitution, the English law of seditious libel prohibited any "unjustified" criticism of the government, its policies, or officials. This was enforced against persons who expressed opinions that were felt to be a threat to the government, such as John Wilkes and the publishers of the Letters of Junius. Nevertheless, ever since the speech of John Milton in the Long Parliament opposing continuation of the censorship laws, there had been a growing argument that the rights of citizens should include a far broader scope for free expression. This had repercussions in the law. In 1792 Fox's Libel Act modified the existing English law of seditious libel by providing that truth would be a defense and that the jury rather than the judge had the power to determine whether the utterance constituted seditious libel.[1]

The First Amendment was drawn up and ratified during this period of transition. Whether the framers intended to abolish outright the English law of seditious libel is a matter of historical dispute. Certainly the First Amendment was adopted by men who had just achieved a successful revolution against autocratic power, who were attempting to establish a popular form of government, and who were aware of the uses to which the law of seditious libel could be put. They had been careful in drafting the treason provision to make sure that expression alone could not be punished under the doctrine of treason. In any event history has since resolved the issue.[2]

Whatever ambiguity there may have been about the meaning of the First Amendment at the time of adoption, the passage of the Alien and Sedition Acts of 1798 brought the matter to a head. Those laws were an attempt by the Federalist administration, then in power, to

1. On the English law background see James F. Stephen, *A History of the Criminal Law of England* (London, Macmillan & Co., 1883), Vol. II, ch. XXIV; Zechariah Chafee, Jr., *Free Speech in the United States* (Cambridge, Harvard University Press, 1941), ch. XIII; Leonard W. Levy, *Legacy of Suppression* (Cambridge, Harvard University Press, 1960); and material collected in Thomas I. Emerson, David Haber, and Norman Dorsen, *Political and Civil Rights in the United States* (Boston, Little, Brown & Co., 3d ed. 1967), pp. 29–35 (hereafter cited in this chapter as *Political and Civil Rights in the United States*).

2. The constitutional provision on treason is discussed in Chapter IV. On the dispute over the original meaning of the First Amendment see Chafee and Levy, *op. cit. supra* note 1. For other material dealing with the adoption of the First Amendment see *Political and Civil Rights in the United States,* pp. 34–35.

eliminate its Republican opposition by means of seditious libel laws. The Sedition Act made it a criminal offense, punishable by a fine up to $2000 or imprisonment up to two years, for any person to

> write, print, utter or publish, or . . . knowingly and willingly assist or aid in writing, printing, uttering or publishing any false, scandalous and malicious writing or writings against the government of the United States, or either house of the Congress of the United States, or the President of the United States, with intent to defame the said government, or either house of the said Congress, or the said President, or to bring them, or either of them, into contempt or disrepute; or to excite against them, or either or any of them, the hatred of the good people of the United States, or to stir up sedition within the United States.

There were at least twenty-five arrests and fifteen indictments under the Act, ranging over every State where Republican strength was substantial. Prosecutions were brought against the editors of the four leading Republican newspapers and against three of the more outspoken Republican officeholders.[3]

The debates in Congress prior to enactment of the Alien and Sedition Acts, the arguments in the Federal courts where prosecutions were brought, and the general controversy that swirled around the legislation, forced full consideration of the constitutional issues. No case reached the Supreme Court, a state of affairs extremely unlikely today. But the Act was sustained by the lower Federal courts, including three Supreme Court justices sitting on circuit. The opposition argument was presented most notably by Jefferson and Madison in the Kentucky and Virginia Resolutions and in the Virginia Report of 1799. There was no final decision while the Sedition Law remained in effect. But subsequent events made the answer clear.

The Federalists were defeated in the election of 1800. The Sedition Act expired the day before Jefferson was inaugurated President in 1801 and was not renewed. No similar legislation was ever again enacted. Finally, in 1964, the Supreme Court officially declared that the Sedition Act had violated "the central meaning of the First Amendment." [4]

It is thus now manifest that the social interest in internal security does not entitle the government to restrict expression sharply critical

3. 1 Stat. 596 (1798). See James M. Smith, *Freedom's Fetters* (Ithaca, Cornell University Press, 1956); John C. Miller, *Crisis in Freedom* (Boston, Little, Brown & Co., 1951); *Political and Civil Rights in the United States,* pp. 37–39.

4. *New York Times v. Sullivan,* 376 U.S. 254, 273 (1964).

of the government or seeking to change government or the institutions of society through democratic procedures. Modern sedition laws have a somewhat different focus. In the first stage, through World War II, they sought to prohibit expression by individuals or organizations that advocated the use of force or violence in effecting political change. More recently they have attempted to punish or outlaw organizations alleged to be anti-democratic in character or subject to foreign control. This legislation raises some difficult and controversial issues. It becomes necessary not only to decide where the line is to be drawn between expression and action, and what degree of protection is to be afforded expression. It is also necessary to confront certain problems relating to the right of association. These include such questions as the extent to which an individual member of an association is to be held responsible for acts of the organization (the guilt by association problem); the extent to which conduct of the organization that is legal must be separated from other conduct that is illegal; and the impact of the fact that political movements are now international in scope.

The constitutional doctrines applicable to these various problems have evolved slowly and often inconsistently. In the light of Federal, State and local experience with specific sedition laws we attempt to reach some conclusions as to the role of these laws in a democratic society and the appropriate doctrines for resolving the constitutional issues under the First Amendment.

B. Sedition Laws Prior to the Smith Act Decisions

Modern sedition laws began to appear early in the twentieth century. The first was passed by New York in 1902, shortly after the assassination of President McKinley. This statute and others that soon followed were the outgrowth of fears aroused by the talk and tactics of militant groups such as the anarchists and the Industrial Workers of the World. Further impetus was given to sedition laws by World War I and the fear of Bolshevism that developed in its wake. Between 1917 and 1921 two-thirds of the States enacted such laws. The first Federal peacetime sedition law after the Alien and Sedition Acts was not passed until 1940.[5]

5. For a collection of materials dealing with sedition laws prior to the Smith Act decisions see *Political and Civil Rights in the United States,* pp. 62, 85–101.

The State sedition statutes were of two general types: criminal anarchy laws, typified by the original New York statute involved in the *Gitlow* case; and criminal syndicalism laws, similar to the California statute dealt with in the *Whitney* case. There were other variations, such as the Oregon statute considered in the *De Jonge* case. They were all alike, however, in that they were directed against the advocacy of force and violence to effect political or social change.

The question of the validity of the sedition laws under the First Amendment reached the Supreme Court in the mid-nineteen-twenties. These cases, following shortly upon the Espionage Act cases, constituted the second main group of decisions in the initial development of First Amendment doctrine. As in the war cases, the Supreme Court was groping toward an adequate theory of the First Amendment and much of what was then decided has long been superseded.

The first such decision of the Supreme Court was rendered in *Gitlow v. New York*. The main provisions of the New York Criminal Anarchy statute declared that any person was guilty of a felony who "[b]y word of mouth or writing advocates, advises or teaches the duty, necessity or propriety of overthrowing or overturning organized government by force or violence, or by assassination of the executive head or of any of the executive officials of government, or by any unlawful means." The chief defendant in the case was Benjamin Gitlow, then a member of the National Council of the Left Wing Section of the Socialist Party, a forerunner of the Communist Party. Gitlow and three associates were charged with violation of the statute in publishing a "Left Wing Manifesto" which is described in Justice Sanford's opinion as follows:

> Coupled with a review of the rise of Socialism [the Manifesto] condemned the dominant "moderate Socialism" for its recognition of the necessity of the democratic parliamentary state; repudiated its policy of introducing Socialism by legislative measures; and advocated, in plain and unequivocal language, the necessity of accomplishing the "Communist Revolution" by a militant and "revolutionary Socialism," based on "the class struggle" and mobilizing the "power of the proletariat in action," through mass industrial revolts developing into mass political strikes and "revolutionary mass action," for the purpose of conquering and destroying the parliamentary state and establishing in its place, through a "revolutionary dictatorship of the proletariat," the system of Communist Socialism. The then recent strikes in Seattle and Winnipeg were cited as instances of a development already verging on revolution-

ary action and suggestive of proletarian dictatorship, in which the strike-workers were "trying to usurp the functions of municipal government"; and revolutionary Socialism, it was urged, must use these mass industrial revolts to broaden the strike, make it general and militant, and develop it into mass political strikes and revolutionary mass action for the annihilation of the parliamentary state.[6]

About sixteen thousand copies of the manifesto were distributed. There was "no evidence of any effect resulting from the publication and circulation of the Manifesto." The Supreme Court, affirming the conviction, developed three important points of doctrine.[7]

The first point was briefly stated and passed almost unnoticed, but it turned out to be the most lasting and significant aspect of the decision. The Court assumed that "freedom of speech and of the press—which are protected by the First Amendment from abridgment by Congress—are among the fundamental personal rights and 'liberties' protected by the due process clause of the Fourteenth Amendment from impairment by the States." This tentative incorporation of the First Amendment in the Fourteenth Amendment was accepted in subsequent decisions and moved from dictum to holding in *Fiske v. Kansas*, the first case to uphold a defendant's claim to protection of the First Amendment. The somewhat casual promulgation of this doctrine in *Gitlow* was all the more surprising in that the Court had stated only three years before in *Prudential Insurance Co. v. Cheek* that the Fourteenth Amendment imposed no restrictions on the States with regard to freedom of speech. In any event the far-reaching proposition that the First Amendment applies to the States through the Fourteenth took form in *Gitlow* and has not been seriously challenged since.[8]

The second doctrinal contribution of the *Gitlow* case was more short-lived. It concerned the basic test for interpretation of the First Amendment. The Court began by saying that the First Amendment "does not confer an absolute right to speak or publish, without responsibility, whatever one may choose." It also rejected the clear and present danger test, which had been accepted in the war cases. That test was suitable, it said, only if the statutory prohibition was couched in

6. *Gitlow v. New York,* 268 U.S. 652, 656–659 (1925).

7. The quotation is from 268 U.S. at 656.

8. 268 U.S. at 666; *Fiske v. Kansas,* 274 U.S. 380 (1927); *Prudential Insurance Co. v. Cheek,* 259 U.S. 530, 543 (1922). The position that the Fourteenth Amendment incorporates the First has been questioned only by Justice Jackson (see *Beauharnais v. Illinois,* 343 U.S. 250, 287–295 [1952]), and Justice Harlan (see *Roth v. United States,* 354 U.S. 476, 501–503 [1957]). For citation of material discussing the issue, see *Political and Civil Rights in the United States,* p. 95.

general (non-speech) terms and the issue was whether certain speech violated the general prohibition. But "where the legislative body itself has previously determined the danger of substantive evil arising from utterances of a specific character," *i.e.*, where the statute is framed in terms of prohibiting certain kinds of speech, the clear and present danger test has no application. The test that the Court thought should be utilized is not entirely clear. It seemed to agree that certain areas would be protected by the First Amendment, namely "utterance or publication of abstract 'doctrine' or academic discussion having no quality of incitement to any concrete action." But the broad principle was laid down that "a State in the exercise of its police power may punish those who abuse this freedom by utterances inimical to the public welfare, tending to corrupt public morals, incite to crime, or disturb the public peace." The Court added: "And, for yet more imperative reasons, a State may punish utterances endangering the foundations of organized government and threatening its overthrow by unlawful means." At times the Court employed qualifying phrases, such as "words . . . urging to action" and "language of direct incitement." But the basic temper of the opinion was that the government may "extinguish the spark without waiting until it has enkindled the flame or blazed into the conflagration." All in all the test has been appropriately described as the "bad tendency" test.[9]

A third matter of doctrine is also of major significance. The function of the Court in applying the First Amendment was held to be a limited one. In the first place the determination of the legislature that the statute was necessary to protect the public safety and welfare "must be given great weight. . . . Every presumption is to be indulged in favor of the validity of the statute." Secondly, once the Court had concluded that the statute was in general constitutional, then the only further question was whether the language used came within the statutory prohibition; "the question whether any specific utterance coming within the prohibited class is likely, in and of itself, to bring about the substantive evil, is not open to consideration." In other words the Court started with a strong presumption in favor of the legislation and then, having once found the statute constitutional, refused to look at the validity of any particular application of the legislation. This approach, of course, was quite different from the clear and present danger doctrine which required a determination that such a danger existed "in every case."[10]

9. 268 U.S. at 666, 671, 667, 669.   10. 268 U.S. at 668, 670.

Justice Holmes dissented in an opinion which Justice Brandeis joined. He rejected a test of "incitement," asserting, "Every idea is an incitement." Applying the clear and present danger test he found "no present danger of an attempt to overthrow the government." And in one memorable sentence, observing that the right of free speech included the right to express beliefs "in proletarian dictatorship," Justice Holmes opened up discussion for the first time in the Court on the fundamental purpose and import of the First Amendment.[11]

In *Whitney v. California* the Court dealt with some of the same issues and some new ones. The California Criminal Syndicalism Act defined criminal syndicalism as the doctrine of "advocating, teaching or aiding and abetting the commission of crime, sabotage . . . or unlawful acts of force and violence or unlawful methods of terrorism as a means of accomplishing change in industrial ownership or control, or effecting any political change." It provided that anyone who "organizes or assists in organizing, or is or knowingly becomes a member of, any organization" which advocates, aids, or abets criminal syndicalism is guilty of a felony. Miss Anita Whitney, a niece of former Supreme Court Justice Stephen J. Field, was indicted for violation of this Act. As a member of the Oakland branch of the Socialist Party, she had attended a convention in Chicago which resulted in the more militant group splitting off to form the Communist Labor Party. At its own meeting this Party adopted a platform which, *inter alia,* rejected parliamentary methods and, along the lines of Gitlow's "Left Wing Manifesto," urged "a revolutionary class struggle." Miss Whitney actively opposed this portion of the platform and voted against it. She nevertheless remained a member of the new party and attended local meetings. Miss Whitney was convicted and sentenced to imprisonment. The Supreme Court affirmed.[12]

Justice Sanford, writing for the majority, found the case no different from *Gitlow.* The *Whitney* case, however, posed a further question of great importance: under what circumstances should an individual member of an organization be held responsible for the conduct of the organization? This was especially in issue here because Miss Whitney

---

11. 268 U.S. at 673. The full quotation from Justice Holmes on "proletarian dictatorship" is given in Chapter III. Benjamin Gitlow and his associates served three years in prison, at the end of which time they were pardoned by Governor Alfred E. Smith. Subsequently Gitlow withdrew from the Communist movement and recanted. The story is told in his book, *I Confess* (E. P. Dutton & Co., 1940).

12. *Whitney v. California,* 274 U.S. 357 (1927).

had actively fought against adoption of the statements for which she was convicted. The majority of the Court did not recognize the problem, Justice Sanford treating it as an ordinary matter of conspiracy. Justice Brandeis, in an opinion with which Justice Holmes concurred, pointed out that associational questions were raised but did not go further to explore or resolve them.

Justice Brandeis' opinion, which was for all practical purposes a dissent, did make a notable contribution to First Amendment theory. For the first time he explained in detail the justification for the clear and present danger test. He pointed out that "a State is, ordinarily, denied the power to prohibit dissemination of social, economic and political doctrine"; that "no danger flowing from speech can be deemed clear and present, unless the incidence of the evil apprehended is so imminent that it may befall before there is opportunity for full discussion"; and that "[o]nly an emergency can justify repression." He also added a new dimension to the clear and present danger test, as it had existed up to then, by declaring that even imminent danger could not justify restriction of speech "unless the evil apprehended is relatively serious." Application of the test would therefore require not only a judgment as to the nearness of the danger emanating from the speech, but also as to the gravity of the substantive evil that the legislature was attempting to prevent.[13]

In reaching these conclusions Justice Brandeis explored the foundations of the First Amendment in a passage that merits quotation at length:

> Those who won our independence believed that the final end of the State was to make men free to develop their faculties; and that in its government the deliberative forces should prevail over the arbitrary. They valued liberty both as an end and as a means. They believed liberty to be the secret of happiness and courage to be the secret of liberty. They believed that freedom to think as you will and to speak as you think are means indispensable to the discovery and spread of political truth; that without free speech and assembly discussion would be futile; that, with them, discussion affords ordinarily adequate protection against the dissemination of noxious doctrine; that the greatest menace to freedom is an inert people; that public discussion is a political duty; and that this should be a fundamental principle of the American government. They recognized the risks to which all human institutions are subject. But they knew that order cannot be secured

13. 274 U.S. at 374, 377.

merely through fear of punishment for its infraction; that it is hazardous to discourage thought, hope and imagination; that fear breeds repression; that repression breeds hate; that hate menaces stable government; that the path of safety lies in the opportunity to discuss freely supposed grievances and proposed remedies; and that the fitting remedy for evil counsels is good ones. Believing in the power of reason as applied through public discussion, they eschewed silence coerced by law—the argument of force in its worst form. Recognizing the occasional tyrannies of governing majorities, they amended the Constitution so that free speech and assembly should be guaranteed.[14]

Two other cases involving State sedition laws were decided in this period. One simply followed *Gitlow* and *Whitney.* But the other, *Fiske v. Kansas,* was of more importance. In it, the Court reversed the conviction of an organizer for the Industrial Workers of the World under the Kansas Criminal Syndicalism law. The only evidence produced was the preamble to the I.W.W. constitution, which stated: "Between these two classes a struggle must go on until the workers of the World organize as a class, take possession of the earth, and the machinery of production and abolish the wage system." The Supreme Court held that the Kansas statute, as applied in this way, violated the Fourteenth Amendment. Fiske was the first claimant to First Amendment protection to succeed in the Supreme Court.[15]

This series of cases, like the decisions a few years earlier in the war cases, represents the first gropings of the Supreme Court for an adequate theory of the First Amendment. Like the war cases they reflected in part the intense feelings and latent fears of the war and its aftermath. The tone of the decisions also indicates a complete unawareness of the functions of freedom of expression in mediating between stability and change. Both the justices and the country seemed totally unprepared to face the urgent realities of the twentieth century, with which the war had brought them face to face. Nor was the Court willing to undertake the role of protecting individual liberty against majority encroachment, particularly when embodied in legislative enactment. In contrast with its attitude when economic liberties were at stake, the majority of the Court was content to relinquish any restraining powers over the legislature with respect to civil and political rights.

14. 274 U.S. at 375–376. Miss Whitney was pardoned by Governor Young of California and did not go to prison.

15. *Burns v. United States,* 274 U.S. 328 (1927); *Fiske v. Kansas,* 274 U.S. 380, 383 (1927). For materials discussing the line of cases beginning with *Gitlow,* see *Political and Civil Rights in the United States,* p. 95.

There was, moreover, a serious failure in legal analysis. Faced with the obvious difficulty that the First Amendment could not literally give immunity to every word uttered, the Court made no effort to formulate a solution in terms of the function of the First Amendment and the underlying distinction between speech and action upon which it was based. The clear and present danger test was originally a chance formulation. It was never really accepted by the majority. In no case was there a serious effort to determine as a factual matter whether a clear and present danger existed or not. It was abandoned in the *Gitlow* case in the very situation where it would presumably have been more useful. The test was put on firmer ground by Justice Brandeis. But it still contained a basic contradiction: the more effective the speech the less the protection given to it. Such an outcome could hardly form the legal foundations of a healthy system of freedom of expression. Finally, the Court had not even begun to consider the problem of formulating its rules in a way that would permit effective judicial administration.

Yet there was some progress. The Court had, almost inadvertently, made the First Amendment applicable to the States. Justices Holmes and Brandeis had commenced the task of exploring the foundations and implications of the First Amendment. The process of creating and refining legal doctrine had started. The times were changing. These factors came to bear fruit with the advent of the Hughes Court.

From 1930, when Charles Evans Hughes was appointed Chief Justice, until the end of World War II, the Supreme Court created a substantial body of law interpreting and expanding constitutional guarantees of individual rights. Many of these cases dealt with First Amendment issues, and several specifically with sedition laws. Of these, the decision in *De Jonge v. Oregon* is particularly important.

De Jonge was convicted under the Oregon Criminal Syndicalism law for violating a provision which made it an offense to preside at or assist in conducting a meeting of an organization that advocated "crime, physical violence, sabotage or any unlawful acts or methods as a means of accomplishing or effecting industrial or political change or revolution." De Jonge, a member of the Communist Party, had presided at a public meeting called by the Communist Party to protest police brutality in a current longshoremen's strike. The meeting was orderly and there had been no advocacy of criminal syndicalism. De Jonge had, however, "asked those present to do more work in obtaining members for the Communist Party." The Supreme Court assumed, for purposes of the decision, that the Communist Party had as its objective advocacy of criminal syndicalism within the meaning of the Oregon law. It held nevertheless that De Jonge "still enjoyed his personal right of free speech and to take part in any peaceable assembly having a lawful purpose, although called by that Party." The essence of Chief Justice Hughes' opinion for a unanimous Court is set forth in the following paragraph:

> These rights [under the First Amendment] may be abused by using speech or press or assembly in order to incite to violence and crime. The people through their legislatures may protect themselves against that abuse. But the legislative intervention can find constitutional justification only by dealing with the abuse. The rights themselves must not be curtailed. The greater the importance of safeguarding the community from incitements to the overthrow of our institutions by force and violence, the more imperative is the need to preserve inviolate the constitutional rights of free speech, free press and free assembly in order to maintain the opportunity for free political discussion, to the end that government may be responsible to the will of the people and that changes, if desired, may be obtained by peaceful means. Therein lies the security of the Republic, the very foundation of constitutional government.[16]

It will be noted that Chief Justice Hughes made no reference to the clear and present danger test. Rather, he assumed that "incitement" to violence would not be protected by the First Amendment and invoked the rule that the statute must be narrowly drawn to meet the particular abuse. This principle came to play a significant role in First Amendment cases. More importantly, however, Chief Justice Hughes laid the foundations for the building of doctrine applicable to problems of associational rights. He refused to attribute the admittedly illegal conduct of the association to one of its members. He made it clear that such illegal conduct on the part of the association had to be separated from the legal conduct for purposes of determining First Amendment rights. The decision also reiterated the proposition that expression not related to force and violence was protected by the First Amendment. It echoed Justices Holmes and Brandeis in looking to the fundamental purposes of the First Amendment as the key to its interpretation.

In other decisions of this period the Court invalidated part of the California red flag law, reversed the conviction of a Communist Party member under a Georgia insurrection statute, and strengthened its

16. *De Jonge v. Oregon,* 299 U.S. 353, 364–365 (1937).

"guilt by association" doctrine by refusing to attribute conduct of the Communist Party to an important member in a denaturalization proceeding. In cases arising in other areas of the First Amendment it established the clear and present danger test as the basic formula for determining the validity of First Amendment claims, confirmed the rule that the statute must be narrowly drawn, frequently invoked the rule against vagueness to invalidate legislation restrictive of expression, and came close to adopting a presumption in favor of the First Amendment. The trend was halted and partially reversed by a series of decisions following shortly upon the end of World War II. Among these decisions were those dealing with the Smith Act.[17]

C. The Smith Act

The Federal effort to deal with radical ideology through prohibiting advocacy of overthrow of the government by force or violence centers around the Smith Act. The Smith Act, named after Representative Howard W. Smith of Virginia, was passed as a rider to the Alien Registration bill in 1940. It received virtually no public attention at the time—Professor Chafee was unaware of its passage until several months later—and very little debate in Congress. Enactment of the bill reflected not so much a deliberate national determination that the measure was necessary to protect internal security as an unwillingness of members of Congress to vote against legislation directed at the Communist Party.[18]

The Smith Act was modeled on the New York Criminal Anarchy Act. The first section, which deals with utterances causing insubordination in the armed forces, has already been discussed. The remainder provides criminal penalties, now set at twenty years and $20,000, for anyone who

17. *Stromberg v. California,* 283 U.S. 359 (1931); *Herndon v. Lowry,* 301 U.S. 242 (1937); *Schneiderman v. United States,* 320 U.S. 118 (1943). The other cases referred to are noted and materials discussing them are collected in *Political and Civil Rights in the United States,* pp. 100–101.

18. The Smith Act as passed is set forth in 54 Stat. 670 (1940). For discussion of its background see Chafee, *op. cit. supra* note 1, pp. 44, 439–490. Other materials are collected in *Political and Civil Rights in the United States,* pp. 105–106.

(1) knowingly or willfully advocates, abets, advises, or teaches the duty, necessity, desirability, or propriety of overthrowing or destroying the government of the United States or the government of any State . . . or . . . any political subdivision therein, by force or violence, or by the assassination of any officer of any such government . . .

(2) organizes or helps or attempts to organize any society, group, or assembly of persons who teach, advocate, or encourage the overthrow or destruction of any such government by force or violence; or becomes or is a member of, or affiliates with, any such society, group, or assembly of persons, knowing the purposes thereof.[19]

The Smith Act was an anachronism at the time of its passage. The militant language and style of the left-wing groups of earlier decades, typified by the manifestos prosecuted in *Gitlow* and *Whitney*, had passed from the scene by the mid-nineteen-thirties. The Communist Party, against which the Smith Act was primarily directed, had by then entered its united front phase. Its constitution provided that any member who conspired to subvert or overthrow American democratic institutions was subject to expulsion. Whatever the problems of internal security may have been in 1940, they did not arise from any public advocacy that the government be overthrown by force or violence.[20]

The Smith Act was invoked twice during World War II, but not against the Communist Party. The first prosecution was against twenty-nine members of the Socialist Workers Party in Minneapolis, eighteen of whom were convicted in 1941 for conspiracy to violate both the insubordination and the advocacy provisions. There is evidence that the impetus for the prosecution came not so much from a threat to the internal security of the United States as from a desire by Attorney General Biddle to test the constitutionality of the Act. In any event the conviction was sustained by the Court of Appeals for the Eighth Circuit on straight *Gitlow* theory. The Supreme Court quietly denied certiorari. The other use of the Smith Act was the abortive prosecution of twenty-eight alleged pro-Nazis in the District of Columbia for conspiracy to violate the insubordination provisions.[21]

---

19. The Smith Act is now incorporated in 18 U.S.C. §2385.

20. See Irving Howe and Lewis Coser, *The American Communist Party* (New York, Frederick A. Praeger, 1962), ch. VIII; Thomas I. Emerson and David M. Helfeld, "Loyalty Among Government Employees," *Yale Law Journal*, Vol. 58 (1948), pp. 1, 61–62.

21. *Dunne v. United States*, 138 F.2d 137 (8th Cir. 1943), cert. denied 320 U.S. 790 (1943). For the circumstances surrounding the prosecution see Francis Biddle, *In Brief Authority* (Garden City, N.Y., Doubleday & Co., 1962), pp. 151–152.

I. THE *DENNIS* CASE

There was no prosecution of the Communist Party during the war. As long as this country was an ally of the Soviet Union in fighting the war such a prosecution would have been incongruous. Indeed, as a gesture of friendship to his capitalist allies, Stalin had dissolved the international organ of Communism, the Comintern, in 1943. The Communist Party of the United States had changed to more innocuous form as the Communist Political Association and toned down its revolutionary theories. In the years after the war, however, the political climate rapidly changed. The Cold War commenced, the Communist Political Association reverted to the Communist Party, and the postwar hysteria known as McCarthyism began to take hold. There was still a substantial question as to how the Smith Act could be applied to the Communist Party. In February 1948 Attorney General Tom Clark indicated to the House Committee on Un-American Activities that there was insufficient evidence on which to base a prosecution of Communist Party leaders under the Smith Act. In July 1948, however, the government obtained an indictment in New York against twelve members of the Central Committee of the Communist Party, the Party directorate, charging conspiracy to violate the advocacy and organizing provisions of the Smith Act. Whether coincidence or not, the indictment was returned a day after the opening of the convention of Henry Wallace's Progressive Party.[22]

After preliminary motions were disposed of, the trial on the merits lasted six months. It was accompanied by considerable publicity, much of which was devoted to a running controversy between Judge Medina and attorneys for the defendants. All the defendants were convicted. The Court of Appeals, in an opinion by Judge Learned Hand, affirmed the conviction. The Supreme Court granted certiorari, but limited its review to constitutional questions and eliminated from consideration any issue of the sufficiency of the evidence.[23]

22. For Attorney General Clark's testimony, see *Hearings before the House Committee on Un-American Activities*, Feb. 5, 1948, pp. 16–37. On the Progressive Party Convention see Curtis D. MacDougal, *Gideon's Army* (New York, Marzani and Munsell, 1965), ch. 22–25.

23. *United States v. Dennis*, 183 F.2d 201 (2d Cir. 1950). Only 11 of the 12 defendants went to trial, the case of William Z. Foster, Party Chairman, being severed because of ill health. On the controversy between Judge Medina and the attorneys see *United States v. Sacher*, 182 F.2d 416 (2d Cir. 1950), 343 U.S. 1 (1952); Fowler V. Harper and David Haber, "Lawyer Troubles in Political Trials," *Yale Law Journal*, Vol. 60 (1951), p. 1.

For a statement of the facts upon which the conviction was based it is necessary to look to the opinion of the Court of Appeals. Coming to the question "whether the evidence was sufficient to support the jury's verdict that the defendants were guilty of the crime charged in the indictment," Judge Hand concluded: "There was abundant evidence, if believed, to show that they were all engaged in an extensive concerted action to teach what indeed they do not disavow—the doctrines of Marxism-Leninism." He went on to say that these doctrines "were set forth in many pamphlets put in evidence at the trial"; that they included overthrow of the existing bourgeois government and establishment of the "dictatorship of the proletariat"; that this "transition period involves use of 'force and violence' . . . and although it is impossible to predict when a propitious occasion will arise, one certainly will arise"; and that, while the defendants contended that "the use of 'force and violence' is no part of their program" except as necessary to protect political power once obtained against counter-revolution, the jury was justified on the evidence in finding against them on this point. It is to be noted that the evidence did not include any conduct on the part of the defendants advocating any specific or immediate acts of force or violence. It was confined to teaching "the doctrines of Marxism-Leninism" as embodied in the various pamphlets and books published and disseminated by them.[24]

The decision of the Supreme Court was one of the most influential in the postwar period. Together with the *Douds* case, considered in the next chapter, it established the judicial framework and the atmosphere in which expression that was related, or could be related, to Communism was tested. In view of this impact it is significant, and somewhat astonishing, that the Court could not agree upon any one doctrine for determining the scope of First Amendment protection. There were five opinions and five theories, ranging over many aspects of First Amendment doctrine. It is instructive to look in some detail at these various efforts to develop a rationale.[25]

Chief Justice Vinson wrote an opinion which received more support than any other, Justices Reed, Burton and Minton joining in it. The doctrine enunciated in this prevailing, but not majority, opinion has come to be known as the Hand-Vinson formula. The trial judge in his charge to the jury had set forth three elements necessary to consti-

24. 183 F.2d at 206.
25. *Dennis v. United States*, 341 U.S. 494 (1951).

tute an offense under the Smith Act: (1) an intent to cause the over-throw of the government by force and violence as speedily as circum-stances would permit; (2) teaching or advocacy of a rule or principle of action, as distinct from utterance of abstract doctrine; (3) the use of language reasonably and ordinarily calculated to incite persons to such action. Although these requirements were put forth as interpreta-tions of the statute, they would presumably be held constitutional re-quirements as well. The trial judge ruled, further, that in order to sat-isfy the demands of the First Amendment it was necessary for the court to "find as a matter of law that there is sufficient danger of a substantive evil that the Congress has a right to prevent." In other words, in addition to finding intent, advocacy as a rule of action, and the language of incitement, there must be a finding of something equivalent to clear and present danger.[26]

The Vinson opinion followed a similar approach. After analysis of the cases it reached the view that, although the majority position in *Gitlow* and *Whitney* had never been "expressly overruled," there was little doubt that "subsequent opinions have inclined toward the Holmes-Brandeis rationale." The Court was therefore "squarely pre-sented with the application of the 'clear and present danger' test, and must decide what that phrase imports." After further consideration of the clear and present danger formula, the Vinson opinion concluded:

> Chief Judge Learned Hand, writing for the majority below, interpreted the phrase as follows: "In each case [courts] must ask whether the grav-ity of the evil, discounted by its improbability, justifies such invasion of free speech as is necessary to avoid the danger." 183 F.2d at 212. We adopt this statement of the rule. As articulated by Judge Hand, it is as succinct and inclusive as any other we might devise at this time. It takes into consideration those factors which we deem relevant, and relates their significances. More we cannot expect from words.[27]

On its face the Hand-Vinson formula seems to emasculate the clear and present danger test. It virtually abandoned the element of "clear," greatly subordinated the element of "present," and overem-phasized the element of the seriousness of the "evil." It has been gen-erally viewed as an abandonment of clear and present danger. Yet there is something to be said for Chief Justice Vinson's claim that the new formula took into consideration the relevant factors and related their significances. The clear and present concept has no application

26. 341 U.S. at 512.   27. 341 U.S. at 510.

unless it is first decided that the evil feared is sufficiently great or of the kind to warrant some control over speech; otherwise the test would permit governmental restrictions in every area, no matter what the "substantive evil." Hence it would seem proper to start with the "gravity of the evil." If a sufficiently grave evil is found, then the "clear and present danger" elements come into play as a limitation on the governmental power of restriction in particular circumstances. Essentially those elements consist of remoteness and probability. The idea could be expressed as "discounted by its improbability." In a sense, therefore, the Hand-Vinson formula is a reasonably accurate restatement of the clear and present danger test.

Chief Justice Vinson seems to be wrong, however, in saying, "More we cannot expect from words." The words employed actually take all the starch out of the clear and present danger test. Both formulations are exceedingly vague and could in most instances yield either result. But the Hand-Vinson formula is so pale in tone and so neutral in emphasis that it is hard to conceive of it as being used effectively to control governmental power over expression. Indeed, this may have been the very reason that Judge Hand devised it and Chief Justice Vinson embraced it. For most observers would have had a difficult time to find a "clear and present danger" of overthrow of the government arising from the teachings of the doctrines of Marxism-Leninism by the Communist Party in 1948 or 1951. But the Vinson opinion shows no hesitation in concluding that the "gravity of the evil, discounted by its improbability" justified the convictions.

The application of the Hand-Vinson formula to the actual situation in the *Dennis* case revealed a further serious drawback in the use of the clear and present danger doctrine. Under either version of the test, the answer reached involved a judgment based upon facts. The decision whether there is a sufficient danger must be resolved "in every case" after examination of all relevant circumstances bearing upon the particular situation before the Court. In the *Dennis* case the facts were numerous and complex, as the opinion of Justice Douglas demonstrated. But there were few facts in the record and the Vinson group was unwilling to treat the matter as a serious factual problem. Relying upon judicial notice it disposed of the question in one sentence:

> The formation by petitioners of such a highly organized conspiracy, with rigidly disciplined members subject to call when the leaders, these petitioners, felt that the time had come for action, coupled with the inflammable nature of world conditions, similar uprisings in other

countries, and the touch-and-go nature of our relations with countries with whom petitioners were in the very least ideologically attuned, convince us that their convictions were justified on this score.[28]

The Hand-Vinson formula seems plainly inadequate to mark the boundaries of First Amendment protection. It is not necessary, however, to pursue the matter further. The formula has never been used again.

Justice Frankfurter, in a concurring opinion, adopted the balancing test. He rejected the Hand-Vinson formula and the clear and present danger test as not including many factors essential to a sound decision, as "not a substitute for the weighing of values." His proposal was that the issue be resolved by a "careful weighing of conflicting interests." But it was not to be a neutral weighing, for the reconciliation of competing interests "is the business of legislatures, and the balance they strike is a judgment not to be displaced by ours, but to be respected unless outside the pale of fair judgment." Moreover, "not every kind of speech occupies the same position on the scale of values"; advocacy of force and violence "ranks low." [29]

Applying his balancing test to the situation before him, Justice Frankfurter first enumerated the factors to be weighed on the side of "the interest in security." He noted from the record that the Communist Party was not an "ordinary political party" and that it had advocated overthrow of the government by force and violence "as a program for winning adherents and as a policy to be translated into action." Observing that "we are not limited to the facts found by the jury," he took judicial notice that Communist doctrines "are in the ascendancy in powerful nations" not friendly to this country; that in 1947, "it has been reliably reported, at least 60,000 members were enrolled in the Party"; that a Canadian Royal Commission had reported that "the Communist movement was the principal base within which the espionage network was recruited"; that the "most notorious spy in recent history [Klaus Fuchs] was led into the service of the Soviet Union through Communist indoctrination"; and that "[e]vidence supports the conclusion that members of the Party seek and occupy positions of importance in political and labor organizations," citing the *Douds* case and an article from *Collier's* magazine.[30]

On the side of the "interest of free speech," Justice Frankfurter

28. 341 U.S. at 510-511.   30. 341 U.S. at 546, 547, 548.
29. 341 U.S. at 544-545.

pointed to some of the functions of freedom of expression in a democratic society, declaring that "[f]reedom of expression is the wellspring of our civilization." Specifically he noted that "criticism of defects in our society" was coupled with the advocacy in this case; that "there may be a grain of truth in the most uncouth doctrine;" and that "[s]uppressing advocates of overthrow inevitably will also silence critics who do not advocate overthrow but fear that their criticism may be so construed." [31]

Coming to the point of balancing the scales, Justice Frankfurter concluded:

> It is not for us to decide how we would adjust the clash of interests which this case presents were the primary responsibility for reconciling it ours. Congress has determined that the danger created by advocacy of overthrow justifies the ensuing restriction on freedom of speech. . . . Can we then say that the judgment Congress exercised was denied it by the Constitution? [32]

Justice Frankfurter's use of the balancing test in *Dennis* affords a good opportunity to observe that test in action. It is not necessary to appraise in detail the particular performance of Justice Frankfurter. One could quarrel with the fact that little consideration was given to the relation between the utterances before the Court and the danger of an attempt at overthrow, or that insufficient attention was devoted to whether the government had alternative ways of safeguarding internal security through exercising control over action rather than expression. The point is that the process was a highly complex one; that, as Justice Frankfurter himself observed, it called for a "judicial reading of events still in the womb of time;" and that, so far as the result was concerned, it could have turned out either way.

It is more important to consider the nature of the weighing process itself. The factors put into the scale on each side were in no way comparable. There was no common ground, or unit of measurement, between the espionage potential of the Communist Party and the dampening effect of the prosecution upon free discussion. The various considerations could be enumerated but not weighed. There was no standard of reference upon which to base a reasoned, functional determination. Ultimately the decision rested upon vague value judgments, most of them unexpressed. Moreover, some of these value judg-

31. 341 U.S. at 550, 549.   32. 341 U.S. at 550-551.

ments—such as whether a particular kind of speech should have a high
or a low rating—are not the kind of judgment which, under the basic
theory of the First Amendment, the government is entitled to make.

The remarkable feature of the Frankfurter opinion is that, in the
end, Justice Frankfurter did not even attempt to strike the balance. He
avoided the problem by falling back upon the legislative judgment.
But this raises more issues than it settles. For one may ask, just what
legislature made what judgment about the balance between internal
security and freedom of speech in instituting the prosecution against
the Communist Party leadership in 1948? Was it the legislature that
passed the bill in 1940? If so, what did it know about the strength of
the Communist Party in 1948, a major factor in the Frankfurter
balancing process? If it was the 1948 legislature, how could it have
made a specific judgment of that kind? The fact is that the Frankfurter
use of the balancing test is a reversion to *Gitlow*. The role of the Court
is merely to say whether the legislature acted reasonably in passing the
legislation initially, and from then on no First Amendment issues are
to be considered. For Justice Frankfurter, the balancing process was
viable because he hardly undertook to balance at all.

Justice Jackson's approach in the *Dennis* case is unique. He considers the clear and present danger test appropriate, as a "rule of reason," in cases involving street meetings or "circulation of a few incen-
diary pamphlets," where the determination "is not a prophecy, for the
danger in such cases has matured by the time of trial or it was never
present." But he holds it impossible of application in a situation such
as *Dennis*, where "we must appraise imponderables, including international and national phenomena which baffle the best informed foreign
offices and our most experienced politicians," and where the "answers
given would reflect our political predilections and nothing more." Justice Jackson finds the key to the *Dennis* issue in the concept of conspiracy, since the principal feature of the problem is that the government
is dealing with "permanently organized, well-financed, semi-secret,
and highly disciplined organizations." He holds that "it is not forbidden to put down force and violence, it is not forbidden to punish its
teaching or advocacy, and the end being punishable, there is no doubt
of the power to punish conspiracy for the purpose." [33]

On one view the Jackson opinion seems superficial; it appears to
assume the answer. The question before the Court was whether or not
"teaching or advocacy"—forms of expression—could constitutionally

33. 341 U.S. at 568, 570, 575.

be punished under the First Amendment. If they could, then conspiracy to teach and advocate could also be punished; if they could not, a conspiracy could not be punished either. This is self-evident. It would seem, therefore, that Justice Jackson was making a different point. What he probably was saying was that the defendants were really being charged with a conspiracy to overthrow the government, not merely to advocate, and that evidence of advocacy could be used to prove such a conspiracy. This position raises crucial questions concerning conspiracy and the First Amendment, matters which are treated in Chapter XI. The indictment in *Dennis* made no charge of conspiracy to overthrow and the Jackson position cannot be sustained against obvious due process objections.

Justice Black, dissenting, rested his opinion upon two grounds. First, pointing out that the defendants were not charged with actual advocacy but only with conspiring or agreeing to advocate at a later date, he found the indictment "a virulent form of prior censorship of speech and press." He would therefore hold the conspiracy section of the Smith Act invalid as a prior restraint. Second, he objected to "jettisoning" the clear and present danger rule, which in his view would have required a reversal of the conviction. "At least as to speech in the realm of public matters," he said, "I believe that the 'clear and present danger' test does not 'mark the furthermost constitutional boundaries of protected expression' but does 'no more than recognize a minimum compulsion of the Bill of Rights.' " [34]

Justice Black's theory of the conspiracy section of the Smith Act as constituting a prior censorship was novel and difficult to fit into the traditional doctrine of prior restraint. In any event, the Court has never pursued the idea further. As to the alternate ground, it is clear that Justice Black did not accept the clear and present danger test as the full measure of First Amendment freedoms, but he did not feel it necessary to go beyond that point.[35]

Justice Douglas accepted the Holmes-Brandeis version of the clear and present danger test and undertook to apply it to the case before him. The precise issue, he said, is whether "the acts charged, *viz.*, the teaching of the Soviet theory of revolution with the hope that it will be realized, have created any clear and present danger to the Nation." He disagreed with the majority that the issue of clear and present danger

34. 341 U.S. at 579, 580.
35. The doctrine of prior restraint is discussed in Chapter XIII.

was one for the Court to decide; he and Justice Black believed it should go to the jury. In either event "there should be evidence of record on the issue." In the absence of such evidence Justice Douglas relied on judicial notice. He agreed with the majority that the "nature of Communism as a force on the world scene would, of course, be relevant to the issue of clear and present danger," but he believed that "the primary consideration is the strength and tactical position of petitioners and their converts in this country." Examining this question in detail, Justice Douglas concluded that as a political party Communists "are of little consequence," that "in America they are miserable merchants of unwanted ideas." He then looked at "[t]heir numbers; their positions in industry and government; the extent to which they have in fact infiltrated the police, the armed services, transportation, stevedoring, power plants, munitions works, and other critical places." And he concluded that "[t]o believe that petitioners and their following are placed in such critical positions as to endanger the Nation is to believe the incredible." [36]

Justice Douglas made a valiant effort to apply the clear and present danger test in the *Dennis* case. But he only scratched the surface of the problem. A serious attempt to make even a half-scholarly inquiry into the question would lead into issues of much wider scope and demand much greater depth. Moreover, there would remain the difficulty of getting the facts before the court or jury. To assemble the necessary material by a judicial process of examining and cross-examining witnesses would be infinitely time-consuming and ultimately impossible. And no one would be sure that the final decision, whether made by judge or jury, would be right or relevant.

From this prolonged analysis of the five opinions in the *Dennis* case, it appears that none of the doctrines employed there provides a workable approach to the First Amendment problem posed by the case. Before attempting to apply the theory of full protection in this area of expression, it is helpful to trace the final outcome of the effort to use the Smith Act against the Communist Party.

After the decision in *Dennis* a series of prosecutions was begun against the secondary leadership of the Communist Party in various parts of the country. Altogether fifteen new conspiracy prosecutions were brought, involving approximately 121 defendants; and eight prosecutions were instituted against individuals under the membership provisions. By 1957, when the *Yates* case was decided, most of these

36. 341 U.S. at 587, 588, 589.

cases had been tried. Normally the trials lasted three to six months and the evidence introduced was the same as or similar to that used in the *Dennis* case. Convictions were secured in every case brought to trial— a total of ninety-six defendants in addition to the eleven *Dennis* defendants—although in four conspiracy cases a total of ten individual defendants were acquitted by the court or by the jury. As the cases began to reach the Courts of Appeals the convictions were uniformly affirmed, with the exception of two defendants for whom a new trial was ordered because of perjured testimony. In the first two cases appealed to the Supreme Court, petition for certiorari was denied. In the spring of 1956, however, the Supreme Court granted certiorari in four cases. The decision in the *Yates* case, which abruptly terminated the whole program, was rendered in 1957.[37]

2. THE *YATES* CASE

The *Yates* case involved the conviction of fourteen defendants in California on charges of conspiracy to advocate overthrow of the government by force and violence, as in the *Dennis* case. The government's evidence that the Communist Party engaged in teaching the doctrines of Marxism-Leninism was very much the same as in *Dennis*. Proof concerning the activities of individual defendants varied, of course, with respect to each person. The Supreme Court's review was not limited, as in *Dennis,* to the bare constitutional issues but rather opened up the whole question of the sufficiency of the evidence. The decision, reversing the conviction by a vote of six to one, marked a major shift in the Court's approach to Smith Act prosecutions.

Justice Harlan, writing for four members of the Court, did not deal with the issues formally in terms of the First Amendment. His decision rested, as far as is relevant here, upon (1) the proper interpretation of the Smith Act and (2) the sufficiency of the evidence to show a violation under the statute. Nevertheless the opinion has important First Amendment implications.

The issue with respect to the interpretation of the statute arose as a question of instructions to the jury. The trial judge had told the jury that "advocacy or teaching which does not include the urging of force and violence as a means of overthrowing and destroying the Govern-

37. *Yates v. United States,* 354 U.S. 298 (1957). For a summary of the prose-cutions up to *Yates* see *Political and Civil Rights in the United States,* pp. 127–129.

ment of the United States" could not constitute a basis for conviction. But he had refused to give instructions "which would have required the jury to find that the proscribed advocacy was not of a mere abstract doctrine of forcible overthrow, but of action to that end, by the use of language reasonably and ordinarily calculated to incite persons to such action." This was held error. "The essential distinction," said Justice Harlan, "is that those to whom the advocacy is addressed must be urged to *do* something, now or in the future, rather than merely to *believe* in something." The statute prohibited, in other words, "advocacy of action," not merely "advocacy in the realm of ideas." [38]

The holding was phrased as a matter of statutory interpretation. There is little doubt, however, that the distinction between "advocacy of action" and "advocacy of ideas" was considered by the Court to have constitutional dimensions. The Smith Act was interpreted in this way in order to avoid constitutional questions. Thus the opinion was offering a further constitutional concept, somewhat different from any specifically proposed in *Dennis*. The new formula, however, is a doubtful contribution to First Amendment theory. Since "advocacy of action" includes advocacy of future action, the formula omits the element of "present" and therefore tends to cut off speech at an earlier point than the clear and present danger test. Although the distinction embodied in the formula has overtones of the distinction between "expression" and "action," it nevertheless is still a distinction between various kinds of "expression." As such it is unrelated to the basic function of the First Amendment and presents no satisfactory standard of reference which makes rational application possible. The distinction thus remains blurred and difficult to apply.

More important than the matter of statutory interpretation was Justice Harlan's appraisal of the evidence. The defect found in the instructions to the jury could be overcome in a new trial or in future prosecutions by a revised set of instructions, which probably would have had little effect upon the jury's decision. But the absence of evidence could not be so easily remedied. Two aspects of the evidence question are significant.

In the first place Justice Harlan found the evidence insufficient to establish that the Communist Party or the Communist Party of California constituted a conspiracy to advocate overthrow of the government by force and violence within the meaning of the Smith Act. There

38. 354 U.S. at 314, 315–316, 320, 324–325. Italics in original.

was abundant evidence of advocacy of ideas but "when it comes to Party advocacy or teaching in the sense of a call to forcible action at some future time we cannot but regard this record as strikingly deficient." This finding had obvious public implications. It also opened an enormous hole in the government's case, since the government then had to establish a special conspiracy in each case rather than rely upon a general Party conspiracy.

Secondly, Justice Harlan examined the evidence concerning each defendant. For five he held that an acquittal must be ordered. All five were leading members of the Communist Party in California, holding offices such as editor of the Party newspaper, educational director, or organizer. "So far as this record shows," Justice Harlan said, "none of them has engaged in or been associated with any but what appear to have been wholly lawful activities, or has ever made a single remark or been present when someone else made a remark, which would tend to prove" their participation in a conspiracy to advocate forcible action. The other nine defendants were remanded for a new trial. There was some evidence linking them with classes or training which might be considered by the jury to have included illegal advocacy. "[W]e are not prepared to say, at this stage of the case," Justice Harlan stated, "that it would be impossible for a jury, resolving all conflicts in favor of the Government and giving the evidence . . . its utmost sweep, to find that advocacy of action was . . . engaged in." [39]

Justices Black and Douglas would have directed that all the defendants be acquitted, on the ground that the Smith Act violated the First Amendment. Justice Black's opinion makes no reference to the clear and present danger test and apparently proceeds upon a theory of according full protection to expression. Justice Clark was the lone dissenter.[40]

With the *Yates* case, prosecutions under the Smith Act collapsed. In the *Yates* case itself the indictment against the nine defendants who had been remanded was dismissed by the trial court on the government's statement that "we cannot satisfy the evidentiary requirements laid down by the Supreme Court in its opinion reversing the convictions in this matter." In all other cases then pending, with the exception of one membership case discussed below (*Scales*), the indictments were ultimately dismissed by the courts or dropped by the government.

39. 354 U.S. at 330–331, 332.
40. Justices Brennan and Whittaker did not participate.

e 141 persons indicted, in the end only twenty-nine served prison
s. These were the eleven defendants in the *Dennis* case, the seventeen defendants in the two post-*Dennis* cases in which the Supreme
Court denied certiorari, and one defendant in a membership case
(Scales). No new prosecutions were instituted after *Yates*. The campaign to prosecute the Communist Party under the Smith Act was
over.[41]

3. APPLICATION OF EXPRESSION-ACTION THEORY TO THE SMITH ACT

In commencing our analysis of the Smith Act in terms of the expression-action theory of the First Amendment, it is useful to recall the
problem with which we are ultimately concerned, that of internal security—protection of the governmental and other institutions of society
against destruction or alteration by methods of force or violence. The
issue is what forms of governmental control should be exercised
against a political or social movement, most likely well organized and
with foreign ties, which advances a program of radical change through
aggressive tactics. The program may be based upon various ideological assumptions about the role of force and violence in social change,
and the tactics may range from orthodox political campaigning
through prophesying, preparing for, or engaging in the use of force or
violence. At what point, consistently with the First Amendment, is the
government entitled to step in and prohibit the conduct of such political associations?

It has been argued above that, with the exception of the position
ultimately reached by Justices Black and Douglas in the *Yates* case,
the various doctrines applied by the Court in the cases just analyzed
are inadequate. The bad tendency test cuts off too much speech too
early. The clear and present danger test has the same result and is
impossibly complex to administer in this situation. The balancing test
is vague and offers no real guidance. The "incitement" and "advocacy
of action" formulae suffer from the same defects. All the tests are in
conflict with the fundamental theory of the First Amendment that expression must be permitted and only subsequent action controlled. We

41. *The New York Times*, Dec. 3, 1957. For a summary of the cases after *Yates*, see *Political and Civil Rights in the United States*, pp. 140–143, 153–155.

reach the question, therefore, how does the full protection theory apply here and is it a viable one in this situation?

The central question is to draw the line between "expression" and "action" in the kind of conduct with which we are here concerned. Clearly a historical account of the function of force and violence in society or an academic discussion of the necessity or propriety of its use would be classified as expression. Similarly, advocating in general terms the use of force or violence at some time in the future must be considered expression. Advocacy of legal forms of action which would put an organization in a more favorable position for later utilization of force and violence, such as forming labor unions in industrial plants, would remain expression. As the communication approached the point of urging immediate and particular acts of violence, it would come closer to being classifiable as action. If such advocacy became merely an incidental part of a program of overt acts the total conduct would cross the boundary line. Instructions on techniques of sabotage, street fighting, or specific methods of violence are well into the area of action. A fortiori, training in para-military operations, including the wearing of uniforms, or organizing groups to engage in acts of violence would fall within the action category. In essence, the line would be drawn between ideological preparation or indoctrination in the use of violence on the one hand, and participation in overt acts of preparation or actual use on the other.

Drawing the line at such a point conforms to the function of a system of free expression and is essential to its effective operation. Plausible as it may seem on the surface, it is simply not possible to cut off expression advocating overthrow of the government by force and violence without curtailing other forms of expression and seriously impairing the whole system. Successful prosecution of a political organization for advocating violence would result in eliminating all criticism or expression of grievances by the group. With the leadership in prison or the organization destroyed, the "high rank" expression on Justice Frankfurter's scale would disappear with the "low rank." Moreover, a militant minority might be suppressed even when its expression did not actually fall within the prohibited zone. The language of politics is filled with terms borrowed from the field of battle and violence, and careful distinction between symbolic and realistic expression, uttered in the heat of controversy, might not be drawn.

Even more important, the suppression would not be confined to

those engaged in the conduct suppressed. Many other participants in
the political process, on the border or near the position taken by those
who have been proceeded against, would feel the repercussions and
fear to speak. The dynamics of repression, the play upon fears and
hates implicit in prosecution of dissenters, would create an atmosphere
hostile to all open discussion. The governmental apparatus built up
around a program of suppression would itself be a repressive factor.
And, finally, the body politic as a whole would find itself concentrating on the wrong problems, using its energies and resources to stamp
out the symptoms of social evil and neglecting the evil itself. In short,
no system of free expression can neatly excise one form of expression,
however noxious, and leave the system unimpaired. The only safe
place to draw the line is at the point that action begins.

There remains one further question. Is allowing protection to expression in this situation a viable position? Can a democratic society
live with such a doctrine, or would it be suicidal? It is perhaps fair to
pose the question another way. Would the Smith Act make the margin
of difference between the Government of the United States continuing
to operate according to democratic procedures and its being overthrown by force and violence? It is difficult to believe that it would.
The national security is protected by numerous laws which control all
those kinds of action which might threaten overthrow. National security is assured even more by measures which seek to meet the needs of
the citizens. One of the strongest supports of a healthy community is
an effective system of freedom of expression. Under these circumstances, dependence on a law punishing advocacy of force and violence as marking the difference between security and insecurity would
only be indicative of the underlying weakness of the society.

4. THE MEMBERSHIP PROVISIONS
AND GUILT BY ASSOCIATION

The Smith Act prosecutions also raised an important problem of
associational rights. The right to form, join, and participate in an association is a crucial aspect of any system of freedom of expression. Increasingly in modern times the only way an individual can be effectively heard is through membership in an organization. Associations
perform other significant functions also, such as affording their members access to information or providing forums for developing and test-

ing ideas. Questions relating to the rights and obligations of associations and their members arise in many forms. At this point we are concerned with problems of the extent to which conduct of an organization should be attributed to one of its members, sometimes called the question of guilt by association.[42]

The Smith Act, as noted above, contains a provision making it an offense to organize "any society, group, or assembly of persons who teach, advocate, or encourage the overthrow or destruction of . . . government by force or violence" and punishing any person who "becomes or is a member of, or affiliates with, any such society, group or assembly of persons, knowing the purposes thereof." Eight prosecutions were commenced against individual members of the Communist Party under this provision and two of them reached the Supreme Court. In one of these the Court reversed the conviction, finding insufficient evidence that the Communist Party had engaged in illegal advocacy under the *Yates* rule. In *Scales v. United States,* however, a majority of the Court did find the evidence of Party advocacy sufficient and reached the question of the circumstances under which an individual member could be convicted of violating the membership clause.[43]

Justice Harlan, writing for the majority, recognized that to impute liability to a member of an organization for the illegal acts of the organization raised serious First Amendment questions: "If there were a . . . blanket prohibition of association with a group having both legal and illegal aims, there would indeed be a real danger that legitimate political expression or association would be impaired." But he held that the Act could be applied to an "active" member of the Party, as distinct from "a nominal, passive, inactive or purely technical" member, who had (1) "the requisite specific intent 'to bring about the overthrow of the government as speedily as circumstances would permit,' " and (2) "knowledge of the proscribed advocacy." Four justices dissented, Justices Black and Douglas objecting on First Amendment grounds.[44]

The protection afforded by the majority to the right of association

42. Other aspects of associational rights connected with freedom of expression are dealt with in subsequent chapters. See, especially, Chapter XII. For a general discussion see Thomas I. Emerson, "Freedom of Association and Freedom of Expression," *Yale Law Journal,* Vol. 74 (1964), p. 1.

43. The membership provision is incorporated in 18 U.S.C. §2385. The decision reversing the conviction is *Noto v. United States,* 367 U.S. 290 (1961). The Scales case is *Scales v. United States,* 367 U.S. 203 (1961).

44. 367 U.S. at 229–230.

in the *Scales* case does not go far enough. Scales was clearly exercising First Amendment rights in joining the organization and participating in various activities that constituted expression. Assuming the Court was correct in holding that some of the conduct of the Party was not protected by the First Amendment (in our terms was "action" rather than "expression"), the question remains whether a particular member may be punished on the basis of intent and knowledge alone, thereby restricting his rights to expression. A sound view of the First Amendment requires that sanctions can be applied only to a member who is shown actually to have participated in the illegal conduct.

Justice Harlan relied primarily upon the requirement of intent as protection for "the member for whom the organization is a vehicle for the advancement of legitimate aims and policies." But the intent with which First Amendment rights are exercised should not determine the existence of those rights. If Scales had not engaged in illegal conduct himself, he was being punished for legal activity in his associational conduct, and the state of his mind should not deprive him of his constitutional rights. In any event the necessity of finding intent is, in practice, a shaky foundation for the support of First Amendment rights. Intent may be inferred from all the circumstances by an unfriendly jury, and the mere association with an unpopular organization would frequently be found to satisfy the requirement. Even in as clear a case as that of Miss Whitney one may doubt that an instruction to the jury on intent would have much helped her.[45]

Nor is the requirement that the member must have knowledge of the illegal conduct a satisfactory safeguard. Proof of knowledge is also an uncertain thing and leaves an unpopular defendant with small protection. Moreover, to impose upon all prospective and existing members an obligation to know about every activity of the organization, or incur the risk of criminal punishment, would effectively deter all but the most dedicated from joining the organization. In addition, the rule that knowledge of association action is the crucial factor in determining guilt allows no room for difference of opinion within the organization. As in the case of Miss Whitney, there is no alternative but to withdraw. Thus the opportunity to change the policies of the organization, indeed the whole system of free expression within the organization, is eliminated.

The critical flaw in the *Scales* rule is that it does not sufficiently

45. See also Justice Douglas' discussion of intent in the *Dennis* case, 341 U.S. at 583 (1951).

separate the illegal conduct of an organization from the legal conduct of its members. The taint of illegality destroys the legal, and may in fact destroy the whole organization. The associational aspects of free expression should, like the individual right, receive the greatest measure of protection possible. As the *De Jonge* case holds, the government's restriction must be directed narrowly to eliminate the abuse, not to crush the right itself. Only a rule that a member cannot be punished for the illegal activities of his organization unless he himself participates in them can be reconciled with the demands of the First Amendment.

D. The Internal Security Act of 1950

Deeming the Smith Act insufficient protection against the Communist movement, Congress enacted the Internal Security Act of 1950, commonly known as the McCarran Act. The legislation was passed before the collapse of the Smith Act prosecutions, and was intended to move beyond the restrictions imposed by that law. The main feature of the new legislation was that it did not rest on prohibiting advocacy of force or violence but sought other forms of control, based on other sources of constitutional power. The Internal Security Act thus raised some novel and crucial issues of First Amendment interpretation.[46]

The Internal Security Act included three major regulatory schemes which are of interest to us here. First, in Title I, designated the Subversive Activities Control Act, an elaborate scheme of registration for certain types of organizations was provided. Second, it contained in Section 4(a) of Title I a separate criminal sedition law. And third, in Title II, designated the Emergency Detention Act, provision was made for the detention of suspected subversives in periods of emergency. The original bill, a product of the House Committee on Un-American Activities, contained only the first two features. The detention provisions were introduced in the Senate as a substitute measure by a group of liberal Senators, headed by Senator Kilgore, who argued that the only danger from the Communist Party would be in

46. 64 Stat. 987 (1950); 50 U.S.C. §§781–798, 811–826. The Act was amended in 1968, as discussed below.

times of emergency. In the course of debate the Kilgore proposal was accepted as an additional measure and on final passage all three features were included in the bill.[47]

Our primary concern is with the registration provisions. This portion of the Act commences with a detailed set of legislative findings, the substance of which is that there exists "a world Communist movement" whose purpose it is, "by treachery, deceit, infiltration . . . , espionage, sabotage, terrorism and any other means deemed necessary," to establish a "Communist totalitarian dictatorship" in countries throughout the world; that the Communist dictatorship of the foreign country controlling the world Communist movement makes use of various organizations in other countries to further its purposes; that in the United States those individuals who participate in the Communist movement "in effect repudiate their allegiance to the United States, and in effect transfer their allegiance to the foreign country" which directs the world Communist movement; and that the Communist movement in the United States presents "a clear and present danger to the security of the United States and to the existence of free American institutions." The Act then sets forth two crucial definitions:

A "Communist-action organization" is any organization in the United States

> which (i) is substantially directed, dominated, or controlled by the foreign government or foreign organization controlling the world Communist movement . . . and (ii) operates primarily to advance the objectives of such world Communist movement.

A "Communist-front organization" is any organization in the United States

> which (A) is substantially directed, dominated or controlled by a Communist-action organization, and (B) is primarily operated for the purpose of giving aid and support to a Communist-action organization, a Communist foreign government, or the world Communist movement.[48]

Upon petition by the Attorney General the Subversive Activities Control Board, created by the Act, was authorized to conduct an administrative proceeding to determine whether an organization was a Communist-action or a Communist-front organization and, if it so

47. For references to the legislative history, see *Political and Civil Rights in the United States,* pp. 169-170.

48. The Act, as amended by the Communist Control Act of 1954, also defines a "Communist-infiltrated organization," but we need not be concerned with this category here.

found, to order the organization to register. The Board's order was subject to court review in accordance with the usual administrative practice. Once the Board's order was final, the organization was required to register with the Attorney General as a Communist-action or Communist-front organization and to file then and yearly thereafter a registration statement. The registration statement was required to include (1) in the case of a Communist-action organization the name and address of every officer and member, and in the case of a Communist-front organization the name and address of every officer; (2) an accounting of all moneys received and expended, including the sources from which received and the purposes for which expended; (3) a listing of all printing presses, mimeograph machines, and other duplicating machinery. The provision for accounting in effect required all organizations to list all dues-paying members. All information filed with the Attorney General was open for public inspection. Furthermore, the organization was required to keep records of all moneys received and expended, and a Communist-action organization was required to keep the names and addresses of all members and all persons actively participating in its affairs.

Various additional sanctions were imposed upon registered organizations and their members. Thus it was a criminal offense for any member to apply for a passport, or to hold any job with the Federal Government, and for a member of any Communist organization to be employed in any defense facility. No organization was permitted to send any communication through the mail to more than two persons or to broadcast any matter over radio or television unless it was labeled as emanating from "a Communist organization." If an organization failed to register or file a registration statement, then the obligation to do so fell upon its officers. Members of a Communist organization who were not registered by the organization must register themselves. Heavy penalties were imposed for failure to register, each day of such failure constituting a separate offense. Penalties were also exacted for failure to file information, for failure to keep records, and for filing false information.

Two crucial aspects of the registration provisions, which frame the constitutional issues, should be noted at this point. In the first place, while the legislation was sometimes referred to as a disclosure statute, it was much closer to a death sentence. Every member of a registered organization was officially branded a traitor, owing his allegiance to a "foreign country." Membership in such an organization not only subjected him to direct sanctions, such as committing a crime by applying for a passport, but rendered him a likely candidate for investigation by a legislative committee or prosecution under the Smith Act. Any such member was likewise vulnerable to all kinds of social and economic pressures, including loss of job and possibly of career. Moreover, in many cases the individual was required to register if the organization did not, and it was evidently contemplated that many individual members would end up in prison.

So far as the organization itself was concerned, it simply would not be able to function. It was forced to make public its membership, its sources of revenue, its expenses, and all who participated in its activities or had any dealings with it. It was required to keep detailed records, and was subject to severe penalties for the slightest infraction. Its leaders were especially marked for reprisal. Under the conditions of the day an organization required to register would almost certainly have to dissolve or go underground.

Secondly, the application of these sanctions did not depend upon a finding that any individual or organization had engaged in force or violence, advocacy of force or violence, or any illegal activity. The only operative factors which called the machinery of the Act into play were the findings that an organization was dominated, directly or indirectly, by a foreign political movement and that it was attempting to bring about a totalitarian form of government. In abandoning the base of force or violence the legislation was closer to the Sedition Act of 1798 than to the Smith Act.

Section 4(a) of the Internal Security Act followed this same pattern. It was made unlawful "for any person to knowingly combine, conspire, or agree with any other person to perform any act which would substantially contribute to the establishment within the United States of a totalitarian dictatorship . . . the direction and control of which is to be vested in, or exercised by or under the domination or control of, any foreign government, foreign organization, or foreign individual." Here the sanction was a direct criminal penalty rather than an administratively imposed registration. Like the registration provisions, however, the offense consisted, not in the use of force or violence or other illegal act, but in any conduct designed to establish a totalitarian form of government under foreign control.

The detention provisions of the Act come into operation only upon proclamation of emergency by the President in the event of invasion, declaration of war, or insurrection in aid of a foreign enemy. When such an emergency was declared, the Attorney General was authorized "to apprehend and by order detain . . . each person as to whom there is reasonable ground to believe that such person probably will engage in, or probably will conspire with others to engage in, acts of espionage or of sabotage." There was no provision for judicial proceedings before detention and only limited review, in which the evidence could be withheld, after detention.

Section 4(a) and the detention provisions of the Internal Security Act have never been invoked. A number of proceedings were, however, brought under the registration provisions. The Act plainly contemplated that the one organization which would qualify as a Communist-action organization was the Communist Party. And it was necessary to find a Communist-action organization before any organization could be found a Communist-front organization. The initial, and principal, proceeding was therefore directed against the Communist Party.[49]

1. THE COMMUNIST PARTY REGISTRATION CASE

In November 1950 the Attorney General filed a petition with the Subversive Activities Control Board for an order requiring the Communist Party to register as a Communist-action organization. After an effort to enjoin the Board from proceeding had failed, hearings were commenced before the Board in April 1951. The Attorney General completed presentation of his case some fourteen months later, in June 1952. The Communist Party defense took three weeks and hearings closed in July 1952. The record consisted of nearly 15,000 pages of testimony and some 507 documentary exhibits. The Board issued its Report in April 1953, ordering the Party to register. Various court proceedings, involving three trips to the Court of Appeals and one to the Supreme Court, occupied seven more years. Finally, on the second time in the Supreme Court a decision was rendered on the merits. This was in June 1961, nearly eleven years after enactment of the statute.[50]

The Supreme Court upheld the Board's order by a five to four vote. The majority passed only upon the validity of the registration requirement itself. It did not reach the questions of self-incrimination

49. For discussion of the Internal Security Act and its administration up to 1967, see *Political and Civil Rights in the United States*, pp. 157–197.

50. *Communist Party v. Subversive Activities Control Board*, 367 U.S. 1 (1961).

involved in compelling organization officers or members actually to file registrations, nor any questions relating to the constitutionality of the various sanctions that became applicable after an order to register had been entered. Although four justices dissented, only Justice Black thought that the registration provisions were in conflict with the First Amendment.

Justice Frankfurter, writing the majority opinion, treated the issue as one of simple disclosure and invoked the balancing test: "Against the impediments which particular governmental regulation causes to entire freedom of individual action, there must be weighed the value to the public of the ends which the regulation may achieve." On the government side of the scales he weighed the Congressional findings, saying, "It is not for the courts to re-examine the validity of these legislative findings and reject them." On the side of freedom of expression he noted only "the public opprobrium and obloquy which may attach to an individual listed with the Attorney General as a member of a Communist-action organization." He had no hesitancy in striking the balance in favor of the regulation.[51]

This conclusion should presumably have ended the matter, but Justice Frankfurter saw fit to address himself to one other point. It had been argued, he said, that if Congress could require the Communist Party to register, it "may impose similar requirements upon any group which pursues unpopular political objectives or which expresses an unpopular political ideology." This outcome he rejected, on the ground that the Act "applies only to *foreign-dominated* organizations which work primarily to advance the objectives of a world movement controlled by the government of a *foreign* country." It would seem, therefore, that in the end Justice Frankfurter found First Amendment considerations outweighed by the factor of foreign domination.[52]

Justice Douglas, with whom Chief Justice Warren and Justice Brennan appeared to concur, agreed that the registration provisions were valid under the First Amendment but he reached that conclusion on different grounds. He started from the position that "no individual may be required to register before he makes a speech"; and "a group engaged in lawful conduct may not be required to file with the Government a list of its members." These principles would normally invalidate the registration provisions. But the findings in this case, he said, "establish that more than debate, discourse, argumentation, propaganda, and other aspects of free speech and association are involved.

51. 367 U.S. at 91, 94, 102.   52. 367 U.S. at 104. Italics in original.

An additional element enters, *viz.*, espionage, business activities, or the formation of cells for subversion, as well as the use of speech, press and association by a foreign power to produce on this continent a Soviet satellite." Such activities, he said, are like picketing, "free speech *plus* . . . and hence can be restricted. . . . These machinations of a foreign power add additional elements to free speech just as marching up and down adds something to picketing that goes beyond free speech." [53]

Justice Black, the lone dissenter on First Amendment grounds, viewed the provisions of the Act as involving more than mere registration: "The plan of the Act is to make it impossible for an organization to continue to function once a registration order is issued against it." The question under the First Amendment, he therefore contended, "is whether Congress has power to outlaw an association, group or party either on the ground that it advocates a policy of violent overthrow of the existing Government at some time in the distant future or on the ground that it is ideologically subservient to some foreign country." In his view neither of these factors justified an invasion of First Amendment rights. As to the first, "under our system of Government, the remedy for this danger [talk about the desirability of revolution] must be the same remedy that is applied to the danger that comes from any other erroneous talk—education and contrary argument. If that remedy is not sufficient, the only meaning of free speech must be that the revolutionary ideas will be allowed to prevail." As to the second, "If there is one thing certain about the First Amendment it is that this Amendment was designed to guarantee the freest interchange . . . of *all* ideas, however such ideas may be viewed in other countries and whatever change in the existing structure of government it may be hoped that these ideas will bring about." And Justice Black concluded:

> The Founders drew a distinction in our Constitution which we would be wise to follow. They gave the Government the fullest power to prosecute overt actions in violation of valid laws but withheld any power to punish people for nothing more than advocacy of their views.[54]

While the order requiring the Communist Party to register was thus upheld, efforts to enforce the order proved fruitless. A prosecu-

53. 367 U.S. at 172–173, 173, 175. Italics in original.

54. 367 U.S. at 141, 147–148, 168. Italics in original.

tion against the Communist Party for failure to register was successful
in the District Court but reversed by the Court of Appeals on the
ground that the Government had failed to show any person available
to register the Party without incriminating himself in violation of the
Fifth Amendment. A second conviction, after a trial in which the Government undertook to prove that two F.B.I. informers in the Party
were available and willing to register the Party, was also reversed on
self-incrimination grounds. The Court of Appeals noted that, in areas
of First Amendment concern, it saw "no inescapable necessity to limit
the reach of the Fifth Amendment by technical theories of artificial
legal personality." Prosecution against individual officers of the Party
for failure to register the Party were dropped, apparently also for self-
incrimination reasons. Finally, proceedings before the Subversive Activities Control Board to require individual members of the Communist Party to register themselves were dismissed by the Supreme Court
as likewise violating the constitutional protection against self-incrimination.[55]

The Supreme Court's decision in *Communist Party v. Subversive
Activities Control Board* therefore remained in effect but inoperative.
The doctrinal aspects of the case, however, are far-reaching and re-
quire further discussion.

On the face of the case, the basis for invalidating the registration
provisions on First Amendment grounds seems virtually unassailable.
There was no question but that the Communist Party, like other political parties, was engaging in conduct that constituted expression within
the meaning of the First Amendment. Nor can it be seriously doubted
that the restrictions imposed by the registration provisions were intended to and would in fact have seriously crippled the organization
and probably forced it wholly underground. To treat the statute as one
that simply required disclosure for purposes of informing the public
and thereby facilitating operation of the system of freedom of expression was pure fiction. Furthermore, the inhibiting restrictions were imposed upon an organization for engaging in ordinary forms of admittedly legitimate expression. The statute did not require a showing of

---

55. *Communist Party v. United States,*
331 F.2d 807 (D.C. Cir. 1963), cert. denied 377 U.S. 968 (1964); *Communist
Party v. United States,* 384 F.2d 957, 968
(D.C. Cir. 1967); *Albertson v. Subversive
Activities Control Board,* 382 U.S. 70
(1965). On the prosecution of individual

officers, see *The New York Times,* Mar.
15 and 17, 1962, Aug. 24, 1964, and May
6, 1966. For a more detailed account of
all these proceedings see *Political and
Civil Rights in the United States,* pp.
189–193.

advocacy of force or violence within the *Dennis* and *Yates* rules, or any other illegal conduct, as a precondition to ordering registration. Nor did the Subversive Activities Control Board find any such conduct on the part of the organization. All that the statute required, and all that the Board found, was that the Communist Party was dominated by a foreign power and engaged in attempting to establish a totalitarian dictatorship in the United States by legal methods of political expression. Under these circumstances the clear and present danger test would appear irrelevant. The balancing test could be applied only if one were frankly reopening the whole question of whether the First Amendment should have been adopted. The only test that makes any sense is the test of extending full protection to expression.

From this analysis the conclusion that the registration provisions were invalid under the First Amendment would inevitably result unless some additional factor changed the initial conclusion. There were three elements in the case which might have had such an effect and which raise important aspects of First Amendment doctrine. These are (1) the contention that First Amendment rights should not be extended to anti-democratic groups; (2) the impact of foreign control or influence; and (3) the question whether other conduct on the part of the association constitutes grounds for limiting expression by the association.

The theory that anti-democratic groups, which would abolish democratic rights upon achieving power, are not entitled to exercise First Amendment rights in their attempt to achieve power, is implicit in the Internal Security Act. This proposition has been considered in an earlier chapter. Suffice it to say here that the courts have never accepted the principle that the First Amendment protects only democratic groups. No justice suggested that possibility in the *Communist Party* case. This element must therefore be ruled out as requiring any change in the initial conclusion.[56]

The element of foreign control was a major, in fact the decisive, factor in the majority opinion of Justice Frankfurter. It also played some part in the Douglas opinion. In view of the increasing internationalization of political movements this issue has come to be of growing significance. But it is not a new problem. Concern over the relations of the Jeffersonian Republicans with Republican France was a crucial element in the enactment of the Alien and Sedition Acts. Unfortunately the Frankfurter and Douglas opinions do little more than

56. See Chapter III.

state a bare conclusion. They offer no explanation of the relation of foreign control to the operations of our system of free expression.

Actually the control found by the Board was, as Justice Black pointed out, entirely ideological. There was no finding of control through force, by some extraterritorial exercise of political power or terrorism. Nor was there evidence of the other chief form of control, the financial. Short of domination by the purse or the sword, foreign influence would not seem an adequate ground for restricting freedom of expression by citizens and residents of the United States.

It was noted in the previous chapter that a foreign political system operates outside our political system and in some respects beyond our system of freedom of expression. Some control of the relations between the two systems, such as registration of paid agents of foreign governments, would not abridge freedom of expression in this country. But the same is clearly not true of ordinary ideological communication entering our system from abroad. In fact, in this age of rapid communication extensive interchange of information and ideas with foreign countries is commonplace. It is also common for organizations engaged in expression to have close ties with organizations in other nations. Numerous associations, including religious, scientific, and political groups, maintain such connections. All of this is an essential feature of our system of freedom of expression. As the Supreme Court held in *Lamont v. Postmaster General,* discussed below, such rights of communication are protected by the First Amendment.

Furthermore, First Amendment rights are infringed for other reasons if ideological communication with a foreign country is made the ground of restriction. In practice such regulations are enforced primarily by searching for a parallelism of ideas and opinions between the foreign and the domestic group. Such a search, indeed, occupied most of the record made before the Subversive Activities Control Board in the *Communist Party* case. This form of inquiry, especially where sanctions result, has a crippling effect upon freedom of belief and expression. In the end many people beyond the area of those directly involved become fearful or circumspect in expressing opinions on subjects that fall within the scope of official concern.

The kind of control revealed in the *Communist Party* case cannot, therefore, be made the ground for restricting freedom of expression in the United States. Regulation of expression based upon such factors would be permissible only where quite different relations existed between the foreign government and the persons exercising First Amendment rights in the United States, or where the regulation would not impair the system of freedom of expression in this country.

The third element which influenced the decision in the *Communist Party* case was the fact that the Party was engaged in other conduct in addition to expression. Justice Douglas based his opinion squarely on the proposition that the Party engaged in "espionage, business activities, or the formation of cells for subversion" as well as in "debate, discourse, argumentation, propaganda." And the Frankfurter opinion, while it relied primarily on the foreign control factor, also argued, "The present statute does not, of course, attach the registration requirement to the incident of speech, but to the incidents of foreign domination and of operation to advance the objectives of the world Communist movement—operation which, the Board has found here, includes extensive, long-continuing organizational, as well as 'speech' activity." Thus conduct by the Party which was adjudged "action" was held to justify the restraint upon the organization's right of expression.[57]

There are two serious faults in this line of reasoning. The first is that the Justices fail to draw the proper line between "expression" and "action." Justice Douglas classifies the "formation of cells" as action and Justice Frankfurter includes "organizational" conduct in that category. But, as we discuss elsewhere, "expression" must include more than the sheer uttering of words or distribution of literature. It must embrace all that ancillary conduct, such as operating a printing press or hiring a hall, which is necessary for effective communication. When an association seeks to exercise First Amendment rights, the term "expression" must include organizational conduct. Otherwise the constitutional guarantee is meaningless. If the government can regulate associational expression on the ground the association engages in organizational activity, the association has no real right of expression, and individuals seeking to make themselves heard through an association are deprived of one of the most effective forms of participation in the system of expression.

The second error in the Douglas and Frankfurter position is that it fails to separate two courses of conduct, one constituting "action" and the other "expression," and thereby restricts expression in the name of controlling action. Such separation is essential in maintaining the rights of an association, or more properly the rights of individuals operating through an association, to freedom of expression. Most or-

57. 367 U.S. at 172, 90.

ganizations engage in "action" as well as "expression." The action may be lawful under existing law, or it may be unlawful. In either event it is subject to governmental regulation. The crucial issue for a system of free expression is whether, or to what extent, the government's power to regulate the action of an association carries with it the power to regulate the expression of the association. Specifically in the *Communist Party* case the question would be whether, if it be assumed that the Party had engaged in "espionage," "business activities," or the use of force or violence, the government could cut off its right of expression by destroying or crippling it through the registration method.

The same issue may arise if it is held, under the clear and present danger test or the balancing test, that a certain communication, even though "expression," is not protected by the First Amendment but is subject to the same regulation as "action." In such a situation the issue would be whether in regulating "illegal expression" the government could also suppress "legitimate expression." Thus in the *Communist Party* case the question would be whether, assuming the Party engaged in the advocacy of force and violence not protected by the First Amendment, the government could by outlawing the organization destroy its right to "legitimate expression." Under the full protection theory, of course, the issue would not arise in this way.

In dealing with this problem the basic principle holds that conduct in the form of "expression" cannot be abridged, directly or indirectly, in the course of regulating other conduct that constitutes "action." An analogy may be drawn to the position of an individual. When a man engages in illegal action, that action alone is punished. His rights of expression remain intact, except of course to the extent that punishment by incarceration may limit them. Similarly an association may be punished for its action in violation of law, but such punishment must be limited to the action and not violate its rights of expression. Otherwise, the right of expression has a precarious existence. For any illegal conduct on the part of the organization could result in its destruction. An organization aggressively pressing an unpopular cause would be especially vulnerable.

The task, therefore, is to separate illegal action by an association from protected expression. In some cases the two may be so interlocked that separation is not possible. But this is not normally the case. Usually control of action can be carefully devised to effectuate that purpose and not interfere, or interfere only remotely, with the right of expression. The Supreme Court indeed has frequently insisted upon such a separation. This was its precise ruling in *De Jonge v. Oregon*. It has imposed the same requirement in cases involving the N.A.A.C.P. But the Court failed to do this in the *Communist Party* case. The reason may be that the Court has never precisely articulated the underlying principle involved. It has reached its conclusions through the doctrine that the statute must be narrowly drawn or that it violates the rule against vagueness. These doctrines are useful in demanding a higher standard of draftsmanship on the part of the legislature. But they do not reach the ultimate issues. The problem requires a careful definition of "expression" and "action" and an insistence that the regulation of action not impinge upon the right of expression.[58]

We conclude, therefore, that the three additional elements that entered into the *Communist Party* case do not lead to the result reached by a majority of the Court. The stark fact remains, as Justice Black insisted, that the Court was sanctioning the outlawry of a political organization for engaging in conduct which was not shown to have gone beyond the bounds of legitimate expression. The decision, in all its aspects, seems fatally inconsistent with the requirements of the First Amendment and the demands of a vigorous system of free expression. It is hard to believe that, if the Court returns to the issues again, it will adhere to its position.

2. THE COMMUNIST-FRONT CASES

Once the Subversive Activities Control Board had ordered the Communist Party to register as a Communist-action organization the way was open to proceed against alleged Communist-front organizations. Beginning in April 1953 the Attorney General filed petitions with the Board against twenty-three organizations. By the end of 1967 all the cases had been disposed of except one, filed against the W.E.B. DuBois Clubs of America in 1966. The outcome of the twenty-two completed proceedings may be summarized as follows:[59]

The Board dismissed eight cases, in all of which the organization had ceased to function. In the remaining fourteen cases the Board

58. *De Jonge v. Oregon*, 299 U.S. 353 (1937), discussed *supra*.

59. The Attorney General also filed petitions against two labor organizations requesting the Board to find them to be Communist-infiltrated organizations. Both petitions were ultimately dismissed. For a full account of these proceedings and the Communist-front proceedings, see *Political and Civil Rights in the United States*, pp. 193–196.

issued orders requiring the organization to register as a Communist-front organization. In three of these fourteen, the organizations had dissolved and no further action was taken. The remaining eleven cases were appealed to the Court of Appeals for the District of Columbia. In seven of these the organization had also ceased to function and no decisive action resulted. In the remaining four cases the issue of dissolution was not raised and the Court of Appeals reached a decision on the merits. In one of the four cases the Court set aside the Board's order on the ground of insufficient evidence. In the three others the Court affirmed the Board's orders. On the First Amendment issues the Court of Appeals relied, without elaboration, upon the Supreme Court's decision in the *Communist Party* case. In one of the three cases the organization became inactive and no further action was taken.[60]

The last two cases reached the Supreme Court. In both, the Supreme Court reversed, per curiam, on the ground that the records were "stale," Justices Black, Douglas, and Harlan dissenting. The Court did not pass on any constitutional issues but noted, "Our Communist Party decision on the Communist-action provisions did not necessarily foreclose petitioner's constitutional questions bearing on the Communist-front provisions." [61]

The net result was that no organization has registered as a Communist-front organization. Of the twenty-two organizations against which proceedings were completed, nineteen ceased to function.

As to the constitutional questions, there has been no Supreme Court decision. With respect to the First Amendment, the argument that the registration provisions violate that guarantee is very much the same as was made above concerning the Communist-action provisions, but substantially stronger. The organizations in question are clearly engaged in expression. The registration provisions, as experience showed, are crippling or fatal. The connection with foreign influ-

60. The Board's order was set aside in *National Council of American-Soviet Friendship v. Subversive Activities Control Board,* 322 F.2d 375 (D.C. Cir. 1963). It was affirmed in *American Committee for Protection of Foreign Born v. Subversive Activities Control Board,* 331 F.2d 53 (D.C. Cir. 1963); *Veterans of the Abraham Lincoln Brigade v. Subversive Activities Control Board,* 331 F.2d 64 (D.C. Cir. 1963); *Weinstock v. Subversive Activities Control Board,* 331 F.2d 75 (D.C. Cir. 1963); Judge Bazelon dissenting in the first two and concurring in the third.

61. *American Committee for Protection of Foreign Born v. Subversive Activities Control Board,* 380 U.S. 503, 505 (1965); *Veterans of the Abraham Lincoln Brigade v. Subversive Activities Control Board,* 380 U.S. 513 (1965). The Subversive Activities Control Board subsequently dismissed both cases.

ence is even more remote. Nor is there a suggestion that any organization has engaged in conduct other than wholly legitimate expression. The possibility of sustaining the Communist-front provisions under the First Amendment seems remote. In any event the self-incrimination decisions of the Supreme Court would preclude enforcement of a registration order.

The holding of the Supreme Court that the records in the two cases it considered were "stale" carries interesting implications. It illustrates one of the difficulties in framing legislation which, like the Internal Security Act, is directed against an ideological position. The political stance of various organizations and groups is constantly changing. It would be very hard, indeed, for a case under the registration provisions to reach the Supreme Court without being stale. As a matter of fact by the end of 1967 the registration provisions themselves were "stale." They were based upon the concept of a monolithic world Communist movement, dominated by the Soviet Union. With the rise of the Chinese Communist Party, and the splitting off of other Communist groups, a single world Communist movement no longer existed and the foundations of the statute were completely undermined.

Despite the precarious hold on constitutionality that the Subversive Activities Control Board possessed by 1967, the Supreme Court would not permit an organization summoned before it to short-circuit the administrative procedures. The DuBois Clubs, the last and only respondent before the Board, sued to enjoin the Board from holding hearings and asked the court to declare the statute unconstitutional. A three-judge District Court refused and the Supreme Court affirmed per curiam, insisting that the DuBois Clubs exhaust their administrative remedies: "The effect would be that important and difficult constitutional issues would be decided devoid of factual context and before it was clear that appellants were covered by the Act." [62]

Justices Black and Douglas dissented on the ground that the statute was unconstitutional on its face. Justice Douglas, apparently withdrawing from his position in the *Communist Party* case, argued that the registration provisions controlled expression, not action, and that such controls violated the First Amendment:

A Communist-front organization, as defined, is not a group engaged in *action* but in *advocacy;* or if *action* is included, so is advocacy, for

62. *DuBois Clubs of America v. Clark,* 389 U.S. 309, 312 (1967).

§781(15) in describing the growth of the Communist movement speaks of those who seek "converts far and wide by an extensive system of schooling and indoctrination." . . .

There is the line between action on the one hand and ideas, beliefs, and advocacy on the other. The former is a legitimate sphere for legislation. Ideas, beliefs, and advocacy are beyond the reach of committees, agencies, Congress, and the courts.[63]

Thus the formal enforcement of the Communist-front provisions came to nothing. Nevertheless, their repressive impact on the right of association, while difficult to measure, was evidently substantial.

3. OTHER PROCEEDINGS UNDER
THE INTERNAL SECURITY ACT

The Internal Security Act provided, as noted above, that once a Communist organization had been ordered to register it became a criminal offense for any member of such organization to apply for a passport or a renewal, or to use a passport. In *Aptheker v. Secretary of State* the Supreme Court held this provision invalid on the ground that it "too broadly and indiscriminately restricts the right to travel and thereby abridges the liberty guaranteed by the Fifth Amendment." Another provision of the Act made it a crime for a member of a Communist-action organization ordered to register "to engage in any employment in any defense facility." The Court struck this down, this time on First Amendment grounds, in *United States v. Robel*. Both cases involved the question of attaching qualifications to a government benefit or position and mark the failure of the additional sanctions provided in the Internal Security Act to survive constitutional attack.[64]

Section 4(a) of the Internal Security Act, the straight sedition provision, makes it unlawful for any person to combine with any other

63. 389 U.S. at 314, 318–319. A further proceeding, seeking a determination of the validity of the Communist-front provisions from a three-judge court, was dismissed in *W.E.B. DuBois Clubs of America v. Clark*, 285 F. Supp. 619 (D.D.C. 1968). The proceeding before the Subversive Activities Control Board, however, was not pressed, apparently because the Department of Justice had used wiretapping or other electronic surveillance in its investigation of the DuBois Clubs. See *The New York Times*, Mar. 20, 1968.

64. *Aptheker v. Secretary of State*, 378 U.S. 500, 505 (1964); *United States v. Robel*, 389 U.S. 258 (1967); both cases are discussed in Chapters VI and VII.

person to perform an act which would substantially contribute to the establishment in the United States of a totalitarian dictatorship under foreign control. One reason this provision has never been invoked is most likely that the Department of Justice considers it unconstitutional on its face. Like the registration provisions, it imposes sanctions, here criminal, on conduct which could consist only of legitimate political expression. The element of foreign influence is even more remote. There seems to be no theory by which the validity of Section 4(a) could be saved.

The detention camp provisions of Title II also have never come into force. Funds were made available in 1951 for the Department of Justice to rehabilitate six World War II installations to serve as detention camps in case of need. The camps were maintained on a standby basis until 1958, at which time they were apparently abandoned or turned to other uses. In 1966 rumors began to circulate that the government was again making the camps ready for use as detention centers in case of an "internal-security emergency." There seemed to be no substantial evidence to support these assertions. The significant issue, however, is not whether detention camps are ready for immediate occupancy; the government could always improvise physical facilities. The question is whether the very existence of the detention camp provisions in Title II has a depressant effect upon the system of freedom of expression. There can hardly be any doubt that they have. Under such circumstances the legal issue is presented whether a suit to have Title II declared unconstitutional, in advance of any use, would be entertained by the courts. Such a suit was initiated in November 1968. If the courts ultimately reach a decision on the merits of the question it is difficult to see how the detention camp provisions can be found valid under any theory of the First Amendment. They could be upheld, if at all, only on some doctrine of martial law superseding normal constitutional rights.[65]

---

65. On the original maintenance and subsequent deactivization of the camps see *The New York Times,* Dec. 27, 1955, and Jan. 1, 1962; *American Civil Liberties Weekly Bulletin,* Jan. 28, 1952, and Feb. 11, 1963. The basis for rumors of revival was primarily Charles R. Allen, Jr., *Concentration Camps, USA* (New York, Marzani and Munsell, 1966). A report of House Committee on Un-American Activities in 1968 suggested the use of detention centers under the McCarran Act "for the temporary imprisonment of warring guerrillas." "Guerrilla Warfare Advocates in the United States," H. Rept. No. 1351, 90th Cong., 2d Sess. (1968), p. 59. Surveys that played down the possibility of detention camps being used include Paul W. Valentine, "Negro Detention Camps: Debunking of a Myth," *Washington Post,* Mar. 3, 1968, pp. A1, A10; William Hedgepeth, "America's Concentration

4. THE 1968 AMENDMENTS

By 1967 the Internal Security Act, apart from the detention camp provisions, had become a virtual nullity. No organization or individual had ever registered under the Act; nor was it likely that one would. After 1956 the Attorney General had filed only two petitions with the Subversive Activities Control Board requesting orders to register, one in 1963 and one in 1966. The Board's only item of business was the *DuBois Clubs* case, which the government was apparently unable to proceed with. The collateral sanctions had been declared invalid in the *Aptheker* and *Robel* cases. No prosecution had ever been brought under Section 4(a). The very foundations of the Act, laid upon the inflexible concept of a monolithic world Communist movement, had disappeared. At this juncture, instead of scrapping the remnants of the Act, Congress voted to attempt a resurrection.

In the fall of 1967 amendments to the Act were pressed in the House by the Committee on Un-American Activities, and in the Senate by Senator Dirksen. They received the support of the Administration, though not of Attorney General Ramsey Clark. There seemed to be no great enthusiasm on the part of most members of Congress but, as usual with such legislation, no disposition to be on record in opposition. The amendments were passed by both houses in December 1967 and approved by President Johnson in January 1968.

The 1968 amendments made a number of alterations in the Act, of which two were of primary significance. One changed the definition of "Communist-front organization" to provide that an organization would be designated such not only if it was directed, dominated, or controlled by a Communist-action organization but if it was directed, dominated, or controlled by "one or more members" of a Communist-action organization. The other eliminated all requirements that organizations or individuals register with the Attorney General or provide

---

Camps: The Rumors and the Realities," *Look Magazine,* May 28, 1968, p. 85. For Attorney General Ramsey Clark's denial, see *Washington Post,* May 13, 1968. The suit challenging Title II is *Bick et al. v. Mitchell* (D.D.C.); government motion to dismiss granted without opinion, May 12, 1969. On the mar-tial law issue see *Korematzu v. United States,* 323 U.S. 214 (1944), and other references in *Political and Civil Rights in the United States,* p. 197. On December 22, 1969, the Senate repealed Title II except for certain findings of fact in section 101. 115 Cong. Rec. S. 17589 (Dec. 22, 1969, daily ed.).

information. Instead, the amendments merely authorized the Board to "keep and maintain records, which shall be open to public inspection, giving the names and addresses of all organizations as to which, and individuals as to whom, there are in effect final orders of the Board" determining that they are Communist-action or Communist-front organizations or members of a Communist-action organization. No effort was made to cure the aging of the Act by changing those provisions which defined the Board's jurisdiction in terms of organizations directed, dominated, or controlled by "the World Communist movement." In an unusual provision, which belied the Congressional finding that the Communist movement presented "a clear and present danger to the security of the United States," it was provided that the Subversive Activities Control Board "shall cease to exist" unless a new proceeding was instituted by the Attorney General and a hearing conducted by the Board before December 31, 1968.[66]

The revised definition of "Communist-front" organization was designed to broaden the Board's power to find organizations falling within that category. But the Attorney General did not file any further petitions against organizations. The Board itself modified its original order against the Communist Party to conform to the new provisions, eliminating from the order any requirement that the Party register or provide information, and merely listing the Party on its records as a "Communist-action organization." In July 1968 the Attorney General filed petitions asking the Board to designate seven individuals as members of the Communist Party. The Board conducted hearings on these petitions, and thereby was kept alive. In November 1968 the Board issued orders against three individuals finding them to be members of a Communist-action organization. In December 1969, however, the Court of Appeals for the District of Columbia set aside the Board's orders on the ground that mere membership in the Communist Party was protected by the First Amendment.[67]

By dropping the self-registration provisions the proponents of the 1968 amendments sought to avoid the self-incrimination problems raised by the original Act. In this they seem to have been successful. But the First Amendment issues remain. Organizations or individuals designated as Communist by the Subversive Activities Control Board are still subjected to that form of exposure to various official and un-

66. 81 Stat. 765 (1968); 50 U.S.C. §§781 et seq.

67. *Boorda v. Subversive Activities Control Board*—F.2d—(D.C. Cir. 1969).

official sanctions and harassments. This plainly impinges upon their rights of expression, including their right of association. In essence, therefore, the First Amendment issues are unchanged.

E. Other Federal Legislation

The last major effort to promote internal security through Federal sedition laws was the Communist Control Act of 1954. Like the Internal Security Act, the Communist Control Act was the product of two proposals, one initiated by conservative members of Congress and the other offered as a substitute by liberal members. The original bill, proposed by Senator Butler, was in the form of an amendment to the Internal Security Act to add a category of "Communist-infiltrated organizations." Senator Humphrey offered a substitute, designed to strike at the "root of the evil," which would have made it a criminal offense to be a member of the Communist Party. The two proposals were combined, other provisions added, and the Humphrey provision modified. The bill passed the Senate unanimously, passed the House with only two dissenting votes, and was signed by President Eisenhower. Omitting the Communist-infiltrated provisions, the major features of the Act are:

(1) Under the heading "Proscribed Organizations," Section 3 provides that the Communist Party of the United States and any successors "are not entitled to any of the rights, privileges, and immunities attendant upon legal bodies created under the jurisdiction of the laws of the United States or any political subdivision thereof; and whatever rights, privileges, and immunities which have heretofore been granted to said party or any subsidiary organization by reason of the laws of the United States or any political subdivision thereof, are hereby terminated."

(2) Section 4 provides that "whoever knowingly and willfully becomes or remains a member of (1) the Communist Party, or (2) any other organization having for one of its purposes or objectives . . . overthrow of the Government . . . by the use of force or violence, with knowledge of the purpose or objective of such organization, shall be subject to all the provisions and penalties of the Internal Security

Act of 1950, as amended, as a member of a 'Communist-action' organization."

(3) Section 5 contains a list of fourteen factors that a jury "shall consider evidence, if presented, as to whether the accused person" is a member of or participates in "the Communist Party or any other organization define in this Act." [68]

The meaning of these provisions is obscure and they have not been invoked in any significant way. Section 3 has figured seriously in only two cases. In one it was used as ground for denying a place on the ballot to a candidate who sought to run under the Communist label in a local New Jersey election. The case never reached the Supreme Court. In the other, the New York Industrial Commissioner relied upon Section 3 to deny unemployment compensation to an employee of the Communist Party and held the Communist Party itself was not covered by the unemployment compensation laws. The New York courts reversed the first ruling and the United States Supreme Court the second. [69]

Section 3 falls short of outlawing the Communist Party in the sense of making membership in it illegal or dissolving it. The section purports to deprive the Communist Party of certain rights, but of what rights is not clear. Certainly it could not deprive the Party of constitutional rights such as the right to due process in court proceedings. But there is no need to search for a meaning. The provision contains all the vices of Section 4(a) of the Internal Security Act and is plainly invalid under the First Amendment. It undertakes to apply sanctions against a political organization engaged, in part at least, in exercising its rights to expression, without a showing that the organization has engaged in illegal conduct of any kind.

The meaning of Section 4 is even more uncertain. It seems to add nothing to existing provisions of the Internal Security Act. Possibly Section 4 could have been intended to accelerate the operation of the registration provisions by requiring that Communist Party members register even before the Subversive Activities Control Board had or-

68. 68 Stat. 775 (1954); 50 U.S.C. §§841–844. For the legislative history see Note, "The Communist Control Act of 1954," *Yale Law Journal,* Vol. 64 (1955), p. 712. For other materials on the Act see *Political and Civil Rights in the United States,* p. 201.

69. *Salwen v. Rees,* 16 N.J.2d 216, 108 A.2d 265 (1954); *In the Matter of the Claim of Albertson,* 8 N.Y.2d 77, 168 N.E.2d 242, 202 N.Y.S.2d 5 (1960); *Communist Party v. Catherwood,* 367 U.S. 389 (1961). See also *Mitchell v. Donovan,* 290 F. Supp. 642 and 300 F. Supp. 1147 (D. Minn. 1969), prob. juris. noted 396 U.S.—(1970).

dered the Party to register; but the provision was never so interpreted.
It has, indeed, never been utilized in any way. Whatever purpose it
may have had, it is now clearly unconstitutional under the Supreme
Court decisions invalidating the passport and defense employment
provisions of the Internal Security Act. Furthermore, Section 4, as
well as Section 3 would undoubtedly be struck down as bills of attainder.[70]

Section 5 was intended as a guide to juries in determining questions of membership or participation in the Communist Party. Beyond
indicating the Congressional frame of mind in 1954 it has served no
significant purpose.

Thus the Communist Control Act has had no direct official impact.
It remains on the books as a monument to the incompetence, irrespon-
sibility, and hysteria of the Eighty-third Congress. Or possibly as a peg
upon which to hang suppression in a future hysteria.

Other Federal legislation designed to protect the national security
against conduct considered seditious is included in the postal and custom laws. These statutes prohibit the mailing or importing of "any
matter advocating or urging treason, insurrection, or forcible resistance to any law of the United States." No Supreme Court decision has
dealt with these provisions. The First Amendment issues are similar to
those arising in connection with the Smith Act.[71]

One further effort by the Federal government to safeguard national security through control of communication needs mention. In
1951 the Government began a program to stop the flow of "foreign
Communist propaganda" into the United States. At first it confiscated
material upon entry. Later, in 1956, it simply held up the material,
asked the addressee if he wished to receive it, and delivered it only if
the recipient formally requested it. In 1961 President Kennedy ordered that the practice be stopped. But the next year Congress enacted
legislation which provided, with certain exceptions, that mail determined by the Secretary of the Treasury to be "communist political
propaganda . . . shall be detained by the Postmaster General upon
its arrival for delivery in the United States . . . and the addressee
shall be notified that such matter has been received and will be delivered only upon the addressee's request." In *Lamont v. Postmaster*

---

70. *Aptheker v. Secretary of State,*
378 U.S. 500 (1964), and *United States
v. Robel,* 389 U.S. 258 (1967), noted in
the preceding section. On the bill of at-

tainder issue see *United States v. Brown,*
381 U.S. 437 (1965), discussed in Chapter VI.

71. 18 U.S.C. §1717; 19 U.S.C. §1305.

General the Supreme Court unanimously invalidated the statute as in conflict with the First Amendment.[72]

The Court could not, however, agree upon its reasons. Justice Douglas, writing for a majority of five, took the position that the requirement of making a formal request for the mail was "almost certain to have a deterrent effect, especially as regards those who have sensitive positions." He went on: "Their livelihood may be dependent on a security clearance. Public officials, like schoolteachers who have no tenure, might think they would invite disaster if they read what the Federal Government says contains the seeds of treason. Apart from them, any addressee is likely to feel some inhibition in sending for literature which federal officials have condemned as 'communist political propaganda.' " Having established that the statute inhibited communication, Justice Douglas moved straight to his conclusion and ended in one sentence: "The regime of this Act is at war with the 'uninhibited, robust, and wide-open' debate and discussion that are contemplated by the First Amendment." [73]

Justice Brennan, with whom Justices Goldberg and Harlan concurred, was unwilling to accept the full protection theory advanced by Justice Douglas. He indicated that the issue was one of balancing: "that only a compelling [governmental] interest in the regulation of a subject within [governmental] constitutional power to regulate can justify limiting First Amendment freedoms." And he ended by applying the rule that the statute must be narrowly drawn: "In the area of First Amendment freedoms, government has the duty to confine itself to the least intrusive regulations which are adequate for the purpose." [74]

The doctrinal aspects of the case are most interesting. No justice suggested the use of the clear and present danger test. Justice Brennan paid lip service to the balancing test but he really did not apply it; he did not go beyond pointing out, as had Justice Douglas, that the requirement was in fact a burden on the exercise of First Amendment rights. Actually it would have been most embarrassing to invoke the balancing test in this situation. For there was nothing to balance unless one assumed that the First Amendment when adopted carried no meaning at all. It is not surprising that three justices in addition to

72. 76 Stat. 840 (1962); *Lamont v. Postmaster General*, 381 U.S. 301 (1965); Justice White did not participate in the decision.

73. 381 U.S. at 307.

74. 381 U.S. at 308–309, 310. See also *Teague v. Regional Commissioner of Customs*, 404 F.2d 441 (2d Cir. 1968), cert. denied 394 U.S. 977 (1969).

Justice Black went along with Justice Douglas on the full protection theory, a total of five. The case is also interesting, it should be noted, as protecting the right to receive, as distinct from sending, communications.

F. State and Local Legislation

State sedition laws, in the form of criminal anarchy or criminal syndicalism laws, have existed since the turn of the century. They were upheld, as we have seen, in the *Gitlow* and *Whitney* cases shortly after World War I. By the time of World War II over two-thirds of the States had some type of sedition law, directed against advocacy of force or violence. Following World War II the States began to pass new kinds of sedition laws, comparable to the Federal Internal Security Act and the Communist Control Act, going far beyond the original prohibitions. Typical of these was the Maryland Ober Law which, in addition to provisions similar to the Smith Act, made it a felony to become or remain a member of a "foreign subversive organization," defined as an organization which is "directed, dominated or controlled directly or indirectly by a foreign government" and which engages in or advocates "activities intended to overthrow, destroy or alter . . . the constitutional form of government" and substitute a government under foreign control. The Ober Law also made it unlawful for a "foreign subversive organization" to "exist or function in the State of Maryland" and any such organization found by a court to be so functioning "shall be seized by and for the State of Maryland." Registration laws similar to the Internal Security Act were passed in eleven States, and eight States outlawed the Communist Party by name or made membership in it a crime. Other varieties of State statutes existed. In addition, upwards of 150 municipalities enacted legislation directed against "subversives," including ordinances requiring registration with the police of members of any "communist organization" or imposing jail sentences on Communist Party members who remained in the city.[75]

75. Md. Ann. Code, Art. 85A, §§1–9 (1957). For a collection of the laws and the materials discussing them see *Political and Civil Rights in the United States*, pp. 207–210.

The impact of the State and local sedition laws was materially curtailed by the decision of the Supreme Court in *Pennsylvania v. Nelson* in 1956, holding that Federal legislation has preempted the field of legislation directed against sedition on a national scale. Steve Nelson, a leading member of the Communist Party, had been convicted under the Pennsylvania Sedition Act and sentenced to imprisonment for twenty years. The Pennsylvania law was very similar to the Federal Smith Act and the evidence against Nelson all dealt with alleged seditious utterances against the United States government rather than the government of Pennsylvania. The Pennsylvania Supreme Court reversed the conviction on the ground that the State law was superseded by the Smith Act and the United States Supreme Court in a six to three vote affirmed. Chief Justice Warren, writing for the majority, ruled that the Pennsylvania act met "each of the several tests of supersession": (1) the scheme of Federal regulation embodied in the Smith Act, the Internal Security Act, and the Communist Control Act was "so pervasive as to make reasonable the inference that Congress left no room for the States to supplement it"; (2) the Federal statutes "touch a field in which the federal interest is so dominant that the federal system [must] be assumed to preclude enforcement of state laws on the same subject"; and (3) "enforcement of state sedition acts presents a serious danger of conflict with the administration of the federal program." [76]

Following *Nelson* all pending proceedings under State sedition laws were dismissed or abandoned. And for several years such laws were seldom, if ever, invoked. But the reach of the *Nelson* case was not entirely clear. Three years later, in *Uphaus v. Wyman*, the Supreme Court partly reversed its field. It held that the *Nelson* doctrine did not apply to a New Hampshire legislative investigation of Dr. Willard Uphaus, "made pursuant to an effort by the Legislature to inform itself of the presence of subversives within the State and possibly to enact laws in the subversive field." And it emphasized that the *Nelson* case had not "stripped the States of the right to protect themselves"; that "a State could proceed with prosecution for sedition against the State itself"; and that "the State had full power to deal with internal civil disturbances." [77]

76. *Pennsylvania v. Nelson,* 350 U.S. 497, 502, 504, 505 (1956).

77. For the effect of *Nelson* on pending State proceedings see *Political and Civil Rights in the United States,* p. 217.

Uphaus v. Wyman, 360 U.S. 72, 76, 77 (1959); see also *DeGregory v. Attorney General of New Hampshire,* 383 U.S. 825 (1966).

In the years following *Uphaus* a gradual revival in the use of State sedition laws took place, both of the internal security variety and of the criminal anarchy and syndicalism variety. Isolated cases of the first type reached the Supreme Court. That tribunal did not find it necessary to pass directly upon any First Amendment issues, however, holding the statutes invalid on other grounds.

Louisiana ex rel. Gremillion v. N.A.A.C.P. involved a Louisiana statute which provided that a "non-trading" association could not do business in the State if it was affiliated with any "foreign or out of state non-trading" association "any of the officers or members of the board of directors of which are members of Communist, Communist-front or subversive organizations, as cited by the House of Congress Un-American Activities Committee or the United States Attorney." An injunction against enforcement of the statute was granted by a Federal District Court and the Supreme Court affirmed, holding the statute void for vagueness. *Dombrowski v. Pfister* invalidated parts of another Louisiana statute, the Subversive Activities and Communist Control Law. One section, requiring registration by members of "a subversive organization," was held unconstitutional on grounds of vagueness in the definition of "subversive organization." Another section required registration of members of a "Communist-front organization" and provided that the fact that any organization had been cited by the United States Attorney General, the Subversive Activities Control Board, or any Committee of Congress as a Communist-front "shall be considered presumptive evidence of the factual status of any such organization." There being no provision for hearing or other procedure in determining whether an organization was a "Communist-front," this provision was stricken as violating due process. In *Stanford v. Texas* the Court held invalid on Fourth Amendment grounds a search warrant issued under the Texas Suppression Act authorizing the seizure of all "books, records, pamphlets, cards, receipts, lists, memoranda, pictures, recordings and other written instruments concerning the Communist Party of Texas, and the operations of the Communist Party in Texas." [78]

These decisions furnish a good example of the umbrella effect of the First Amendment. In none of them did the result turn squarely on a determination that the legislation violated the First Amendment. But the Court made clear in all that First Amendment considerations were

78. *Louisiana ex rel. Gremillion v. N.A.A.C.P.*, 366 U.S. 293 (1961); *Dom-* *browski v. Pfister*, 380 U.S. 479 (1965); *Stanford v. Texas*, 379 U.S. 476 (1965).

an important factor in leading it to enforce other constitutional safeguards with particular stringency. Such considerations undoubtedly also influenced the Court in *Pennsylvania v. Nelson*. Thus the First Amendment played a supporting, though not principal, role.

The revival of the State criminal anarchy and criminal syndicalism laws was a matter of more significance. As the fear of Communism diminished in the nineteen-sixties the threat to internal security appeared to lie more in the activities of civil-rights workers, black militants, aggressive peace marchers, and the New Left generally. The internal security laws were not relevant to these problems. Most of the new radicals did not adhere to the Communist Party, or indeed to any orthodox ideology, and were largely unorganized. Much of their language and style, however, was openly militant, in some ways reminiscent of the left-wing manifestos of the twenties. In any event the States began to look once more to the criminal anarchy and criminal syndicalism laws as a device to control the utterances and actions of these groups. Most of the cases dealt with local issues of law and order, rather than national security matters, and are discussed in Chapter IX. But they raised sharply the broader question whether the antiquated sedition laws, originally upheld in *Gitlow* and *Whitney*, could survive the later developments of First Amendment doctrine. An increasing number of lower Federal courts began to find the State laws invalid as vague and overbroad. In 1969 the Supreme Court returned to the problem.[79]

During the 1968–1969 term the Court had accepted for consideration five cases involving State sedition and unlawful assembly laws. At the end of the term, in June 1969, it ordered four of these cases set

---

79. State sedition laws were invalidated in *Ware v. Nichols*, 266 F. Supp. 564 (N.D. Miss. 1967) (Mississippi criminal syndicalism statute, applied to civil-rights workers); *Carmichael v. Allen*, 267 F. Supp. 985 (N.D. Ga. 1966) (Georgia insurrection statute); *Harris v. Younger*, 281 F. Supp. 507 (C.D. Calif. 1968) (California criminal syndicalism statute, upheld in *Whitney*); *McSurely v. Ratliff*, 282 F. Supp. 848 (E.D. Ky. 1967) (Kentucky criminal syndicalism statute); *Baker v. Bindner*, 274 F. Supp. 658 (W. D. Ky. 1967) (same). State laws were upheld in *People v. Epton*, 19 N.Y.2d 496, 281 N.Y.S.2d 9, 227 N.E.2d 829 (1967), cert. denied and app. dis. 390 U.S. 29 (1968), Justices Douglas and Stewart dissenting (New York criminal anarchy law, upheld in *Gitlow*); *Samuels v. Mackell*, 288 F. Supp. 348 (S.D.N.Y. 1968) (same); *Brandenburg v. Ohio* (not reported; Ohio 1968) (Ohio criminal syndicalism law). Most of the above cases are discussed in Note, Paul Harris "Black Power Advocacy: Criminal Anarchy or Free Speech," *California Law Review*, Vol. 56 (1968), p. 702. For earlier cases see *Political and Civil Rights in the United States*, pp. 227–228. The New York statute was amended in 1967 to narrow its provisions and confine its reach to advocacy of overthrow of the State Government. N.Y. Penal Law, §240.15.

down for reargument in the new term beginning the following October. But it did decide one of them—*Brandenburg v. Ohio*.[80]

The *Brandenburg* case involved the Ohio Criminal Syndicalism statute, similar in text to the California Criminal Syndicalism Act upheld in *Whitney v. California*. Brandenburg, a leader of a Ku Klux Klan group, had been convicted under the Ohio law, and sentenced to imprisonment for one to ten years, primarily on the basis of a speech which he had made at a Klan rally. The nearest Brandenburg had come to advocacy of violence was the statement: "We're not a revengent organization, but if our President, our Congress, our Supreme Court, continues to suppress the white, Caucasian race, it's possible that there might have to be some revengeance taken." The appellate court and Supreme Court of Ohio affirmed the conviction, neither writing an opinion. The United States Supreme Court, in a short per curiam opinion, unanimously reversed.

The Court began by saying that the *Whitney* case "has been thoroughly discredited by later decisions," citing *Dennis*. And it went on to state what must be taken as its 1969 rule: "These later decisions have fashioned the principle that the constitutional guarantees of free speech and free press do not permit a State to forbid or proscribe advocacy of the use of force or of law violation except where such advocacy is directed to inciting or producing imminent lawless action and is likely to incite or produce such action." In the case before them "[n]either the indictment nor the trial judge's instructions to the jury in any way refined the statute's bald definition of the crime in terms of mere advocacy not distinguished from incitement to imminent lawless action." Accordingly the statute "falls within the condemnation of the First and Fourteenth Amendments." Finally, "[t]he contrary teaching of *Whitney v. California* . . . cannot be supported, and that decision is therefore overruled." [81]

Justice Douglas joined the Court's opinion but wrote an extensive concurrence. In it he reviewed numerous First Amendment cases and concluded: "The line between what is permissible and not subject to control and what may be made impermissible and subject to regulation is the line between ideas and overt acts." Justice Black, agreeing with Justice Douglas, also joined the majority opinion on the understanding

80. *Brandenburg v. Ohio*, 395 U.S. 444 (1969). The cases ordered reargued were *Harris v. Younger* and *Samuels v. Mackell*, cited in note 79, and *Boyle v. Landry*, 280 F. Supp. 938 (N.D. Ill. 1968), and *Gunn v. University Committee to End the War in Vietnam*, 289 F. Supp. 469 (W.D. Tex. 1968), noted in Chapter IX.

81. 395 U.S. at 447, 448–449.

it "does not indicate any agreement on the Court's part with the 'clear and present danger' doctrine on which *Dennis* purported to rely." [82]

Thus a majority of the Court came to settle on an incitement test as the measure of the validity of State sedition laws. There remained unresolved the question whether these laws were invalid on their face as vague and overbroad, or were still capable of being applied, on a narrowed basis, in particular prosecutions. In general it would appear that such State laws, whether in their present form or rewritten to conform to *Brandenburg,* are not likely to be a major factor in the area of internal security but may well play an important role with respect to local problems of internal order.

The revival by the States of their sedition laws, coupled with the strong likelihood that the laws were no longer valid, brought to the fore an important issue of Federal-State relations. The question is whether the general validity of State statutes, or their enforcement in particular instances, can be tested by suit in the Federal courts prior to initiation or completion of prosecution in the State courts. The matter is of particular significance to the system of freedom of expression. State sedition laws can readily be utilized to suppress radical or unpopular individuals and if such persons are forced to undergo lengthy State proceedings to vindicate themselves crucial First Amendment rights will be lost in the process. On the other hand Federal courts have always been reluctant, and properly so, to interfere with State proceedings in progress or to decide cases in advance of a full and specific record.

Earlier Supreme Court decisions had indicated that the constitutional issues growing out of State criminal prosecutions could be raised in Federal courts only after conviction in the State court. But in 1965, in *Dombrowski v. Pfister,* the Supreme Court took another look at the problem. In *Dombrowski* suit was brought by the Southern Conference Educational Fund and three individuals to enjoin enforcement of Louisiana sedition legislation. The complaint alleged that Louisiana officials had arrested the individual plaintiffs, raided their homes and offices, raided the S.C.E.F. office, and seized their files and records. A State judge had quashed the arrest warrant and held the seizures illegal. Nevertheless the Louisiana authorities convened a grand jury and threatened plaintiffs with prosecution. The plaintiffs further alleged that the statutes were void on their face as overbroad, and that the

82. 395 U.S. at 456, 450.

threats to enforce the statutes were not made "with any expectation of securing valid convictions, but rather as part of a plan . . . to harass [plaintiffs] and discourage them and their supporters from asserting and attempting to vindicate the constitutional rights of Negro citizens in Louisiana." After the complaint was filed indictments were returned by the grand jury. The Supreme Court, by a margin of five to two, held that the complaint alleged sufficient irreparable injury to justify equitable relief and that the doctrine of abstention should not be applied. The majority opinion pointed out "the chilling effect on free expression of prosecutions initiated and threatened," and concluded: "We believe that those affected by a statute are entitled to be free of the burdens of defending prosecutions, however expeditious, aimed at hammering out the structure of the statute piecemeal." [83]

Following *Dombrowski,* numerous attempts were made to obtain relief in the Federal courts, either by way of declaratory judgment or injunction, against enforcement of many kinds of State laws which affected First Amendment rights. Most of these efforts were unsuccessful. In several subsequent decisions the Supreme Court undertook to bring some order to a chaotic situation, but the scope of the *Dombrowski* rule has remained uncertain. In general it appears that the Federal courts will grant declaratory relief if the State statute is invalid on its face, a substantial likelihood of attempted enforcement exists, and no special countervailing circumstances are present, such as the susceptibility of the statute to a construction by the State courts which would eliminate the constitutional defect. The Federal courts are more reluctant to grant an injunction against a threatened or pending prosecution in the State courts. In such a situation the potential defendant must establish that defense of the State prosecution will not assure adequate vindication of his constitutional rights. This can be shown when the State statute is invalid on its face, especially by reason of vagueness or overbreadth, and the person involved should be free of the burden of making a defense. Or it can be shown, whether the statute is valid or invalid, if it is established that the State prosecution is brought in bad faith, for purposes of harassment, with no intention of pressing the charges or expectation of securing a conviction.[84]

---

83. *Dombrowski v. Pfister,* 380 U.S. 479, 482, 487, 491 (1965). For the earlier view of the Supreme Court see *Douglas v. City of Jeanette,* 319 U.S. 157 (1943).

84. See *Cameron v. Johnson,* 381 U.S. 741 (1965), and 390 U.S. 611 (1968);

Zwickler v. Koota, 389 U.S. 241 (1967). Cf. *W.E.B. DuBois Clubs of America v. Clark,* 389 U.S. 309 (1967). The *Dombrowski* doctrine has also been important in connection with State statutes affecting the right of assembly. See Chapter IX.

Taken as a whole the *Dombrowski* rule would seem to afford substantial promise of obtaining relief in the Federal courts against State sedition laws that are unconstitutional on their face. However, if the State law is valid on its face but is being utilized for harassment the proof required by the Federal courts is difficult to provide. Further development of the possibilities of securing Federal protection in these circumstances is essential to maintaining a more effective system of freedom of expression.[85]

G. An Appraisal of Sedition Laws

Experience with sedition laws in the United States has demonstrated that they are not needed to protect internal security and are incompatible with the democratic process. The Sedition Act of 1798, designed to eliminate all criticism which brought the Federalist government into "disrepute," was repudiated as error in the election of 1800, a judgment repeatedly confirmed since then. No sedition laws were deemed necessary again until the twentieth century. The new laws, directed more specifically at advocacy of violent overthrow of government, were employed mainly in the post–World War I Red Scare, another period now viewed as one of regrettable hysteria. The Smith Act, the anachronistic Federal copy of State advocacy laws, was rendered inoperative in the *Yates* case without any noticeable effect upon the security of the nation. The Internal Security Act and the Communist Control Act, using the concept of foreign control as the basis for suppressing a political movement, have likewise proved unworkable, again with no apparent danger to the country. The use of this Federal legislation coincided with the era of McCarthyism, a third period of irrational response to imagined fears. State sedition laws, as far as national security is concerned, have been largely nullified by Federal preemption.

Thus the sedition laws have, in fact, been unnecessary for the safe-

---

For material discussing the *Dombrowski* doctrine see *Political and Civil Rights in the United States,* D'Army Bailey, "Enjoining State Criminal Prosecutions Which Abridge First Amendment Freedoms," *Harvard Civil Rights–Civil Liberties Law Review,* Vol. 3 (1967), p. 67; Note, "The Chilling Effect in Constitu-

tional Law," *Columbia Law Review,* Vol. 69 (1969), p. 808.

85. Various cases pending before the Supreme Court during the 1969–1970 term, including those cited in Note 80, *supra,* raise issues under the *Dombrowski* rule.

guarding of our internal security. When put into actual operation, they have been revealed as wholly inconsistent with the basic assumptions of a democratic body politic. Fortunately, in this conflict up to now, democratic procedures have largely prevailed and the sedition laws failed. Yet in the process much harm has been done.

The fact is that sedition laws are, in the final analysis, a relic of government by monarchy. They are designed to destroy political opposition. Yet popular participation in the governing process implies that social and political movements aimed at basic change in society must be allowed to exist and have their say. For both theoretical and practical reasons this remains true even when the opposition goes to the length of advocating change by force and violence if necessary. The answer to such a challenge, in a democratic community, is to punish overt action if and when it occurs, and to maintain the social and economic conditions necessary for a viable society. Suppression of political groups, apart from any use of violence, cannot be reconciled with constitutional government.

From this it follows that the First Amendment must be viewed as operating to protect all expression, confining governmental controls to the stage of action. Other legal doctrines, as experience in the sedition cases has shown, are inadequate to carry out the fundamental design of affording effective constitutional protection. This basic doctrine of full protection to expression must be supported by additional rules that will spell out the distinction between "expression" and "action," separate legal expression from illegal action in associational conduct, protect the individual from guilt by association, and otherwise cope with such problems as the impact of foreign control upon the right to function within our system of freedom of expression.

The part played by the Supreme Court in the development of First Amendment doctrine in the sedition cases has been a mixed one. It has not met the problems head on. Faced with decision on the basic incompatibility of the Smith Act and the Internal Security Act with the First Amendment it has backed away. Then, by a somewhat circuitous route, it has undercut the actual administration of those laws. The Court's method of operation is understandable. It started, not so long ago, from a point where First Amendment doctrine was wholly undeveloped and public comprehension somewhat limited. Yet, having traversed its winding route and had the opportunity to educate itself and the nation, the Court may now have reached the place where it is ready to face the issues fully and without unnecessary caution.

VI

Internal Security: Expression as a Ground for Denying Benefits or Positions

The state frequently seeks to protect its interest in internal security not only through direct prohibitions on conduct but through denial of benefits, privileges or positions of influence to persons thought to be "subversive." We are concerned here, of course, only with those regulations which impose such disqualifications on the basis of "expression," not with those whose basis is "action." Restrictions of this sort have existed throughout history, most frequently in the form of loyalty oaths. But they have become of increasing concern with the expansion of social control over individual affairs. In the last several decades, they have been employed not only in extensive loyalty-security qualifications for government employment, but in numerous programs establishing qualifications for participating in labor organizations, for engaging in various professions or occupations, for receiving governmental financial

161

or welfare aid, for obtaining a passport, and for functioning in many other capacities. This form of restriction poses special problems for a system of freedom of expression.[1]

At the outset it is again necessary to define precisely the social interest involved. In most of the regulations with which we are here concerned the social interest at stake is said to be the interest in internal security. It should be remembered that this is an interest in protecting the government and the institutions of society against destruction or alteration by non-democratic methods, essentially force and violence; it does not encompass, certainly where control over expression is exercised, the power to forestall change by democratic processes. This interest in internal security is clearly dominant in some forms of regulation, such as the non-Communist affidavit of the Taft-Hartley Act or the port security program. That interest tends to diminish or almost disappear, however, in other forms of regulation, such as the exclusion of Communist Party members from the practice of law or from welfare benefits. In such situations other social interests may be invoked as, for instance, the more effective administration of a welfare program. But it is seldom argued that these other social interests should overcome the right to freedom of expression. We are primarily concerned, therefore, with the interest in internal (or at times external) security.

The effect on freedom of expression from withholding benefits or positions is apparent. To some extent the impact is direct, as when a person deliberately foregoes some form of expression in order to be eligible for a benefit or position. More frequently the impact is indirect. Numerous other persons seek to avoid future trouble by steering clear of controversial opinions or associations. These repercussions extend particularly to young persons, studying for or just entering a career. The more extensive the restrictions and the longer they remain in operation the more pervasive becomes the dampening effect. Over a period of time the whole ethos of political life may be drastically altered.

There are, moreover, certain features of this kind of restriction which accentuate the impact upon the system of free expression. In the

1. For a general collection of materials and references, see Thomas I. Emerson, David Haber and Norman Dorsen, *Political and Civil Rights in the United States* (Boston, Little, Brown & Co., 3d ed. 1967), pp. 228–337 (cited hereafter in this chapter as *Political and Civil Rights in the United States*). See also Note, "Civil Disabilities and the First Amendment," *Yale Law Journal,* Vol. 78 (1969), p. 842.

first place the regulations are, even more clearly than in most controls of expression, a form of preventive law. No harm has yet been done. The scheme is to avoid injury by weeding out in advance those persons who might possibly cause the injury some time in the future. Such restrictions almost inevitably suffer from overbreadth, in design and in application. In order to avoid the bad risks they tend to eliminate many of the good risks.

Secondly, the restrictions are usually framed as administrative regulations rather than criminal offenses. Hence the safeguards of a criminal proceeding are lacking. Rules relating to the burden of proof, the admission of evidence, the necessity of a judicial tribunal, are all relaxed or abandoned. It is possible, moreover, to initiate a proceeding or disqualify an applicant on a showing substantially less than is required to commence a criminal prosecution. The administrative system may, therefore, be a much tighter, more pervading form of restriction.

Finally, the system of restriction is normally one of low visibility. Decisions are frequently informal, made without public hearing, and indeed without publicity. Official findings of fact and reasons are usually not given. Such procedures are particularly likely when the person affected is an applicant rather than an incumbent. Thus an air of mystery and uncertainty permeates the process. The imagined impact of the restriction may be the most repressive feature of all.

One further matter should be noted by way of preliminary. Even more than in the case of sedition laws, the courts here deal with First Amendment problems without relying upon First Amendment doctrines. Nevertheless the presence of First Amendment factors influences the manner in which the courts apply non–First Amendment principles. It is not possible to explore all the ramifications of the umbrella effect of the First Amendment in this area. Yet its impact must not be ignored if the full picture is to be seen.

A. Labor Organizations

The constitutional issues involved in denying benefits or positions on the basis of expression were initially raised in connection with restrictions imposed on labor organizations. This was no accident. Radical political theories and radical political movements, along with the fears engendered by them, had long been associated in the United States with the labor movement. At the end of World War II public concern over the spread of Communism coincided with a growing reaction to the political and economic strength of labor. The result was the Taft-Hartley Act. Enacted in 1947, this legislation sought generally to curb the power of labor and specifically to eliminate Communist influence from the labor movement.

The Taft-Hartley Act amended the National Labor Relations Act by adding Section 9(h). This provided that no labor organization could obtain the benefits of that Act (governmental enforcement of the right to self-organization and collective bargaining) unless there was filed with the National Labor Relations Board an annual affidavit from each officer of the union declaring "that he is not a member of the Communist Party or affiliated with such party, and that he does not believe in, and is not a member of or supports any organization that believes in or teaches, the overthrow of the United States Government by force or by any illegal or unconstitutional methods." The constitutionality of this provision reached the Supreme Court in *American Communications Association v. Douds*. The Court upheld the first part of the oath by a vote of five to one and divided three to three on the belief provisions.[2]

The decision in the *Douds* case was one of the most important rendered by the Vinson Court. Coming a year before the *Dennis* decision upholding the Smith Act, the *Douds* case established the basic position of the courts toward the growing mass of postwar restrictions designed to curb alleged Communist and pro-Communist activities. In doing so the decision also marked a fundamental shift of direction in the development of First Amendment doctrine.[3]

The majority opinion in *Douds*, representing the views of four members of the Court, was written by Chief Justice Vinson. The Vin-

2. *American Communications Association v. Douds*, 339 U.S. 382 (1950). See Chapter II for a discussion of the decision on the belief provisions. Justices Douglas, Minton and Clark did not participate in the *Douds* decision. In a similar case decided a month later, however, Justice Minton voted to uphold both parts of the oath, Justice Douglas thought the belief provisions were unconstitutional and did not reach the issues as to the first part, and Justice Clark did not partici-

pate. The result was that the first part of the oath was upheld six to one, and the vote on the belief provisions remained equal at four to four. *Osman v. Douds*, 339 U.S. 846 (1950). For material on the background and legislative history of the non-Communist affidavit provision, see *Political and Civil Rights in the United States*, p. 248.

3. The *Dennis* case is discussed in Chapter V.

son opinion first established the constitutional justification for the non-Communist oath, apart from any First Amendment issues. It noted that the purpose of the provision was to prevent obstruction to interstate commerce by eliminating "political" strikes, and held that this was within the commerce power. It also ruled that the means used to accomplish this—the removal of Communist Party members as leaders of labor unions—were reasonable: "Congress could rationally find that the Communist Party is not like other political parties in its utilization of positions of union leadership as means by which to bring about strikes and other obstructions of commerce for purposes of political advantage." The opinion acknowledged, however, that the method used had an adverse effect upon freedom of expression: "By exerting pressures on unions to deny office to Communists and others identified therein, §9(h) undoubtedly lessens the threat to interstate commerce, but it has the further necessary effect of discouraging the exercise of political rights protected by the First Amendment." The opinion then turns to a solution of the First Amendment problem.[4]

Chief Justice Vinson begins his analysis at the same point that Justice Holmes did in the *Schenck* case. He starts with the proposition that the First Amendment could not mean that all speech is protected: "Freedom of speech thus does not comprehend the right to speak on any subject at any time." The question then is "not whether, but how far, the First Amendment permits the suppression of speech which advocates conduct inimical to the public welfare." He notes that some have answered this question by using the "reasonable tendency" test, but appears to agree that the Holmes-Brandeis clear and present danger test has superseded "reasonable tendency." He then rules, however, that the clear and present danger test is not applicable to the problem before him. The reason is that Congress is not here concerned directly with the effects of the speech involved, but with preventing conduct caused by the kind of people who engage in the speech in question: "Section 9(h) . . . does not interfere with speech because Congress fears the consequences of speech; it regulates harmful conduct which Congress has determined is carried on by persons who may be identified by their political affiliations and beliefs." In other words, the regulation is addressed to other conduct and its effect upon speech is only indirect.[5]

By this reasoning Chief Justice Vinson reached the conclusion that the test must be one of balancing interests: "When particular conduct

4. 339 U.S. at 391, 393.   5. 339 U.S. at 394–395, 396.

is regulated in the interest of public order, and the regulation results in an indirect, conditional, partial abridgment of speech, the duty of the courts is to determine which of these two conflicting interests demands the greater protection under the particular circumstances presented." This was the first time that the balancing test had received such specific and carefully reasoned endorsement. From this beginning it was to become the principal doctrine employed in deciding First Amendment cases.[6]

The Vinson opinion then goes on to apply the balancing test to the situation before him. On the side of "the interest of public order" he first makes clear that "this Court is in no position to substitute its judgment as to the necessity or desirability of the statute for that of Congress." He then observes that "the problem of political strikes" is more significant and complex than regulations "dealing with littering of the streets or disturbance of householders by itinerant preachers." Finally he notes that Section 9(h) is "part of some very complex machinery set up by the Federal Government for the purpose of encouraging the peaceful settlement of labor disputes"; that under this scheme the unions having a majority are given the right to represent all employees; that "power is never without responsibility"; and therefore "the public interest in the good faith exercise of that power is very great." [7]

On the other side of the equation—the interest in freedom of speech—the Vinson opinion focuses on the limited nature of the restriction. The gist of the opinion on this issue is: "Section 9(h) touches only a relative handful of persons, leaving the great majority of persons of the identified affiliations and beliefs completely free from restraint. And it leaves those few who are affected free to maintain their affiliations and beliefs subject only to possible loss of positions which Congress has concluded are being abused to the injury of the public by members of the described groups." [8]

The issue is resolved in favor of the interest in public order. Chief Justice Vinson also rejects three other arguments. He holds that the statute is not too broadly drawn, that it is not void for vagueness, and that it does not constitute a bill of attainder.

Justice Frankfurter agreed generally with the Vinson opinion. Justice Jackson, also concurring, stressed that the oath provisions could be applied to the Communist Party, but not to the Republican, Democratic or Socialist parties, because "Congress could rationally con-

---

6. 339 U.S. at 399.   8. 339 U.S. at 404.
7. 339 U.S. at 400–401, 402.

clude that, behind its political party façade, the Communist Party is a conspiratorial and revolutionary junta, organized to reach ends and use methods which are incompatible with our constitutional system." [9]

Justice Black dissented. He pointed out that the majority admitted that the "proscriptions" of Section 9(h) rest on "beliefs and political affiliation" and that Congress had "undeniably discouraged the lawful exercise of political freedoms" which are "protected by the First Amendment." "These inescapable facts," he said, "should compel a holding that §9(h) conflicts with the First Amendment." He added:

> Like anyone else, individual Communists who commit overt acts in violation of valid laws can and should be punished. But the postulate of the First Amendment is that our free institutions can be maintained without proscribing or penalizing political belief, speech, press, assembly, or party affiliation. This is a far bolder philosophy than despotic rulers can afford to follow. It is the heart of the system on which our freedom depends. [10]

Chief Justice Vinson was sound in his rejection of the "reasonable tendency" test. He would also seem to have been correct in maintaining that the clear and present danger test is not applicable to cases in which the infringement on First Amendment rights results from using expression as the basis for disqualification from a benefit or position. In such a situation it is not the expression itself which creates or leads to the evil. Rather expression is being used as the measure of a person's proneness to commit the evil. Hence a test that seeks to measure how close the expression is to producing the evil is simply not addressed to the problem. One could utilize a modified form of the clear and present danger test in benefit and position cases. It would run as follows: Is there a clear and present danger that A, who has uttered expression X, will engage in the conduct feared? The test would be a substitute for the "reasonable relation" test of due process, which would normally govern such an issue. But it would not have the same meaning as the original test, primarily because it omits the element of "present." Furthermore, it would be useful only in solving the due process issue, not the First Amendment problem.

Chief Justice Vinson's use of the balancing test had, as stated above, far-reaching consequences. It established a process of decision making that rendered it most difficult for a court to uphold First Amendment rights against the mandate of the legislature. The interest

9. 339 U.S. at 424.   10. 339 U.S. at 446, 452–453.

in internal security, considered by itself, is so powerful and pressing that it almost automatically overwhelms the less immediately demanding interest in freedom of expression. Moreover, the formula is so loose and open-ended, so lacking in judicial guidelines, that the Court is hardly making a judicial determination; it is acting more in the capacity of a legislature. In addition, the balancing test deprives the courts of the power, embodied in the clear and present danger test, to decide the constitutional issue on the facts "in each case." Rather, as in *Gitlow,* the Court upholds the general validity of the law and the only issue thereafter is whether the facts of each case fit into the meaning of the statute.

Furthermore, the manner in which the Court applied the balancing test in *Douds* could hardly have given rise to any optimism that First Amendment rights would be adequately protected. In holding at the outset that it could not make any independent judgment on "the necessity or desirability" of the restriction the Court had already heavily weighted the scales in favor of the legislation. The actual weighing done in the opinion can only be described as cursory. There is a comparison to littering and canvassing regulations, a reference to the responsibility given the union as representative of the employees, an argument that the infringement affects only a few persons in a partial way—and that is all. Moreover, even if the Court had attempted a more careful weighing it could not have found comparable factors to place on each side of the scales. One is left with no confidence that the balancing test could serve a useful purpose in maintaining an effective system of freedom of expression.

The Vinson opinion starts from the premise that the First Amendment could not possibly be read as protecting every instance of speech and that therefore some kind of limiting test must be devised. This was the common approach in seeking to develop First Amendment doctrine, and embraced the common fallacy. Chief Justice Vinson apparently gave no thought to another possibility—that of defining more carefully, in the light of First Amendment purposes, the meaning of "speech" and "abridge," and then giving full effect to the provision. Justice Black had now reached this position, although he did not fully articulate it. Before considering this approach to the Taft-Hartley problem, however, let us look briefly at subsequent developments in the effort to remove persons from union leadership on the basis of political affiliation.

The only other Supreme Court decision that dealt with First Amendment issues was *Killian v. United States*. In that case Killian, a union officer, was convicted for swearing falsely in an affidavit filed under Section 9(h) that he was not a "member" of the Communist Party or "affiliated" with it. The Supreme Court reversed for failure of the prosecution to produce certain documents, but it went on to consider some problems of associational rights involved in determining "membership" and "affiliation." Justice Whittaker, writing for the majority of five, upheld instructions to the jury that defined membership as "a status of mutuality between the individual and the organization," that is, "the desire on the part of the individual to belong to the Communist Party and a recognition by that Party that it considers him as a member." The trial judge had rejected Killian's request to charge that the jury had to find "a definite objective factual phenomenon [of joining]" or "a specific formal act of joining." Justice Whittaker said that "the very nature of the case—claimed membership in an underground or secretly operating organization . . . precludes the possibility of such evidence," and that proof of "the ultimate subjective fact of membership" was all that was required.[11]

As to "affiliation," the Court held that this was satisfied by proof of "a close working alliance or association between [the defendant] and the organization, together with a mutual understanding or recognition that the organization can rely and depend upon him to cooperate with it, and to work for its benefit." The Court ruled out a definition that would have required a showing that the defendant was a member of another organization that was in turn affiliated with the Party. It rejected, as it had in connection with the definition of membership, Killian's contention that the instructions to the jury "erroneously defined the phrase 'affiliation with' only in subjective terms and without objective criteria." Justice Brennan dissented from the rulings on both membership and affiliation.[12]

The Court in *Killian* passed also upon another aspect of associational rights. It rejected the contention that proof of membership or affiliation could not be based "upon statements or acts that are protected by the First Amendment." It did so on the ground that Killian "was not charged with criminality for being a member of or affiliated with the Communist Party, nor with participating in any criminal ac-

11. *Killian v. United States,* 368 U.S.   12. 368 U.S. at 255, 257.
231, 247–249 (1961).

tivities of or for the Communist Party," but only with having submitted a false affidavit. The majority therefore distinguished the case
from *Scales*.[13]

Justice Douglas, with whom Chief Justice Warren and Justice
Black concurred, dissented on this issue:

> [U]nless we toss to the winds the tolerance which a Free Society shows
> for unorthodox, as well as orthodox, views, the fact that a person em-
> braces lawful views of the party should not establish that he is a
> "member" of the party within the meaning of the Act. Membership,
> as that word is used in the Act, should be proved by facts which tie
> the accused to the illegal aims of the party. If beliefs are used to con-
> demn the individual, we have ourselves gone a long way down the to-
> talitarian path.[14]

The problems raised by *Killian* reveal sharply the practical impact
of regulations denying benefits or positions upon a system of free expression. Such restrictions are frequently cast in terms of disqualification for membership in or affiliation with certain organizations. The
concept of membership or affiliation, however, turns out to be a somewhat elusive one. It is a "subjective," not an "objective," fact. Persons
having any relation to a questioned organization cannot be sure it
will not be interpreted by some security officer or jury as membership
or affiliation. Moreover, the rule that membership or affiliation can be
proved by legitimate as well as illegitimate conduct removes the possibility that a person may avoid trouble so long as his own conduct is
within the law, and thereby greatly discourages any cooperation or
connection with unorthodox associations. The fact that "expression"
can be used as evidence in proof of membership or affiliation similarly
operates to inhibit freedom of speech and association.[15]

In doctrinal terms *Killian* does not seem to add very much to
Douds. The dissenters contended vigorously that, in failing to separate
legal conduct within an association from illegal conduct, the *Killian*
decision repudiated *Douds*. But this would not seem to be so. It is true
that the Vinson opinion in *Douds*, though not the Jackson opinion, did
separate legal from illegal conduct. But the *Douds* decision then refused to protect the legal conduct, and the majority in *Killian* were

13. 368 U.S. at 253, 254. For discussion of *Scales* see Chapter V.

14. 368 U.S. at 263–264.

15. For further discussion of the use
of expression as evidence in applying
sanctions directed ultimately at action,
see Chapter XI.

doing no more than carrying out the implications of this holding. It is interesting to note, however, that a majority of the Court could not be mustered, as it had been in *Yates,* for a narrow interpretation of the statute, which would have made the government's enforcement problem far more difficult, if not impossible. Perhaps a potential majority for that view thought it unnecessary; by the time of the *Killian* decision Section 9(h) had already been repealed.

Section 9(h) proved unsatisfactory in operation. The Supreme Court held that the National Labor Relations Board had no jurisdiction to decide whether an affidavit filed with it was false or not; that question could be determined only in a separate criminal prosecution for false swearing. This eliminated enforcement through the administrative process. Many violations were suspected, but only eighteen prosecutions were brought. Convictions were easily obtained in these cases but, as in *Killian* itself, frequently reversed on some technical ground. Evasion of the provision, by resignation from the Communist Party, by "fronting" devices, and by other methods, was not uncommon.[16]

Congress first attempted to buttress Section 9(h) through providing in the Communist Control Act of 1954 for the designation of "Communist-infiltrated organizations" by the Subversive Activities Control Board. Only two proceedings were brought under these provisions, one against the United Electrical, Radio and Machine Workers, and the other against the International Union of Mine, Mill and Smelter Workers. Both were ultimately dismissed. Finally in 1959, when Congress enacted the Labor-Management Reporting and Disclosure Act, it repealed Section 9(h) and substituted a new provision. The new enactment, Section 504, made it a criminal offense for any person "who is or has been a member of the Communist Party" during the preceding five years to serve as an officer or employee "of any labor organization."[17]

16. The decisions withholding enforcement powers from the N.L.R.B. are *Leedom v. International Union of Mine, Mill and Smelter Workers,* 352 U.S. 145 (1956), and *Amalgamated Meat Cutters v. N.L.R.B.,* 352 U.S. 153 (1956). For materials on the other problems in administration of Section 9(h), see *Political and Civil Rights in the United States,* 2d ed., pp. 469–471, and 3d ed., pp. 247–252.

17. The Communist Control Act provisions are found at 68 Stat. 775 (1954), 50 U.S.C. §§782, 792a. For an account of the proceedings before the S.A.C.B. under these provisions, see *Political and Civil Rights in the United States,* pp. 195–196. The repeal of Section 9(h) is found at 73 Stat. 525 (1959). The new provision became 29 U.S.C. §504.

Section 504 was declared unconstitutional by the Court of Appeals for the Ninth Circuit on First Amendment grounds in *Brown v. United States*. That Court held that a direct criminal sanction could not validly be imposed upon membership "in the absence of a specific intent to accomplish that which Congress seeks to prevent," and therefore the provision was "unreasonably" broad. The Supreme Court, in a five to four division, likewise found Section 504 unconstitutional, but as a bill of attainder, without passing on First Amendment issues. Chief Justice Warren, writing for the majority, argued:

> The statute does not set forth a generally applicable rule decreeing that any person who commits certain acts or possesses certain characteristics (acts and characteristics which, in Congress' view, make them likely to initiate political strikes) shall not hold union office, and leave to courts and juries the job of deciding what persons have committed the specified acts or possess the specified characteristics. Instead, it designates in no uncertain terms the persons who possess the feared characteristics and therefore cannot hold union office without incurring criminal liability—members of the Communist Party.[18]

Justice White and the dissenters took issue with this proposition, contending that the classification was a sufficiently general one and that the majority view would invalidate many other disqualification statutes, such as those disbarring felons from practicing medicine. Chief Justice Warren's reply is most interesting. He declared that to use the Communist Party classification as "shorthand" for describing certain disqualifying characteristics could not be tolerated because it rested on "the fallacy . . . that membership in the Communist Party, or any other political organization, can be regarded as an alternative, but equivalent, expression for a list of undesirable characteristics." This would not be tolerable because, quoting *Schneiderman v. United States,* "under our traditions beliefs are personal and not a matter of mere association and . . . men in adhering to a political party or other organization notoriously do not subscribe unqualifiedly to all of its platforms or asserted principles." Thus, the crucial distinction between an enumeration which constitutes a bill of attainder and one which does not was based upon First Amendment factors. The *Brown* decision is a striking example of those cases in which the Court's appli-

---

18. *Brown v. United States,* 334 F.2d 488, 495 (9th Cir. 1964). The case was heard *en banc*, with five judges concurring on the constitutional issue, two dissenting, and one not reaching the point. In the Supreme Court the case became *United States v. Brown,* 381 U.S. 437, 450 (1965).

cation of constitutional doctrine is strongly influenced by First Amendment considerations.[19]

While the Court did not expressly overrule *Douds* on the bill of attainder issue, the effect of the decision would seem to be to eliminate disqualifications based upon membership in a named organization. Such regulations could thenceforth only be framed in terms of describing or defining a type of organization, leaving it up to the executive or judicial branch to determine whether any particular organization fitted the category. This immediately raises some important administrative problems. The making of such a determination in the case of each individual, for instance, is a cumbersome process. One solution is to compile a master list of organizations that come within the disqualifying classification. This in turn adds to the impact of the regulation on freedom of expression.[20]

In any event the *Brown* case marked the end of the effort to disqualify persons from union leadership on the basis of political affiliation or belief. We return, then, to the problem of applying the expression-action theory to this situation.

Both Section 9(h) and Section 504 raise two preliminary problems of associational rights. The first is to what extent the conduct of a person in forming, joining or participating in an association is to be classified as "expression" rather than "action." In creating an association the individual, or group of individuals, seeks to make individual expression more effective through reaching a larger audience with more persuasive communication. Hence all ordinary conduct necessary to communication through the means of an association must be classified as expression. This includes not only speaking at a meeting or distributing literature issued by the association, but making preparations for the meeting, soliciting members, serving on committees, keeping organizational records, and the like. Membership or affiliation with an organization engaged in communication therefore necessarily involves conduct that is entitled to protection under the First Amendment as "expression." The courts, indeed, have never questioned this initial proposition.[21]

---

19. 381 U.S. at 455, 456; *Schneiderman v. United States*, 320 U.S. 118, 136 (1943).

20. See Chapter VII. The question whether *Brown* overruled *Douds* was left undecided by the Supreme Court in *Bryson v. United States*, 396 U.S. 990 (1969).

21. For a fuller development of this matter see Thomas I. Emerson, "Freedom of Association and Freedom of Expression," *Yale Law Journal*, Vol. 74 (1964), p. 1. See also the discussion of the right of association in Chapter XII.

The second problem of associational rights relates to the separation of "expression" and "action" when an organization engages in both forms of conduct. A system of freedom of expression demands that in such a situation, as far as possible, the expression be isolated so that it may be protected. This is the principle of the *De Jonge* case. Actually, though he did not articulate the position, Chief Justice Vinson recognized the fact of separation in the *Douds* case. He reasoned that, although Congress had found that the Communist Party used "positions of union leadership as means by which to bring about strikes and other obstructions of commerce for purposes of political advantage," nevertheless "Communists, we may assume, carry on legitimate political activities"; and since the regulation impinged on these legitimate activities it raised First Amendment questions. Chief Justice Vinson disposed of the problem, however, simply by applying the balancing test and refusing to protect the expression. The majority in *Killian* followed the same course. On the other hand, Justice Jackson in *Douds* did not recognize the issue; he lumped together all activities of the Communist Party and justified restriction on expression as part of the regulation of the total conduct.[22]

If, then, we recognize that associational conduct in the form of expression is involved, and that expression must be separated from action in the affairs of the Communist Party, the application of the full protection theory is not difficult. Both Section 9(h) and Section 504 plainly "abridged" expression. This was recognized by all members of the Court in *Douds*. The fact that the abridgment was "incidental" to achieving another purpose is not material. The government may not seek to advance other social interests, directly or indirectly, through curtailment of expression. Such being the case, the infringing regulation must be declared invalid as in conflict with the First Amendment.

Once again the question may be asked, is the application of the full protection theory to this area sensible or suicidal? Is it recklessly impracticable, in other words, to insist that conduct amounting to expression can never be taken into account, when the result is to impair our system of free expression, in imposing conditions for obtaining benefits or holding positions? This question need not be answered across the board at this point. We may look at particular aspects of it as we go along.

As far as the qualifications for union leadership are concerned, the

22. *De Jonge v. Oregon*, 299 U.S. 353 (1937), discussed in Chapter V. The Vinson quotations are taken from 339 U.S. at 391, 393.

answer, in light of the actual event, would appear to be that our internal security successfully survived the continuous failure of the program. This is not conclusive, but the experience does indicate that the threat to internal security was, as usual, exaggerated. Moreover, there is no convincing evidence that, if the threat had proved powerful, the measures taken in Sections 9(h) and 504 would have effectively warded off the danger of political strikes. Had the Communist Party captured the allegiance of important sectors of the rank and file in the labor movement, it is doubtful that these provisions would have had much impact. The experience of France and Italy with massive Communist influence in labor unions indicates otherwise. It can be argued, of course, that the existence of Sections 9(h) and 504 prevented American labor from going Communist. But surely that outcome must be attributed to more general and more potent factors.

Nor can the restriction upon expression be justified on the ground that it prevents clandestine infiltration of the labor movement by the Communist Party. Rank and file ignorance of the political connections of union officials may facilitate the calling of an isolated political strike. But a serious threat to national security through massive political strikes could hardly occur if the political views and affiliations of union officers remained undisclosed to the union membership.

The power of the government to meet the feared danger through control of action, an alternative always open, must also be taken into account. It would have been possible, of course, to impose a direct prohibition on "political strikes," thus meeting the issue head on. Or the government could have framed its regulation in terms of declaring ineligible for union leadership persons who had engaged in specific overt actions, or had been convicted of a crime. These measures are not guaranteed to achieve success. But it is by no means clear that any repressive measures of a constitutional character could prevent the labor movement from going Communist if the basic forces at work in the nation turned in that direction. Only a police state could accomplish this.

On the other hand the method actually employed here set a dangerous precedent. The Supreme Court's decisions developed no doctrine that would have set up a stopping place. Only the balancing test, heavily weighted on the legislative end, would be available to prevent the elimination of labor union leadership for any views the government may think are a threat to the *status quo*. Moreover, the price paid for the legislation may have been an exorbitant one. The present quiescent attitude of the labor movement in face of the urgent problems of the day is probably not unrelated to the dampening impact of the Taft-Hartley non-Communist affidavit law.

B. Professions and Occupations

Qualifications upon the right to engage in a profession or occupation are common. In most instances these restrictions are administered through licensing or permit systems, although they may appear as loyalty oaths or in other guises. Ordinarily such requirements do not present any question under the First Amendment, even if conduct in the form of expression is considered in determining whether a person meets the qualifications. It is only when reliance upon expression adversely affects our system of free expression—"abridges" freedom of expression—that a First Amendment issue arises. Thus, if the social interest to be protected is assurance to the public of competency in a profession, qualifications based upon expression would not normally abridge freedom of expression. Rejection of an applicant for admission to the bar on the ground that the views expressed in his bar examination were puerile or unsupportable would not create any problem under the First Amendment. Sometimes the issue of whether the use of expression has resulted in an abridgment may be difficult to decide. In practice, however, such questions have seldom come up. So far as appears, the issue has received judicial attention only in those cases in which qualifications have been imposed for protection of the interest in national security.[23]

1. PRACTICE OF LAW

One might consider it unlikely that our internal security would be jeopardized by the absence of security measures in the requirements for admission to the practice of law. Yet the issue arose in the wake of both world wars. Indeed, until the *Robel* case in 1967, the only Su-

23. For general discussion of occupational licensing see Lawrence M. Friedman, "Freedom of Contract and Occupational Licensing 1890–1910," *California Law Review*, Vol. 53 (1965), p. 487;

Walter Gellhorn, *Individual Freedom and Governmental Restraints* (Baton Rouge, La., Louisiana State University Press, 1956), ch. 3.

preme Court decisions on the First Amendment aspects of professional and occupational qualifications dealt with this problem.[24]

Some of the qualifications imposed on the legal profession involved the right of persons already members of the bar to continue in the practice of law. After World War I there were some instances in which attorneys were disbarred from practice on loyalty grounds. Following World War II several states adopted legislation or regulations providing for the disbarment of attorneys who advocated overthrow of the government by force and violence or were "subversive persons." In 1950 the American Bar Association adopted a resolution urging that "all licensed to practice law in the United States of America" be required to attest to their "loyalty to our form of government by anti-communist oath." A year later it proposed that the "appropriate authorities immediately commence disciplinary actions of disbarment" against any lawyer "who is a member of the Communist Party of the United States, or who advocates Marxism-Leninism." A similar resolution was adopted by the American Bar Association in 1953 and by some State and local bar associations. Actual proceedings to disbar lawyers on such grounds were rare; only three instances were reported, none of which was successful. In none of these proceedings did the courts find it necessary to reach First Amendment issues.[25]

More widespread and more vigorously enforced were the qualifications imposed by the States upon admission to the bar. In the post–World War II period virtually all the States had some form of loyalty test for applicants to the bar, either in the form of requiring an oath, asking questions on application blanks, or making investigation through committees on character and fitness. A series of cases began to make their way to the Supreme Court. In 1954 the Court refused to grant certiorari to George Anastaplo, who had been denied admission to the Illinois bar for declining to answer questions as to whether he was a member of the Communist Party or any organization on the Attorney General's List. In 1957, however, the Supreme Court decided two cases, in both upholding the applicant but not reaching constitutional issues. Finally in 1961 the Court came to grips with the problem.[26]

24. *United States v. Robel*, 389 U.S. 258 (1967). There were, of course, a number of decisions on loyalty qualifications for government employment, considered in the next chapter.

25. For a summary of these matters and a collection of references see *Political and Civil Rights in the United States*, pp. 262–266.

26. See Ralph S. Brown and John D. Fassett, "Loyalty Tests for Admission to the Bar," *University of Chicago Law Re-*

The major decision was in *Konigsberg v. State Bar of California*. Under California law, in order to be certified as qualified for admission to the bar an applicant had to satisfy the Committee of Bar Examiners that he was of "good moral character" and not a person "who advocates the overthrow of the Government of the United States or of this State by force, violence, or other unconstitutional means." In appearing before the Committee Konigsberg had testified that he did not believe in violent overthrow of government, and that he had never knowingly been a member of any organization which advocated such action. He refused, however, to answer any question pertaining to membership in the Communist Party, asserting that such questions violated his First Amendment rights. The Committee declined to certify him upon the ground that his refusal to answer had obstructed a full investigation into his qualifications. In a five to four decision the Court rejected Konigsberg's position.[27]

The *Konigsberg* case furnished the occasion for a major debate within the Court on First Amendment doctrine. Justice Harlan, writing for the majority, held that in cases involving "general regulatory statutes, not intended to control the content of speech but incidentally limiting its unfettered exercise" the balancing test applied. Justice Black, in an opinion with which Chief Justice Warren and Justice Douglas joined, strongly protested the use of balancing to resolve First Amendment issues. He took the position that the admitted fact that California had subjected "speech and association to the deterrence of subsequent disclosure" was "sufficient in itself to render the action of the State unconstitutional." Justice Brennan dissented on burden of proof grounds.[28]

It is not necessary to review here the various arguments on doc-

---

view, Vol. 20 (1953), p. 480; Ralph S. Brown, *Loyalty and Security* (New Haven, Conn., Yale University Press, 1958), pp. 109–111; *Political and Civil Rights in the United States,* pp. 266–268. These programs continue in most States on a less intensive basis. The Anastaplo case is *In re Anastaplo,* 3 Ill. 2d 471, 121 N.E.2d 826 (1954), cert. denied 348 U.S. 946 (1954). The two 1957 cases are *Schware v. Board of Bar Examiners of New Mexico,* 353 U.S. 232 (1957); *Konigsberg v. State Bar of California,* 353 U.S. 252 (1957). The Schware case was particularly significant in that the majority,

through Justice Black, held that Schware's membership in the Communist Party 15 years before, with no showing that the membership involved any illegal conduct on his part, did not "justify an inference that he presently has bad moral character." 353 U.S. at 246. See also *In re Patterson,* 353 U.S. 952 (1957).

27. *Konigsberg v. State Bar of California,* 366 U.S. 36 (1961). The case involved the same applicant as in the 1957 case, cited in the previous note. It came back to the Supreme Court after further proceedings in California.

28. 366 U.S. at 50–51, 60–61.

trine advanced in *Konigsberg*. The main contentions have been discussed at other points. But it is important to examine more closely the
issues raised by the case and the manner in which the Justices resolved
them.

The issue started out as one of determining what qualifications
may be imposed, consistently with the First Amendment, upon
admission to the bar. Justice Harlan's opinion, however, did not deal
at any length with this problem. He indicated, without expressly saying
so, that "bare, innocent membership" in the Communist Party would
not have constituted grounds for disqualification, thereby moving
away from the *Douds* case. But he accepted the proposition, which
indeed Konigsberg did not contest, that "advocating the violent overthrow of government" would be an important consideration "in determining the fitness of applicants for membership in a profession in
whose hands so largely lies the safekeeping of this country's legal and
political institutions." Justice Harlan did not find it necessary to go
beyond this point with respect to the qualification question. He moved
at once to the further issue which grew out of his decision on the first:
in determining whether a person possesses the proper qualifications,
how far can the government go in inquiring into matters that affect
First Amendment rights?

The issue is a crucial one in the administration of qualification
programs established to protect the social interest in internal security.
Freedom of expression may be seriously impaired when persons are
forced to make public disclosure of beliefs, opinions, associations or
other matters of an unorthodox or unpopular nature. Moreover, as a
practical matter, the person under inquiry is placed in a most difficult
position. If he refuses to answer he automatically loses the privilege or
relinquishes the position. He can regain his rights, if at all, only after
long and protracted proceedings. In addition, the more he is required
to answer questions on such matters, the more vulnerable he becomes
to charges of concealment or to prosecution for perjury. Under these
circumstances many people are disinclined to seek the benefit or position or, if not already committed beyond repair, curtail their expression in order to avoid trouble. Thus the sheer power to compel answers
to questions may have as great an impact upon freedom of expression
as do the qualifications themselves. This problem has loomed large in
the administration of loyalty programs.

Justice Harlan's position was that "it is difficult . . . to imagine a
view of the constitutional protections of speech and association which

would automatically and without consideration of the extent of the deterrence of speech and association and of the importance of the state function, exclude all reference to prior speech or association on such issues as character, purpose, credibility, or intent." He therefore applied the balancing test and concluded: "we regard the State's interest in having lawyers who are devoted to the law in its broadest sense, including not only its substantive provisions, but also its procedures for orderly change, as clearly sufficient to outweigh the minimal effect upon free association occasioned by compulsory disclosure in the circumstances here presented." Apart from the above conclusion, the only factors he weighed in the balance were that there was "no likelihood that deterrence of association may result from foreseeable private action . . . for bar committee interrogations such as this are conducted in private"; and there was no "possibility that the State may be afforded the opportunity for imposing undetectable arbitrary consequences upon protected association . . . for a bar applicant's exclusion by reason of Communist Party membership is subject to judicial review." [29]

Justice Black held to the view that exercise of the right of speech or association, including advocacy of forcible overthrow or membership in the Communist Party, could not constitute a ground for excluding an applicant from the bar. Konigsberg therefore had no need to answer questions on these matters. With respect to the scope of the inquiry power, as the issue was framed by Justice Harlan, Justice Black rejected the use of the balancing test and would have found a violation of the First Amendment in the fact that any "deterrence" to expression eventuated from the questioning. He also challenged Justice Harlan's application of the balancing test. He pointed out that Konigsberg had testified, without contradiction, that he "does not now, and never will advocate the overthrow of the Government of this country by unconstitutional means," and hence "[a]ll we really have on the State's side of the scales is its desire to know whether Konigsberg was ever a member of the Communist Party." As to the interest on the other side of the scales, Justice Black observed that answers to the committee's interrogations were not required to be kept private and would inevitably leak out; and that exercise of the right to judicial review would give them further publicity. Finally, he objected that the majority had not considered at all "the interest of all the people in having a society in which no one is intimidated with respect to his beliefs or associations":

29. 366 U.S. at 51, 52, 52–53.

It seems plain to me that the inevitable effect of the majority's decision is to condone a practice that will have a substantial deterrent effect upon the associations entered into by anyone who may want to become a lawyer in California. If every person who wants to be a lawyer is to be required to account for his associations as a prerequisite to admission into the practice of law, the only safe course for those desiring admission would seem to be scrupulously to avoid association with any organization that advocates anything at all somebody might possibly be against . . . In addition it seems equally clear that anyone who had already associated himself with an organization active in favor of civil liberties before he developed an interest in the law, would, after this case, be discouraged from spending the large amounts of time and money necessary to obtain a legal education in the hope that he could practice law in California.[30]

On the same day it decided *Konigsberg* the Supreme Court also decided another bar admission case, *In re Anastaplo.* Anastaplo had been refused admission to the Illinois bar because he declined to answer questions of the Committee on Character and Fitness "as to his possible membership in the Communist Party or in other allegedly related organizations." The issues were the same as in *Konigsberg,* with one exception: "[I]n *Konigsberg* there was some, though weak, independent evidence that the applicant had once been connected with the Communist Party, while here there was no such evidence as to Anastaplo." The Court, by the same margin, reached the same conclusion as in *Konigsberg,* saying "it is of no constitutional significance whether the State's interrogation of an applicant on matters relevant to [the requisite] qualifications—in this case Communist Party membership —is prompted by information which it already has about him from other sources, or arises merely from a good faith belief in the need for exploratory or testing questioning of the applicant." [31]

The application of the full protection theory in determining the validity of qualifications for admission to the bar, certainly if the social interest to be preserved is internal security, would not seem to pose any serious problem. There can be no doubt that freedom of expression is "abridged" by imposing qualifications based upon political opinions or associations. Action inimical to internal security can safely be controlled by direct regulation, without trying to eliminate it in advance by restrictions on expression. Indeed, governmental power to

30. 366 U.S. at 71–72, 73–74.
31. *In re Anastaplo,* 366 U.S. 82, 86, 89–90 (1961). This case involved the same applicant as the 1957 case, cited above.

deal with action in this situation is almost unprecedented in scope and
ease of application. It includes, in addition to criminal and other traditional forms of sanction, the authority to punish for contempt, to disbar, and to discipline. Moreover, members of the bar operate within a
professional framework that provides considerable unofficial scrutiny
and control over their conduct. The danger that lawyers will slip
through the admission process and subvert our judicial institutions unless applicants are put to a political test seems chimerical.[32]

If qualifications based upon political expression are held to be excluded by operation of the First Amendment, the secondary problem
of limiting governmental inquiry in areas that affect First Amendment
rights is substantially reduced. It would not, for instance, have arisen
in *Konigsberg* or *Anastaplo*. Yet to some extent the problem would
persist. For an inquiry into areas of action might also impinge upon
areas of expression. The answer would not seem to lie in the balancing
test, which affords no logical or functional basis for resolving the issue.
Justice Harlan's effort in *Konigsberg* is hardly reassuring. Rather the
solution must be found in rules for separating expression from action
in the investigating process. With respect to isolated individual conduct, this would not seem to be a complex task. The difficulties arise
mostly where an association is involved. Here the answer would turn
in large part upon the rules developed for dealing with associational
rights. If the conduct of the association were not to be attributed to
any individual member for this purpose, but significance attached only
to individual conduct, the issues would again be susceptible of solution. For in such a case only questions related to individual action, not
mere membership or association, would be relevant or at least constitutionally permitted. A supplementary technique for solving the inquiry problem might be the one rejected in *Anastaplo*, namely that
some substantial foundation be laid before questions are allowed in a
possibly protected area. All these matters are considered at greater
length in Chapter VIII, dealing with legislative investigating committees, and will not be pursued further here.

32. That some change in attitude of
the courts has taken place in recent years
may be deduced from *Hallinan v. Committee of Bar Examiners*, 65 Calif. 2d
447, 65 A.C. 485 (1966). See also *Law
Students Civil Rights Research Council v.
Wadmond*, 299 F. Supp. 117 (S.D.N.Y.
1969). Similar issues are again before the
Supreme Court in *Baird v. Arizona* (Ariz.
Sup. Ct. 1969, unreported), cert. granted
394 U.S. 957 (1969); *In re Stolar*, (Ohio
Sup. Ct.), cert. granted 396 U.S. 816
(1969); and the *Wadmond* case.

2. OTHER PROFESSIONS AND OCCUPATIONS

Qualifications based upon expression have been imposed on many occupations and professions in addition to the law. For example, a 1951 Texas statute required every person seeking a license as a pharmacist to take an oath similar to the Taft-Hartley non-Communist affidavit. Insurance salesmen in the District of Columbia have been compelled to disclose whether they were or ever had been members of the Communist Party or any organization on the Attorney General's List. In Indiana professional wrestlers and boxers have been subjected to a loyalty oath. Most of these regulations, even without regard to First Amendment issues, violate due process of law as lacking any reasonable relation between the objective sought and the means used. But some do pose closer questions. One form of qualification that has received attention in the courts, though it has not elicited a Supreme Court opinion, is that imposed by the Federal Communications Commission upon applicants for radio and television licenses. As illustrating the more serious questions that arise in the field of occupational qualifications, the F.C.C. cases deserve brief attention.[33]

The Federal Communications Act empowers the Commission to issue licenses on the basis of "public interest, convenience, or necessity." The Commission has never adopted formal regulations on the subject but it has followed the practice, in some cases, of requiring an applicant for an operator's or broadcasting license to answer questions concerning past and present Communist membership and associations. The major decision is *Borrow v. Federal Communications Commission.* In that case Borrow applied for renewal of his radio operator's license, entitling him to operate transmitter apparatus at radio and television stations, aboard vessels of the Merchant Marine, and at Coast Guard stations. He refused to answer questions as to whether he was or had been (1) a member of the Communist Party, or (2) a member of any organization advocating overthrow of the Government by force or violence. After hearing, the Commission denied the re-

---

33. The Texas statute is Tex. Rev. Stat. Ann., Art. 4542a, §9. The District of Columbia requirement is described in American Civil Liberties Union, *Weekly Bulletin* for Feb. 4 and Oct. 28, 1957, and *Annual Report* for 1954–1955, p. 39. The Indiana regulation and other examples are noted in Gellhorn, *op. cit. supra* note 23, pp. 129–130. Cases holding such laws invalid on due process grounds are referred to in footnote 47, *infra*.

newal. The Court of Appeals affirmed, on the basis of the *Douds* case, saying:

> It seems to us it would be difficult to imagine a question more rele-
> vant or more material to the qualification of a radio operator under the
> statutory criteria than is the second of the two questions asked. Radio
> beams are the operational essence of quick modern communication and
> of the control of modern weapons. Not only the power to use these
> electronic devices but the power to interfere with waves being used by
> others should, it might properly seem to the Commission, be lodged
> in those whose loyalty to the United States is made to appear. Surely
> no such power should knowingly be accorded to those who belong to
> organizations advocating or teaching the overthrow of this govern-
> ment by force or violence. At the very least the Commission is entitled
> to know whether those whom it licenses to control these devices belong
> to such an organization. Any program less than that simple necessity
> would be not only short-sighted but dangerous to the national security.[34]

Judge Washington, dissenting, took the position that the Commission could not act as it had without express legislative authorization:

> I do not doubt that there are strong reasons of public policy for
> seeking to insure that radio operators will be loyal and trustworthy at
> all times, and particularly in the event of a national emergency. But
> the same is true of a large part of our population, given the times in
> which we live. Railroad engineers, airline pilots, electrical system opera-
> tors, reservoir inspectors, gas pipeline controllers—the list of people
> who can play vital roles in the functioning or nonfunctioning of our
> system is well-nigh endless. If these people are required to be licensed
> by some federal, state or local agency—and many of them are—does
> it follow that the licensing authority can ask them about possible Com-
> munist connections and deny them a license (and possibly a livelihood)
> for failure to answer? Or for giving an unacceptable answer? Perhaps
> we will come to that. But if we do, it should be a legislative and not an
> administrative decision: a decision made after careful consideration of
> the needs of the national security, and of the possible consequences on
> the availability, mobility and self respect of our people.[35]

---

34. *Borrow v. Federal Communications Commission*, 285 F.2d 666, 668–
669 (D.C. Cir. 1960), cert. denied 364
U.S. 892 (1960). For a summary of the
F.C.C. practices and the court decisions,
see *Political and Civil Rights in the
United States*, pp. 309–313; Ralph S.
Brown, "Character and Candor Requirements for F.C.C. Licensees," *Law and*

Contemporary Problems, Vol. 22 (1957),
p. 644.

35. 285 F.2d at 670. The Court of Appeals also upheld the F.C.C. in two other
similar cases: *Cronan v. Federal Communications Commission*, 285 F.2d 288
(D.C. Cir. 1960), cert. denied 366 U.S.
904 (1960) (failure of F.C.C. to adopt
regulations on the subject not material);

The full protection theory of the First Amendment would, of course, preclude the Federal Communications Commission's establishing qualifications based on membership, association, or other forms of expression, and asking questions pertaining to such matters. Is the result one that a modern democratic society cannot live with? The answer must be in the negative. It should be remembered that we are not here dealing with radio operators in military service, a matter outside the civilian system of freedom of expression. Undoubtedly the basic concern of the Federal Communications Commission is with the actions of licensed operators in the event of war with a foreign country. Yet in a minor war the damage done could hardly be fatal and in a nuclear war the problem would be academic. More significant, perhaps, is the possible danger in case of domestic insurrection. But is not Judge Washington correct? A technological society is extremely vulnerable to disruptive tactics. Damage can be inflicted by persons occupying thousands of different positions. A nation that seeks its security in loyalty tests for all such persons is well on the road to disintegration. If it does continue to exist it will not be as a democracy.

The Federal Communications Commission has also, on occasion, made inquiries about Communist affiliations in connection with the issuance or renewal of broadcasting licenses. The issue was brought to public attention in the cases of Edward Lamb in 1954 and the Pacifica Foundation in 1963. In both instances the license was ultimately granted and the problem did not reach the courts. The validity of the full protection theory seems even clearer in this situation. By definition broadcasting consists only of expression. Any possible use of the station in connection with a domestic insurrection can hardly be grounds for instituting what could only amount, especially if applied to the right as well as to the left, to an elaborate system of government censorship.[36]

The Supreme Court dealt with another aspect of occupational qualifications in *United States v. Robel.* The decision, rendered in

---

Blumenthal v. Federal Communications Commission, 318 F.2d 276 (D.C. Cir. 1963), cert. denied 373 U.S. 951 (1963), Justices Black, Douglas and Brennan dissenting (applicant invoked the privilege against self-incrimination). See also *Homer v. Richmond,* 292 F.2d 719 (D.C. Cir. 1961).

36. For a summary of the *Lamb* and *Pacifica* cases see *Political and Civil Rights in the United States,* pp. 309, 312–313. The government does, of course, exercise extensive controls over radio and television, on theories discussed in Chapter XVII. But those powers would not authorize the government to discriminate among various users of the medium on the basis of political views or associations.

1967, reflects important developments in the Court's attitude toward the problem since the *Douds* and *Konigsberg* cases.[37]

The *Robel* case involved the validity of Section 5(a)(1)(D) of the Internal Security Act. This provided that, when a Communist-action organization had been ordered to register by the Subversive Activities Control Board, it became unlawful for any member of the organization "with knowledge or notice . . . that such order had become final . . . to engage in any employment in any defense facility." Robel, a member of the Communist Party, was employed as a machinist in the Todd Shipyards in Seattle. He continued to work there after the Supreme Court had upheld the order requiring the Communist Party to register as a Communist-action organization and after the Secretary of Defense had designated Todd Shipyards as a "defense facility." Robel was indicted for violating Section 5(a)(1)(D). The District Court dismissed the indictment on the ground that it did not allege that Robel was an active member of the Communist Party and had the specific intent to further illegal goals of that organization, within the doctrine of the *Scales* case. Robel went back to work and the Government appealed. The Supreme Court, by a six to two vote, affirmed dismissal of the indictment, but on different grounds.

Chief Justice Warren, speaking also for Justices Black, Douglas, Stewart and Fortas, ruled that Section 5(a)(1)(D) could not be construed narrowly to apply only to active membership with specific intent. Taking the provision in its broad scope, he concluded that it "sweeps indiscriminately across all types of associations with Communist-action groups" and hence "runs afoul of the First Amendment." "The statute quite literally," said Chief Justice Warren, "establishes guilt by association alone, without any need to establish that an individual's association poses the threat feared by the Government in proscribing it." The opinion added in elaboration:

> It has become axiomatic that "[p]recision of regulation must be the touchstone in an area so closely touching our most precious freedoms." . . . Such precision is notably lacking in §5(a)(1)(D). That statute casts its net across a broad range of associational activities, indiscriminately trapping membership which can be constitutionally punished [citing *Scales*] and membership which cannot be so proscribed. It is made irrelevant to the statute's operation that an individual may be a passive or inactive member of a designated organization, that he may be unaware

37. *United States v. Robel,* 389 U.S. 258 (1967).

of the organization's unlawful aims, or that he may disagree with those unlawful aims. It is also made irrelevant that an individual who is subject to the penalties of §5(a)(1)(D) may occupy a nonsensitive position in a defense facility. Thus, §5(a)(1)(D) contains the fatal defect of overbreadth because it seeks to bar employment both for association which may be proscribed and for association which may not be proscribed consistently with First Amendment rights. . . . This the Constitution will not tolerate.[38]

The opinion then went on to say that the Court was "not unmindful of the congressional concern over the danger of sabotage and espionage in national defense industries"; and nothing said in the opinion "should be read to deny Congress the power under narrowly drawn legislation to keep from sensitive positions in defense facilities those who would use their positions to disrupt the Nation's production facilities." Whether an industrial security screening program or other measures were employed was up to Congress, so long as it did not exceed "the bounds imposed by the Constitution when First Amendment rights are at stake." [39]

Justice Brennan was "not persuaded to the Court's view that overbreadth is fatal to this statute." But he concurred on the ground that "the congressional delegation of authority to the Secretary of Defense to designate 'defense facilities' creates the danger of overbroad, unauthorized, and arbitrary application of criminal sanctions in an area of protected freedoms and therefore, in my view, renders this statute invalid." Justices White and Harlan, dissenting, would have upheld "the judgment of Congress and the Executive Branch that the interest of appellee in remaining a member of the Communist Party, knowing that it has been adjudicated a Communist-action organization, is less substantial than the public interest in excluding him from employment in critical defense industries." As to the problem of overbreadth, the dissenters thought that Congress should be entitled to take "suitable precautionary measures": "Some Party members may be no threat at all, but many of them undoubtedly are, and it is exceedingly difficult to identify those in advance of the very events which Congress seeks to avoid." [40]

The *Robel* decision is significant in several respects: In the first place, the Court's use of the technique of refining the issues—of breaking down the regulation into its various applications and holding the

38. 389 U.S. at 262, 265, 266.   40. 389 U.S. at 272, 285, 287.
39. 389 U.S. at 266, 267.

whole regulation invalid if some applications are found to infringe a constitutional right—has important implications. For one thing it disposes of the particular restriction before the Court, which may never be renewed. It also, of course, greatly narrows the scope of the restriction. This is particularly significant if, as the dissenters point out, the purpose of the legislation is "precautionary" or preventive, and is likely by its very nature to be overinclusive. Furthermore, the technique tends to force the government into more refined administrative procedures. It precludes the possibility of using readily provable criteria, such as simple membership in an association, and imposes more particularized standards. The *Robel* case, for example, comes close to requiring individual screening procedures. This in turn not only enforces the limitations on scope but adds to the burden of administration, facilitates the development of a case law, and enlarges the possibility of judicial supervision. This technique and others like it were developed mainly in loyalty cases and will be considered further in the next chapter.

Secondly, the doctrinal aspects of the *Robel* case are intriguing, and may even foreshadow a major shift in the Court's position on the balancing test. In holding that the statute was overbroad the majority opinion necessarily held that in some of its applications the statute violated the First Amendment. The complete area of invalidity was not delineated, but it included extension of the prohibition to innocent or passive membership and to non-sensitive positions. On what theory of the First Amendment did this conclusion rest? Nothing was said about clear and present danger, and the opinion, in a footnote, expressly repudiated the use of balancing:

> It has been suggested that this case should be decided by "balancing" the governmental interests expressed in §5(a)(1)(D) against the First Amendment rights asserted by the appellee. This we decline to do. We recognize that both interests are substantial, but we deem it inappropriate for this Court to label one as being more important or more substantial than the other. Our inquiry is more circumscribed.[41]

The majority opinion went on to say: "Faced with a clear conflict between a federal statute enacted in the interests of national security and an individual's exercise of his First Amendment rights, we have confined our analysis to whether Congress has adopted a constitu-

41. 389 U.S. at 268.

tional means in achieving its concededly legitimate legislative goal." It concluded: "We have ruled only that the Constitution requires that the conflict between congressional power and individual rights be accommodated by legislation drawn more narrowly to avoid the conflict." It remains unclear what theory the Court was adopting. The dissenters seemed to have thought the majority was still using the balancing test. Possibly the majority was adopting an extreme form of the requirement that the legislature must seek other alternatives if the one chosen impinges upon First Amendment rights. Possibly it was employing the full protection doctrine. In any event the statement that balancing was "inappropriate for this Court" suggests that five members of the Court favored abandonment of the balancing test.[42]

Thirdly, the Court did not make clear how far it intended to go in forbidding the consideration of expression, protected by the First Amendment against direct sanctions, as a criterion in determining qualifications for holding a position. At times it seemed to take the view that all such consideration was prohibited, as when it said that Section 5(a)(1)(D) was fatally defective because it sought to bar employment "for association which may not be proscribed consistently with First Amendment rights." This would eliminate all qualifications based upon protected expression and completely wipe out *Douds,* though possibly not *Konigsberg.* On the other hand, the Court said it was not denying Congress power to keep from sensitive positions in defense plants "those who would use their positions to disrupt the Nation's facilities." This formulation did not necessarily rule out reliance upon conduct in the form of expression as proof of proneness to disrupt. The issue is, of course, closely related to the doctrinal question just considered.[43]

Finally, there may be some future in the suggestion of Justice Brennan that the doctrine of excessive delegation of legislative power still has some blood in it when invoked to protect First Amendment rights. None of the other Justices agreed. While the delegation doctrine is still used in the State courts, it has not been used to invalidate Federal legislation since the *Schechter* case in 1935. Nevertheless, Justice Brennan's opinion has raised the possibility that the delegation principle may be added to the growing list of substantive and proce-

---

42. 389 U.S. at 268. On the rule requiring the use of alternatives which do not affect First Amendment rights see Note, "Less Drastic Means and the First Amendment," *Yale Law Journal,* Vol. 78 (1969), p. 464.

43. 389 U.S. at 266, 267.

dural doctrines that take on special strength when called into the service of supporting the First Amendment.[44]

The second case in which the Supreme Court has dealt with the problem of occupational qualifications is *Schneider v. Smith,* decided in 1968. Like *Robel,* the *Schneider* decision came after significant developments in the government employee loyalty cases and must be read in connection with those cases. Also like *Robel, Schneider* involved an attack on a government program imposing qualifications upon the employees of private employers, in this case the port security program. Under the Magnuson Act the President was authorized to "safeguard against destruction, loss, or injury from sabotage or other subversive acts, accidents, or other causes of a similar nature, vessels, harbors, ports and waterfront facilities in the United States." Pursuant to this provision the President delegated power to the Coast Guard to institute a security program, under which all prospective seamen must obtain certification from the Coast Guard that their employment on American merchant vessels "would not be inimical to the security of the United States." Schneider applied to the Coast Guard for clearance and, in response to questions, admitted he had once been a member of or associated with various organizations on the Attorney General's List of "subversive" organizations. He stated, however, that he had never advocated violent overthrow of the Government and had not been a member of or participant in the activities of the organizations in question for ten years. Schneider was then asked a series of detailed questions which included a request for "full particulars" concerning his participation in all "political and social organizations" to which he had belonged, and his "present attitude" towards the Communist Party, the "principles and objectives of Communism," and the "form of Government of the United States." Schneider refused to answer and brought suit to test the authority of the Coast Guard to bar him from employment. The District Court dismissed the complaint, but the Supreme Court unanimously reversed.[45]

Justice Douglas, writing for the Court, held that the Magnuson Act must be "read narrowly so as to avoid questions concerning . . . 'associational freedom' . . . and concerning other rights within the purview of the First Amendment." He therefore refused to give the

44. *Schechter Poultry Corp. v. United States,* 295 U.S. 495 (1935).

45. *Schneider v. Smith,* 390 U.S. 17 (1968). Justice Marshall did not par-

ticipate. Aspects of the case touching on freedom of belief have been discussed in Chapter II.

Act a construction that would authorize the government to "probe the reading habits, political philosophy, beliefs, and attitudes on social and economic issues of prospective seamen on our merchant vessels." Justices Fortas, Stewart and Black, concurring, took the flat position, but without elaboration, that "the interrogatories which petitioner refused to answer offend the First Amendment." Justices White and Harlan concurred in the decision without expressing an opinion on the constitutional issues.[46]

Like *Robel,* the *Schneider* decision makes clear that qualifications for employment based on conduct within the coverage of the First Amendment are no longer favored by the Court and will be held within narrower bounds. It does not indicate, however, whether all such qualifications are to be outlawed or, if allowed, how much infringement of First Amendment rights will be permitted. Justice Fortas, speaking also for Justice Stewart, took pains to observe, "Needless to say, Congress has constitutional power to authorize an appropriate personnel screening program." Nor does the decision enlighten us on any doctrinal points. The technique of construing the statute to avoid First Amendment problems is to be noted as another device, indeed a common one, for striking down particular legislative or executive action without dealing squarely with First Amendment issues.

The substantive question raised by the *Robel* and *Schneider* cases is how far the government can go in establishing a loyalty-security program for employees of private employers. Discussion of the application of the full protection doctrine in this situation is reserved until the next chapter.

C. Tax and Social Welfare Legislation

Efforts to impose qualifications based upon expression as a condition for obtaining benefits under social welfare or tax legislation appeared rather frequently in the post–World War II period, tapering off substantially in the nineteen-sixties. The matter is one of enormous potential significance. If the government can control expression, directly or indirectly, through its welfare and tax laws it possesses an instrument of almost unlimited reach and power. That weapon would in-

46. 390 U.S. at 27, 24, 27.

crease in effectiveness as the country moved further in the direction of a "welfare state." Such proposals as the guaranteed annual wage or the negative income tax would be fraught with danger unless they were framed and administered in accordance with ironclad principles that no benefit due under them would be diminished or withheld on the basis of any exercise of the right to freedom of expression.

On the whole, attempts to utilize the welfare and tax laws as means of controlling expression have not been well received by the courts, although the decision has usually not been based on First Amendment grounds. Thus the Emergency Relief Act of 1941, which prohibited relief employment of any "communist" or "member of any Nazi Bund organization," was held unconstitutional on the ground there was no reasonable connection between political beliefs and financial distress. The Gwinn Amendment, a rider incorporated in Federal appropriation acts in 1952 and 1953, provided that no housing unit constructed under the Housing Act of 1937 "shall be occupied by a person who is a member of an organization designated as subversive by the Attorney General"; it was held invalid on First Amendment grounds by the Wisconsin Supreme Court and on other grounds by other courts. The effort to cut off veterans' benefits under a 1943 amendment to the veterans' laws, authorizing forfeiture of benefits to veterans who "rendered assistance to an enemy," was thwarted as to two members of the Communist Party on statutory interpretation grounds. Likewise the provision of the Medicare Law of 1965 withholding benefits from persons who were members of any organization ordered to register under the Internal Security Act was invalidated. On the other hand, an Ohio Unemployment Compensation law denying benefits to any person who "advocates, or is a member of a party which advocates, overthrow of our government by force" was upheld by an Ohio court. Also, Section 11 of the Internal Security Act, denying tax exemption to any organization ordered to register under that law, has never been tested.[47]

---

47. *United States v. Schneider*, 45 F. Supp. 848 (E.D. Wis. 1942) (Emergency Relief Act); *Lawson v. Housing Authority of the City of Milwaukee*, 270 Wis. 269, 70 N.W.2d 605 (1955), cert. denied 350 U.S. 882 (1955); and *Rudder v. United States*, 226 F.2d 51 (D.C. Cir. 1955) (Gwinn Amendment); *Wellman v. Whittier*, 259 F.2d 163 (D.C. Cir. 1958); and *Thompson v. Gleason*, 317 F.2d 901 (D.C. Cir. 1962) (veterans' benefits); *Reed v. Gardner*, 261 F. Supp. 87 (C.D. Cal. 1966) (medicare; the government conceded and declined to appeal, *The New York Times*, Jan. 5, 1967); *Dworken v. Collopy*, 91 N.E.2d 564 (Ct. C.P. Ohio 1950) (Ohio Unemployment Compensation Law); 50 U.S.C. §790 (Section 11 of Internal Security Act). For a collection of cases and materials,

The United States Supreme Court has dealt with these issues on two occasions. In neither case did the Court give a decisive answer to the First Amendment questions. But the decisions touched on significant collateral issues.

Flemming v. Nestor involved a challenge to that section of the Social Security Act which provided for the termination of old age benefits payable to an alien who was deported on grounds of membership in the Communist Party. Nestor, the alien, had lived in the United States since 1913 and was a member of the Communist Party from 1933 to 1939. In 1956 he was deported because of this past membership and his social security benefits were terminated. In a five to four decision the Court upheld the provision in dispute. Justice Harlan, writing for the majority, ruled that there was no denial of due process because the provision could serve the purposes of the social security system by cutting off benefits where they were not being used to increase purchasing power in the United States; and, the denial of benefits not being a "punishment," there was no violation of the constitutional provisions against punishment without trial, bill of attainder, or ex post facto laws. The dissenters disagreed on one or both grounds. There was no discussion of the First Amendment, except by Justice Black, who thought that the decision was "part of a pattern of laws all of which violate the First Amendment." [48]

The First Amendment issue was complicated by the fact that the denial of benefits was technically attached to deportation, not to membership in the Communist Party, and by the fact that Nestor was an alien. It may have been thought that, if Nestor could be deported for past membership in the Communist Party despite the First Amendment, that provision would likewise not protect him against losing his social security benefits. Nevertheless, it is puzzling that so little attention was paid to the First Amendment. On any realistic analysis, as Justice Black pointed out, "[t]he basic reason for Nestor's loss of his insurance payments is that he was once a Communist." Such being the case, it would seem clear that this could not be done consistently with the First Amendment. Even on the balancing test it is difficult to see any interest in internal security or in the effective administration of the

see *Political and Civil Rights in the United States*, pp. 285–309. See also *Holt v. Richmond Redevelopment and Housing Authority*, 266 F. Supp. 397 (E.D. Va. 1966); *Thorpe v. Housing Authority of the City of Durham*, 393 U.S. 268 (1969).

48. *Flemming v. Nestor*, 363 U.S. 603, 628 (1960).

social security system that could be thought to outweigh the First Amendment right. The same result would be reached, of course, under the full protection doctrine.[49]

The decision in *Flemming v. Nestor* displays a niggardly attitude towards the constitutional rights of the individual under the welfare system. But it must be regarded as aberrational. Three years later the Court took a different view in holding that a Seventh-Day Adventist could not be denied unemployment compensation because she refused to accept employment on Saturday, the Sabbath Day of her faith. Finding that the disqualification imposed a "burden upon the free exercise of religion," the Court emphasized that "conditions upon public benefits cannot be sustained if they so operate, whatever their purpose, as to inhibit or deter the exercise of First Amendment freedoms." [50]

Speiser v. Randall involved the validity of conditions attached to obtaining a property tax exemption allowed by California law to honorably discharged veterans. The California Constitution provided that no person who "advocates the overthrow of the Government . . . by force or violence or other unlawful means or who advocates support of a foreign government against the United States in the event of hostilities" could receive any tax exemption. The California Supreme Court had interpreted this provision to deny exemption "only to claimants who engage in speech which may be criminally punished consistently with the free speech guarantees of the Federal Constitution." No direct issue under the First Amendment was therefore raised. But the California tax laws and regulations provided that claimants could obtain the exemption only by subscribing to an oath or declaration, framed in the words of the Constitution; and that if the tax assessor believed the claimant was not qualified he could deny the exemption and require the claimant, on judicial review, to prove the incorrectness of that determination. The question to which the Supreme Court addressed itself was whether putting the burden of proof and persuasion on the taxpayer in this manner violated his constitutional rights to due process of law. The Court held, in a seven to one vote, that it did.[51]

Justice Brennan, writing for the majority, stated the underlying principle: "When we deal with the complex of strands in the web of freedoms which make up free speech, the operation and effect of the method by which speech is sought to be restrained must be subjected to

---

49. 363 U.S. at 626–627.

50. *Sherbert v. Verner*, 374 U.S. 398, 404–405 (1963).

51. *Speiser v. Randall*, 357 U.S. 513 (1958). Chief Justice Warren did not participate. Justice Clark dissented.

close analysis and critical judgment in the light of the particular circumstances to which it is applied." He went on to point out the significance of the fact-finding process, and particularly the burden of proof, to the outcome of litigation. He concluded:

> The vice of the present procedure is that, where particular speech falls close to the line separating the *lawful and the unlawful, the possibility of mistaken fact-finding—inherent in all litigation—will create the danger that the legitimate utterance will be penalized. The man who knows that he must bring forth proof and persuade another of the lawfulness of his conduct necessarily must steer far wider of the unlawful zone than if the State must bear these burdens. This is especially to be feared when the complexity of the proofs and the generality of the standards applied, cf. *Dennis v. United States* [341 U.S. 494], provide but shifting sands on which the litigant must maintain his position. How can a claimant whose declaration is rejected possibly sustain the burden of proving the negative of these complex factual elements? In practical operation, therefore, this procedural device must necessarily produce a result which the State could not command directly. It can only result in a deterrence of speech which the Constitution makes free.[52]

Justices Black and Douglas, while agreeing with the Brennan opinion, would have invalidated the California provision as "a palpable violation of the First Amendment." "Advocacy which is in no way brigaded with action," said Justice Douglas, "should always be protected by the First Amendment." [53]

The *Speiser* decision broke new paths in its recognition of the importance of taking into account the dynamics of a system of freedom of expression. It began the search for legal doctrine that would protect the system in its actual working as well as expound its underlying principles. Together with the later opinions in *New York Times v. Sullivan* and *Dombrowski v. Pfister,* both also the work of Justice Brennan, the *Speiser* opinion laid the foundations for a realistic judicial support of the system as it operates in practice.[54]

How far the specific rule of the *Speiser* case carries is by no means clear. The rule was not applied in *Konigsberg,* decided three years later, over the vigorous objection of Justice Black and the other three dissenters. The majority held that, although California had placed on

---

52. 357 U.S. at 520, 526.
53. 357 U.S. at 530, 536–537.
54. *New York Times v. Sullivan,* 376 U.S. 254 (1964), discussed in Chapter XIV; *Dombrowski v. Pfister,* 380 U.S. 479 (1965), discussed in Chapter V.

Konigsberg the burden of proving "good moral character," it had not unequivocally placed on him the burden of proving "nonadvocacy of violent overthrow." It also ruled that the *Speiser* doctrine "was explicitly limited so as not to reach cases where, as here, there is no showing of an intent to penalize political beliefs." The majority in *Konigsberg* seem unnecessarily rigid, certainly in the second ground of their decision. The rationale of the Court in *Speiser* would make the rule applicable in any situation where the burden of proof was on the individual to take himself out of a category of conduct consisting of unprotected expression or action bordering on expression. Of course, under the doctrine of full protection for expression the rule of the *Speiser* case would be applicable much less frequently.[55]

Returning to the general problem of welfare and tax legislation, the conclusion is difficult to escape that under no circumstances should the benefits of such measures be diminished or denied on the basis of expression. The social interest in internal security does not even reach to such a situation. Nor would the social interest in effective administration constitute a valid reason for abridging First Amendment rights. Indeed, the regulations which have raised the question in this field have been rather open uses of the tax or spending power as direct sanctions against unwanted expression. In any event there is no reason for not applying the full protection rule. Actually the courts have reached this result, though without articulating First Amendment grounds.

D. Other Areas

The courts have dealt with the denial of rights or privileges for conduct consisting of expression in two other important areas: the right to travel abroad and the right to appear on the ballot. In neither of these situations, however, has the Supreme Court thus far ruled directly on First Amendment grounds.[56]

55. *Konigsberg v. State Bar of California,* 366 U.S. 36, 54 (1961), discussed above in section B of this chapter.

56. Questions relating to the denial of public facilities for purposes of assembly are treated in Chapter IX. Problems concerned with the admission, deportation, naturalization and denaturalization of aliens are not dealt with in this book.

1. PASSPORTS

Travel abroad should probably be classified as "action" rather than "expression." In common-sense terms travel is more physical movement than communication of ideas. It is true that travel abroad is frequently instrumental to expression, as when it is undertaken by a reporter to gather news, a scholar to lecture, a student to obtain information, or simply an ordinary citizen in order to expand his understanding of the world. Nevertheless, there are so many other aspects to travel abroad and functionally it requires such different types of regulation that, at least as a general proposition, it would have to be considered "action." As action, it is a "liberty" protected by the due process clause of the Fifth and Fourteenth Amendments. The First Amendment is still relevant in two ways: (1) there are sufficient elements of expression in travel abroad so that the umbrella effect of the First Amendment comes into play, thereby requiring the courts to apply due process and other constitutional doctrines with special care; (2) conditions imposed on travel abroad based on conduct classified as expression impair freedom of expression and hence raise direct First Amendment questions.

For many years, and notably after the end of World War II, it was the practice of the State Department to restrict travel abroad, through control of passports, whenever it decided that such travel would not be in the "best interests of the United States." This phrase was construed to mean that passports should be denied to various persons or classes of persons on the basis of their political beliefs, opinions or associations. In 1952, for example, the State Department issued regulations providing for the revocation or refusal of passports to members of the Communist Party, persons who "engage in activities which support the Communist movement" as a result of "direction, domination or control exercised over them by the Communist movement," and persons "going abroad to engage in activities which will advance the Communist movement." The regulations also provided that an applicant "may be required" to take an oath "with respect to present or past membership in the Communist Party." The State Department policies were challenged in a number of cases and the issue finally reached the Supreme Court in 1958 in *Kent v. Dulles.*[57]

57. *Kent v. Dulles,* 357 U.S. 116 (1958). The 1952 regulations may be found in 17 Fed. Reg. 8013 (1952). For a detailed account of the State Depart-

The suit was brought by Rockwell Kent, who had desired to go to England and to attend a meeting of the World Council of Peace in Finland. His application for a passport was denied on grounds (1) that he was a Communist, and (2) that he had "a consistent and prolonged adherence to the Communist Party line." Justice Douglas, writing for a majority of five, declared that the "right to travel is part of the 'liberty' of which a citizen cannot be deprived without due process of law under the Fifth Amendment." He found it unnecessary to decide any constitutional issues, however, because he concluded that the governing statutes did not authorize the Secretary of State "to withhold passports to citizens because of their beliefs and associations." The Court thus did not pass directly on the First Amendment question, but First Amendment considerations were clearly influential on the issue of statutory construction.[58]

Following the *Kent* decision the State Department abandoned its policy of refusing passports on the grounds stated in the 1952 regulations. In 1961, however, the Supreme Court upheld the order of the Subversive Activities Control Board requiring the Communist Party to register as a "Communist-action organization" and that brought into operation Section 6 of the Internal Security Act. This provision made it a criminal offense for any member of a "Communist organization" ordered to register under the Internal Security Act to make application for or use a passport. The State Department reinstituted its ban on members of the Communist Party and again began to require applicants to take an oath of non-membership.[59]

In *Aptheker v. Secretary of State* the Supreme Court, by a six to three margin, held Section 6 of the Internal Security Act invalid. Again the decision was not put on First Amendment grounds. But Justice Goldberg, writing for the majority, did note that First Amendment rights were involved: "Since freedom of association is itself guaranteed in the First Amendment, restrictions imposed upon the right to travel [on the basis of association] cannot be dismissed by asserting that the right to travel could be fully exercised if the individual would first yield up his membership in a given association." He then went on to point

ment's policies and practices on passports see *Political and Civil Rights in the United States*, pp. 1273–1304. For later material see Thomas Ehrlich, "Passports," *Stanford Law Review*, Vol. 19 (1966), p. 129.

58. 357 U.S. at 125, 130.
59. *Communist Party v. Subversive Activities Control Board*, 367 U.S. 1 (1961); 50 U.S.C. §785.

out that the prohibition of Section 6 applied to all members of the Communist organization regardless of the individual's "knowledge, activity or commitment" in the organization, regardless of "the purposes for which an individual wishes to travel," and regardless of "the security-sensitivity of the areas in which he wishes to travel." He further observed that "it is also important to consider that Congress has within its power 'less drastic' means of achieving the congressional objective of safeguarding our national security," namely, a more refined security program. He concluded: "The section, judged by its plain import and by the substantive evil which Congress sought to control, sweeps too widely and too indiscriminately across the liberty guaranteed in the Fifth Amendment." Justice Black would have declared Section 6 unconstitutional on First Amendment grounds and Justice Douglas on grounds that it violated the "privileges and immunities of national citizenship." Justices Clark, Harlan and White dissented.[60]

The *Kent* and *Aptheker* decisions removed the power of the State Department to refuse passports to individuals on grounds of political belief, opinion or association, at least under existing legislation. The Department has also over many years exercised authority to refuse passports to any person for travel to particular countries or areas. These area restrictions were upheld, in the case of a ban on travel to Cuba, in *Zemel v. Rusk*. The argument was advanced in the *Zemel* case that the right of travel was a First Amendment right and was violated by the area restriction. None of the Justices accepted this view. But the contention did require them to address themselves to the distinction between "expression" and "action," a rare event. Chief Justice Warren, writing for the majority of seven, explained his position:

> We must agree that the Secretary's refusal to validate passports for Cuba renders less than wholly free the flow of information concerning that country. While we further agree that this is a factor to be considered in determining whether appellant has been denied due process of law, we cannot accept the contention of appellant that it is a First Amendment right which is involved. For to the extent that the Secretary's refusal to validate passports for Cuba acts as an inhibition (and it would be unrealistic to assume that it does not), it is an inhibition of action. There are few restrictions on action which could not be clothed by ingenious argument in the garb of decreased data flow. For example, the prohibition of unauthorized entry into the White House diminishes the citizen's opportunities to gather information he

60. *Aptheker v. Secretary of State,* 378 U.S. 500, 507, 514, 511, 512 (1964).

might find relevant to his opinion of the way the country is being run, but that does not make entry into the White House a First Amendment right. The right to speak and publish does not carry with it the unrestrained right to gather information.[61]

Justice Douglas, dissenting with Justice Goldberg, observed: "As I have said, the right to travel is at the periphery of the First Amendment, rather than its core, largely because travel is, of course, more than speech: it is speech brigaded with conduct." He laid down the rule: "Restrictions on the right to travel in times of peace should be so particularized that a First Amendment right is not precluded unless some clear countervailing national interest stands in the way of its assertion."[62]

For reasons already stated, the Supreme Court seems correct in considering the right of travel to be a "liberty" under the Fifth Amendment rather than "expression" under the First. It is unfortunate, however, that the Court has not made its position clear on the constitutional power of the government to condition the issuance of passports to individuals on the basis of conduct protected under the First Amendment as expression. The only legitimate aspect of national security that would seem to be served by passport limitations on individuals is an interest in preventing espionage by curtailing opportunity for communication. Yet other counterespionage methods that do not curtail freedom of expression are available to the government, and the State Department has never been convincing in its position that denying passports to suspected "subversives" is of substantial aid in solving the espionage problem. Application of the full protection doctrine in this situation can hardly be cause for alarm.

61. *Zemel v. Rusk,* 381 U.S. 1, 16–17 (1965). The argument that the right to travel is expression protected by the First Amendment is made in Lawrence R. Velvel, "Geographical Restrictions on Travel: The Real World and the First Amendment," *Kansas Law Review,* Vol. 15 (1966), p. 35.

62. 381 U.S. at 26. Although the Supreme Court has upheld area restric- tions, under existing legislation such re- strictions cannot be enforced either by criminal prosecution, *Worthy v. United States,* 328 F.2d 386 (5th Cir. 1964); *United States v. Laub,* 385 U.S. 475 (1967); *Travis v. United States,* 385 U.S. 491 (1967); or by revocation of the passport, *Lynd v. United States,* 389 F.2d 940 (D.C. Cir. 1967).

2. ACCESS TO THE BALLOT

The right of a political party or a candidate to appear on the ballot in an election would not seem to be in itself a right of expression covered by the First Amendment. Such a right of access to the ballot is, of course, protected by other constitutional guarantees. But access to the ballot is largely governed by factors different from those relevant to maintaining a system of freedom of expression. On the other hand, when the right of access is conditioned upon not engaging in certain kinds of expression, direct First Amendment issues are presented.[63]

Conditions on access to the ballot based upon expression have usually taken the form of the exclusion of a political party from the ballot or the requirement that individual candidates meet certain qualifications or take some kind of disclaimer oath. In the first category, Section 3 of the Communist Control Act of 1954, providing that the Communist Party is "not entitled to any of the rights, privileges, and immunities attendant upon legal bodies," was apparently intended to remove the Communist Party from the ballot in all elections. It has been applied in only one case, which became moot after the election and was never taken to the Supreme Court. About half the States have legislation on the books excluding from the ballot "subversive organizations," variously defined, or the Communist Party by name. Such laws were sustained in some States during the nineteen-forties, but the issue has not been decided by the United States Supreme Court. Because the Communist Party and other parties likely to be challenged have seldom attempted to get on the ballot since World War II the constitutional questions have received little attention.[64]

The second form of restriction appears in the laws of more than a

63. In *Williams v. Rhodes,* 393 U.S. 23 (1968), the Supreme Court, by a vote of six to three, held invalid Ohio election laws restricting access of new and minority parties to the ballot. Justice Black, writing for himself and three others, thought the legislation denied equal protection of the laws in discriminating against "the right of individuals to associate for the advancement of political beliefs" and the right of voters "to cast their votes effectively." 393 U.S. at 30. Justices Douglas and Harlan, concurring, apparently considered the right of access to the ballot a direct First Amendment right. The other Justices, however, did not accept this position.

64. 50 U.S.C. §842; *Salwen v. Rees,* 16 N.J.2d 216, 108 A.2d 265 (1954). For discussion of the Communist Control Act see Chapter V. Cases and materials on the exclusion of political parties from the ballot are collected in *Political and Civil Rights in the United States,* pp. 315–318. The impact of the Communist Control Act is before the Supreme Court in *Mitchell v. Donovan,* 290 F. Supp. 642 and 300 F. Supp. 1145 (D. Minn. 1969), prob. juris. noted 396 U.S.——(1970).

score of States. There have been only scattered judicial decisions, but the United States Supreme Court did touch on the problem in *Gerende v. Board of Supervisors*. In that case it affirmed per curiam a decision of the Maryland Court of Appeals denying a place on the ballot in a municipal election to a candidate who refused to take the oath prescribed by the Maryland Ober Law. The Maryland Court had construed the law to mean that "a candidate need only make oath that he is not a person who is engaged 'in one way or another in the attempt to overthrow the government by *force and violence*,' and that he is not knowingly a member of an organization engaged in such an attempt." The conditions of the oath can be read as referring only to action, and hence the decision cannot be taken as a precedent for conditions based on expression. In any event the *Gerende* case has been overruled or modified by later decisions in the cases involving loyalty oaths for government employees.[65]

Qualifications for access to the ballot grounded upon conduct otherwise protected as expression would seem to present the clearest possible case for application of the full protection rule. It is difficult to see how the social interest in internal security is served by exclusion of a political party from the political process. On the contrary, the danger to the State or nation would surely be enhanced by denying to any party or group the possibility of redressing their grievances through democratic procedures.

E. Conclusions

This review of the problems raised by imposing disqualifications for benefits or positions upon the basis of expression reveals a shifting course of judicial development. At the beginning of the process in *Douds* (1950), faced with the apparently inescapable conclusion that speech could not be "unlimited," and finding the clear and present danger test inapplicable, the Supreme Court established the balancing test as the chief instrument of First Amendment interpretation.

---

65. *Gerende v. Board of Supervisors of Elections of Baltimore*, 341 U.S. 56 (1951); italics in original. For discussion of the cases and collection of the materials, see *Political and Civil Rights in the United States*, pp. 318–319. The government employee loyalty cases are discussed in Chapter VII.

Applying this doctrine it upheld a disqualification based upon simple membership in the Communist Party, and even divided equally on the validity of a disqualification based upon mere beliefs. In *Killian* (1961), it adhered to this position by a reduced majority, even though some of the associational problems implicit in the *Douds* position began to surface. In *Konigsberg* (1961), the Court extended the impact of the disqualifying process substantially further by approving, also on the basis of the balancing test, a virtually unlimited right of inquiry.

Meanwhile, however, countertrends had set in. The Court had begun a selective withdrawal, employing doctrines not directly derived from the First Amendment. In *Speiser* (1958), it invalidated on due process grounds a requirement not based on expression but administered in a way that impinged upon expression. In *Aptheker* (1964), it started a process of demanding, again on due process grounds, that the disqualifications be narrowly drawn to meet specific dangers. In *Brown* (1965), it utilized the bill of attainder provision to prohibit disqualification based upon a named organization, thereby requiring the government to define the type of organization and adding to the burdens of administration. The *Robel* case (1967), carried the process of refinement still further, greatly narrowing the range of associational relationships that were permissible grounds for disqualification. Even more important, the *Robel* decision proceeded directly on First Amendment grounds and may even have marked the demise of the balancing test itself. Finally, in *Schneider* (1968), the Court took steps to limit the scope of inquiry, which had been left wide open in *Konigsberg*.

The net effect of this advance and retreat has been to leave the field of battle in some confusion. Certainly, not much remains of *Douds*, the starting position. The area in which disqualification based on expression will now be permitted is greatly narrowed. It is likely that loyalty conditions will never be tolerated in the tax and welfare laws, for example. Where permitted, disqualifications based on associational relations are limited at least to active membership, with knowledge of the organization's illegal aims, and specific intent to achieve them. The organization itself cannot be named but only described. Probably a process of individual adjudication is required.

Yet disqualifications based upon expression have not been completely wiped out. Some members of the Communist Party, under some circumstances, can apparently be denied passports. Some form of industrial security screening seems to be permissible, and a port security program is not entirely outlawed.

It is thus not possible to state precisely how far the Court will permit disqualifications based on expression to be utilized in the future. Many of the questions left open are similar to those raised in the operation of the loyalty programs for government employees, discussed in the following chapter. A final judgment on the position of the Court must await a consideration of those problems.

As far as concerns the application of the full protection theory in this area, analysis of the Supreme Court's decisions and experience with actual operation of the programs supply strong support for its acceptance. No competing doctrine proves itself satisfactory. The clear and present danger test is not relevant. The balancing test is demonstrated to be an empty formula, not seriously applied, and apparently abandoned by a majority. In terms of actual results, the attempts to increase our internal security by imposing disqualifications based upon expression have led to no ascertainable advantage. The initial and major efforts, among the labor organizations, proved a series of failures. Qualifications for admission to the professions, in tax and welfare systems, as a condition of obtaining a passport, and for access to the ballot have little or no justification. A plausible case for such disqualifications can be made out only in one limited area: certain aspects of defense employment, a special question discussed in the next chapter. Apart from this, if one looks closely at each particular situation where such disqualifications are imposed, the doctrine of full protection emerges as not only a viable policy but as one essential to the maintenance of a system of freedom of expression.

VII

Internal Security: Loyalty Qualifications for Employment

Loyalty tests for government employment have not been unknown in American history. They were imposed during the Revolutionary War and again during the Civil War. Many States began to require loyalty oaths of teachers, and sometimes others, during World War I and its aftermath. During the nineteen-twenties the Federal Government for a time again instituted loyalty qualifications for its employees. Yet it was not until the period following World War II that loyalty tests for government employees assumed a permanent, rather than episodic, place in American life, and took on the pervading bureaucratic qualities they now possess. At the same time loyalty programs spread into many non-government areas, to employees of government contractors, maritime workers, and others.[1]

1. For the history of loyalty tests in the United States see Harold M. Hyman, *To Try Men's Souls: Loyalty Tests in American History* (Berkeley, University of California Press, 1959). Generally on the current problems see Ralph S. Brown, *Loyalty and Security* (New Haven, Conn., Yale University Press, 1958). An extensive bibliography may be found in Thomas I. Emerson, David Haber, and

Loyalty qualifications for employment have taken two main forms. One form is the loyalty oath, in which the prospective employee swears or affirms that he is not disqualified on various assigned grounds. Such a disclaimer oath may also include a promise not to engage in specified conduct in the future. The employee may be required to renew the oath at yearly or other intervals. The other form is the loyalty program, in which various loyalty qualifications are prescribed and an investigation is made to determine whether the prospective or incumbent employee meets the specified standards. Such investigation may be elaborate or casual, or undertaken only if some question is raised about a particular applicant or employee. There are, of course, many variations and mixtures of the two forms.[2]

Loyalty tests for government employees and government-imposed tests for non-government employees have become of increasing significance as government functions and employment have multiplied. There are nearly 3,000,000 Federal government employees at any one time, virtually all of whom are subject to loyalty tests. Out of some 9,000,000 State and local government employees probably two-thirds, about 6,000,000, engage in work for which a loyalty oath or other loyalty test is required. In addition, about 5,000,000 non-government employees are under Federal loyalty programs such as the industrial security program. Thus a total of 14,000,000, out of a working force of 70,000,000, are directly affected. In other words, more than one out of every five persons is required, as a condition of his current employment, to meet government loyalty qualifications. To this should be added about 3,500,000 members of the armed forces. Moreover, if the turnover in employment and military service and the involvement of families and dependents are taken into account, it will be seen that the

---

Norman Dorsen, *Political and Civil Rights in the United States* (Boston, Little, Brown & Co., 3d ed. 1967), pp. 338–340 (cited hereafter in this chapter as *Political and Civil Rights in the United States*). Later material includes Jerold H. Israel, "Elfbrandt v. Russell: The Demise of the Oath?," *Supreme Court Review*, Vol. 1966 (1966), p. 193; Note, "Loyalty Oaths," *Yale Law Journal*, Vol. 77 (1968), p. 739. On the British experience see David Williams, *Not in the Public Interest* (London, Hutchinson, 1965).

2. We reserve for discussion at the end of this chapter the subsidiary problem of the so-called positive oath, in which the individual swears to support the Constitution and laws but is not required to make any negative disclaimer of beliefs, opinions or associations. We do not consider in this book loyalty qualifications for employment imposed by private employers under no compulsion from the government. On those issues see Brown, *op. cit. supra* note 1, chs. 5 and 18; *Political and Civil Rights in the United States*, pp. 422–426.

loyalty tests have even more widespread ramifications. The overall impact upon freedom of expression can scarcely be exaggerated.[3]

In exploring the question whether, or to what extent, loyalty qualifications for employment are compatible with our system of freedom of expression, we first examine the problem in terms of the effect of loyalty tests upon freedom of expression, the need of the government for imposing loyalty qualifications, and the kind of program required to satisfy the social interest in national security without impairing the system of free expression. Thereafter we consider to what extent the courts have shaped their decisions, on both Federal and State loyalty tests, to meet these requirements.

A. An Analysis of the Problem

Our only concern here is with qualifications for employment based on beliefs, opinions, or associations, that is, upon "expression." We are not concerned with qualifications grounded upon "action." Hence various kinds of disqualification could be imposed in the interests of national security, such as ineligibility for commission of a crime, which would not hamper freedom of expression.

Within this narrower framework, it is first necessary to review briefly the impact of loyalty qualifications upon the system of expression. Generally speaking, cutting a person off from employment or career because of his beliefs, opinions, or associations has a grossly inhibiting effect upon the free exercise of expression by that person and by many others. Where, as in this country, loyalty qualifications are demanded for a substantial proportion of available employment, the impact is widespread and deep. Moreover, certain aspects of loyalty oaths and loyalty programs magnify the total effect.

Inevitably couched in ambiguous language, the loyalty oath, as mentioned in the discussion on freedom of belief, tends to bar the more conscientious and invite the less scrupulous to pass. "Self-

3. The estimates of the number of persons subject to government loyalty tests are based upon calculations, brought up to date, made by Professor Brown in 1958. See Brown, *op. cit. supra* note 1, ch. 6. They are, of course, rough approximations. Likewise they do not take into account the impact of recent court decisions discussed below.

executing" by its nature, it places the burden upon the person taking the oath to interpret its requirements, recall all past events in his life, and decide what current or future administrators of the oath may consider relevant, all at his peril. It operates as a blanket prohibition, leaving no room for individual differences. Enforced by perjury prosecution or dismissal, it places the oath-taker at the continuing mercy of the oath-giver. It is inherently demeaning to a free people.

The loyalty program may be even more inhibiting. In the first place, it is most difficult to place any logical limits on the standard of loyalty to be required. If the test is aimed at those who advocate violent overthrow of government, the investigators soon find themselves delving into questions of Marxism, Leninism, Stalinism, and other ideologies; into attitudes toward violence in the civil-rights movement; into problems of civil disobedience; and beyond. If the standard forbids membership in an organization, the questioning soon leads to matters of affiliation, front organizations, support to the organization, parallelism of ideas, and beyond. Even if the person investigated is finally found qualified, word of the interrogation spreads around and has a depressing effect.

Furthermore, a loyalty program involves administration through a bureaucracy. This means that subtle distinctions or sensitive judgments are unlikely to prevail down through the ranks. Security officials, by their very nature, are motivated by a zest for the job of ferreting out disloyalty, and are prone to fears that tend to drive the program to excess. An apparatus of investigators, professional informers, amateur informers, blacklists of organizations, files and crossfiles is created. The whole operation is scarcely visible to the public or the courts, for it is conducted in secret, with no hearings open, findings made, or reasons given. Particularly is there small chance of control over the treatment of those who are in the vulnerable position of being mere applicants for a job.

For these and similar reasons, loyalty oaths and loyalty programs have a destructive impact upon freedom of expression that extends far beyond what may seem to be their limited scope on paper. Since World War II, within the government service they have resulted in a blanketing of new ideas and an absence of new blood; outside the government they have seriously impaired our ability to understand and meet new problems. Indeed there is evidence that government loyalty oaths and programs are in part responsible for the feeling among many of our youth that existing institutions are incapable of coping with the current ills of our society. In any event, whatever may be the exact effects of the loyalty tests, it is clear that the costs have been high.[4]

In formulating rules for measuring the validity of government loyalty tests against the requirements of the First Amendment, however, certain important considerations must be borne in mind. Under some circumstances the consideration of expression in determining qualifications for government employment may not in fact impair the system of freedom of expression. To take an extreme example, a leading member of the Democratic Party would not feel that his freedom of expression had been infringed if he was passed over, because of his political opinions and associations, for a position in the cabinet of a Republican President. The impact depends upon the nature and needs of the government organization and the common expectations of citizens concerning its operation.

The government is of course entitled to carry on its functions through organizational forms. Such organization is indeed necessary to support the system of freedom of expression and to give effect to decisions that are the product of the system. Inherent in the organizational form are certain requirements essential to effective performance. One is that at times the holding of specific opinions is an affirmative prerequisite for doing a particular job. In a sense this special viewpoint becomes a bona fide occupational qualification. Recognition of this need does not curtail freedom of expression on the part of others holding different opinions.

These special needs of the government in the conduct of its delegated functions are broadly accepted by participants in the system of freedom of expression. In one sense freedom of expression may be restrained by the private pressures of the society; a person joining a radical organization knows he is shutting certain doors that might otherwise be open to him. Yet such effects are not ordinarily prevented by the First Amendment; they are part of the workings of a democratically organized society. In a similar manner, under some conditions the fact that the government takes into account the views or associations of an individual in determining his qualifications for a government position is not felt to be an unwarranted infringement of the right

4. For material dealing with the impact of the loyalty tests see Marie Jahoda and Stuart W. Cook, "Security Measures and Freedom of Thought: An Exploratory Study of the Impact of Loyalty and Security Programs," *Yale Law Journal,* Vol. 61 (1952), p. 295; Arval A. Morris, "Academic Freedom and Loyalty Oaths," *Law and Contemporary Problems,* Vol. 28 (1963), p. 487; *Political and Civil Rights in the United States,* pp. 390–395.

to expression. To give another example, a rabid member of the Ku Klux Klan would hardly expect to be appointed as head of the Civil Rights Commission. Nor would a scientist of unorthodox views feel that his right to dissent was impaired if he was not called in as a consultant on a government project framed on theories not shared by him.

In constitutional terms all this means that in a limited area, measured by the common-sense requirements of the organization, occupational qualifications for government employment based on opinions or associations do not "abridge" freedom of expression. Moreover, what is true of direct government employment may be true, in some degree, of private employment in effect devoted to governmental tasks. Employees of government contractors may, under certain circumstances, be the equivalent of government agents. In this situation, too, opinions as revealed by expression may be bona fide occupational qualifications. Here also, as commonly recognized, there would be no "abridgment" of the system of freedom of expression.

The next task is to examine in some detail what social interests the government may seek to protect through a loyalty program and the extent to which qualifications based upon expression might be considered necessary or appropriate for safeguarding those interests. We are primarily concerned with the interest in internal security (or national security) but other kinds of interests also come into the picture.

The starting point is to reject the proposition that the government is entitled to refuse employment to persons who are "disloyal," in the sense of being critical of American institutions, and therefore do not deserve to share in the benefits of government largess. For many people, loyalty tests are built substantially on this premise. But such a social interest, if it can be called that, has no constitutional weight. To give it any effect would, on its face, violate the fundamental concept of the First Amendment, and due process as well. No court has ever supported such a proposition.

We may also put aside that part of the problem embraced within the system of military operations. This would exclude from consideration any loyalty qualifications required of military personnel functioning within the armed services. It would also exclude some civilian personnel employed by the military in military operations to the extent that such persons are part of the military system. The separation of the civilian system of freedom of expression from the system of military operations does not imply that the First Amendment has no application to the military system. It does mean that the principles governing a civilian system of freedom of expression do not necessarily hold under the totally different circumstances at work in a system of military operations.[5]

Accepting the foregoing premises, the legitimate needs of the government service would seem to fall into four main categories:

(1) One of the main concerns of the government in framing its loyalty tests has been that employees with certain beliefs, opinions, or associations would be more likely to engage in acts of sabotage or physical obstruction in times of crisis. It would seem most doubtful that any democratic government could avoid fifth column activities in a period of emergency by imposing loyalty tests upon the great mass of its employees. A state of perfect security cannot be achieved by any government, even a government using police state methods to obtain it, and there is no point in attempting the impossible. Accepting some risk, therefore, it seems unlikely that the danger would be materially reduced by examining the opinions and associations of all current and prospective employees, with no overt actions to go on. Certainly a government facing a crisis attended by fifth column activities on a broad scale would not be safe in relying upon loyalty tests for its employees. Such problems must be dealt with on another level.

If the problem of potential sabotage in the government service were to be handled on a more common-sense basis, the most that would be required would be the application of limited tests of ordinary suitability to a few especially sensitive positions. Thus a person who himself advocated the immediate use of violence to achieve political goals would not be a satisfactory employee in an installation, such as a nuclear power plant, where sabotage is to be particularly feared. Eligibility requirements based on expression would not need to go beyond this. The use of such qualifications would not seem to pose any problem for a system of freedom of expression. Neither a person expressing such views nor other persons would feel that their right of expression was curtailed if the holding of certain government posts was foreclosed under these circumstances. No elaborate administrative machinery would be necessary to carry out such eligibility requirements. The problem would not arise very often and could be covered by normal methods of ascertaining suitability. Hence the dampening effects of a farflung loyalty program would not impinge upon the system of free expression.

5. For further discussion see Chapter III.

(2) Another factor that has played an important part in the formulation of loyalty tests has been the effort to protect the government against espionage or the divulging of secret information. Experience with loyalty qualifications up to now, however, has not demonstrated any relation between the loyalty tests and the prevention of espionage. There seems to be no recorded instance in which the loyalty tests have revealed or excluded a spy. The problem of espionage would seem more effectively handled through the usual methods of counterespionage. So far as concerns the problem apart from espionage, there would likewise seem to be no general relation between expression and the revealing of secret information. An elaborate program for weeding out, on the basis of opinions or associations, persons who may give away government secrets would therefore be misdirected. The usual inquiries concerning honesty and integrity, plus the punishment of actual action, would be the more effective way to meet this problem.

Here again, however, some exception to the general principle may be warranted in the case of a few sensitive positions. A person whose opinions or associations indicate a strong ideological commitment to a foreign country might not be suitable for a position involving access to important military secrets. The problem of safeguarding most military secrets falls under the jurisdiction of the military system, but the issue could arise in a few civilian areas, such as the Atomic Energy Commission, or in the case of government contractors. A similar question would be presented by a position in which the incumbent had access to secrets relating to foreign affairs. A carefully drawn program to deal with these particularly sensitive positions would not seem to interfere with freedom of expression. The relation between expression and the government position is such that most participants in the system would not feel that freedom of expression was abridged. The administration of such qualifications, especially insofar as they involved associational ties, might create more of a problem. Yet the program would be limited to a small number of persons, and could be administered in such a way that it would not impair the system of freedom of expression.

(3) A third concern of the government in establishing loyalty tests for employment has been to exclude persons who will not adhere to official policy in performing their duties, but will decide questions in a way most favorable to their ideological or associational interests. Thus it is frequently said that a member of the Communist Party in a government position would make decisions in a manner that would

promote Communist Party interests and would favor Communist Party members in hiring employees. The basic problem is an important one for the government service but it is not solved by loyalty tests. The tendency to use a government position to forward one's own personal or associational interests is not limited to persons having any particular opinion or membership. It applies to Democrats, Republicans and Socialists, to Protestants, Catholics and Jews, and to persons having other kinds of interests and connections. The solution is therefore not a test designed to eliminate persons of any particular views or associations, but an application of the usual methods available to a bureaucracy to make sure that employees follow its policy, including discharge, transfer, or other discipline when improper action in fact occurs.

There are, however, a few situations in which opinions or associations are integrally related to the job to be performed. Thus a position in the State Department in which it was necessary to deal on friendly terms with Arab countries might not be suitable for a Jew, or a position on the African desk for a white racist. Since there is a close and direct relation between the opinion expressed and the job to be done, the selection of a suitable person to do the job does not discourage freedom of expression. The foreclosure of such opportunity is an accepted aspect of any system of free expression. The process of selection, also, need not have any deleterious effect upon the system.

(4) A final interest of the government is in the competence of its employees. The selection of competent employees is an important matter, but clearly not one that demands the use of loyalty tests. Ordinarily political belief, opinion, or association has no bearing on the ability of the prospective employee to perform in the designated position. Yet it is political expression that the loyalty test is primarily aimed at. Occasionally, for particular jobs, political opinions, and even beliefs, may be directly related to the function of the position, and hence relevant. Qualifications based to that extent upon expression do not, for reasons already stated, abridge freedom of expression. Those qualifications can be ascertained, in proper cases, without relying upon the paraphernalia of loyalty oaths or programs.

In light of these considerations, we come to the crucial question: What kind of loyalty qualifications are compatible with a system of freedom of expression? Or to ask the question another way, what rules of law governing loyalty tests are required to give full protection of the First Amendment to freedom of expression? The issue is put in this form because, under the basic theory of the First Amendment here being proposed, the legal principles necessary to sustain an effective system of freedom of expression prevail even though there be some risk to other social interests. Nevertheless we believe that, for reasons stated above, the risks to other interests are minimal.

The general principle with which we start is that no qualifications for employment based upon expression are valid under the First Amendment if the use of the criterion or the manner of its administration would "abridge" freedom of speech, that is, materially impair the system of freedom of expression. This principle applies to all government employment and all non-government employment upon which the government loyalty tests are imposed. The rule would, however, allow qualifications based upon expression to be used in limited situations, such as if (1) the position is a sensitive one in terms of possible sabotage and the standard is personal advocacy of immediate violence; (2) the position involves access to military or foreign relations secrets and the standard is a strong ideological commitment to a foreign country; (3) the position is one that entails application of a particular policy or requires a particular competence and the test of expression is clearly and directly related to performance in that position. In all such and similar cases, for the reasons given, there would be no impairment of the system of free expression. In addition, the rule would not be applicable to qualifications imposed upon employment in the military system.

More specifically, the application of the above principles would require that:

(1) Loyalty tests across the board, covering all employees of the government, would not be permitted. The test would have to be confined to a limited number of jobs, carefully defined.

(2) A precise enumeration of the standards would be necessary, tailored to the requirements of each position or group of positions.

(3) Application of the standards in such a way as to reach a particular decision on the individual case would be essential. This would eliminate the loyalty oath altogether. It would also eliminate the broad tests of guilt by association. Only personal participation in the affairs of an organization would be considered relevant.

(4) Procedures would have to be carefully devised to eliminate any direct or indirect impact upon the system of freedom of expression. This would require the full procedural protections of the administrative process, including judicial review; procedural devices to cushion

the effect on the individual, such as payment of salary during the proceeding, the furnishing of costs of obtaining counsel, and transfer to another position where feasible; maximum visibility to assure critical appraisal of the system; and development of rules for limitation upon the scope of the inquiry that would protect the employee involved.

It is not urged that the foregoing proposals embody a perfect plan or represent the final word. It is suggested, however, that they present the kind of approach that is necessary to accommodate the social interests involved to an effective system of freedom of expression. We turn now to a consideration of the extent to which the courts, in dealing with the loyalty test problem, have accepted or followed such an approach.

B. Federal Loyalty Tests

Under the original Civil Service Rule I, issued in 1884, no inquiry could be made of "the political or religious opinions or affiliations of any applicant" for employment in the Federal Government covered by civil service. The position of the Federal employee was strengthened by the Lloyd-LaFollette Act of 1912 which gave civil service employees the right to notice of charges and an opportunity to reply in writing before dismissal. That Act, and the Civil Service regulations issued under it, also provided for the removal or discipline of employees "for such cause as will promote the efficiency of the service." This provision was not, so far as appears, used as the basis for imposing loyalty qualifications prior to World War II.[6]

Modern loyalty tests for employees of the Federal Government began with passage of the Hatch Act in 1939. That legislation made it unlawful for any Federal employee "to have membership in any political party or organization which advocates the overthrow of our constitutional form of government in the United States." From 1941 on Congress included in virtually all appropriation acts a rider specifying that none of the funds could be used to pay the salary or wages of "any person who advocates, or who is a member of an organization that

6. For Civil Service Rule I, see 5 C.F.R. 1.2 (1939 ed.). The Lloyd-LaFollette Act is 37 Stat. 555 (1912), 5 U.S.C. §652, and the Civil Service regulation issued under it is Civil Service Rule XII, §1, 5 C.F.R. 12.1 (1939 ed.).

advocates, the overthrow of the Government of the United States by force or violence." In 1942 the Civil Service Commission broadened the program by adopting a regulation that an applicant would be disqualified or an employee removed if there were "reasonable doubt as to [the] loyalty [of the person involved] to the Government of the United States." During the war enforcement of these provisions was sporadic and little administrative machinery was established.[7]

The Federal loyalty program began to assume its present proportions with the promulgation of Executive Order 9835 by President Truman in March 1947. This order called for a loyalty investigation of all applicants for employment and all existing employees in the executive branch of the Federal Government. The basic standard to be applied was whether "on all the evidence, reasonable grounds exist for the belief that the person involved is disloyal to the Government of the United States." An amendment in 1951, intended to tighten the program, changed the standard to whether "on all the evidence, there is a reasonable doubt as to the loyalty of the person involved to the Government of the United States." More specifically the order provided that the "activities and associations" to be considered in determining loyalty were to include (a) sabotage, espionage or knowingly associating with spies or saboteurs; (b) treason or sedition or advocacy thereof; (c) advocacy of revolution or force or violence to alter the constitutional form of government; (d) intentional, unauthorized disclosure of confidential documents or information; (e) performing duties or acting "so as to serve the interests of another government in preference to the interests of the United States"; and, as the most far-reaching,

> (f) Membership in, affiliation with or sympathetic association with any foreign or domestic organization, association, movement, group or combination of persons, designated by the Attorney General as totalitarian, fascist, communist, or subversive, or as having adopted a policy of advocating or approving the commission of acts of force or violence to deny other persons their rights under the Constitution of the United States, or as seeking to alter the form of government of the United States by unconstitutional means.[8]

7. The Hatch Act is 53 Stat. 1147, 1148 (1939), now 5 U.S.C. §7311. For an example of the appropriation riders see 55 Stat. 5, 6 (1941). The 1942 Civil Service regulation is Civil Service War Regulations §18.2(c), 7 Fed. Reg. 7723, now Civil Service Regulations §731.201, 5 C.F.R. 731.201.

8. Executive Order 9835, 12 Fed. Reg. 1935 (1947), amended by Executive Order 10241, 16 Fed. Reg. 3690 (1951).

Meanwhile Congress, beginning in 1940, had passed a series of measures giving certain "sensitive agencies" the right of summary dismissal. This form of legislation culminated in Public Law 733, enacted in 1950. Under this enactment the heads of certain agencies were authorized to suspend summarily and thereafter terminate the employment of any employee "whenever he [the agency head] shall determine such termination necessary or advisable in the interest of the national security of the United States." The employee was to be notified of the reasons only to the extent that the agency head "determines that the interests of national security permit." The law was applicable to eleven named agencies, including the Departments of State, Justice, Defense and Commerce, but could be applied to such other agencies "as the President may, from time to time, deem necessary in the best interests of national security." [9]

When the Eisenhower administration came to power in 1953 it commenced a review of the Truman loyalty program and in April of that year superseded the Truman Order with Executive Order 10450. The new order provided that Public Law 733 should be applied to all agencies of the government. It made the head of each agency responsible for establishing "an effective program to insure that the employment and retention" of any employee within the agency "is clearly consistent with the interests of the national security." It listed as relevant to the determination of the latter issue the same matters, with some elaboration, as set out in the Truman Order. The Eisenhower Order made one further change of major importance. It directed the agency head to consider not only issues of loyalty, but also whether the employee was reliable or trustworthy, used intoxicants to excess, was subject to mental illness, and the like. In other words the Eisenhower Order transformed the loyalty program into a loyalty-security program. [10]

In 1955 Congress combined the Hatch Act and the appropriation provisions into a single provision, thereafter dropping the appropriation riders. The 1955 codification also added an oath requirement providing that every person "who accepts office or employment in the Government of the United States . . . shall . . . execute an affidavit that his acceptance and holding of such office or employment does

---

9. Public Law 733, 81st Cong., 2d Sess. (1950), 64 Stat. 476, 5 U.S.C. §22–1 to 22–3.

10. Executive Order 10450, 18 Fed. Reg. 2489 (1953), 3 C.F.R. 1949–1953 Comp. p. 936, 5 U.S.C. §631 note.

not or . . . will not constitute a violation" of the Hatch Act provision.[11]

The Eisenhower Order was drastically curtailed by the decision of the Supreme Court in *Cole v. Young,* rendered in 1956. That case held that an employee could be discharged under Public Law 733 only if he occupied a "sensitive" position. The effect of the decision was that the Eisenhower Order became inapplicable to most Federal employees.[12]

Thereafter, no new executive order was issued and no new legislation enacted. The loyalty program continued, however, upon much the same basis as before, except that the standards and summary procedures of Public Law 733 applied only to employees in "sensitive" positions. The result is that the loyalty program for Federal employees now rests upon the following basis:

(1) An applicant or employee under the civil service is subject to rejection or removal under the Lloyd-LaFollette Act "cause" provision, the Hatch Act as amended in 1955, and the Civil Service "reasonable doubt" regulation of 1942.

(2) Employees in "sensitive" positions are also subject to suspension and termination under Public Law 733.

(3) An applicant or employee not under civil service is subject to rejection or removal without regard to any statute, limited only by constitutional restrictions.[13]

In addition to its major program for Federal employees the Federal Government administers various other loyalty programs. These include the military personnel security program, the Atomic Energy Commission program, the program for employees of international agencies, the industrial security program for employees of government contractors having access to classified material, the port security program for maritime workers, and others. While all these programs have special features, the standards of loyalty and the procedures for determining it are roughly comparable to those of the basic program just described.[14]

The actual operations of the Federal loyalty program are shrouded in obscurity. Proceedings are not made public. Decisions, containing

11. 69 Stat. 624 (1955), 5 U.S.C. §118, p, q and r.

12. *Cole v. Young,* 351 U.S. 536 (1956).

13. For a summary of the laws and regulations, and a collection of materials,

see *Political and Civil Rights in the United States,* pp. 337–349.

14. For a summary of the other programs, see *Political and Civil Rights in the United States,* pp. 349–353.

findings of fact and reasons, are not available. There is no way of knowing, much less studying, what is going on. Such information as is available has been revealed in bits and pieces by occasional applicants or employees who have been through the process. Even they, however, do not usually know the full story.

It is therefore not possible to analyze in detail the standards of loyalty applied under the Federal loyalty program at any time. It is clear, however, that many forms of expression which the First Amendment admittedly protects against direct infringement have been used as grounds for disqualification from Federal employment, without regard to the nature of the position involved. Such expression has included the reading of books, such as those by Louis Adamic; subscribing to magazines, such as *The Nation* or *The New Republic;* unorthodox opinions, especially about foreign policy or race relations; friendship or acquaintance with other suspected persons; and even "exhibiting a hypercritical attitude toward society." The ground for disqualification most frequently invoked has probably been membership, affiliation or support of a "subversive" organization. Certainly membership in the Communist Party has been automatic ground for rejection. Any relation to one of the several hundred organizations on the Attorney General's List has also been fatal or near fatal. As the McCarthy period tapered off in the late nineteen-fifties the standards were undoubtedly relaxed. But what they were then or what they are now cannot be known.[15]

The Federal loyalty program is accompanied by elaborate administrative machinery that greatly magnifies its effect upon the system of freedom of expression. Under the Truman Order there were loyalty boards in every agency, and an appellate Loyalty Review Board. The Eisenhower Order abolished the loyalty boards but a sizable force of security officers remains. When any "derogatory information" is uncovered about any person a "full field" investigation is made by the F.B.I. or some other intelligence agency, in which all aspects of the person's life, beginning with family background and early school days, are thoroughly probed. Informers, both amateur and professional, are extensively employed. Much information used in making the decision is withheld from the employee. Prosecution for false statements is infrequent, but the few that occur are sufficiently well publicized to convey the message. In short, any person whose loyalty is

15. For further details on the standards applied, and a collection of materials on the subject, see *Political and Civil Rights in the United States,* pp. 354–360.

questioned faces a prolonged and agonizing experience. It becomes well known, particularly in university circles, that unconventional ideas or opinions are not advisable for those considering careers in government service. Again, the outward manifestations of the loyalty-security programs receded into the background toward the end of the nineteen-fifties. Yet an extensive apparatus still exists.[16]

It is thus apparent that the Federal loyalty program, in the extent of its coverage, in the standards it applies, and in its methods of administration, has been and is in conflict with First Amendment rights. This is certainly true under the principles derived from applying the doctrine of full protection to the loyalty problem. It would probably also be true for many aspects of the program under other tests of the First Amendment. Yet until the *Robel* decision in 1967 there was no court decision invalidating any part of the Federal loyalty program upon First Amendment grounds.

The first major challenge to the Federal loyalty program was *Bailey v. Richardson,* in 1950. Dorothy Bailey, a training officer in the United States Employment Service, was discharged under the Truman Order upon a finding by a loyalty board that "reasonable grounds exist for belief that [she] is disloyal to the Government of the United States." She brought suit for declaratory judgment and reinstatement in the District of Columbia and lost. The chief controversy was over the procedure employed by the loyalty board—the evidence against her was not made available to her—but the Court of Appeals also dealt with the straight First Amendment issue. Judge Prettyman, writing for the majority, held that "so far as the Constitution is concerned there is no prohibition against dismissal of Government employees because of their political beliefs, activities or affiliations." "The situation of the Government employee," he said, "is not different in this respect from that of private employees." Judge Edgerton, in dissent, contended that dismissal based upon opinions, having no relation to the efficiency of the government service, constituted a restraint on freedom of speech, and that the attribution of guilt by association violated freedom of assembly.[17]

16. On the administrative aspects of the Federal loyalty programs, see *Political and Civil Rights in the United States,* pp. 388–395.

17. *Bailey v. Richardson,* 182 F.2d 46, 59, 60 (D.C. Cir. 1950). A similar result was reached in *Washington v.* *McGrath,* 182 F.2d 375 (D.C. Cir. 1950). An earlier case, likewise decided against the employee, but not squarely dealing with the constitutional issues, was *Friedman v. Schwellenbach,* 159 F.2d 22 (D.C. Cir. 1946), cert. denied, 330 U.S. 838 (1947).

The Supreme Court affirmed the *Bailey* case on an evenly divided vote, Justice Clark not participating. There was thus no opinion written in *Bailey*. Some of the Justices, however, took the opportunity to express their individual views in a case decided the same day, *Joint Anti-Fascist Refugee Committee v. McGrath,* involving the power of the Attorney General to put an organization upon his list of "subversive organizations." It appeared that Chief Justice Vinson and Justices Reed and Minton considered the Federal loyalty program valid, while Justices Black, Douglas and Jackson thought it violated the First Amendment in various ways. This is as close as the Supreme Court came to expressing its position directly upon the First Amendment aspects of the Federal loyalty program until *Robel*. The Prettyman doctrine that the First Amendment did not apply to government employment did not long survive. But the *Bailey* case supported the general validity of the Federal program for many years.[18]

In four decisions after *Bailey* the constitutional issues were raised but not reached. The Supreme Court decided in favor of the employee in all the cases, but on technical or statutory grounds. The most important of these was *Cole v. Young,* discussed above, which held that Public Law 733 applied only to "sensitive" positions. The opinion implies that the Court would make a constitutional distinction between sensitive and non-sensitive positions, but the import of this for the Federal loyalty program was not made clear. A fifth case involved the industrial security program, and the Court, again upholding the employee, avoided constitutional issues by ruling that the authorizing statute could not be construed to permit the use of secret evidence.[19]

The Court decided against the employee, for the first and only time, in *Cafeteria and Restaurant Workers Union v. McElroy*. The question here was whether the Rear Admiral in charge of the Naval Gun Factory could revoke the admittance privileges of a short-order cook employed by a private contractor who furnished meals at the Factory. The result of the Admiral's action was to deprive the cook of her employment. The operations of the Factory included "the development of weapons systems of a highly classified nature." The Admiral acted on grounds of national security but gave no further detail. The

18. The Supreme Court's action in the *Bailey* case is reported at 341 U.S. 918 (1951). *Washington v. McGrath* was also affirmed by an equal vote, 341 U.S. 923 (1951). The *Joint Anti-Fascist* case is reported at 341 U.S. 123 (1951).

19. *Peters v. Hobby,* 349 U.S. 331 (1955); *Cole v. Young,* 351 U.S. 536 (1956); *Service v. Dulles,* 354 U.S. 363 (1957); *Vitarelli v. Seaton,* 359 U.S. 535 (1959); *Greene v. McElroy,* 360 U.S. 474 (1959).

Court in a five to four decision found there had been no violation of statutory or constitutional rights. The principle upon which the conclusion is based, and consequently the scope of the decision, is by no means clear. It should be noted, however, that the result is consistent with our theory that loyalty programs in a military system are not governed by the rules applicable to the civilian sector.[20]

One particular feature of the Federal loyalty program merits brief attention—the Attorney General's List of "subversive organizations." Shortly after the passage of the Hatch Act and early in the loyalty program the Attorney General had prepared a list of organizations association with which was considered to cast doubt upon loyalty. The Truman Order formally required the Attorney General to compile a list of organizations he considered "totalitarian, fascist, communist or subversive," and in November of 1947 he furnished the Loyalty Review Board with a list of eighty-two organizations. The list was made public. Thereafter the Attorney General from time to time made additions to the list until it contained the names of about 275 organizations. The Attorney General's List was extensively used in the administration of the Federal loyalty program; in fact, as already noted, most cases involved charges of association with one or more of the organizations on the list. It was also widely utilized outside the Federal loyalty program, by State and local governments and by private groups, as an official tabulation of "subversive organizations." [21]

The Attorney General's List was created in response to demands that inhere in every loyalty program. Much of the evidence of "disloyalty" is inevitably concerned with the relations of individuals to various organizations. Since the administrators of the loyalty program would find it difficult to make a *de novo* determination in each case as to whether a particular organization were "subversive" or not, it becomes imperative to have some procedure for preparing and maintaining a master list.

Any such process, however, raises a host of First Amendment problems. What standards are to be used in determining whether an organization is "subversive"? What right does an individual employee have to challenge the presence on the list of a particular organization? If such a list is kept secret, there is no opportunity to challenge it; but if

20. *Cafeteria and Restaurant Workers Union v. McElroy*, 367 U.S. 886 (1961).

21. For a summary of the development of the Attorney General's List and the manner in which it was used, see *Political and Civil Rights in the United States*, pp. 385–388.

it is made public it immediately becomes an official blacklist. If no hearing is held before listing, the organization listed has no chance to defend itself; if a hearing is held the very process is expensive, time-consuming and publicly damaging. The total impact is that the government has virtually life and death power over which organizations are allowed to exist and which not.

The Supreme Court has never dealt directly with the validity of the Attorney General's List under the First Amendment. It did rule in the *Joint Anti-Fascist* case, as already noted, that the Attorney General could not place an organization on the list without first affording it the opportunity for a hearing. Thereafter the Attorney General did not add any more names to the list, and three organizations were dropped. But the Attorney General's List remains in existence and is still utilized both in the Federal loyalty program and in other connections.[22]

The failure of the Supreme Court throughout this period to come to grips with the First Amendment issues in the Federal loyalty program is somewhat surprising. The program was operating on all fronts in full force. Yet only isolated cases reached the Supreme Court. In all of these, except when the issue involved exclusion from a military installation, the Court ruled against the program, but on nonconstitutional grounds.

Finally, in the 1967 Term, the Supreme Court decided two cases that indicated it was at last prepared to apply First Amendment doctrine in a manner that would substantially narrow the operation of the Federal loyalty program. Both cases involved employees in private industry and therefore less subject to the restrictions that might be placed on government employees. But the principles enunciated or implied in the two cases would seem also applicable to those parts of the Federal program that affect government employees.

The *Robel* case, as noted in the previous chapter, invalidated the provision of the Internal Security Act which made it an offense for a

22. *Joint Anti-Fascist Refugee Committee v. McGrath,* 341 U.S. 123 (1951). The current Attorney General's List may be found in Bureau of National Affairs, *Manual of Government Security and Loyalty* 15: 112–119; House Committee on Un-American Activities, *Guide to Subversive Organizations and Publications,* App. II (1961). For court decisions dealing with the legal status of, and the effect of membership in, an organization on the Attorney General's List, apart from the Federal loyalty program, see *Political and Civil Rights in the United States,* pp. 387–388. Two recent efforts to challenge the List as a violation of the First Amendment were decided on other grounds in *Industrial Workers of the World v. Clark,* 385 F.2d 687 (D.C. Cir. 1967), cert. denied 390 U.S. 948 (1968); and *Veterans of the Abraham Lincoln Brigade v. Attorney General,* 409 F.2d 1139 (D.C. Cir. 1969).

member of an organization ordered to register as a Communist-action organization "to engage in any employment in any defense facility." The decision, refusing to apply the balancing test, rested on the proposition that the provision covered too much ground. In sorting out those factors which could validly result in disqualification from those which could not, the opinion of Chief Justice Warren indicates (1) membership of the character found in the *Scales* case, that is, active membership with a specific intent to further the unlawful goals of the organization, could be a basis for disqualification, at least for sensitive positions; (2) membership that was passive or inactive, or by a person unaware of the organization's unlawful aims, or by one who disagreed with those aims, could not be a ground for disqualification, at least for non-sensitive positions; and (3) the sensitivity or non-sensitivity of the position had to be taken into account, though the opinion did not make clear in what way this would have to be done.[23]

The *Schneider* case, also noted in the previous chapter, did not rest on First Amendment grounds directly but on grounds of statutory interpretation. Nevertheless it hints at far-reaching First Amendment limitations on loyalty programs. Regulations issued by the President under the Magnuson Act incorporated standards or qualifications very similar to those set forth in the Truman and Eisenhower Executive Orders. Pursuant to these regulations the seaman applying for clearance was asked detailed questions described by Justice Douglas as a "probe [of] reading habits, political philosophy, beliefs, and attitudes on social and economic issues." Justice Douglas, writing the prevailing opinion, held that if the Act were construed to authorize "a type of screening program directed at 'membership' or 'sympathetic association'" it would present serious First Amendment questions. He added that the Act "speaks only in terms of actions, not ideas or beliefs or reading habits or social, educational, or political associations." He therefore concluded that the investigation conducted in the case before him was not authorized by the Act. There is no doubt that Justice Douglas was talking in constitutional terms. But it is not possible to disentangle the terms of the statute, the standards in the regulations, and the actual investigation sufficiently to say exactly how far his First Amendment objections went. His opinion can be construed as applying the full protection theory to the port security program, thereby requir-

23. *United States v. Robel,* 389 U.S. 258 (1967).

ing that disqualification be based only on actions, not on expression. But it seems unlikely that a majority of the Court was ready to go that far.[24]

C. State and Local Loyalty Tests

Most State and local loyalty tests have taken the form of loyalty oaths. The oaths have been primarily concerned with forswearing association with designated or described organizations. The Supreme Court decisions have thus centered around these two problems of oath-taking and associational rights. As is to be expected, various doctrines other than those pertaining to the First Amendment have been utilized in disposing of the cases; yet First Amendment considerations have at all times shaped the application of those doctrines. In general, the Supreme Court decisions fall into two periods. The decisions prior to 1960 sustained the loyalty tests, albeit within a relatively confined area. Thereafter the Court went out of its way to overturn State loyalty tests, though usually not on First Amendment grounds. Beginning with *Shelton v. Tucker* in 1960, every State loyalty test to come before the Court has been struck down. ◦

The line of development begins in 1951 with a case that did not involve a loyalty test for government employees. *Gerende v. Board of Supervisors of Elections of Baltimore* concerned a provision of the Maryland Ober Law which provided that, in order to obtain a place on the ballot, the candidate must take an oath that he was not a "subversive person" within the meaning of that statute. The Supreme Court construed the Maryland decision upholding this provision as meaning

24. *Schneider v. Smith*, 390 U.S. 17, 24, 25 (1968). In *Soltar v. Postmaster General*, 277 F. Supp. 579 (N.D. Cal. 1967), questions asked on Civil Service application forms were held invalid, and in *Haskett v. Washington*, 294 F. Supp. 912 (D.D.C. 1968), the District of Columbia oath was held invalid, both decisions resting on grounds of overbreadth. Subsequently a three judge court in the District of Columbia ruled that the Hatch Act provision (5 U.S.C. §7311) and the oath required under that provision were unconstitutional as overbroad. *Stewart v. Washington*, 301 F. Supp. 610 (D.D.C. 1969). The Government did not appeal the decision and the Civil Service Commission abandoned the oath. *The New York Times*, January 7, 1970.

that "a candidate need only make oath that he is not a person who is engaged 'in one way or another in the attempt to overthrow the government *by force or violence*,' and that he is not knowingly a member of an organization engaged in such an attempt." Even as thus limited the oath contained some problems which would later trouble the Court, such as whether "engaged" included expression as well as action, and whether "knowingly a member" included passive membership or some more active form. The Court, however, did not stop to consider these refinements. In a per curiam opinion, and without discussion, it affirmed the Maryland court.[25]

The first case actually involving a loyalty test for government employees was *Garner v. Board of Public Works of Los Angeles,* decided two months after *Gerende*. In that case every employee of the City of Los Angeles was required to take an oath that he (1) did not "advise, advocate or teach," and had not done so within five years prior to the passage of the law, "the overthrow by force, violence or other unlawful means" of the government; and (2) was not, and had not been within the five-year period, "a member or affiliated with" any organization which so advised, advocated or taught; and (3) would not, while in the service of Los Angeles, so advise, advocate or teach, or become a member of or affiliated with an organization that did. Justice Clark, speaking for five members of the Court, had no difficulty in upholding this oath. "We assume," he said, that the oath is valid as "a reasonable regulation to protect the municipal service by establishing an employment qualification of loyalty to the State and the United States," and that it is "reasonably designed to protect the integrity and competency of the service." The only limitation he placed upon this sweeping validation of loyalty oaths was a further assumption that the oath would not be construed "as affecting adversely those persons who during their affiliation with a proscribed organization were innocent of its purpose, or those who severed their relations with any such organization when its character became apparent, or those who were affiliated with organizations which at one time or another during the period covered by the ordinance were engaged in proscribed activities but not at the time of affiant's affiliation." Justice Clark made no reference to the First Amendment. The bulk of his opinion was taken up

---

25. *Gerende v. Board of Supervisors* (1951). Italics in original. Discussed also
of Elections of Baltimore, 341 U.S. 56   in Chapter VI.

with a discussion of the contention that the oath constituted a bill of attainder, an argument he rejected on the ground that no punishment of specified persons was involved.[26]

The Los Angeles ordinance also required that every employee execute an affidavit "stating whether or not he is or ever was a member of the Communist Party . . . and if he is or was such a member, stating the dates when he became, and the periods during which he was, such a member." Again Justice Clark saw no constitutional problem in the city's "inquiring of its employees as to matters that may prove relevant to their fitness and suitability for the public service." Yet he also pointed out that "the question whether the city may determine that an employee's disclosure of such political affiliation justifies his discharge" was not before them.[27]

Justice Douglas, with Justice Black concurring, dissented on the ground that the oath constituted a bill of attainder. "Petitioners were disqualified from office," he said, "not because of any program they currently espouse . . . not because of standards related to fitness for the office . . . but for what they once advocated. They are deprived of their livelihood by legislative act, not by judicial process."[28]

Justice Frankfurter agreed with the majority that the city could inquire about Communist affiliations of its employees: "In the context of our time, such membership is sufficiently related to effective and dependable government, and to the confidence of the electorate in its government." But he thought that the oath was invalid because it was couched in too uncertain language. Recognizing that a disclaimer oath, by its very nature, put a difficult burden on the employee to decide on pain of perjury whether his past conduct placed him inside or outside its terms, Justice Frankfurter pointed out the dilemma of the employee and the effect of the oath on freedom of expression:

> The oath thus excludes from city employment all persons who are not certain that every organization to which they belonged or with which they were affiliated (with all the uncertainties of the meaning of "affiliated") at any time since 1943 has not since that date advocated the overthrow by "unlawful" means of the Government . . .
> If this ordinance is sustained, sanction is given to like oaths for

26. *Garner v. Board of Public Works of Los Angeles,* 341 U.S. 716, 720–721, 723 (1951).

27. 341 U.S. at 720.

28. 341 U.S. at 735–736.

every governmental unit in the United States. Not only does the oath make an irrational demand. It is bound to operate as a real deterrent to people contemplating even innocent associations. How can anyone be sure that an organization with which he affiliates will not at some time in the future be found by a State or National official to advocate overthrow of government by "unlawful means"? All but the hardiest may well hesitate to join organizations if they know that by such a proscription they will be permanently disqualified from public employment. These are considerations that cut deep into the traditions of our people.[29]

The *Garner* case was decided the same day that the Court upheld the Smith Act in *Dennis v. United States.* Like the *Dennis* case it dealt in broad strokes with advocacy of violent overthrow, upholding disqualification from government employment for engaging in such advocacy or being associated with an organization that did. This undifferentiated approach to the problem was followed in the next case, *Adler v. Board of Education,* decided the following year. *Adler,* unlike *Gerende* and *Garner,* dealt with a loyalty program rather than an oath. The Court considered some of the problems involved in the administration of such an investigatory program. But the case arose in a suit for injunction against the program as a whole, and did not involve the application of the program to any particular employee.[30]

The substantive provision at issue in *Adler* was Section 12-a of the Civil Service Law of New York. This section made ineligible for government service, including the public school system, any person who (1) "advocates, advises or teaches the doctrine that the government . . . should be overthrown or overturned by force, violence or any unlawful means," or (2) "organizes or helps to organize or becomes a member of any society or group" which teaches or advocates such overthrow. In 1949 Section 3022 of the Education Law, known as the Feinberg Law, was passed to implement Section 12-a. This provision directed the Board of Regents to adopt and enforce regulations to provide for the disqualification of persons ineligible under Section 12-a. It specifically required the Board, after notice and hearing, to "make a listing of organizations" advocating or teaching violent overthrow and to provide in its regulations that membership in any listed organization "shall constitute prima facie evidence of disqualification" for

29. 341 U.S. at 725, 726, 727–728.   30. *Adler v. Board of Education,* 342
Justice Burton also dissented in part.   U.S. 485 (1952).

appointment or retention in the school system. The Supreme Court, with Justices Black and Douglas dissenting on the merits and Justice Frankfurter dissenting on a procedural ground, upheld both the standards for eligibility and the procedures established by the Feinberg Law.

With respect to the standards, Justice Minton, writing for the Court, stated that ineligibility based upon advocacy had not been questioned, citing *Gitlow,* and that ineligibility for membership was governed by *Garner.* Stressing the point that a person was entitled to work for the school system only upon "reasonable terms laid down by the proper authorities in New York," Justice Minton said:

> If, under the procedure set up in the New York law, a person is found to be unfit and is disqualified from employment in the public school system because of membership in a listed organization, he is not thereby denied the right of free speech and assembly. His freedom of choice between membership in the organization and employment in the school system might be limited, but not his freedom of speech or assembly, except in the remote sense that limitation is inherent in every choice. Certainly such limitation is not one the state may not make in the exercise of its police power to protect the schools from pollution and thereby to defend its own existence.[31]

On the question of making membership in a listed organization prima facie evidence of disqualification Justice Minton noted that the New York courts had construed the statutes to require that only an employee who had knowledge of the organization's purpose could be disqualified. Under such circumstances, he said, membership in the organization "is a legislative finding that the member by his membership supports the thing the organization stands for, namely, the overthrow of government by unlawful means," and "[d]isqualification follows therefore as a reasonable presumption from such membership and support." [32]

The dissent of Justices Black and Douglas was placed upon broad First Amendment grounds. Justice Black declared that, under the First Amendment, "public officials cannot be constitutionally vested with powers to select the ideas people can think about, censor the public views they can express, or choose the persons or groups people can associate with." Justice Douglas asserted that the Feinberg law vio-

31. 342 U.S. at 493.   32. 342 U.S. at 494–495.

lated the principle of guilt by association because a teacher could be disqualified for membership in an organization found to be "subversive" in a "proceeding to which the teacher is not a party." He went on to give a vivid description of the impact of the loyalty program upon freedom of expression.[33]

The limitation on loyalty tests noted by the Court in *Garner* and *Adler* resulted in the invalidation of an Oklahoma loyalty oath in *Wieman v. Updegraff,* decided later in 1952. The oath, required of all State employees including faculty and staff of the State universities, provided that an employee must swear he had not in the past five years been a member of the Communist Party, of any organization on the Attorney General's List, or of any other organization advocating violent overthrow. The Oklahoma Supreme Court had interpreted the oath as disqualifying persons "solely on the basis of organizational membership, regardless of their knowledge concerning the organizations to which they belonged." The United States Supreme Court held that the oath, as thus construed, violated due process of law. Justice Clark, writing for the Court, also described the effect of loyalty tests on the system of freedom of expression:

> There can be no dispute about the consequences visited upon a person excluded from public employment on disloyalty grounds. In the view of the community, the stain is a deep one; indeed, it has become a badge of infamy. Especially is this so in time of cold war and hot emotions when "each man begins to eye his neighbor as a possible enemy" [quoting Judge Learned Hand]. Yet under the Oklahoma Act, the fact of association alone determines disloyalty and disqualification; it matters not whether association existed innocently or knowingly. To thus inhibit individual freedom of movement is to stifle the flow of democratic expression and controversy at one of its chief sources. We hold that the distinction observed between the case at bar and *Garner, Adler* and *Gerende* is decisive. Indiscriminate classification of innocent with knowing activity must fall as an assertion of arbitrary power. The oath offends due process.[34]

The *Wieman* decision, for the time being, represented the only restriction imposed by the Supreme Court upon State loyalty tests. A few years later the Court greatly expanded the impact of loyalty tests by a

33. 342 U.S. at 497, 508, 510.

34. *Wieman v. Updegraff,* 344 U.S. 183, 190–191 (1952). Justices Black and Frankfurter concurred in separate opinions, both of which Justice Douglas joined. Justice Burton concurred in the result. Justice Jackson did not participate.

series of decisions concerned with the right of government employees to refuse to answer questions about their political opinions and associations. The power to inquire into such matters, potentially extending beyond the kinds of expression that would have resulted in disqualification, posed a significant threat to freedom of expression in itself. Many persons refused to answer questions on grounds of principle, quite apart from their capacity to qualify under the substantive requirements of the loyalty oath or program. The result was that numerous dismissals under State loyalty tests, especially among university faculties, were based upon the refusal to answer questions rather than upon any proven failure to meet existing standards of eligibility.[35]

The Supreme Court had, of course, held in *Garner* that a State employee could be required to file an affidavit giving information about his membership in the Communist Party. Some doubt had been introduced, however, by the Court's decision in *Slochhower v. Board of Higher Education of New York City* that a summary dismissal of a faculty member of a city college for invoking the Fifth Amendment privilege against self-incrimination before a Congressional committee constituted a denial of due process within the prohibition of *Wieman*. The issues came up for full consideration in two cases reaching the Court in 1958.[36]

In *Beilan v. Board of Public Education* a public school teacher in Philadelphia refused to answer questions concerning Communist associations before the Superintendent of Schools and later before the House Committee on Un-American Activities, in the latter instance relying upon the privilege against self-incrimination. He was discharged on grounds of "incompetency," a term construed by the State court to cover his "deliberate and insubordinate refusal to answer the questions of his administrative supervisor in a vitally important matter pertaining to his fitness." In *Lerner v. Casey* a subway conductor on the New York City transit system refused to tell the city Commissioner of Investigation whether he was a member of the Communist Party, also relying upon the Fifth Amendment. He was discharged under the New York Security Risk Law as being a person "of doubtful trust and reliability." In five to four decisions the Supreme Court affirmed the validity of both dismissals. The majority took the position that the em-

35. See Ralph S. Brown, *op. cit. supra* note 1, pp. 122–131.

36 *Slochower v. Board of Higher Education of New York City*, 350 U.S. 551 (1956).

ployees had not been discharged for invoking the Fifth Amendment; nor had any adverse inference been drawn from the fact that they had pleaded the Fifth Amendment. The dismissals were based upon "incompetence" and "unreliability," and nothing in the Constitution prevented the government from taking such action.[37]

Justices Black and Douglas, in an opinion by the latter, dissented on First Amendment grounds:

> The fitness of a subway conductor for his job depends on his health, his promptness, his record for reliability, not on his politics or his philosophy of life. The fitness of a teacher for her job turns on her devotion to that priesthood, her education, and her performance in the library, in the laboratory, and the classroom, not on her political beliefs. Anyone who plots against the government and moves in treasonable opposition to it can be punished. Government rightly can concern itself with the actions of people. But it's time we called a halt to government's penalizing people for their beliefs. To repeat, individuals and private groups can make any judgments they want. But the realm of belief—as opposed to action—is one which the First Amendment places beyond the long arm of government.[38]

By virtue of the Supreme Court's decisions up to this point, State loyalty tests had been established upon a reasonably firm and rather comprehensive basis. The Court had not approved standards of loyalty that went beyond disqualification for advising, advocating or teaching the overthrow of the government by force, violence or illegal means, or knowingly being a member of or affiliated with an organization which so advised, advocated or taught. Yet this was a sufficient foundation upon which to build a program that could range widely into most areas left of center. Moreover, the Court had approved a vital part of the administrative machinery necessary to maintain such a program—compilation of a list of "subversive organizations," membership in which was prima facie evidence of disqualification. It had given considerable extra scope to the program by allowing interrogation into

37. *Beilan v. Board of Public Education*, 357 U.S. 399 (1958); *Lerner v. Casey*, 357 U.S. 468 (1958).

38. 357 U.S. at 415–416. Justice Brennan dissented on the ground that the real basis for dismissal in each case was not incompetence or unreliability but disloyalty, and that there was no evidence to support a finding of disloyalty in either case. Chief Justice Warren agreed with Justice Brennan in the *Lerner* case, and dissented in the *Beilan* case on the ground that the dismissal was essentially because of the invocation of the Fifth Amendment and hence invalid under *Slochhower*.

The *Beilan* and *Lerner* cases were reaffirmed in *Nelson v. County of Los Angeles*, 362 U.S. 1 (1960), as to a temporary employee. But the Court divided four to four in the same case on similar issues involving a permanent employee, Chief Justice Warren not voting.

political opinion and association that carried beyond the permissible range of disqualification and, indeed, did not even have to be founded upon a formal loyalty oath or program.

Beginning with its decision in *Shelton v. Tucker* in 1960, however, the Supreme Court began to chip away at State loyalty tests until they had been reduced in number, scope and significance. The *Shelton* case introduced a new factor, for it dealt with a program to purge or harass, not political "subversives," but advocates and supporters of civil rights. At issue in the case was an Arkansas law which required every teacher, as a condition of employment in a public school or State college, to file yearly an affidavit listing every organization to which he had belonged or regularly contributed during the preceding five years. The provision was aimed primarily at uncovering and exposing members of the N.A.A.C.P. The Supreme Court, in a five to four decision, struck down the statute as overbroad. Justice Stewart, writing for the majority, pointed out, first, that "there can be no question" of the right of the State to inquire "into the fitness and competence of its teachers"; and second, that "[i]t is not disputed that to compel a teacher to disclose his every associational tie is to impair that teacher's right of free association, a right closely allied to freedom of speech and a right which, like free speech, lies at the foundation of a free society." He then resolved the conflict by holding that, since the statute required "every one of its teachers to disclose every single organization," many of such relationships "could have no possible bearing upon the teacher's occupational competence or fitness." Thus the "unlimited and indiscriminate sweep of the statute . . . goes far beyond what might be justified in the exercise of the State's legitimate inquiry into the fitness and competency of its teachers." [39]

Justice Frankfurter, with whom Justices Clark, Harlan and Whittaker concurred, dissented on the ground that he was "unable to say, on the face of this statute, that Arkansas could not reasonably find that the information which the statute requires—and which may not be otherwise acquired than by asking the question which it asks—is germane to that selection." In another opinion, with which all the dissenters agreed, Justice Harlan objected also that it was "impossible to determine *a priori* the place where the line should be drawn between what would be permissible inquiry and overbroad inquiry in a situation like this"; and that he could not understand how the school au-

---

39. *Shelton v. Tucker*, 364 U.S. 479, 485–486, 487–488, 490 (1960).

thorities could "be expected to fix in advance the terms of their inquiry so that it will yield only relevant information." [40]

The majority decision in *Shelton* was technically a narrow one. Moreover, by implication at least, it treated the First Amendment right (or the right of association) as purely a due process right, to be protected only against arbitrary or unreasonable restrictions. Nevertheless, the decision was of considerable significance. It introduced the requirement that a State oath or program would have to be carefully tailored to cover only those areas that appeared to the Court clearly relevant. Furthermore, in brushing aside the very plausible objections of the dissenters, it foreshadowed an attitude of increasing hostility toward State loyalty tests. Both of these tendencies were pushed further in the next two cases.

Cramp v. Board of Public Instruction brought up the validity of a Florida statute requiring all State employees to take an oath that included the language: "I have not and will not lend my aid, support, advice, counsel or influence to the Communist Party." The Supreme Court unanimously held the requirement void for vagueness. Justice Stewart, after speculating freely and imaginatively on possible meanings of "aid," "support," "advice," "counsel" and "influence," pointed out the effect of such ambiguities in the context of oath-taking:

> With such vagaries in mind, it is not unrealistic to suggest that the compulsion of this oath provision might weigh most heavily upon those whose conscientious scruples were the most sensitive. While it is perhaps fanciful to suppose that a perjury prosecution would ever be instituted for past conduct of the kind suggested, it requires no strain of the imagination to envision the possibility of prosecution for other types of equally guiltless knowing behavior. It would be blinking reality not to acknowledge that there are some among us always ready to affix a Communist label upon those whose ideas they violently oppose. And experience teaches that prosecutors too are human.[41]

The rule against vagueness was extended further in *Baggett v. Bullitt*. With two members of the Court dissenting this time, a majority invalidated two Washington statutes on vagueness grounds. One required all teachers to swear that they "will by precept and example promote respect for the flag and the institutions of the United States of

---

40. 364 U.S. at 496, 498–499.
41. *Cramp v. Board of Public Instruction*, 368 U.S. 278, 286–287 (1961). Justices Black and Douglas stated that they joined in the opinion but also adhered to their views expressed in *Garner, Adler* and *Wieman*.

America and the State of Washington, reverence for law and order and undivided allegiance to the government of the United States." The second oath, applicable to all State employees, required swearing that one was not a "subversive person." That term was defined to mean "any person who commits, attempts to commit, or aids in the commission, or advocates, abets, advises or teaches by any means any person to commit, attempt to commit, or aid in the commission of any act intended to overthrow, destroy or alter, or to assist in the overthrow, destruction or alteration of, the constitutional form of the government . . . by revolution, force, or violence"; or who "with knowledge" of the nature of the organization "becomes or remains a member of a subversive organization or a foreign subversive organization." The Act defined "subversive organization" and "foreign subversive organization" in similar terms and declared the Communist Party a subversive organization. Justice White, writing for the majority, stressed the ambiguity of "aiding" the Communist Party; "advising" or "teaching" a member of the Communist Party; abetting or advising "another in aiding a third person to commit an act which will assist yet a fourth person in the overthrow or alteration of constitutional government"; and "revolution." He concluded:

> It will not do to say that a prosecutor's sense of fairness and the Constitution would prevent a successful perjury prosecution for some of the activities seemingly embraced within the sweeping statutory definitions. The hazard of being prosecuted for knowing but guiltless behavior nevertheless remains. . . . Well-intentioned prosecutors and judicial safeguards do not neutralize the vice of a vague law. Nor should we encourage the casual taking of oaths by upholding the discharge or exclusion from public employment of those with a conscientious and scrupulous regard for such undertakings.[42]

The next loyalty case to reach the Supreme Court—*Elfbrandt v. Russell*—involved an oath that had been carefully drafted, after *Cramp* and *Baggett,* to avoid the vice of vagueness. Nevertheless, the Court continued on its course of invalidation, this time concentrating on some of the associational problems. The actual oath, taken by all State employees in Arizona, was simply a traditional oath of office by which the employee swore to uphold the constitution and faithfully discharge his duties. In 1965, however, the Arizona legislature passed

42. *Baggett v. Bullitt,* 377 U.S. 360, 369, 373–374 (1964). Justices Clark and Harlan dissented.

a law providing that any employee who took the oath would, under certain conditions, be guilty of perjury. Among the conditions were that the employee, at the time of taking the oath or at any time during his term of office or employment, (1) knowingly and willfully "advocates the overthrow by force or violence of the government"; or (2) "knowingly and wilfully becomes or remains a member of the communist party of the United States or its successors or any of its subordinate organizations or any other organization having for its purposes the overthrow by force or violence of the government" with "knowledge of said unlawful purpose of said organization." The vote to strike down the oath, as thus enlarged, was five to four.[43]

Justice Douglas, writing for the majority, confined his attention to the membership provisions of the oath. He found these provisions invalid because they included membership "which was not accompanied by a specific intent to further the unlawful aims of the organization." In reaching this conclusion Justice Douglas relied first upon cases that had imposed a similar requirement when membership in an organization was subject to criminal punishment. These were the *Scales* and *Noto* cases, upholding the membership provision of the Smith Act as thus interpreted, and the *Aptheker* case, invalidating the passport provision of the Internal Security Act for lack of such a requirement. Secondly, Justice Douglas relied upon *Cramp* and *Baggett*, pointing out the uncertainty for an employee in the absence of an intent requirement. Thirdly, he invoked *Speiser v. Randall*, saying that the Arizona statute went even further than putting the burden of proof on the employee that he was not engaging in criminal advocacy. Justice Douglas summed up his position in the following language:

> Those who join an organization but do not share its unlawful purposes and who do not participate in its unlawful activities surely pose no threat, either as citizens or as public employees. Laws such as this which are not restricted in scope to those who join with the "specific intent" to further illegal action impose, in effect, a conclusive presumption that the member shares the unlawful aims of the organization.[44]

Justice White, on behalf of the minority, pointed out that the majority opinion "does not mention or purport to overrule" the line of

43. *Elfbrandt v. Russell*, 384 U.S. 11 (1966).

44. *Scales v. United States*, 367 U.S. 203 (1961), and *Noto v. United States*, 367 U.S. 290 (1961), discussed in Chapter V; *Aptheker v. Secretary of State*, 378 U.S. 500 (1964), discussed in Chapter VI; *Speiser v. Randall*, 357 U.S. 513 (1958), discussed in Chapter VI. The quotation of Justice Douglas is from 384 U.S. at 17.

cases from *Gerende* through *Beilan* and *Lerner*. He objected to the treatment of the Arizona law as a statute imposing criminal penalties on membership. In his view it was an ordinary perjury statute, punishing false swearing, and the validity of the loyalty provisions embodied in it should be governed by principles established in prior loyalty cases. Under these "unequivocal prior holdings of this Court," he declared, "a State is entitled to condition public employment upon its employees abstaining from knowing membership in the Communist Party and other organizations advocating the violent overthrow of the government which employs them; the State is constitutionally authorized to inquire into such affiliations and it may discharge those who refuse to affirm or deny them." [45]

The *Elfbrandt* decision, while ambiguous in some respects, was far-reaching in its impact. It made clear that in the future no loyalty test would be sustained that imposed disqualification for membership in an organization, unless that membership was (1) active, (2) with knowledge of illegal objectives of the organization, and (3) with "specific intent" to further those purposes. To this extent the *Gerende, Garner* and *Adler* cases were modified. The ambiguity consisted in hints that (1) the membership would also have to include personal participation in the organization's unlawful activities; (2) disqualification from government employment could only be based upon conduct that could be criminally punished; and (3) disclaimer loyalty oaths as a whole were invalid because they place an unconstitutional burden on the oath-taker to exculpate himself.

The New York loyalty program returned to the Court, after fifteen years, in *Keyishian v. Board of Regents of the University of the State of New York*. On the second round there were some new provisions and some new issues. In another five to four decision the Court, speaking through Justice Brennan, held the major features of the New York program invalid:[46]

Four provisions of the New York laws were found void for vagueness, an issue not raised in *Adler*. These were provisions which required removal:

(a) for "the utterance of any treasonable or seditious word or words." This was summarily outlawed as "dangerously uncertain."

(b) for utterance of "the doctrine that organized government

45. 384 U.S. at 19. Justices Clark, Harlan and Stewart concurred in Justice White's opinion.

46. *Keyishian v. Board of Regents of the University of the State of New York*, 385 U.S. 589 (1967).

should be overthrown by force or violence, or by assassination . . . or by any unlawful means." This fell because the "teacher cannot know the extent, if any, to which [the] utterance must transcend mere statement about abstract doctrine, the extent to which it must be intended to and tend to indoctrinate or incite to action in furtherance of the defined doctrine."

(c) if the teacher "by word of mouth or writing willfully and deliberately advocates, advises or teaches the doctrine" of forceful overthrow of government. This was ambiguous as to whether it included abstract doctrine or incitement to action, "mere advising" or advising another to support, teaching about the doctrine or advocating it.

(d) for distribution of written material "containing or advocating, advising or teaching the doctrine" of forceful overthrow and engaging in conduct that "advocates, advises, teaches, or embraces the duty, necessity or propriety of adopting the doctrine." This, also, included "mere advocacy of abstract doctrine," might bar distribution of histories of revolutions, and could "reasonably be construed to cover mere expression of belief." [47]

The New York program retained the provision, sustained in *Adler*, that an employee would be disqualified if he "organizes or helps to organize or becomes a member of" any organization that teaches or advocates forcible overthrow of government. After *Adler*, the Board of Regents, pursuant to the Feinberg Law also sustained in *Adler*, had listed the Communist Party as a "subversive" organization falling within the above provision. Thereafter the legislature had amended the law to provide specifically that "membership in the Communist Party . . . shall constitute prima facie evidence of disqualification." On this issue the Court expressly overruled *Adler*, saying it was based upon the false premise "that public employment, including academic employment, may be conditioned upon the surrender of constitutional rights which could not be abridged by direct government action." The Court then went on to find the above provision invalid under the *Elfbrandt* doctrine: "legislation which sanctions membership unaccompanied by specific intent to further the goals of the organization or which is not active membership violates constitutional limitations." [48]

Justice Clark, with whom Justices Harlan, Stewart and White concurred, objected that not only *Adler*, but *Garner, Beilan* and *Lerner* had in effect been overruled. The effect of the *Keyishian* decision on

47. 385 U.S. at 597, 598, 599, 600   48. 385 U.S. at 608.
and 601.

Beilan and *Lerner,* involving the right to ask questions, was not clear. But it was clear that, at a minimum, loyalty tests would have to be couched in exceedingly precise language in order to survive Court scrutiny. Furthermore, in the language of Justice Brennan rejecting the *Adler* doctrine, in his reasons for holding the force and violence provisions too vague, and in his confirmation of the *Elfbrandt* rule on intent, there were strong suggestions that standards for disqualification from employment would have to meet the standards for application of criminal sanctions.

The decision in *Whitehill v. Elkins,* nullifying the Maryland Ober Law oath, virtually completed the circle. Whitehill, who had been offered a teaching position at the University of Maryland, was asked to take an oath that "I am not engaged in one way or another in the attempt to overthrow the Government . . . by force or violence." This language was the same as that upheld, with respect to candidates for office, in the *Gerende* case, except that it omitted the membership provision, which had been removed after *Elfbrandt*. The Court, without overruling the *Gerende* case, said that the oath had to be read in connection with the remainder of the Ober Law, which prohibited employment of a "subversive person" as defined. This included persons who would "alter" the form of government "by revolution, force, or violence" and those who were members of an organization that would do so. Even if these provisions were not considered, the Court said, the phrase "in one way or another" might include a member of an organization "out to overthrow the Government by force and violence" though the individual "was ignorant of the real aims of the group and wholly innocent of any illicit purpose." Hence the oath was overbroad and invalid within the doctrines of *Baggett, Elfbrandt* and *Keyishian*.[49]

Justices Harlan, Stewart and White dissented, saying that the oath should be taken as written, without reference to other parts of the statute, and in that form would be admittedly valid. There would seem to be some substance to the dissenters' complaint: "The only thing that does shine through the opinion of the majority is that its members do not like loyalty oaths." [50]

49. *Whitehill v. Elkins,* 389 U.S. 54, 59 (1967).

50. 389 U.S. at 63. In *James v. Gilmore,* 389 U.S. 572 (1968), the Supreme Court affirmed per curiam a decision of a three-judge court holding invalid, primarily on the basis of *Elfbrandt*, a Texas loyalty oath. In addition State loyalty tests have been invalidated by lower Federal courts, State courts, or State officials in California, Colorado, Kansas, Nebraska, New Hampshire, New Jersey and Oregon: *Vogel v. County of Los Angeles,* 68 Cal. 2d 18, 64 Cal. Rptr. 409, 434 P.2d 961 (1967); *Gallagher v. Smiley,* 270 F. Supp. 86 (D. Colo. 1967); *Ehrenreich v. Lon-*

D. Appraisal of the Supreme Court's Position

It is now possible to draw together the threads in the Supreme Court's decisions on loyalty tests, both Federal and State, and attempt an appraisal of how far the Court has come and what point has been reached. It is particularly interesting to compare the position of the Supreme Court with the position outlined in the first part of this chapter based on the full protection theory of the First Amendment applied in the context of the social interest in internal security.

I. LOYALTY OATHS

The Supreme Court, while not officially saying so, has made it virtually impossible for either the Federal or a State government to impose a meaningful loyalty oath upon its employees. This outcome results from the cumulative impact of the Court's decisions upon various features of disclaimer oaths.

In the first place, the standards of loyalty or qualifications the Supreme Court would permit the oath to impose have been greatly narrowed. The Court has never approved a standard other than one tied to "force and violence." Nor is it likely to do so. So far as the standard of "force and violence" is concerned, the Court has limited its use to advocacy of the type that would be prohibited by the Smith Act (*Keyishian*). This would presumably include not only the *Yates* requirement that it be "advocacy of action," but the *Dennis* requirement that it create some sort of probable danger. The incorporation of these elements in a loyalty oath would present an awkward problem, since they can really be ascertained only on a case-by-case, rather than a blanket, basis.

Secondly, the Supreme Court has interposed various limitations upon the use of membership or other associational relationships in loyalty oaths. The Court never returned to an exploration of the bill of

---

derholm, 273 F. Supp. 178 (D. Kan. 1967); *The New York Times*, April 19, 1967 (Lancaster County Court, Neb.); Opinion of the Justices, 108 N.H. 62, 228 A.2d 165 (1967); *The New York Times*, October 10, 1967 (opinion of N.J. Attorney General); *Brush v. State Board of Higher Education*, 245 Ore. 373, 422 P.2d 268 (1966). See also the *Soltar*, *Haskett* and *Stewart* decisions, cited in footnote 24, *supra*.

attainder problem after *Garner,* but the decision in *United States v. Brown* would seem to preclude reference in the oath to organizations designated by name rather than by description. More important, the associational relation must be (1) a knowing rather than an innocent one (*Wieman*); (2) active rather than passive (*Robel, Elfbrandt, Keyishian*); and (3) with the specific intent to achieve the unlawful objectives of the organization (*Elfbrandt, Keyishian*). These requirements are rather difficult to include in the oath form of loyalty test. In addition, there is some indication that the Court would insist upon actual personal participation in illegitimate activities (*Elfbrandt, Robel, Schneider*). This, of course, would eliminate the membership factor altogether.[51]

Thirdly, the Court has consistently applied the most exacting standards of precision. Recognizing from the beginning that the "self-executing" features of the loyalty oath created acute problems for the oath-taker (Frankfurter in *Garner*), the Court has invoked the rule against vagueness with a determination and imagination unequaled in any other area (*Cramp, Baggett, Whitehill*). Coupling the need for precision with the requirements concerning standards and associational relationships, the problem of drafting a constitutional oath becomes almost insuperable.

Finally, the Court has shown signs of feeling that the "self-executing" factor, which in effect imposes on the oath-taker the burden of exculpating himself, is sufficient in itself to invalidate the oath technique (*Speiser, Elfbrandt, Keyishian*). The Court has never taken this position outright, but the inclination seems to lurk beneath the surface.

What all this comes down to is that the disclaimer oath is beset with constitutional requirements almost impossible to meet. Here the Court is very close to the position suggested in the analysis based upon the full protection theory, namely, that disqualification for employment must be imposed on a case-by-case basis and not through the medium of a blanket loyalty oath.

51. *United States v. Brown,* 381 U.S. 437 (1965).

2. LOYALTY PROGRAMS

The impact of the Court's decisions on loyalty programs is less clear. The Court has strongly expressed the view, however, that loyalty programs must distinguish between sensitive and non-sensitive employment (*Cole, Robel*). It is probably close to the position that loyalty programs are valid only when applied selectively to particular sensitive jobs.

As to non-sensitive employment, the requirements respecting the standards of individual conduct and associational relationships, noted above in connection with loyalty oaths, would apply to loyalty programs. So would the rule against vagueness, though perhaps on a less exacting basis. (Objections based on the "self-executing" character of the oath would not, of course, be applicable.) The practical effect of this would be that probably no blanket loyalty program could be put into operation.

In the non-sensitive area, moreover, it is not unlikely that the Court would follow through on the suggestion made in several cases that the loyalty program could not impose more stringent qualifications upon expression than the government could impose through criminal sanctions (*Elfbrandt, Keyishian, Schneider*). If this position were adopted, there would still be a gap between the Supreme Court and the full protection theory. Thus advocacy prohibitable under the Smith Act decisions, and membership of the type involved in *Scales*, would be grounds for disqualification in non-sensitive positions. Yet not many problems of this nature would arise. Taken as a whole, therefore, the result would not be far different from that reached under the full protection theory.

As to sensitive positions, Chief Justice Warren in *Robel* and Justice Fortas in *Schneider* probably spoke for a majority of the Court in stating that a screening program based on narrow and precise standards would be constitutionally permissible (see also *Aptheker*). The Court has never, however, stated what test the standards utilized in such a selective program would have to meet. Presumably the Court would require more than relevance (despite *Shelton*). Presumably also, the test would not be balancing (*Robel*). But the question remains open. Under the full protection theory, the issue would be governed by excluding other systems, such as the military, and within the system of free expression looking to the definition of "abridge." A majority of the Supreme Court is probably not very far from this position.

Two other problems require brief mention: Even if, under the Supreme Court view, loyalty programs were restricted to an individual screening program for sensitive positions, there would still be a demand for a list of "subversive organizations" comparable to the Attorney General's List. The Court's reaction to this problem is not clear. *Keyishian* did not squarely overrule *Adler* on this point. Under the full protection rule the need for such a list would be obviated; only personal conduct, rather than any attribution from association, would be relevant. The Supreme Court has hinted at such a rule (*Elfbrandt, Robel, Schneider*). The possibility of eliminating the list of "subversive organizations," a serious threat to any system of freedom of expression, provides another strong reason for moving to this position.

The interrogation problem, raised by *Beilan* and *Lerner,* was considered again in *Schneider*. But *Schneider* was perhaps an extreme case and the Court did not take the occasion to refine its position. The question thus stands unresolved. Of course, issues concerning the extent of allowable interrogation become less important as the loyalty oath is eliminated and the loyalty program narrowed. But they remain as long as any form of loyalty program persists. The issues presented are raised most acutely in connection with legislative investigations and are considered at length in the next chapter.

3. CONCLUSION

The Supreme Court has moved a long way from *Bailey, Garner* and *Adler*. It has done so in substantial part by the use of supplementary doctrines, such as the rule against vagueness, or by statutory interpretation. It has also, in the later decisions, come to rest more directly upon First Amendment grounds. Yet its basic theory of the First Amendment remains obscure. The gap between the Supreme Court's view and the full protection theory does not, however, appear to be very wide. With a small adjustment the Court could reach this position.

E. "Positive" Oaths

The "positive" oath, in which the individual is asked to make an affirmative promise or commitment in undertaking governmental duties or accepting government benefits, raises some different questions from the disclaimer or "negative" oath. The most common form of positive oath is the traditional oath of office, in which a government officer or employee swears to support the Constitution and laws and faithfully discharge his duties. As pointed out in Chapter II, the officer or employee here simply promises to carry out in the future the functions which he is obligated by law to perform. There is no test of his qualifications, no disclaimer of beliefs, opinions or associations, and no commitment beyond his official duty. In any event these oaths have not posed any serious threat, at least up to the present, to our system of freedom of expression.[52]

In another form, however, the positive oath may require an affirmation of belief. The National Defense Education Act oath, demanding that an applicant for fellowship aid swear that he bears "true faith and allegiance to the United States," is of this character. For the reasons stated in Chapter II these oaths are an infringement upon freedom of belief and invalid under the doctrine of the *Barnette* case.[53]

There remain for consideration certain other types of positive oaths. The most common is similar to the customary oath of office, but is required from the recipient of a governmental privilege or benefit, or persons engaged in a particular occupation. Thus the National Defense Education Act oath also requires that the applicant swear that he "will support and defend the Constitution and laws of the United States against all its enemies, foreign and domestic." A New York statute requires that teachers in private tax-exempt educational institutions swear "that I will support the constitution of the United States of America and the constitution of the State of New York, and that I will faithfully discharge, according to the best of my ability, the duties of the position of [title and name of school], to which I am now assigned." In *Knight v. Board of Regents* a group of faculty members at

---

52. As noted in Chapter II, the Constitution itself requires an oath of office from all Federal and State officials. State oaths of office were upheld in *Bond v. Floyd,* 385 U.S. 116 (1966).

53. The N.D.E.A. oath is set forth in 20 U.S.C. §581(f). *West Virginia State Board of Education v. Barnette,* 319 U.S. 624 (1943).

Adelphi University, a private institution, challenged the validity of the New York oath. A three-judge District Court upheld the requirement, saying that the "statutory language of support of the constitutional governments can be substantially equated to that allegiance which, by the common law, every citizen was understood to owe his sovereign." The Supreme Court affirmed without opinion.[54]

Despite the Supreme Court's casual disposition of the *Knight* case, the issue raised by such positive oaths is a serious and difficult one. In the case of an attorney, who is an "officer of the court" and therefore close to being an official of the government, the requirement of an oath of this nature on admission to the bar may be justified. But the faculty member of a private university, and the student in need of funds to pursue his studies, are in a different situation. The underlying rationale for the oath of office does not apply to them; they are not entering upon a government position in which they are committing themselves to discharge their official duties in accordance with the laws of the land and the needs of a governmental organization. The reason for imposing a positive oath in their case is the same as that which motivates the disclaimer oath. It is an attempt, through the oath device, to assure "loyalty," or conformity, to orthodox beliefs, opinions, and associations. This is normally evident, indeed, from the circumstances in which the oath requirement is adopted. In such a situation the positive oath is the equivalent of the negative oath and subject to the same First Amendment objections. The fact that positive oaths are rarely enforced does not save them. For either the cautious or the conscientious, the impact is the same.

The requirement that teachers in a public school or public university take a positive oath falls into a borderline constitutional area. The laws of some thirty States now impose such oaths. In *Hosack v. Smiley*, teachers and employees at the University of Colorado sought relief against a University requirement that they take an oath to support the Constitution and laws of the United States and of Colorado. As in *Knight*, a three-judge District Court found no violation of the First

54. *Knight v. Board of Regents*, 269 F. Supp. 339, 341 (S.D.N.Y. 1967), aff'd 390 U.S. 36 (1968). In *Pedlosky v. Massachusetts Institute of Technology*, the Massachusetts Supreme Court held invalid a Massachusetts statute which required every teacher in private educational institutions to take an oath that he would support the United States and Massachusetts Constitutions and "faithfully discharge the duties" of his position "according to the best of his ability." The Massachusetts Court held the latter requirement "altogether too vague a standard to enforce judicially." 224 N.E.2d 414, 416 (1967). See also *Baggett v. Bullitt*, 377 U.S. 360 (1964), discussed *supra*.

Amendment: "Recognition of and respect for law in no way prevents the right to dissent and question repugnant laws." Again, the Supreme Court summarily affirmed.[55]

Yet the problem is by no means so clear-cut. Strictly speaking, teachers in public educational institutions are government employees and the usual oath of office might therefore be acceptable. But public teachers are not ordinary government employees. The function of educational institutions, particularly in higher education, is not only to transmit knowledge but to advance knowledge and criticize society. To perform that function, as the principles of academic freedom emphasize, educational institutions should be to some extent separate from and independent of the ordinary political forces in the government bureaucracy. Public teachers therefore have a strong claim to remain free of the inhibitions inherent in any kind of oath-giving and oath-taking.[56]

55. *Hosack v. Smiley,* 276 F. Supp. 876 (D. Colo. 1967), aff'd 390 U.S. 744 (1968). See also *Ohlson v. Phillips,* 304 F. Supp. 1152 (D. Colo. 1969).

56. See the discussion of academic freedom in Chapter XVI.

VIII

Internal Security: Legislative Investigating Committees

Legislative investigating committees have always played an important role in American political life. The scope and intensity of their operations have steadily increased as the function of the legislature has shifted from formulating policy and initiating legislation to approving proposals of the executive branch, overseeing the government bureaucracy, and generally registering public opinion. It was not until the late nineteen-thirties, however, that legislative committees began to pose serious problems for our system of freedom of expression. The New Deal had given considerable impetus to the growth of the legislative investigating committee, using it to expose the operation of the securities markets, the public utility holding companies, labor spies and professional strikebreakers, lobbyists, and other features of our economic and social institutions that seemed to need reform. As the New Deal ebbed, the techniques it had fostered were turned against it, but at a new and different level. Beginning with the creation of the Dies Committee in 1938, legislative investigating committees started to probe into political opinions and associations, first in government and then throughout the country. For many years this form of investigation commenced with Communist Party membership and activities, and spread from there in a widening circle into other shades of unpopular opinion. More recent committees have been concerned with "subversive influences" in the civil-rights movement, the "black revolution," and the New Left.[1]

The extension of legislative investigations to the field of political expression has been accompanied by a significant advance in the technique and scope of operations of the committees. Legislative investigating committees generally have greatly improved their methods of investigation, their presentation of material, and their ability to command public attention. Equally important, they have taken on the characteristics of a permanent bureaucracy. With more funds available, larger staffs, organized on a continuing basis, they have become established institutions with a life and direction of their own. As a result, their impact upon freedom of expression has been substantially strengthened.

It is not to be supposed, however, that the operations of most legislative investigating committees create any threat to our system of freedom of expression. A major part of legislative fact finding is concerned with the collection of general information genuinely designed to throw light on pending legislation. The material sought and obtained consists of statistical data, reports of scientific studies, analysis of comparative legislation, the opinions of experts, and the views of interested parties. Witnesses are voluntary, appearing upon invitation or by their own request, and no element of compulsion is present. Another large segment of legislative investigation involves inquiry into some phase of the operations or policies of the executive branch. Here the probe may concern more specific facts or relate to specific individuals, but it is directed toward action, or to opinions freely given and defended. The problems for a system of freedom of expression arise in a relatively narrow area in which the legislative committee is seeking information about the political opinions, attitudes or associations of particular individuals. Since the information sought relates to unorthodox or unpopular positions these proceedings become adversary or adjudicative in nature, rather than broadly legislative. The subject matter is expres-

1. For a collection of materials on legislative investigating committees see Thomas I. Emerson, David Haber and Norman Dorsen, *Political and Civil Rights in the United States* (Boston, Little, Brown & Co., 3d ed. 1967), pp. 426–511, bibliography at pp. 428–431 (hereafter cited in this chapter as *Political and Civil Rights in the United States*). Later material includes Walter Goodman, *The Committee* (New York, Farrar, Straus and Giroux, 1968); Allen B. Moreland, "Congressional Investigations and Private Persons," *Southern California Law Review*, Vol. 40 (1967), p. 189.

sion, not action, and the social interest in the name of which the right of expression is invaded is usually the interest in internal security.

Nearly all the major controversies that have raged over interference with freedom of expression by Federal legislative investigations have arisen out of the operations of three committees. These have been the House Committee on Un-American Activities, now the House Committee on Internal Security; the Subcommittee on Internal Security of the Senate Judiciary Committee, which has functioned under the chairmanship of Senators McCarran, Jenner and Eastland; and the Subcommittee on Investigations of the Senate Committee on Government Operations, as it operated during the Eisenhower administration under Senator Joseph McCarthy. At the State and local level, also, virtually all the problems have emanated from particular committees of similar design and attitude. Many other types of legislative investigating committee can, and occasionally do, raise issues that touch on freedom of expression. Most committee hearings of the adversary or adjudicatory type also present serious issues of other individual rights. Yet, the conflict between legislative investigations and freedom of expression has concerned only a very small fraction of the legislative fact-finding process.

Within this area, of course, the conflict has been acute. This is evident from mere perusal of the mandates of the two Federal committees recently most active. The investigatory powers of the House Un-American Activities Committee, until altered in 1969, encompassed:

(1) The extent, character, and objects of un-American propaganda activities in the United States, (2) the diffusion within the United States of subversive and un-American propaganda that is instigated from foreign countries or of a domestic origin and attacks the principle of the form of government as guaranteed by our Constitution, and (3) all other questions in relation thereto that would aid Congress in any necessary remedial legislation.[2]

When its name was changed to Committee on Internal Security in 1969 and its authority redefined, the Committee retained much of its power to probe into areas of expression. The new mandate authorizes it to investigate:

(1) the extent, character, objectives, and activities within the United States of organizations or groups, whether of foreign or domestic origin,

2. Rule XI, Clause 19, of the Standing Rules of the House of Representatives (1946 to 1969). See 60 Stat. 823, 828.

their members, agents, and affiliates, which seek to establish, or assist in the establishment of, a totalitarian dictatorship within the United States, or to overthrow or alter, or assist in the overthrow or alteration of, the form of government of the United States or of any State thereof, by force, violence, treachery, espionage, sabotage, insurrection, or any unlawful means, (2) the extent, character, objectives, and activities within the United States of organizations or groups, their members, agents, and affiliates, which incite or employ acts of force, violence, terrorism, or any unlawful means, to obstruct or oppose the lawful authority of the Government of the United States in the execution of any law or policy affecting the internal security of the United States, and (3) all other questions, including the administration and execution of any law of the United States, or any portion of law, relating to the foregoing that would aid the Congress or any committee of the House in any necessary remedial legislation.[3]

The Subcommittee on Internal Security of the Senate Judiciary Committee operates under a Senate resolution, passed in 1950, which authorizes investigation into:

(1) the administration, operation, and enforcement of the Internal Security Act of 1950; (2) the administration, operation, and enforcement of other laws relating to espionage, sabotage, and the protection of the internal security of the United States; and (3) the extent, nature and effects of subversive activities in the United States. . . .[4]

The effect that legislative investigations of this character have upon freedom of expression is well-known and requires no elaboration. The mere fact of forcing a person to appear before an official tribunal of the government and there defend his political opinions and associations against hostile inquisitors, amidst glaring publicity, and under the threat of perjury if he momentarily slips, is a terrifying experience for the ordinary citizen. Even the most politically sophisticated find it an ordeal. The resulting exposure, in which the witness is cast in the role of a disloyal or even traitorous citizen, multiplies the effect and extends it over an indefinite period of time. The witness may lose his job, even his career; he may suffer other forms of economic reprisal, such as inability to obtain insurance or a mortgage; he is subject to great social pressures, which operate also against his entire fam-

---

3. Rule XI, Clause 11, of the Standing Rules of the House, as amended by H. Res. 89, 91st Cong., 1st Sess. (1969), 115 *Cong. Rec.* H. 958–980 (daily ed. Feb. 18, 1969).

4. Sen. Res. 366, 81st Cong., 2d Sess. (1950), 96 *Cong. Rec.* 16872.

ily. The personal strain of such an experience may be unbearable, and the lesson is not lost on others.

Moreover, the legislative investigating committee that undertakes to root out "Un-American" or "subversive" activities tends to develop an elaborate machinery of surveillance that keeps perpetual watch for signs of unorthodox expression. Thus the Committee on Un-American Activities maintained files on millions of American citizens, the contents of which were available to groups or individuals sharing the Committee's viewpoint. It had a permanent staff of investigators, who by their mere appearance on the scene could smother a new organization or stifle some outcropping of unorthodox opinion. It supported a system of informers, some of whom it kept on its payroll. It conducted hearings in a manner that tended to stimulate hysteria. It issued reports, with or without prior hearing, that condemned certain conduct as disloyal. It functioned, in short, as a sort of modern Inquisition, attempting to stamp out heresy in the nation. The Committee has continued to operate in much the same manner under its new name.[5]

The description just given does not apply to every legislative committee that inquires into matters of expression, or to every investigation conducted by the major committees that specialize in this area. But it does indicate the degree of pressure some committees have put upon the system of freedom of expression, and it also indicates the kind of pressure any such committee continually exerts. It is quite possible, indeed, that in the period since World War II legislative investigating committees have had more impact upon freedom of expression in this country than any other force.

The question for consideration here is to what extent the law and legal institutions can protect the system of freedom of expression against interference by legislative investigating committees. Several general observations should be made at the outset. In the first place the efforts of the courts to limit the functioning of legislative investigating committees have been largely confined to those aspects of committee operations that involve the use of compulsory process to obtain testimony or other evidence. When a legislative committee undertakes to compel a person to appear before it and answer questions, or produce documentary evidence, or attempts to obtain the records of an associ-

---

5. Materials discussing the operations of the major committees concerned with investigation into areas of expression are collected in *Political and Civil Rights in the United States*, pp. 429–430,

103. See also the debates in the House of Representatives on the Committee on Un-American Activities, *e.g.* 112 *Cong. Rec.* 27444–27448 (1966); 114 *Cong. Rec.* 6270–6275 (1968).

ation, procedures for review of such committee action are available in the courts, at least at some stage. But other features of the committee's operation, such as its power to send investigators in search of information, to conduct hearings if the evidence is produced voluntarily, or to issue reports, have been considered largely beyond the capacity of courts to review. Most of the discussion, therefore, will relate to judicial supervision over the use of compulsory procedures to obtain information.

In the second place, even within this narrow area of judicial supervision, the formulation of theory by which to control the scope of legislative committee investigation is beset with difficulties. By its very nature an investigation has no precise limits that can be readily defined in advance of the outcome. It may be necessary to exceed the tentatively prescribed boundaries in order to ascertain them, or to understand the full scope of the problem, or to check out provisional answers. The court is thus confronted with a complex doctrinal problem at the outset of its deliberations.

Thirdly, the institutional techniques available for accommodating opposing interests in this area are not well designed to carry out that task effectively. The judiciary is particularly reluctant to interfere with the legislative branch at this stage in its operations. The interposition of judicial review in the middle of an on-going investigation raises some difficult problems. Methods of adequately protecting the witness, without at the same time seriously interrupting the investigation, have been slow to evolve.

A. The Limits of the Legislative Investigating Power

1. THE POWER TO COMPEL THE PRODUCTION OF EVIDENCE

A major portion of the legislative investigating power rests upon the authority of the legislature or its committees to compel the production of evidence, either oral or documentary. That authority can be exercised in two ways. A refusal to appear and answer questions or to produce documents can be punished directly by the legislature itself, or by either house, as a contempt of the legislature. Under this procedure the offender is adjudged guilty or not guilty by vote of the legislative body and, if guilty, is taken into custody and held in confinement by officials of the legislature. He cannot be held, however, beyond the end of the legislative session. This procedure, it can be seen, is cumbersome and time-consuming for the legislature, as well as limited by the length of the legislative term. The more usual method of enforcing the legislative power to compel production of evidence is through passage of a statute making it an offense punishable through regular court procedures for any person to refuse to comply with the legislative mandate. Thus the existing Federal statute on the subject, Section 192 of Title 2 of the U.S. Code, makes it a misdemeanor, punishable by a fine of not more than $1000 or less than $100 and imprisonment for not less than one month or more than twelve months, for any person who, "having been summoned as a witness by authority of either House of Congress to give testimony or to produce papers upon any matter under inquiry before either House . . . willfully makes default, or who, having appeared, refuses to answer any question pertinent to the question under inquiry." Under either procedure, it is now well established, the courts may review the contempt issue, through habeas corpus proceedings in cases of direct citation for contempt and through the usual methods if the statute has been invoked. Thus the courts have ultimate jurisdiction to decide whether the legislative power to compel evidence has been validly exerted.[6]

The validity of the exercise of legislative authority depends in the first instance, in theory at least, upon whether that authority may be found within the affirmative powers of the legislature to require the production of evidence. The established doctrine is that, while the legislature may not compel the production of evidence merely for its own sake, it does have constitutional power to do so in aid of any of its functions. These functions include not only the primary one of enacting laws, but also such ancillary powers as judging the election of its members, expelling or disciplining members, impeaching government officials, approving appointments (in the case of the Senate), and such implied functions as protecting its own integrity by punishing those who would attempt to bribe its members. The potential range of these functions is so broad that any attempt to limit the scope of legislative investigation by a narrowing construction of the basic affirmative

6. For an account of the development of the legislative contempt power and the right of judicial review see *Watkins v. United States,* 354 U.S. 178, 188–198 (1957). See also Carl Beck, *Contempt of Congress* (New Orleans, Hauser Press, 1959); Ronald L. Goldfarb, *The Contempt Power* (New York, Columbia University Press, 1963), ch. IV.

power poses serious difficulties. Even the Federal Congress, operating under the doctrine of enumerated powers, may investigate in aid of the spending power, the appropriating power, the power to assure the States a republican form of government, perhaps even the amending power. The State legislatures are not confined by anything except the possibility of conflict with Federal power. To forge a connection between the obtaining of information on virtually any subject and possible legislation is therefore not a difficult task. The suspicion that the connection is a spurious one, designed only as a cover for probing into other areas, can be translated into a legal prohibition only if the courts are willing to delve into the recesses of legislative motives, a task they normally shrink from undertaking.[7]

A second limitation upon legislative investigating powers derives not from seeking the outermost limits of the affirmative power but from looking to specific constitutional limitations, such as those embodied in the Bill of Rights, which cut across and limit the affirmative power at the point where the two conflicting principles intersect. The main task in limiting the legislative investigating power in the interests of freedom of expression is to formulate rules for applying the constitutional limitations found in the First Amendment. A cluster of other constitutional doctrines can be employed for the same purpose; so can various nonconstitutional techniques of statutory construction or procedural niceties. These devices should be noted, though they cannot here be fully explored.

The First Amendment was initially called into service as a limitation on Congressional investigating power in two cases considered by the Court of Appeals but not by the Supreme Court. In the first of these, *United States v. Josephson,* the defendant had been called before the House Committee on Un-American Activities and had refused to be sworn or to testify. Upon being prosecuted for violation of Section 192 he invoked the First Amendment, asserting that, since Congress was "prohibited from legislating on matters of thought, speech or opinion," it had no authority to investigate such matters. The majority of the Court of Appeals for the Second Circuit rejected the position out of hand, saying that Congress could use the information in deciding whether to pass legislation and no infringement of the First Amendment could be involved unless Congress did pass legislation that violated it. The majority, in fact, completely missed the point

7. A discussion of this problem may be found in Martin M. Shapiro, *Law and* *Politics in the Supreme Court* (New York, Free Press of Glencoe, 1964), ch. 2.

of why the First Amendment was applicable at all to a legislative investigation, as distinct from the subsequently enacted legislation. It declared: "[T]here is no restraint resulting from the gathering of information by Congress in aid of its power and duty to legislate which does not flow wholly from the fact that the speaker is unwilling to advocate openly what he would like to urge under cover." [8]

Judge Charles E. Clark, dissenting, explained the basis for application of the First Amendment to the investigating process and attempted to formulate a theory by which to apply it. His view was that "the scope of the investigation [cannot] be broadened beyond the point of any possible valid legislation." Since a statute prohibiting the conduct which the Committee was authorized to investigate would have been clearly invalid, the investigation was invalid. Judge Clark apparently recognized that a rule limiting the area of investigation to the area of valid legislation still left certain problems unanswered. For instance, since the measure of the validity of legislation impinging upon expression was then the clear and present danger test, would the Committee be authorized to investigate opinions and associations to determine whether they presented a clear and present danger? To this Judge Clark's reply seems to have been that the Committee could not go excessively beyond the area of permissible legislation: "[T]he *excess* is the important question here." [9]

The second case involved the refusal of Dr. Edward K. Barsky and other members of the executive committee of the Joint Anti-Fascist Refugee Committee, an organization collecting and disbursing funds for relief of refugees from Spain and elsewhere, to produce records of the organization before the Committee on Un-American Activities. The records were withheld because of fear that their disclosure would injure political refugees in foreign countries. But the First Amendment issue turned on the contention that the members of the executive committee, if called before the Committee, would be compelled to answer questions as to whether they "were believers in Communism or members of the Communist Party." The majority of the Court of Appeals for the District of Columbia ruled that such questions could be asked. Their view was that the power of legislative investigation was not limited to "activities which might be regulated"; that the legislature could inquire into threats to the existing form of government without regard to whether a clear and present danger existed; and that, while "public

8. *United States v. Josephson,* 165 F.2d 82, 92 (2d Cir. 1947).

9. 165 F.2d at 98. Italics in original.

revelation at the present time of Communist belief and activity . . . would result in embarrassment and damage," that factor did not "outweigh the public necessities in this matter." The Court thus rejected the clear and present danger test and applied a balancing test.[10]

Judge Edgerton, dissenting, gave a detailed analysis of how the Committee's operations in fact restricted freedom of speech. The thrust of his opinion from that point on is less clear. His ultimate position seems to be: "Congressional action that is either intended or likely to restrict expression of opinion that Congress may not prohibit violates the First Amendment. Congressional action in the nature of investigation is no exception." But his answer to the contention that Congress "may punish propaganda that advocates overthrow of the government by force or violence" and that it "may therefore investigate to determine whether such legislation is necessary," seems to be partly that the investigation was not necessary because the problem was already being taken care of by the Smith Act, and partly that the Committee investigation had in fact carried much beyond this. Thus the dissents in both *Barsky* and *Josephson* seem ultimately to come down to the proposition that the Un-American Activities Committee was authorized to and did probe too broadly into protected areas, but they did not make entirely clear how far the Committee should be permitted to go.[11]

The Supreme Court denied petitions for certiorari in both the *Josephson* and *Barsky* cases, Justices Douglas, Murphy and Rutledge dissenting in *Josephson*. It continued to do so in subsequent cases until it reached the issue, obliquely, in *United States v. Rumely,* decided in 1953. The *Rumely* case involved the House Select Committee on Lobbying Activities, which operated under a resolution authorizing investigation into "all lobbying activities intended to influence, encourage, promote, or retard legislation." Rumely, executive secretary of the Committee for Constitutional Government, refused to give the Lobbying Committee the names of persons who had made bulk purchases of books, such as John Flynn's *The Road Ahead,* which were then distributed by the Committee for Constitutional Government. The Supreme Court unanimously reversed Rumely's conviction for contempt, a majority by construing the resolution as not intended to cover such material. The Court observed that to interpret the resolution otherwise would raise "grave constitutional questions":

10. *Barsky v. United States,* 167 F.2d 241, 244, 245, 249 (D.C. Cir. 1948).   11. 167 F.2d at 259, 256.

Surely it cannot be denied that giving the scope to the resolution for which the Government contends, that is, deriving from it the power to inquire into all efforts of private individuals to influence public opinion through books and periodicals, however remote the radiations of influence which they may exert upon the ultimate legislative process, raises doubts of constitutionality in view of the prohibition of the First Amendment.[12]

The Supreme Court thus made clear that the First Amendment would, at some point, interpose a limit to the scope of Congressional inquiry. It did not make clear, however, exactly where that point lay. In *Quinn v. United States,* a case upholding the right of a witness to invoke the privilege against self-incrimination before a legislative committee, the Court in dictum came closer to stating a theory of limitation. Citing *Rumely* the Court observed: "Nor does [the power to investigate] extend to an area in which Congress is forbidden to legislate." But the Court was still far from taking a decisive position, much less expounding a coherent doctrine, as to what the limiting role of the First Amendment might be.[13]

When the Supreme Court decided the *Watkins* and *Sweezy* cases in 1957 it seemed for a moment that it was ready to fill the gap. But the opinions in both cases veered off at the last minute, leaving the First Amendment position still obscure. In *Watkins,* the Committee on Un-American Activities was investigating Communist activity in labor unions. Watkins testified freely about himself, saying he had cooperated with the Communist Party though he had not been a member. He refused, however, to answer questions concerning certain other persons who he felt might once have been Communist Party members but no longer were. The Supreme Court, with only Justice Clark dissenting, reversed a conviction under Section 192. Chief Justice Warren, writing also for Justices Black, Douglas, Harlan and Brennan, traced the source of the legislative contempt power, the history of Congressional investigations, and the course of judicial decisions. He noted the application of the privilege against self-incrimination, and finally reached the First Amendment. Chief Justice Warren's opinion reaffirmed the position that the First Amendment constituted a limitation on the legislative investigating power: "Clearly, an investigation is

12. The denials of certiorari in *Josephson* and *Barksy* are reported in 333 U.S. 838 (1948), and 334 U.S. 843 (1948). For reference to the other cases see *Political and Civil Rights in the United States,* pp. 432–433. The *Rumely* case is reported in 345 U.S. 41, 46 (1953).

13. *Quinn v. United States,* 349 U.S. 155, 161 (1955).

subject to the command that the Congress shall make no law abridging freedom of speech or press or assembly." He went on to give a cogent summary of how the operations of a legislative committee affected First Amendment rights:

> The mere summoning of a witness and compelling him to testify, against his will, about his beliefs, expressions or associations is a measure of governmental interference. And when those forced revelations concern matters that are unorthodox, unpopular, or even hateful to the general public, the reaction in the life of a witness may be disastrous. This effect is even more harsh when it is past beliefs, expressions or associations that are disclosed and judged by current standards rather than those contemporary with the matters exposed. Nor does the witness alone suffer the consequences. Those who are identified by witnesses and thereby placed in the same glare of publicity are equally subject to public stigma, scorn and obloquy. Beyond that, there is the more subtle and immeasurable effect upon those who tend to adhere to the most orthodox and uncontroversial views and associations in order to avoid a similar fate at some future time. That this impact is partly the result of non-governmental activity by private persons cannot relieve the investigators of their responsibility for initiating the reaction.[14]

Chief Justice Warren moved on to consider "[a]ccommodation of the congressional need for particular information with the individual and personal interest," which he noted was "an arduous and delicate task for any court." His formulation of the legal doctrine was couched in terms of balancing:

> The critical element is the existence of, and the weight to be ascribed to, the interest of the Congress in demanding disclosures from an unwilling witness. We cannot simply assume, however, that every congressional investigation is justified by a public need that overbalances any private rights affected. To do so would be to abdicate the responsibility placed by the Constitution upon the judiciary to insure that the Congress does not unjustifiably encroach upon an individual's right to privacy nor abridge his liberty of speech, press, religion or assembly.[15]

Having come this far, the Court concluded that the "arduous and delicate task" need not be performed in the case before them, and disposed of the matter on the due process ground that Watkins had not

---

14. *Watkins v. United States,* 354 U.S. 178, 197–198 (1957). Justice Frankfurter wrote a concurring opinion; Justices Burton and Whittaker did not participate.

15. 354 U.S. at 198–199.

been adequately informed of the pertinency of the questions to the subject under inquiry.

The Court followed much the same process in the *Sweezy* case, decided the same day as *Watkins*. Sweezy had refused to answer questions before the Attorney General of New Hampshire, who had been delegated the legislative power to investigate whether there were "subversive persons" in the State. Sweezy had testified that he was not a member of the Communist Party or a part of any program to overthrow the government by force and violence. But he would not respond to inquiries concerning the Progressive Party (the Henry Wallace party) or the contents of a lecture on socialism which he had delivered at the University of New Hampshire. Chief Justice Warren again wrote the opinion, this time joined by Justices Black, Douglas and Brennan. He pointed out that "there unquestionably was an invasion of petitioner's liberties in the areas of academic freedom and political expression." He noted that the New Hampshire Supreme Court had recognized this but had "concluded that the need for the legislature to be informed on so elemental a subject as the self-preservation of government outweighed the deprivation of constitutional rights that occurred in the process." Chief Justice Warren then went on to say: "We do not now conceive of any circumstances wherein a state interest would justify infringement of rights in these fields." But it was not necessary "to reach such fundamental questions of state power to decide this case," he concluded. The delegation to the Attorney General was so vague that the interest of New Hampshire in eliciting the information required could not be ascertained, and hence punishment of Sweezy for refusing to give it would deprive him of due process.[16]

Justice Frankfurter concurred in an opinion which Justice Harlan joined. They would have decided the case squarely on First Amendment grounds, applying the balance of interests test. With respect to questions addressed to the lecture at the University of New Hampshire, Justice Frankfurter concluded: "When weighed against the grave harm resulting from governmental intrusion into the intellectual life of a university, such justification for compelling a witness to discuss the contents of his lecture appears grossly inadequate." As to the questions concerning the Progressive Party, Justice Frankfurter said: "For a citizen to be made to forego even a part of so basic a liberty as his political autonomy, the subordinating interest of the State must be

16. *Sweezy v. New Hampshire*, 354 U.S. 234, 250, 251 (1957).

compelling." He could find no such State interest "in the remote, shadowy threat to the security of New Hampshire allegedly presented in the origins and contributing elements of the Progressive Party and in petitioner's relations to these." [17]

The *Watkins* and *Sweezy* decisions were interesting on several grounds. From the viewpoint of doctrine, it would appear that Chief Justice Warren had abandoned his "area" theory of affirmative power announced in the *Quinn* case. He had now switched to a theory based upon the First Amendment as negatively restricting the investigating power and, as the measure of the First Amendment limitation, he applied the balancing test. Justices Black and Douglas, rather surprisingly, did not overtly object to this. Justice Frankfurter had also altered his position. Instead of a balancing test heavily weighted in favor of the legislative judgment, he now called for one in which "the subordinating interest of the State must be compelling," thus reversing his presumption of constitutionality. The Court, in other words, seemed to be having a difficult time working out a satisfactory theory for application of the First Amendment to legislative investigations.

In their immediate impact, the *Watkins* and *Sweezy* cases seemed to convey a clear warning to legislative committees that their operations would have to be severely curtailed, at least with respect to inquiry into opinion or association. Several cases pending in the Supreme Court that raised similar issues were remanded to lower courts for consideration in light of *Watkins* and *Sweezy*. Thereafter the lower courts moved perceptibly in the direction of upholding the claims of the witness against the demands of the Committee.[18]

The *Watkins* and *Sweezy* cases were decided in the same term of Court as the *Yates* case and *Pennsylvania v. Nelson*. The response in Congress was the introduction of legislation to curb the powers of the Court. One bill, introduced by Senator Jenner, proposed to withdraw the jurisdiction of the Supreme Court in cases involving contempt of Congress, as well as in cases relating to loyalty programs and State anti-sedition laws. These bills were the center of a major struggle in and out of Congress for over a year. In the end restrictions on the Supreme Court were defeated, but by a narrow margin. The Jenner bill itself was tabled in the Senate only by a vote of 49 to 41.[19]

---

17. 354 U.S. at 261, 265. Justices Clark and Burton dissented.

18. See the cases collected in *Political*

and Civil Rights in the United States, pp. 447–448.

19. The *Yates* and *Nelson* cases are

The indication in *Watkins* and *Sweezy* that the Supreme Court was prepared to develop effective First Amendment safeguards against legislative committees did not materialize. The turning point was *Barenblatt v. United States,* decided in 1959.[20]

Barenblatt was, shortly before he was called by the Committee on Un-American Activities, an instructor in psychology at Vassar College. He declined to answer whether he was or had been a member of the Communist Party, or whether he had been a member of the Haldane Club of the Communist Party while attending the University of Michigan. He also refused to say whether he had known one Francis Crowley "as a member of the Communist Party" and whether he (Barenblatt) had been a member of the University of Michigan Council of the Arts, Sciences and Professions. Barenblatt was convicted under Section 192 and the conviction was sustained by the Supreme Court on a five to four vote. Justice Harlan, speaking for the majority, dealt only with the validity of the conviction for refusing to answer the first set of questions, finding it unnecessary to pass on the second set. He commenced by accepting the balancing test: "Where First Amendment rights are asserted to bar governmental interrogation resolution of the issue always involves a balancing by the courts of the competing private and public interests at stake in the particular circumstances shown." He then launched into a long discussion of "whether this investigation was related to a valid legislative purpose." Justice Harlan's reason for treating this issue of the affirmative power to conduct the inquiry as part of the First Amendment question is not clear; analytically they would seem to be different issues. In any event, he found that the questions asked did serve a valid legislative purpose, and he refused to inquire whether the real purpose of the Committee was simply to expose. At this point he should have come back to the balancing test and weighed the competing interests. Instead, he summarily stated that the questions asked did serve a valid legislative purpose, and he sometimes lead to the conclusion that the individual interests at stake were not subordinate to those of the state," pointing out that there was no attempt to pillory the witness or to summon witnesses on an "indis-

discussed in Chapter V. For reference to the legislation see *Political and Civil Rights in the United States,* pp. 217–218.

20. *Barenblatt v. United States,* 360 U.S. 109 (1959). There were three cases decided in the interval before *Barenblatt,* in all of which a conviction for contempt was reversed on nonconstitutional grounds. See *Political and Civil Rights in the United States,* pp. 447–448.

criminate dragnet" basis. He concluded that "the balance between the individual and the governmental interests here at stake must be struck in favor of the latter." [21]

In the course of his discussion on whether the questions asked were authorized under the affirmative power of the legislature, Justice Harlan touched upon the issue of separating the conduct which might be open to investigation from that which might not. He recognized that "the Communist Party may also sponsor peaceable political reforms," that is, engage in conduct beyond the power of Congress to prohibit. But he saw no reason why this fact should limit the Committee's power: "An investigation of advocacy of or preparation for overthrow certainly embraces the right to identify a witness as a member of the Communist Party . . . and to inquire into the various manifestations of the Party's tenets." He added: "The strict requirements of a prosecution under the Smith Act [citing *Dennis* and *Yates*] are not the measure of the permissible scope of a congressional investigation into 'overthrow', for of necessity the investigatory process must proceed step by step." He thus had no trouble disposing of the separation problem as a question of the extent of the affirmative powers of investigation. He did not consider the matter in connection with the First Amendment issue. Indeed, under the balancing test the problem could scarcely arise.[22]

Justice Black, in an opinion with which Chief Justice Warren and Justice Douglas agreed, dissented on the ground that the Committee's resolution was so sweeping that it violated the procedural requirements of due process, that compelling an answer to the questions violated the First Amendment, and that the Committee's program was essentially one of punishment by exposure. On the First Amendment issue Justice Black took the flat position that the Committee's activities abridged freedom of speech "through exposure, obloquy, and public scorn," and therefore violated the First Amendment. He reiterated his opposition to the balancing test as the measure of First Amendment rights where the governmental action was "directly aimed at curtailing speech and political persuasion." Such was the case here, he said, because the Committee's authorizing resolution "on its face and as here applied . . . attempts inquiry into beliefs, not action—ideas and associations, not conduct." Assuming the balancing test were to be applied, Justice Black declared that the majority "after stating the test ignores it completely." Furthermore the balancing done by the Court

21. 360 U.S. at 126, 127, 134.   22. 360 U.S. at 128, 130.

"mistakes the factors to be weighed"; particularly it "leaves out the real interest in Barenblatt's silence, the interest of the people as a whole in being able to join organizations, advocate causes and make political 'mistakes' without later being subjected to governmental penalties for having dared to think for themselves." Finally, Justice Black objected to the majority's blanketing together "those aims of communism which are illegal" with those that "are perfectly normal political and social goals." The result is to outlaw the Party because of its "political aims or ideas," and when that is done "no group is safe." [23]

Justice Brennan also dissented, agreeing with Justice Black that the record showed no purpose for the investigation except exposure: "An investigation in which the processes of law-making and law-evaluating are submerged entirely in exposure of individual behavior —in adjudication, of a sort, through the exposure process—is outside the constitutional pale of congressional inquiry." [24]

On its facts *Barenblatt* was distinguishable from *Watkins* and *Sweezy*. *Barenblatt* dealt with the stark question whether a legislative committee could ask a witness whether he was or ever had been a member of the Communist Party. In both *Watkins* and *Sweezy* the witness answered that question. The issue in *Watkins* was whether he could be forced to testify about others who had left the Party, and in *Sweezy* the questions not answered did not involve direct membership in the Communist Party at all. Nevertheless, the whole temper of the opinions in *Barenblatt* indicated that the Court had withdrawn from the position it assumed in *Watkins* and *Sweezy*. This was confirmed by the decision in *Uphaus v. Wyman*, handed down the same day as *Barenblatt*.

Dr. Willard Uphaus, Executive Director of World Fellowship, Inc., conducted a summer camp in New Hampshire. A major feature of the camp was to provide discussion programs on political, economic, and social issues, led by guest speakers and open to public attendance. Operating under the same legislative authority as in *Sweezy*—to investigate the presence of "subversive persons" in New Hampshire—the Attorney General of New Hampshire summoned Dr. Uphaus to testify and produce records of the camp. Dr. Uphaus answered questions concerning himself but refused to produce the names of the persons who had attended the camp over the past two years. His conviction for

23. 360 U.S. at 141, 142, 144, 149, 150.   24. 360 U.S. at 166.

contempt, and an order that he be confined until he produced the documents, was affirmed by the Supreme Court by the same five to four vote as in *Barenblatt*. Justice Clark, writing for the majority, distinguished the *Sweezy* case on the ground that neither a university nor a political party was involved and that, in this case, the New Hampshire courts had expressly decided that the legislature had delegated the authority to the Attorney General to obtain the information he requested. Applying the balancing test, Justice Clark noted: "The record reveals that appellant had participated in 'Communist-front' activities and that '[n]ot less than nineteen speakers invited by Uphaus to talk at World Fellowship had either been members of the Communist Party or had connections or affiliations with it or with one or more of the organizations cited as subversive or Communist controlled in the United States Attorney General's list.' " He noted further that the guests had been required by New Hampshire law, on arrival at the camp, to sign their names to a register that was open to inspection by sheriffs and police officers. He concluded: "[T]he governmental interest in self-preservation is sufficiently compelling to subordinate the interest in associational privacy of persons who, at least to the extent of the guest registration statute, made public at the inception the association they now wish to keep private." [25]

Justice Brennan, joined by Chief Justice Warren and Justices Black and Douglas, dissented. In his view the investigation had been conducted "purely for the sake of exposure," and hence there was no "showing of any requisite legislative purpose or other state interest that constitutionally can subordinate appellant's rights." Justices Black and Douglas added that they would also dissent on grounds not utilizing the balancing test. Dr. Uphaus served a year in prison.[26]

The *Barenblatt* decision was followed in the *Braden* and *Wilkinson* cases, decided in 1961. Both cases raised, in different form, the question of separating protected from unprotected conduct in legislative committee investigations. The cases arose out of hearings held by a subcommittee of the Un-American Activities Committee in Atlanta for the purpose of investigating "Communist infiltration into basic industry in the South" and "Communist Party propaganda in the South." Frank Wilkinson had gone to Atlanta as representative of the Emergency Civil Liberties Committee, an organization then engaged in an

25. *Uphaus v. Wyman*, 360 U.S. 72, 26. 360 U.S. at 82.
79, 81 (1959).

active campaign to abolish the Un-American Activities Committee, in order to mobilize opposition to the Committee. After his arrival in Atlanta he was called before the Committee. Wilkinson gave his name, but refused to answer any other questions. He was charged with contempt and convicted for refusing to answer the question: "Are you now a member of the Communist Party?"

Justice Stewart wrote for the majority of five. He rejected the contention that the Committee had called Wilkinson solely to expose him because of his activities against the Committee, pointing out that at a prior Committee hearing a witness had identified Wilkinson as a member of the Communist Party, that he was representative of a group the Committee "believed to be Communist-dominated," and that his very presence in Atlanta indicated he was connected with the "subject under inquiry—Communist Party propaganda activities in that area of the country." Wilkinson was thus "not summoned to appear as a result of an indiscriminate dragnet procedure, lacking in probable cause for belief that he possessed information which might be helpful to the subcommittee." On the First Amendment issue Justice Stewart held *Barenblatt* controlling. That case could not be distinguished, he said, on the ground that Wilkinson was engaged in protected conduct at the time he was questioned: "[W]e cannot say that, simply because the petitioner at the moment may have been engaged in lawful conduct, his Communist activities in connection therewith could not be investigated." [27]

Carl Braden, a field secretary of the Southern Conference Educational Fund, was called by the subcommittee to testify about his conduct in organizing opposition to the Atlanta hearings and to legislation pending in Congress that would overturn the Supreme Court's decision in *Pennsylvania v. Nelson*. He refused to answer any questions and was convicted for contempt. The Supreme Court's decision turned upon the validity of the question: "Were you a member of the Communist Party the instant you affixed your signature to that letter?" The letter referred to was one which Braden and his wife had composed and circulated, urging others to write their Congressmen in opposition to the pending legislation. Justice Stewart, speaking for the same majority as in *Wilkinson*, again held that the case was ruled by *Barenblatt*. He rejected a contention that *Barenblatt* was distinguish-

27. *Wilkinson v. United States,* 365 U.S. 399, 411–412, 414 (1961).

able because here the Committee did not have a proper legislative purpose in that it was inquiring into protected activity, that is, a petition for redress of grievances:

> But *Barenblatt* did not confine congressional committee investigation to overt criminal activity, nor did that case determine that Congress can only investigate the Communist Party itself. Rather the decision upheld an investigation of Communist activity in education. Education, too, is legitimate and protected activity. Communist infiltration and propaganda in a given area of the country, which were the subjects of the subcommittee investigation here, are surely as much within its pervasive authority as Communist activity in educational institutions. The subcommittee had reason to believe that the petitioner was a member of the Communist Party, and that he had been actively engaged in propaganda efforts. . . . Information as to the extent to which the Communist Party was utilizing legitimate organizations and causes in its propaganda efforts in [the South] was surely not constitutionally beyond the reach of the subcommittee's inquiry.[28]

Justice Black, with whom Chief Justice Warren and Justice Douglas concurred, dissented in both cases, urging that *Barenblatt* be overruled and stating again his objections to the balancing test. He warned:

> The very foundation of a true democracy and the foundation upon which this Nation was built is the fact that government is responsive to the views of its citizens, and no nation can continue to exist on such a foundation unless its citizens are wholly free to speak out fearlessly for or against their officials and their laws. When it begins to send its dissenters, such as Barenblatt, Uphaus, Wilkinson, and now Braden, to jail, the liberties indispensable to its existence must be fast disappearing. . . . Only by a dedicated preservation of the freedoms of the First Amendment can we hope to preserve our Nation and its traditional way of life.[29]

Justice Brennan dissented in both cases on the ground that the Committee had not laid an adequate foundation for the questions and that its dominant purpose was exposure. Justice Douglas also dissented in *Wilkinson* on the ground that the authorizing resolution could not be interpreted to empower the Committee to investigate criticism of itself. The other dissenters joined one or both of these opinions.[30]

---

28. *Braden v. United States*, 365 U.S. 431, 435 (1961).

29. 365 U.S. at 444.

30. During the same term the Supreme Court decided three other contempt cases, upholding a conviction in

The Supreme Court did not deal with First Amendment issues in legislative investigations again until *Gibson v. Florida Legislative Investigation Committee,* decided in 1963. Here a new element entered the picture. The investigation was directed against a civil-rights organization. Moreover, time had brought a change in the personnel of the Court, Justices White and Goldberg replacing Justices Whittaker and Frankfurter. Whatever the reason, the Court now undertook to work out a refinement of doctrine that would offer more protection to witnesses relying upon First Amendment guarantees.[31]

In *Gibson* the Florida legislature had in 1959 authorized the Legislative Investigation Committee to make an investigation "of all organizations whose principles or activities include a course of conduct on the part of any person or group which would constitute violence, or a violation of the laws of the state, or would be inimical to the well-being and orderly pursuit of their personal and business activities by the majority of the citizens of this state." Pursuant to this authority the Committee began an investigation of "Communist infiltration" into various organizations including the Miami branch of the N.A.A.C.P. The Committee had information that fourteen persons who had been members of or affiliated with the Communist Party also were or had been members of or active in the Miami branch. It thereupon ordered Gibson, president of the Miami branch, to appear before it and to bring records showing the names of the organization's members and contributors. Gibson appeared but refused to produce the records, or to check the names of suspected Communists against the records. He was convicted of contempt. The Supreme Court reversed five to four, Justice Goldberg writing the opinion of the Court.

Justice Goldberg adopted as the governing principle the form of the balancing test originally enunciated by Justice Frankfurter in his concurring opinion in *Sweezy.* Quoting from *Bates v. City of Little Rock,* he phrased it: "Where there is a significant encroachment upon personal liberty, the State may prevail only upon showing a subordinating interest which is compelling." As applied in this case, Justice Goldberg said, the issue was whether the record showed "a substantial connection between the Miami branch of the N.A.A.C.P. and Com-

one, and reversing in the other two. In none of these cases did the Court consider basic constitutional issues. See *Political and Civil Rights in the United States,* p. 466.

31. *Gibson v. Florida Legislative Investigation Committee,* 372 U.S. 539 (1963).

munist *activities*"; otherwise there would be no "immediate, substantial and subordinating state interest necessary to sustain its right of inquiry into the membership lists of the association." He found the case different from *Barenblatt, Wilkinson* and *Braden* because those cases involved a refusal to answer questions concerning the witness's *"own"* membership *"in the Communist Party";* because the Communist Party is "not an ordinary or legitimate political party" no further "demonstration of compelling government interest was deemed necessary." In *Uphaus,* Justice Goldberg said, "a sufficient connection between subversive activity . . . and the World Fellowship" had been shown. Justice Goldberg then proceeded to examine the evidence offered by the Committee as probable cause for thinking that fourteen Communists were members of or active in the Miami branch. Looking at this material with a very jaundiced eye, Justice Goldberg found it insufficient. There being no "adequate foundation" laid, the Committee had failed to establish the necessary "compelling and subordinating government interest essential to support" its inquiry. Justice Goldberg summed up his position in the following words:

> Nothing we say here impairs or denies the existence of the underlying legislative right to investigate or legislate with respect to subversive activities by Communists or anyone else; our decision today deals only with the manner in which such power may be exercised and we hold simply that groups which themselves are neither engaged in subversive or other illegal or improper activities nor demonstrated to have any substantial connections with such activities are to be protected in their rights of free and private association.[32]

Justices Black and Douglas wrote additional opinions. Justice Black's view was that "the constitutional right of association includes the privilege of any person to associate with Communists or anti-Communists, Socialists or anti-Socialists, or, for that matter, with people of all kinds of beliefs, popular or unpopular"; and that Florida had no "constitutional authority" to "compel answers to questions which abridge that right." Justice Douglas undertook a more elaborate analysis of his position. It began with the "area" theory of affirmative powers: "When the State or Federal government is prohibited from dealing with a subject, it has no constitutional privilege to investigate it. . . . That is to say, investigations by a legislative committee which 'could result in no valid legislation on the subject' are beyond the

32. 372 U.S. at 546, 551, 547, 550, 557–558. Italics in original.

pale." Justice Douglas then went on to assert: (1) "the associational rights protected by the First Amendment . . . cover the entire spectrum in political ideology as well as in art, in journalism, in teaching and in religion"; (2) the government is therefore precluded from probing into these associational rights; (3) "an investigating committee [cannot] ascertain whether known Communists or criminals are members of an organization not shown to be engaged in conduct properly subject to regulation," any more than it could "probe to ascertain what effect they have had on the other members." [33]

Justice Harlan, joined by Justices Clark, Stewart and White, dissented. He could see no reason for "any difference in the degree of governmental investigatory interest as between Communist infiltration *of* organizations and Communist activity *by* organizations." Unless the government were required "to prove in advance the very things it is trying to find out," he could not understand "how it can be said that the information preliminarily developed by the Committee's investigator was not sufficient." Justice White added: "The net effect of the Court's decision is, of course, to insulate from effective legislative inquiry and preventive legislation the time-proven skills of the Communist Party in subverting and eventually controlling legitimate organizations." [34]

Two decisions following *Gibson* complete the First Amendment picture. In 1966 the New Hampshire investigation of Hugh DeGregory, which had been going on for many years, again reached the Supreme Court. In the latest episode DeGregory, interrogated by the New Hampshire Attorney General in 1960, had answered questions concerning Communist activities since 1957 but had refused to testify about earlier periods. Committed to jail until he purged himself of contempt, DeGregory obtained a reversal in the Supreme Court. Justice Douglas, writing for the Court, held that "the staleness of both the basis for the investigation and its subject matter" removed any compelling state interest that "would warrant intrusion into the realm of political and associational privacy protected by the First Amendment." Justices Harlan, Stewart and White dissented. Also in 1966 the *Gojack* case, which had been pending since 1955, reached a final decision, resulting in a reversal of the conviction on non-constitutional grounds. Gojack's counsel had asked the Court to overrule *Barenblatt*. The Court did not find it necessary to reconsider *Barenblatt*, but it hinted

33. 372 U.S. at 559, 561–562, 565–566.

34. 372 U.S. at 579, 580, 585. Italics in original.

that the question was open, saying: "Since we decide the present case on other grounds, it is not necessary nor would it be appropriate to reach the constitutional question." [35]

The position taken by the courts on First Amendment issues in legislative investigation cases must be evaluated in the broader context of the total impact of judicial review upon legislative committee operations. Other constitutional restrictions upon legislative committee powers have been recognized by the courts and, at least in case of the privilege against self-incrimination, vigorously and generously enforced. Moreover, the courts have utilized or invented numerous procedural or technical rules to upset particular contempt citations. The Supreme Court itself has reversed convictions on the ground that the inquiry was not authorized by the legislature; that the questions asked were not pertinent to the inquiry; that the matter under inquiry and the pertinency of the question were not made clear to the witness; that the question asked by a subcommittee was not within the scope of the inquiry authorized by the full committee; that the committee did not insist upon an answer; and that the committee did not follow its own rules. The lower courts have employed these and other devices for the same purpose.[36]

The results of all this have been somewhat surprising. From a compilation made by Carl Beck in 1959 it appears that out of 226 contempt citations voted by Congress from 1944 to 1957, the contempt was upheld judicially in only 44 cases. Of the remainder, 122 cases resulted in acquittal or dismissal, 35 were never prosecuted, and 25 were still pending. Most of the contempt citations resulting from the hearings of the Kefauver Committee investigating organized crime ended in acquittals or reversals. None of the seven prosecutions for contempt in refusing to answer questions of the McCarthy Committee was successful. The House Committee on Un-American Activities has won only one contempt case in court since the *Wilkinson* and *Braden* cases in 1961; in that case, involving the Ku Klux Klan, First Amendment issues were not squarely raised. With the exception of Dr. Uphaus, no witness who testified about his own conduct but refused to testify about other persons has gone to jail.[37]

35. *DeGregory v. Attorney General of New Hampshire,* 383 U.S. 825, 828–829 (1966); *Gojack v. United States,* 384 U.S. 702, 706 (1966).

36. For a collection of the cases see *Political and Civil Rights in the United States,* pp. 480–490, 493–500.

37. See Carl Beck, *Contempt of Congress* (New Orleans, Hauser Press, 1959), p. 243; Leonard B. Boudin, "The Im-

The technique of the courts has thus been to keep the legislative committees under constant scrutiny without confronting them with an attack upon their basic powers. Undoubtedly First Amendment considerations played an important part in this process. It can be argued that the strategy of control by technical niceties rather than by outright application of First Amendment doctrine is a sound and statesmanlike approach. Yet one cannot help but have reservations. In the long run it might be more conducive to good relations between the legislative and judicial branches, and more healthy for our society as a whole, if the courts undertook to establish, directly and openly, the principles that legislative committees must follow to bring their operations within the constitutional guarantees of the First Amendment.

As noted, there are two main approaches to the problem of limiting the power of legislative investigation in the interest of maintaining a system of freedom of expression. One is to search for the limits of the affirmative power to investigate in aid of legislative functions. The other is to utilize the restriction of the First Amendment as a countervailing principle to cut off the affirmative power, before it has exhausted its own force, at the point where it conflicts with effective operation of the system of freedom of expression. The Supreme Court, and its various members, have taken both approaches, usually without distinguishing between them. They are not necessarily inconsistent, but the second has proved more fruitful.

The first approach proceeds from the principle that the legislative power to investigate exists to the extent that it is necessary or appropriate in aid of some legislative function. The primary function, and the one which the decided cases have been concerned with, is the function of lawmaking. The result of the lawmaking process, namely legislation, is of course limited by the requirements of the First Amendment. Consequently, the argument runs, if the contemplated legislation is in an area forbidden by the First Amendment, there would be no power to legislate and hence no power to investigate. This is the "area" theory of limitation, that the legislature cannot investigate in an "area" in which it cannot validly legislate. It was invoked by Judge Clark in the first effort, made in the *Josephson* case, to work out a theory of First Amendment limitation. It was also the theory advanced by Chief Jus-

---

munity Bill," *Georgetown Law Journal*, Vol. 42 (1954), pp. 497, 504, n. 31 (collecting the Kefauver cases). The KKK case is *Shelton v. United States*, 404 F.2d 1292 (D.C. Cir. 1968), cert. denied 393 U.S. 1024 (1969).

tice Warren in the *Quinn* dictum, utilized in part by Justice Harlan in *Barenblatt* and Justice Stewart in *Braden,* and accepted by Justice Douglas concurring in *Gibson.*

The problems of attempting to apply the area theory have already become apparent. In the first place, the investigating process is such that, even if the theoretical limits of the legislation are prescribed by the First Amendment, it may still be necessary or appropriate to probe beyond the boundary in order to discover where the boundary is. To take an example from another field, Congress is limited under the commerce power to regulating matters which affect interstate commerce, but it may well be that Congress would be justified in investigating widely into matters of intrastate commerce in order to determine whether they do or do not affect interstate commerce. The difficulty is accentuated if the validity of the legislation is determined by the First Amendment and the First Amendment itself is applied by looking to see if the expression creates a clear and present danger or whether the value of the expression is overbalanced by other social interests.[38]

Secondly, at the time the investigation is in progress, what legislation might result is not known, or at least its precise form is not ascertainable. This introduces a pervading ambiguity into the issue of whether the unformulated legislation would be valid or not under the First Amendment; in fact it makes the hypothetical decision almost impossible. Thus it is hard for a court to apply the area rule seriously. In addition, the person objecting to the investigation is put in the position of proving a difficult negative—that no valid legislation of any kind is possible to conceive.

Thirdly, there is the possibility that the legislature may want to investigate in order to amend the Constitution. It may wish to consider abolishing the First Amendment, for example, or modifying its impact upon legislative investigations.

The crux of the difficulty is, in short, that the function of lawmaking tends to reach into broader areas than would be allowed in the resulting legislation. Under such circumstances the area theory does not quite meet the needs of the situation. Even if it did, the theory would be so vague and difficult of application as to give the committees, the witness, and the courts little guidance.

38. On the power of Congress to obtain information in areas of intrastate commerce see *Interstate Commerce Commission v. Goodrich Transit Co.,* 224 U.S. 194 (1912).

It is not surprising, therefore, that the area theory has in fact proved an unsatisfactory basis for limiting the legislative investigating power. Judge Clark in *Josephson* was forced into the position of admitting that the investigation could go beyond the area of valid legislation, as long as the breach was not "excessive." From the other point of view, Justice Harlan had no trouble demonstrating in *Barenblatt* that the expression or associations of Communists were matters well within the area of potentially valid legislation. Moreover, this could be done with almost any conduct not patently protected by the First Amendment.

Even if one accepts the full protection theory as the measure of the First Amendment right, and thereby eliminates the need for determining clear and present danger or for balancing interests, difficulties remain. The effort of Justice Douglas to apply the area theory in *Gibson*, for example, is not very convincing. Justice Douglas gives no explanation for jumping from the proposition that all associational rights involving expression are protected under the First Amendment to the proposition that a legislative committee cannot inquire whether "Communists or criminals" (the latter of whom at least presumably engage in action) are members of an organization. The fact is that the area theory tends to be abstract and sterile because it does not focus on the main problem. The most important question is not whether various forms of potential or inchoate legislation would be constitutional, but the effect of the investigation upon the system of freedom of expression.

Another doctrine based upon the approach of limiting the affirmative powers of investigation is the "exposure" theory. The position is that a legislative investigating committee may not "expose for the sake of exposure." This proposition is theoretically sound. The power to investigate does not include the power to expose as such, and hence a committee engaged in such a pursuit would not be exercising any valid power. Its practical drawbacks, though, are virtually fatal. Since it is always possible to conjure up some potential legislation as the source of the committee's authority, the exposure position is reduced to the contention that the committee is not "really" interested in legislation but is using that only as an excuse for exposure. The lack of power, then, depends on the motive of the legislature or the committee. The Supreme Court is, as noted, extremely reluctant to probe into legislative motives, good or bad. Moreover, proof of motive is often impossible to obtain. Finally, even if the Court were willing to appraise motives and the necessary showing could be made, the legislature or committee could readily evade the doctrine by taking a few simple precautions in conducting its hearings.

The difficulties of the exposure rule are evident from the *Wilkinson* case. The motive of exposure could scarcely have been more apparent on the face of the record than it was in that case. Yet the Court could not be persuaded. Indeed Justice Brennan is the only member of the Court who has invoked the exposure doctrine as the sole basis for finding a lack of legislative power. He has not been able to convince his colleagues, even those who agree with his conclusions. Proof that the committee was bent on exposure for exposure's sake is valuable in setting a tone, or as an element in a balancing test, but the burden of proving improper legislative motive is too heavy for a witness to carry.[39]

This brings us to the second approach, that of using the First Amendment as a countervailing principle that directly blocks off the affirmative power to investigate even though that power would not yet otherwise have been exhausted. The use of the First Amendment in this way is now fully recognized, and has been by every court since *Barsky.* The basis of its application is that the process of investigating into beliefs, opinions, and associations seriously impairs the right of free political discussion. This argument was first fully developed, though not ultimately utilized, by Chief Justice Warren in *Watkins* and *Sweezy.* It formed the basis of the Goldberg opinion in *Gibson,* and it has consistently been the ground for Justice Black's position in every case since *Watkins* and *Sweezy.* This approach has the immense advantage of being entirely functional. It focuses attention upon the real issue—the effect of the legislative action upon the system of freedom of expression.

Looking at the problem from this point of view, the court is immediately confronted with the traditional question: Recognizing that the legislative action abridges First Amendment rights, what test of the force of the First Amendment is to be applied? No court or judge has attempted to resolve this problem by use of the clear and present danger test. The reasons for this are not hard to fathom. The issue posed to the court is not whether the expression in question has in fact created a clear and present danger of some substantive evil, but whether the legislature is entitled to obtain the information in aid of its lawmaking or

---

39. See, in addition to the cases involving freedom of expression cited in the text, *Hutcheson v. United States,* 369 U.S. 599 (1962).

other function even though the process "incidentally" infringes on First Amendment rights. In this respect the issue is similar to that raised in the cases involving denial of benefits or positions upon the basis of expression. The clear and present danger test, therefore, is not relevant. Furthermore, it would be difficult or impossible to apply the clear and present danger test in advance of knowing what the expression in fact was. For these and other reasons the clear and present danger test has never been employed in this connection.

The majority position has been to apply the balancing of interests test. Strangely enough, this test has not been used in its original *Douds* form, in which heavy weight is placed upon the legislative judgment. Possibly the Court has felt that the judgment of a legislative committee is not entitled to the weight accorded the judgment of the full legislature, though the contempt citation presumably represents the judgment of at least one house of the legislature. Or possibly the Court has simply followed the lead of Justice Frankfurter, the chief exponent of the balancing test, in *Sweezy*. Or, more likely, the balancing test as a whole has undergone transformation as the Court has come to give greater weight to the First Amendment side of the balance. In any event the balancing test has taken the form of requiring the government to show a "subordinating" interest that is "compelling." In this version the test comes close to putting the burden of persuasion on the government and establishing a presumption in favor of First Amendment rights. The test as thus phrased was first used in a majority opinion by Justice Harlan in *Barenblatt*. The new form was given emphasis by Justice Goldberg in *Gibson*.

The usual objections to the balancing test apply when it is used as the formula for determining the power of legislative investigating committees to infringe First Amendment rights. It is still vague; it attempts to weigh factors that are not comparable; it puts the court in the position of opposing the legislature on the legislature's own grounds. All these objections are, indeed, intensified in the case of legislative investigating committees. The vagueness is particularly damaging to a witness who must decide on the spur of the moment, at the risk of prison if he reaches the wrong conclusion, whether the balancing test would be construed by a court to permit the question with which he is confronted. The social interest in internal security, the type of interest usually invoked in legislative committee cases, is very likely to get the nod over the more amorphous interest in free expression. The courts are dealing with an especially acute area of legislative relations, since the investigating power has come to be the most cherished instrument of many individual members of the legislature.

Actual experience with the use of the balancing test in legislative committee cases confirms these observations. Justice Harlan made no serious effort to balance interests in the *Barenblatt* case; indeed he conceived of the interest on the First Amendment side of the scales as not a social interest at all but merely the interest of one individual, to be weighed against the broad and ponderous interest of the state. Justice Clark's balancing in the *Uphaus* case is even less convincing; it mistakenly assumed that the First Amendment interest had in effect been waived. Furthermore, the balancing test has never thus far been used in a Federal committee case to hold that the interest of the government was outweighed by the First Amendment interest. That result has been reached, by Justice Goldberg in *Gibson,* by Justice Douglas in *DeGregory,* and by Justice Frankfurter in *Sweezy,* only in State committee cases. All in all the balancing test must be adjudged too weak and ineffective to afford adequate protection to the system of freedom of expression.

Before considering the full protection test mention should be made of the "probable cause" doctrine—the requirement that some prima facie case be made out before inquiry into matters of expression will be permitted. The rule has been applied in two ways. In *Barenblatt* Justice Harlan was careful to point out that the Committee had not proceeded on any "indiscriminate dragnet" basis, but had probable cause to believe that Barenblatt possessed information which would be helpful to the Committee; and Justice Stewart stressed the same point in *Wilkinson* and *Braden.* It is not clear from these dicta, however, what kind of preliminary showing the majority would demand, or indeed whether such a showing is an absolute condition to an inquiry into the area of expression. In *Gibson* Justice Goldberg used the probable cause requirement in a somewhat different manner. In that case, the presence or absence of probable cause was an aspect of the balancing test, a factor to be considered in determining the weight of the government interest in obtaining the information.

The probable cause rule is valuable as an ameliorating principle to lessen the impact of legislative investigation upon freedom of expression. It would, for instance, prevent or reduce the likelihood of mass fishing expeditions. It may also be a useful device in controlling legislative investigations into areas of mixed expression and action. But it has little value otherwise. Justice Black pointed out in the *Wilkinson* case how tenuous was the probable cause upon which the Committee acted. The only information the Committee had was a "flat conclusory statement" by a single informant, accompanied by no detail and with no opportunity for cross-examination. In Justice Black's view the protection afforded by the probable cause rule was "almost totally worthless." The rule did not protect Dr. Uphaus and it helped Gibson only because Justice Goldberg subjected it to unusual strain. In short, the probable cause rule would not in practice seriously limit the investigating power in most cases that involved committee probes of the opinions or associations of any person with politically unorthodox views. As a matter of theory it does not reach to the important issues. The presence of probable cause that the witness holds particular views or has particular associations does not, of course, warrant investigation into these matters.[40]

The full protection test would prohibit a legislative investigating committee from making any inquiry that abridges First Amendment rights, regardless of the extent to which the information sought would aid the legislature in performing a legislative function. Specifically this would mean that no questions could be asked concerning a person's beliefs, opinions, or the associations he has engaged in for purposes of expression; in short no inquiry could be made into the conduct of an individual classifiable as expression. The prohibition would apply whether the question was designed to elicit information of direct use to the committee, to obtain leads to other information to which the committee was entitled, or to check the accuracy of other information already given. It would apply to non-political as well as to political expression. But the rule would not be applicable, of course, to situations that involved no "abridgment."

The same rule would govern if the inquiry pertained to conduct of an association that took the form of expression. Thus membership lists, finances, minutes of meetings, and all the other aspects of expression emanating from an association formed for purposes of engaging in expression, would be protected. This right of association follows from the right of the individual to enlarge the impact of his expression by organizing or joining an association. As before, inquiry which did not "abridge" freedom of expression would not be foreclosed to an investigating committee.

Since all matters of expression would be banned from inquiry, and

40. *Wilkinson v. United States,* 365 U.S. at 418–419.

not just expression that did not create a clear and present danger or overbalance other interests, the full protection rule would be reasonably definite and relatively easy to apply. The only serious problems that might be encountered are those that arise in situations in which the individual or association has engaged in both expression and action, and the legislative inquiry is directed to the action but also invades the realm of expression. The basic principle here, as usual, is to separate the action and the expression as far as possible, and protect the expression. If an individual alone is involved this would normally not be difficult. But more troublesome questions are presented in the case of the association.

The associational problem might arise in two different aspects. One involves the direction of a legislative inquiry at an individual who is associated with an organization that has engaged in both expression and (legal or illegal) action. The other involves the inquiry aimed at the conduct of such an association itself. As to the first, the principle of separation would require that an inquiry into the associational conduct of an individual be limited to personal conduct classifiable as action. This would rule out, at least in the first instance, the multifaceted question of membership, which combines elements of both expression and action. It would also eliminate questions concerning the expression of other members or of the association itself. Only after the inquiry had established that the individual himself had engaged in action could associational conduct incidental to the action be open to inquiry. Such a rule would resemble the "probable cause" requirement of the *Gibson* case. It might more appropriately, however, be considered a rule of order of proof.

The same rule of order of proof would apply to the conduct of the association itself. Mixed questions on membership would not be permitted. Nor would questions concerning contributions, finances, or similar matters that related to both expression and action. There must first be a showing that the organization had engaged in action. Once action had been shown, questions incidentally involving combined associational conduct would be in order.

These rules would solve the problem raised in *Barenblatt:* whether the committee can ask a witness if he is a member of the Communist Party; and the issue presented in *Gibson:* whether it can ask the organization if its members are also members of the Communist Party. Both inquiries clearly related to expression. For the Communist Party, whatever else it may be doing, engages in various forms of legitimate expression; and the questions put are, in the phrase of Dr. Alexander Meiklejohn, "complex" ones, relating to various kinds of conduct, some of which is protected as an exercise of the right to expression. The legislative committee may properly inquire into alleged activities of the witness or the Communist Party that constitute "action," including espionage, sabotage, violence, preparations for violence, and the like. But in the absence of evidence of such action it should not, by lumping different forms of conduct together in one question, abridge freedom of expression.

There remains only the final question, whether such rules are so quixotic that we are compelled to abandon the full protection theory as the guiding principle of the First Amendment. Again the answer seems clearly in the negative. The intrusion of legislative committees upon First Amendment rights has taken place only in connection with the lawmaking function. Legislative investigation in aid of other functions, including election contests, impeachment, and government corruption, has not created these issues; indeed in such cases the problem is no different from that presented in an ordinary judicial proceeding. The essential question, therefore, is whether the legislature has need of specific facts about an individual, extracted from him or his friends by compulsory process, in order to frame general legislation. All our experience points to the conclusion that the power to conduct an adversary proceeding of this kind is not essential to the legislative process, at least when it infringes upon freedom of expression. The overwhelming proportion of Federal and State legislation is framed in committees that do not use adversary hearings or invoke compulsory process at all. Those committees that do conduct such proceedings in the field of expression are notorious for the paucity of legislation they produce; and most of what they have produced has been unconstitutional. Moreover, the full protection rule does not preclude a legislative committee investigation in the field of action. There are, in short, other methods of fact finding available to legislative bodies. The British have never utilized any instrument comparable to our legislative committees that engage in adjudicatory hearings in the field of expression. The adversary hearing does produce a dramatic effect, and may be useful for educational purposes. Or it may be helpful to an individual legislator who seeks public attention. But these reasons are scarcely sufficient to justify the devastating impact of legislative committees upon freedom of expression in the past few decades.

2. OTHER POWERS OF LEGISLATIVE INVESTIGATION

Apart from the authority to compel the production of evidence, the powers of legislative investigating committees have thus far been subject to little control by the judicial process. The committee's use of its staff to make inquiries concerning a person or group, as long as no compulsory process is employed, is not ordinarily open to challenge in the courts. Hence there is little chance through court action to prevent a committee from maintaining a general surveillance over those forms of public expression, such as the civil-rights movement or antiwar protest, which the committee may decide to concern itself about. Under unusual circumstances, suit against agents of the committee might be brought to enjoin undue or persistent harassment of a particular person or group. But no such litigation has so far been attempted.

There is also small likelihood of obtaining judicial relief from the holding of committee hearings when witnesses appear on a voluntary basis. No court has so far interfered with the committee practice of maintaining files, open or closed to the public, or furnishing information about persons with viewpoints held in disfavor by the committee. Nor have the courts undertaken to review statements issued by committees, or findings or reports published by them, however damaging to an individual or group. Only one effort to prevent committee action of this sort through the judicial process appears to have been made. In 1956 the Methodist Federation for Social Action brought suit against the Senate Internal Security Subcommittee to enjoin it from publishing a report in which it made findings, without hearings, that the Federation was a Communist front. The proceeding was dismissed, in an opinion by Judge Edgerton, on the ground that to enjoin publication of a legislative report "would invade the constitutional separation of powers." [41]

Protection of First Amendment rights in this area rests primarily with the legislative branch itself, and the primary remedy for abuse of power remains in the political process. This need not be fatal to the system of freedom of expression. The power of the courts to supervise use of the compulsory process gives them authority to deal with the

41. *Methodist Federation for Social
Action v. Eastland*, 141 F. Supp. 729, 731
(D.D.C. 1956).

most hurtful aspects of the legislative investigating operation. The legislative branch has a right to engage in political expression. Assuming a modicum of respect for First Amendment rights by legislative committees the system of free expression should be able to withstand any likely shock and remain viable.

B. The Effectiveness of Judicial Controls

Judicial controls over the legislative investigating power, even though limited in scope, are of critical importance. It is necessary, therefore, to look briefly at some of the factors that determine the effectiveness of those controls in protecting the system of freedom of expression.

In general the questions have involved the timing of judicial review and the availability of certain forms of relief. Three specific problems have emerged: To what extent, if any, can a person summoned as a witness obtain judicial review of the committee's authority prior to his actual appearance before the committee? When a witness does appear before the committee, is there any way he can obtain a judicial determination of the committee's right to oral or documentary evidence except by refusing the committee's demand and thereby incurring a criminal penalty if he proves to be wrong? What relief is available when documents have been illegally seized, by the committee or by someone else, and are about to be used in a committee proceeding? In the past, for various reasons, the courts have by and large been unable or unwilling to grant effective review in these situations. But the development of committee powers and the increasing concern of the courts for individual rights have forced a general reconsideration of the judicial role.

The right to challenge the authority of a legislative committee by injunction or declaratory judgment prior to appearing at a committee hearing is a matter of great import to the person called as a witness. It will be remembered that the impact on First Amendment rights arises in large part out of the very fact of being summoned before the committee. Moreover, the person served with a committee subpoena has no way to test the committee's authority except by refusing to appear and running the risk of a criminal prosecution. On the other hand, both separation of powers doctrine and concern over a political confrontation make the courts hesitant to prohibit in advance or even delay the operations of a committee of the legislature.

Sporadic efforts over the years to persuade lower Federal courts to examine the powers of Federal legislative committees or the validity of their subpoenas, prior to committee hearing, have been unsuccessful. The Federal courts have taken the position that judicial interference with the actual operations of the legislative branch in this manner would constitute an unwarranted violation of the principle of separation of powers. The legislative committees have furthermore given strong indications that they would not brook such judicial intrusion in their affairs. So far a confrontation has been avoided. Yet some State courts have been willing to undertake the task with respect to State legislative committees. The Federal courts have also on occasion afforded advance judicial review of the operations of State committees. The issues were pressed again in the Federal courts in a series of cases involving the House Committee on Un-American Activities, shortly before its change of name and mandate. The Supreme Court has not made a decision on the merits, however, and the question remains unresolved.[42]

The reluctance of the Federal courts to enjoin the proceedings of Federal investigating committees is understandable. Any rule of law permitting judicial intervention on an extensive scale or as a routine matter would undoubtedly violate the principle of separation of powers. Yet there would seem to be occasions when the issues were sufficiently fundamental to the operation of the committee, and the questions were sufficiently crystalized, that judicial review would be

42. A collection of the earlier Federal and State cases may be found in *Political and Civil Rights in the United States*, pp. 501–502. Later cases in which Federal courts have granted advance review of State committees are *Liveright v. Joint Committee of the General Assembly of Tennessee*, 279 F. Supp. 205 (M.D. Tenn. 1968); *Goldman v. Olson*, 286 F. Supp. 35 (W.D. Wis. 1968); cf. *Black Unity League of Kentucky v. Miller*, 394 U.S. 100 (1969). The H.U.A.C. cases include *Krebs v. Ashbrook*, 275 F. Supp. 111 (D.D.C. 1967), 407 F.2d 306 (D.C. Cir. 1968), cert. denied 393 U.S. 1026 (1969); *Stamler and Hall v. Willis*, 415 F.2d 1365 (7th Cir. 1969); *Davis v. Willis* (D.C. Cir.

pending). In the *Stamler* case the Court of Appeals for the Seventh Circuit, while dismissing the case as to members of the Committee, ordered the District Court to proceed to trial against the Attorney General and members of the Committee's staff on the constitutional issues raised by the plaintiffs in their suit for injunction and declaratory judgment. See also *Cole v. Trustees of Columbia University*, 300 F. Supp. 1026 (S.D.N.Y. 1969). For discussion of the subject see Note, "HUAC and the 'Chilling Effect': The *Dombrowski* Rationale Applied," *Rutgers Law Review*, Vol. 21 (1967), p. 679. Compare *Powell v. McCormack*, 395 U.S. 486 (1969), noted in Chapter XIX.

appropriate at the threshold of the committee proceedings. Thus a challenge to the total jurisdiction of a legislative committee, on the ground that its mandate was excessively vague or patently infringed First Amendment rights, would constitute the kind of question that should be disposed of at the outset. Similarly the power of a committee to subpoena a particular document might pose a specific and matured issue that could be appropriately decided without putting the witness to the peril of a contempt citation. It is unlikely, in view of the political forces at work, that such intervention by the courts would unduly interfere with committee operations. Cases could be given expeditious treatment, stays granted rarely, and jurisdiction asserted only if a serious claim to immediate relief were advanced. In return for a minor impact upon the legislative investigating function an important protection for the system of freedom of expression could be achieved.

The problem of protecting the witness actually before a committee raises more difficult issues for the courts. There is no doubt about the dilemma in which the witness is placed when he seeks to exercise his constitutional right not to respond to the demand that he answer certain questions or produce certain documents. At this point he or his attorney must make an intricate decision, usually on the spur of the moment, as to what his legal rights are. If he does decide to refuse the committee request he is subject to the charge of contempt and, unless he turns out to be correct, he will be found guilty. This is true whether the contempt is enforced by direct act of the legislature or by prosecution under a statute such as Section 192. The unfortunate position in which the witness is placed seriously impairs the practical possibility of realizing his constitutional rights.

There is no easy judicial way out of this dilemma. The court does not control the legislative hearing in the same way it does a grand jury hearing, in which the proceeding can be interrupted long enough to get a ruling from the court on the legal obligation to answer a question. It is, moreover, unlikely a court would consent to force suspension of committee operations pending judicial review of the committee's demand for information. The problem could be solved, however, by action of the legislature itself. There are various methods by which the legislature could provide for a judicial test before the witness incurs any liability for refusal to answer. An interlocutory review of this sort would entail some delay in committee proceedings, even if it were limited to consideration of the issue by a single court. Nevertheless, accelerated forms of procedure could be worked out. If it is correct that adversary hearings are not essential for legislative fact finding, the delay would not seriously disrupt committee operations. In any event the delays would diminish as more specific rules governing the rights of committee witnesses were devised by the courts. Some States have adopted procedures that allow preliminary judicial review. With important constitutional rights at stake, a solution along these lines does not seem to be asking too much of the legislative branch.[43]

The question of illegally seized files, records, or other documents also poses difficult practical problems. When such materials are already in the hands of the committee the courts have followed their usual rule and refused to enjoin use of the material by the committee. Apart from this situation, however, the courts have some leeway. They have always been more ready to entertain legal proceedings against staff members or agents of the committee than against members of the legislature itself. In seizure cases, therefore, suits for damages have been upheld against staff members who participated in an illegal seizure. There have also been indications that the courts would enjoin staff members from seizing documents if suit is brought in advance of the seizure. These remedies are important, but they still leave the individual or group without recourse once the seized materials have come into possession of the committee.[44]

All in all the practical possibility of enforcing protection of First Amendment rights against invasion by legislative committees has distinct limitations. Hope must be placed in developing rules that will give more clear-cut guidance to all the parties involved. When this has been done the procedural problems will probably be more amenable to solution. Yet the task of reconciling the divergent interests of the legislative and judicial branches in this area will remain. Only a full acceptance by both branches of the basic principles underlying the First Amendment will permit unhampered operation of the system of freedom of expression.

43. For a discussion of these problems and proposed solutions see *Political and Civil Rights in the United States*, pp. 501–502.

44. See *Hearst v. Black*, 87 F.2d 68 (D.C. Cir. 1936); *Dombrowski v. Eastland*, 387 U.S. 82 (1967); cf. *Wheeldin v. Wheeler*, 373 U.S. 647 (1963); *McSurely v. Ratliff*, 398 F.2d 817 (6th Cir. 1968). In *Dombrowski v. Pfister*, discussed in Chapter V, the Supreme Court ordered the Louisiana officials to make "immediate return of all papers and documents seized." 380 U.S. 479, 497 (1965). See generally *Political and Civil Rights in the United States*, pp. 493–494. On legislative immunity see Chapter XIX. Similar issues are pending in *McSurely v. McClellan* (D. Ky.) and *National Conference for New Politics v. Eastland* (D.D.C.).

IX

*Internal
Order:
Meetings,
Demonstrations,
Canvassing*

Maintenance of internal order is an elementary and essential requirement of any community. The adjustment between an effective system of freedom of expression and this basic interest has always posed a primary challenge for the society that seeks to assure maximum individual freedom for its members. Issues of this sort have indeed provided the main points of controversy in the long evolution of the theory and practice of freedom of expression. While other concerns have now come to the fore, these problems still remain as significant and as troublesome as ever.

The social interest here is not the overall need for national security, but the requirement of law and order in the immediate community. It is concern with the elementary right of the ordinary citizen to go about his business without fear for his safety, injury to his property, or invasion of his personality. In general it relates to those functions of government exercised through what were formerly termed the "police powers"—protection of health, safety, morals and basic good order. This is normally the function of the State or local, rather than the Federal, government.

The system of freedom of expression may impinge upon this social interest in internal order at various points. The major source of tension is that arising from exercise of the right of assembly and petition. Communication of this nature takes the form of meetings, parades, picketing, demonstrations, distribution of leaflets, canvassing, and the like. Roughly speaking, it is communication addressed directly, in face-to-face encounter, to a mass audience in public, usually in the streets or other open places.[1]

The various modes of public assembly and petition play a vital role in a modern system of free expression. Such forms of expression—particularly parades—are frequently employed by groups representing conventional opinion, or minority but easily tolerated views, to reiterate or dramatize accepted or noncontroversial ideas, attitudes and values. But they are of special and crucial significance for radical, unpopular or underprivileged individuals and groups. For these persons do not normally have access to the mass media of communication. The public assembly is essential to their reaching a wider audience, or any audience at all. The reporting of their activities in the mass media, despite the unfavorable slant which may be given, further enlarges the area of communication. Indeed these forms of expression constitute one of the chief methods by which, under prevailing institutions of communication, some semblance of a "market place of ideas" can in practice be realized.

Furthermore, public assemblies possess important advantages for effective expression that do not inhere in other forms of communication. They permit face-to-face contact between the speaker and his audience, thereby increasing the flexibility of the interchange and enhancing the power of the communication. For the participants they evoke feelings of solidarity and mutual support. For the audience they evidence the intensity and dedication with which the views expressed are held. All in all, the public assembly has a dynamic quality achieved by no other form of communication.

Public assemblies also have an important impact upon the broader community, extending beyond the range of those who see or hear in person. If the message is an unpopular one, or one that the dominant element in the community would prefer to ignore, the mass assembly

---

1. I am using the term "internal order" in a somewhat different sense from that employed in *Toward a General Theory of the First Amendment*, where it included some aspects of national security. For a collection of materials and references on the problems of this chapter see Thomas I. Emerson, David Haber and Norman Dorsen, *Political and Civil Rights in the United States* (Boston, Little, Brown & Co., 3d ed. 1967), ch. IV (cited hereafter in this chapter as *Political and Civil Rights in the United States*).

has an unsettling or disruptive effect. Long before Marshall McLuhan, it was understood that this medium carried a special message. If the pressure is continued over a period of time the community may become uncomfortable, restless and tense. It may no longer be possible for individuals to consider themselves innocent bystanders, or for the leadership to sweep the underlying problems beneath the rug. The community may thus be forced to pay attention to the views expressed by the demonstrators, and perhaps become involved in an effort to redress grievances.

If the dissenting group is large enough, or militant enough, it may use the technique of the public assembly to press toward "creative disorder," violent disorder, or revolution. At this point, of course, the public assembly has moved beyond the area of expression. The threat of such a development may, however, have an impact at the earlier stage.

It is therefore not surprising to find that, from the very beginnings of free expression, the public assembly has provided an essential technique for the propagation of new, minority or unconventional opinion. In England it figured prominently in political reform movements from the time that political opposition became legitimate, as well as in the activities of such groups as the Salvation Army and the suffragettes. In the United States it has been the indispensable instrument of virtually all minority movements. Thus the abolitionists, the suffragettes, and minority political parties all relied heavily on various forms of public assembly to advance their viewpoints. Likewise, without the public assembly the labor movement could hardly have been successful in its struggle for wider acceptance and political support.[2]

In recent times the public assembly has been extensively utilized by the civil-rights movement, by peace groups, by the black community, by students, and by other radicals of the New Left. In fact one of the striking developments of the last decade has been the widespread employment of new forms of public assembly and the refurbishing of old ones. There have seen sit-ins at drug stores, restaurants, draft boards, offices of public officials, and many other places; pray-ins at churches; lie-ins in front of trucks, bulldozers and troop trains; vigils of varying duration; blockages of traffic at various points; shop-ins, love-ins and

2. On the history and significance of the public assembly in political affairs see Max Beloff, *Public Order and Popular Disturbances, 1660–1714* (London, Oxford University Press, 1938); George F. Rudé, *The Crowd in History* (New York, J. Wiley, 1964); Glenn Abernathy, *The Right of Assembly and Association* (Columbia, University of South Carolina Press, 1961).

be-ins. Most of these forms of public protest have been a response to the conviction that customary methods of persuasion have been ineffective, and are designed to employ "direct action" as a means of obtaining political goals. The extent to which they can be regarded as "expression," rather than "action," is considered below. Whether part of the system of freedom of expression or not, they form the background of our problems in internal order.[3]

The values that a community seeks from internal order are quite apparent. Indeed law and order are essential to the existence of the system of freedom of expression itself. The dynamics of disorder are apparent too. Once the degree of compliance with law declines below a certain threshold, rapid deterioration may set in. Law and order depend upon general acceptance of the community, and that acceptance is given on the basis of fair and impartial administration of the governing rules. Violation of law, especially by the use of force, negates the whole principle upon which the structure rests. Popular acquiescence is withdrawn, institutions become corrupt and demoralized, the prestige of the government is undermined, and the community as a whole is riven and disorganized.

There are certain general relationships between a system of freedom of expression and the interest in internal security, however, that require further exploration. In the first place it cannot be expected that the system of freedom of expression will function in such a way as never to result in any violation of law and order. Freedom of expression implies controversy, and in this situation the controversy takes place in the public arena. It often involves large masses of people, hostile forces opposing each other face to face, high emotions, and unforeseeable consequences. Street meetings, demonstrations, and other public assemblies are not always guided by the canons of middle-class politeness; they may be rough, aggressive and turbulent. Even the most peaceful beginning can end in disorder. To exact a guarantee as a condition of assembling that no violation of law will be forthcoming, is to eliminate the public assembly altogether. Some impairment of inter-

3. With respect to modern uses of the public assembly see L. Griffin, "The Rhetorical Structure of the 'New Left' Movement: Part I," *Quarterly Journal of Speech*, Vol. 50 (1964), p. 113; Mulford Q. Sibley, "Direct Action and the Struggle for Integration," *Hastings Law Journal*, Vol. 16 (1965), p. 351; Franklyn S. Haiman, "The Rhetoric of the Streets: Some Legal and Ethical Considerations," *Quarterly Journal of Speech*, Vol. 53 (1967), p. 99; Arthur I. Waskow, *From Race Riot to Sit-In, 1919 and the 1960s* (Garden City, N.Y., Doubleday, 1966).

nal order is the unavoidable price of maintaining a lively, dynamic system of expression.

Furthermore, any minority seeking to force a significant social change upon a reluctant establishment may find its efforts approaching the borderline of disorder. In relation to social change, law and order are scarcely neutral. For many reasons the existing system of law favors the *status quo*. The assumptions upon which it operates, expressed and unexpressed, embody prevailing values and attitudes, and protect existing interests. All the forces of inertia are ranged on its side. The very proliferation of legal procedures, which are essential to the fair administration and hence popular acceptance of the existing system of law, make it easier to delay or block change than to achieve it. Powerful psychological pressures, including fear of the unknown, support the prevailing order. Hence individuals and groups proposing change are often driven to aggressive, even militant, conduct. By necessity highly motivated, impatient of delay, perhaps frustrated and angry, with the leadership pressed hard from below, the forces seeking change find it difficult to stay within the confining bounds of peaceful and lawful action. This has been the history of all important social and political movements in this country, from the Boston Tea Party to the "Black Revolution."

In spite of this tendency to militancy on the part of groups struggling for social change, most of the physical violence emanating from public assemblies has resulted from hostile action by opposition groups or the efforts of the government to suppress the assembly. There are relatively few instances when those participating in an assembly, with a view to exercising their rights of expression, have independently gone on to engage in acts of violence against either persons or property. When conduct involving the use of force has taken place, as in the ghetto riots or student occupation of buildings, it has usually not been the direct outcome of a public assembly.[4]

4. For recent studies of violence in the United States see, *e.g., Report of The National Advisory Commission on Civil Disorders* (New York, Bantam Books, 1968) (the Kerner Report); the various staff reports of The National Commission on the Causes and Prevention of Violence, especially Hugh Davis Graham and Ted Robert Gurr, *Violence in America: Historical and Comparative Perspectives* (New York, Bantam Books, 1969), and Jerome H. Skolnick, *The Politics of Protest* (New York, Simon and Schuster, 1969); *Crisis at Columbia: Report of the Fact-Finding Commission Appointed to Investigate the Disturbances at Columbia University in April and May 1968* (New York, Random House, 1968) (the Cox Commission Report); Robert H. Connery (ed.), *Urban Riots: Violence and Social Change* (New York, The Academy of Political Science, 1968); "Anatomy of a

Finally, the use of violence or disorder in political conflict often serves an important social function. It warns society that ordinary institutions for effecting social change are not operating. It may shock the bureaucracy and the public into some remedial action. Throughout history much of the social reform granted by dominant groups to upwardly rising groups has been yielded in the face of violence or threat of violence.[5]

In any event the essential point is that, in the long run, the community will not achieve greater internal order by suppressing freedom of assembly. Expression that ends up in disorder generally originates in some kind of grievance. The underlying threat to internal order is not removed by eliminating its outward manifestations. On the contrary the basic function of freedom of expression is to facilitate the peaceful process of social change.

Legal protection of the right to public assembly must have been very much in the minds of the framers of the First Amendment. Public assemblies had played an important role in English political history throughout the eighteenth century, and the experience of the colonists themselves in the conflict that led up to the Revolution certainly formed a vivid background to their thinking. It is of considerable significance, therefore, that the First Amendment expressly forbids abridgment of the right of the people to assemble and petition for redress of grievances, making the right subject only to the qualification that it be exercised peaceably. The specific extent to which the First Amendment was intended to modify the existing English law of unlawful assembly and breach of the peace is not clear. But that it was meant to protect a broad right of assembly and petition as a vital part of a system of freedom of expression cannot be open to doubt.

The Supreme Court did not have occasion to consider the right of assembly or petition under the First Amendment until late in the nineteen-thirties, well after the Hughes Court had begun its trend of liberal decisions at the beginning of the decade. The reason for this, apart from circumstances that delayed all development of First Amendment

---

Riot: An Analytical Symposium of the Causes and Effects of Riots," *Journal of Urban Law* (Vol. 45, No. 3 and 4, 1968); "Protest in the Sixties," *The Annals of the American Academy of Political and Social Science*, Vol. 382 (March 1969).

    5. See Lewis A. Coser, *The Functions of Social Conflict* (Glencoe, Ill., Free Press, 1956), and *Continuities in the Study of Social Conflict* (New York, Free Press, 1967); "Patterns of Violence," *The Annals of the American Academy of Political and Social Science*, Vol. 364 (March 1966); H. I. Nieburg, "The Threat of Violence and Social Change," *American Political Science Review*, Vol. 56 (1962), p. 865, and *Political Violence* (New York, St. Martin's Press, 1969).

doctrine, undoubtedly lay in the fact that issues of this nature arose almost exclusively under State or municipal law, and the First Amendment was not made applicable to the States and their political subdivisions until the *Gitlow* decision in 1925. At any rate the Supreme Court did take up the problems in a series of cases beginning in 1938 and running through the nineteen-forties, most of them dealing with the rights of Jehovah's Witnesses. In these cases the Court made important advances in the doctrines of clear and present danger, prior restraint, vagueness, and overbreadth, and came close to establishing the principle that First Amendment freedoms enjoyed a "preferred position." Only occasional cases reached the Court in the nineteen-fifties. The most important came at the beginning of the McCarthy era and marked an end to the liberal trend. The civil-rights movement produced a new series of cases in the nineteen-sixties and a steady stream has continued to flow to the Court since then. Despite a significant volume of decisions, however, the development of the law has been sporadic. Many basic issues remain unresolved and no comprehensive theory has evolved.[6]

The formulation of legal doctrine on this subject presents some special difficulties. The problems involve supervision over the lowest echelons of the government apparatus—the policeman, the local prosecuting officials and magistrates, the local authorities empowered to issue permits and licenses. The legal instruments of control—breach of the peace, disorderly conduct, permit systems—are usually broad and vague, giving enormous discretion to the administering officials. The cases are numerous and mostly ad hoc in nature; each case must be dealt with on its own particular facts, with little opportunity for judicial disposition of multiple cases in a single broad decision. Delay in vindication of rights is equivalent to denial. Pressures for suppression of expression, particularly through preventive devices, may be severe. The persons seeking to communicate are likely to be the most deprived members of the society, with few resources for obtaining legal redress and small influence in the community.

In approaching these problems it is first necessary to consider more precisely than the courts have hitherto attempted what the basic rights of assembly and petition embrace (Section A). We then turn to issues involved in maintaining those rights where the social interest at stake is the preservation of the public peace (Section B). After that we con-

6. For a general account of the legal developments, see *Political and Civil* *Rights in the United States*, pp. 67–68, 512–533, 550–553, 582–601.

sider other aspects of the interest in internal order (Section C) and the allocation of physical facilities (Section D). Finally we deal with the critical problem of administration of the controls, particularly the operation of permit systems (Section E).

A. Basic Rights of Assembly and Petition

It is useful to commence with a discussion of the basic rights that the First Amendment's guarantee of assembly and petition confer upon the individual citizen. Strangely enough, the fundamental structure of these rights has never been fully explicated by the Supreme Court and stands today in a state of great uncertainty. The main problems have concerned, first, what forms of conduct are protected by the First Amendment and what forms are not; and, second, in what kinds of places the rights of assembly and petition may be exercised.

1. THE DIVISION BETWEEN EXPRESSION AND ACTION

The question of what forms of conduct, in the nature of assembly and petition, are protected by the First Amendment can only be answered in terms of drawing the distinction between "expression" and "action." This is true regardless of what doctrine is later applied to determine the extent of protection afforded by the First Amendment to conduct that is found to fall within its shelter. Whether a test of incitement, clear and present danger, balancing, or full protection is employed, it is first necessary to decide that the conduct for which the claim of protection is made does come within the coverage of the First Amendment. This determination, if it is to have a rational basis, must be made in light of the general functions performed by the system of freedom of expression, the particular purpose served by assembly and petition, the dynamics of administering a system for protection of those rights, and the role played by the courts in the whole process.

The problem of drawing the line between "expression" and "action" presents particular difficulties with regard to assembly and petition. Much of the conduct involved, such as marching in a parade, embraces nonverbal as well as verbal elements. Equally troublesome, by the very nature of a public assembly, verbal or nonverbal expression moves rapidly and indistinguishably into verbal and nonverbal action. In the face-to-face encounter between speaker and audience the effect of the communication is more immediate. Time and opportunity for countervailing opinion to take effect are minimized. The fact that large numbers of people may congregate together, especially in tense situations, sets the stage for subsequent action, at times of a violent character. All these factors make the determination a troublesome one, not only for the courts but for other officials, participants and the public.

The framers of the First Amendment clearly intended to extend its protection beyond sheer verbal communication. They included in the guarantee not only freedom of speech and the press but in addition the right of assembly and petition. Plainly they meant to embrace more than the individual speaker or the written word, and to establish the kind of spirited and even turbulent system that included meetings, marches, demonstrations, and similar aspects of assembly. Beyond this, however, we must look for guidance to the requirements of a modern system of freedom of expression.

In general all forms of verbal communication customarily used in public assemblies must be classified as "expression." This would include speech, writing, signs, singing, dramatic performances, the shouting of slogans, and the like. In addition, all nonverbal conduct that is an integral part of assembly would normally be considered "expression." This would include the holding of a meeting, marching, carrying signs, gestures, display of symbols, door-to-door canvassing, and similar conduct. Patrolling up and down or picketing would also constitute "expression" except insofar as it amounted to a signal for the exertion of organized economic pressure. The presence of people in the street or other open public place for the purpose of expression, even in large numbers, would also be deemed part of the "expression."

On the other hand, the use of physical force or violence, against person or property, would be considered "action." A sit-in, lie-in, or chain-in, in which the physical occupation of territory is used as a form of pressure, would normally constitute "action." So would the obstruction of traffic, or obstruction of ingress or egress, when undertaken for the purpose of physical interference. Disruption of a meeting by moving about or making noise must also be counted as "action." Likewise, wearing of masks or uniforms under circumstances implying the use of force or violence would be put in the same category. Some conduct of a purely verbal nature, such as the issuance of a command or directions to engage in violence, would also come within the definition of "action."

There are, of course, many intermediate forms of conduct for which it cannot be so readily decided whether verbal communication is a verbal act, or non-speech is an integral part of expression. Some of these matters are considered later. The essential point here is that an effective right of assembly and petition demands that conduct extending beyond mere speech be protected, and that the determination of where the line is drawn be made by the kind of analysis just indicated.

The courts have never pursued the problem along these lines. In some of their earlier decisions the Supreme Court apparently recognized that in assembly cases the First Amendment protects a wider area of expression than mere verbal communication. Thus it upheld the right to hold a meeting in *De Jonge v. Oregon,* the right to picket in *Thornhill v. Alabama,* the right to solicit membership in *Thomas v. Collins,* and the right to march in *Edwards v. South Carolina.* Indeed in the *Edwards* case Justice Stewart, writing for all members of the Court except Justice Clark, referred to a demonstration by 187 students on the State Capitol grounds as an exercise of the rights of free speech, free assembly, and freedom to petition for redress of grievances "in their most pristine and classic form." The Court has also held that other forms of nonverbal conduct are covered by the First Amendment. These include the right to display a red flag in *Stromberg v. California,* the right not to salute the flag in *West Virginia State Board of Education v. Barnette,* and the right of a civil-rights organization to engage in the solicitation of legal business in *N.A.A.C.P. v. Button.* But the Court never articulated its reasoning, or even addressed itself seriously to the problem. In its more recent decisions, the Court has adopted a two-level theory that undertakes to distinguish in assembly cases between "pure speech" and "speech plus," the latter receiving a lesser degree of protection under the First Amendment.[7]

---

7. *De Jonge v. Oregon,* 299 U.S. 353 (1937); *Thornhill v. Alabama,* 310 U.S. 88 (1940); *Thomas v. Collins,* 323 U.S. 516 (1945); *Edwards v. South Carolina,* 372 U.S. 229, 235 (1963); *Stromberg v. California,* 283 U.S. 359 (1931); *West Virginia State Board of Education v. Barnette,* 319 U.S. 624 (1943); *N.A.A.C.P. v. Button,* 371 U.S. 415 (1963). Legal solicitation was also upheld as a First Amendment right in *Brotherhood of R.R. Trainmen v. Virginia,* 377 U.S. 1 (1964); *United Mine Workers of America v. Illinois State Bar Association,* 389 U.S. 217 (1967). For lower court cases holding that sit-ins, lie-ins, and similar conduct are not protected by the First Amendment see *Political and Civil Rights in the United States,* pp. 572–573. The characterization of the Supreme Court's position as a "two-level" theory was first made by Professor Harry Kalven, Jr. See "The

The Supreme Court's two-level theory had its origin in the labor picketing cases. But it first appeared with broader application in the opinions rendered in two cases decided in 1965. The cases, each entitled *Cox v. Louisiana*, dealt with three convictions of a single defendant growing out of a civil-rights demonstration in Baton Rouge. The convictions were for violation of Louisiana statutes prohibiting breach of the peace, obstructing public passages, and picketing a courthouse. Justice Goldberg, writing for five members of the Court, upheld the Louisiana statute that prohibited picketing "in or near" a courthouse. Answering claims that the statute violated First Amendment rights to freedom of speech and assembly, Justice Goldberg argued: "The conduct which is the subject of this statute—picketing and parading—is subject to regulation even though intertwined with expression and association." Citing examples of holdings by the Court "that certain forms of conduct mixed with speech may be regulated or prohibited," primarily labor picketing cases, he went on to say: "We are not concerned here with such a pure form of expression as newspaper comment or a telegram by a citizen to a public official. We deal in this case not with free speech alone, but with expression mixed with particular conduct." [8]

Justice Goldberg restated this proposition, even more strongly, in the other *Cox* case. Addressing himself to the validity of the statute prohibiting the obstruction of public passages, he said:

> We emphatically reject the notion urged by appellant that the First and Fourteenth Amendments afford the same kind of freedom to those who would communicate ideas by conduct such as patrolling, marching, and picketing on streets and highways, as these amendments afford to those who communicate ideas by pure speech.[9]

Justice Black, in a concurring opinion, went even further. He took the position that marching or picketing was conduct entirely outside the protection of the First Amendment; that such conduct was subject to governmental regulation, including prohibition; and that if the regulation indirectly infringed upon freedom of speech it was subject to

---

Concept of the Public Forum: *Cox v. Louisiana," Supreme Court Review,* Vol. 1965 (1965), pp. 1, 13–21.

8. *Cox v. Louisiana,* 379 U.S. 559, 563, 564 (1965). It will be noted that the Supreme Court sometimes uses the term "conduct" to refer to nonverbal activity. As used in this book the term

"conduct" embraces all activity, verbal and nonverbal, and hence embraces both "expression" and "action." For discussion of the labor picketing cases see Chapter XII.

9. *Cox v. Louisiana,* 379 U.S. 536, 555 (1965).

constitutional limitation only under the balancing test. Referring to the breach of peace statute he said:

> A state statute . . . regulating *conduct*—patrolling and marching—as distinguished from *speech,* would in my judgment be constitutional, subject only to the condition that if such a law had the effect of indirectly impinging on freedom of speech, press, or religion, it would be unconstitutional if under the circumstances it appeared that the State's interest in suppressing the conduct was not sufficient to outweigh the individual's interest in engaging in conduct closely involving his First Amendment freedoms.[10]

And, again, with respect to the statute forbidding obstruction of public passages: "I have no doubt about the general power of Louisiana to bar all picketing on its streets and highways. Standing, patrolling, or marching back and forth on streets is conduct, not speech, and as conduct can be regulated or prohibited." [11]

A year after *Cox,* in *Brown v. Louisiana,* Justice Fortas, who had replaced Justice Goldberg, joined by Chief Justice Warren and Justice Douglas, held to the view that the conduct of Negroes who remained standing or sitting in a library after being refused service, constituted expression within the protection of the First Amendment:

> As this Court has repeatedly stated, these rights [of freedom of speech, assembly and petition] are not confined to verbal expression. They embrace appropriate types of action which certainly include the right in a peaceable and orderly manner to protest by silent and reproachful presence, in a place where the protestant has every right to be, the unconstitutional segregation of public facilities.[12]

Whatever doubts there may have been about the Supreme Court's acceptance of the Goldberg position, however, were set at rest in the next few years. In 1967, in *Walker v. City of Birmingham* Justice Stewart quoted the language of the *Cox* case with full approval. The following year in *Cameron v. Johnson* Justice Brennan, speaking for all members of the Court except Justices Douglas and Fortas, reaffirmed that an anti-picketing statute regulated "conduct" which is "intertwined with expression." In *Amalgamated Food Employees*

---

10. 379 U.S. at 577. Italics in original.
11. 379 U.S. at 581. Justice Black had previously taken a similar position in *N.L.R.B. v. Fruit and Vegetable Packers and Warehousemen, Local 760,* 377 U.S. 58, 77–78 (1964). Justices Clark, Harlan

and White did not touch on the issue in the *Cox* cases.
12. *Brown v. Louisiana,* 383 U.S. 131, 141–142 (1966). For a similar statement made earlier by Justice Harlan see *Garner v. Louisiana,* 368 U.S. 157, 201 (1961).

Union v. Logan Valley Plaza, Inc., Justice Marshall further elaborated
on the concept. That case raised the question whether picketing within
a shopping center was protected by the First Amendment. Justice
Marshall pointed out that the Court had previously held that "picketing involves elements of both speech and conduct, *i.e.* patrolling, and
has indicated that because of this intermingling of protected and unprotected elements, picketing can be subjected to controls that would
not be constitutionally permissible in the case of pure speech." He also
observed, "Handbilling, like picketing, involves conduct other than
speech, namely, the physical presence of the person distributing
leaflets on municipal property." Justice Marshall then proceeded to
decide whether prohibition of picketing and handbilling was a "permissible regulation" under the First Amendment by applying the balancing test, resolving the balance in this case in favor of the First
Amendment rights. Justice Douglas concurred, saying: "Picketing is
free speech *plus,* the *plus* being physical activity that may implicate
traffic and related matters. Hence the latter aspects of picketing may
be regulated." [13]

Subsequent decisions have adhered to the two-level theory. In
Tinker v. Des Moines Independent Community School District Justice
Fortas classified wearing black armbands in protest of the Vietnam
war as conduct "closely akin to 'pure speech'," citing *Cox.* Justice
Stewart repeated the *Cox* dictum in *Shuttlesworth v. City of Birmingham.* In *Gregory v. City of Chicago* Justice Black restated his position
with Justice Douglas concurring. [14]

The Supreme Court thus seems, temporarily at least, to have settled on the proposition that exercise of the right of assembly involves
both "pure speech" and other forms of conduct entitled to a lesser
degree of protection under the First Amendment. The Court's analysis
is both confusing and destructive of First Amendment rights. First of
all the distinction is only a semantic one. Virtually all expression contains some mixture of nonverbal "conduct," and the Court's
formulation affords no functional basis for deciding what is "pure
speech" and what is other "conduct," or for differentiating between the

13. *Walker v. City of Birmingham,*
388 U.S. 307, 316 (1967); *Cameron v.
Johnson,* 390 U.S. 611, 617 (1968);
*Amalgamated Food Employees Union v.
Logan Valley Plaza, Inc.,* 391 U.S. 308,
313, 315–316, 321, 326 (1968) (italics in
original).

14. *Tinker v. Des Moines Independ-*
ent Community School District, 393 U.S.
503 (1969); *Shuttlesworth v. City of
Birmingham,* 394 U.S. 147, 152 (1969);
Gregory v. City of Chicago, 394 U.S.
111, 124–126 (1969). See also the discussion of similar issues as raised in the
draft card burning and flag burning cases
in Chapter IV.

kind of protection that should be extended to one but not the other. Furthermore, the Court gives a minimum of protection to "speech plus" and hence also to the right of assembly and petition. Of course, if the balancing test is used for both "pure speech" and other "conduct," the result is simply that the latter is given less weight in the balance. Under these circumstances the distinction may not be of much significance, though it would be both unnecessary and misleading. Under any doctrine, however, it is hard to believe that the second-class protection afforded other "conduct" would prove very effective. The formula would, in short, remove a large segment of the right of assembly and petition, as well as other vital forms of expression, from any real protection under the First Amendment.

Justice Black's position expressly accomplishes this. It takes "conduct," as distinct from "speech," completely outside the First Amendment. "Conduct" is defined as including "standing," "patrolling," and "marching." It is perhaps not an accident that Justice Black, in listing First Amendment rights in the *Cox* case, mentions speech, press and religion, but not assembly or petition. On his formulation there is very little left to the right of assembly or petition.

2. THE PROBLEM OF PLACE

A second basic aspect of the right to assemble and petition concerns the place where such activities may be carried on. It has always been assumed that, as a general proposition, there is no right under the First Amendment to engage in any form of expression upon private property without the consent of the owner, express or implied. The prohibition is enforced by trespass and other laws. Moreover, it is absolute, not governed by any balancing test. The reason for the law's position on this issue has never been fully explained by the courts. Undoubtedly it rests primarily upon the fact that the function of private property is to give the owner protection from outside intrusions, including persons seeking access to an audience. If the property is dedicated to this purpose, or is devoted to other purposes incompatible with exercise of the right of expression, protection of the property owner does not "abridge" freedom of expression as the system of free expression has functioned and should function. These considerations do not apply to property serving other functions, however, and it is here that the issues of place arise.

The problem of place, or location, is particularly crucial in connection with the right of assembly and petition. Exercise of that right, by its very nature, brings together large numbers of people, thus requiring a place where they can be accommodated. Equally important, this form of expression must bring the communication to other persons where they can be found and reached. The process involves searching out potential recipients of the communication, inviting them to accept the communication and even, to some extent, forcing it upon their attention. Carried far enough, this raises the question of a "captive audience," and it is this factor that concerns those who, like Justice Black, would closely limit the places in which the right of expression may be exercised. Nevertheless, our traditions of public assembly, leaflet distribution, and canvassing have always allowed for a substantial right of access to the potential audience and an opportunity to secure public attention.

It is therefore essential that persons seeking to exercise the right of assembly and petition have the use of places or areas where large groups of people can be participants or spectators, and where the potential audience can be approached. Primarily this involves the right to use the street, parks and similar open public places. It also raises questions as to the use of other public facilities, open or enclosed, and to some extent the use of privately owned places or facilities which have some public or quasi-public character. We are concerned at this point only with the general right to use such places or facilities for assembling, petitioning or canvassing. The right of the government or others to impose particular limitations, or regulate use through permit devices, is dealt with subsequently.

a. Streets, Parks, and Similar Open Public Places The Supreme Court initially refused to recognize any constitutional right of citizens to use the streets, parks, and similar public places for purposes of assembly. The issue arose in *Davis v. Massachusetts,* a case decided in 1897. The defendant in that case had been charged with making a speech on Boston Common in violation of a city ordinance which made it an offense for any person to "make any public address, discharge any cannon or firearm, expose for sale any goods," etc., on "any public grounds" without a permit from the mayor. The Massachusetts Supreme Judicial Court upheld a conviction, in an opinion by Justice Holmes, then a member of that Court. The Massachusetts Court's view of the case was simple: "For the legislature absolutely or conditionally to forbid public speaking in a highway or public park is no more an infringement of the rights of a member of the public than for the owner of a private house to forbid it in his house." The United States Supreme Court affirmed, fully accepting the Holmes view, and saying that the Fourteenth Amendment "does not have the effect of creating a particular and personal right in the citizen to use public property in defiance of the constitution and laws of the State." The Supreme Court did not expressly consider any First Amendment issue, and indeed at that time the First Amendment had not been made applicable to the States through the Fourteenth.[15]

The *Davis* case was hardly conclusive and indeed was overtaken and superseded by the development of First Amendment doctrine in the nineteen-thirties. The classic exposition of the other view came in *Hague v. C.I.O.*, decided in 1939. The case arose out of the efforts of Mayor Hague to break up an organizing campaign by the C.I.O. in Jersey City. The tactics employed included both physical harassment of organizers and the enforcement of municipal legislation to prevent organizers from holding meetings or distributing literature. The Supreme Court affirmed a lower court decision granting an injunction. Justice Roberts, in an opinion that Justice Black joined and with which Chief Justice Hughes concurred, held that the actions of the Jersey City officials violated the privileges and immunities of citizens under the Fourteenth Amendment. It had been contended that "the city's ownership of streets and parks is as absolute as one's ownership of his home, with consequent power altogether to exclude citizens from the use thereof," relying upon the *Davis* case. To this Justice Roberts replied:

> We have no occasion to determine whether, on the facts disclosed, the *Davis* case was rightly decided, but we cannot agree that it rules the instant case. Wherever the title of streets and parks may rest, they have immemorially been held in trust for the use of the public and, time out of mind, have been used for purposes of assembly, communicating thoughts between citizens, and discussing public questions. Such use of the streets and public places has, from ancient times, been a part of the privileges, immunities, rights, and liberties of citizens. The privilege of a citizen of the United States to use the streets and parks for communication of views on national questions may be regulated in the interest of all; it is not absolute, but relative, and must be exercised in

15. *Davis v. Massachusetts,* 167 U.S. 43, 47–48 (1897).

subordination to the general comfort and convenience, and in consonance with peace and good order; but it must not, in the guise of regulation, be abridged or denied.[16]

Justice Roberts spoke only for a minority of the Court in the *Hague* case. Nevertheless his views came to be accepted as the prevailing doctrine, both in later decisions and by legal commentators.[17]

In 1965, however, Justice Goldberg's opinion in *Cox v. Louisiana* reopened the question. The Louisiana statute prohibiting obstruction of public passages would, on its face, have precluded all "street assemblies and parades." The Court was thus faced with the possibility of reaffirming *Hague* or repudiating it. Justice Goldberg chose to avoid the issue: "We have no occasion in this case," he said, "to consider the constitutionality of the uniform, consistent, and nondiscriminatory application of a statute forbidding all access to streets and other public facilities for parades and meetings." City officials, he found, had in fact permitted some meetings and parades, and thus the situation was the same as if the statute had permitted "parades or demonstrations in the unbridled discretion of the local officials." He concluded: "It is clearly unconstitutional to enable a public official to determine which expressions of view will be permitted and which will not or to engage in invidious discrimination among persons or groups either by use of a statute providing a system of broad discretionary licensing power or, as in this case, the equivalent of such a system by selective enforcement of an extremely broad prohibitory statute." [18]

Justice Black, again going further than his colleagues, made it entirely clear that in his present view there was no First Amendment right to use the streets for public assembly, at least so far as standing, marching or patrolling was concerned:

The First and Fourteenth Amendments, I think, take away from government, state and federal, all power to restrict freedom of speech, press, and assembly *where people have a right to be for such purposes.* This does not mean, however, that these amendments also grant a

16. *Hague v. C.I.O.*, 307 U.S. 496, 515–516 (1939). Justices Stone and Reed concurred in the result on due process grounds; Justices McReynolds and Butler dissented; Justices Douglas and Frankfurter did not participate.

17. Thus the Roberts view was restated in *Schneider v. State*, 308 U.S. 147, 163 (1939); *Cox v. New Hampshire*, 312 U.S. 569, 574 (1941); *Jamison v. Texas*, 318 U.S. 413, 415–416 (1943); *Kunz v. New York*, 340 U.S. 290, 293 (1951); *Edwards v. South Carolina*, 372 U.S. 229 (1963). It is true, however, that the restatement was sometimes less broad or forceful than the original. See Kalven, *op. cit. supra* note 7, pp. 13–21.

18. *Cox v. Louisiana*, 379 U.S. 536, 555, 557–558 (1965).

constitutional right to engage in the conduct of picketing or patrolling, whether on publicly owned streets or on privately owned property. . . . Were the law otherwise, people on the streets, in their homes and anywhere else could be compelled to listen against their will to speakers they did not want to hear.[19]

The issues were again raised two years later in *Adderley v. Florida*. In that case a group of students were convicted under a Florida trespass statute for conducting a peaceful demonstration on the grounds of a county jail. They were protesting the arrest of some of their fellows in a prior demonstration against segregation. The Supreme Court affirmed the conviction by a vote of five to four. Justice Black, writing for the majority, distinguished the *Edwards* case, which had upheld a demonstration on the grounds of the South Carolina State Capitol: "Traditionally, state capitol grounds are open to the public. Jails, built for security purposes, are not." Later in the opinion, however, Justice Black moved onto broader ground, reminiscent of *Davis*:

> The State, no less than a private owner of property, has power to preserve the property under its control for the use to which it is lawfully dedicated. For this reason there is no merit to petitioners' argument that they had a constitutional right to stay on the property, over the jail custodian's objections, because this "area chosen for the peaceful civil rights demonstration was not only 'reasonable' but also particularly appropriate. . . ." Such an argument has as its major unarticulated premise the assumption that people who want to propagandize protests or views have a constitutional right to do so whenever and however and wherever they please. That concept of constitutional law was vigorously and forthrightly rejected in [*Cox v. Louisiana*]. We reject it again. The United States Constitution does not forbid a State to control the use of its own property for its own lawful nondiscriminatory purpose.[20]

The minority, consisting of Chief Justice Warren and Justices Douglas, Brennan and Fortas, in an opinion by Justice Douglas, protested that the majority was refusing to recognize the traditional rights of assembly and petition:

> The jailhouse, like an executive mansion, a legislative chamber, a courthouse, or the statehouse itself . . . is one of the seats of government,

19. 379 U.S. at 578. Italics in original.
20. *Adderley v. Florida*, 385 U.S. 39, 41, 47–48 (1966).

whether it be the Tower of London, the Bastille, or a small country jail. And when it houses political prisoners or those who many think are unjustly held, it is an obvious center for protest. . . .

There may be some public places which are so clearly committed to other purposes that their use for the airing of grievances is anomalous. There may be some instances in which assemblies and petitions for redress of grievances are not consistent with other necessary purposes of public property. A noisy meeting may be out of keeping with the serenity of the statehouse or the quiet of the courthouse. No one, for example, would suggest that the Senate gallery is the proper place for a vociferous protest rally. And in other cases it may be necessary to adjust the right to petition for redress of grievances to the other interests inhering in the uses to which the public property is normally put. . . . But this is quite different from saying that all public places are off limits to people with grievances.[21]

The *Adderley* case left it uncertain how far Justice Black's colleagues in the majority intended to accept his limited view of the right of assembly and petition. The question remained unresolved in *Cameron v. Johnson.* But in the *Logan Valley Plaza* decision the Court definitely returned to the *Hague* doctrine. There Justice Marshall, speaking for a majority of five and with Justices Douglas and White clearly concurring, cited *Hague* and the early leaflet distribution cases, and concluded: "The essence of those opinions is that streets, sidewalks, parks, and other similar public places are so historically associated with the exercise of First Amendment rights that access to them for the purpose of exercising such rights cannot constitutionally be denied broadly and absolutely." [22]

Subsequently in *Shuttlesworth v. City of Birmingham* Justice Stewart clinched the matter by reciting in full the Roberts quotation from *Hague.* Thus it may now be assumed that the Court has finally accepted the position that there is a basic constitutional right to use the streets, parks and public open places for purposes of assembly and petition.[23]

To some degree the practical importance of recognizing a constitutional right to use the streets and other open places is lessened by the principle that, if such places are made available to anyone for purposes

21. 385 U.S. at 49, 54.

22. *Amalgamated Food Employees Union v. Logan Valley Plaza, Inc.,* 391 U.S. 308, 315 (1968). Justice Harlan did not pass on the place issue. Justice Black dissented on other grounds.

23. *Shuttlesworth v. City of Birmingham,* 394 U.S. 147, 152 (1969), Justices Black and Harlan concurring and Justice Marshall not participating.

of assembly, they must be open to all on an equal basis. This doctrine had been laid down in *Fowler v. Rhode Island* and was reiterated in *Cox v. Louisiana*. Since everyone loves a parade, and since many different kinds of groups customarily use the streets and parks for assemblies, the possibility of excluding unpopular or unorthodox groups is diminished. Yet this is by no means a complete answer. It is not at all clear how far a municipality could legitimately go, despite equal protection safeguards, in distinguishing not between *users* but between *uses*. Could it, for example, allow all religious groups to assemble on public property but exclude all political groups? Or could it put a time limit on each group, permitting one meeting a year? If the only consideration is to avoid discrimination, the outcome of such cases might not be certain. Moreover, under the nondiscrimination doctrine it would always be open to a community to close its streets and parks to all assemblies, at least for a time. Experience with the civil-rights movement in the South and with other communities engaged in serious controversy indicates that such a complete obliteration of the right of public assembly might frequently be the course of action chosen by the majority or the dominant element of a community.[24]

It is also true that the basic right to use the streets and public open places is subject to many limitations. It has been suggested that the area of restriction is so broad that there is little left to the basic right, and that whether it exists or not is more a theoretical than a realistic issue. But such an argument ignores both the legal and psychological advantages of judicial recognition that the right exists. However many the limitations, a system of freedom of expression is more firmly founded when it rests on the strongly held premise that a constitutional right to use the streets and open places is the starting point from which discussion of limitations begins.

b. Other Public Facilities   If it be assumed that there is a basic constitutional right to use the streets, parks and similar places for purposes of expression, further questions arise. There are many other kinds of public facilities, ranging from grounds in front of a public building to the private office of the Chief Executive. To what extent does there exist a constitutional right under the First Amendment to use any of these facilities?

24. *Fowler v. Rhode Island*, 345 U.S. 67 (1953) (refusal to allow Jehovah's Witnesses to conduct religious services in a park, although other religious groups were permitted to do so, held to violate the First Amendment); *Cox v. Louisiana*, 379 U.S. 536, 553–558, discussed above.

As a general proposition it would seem that the constitutional right recognized by Justice Roberts would extend to any public facility where roughly the same conditions prevailed as in the case of streets and parks and the use serves the same underlying purposes. This would seem to occur in at least two situations. One is when there are public open places which are not devoted to uses that exclude an assemblage of persons and which furnish an appropriate site for exercise of such rights. Under these circumstances the public facility would fulfill the purpose of supplying a physical area where expression in the form of assembly and petition could take place. This would seem to be the situation in *Adderley*. The jailhouse grounds were an open area, not devoted to inconsistent uses, and affording a peculiarly relevant location for the demonstration. Indeed the jailhouse was perhaps the prime symbol of the enforced system of segregation against which the protest was directed. Exercise of the basic right to use the facility would, of course, be subject to various forms of limitation. The security of the jail, essential to the use for which the public facility was primarily designed, would certainly furnish grounds for such limitation. But there was no showing in the *Adderley* case that this consideration precluded use of the grounds for the peaceful demonstration that in fact took place.

The second situation involves the use of a public facility, whether open or enclosed, by the public in much the same way as the streets and parks, for passing to and fro, congregating, or conversing. Here use of the facility fulfills the other major purpose underlying the constitutional right, namely, it makes available an audience that could not otherwise be reached. The Supreme Court has not had occasion to pass upon the issues in this form. But the Court of Appeals for the Second Circuit has upheld the right of citizens to distribute antiwar leaflets and discuss their views in the Port of New York Authority bus terminal. The Court pointed to the kind of factors that govern in this situation when it said: "The Terminal building is an appropriate place for expressing one's views precisely because the primary activity for which it is designed is attended with noisy crowds and vehicles, some unrest and less than perfect order." [25]

Other types of public facilities pose less clear questions. Perhaps the most significant is whether there is a constitutional right to use

---

25. *Wolin v. Port of New York Authority*, 392 F.2d 83, 90 (2d Cir. 1968), cert. denied 393 U.S. 940 (1968). See also *In re Hoffman*, 67 Calif. 2d 845, 64 Calif. Rptr. 97, 434 P.2d 353 (1967).

public facilities suitable for indoor meetings, such as public auditoriums, town halls, firehouses, civic centers, and the like. There are no decisions, so far as appears, that impose an obligation on the government to make such facilities available to private individuals or groups seeking to exercise First Amendment rights. The courts have indeed tended to assume otherwise. But a strong argument can be made that the First Amendment does impose such an obligation on the government, at least where no other facilities are available. The energizing principle which defines the constitutional right to use the streets and parks for assembly and petition is that the government must make available the opportunity for the exercise of this crucial form of expression. This principle would certainly extend to the right of indoor as well as outdoor assembly. The proposition could also be placed upon broader grounds. If the purpose of the First Amendment is to assure an effective system of free expression, then the failure of the government to maintain facilities for exercise of the elemental right to hold a public meeting could be construed as abridgment of the constitutional guarantee.[26]

Other kinds of public facilities would not seem to lend themselves to use for public assembly or most other forms of expression. Yet the right to petition for redress of grievances certainly provides some constitutional basis for access to government buildings. That right includes an opportunity for citizens to take their petition to the seat of government and to the office of the public official directly involved. At some point in time, access gained by the right of petition would expire and a prolonged stay, amounting to a sit-in, would not be protected expression. Until such a point has been reached, however, a group presentation of grievances at the appropriate public facility would constitute an exercise of the right of petition. The prevailing opinion in *Brown v. Louisiana*, upholding the presence in a library of a group protesting racial discrimination, seems to recognize the operation of the right of petition in this manner.[27]

The doctrine that the use of public facilities for purposes of expres-

26. For statements that there is no obligation on the part of the government to make public buildings available for assembly see, *e.g.*, *Danskin v. San Diego Unified School District*, 20 Calif. 2d 536, 545, 171 P.2d 885, 891 (1946); *East Meadow Community Concerts Association v. Board of Education*, 18 N.Y.2d 129, 133, 272 N.Y.S.2d 341, 344, 219 N.E.2d 172, 174 (1966); *Madole v. Barnes*, 20 N.Y.2d 169, 173, 282 N.Y.S. 2d 225, 228, 229 N.E.2d 20, 22 (1967). For discussion of the affirmative character of the First Amendment see Chapter XVII.

27. *Brown v. Louisiana*, 383 U.S. 131 (1966).

sion may not be withheld on a discriminatory basis is, of course, applicable in this area. Indeed the doctrine is of substantial importance here because the practice of making available public schools, civic 'centers, and other buildings to various groups for meetings or other activities is widespread, both by statute and by custom. The same sorts of issues arise as in the case of streets and parks with respect to the kinds of distinction between uses that may validly be made. Because public buildings are designed for varying purposes, it is perhaps more likely that reasonable grounds exist for differentiating between the uses for which they are opened to the public. A room designed for chamber music may perhaps not be suitable for a political rally. In most situations, however, no rational basis for distinguishing between different kinds of use for expression can be demonstrated, and the effort to do so is in essence a discrimination based upon content. As such it would violate the First Amendment.[28]

c. Quasi-Public Places   The system of freedom of expression does not contemplate that the right of expression can be exercised upon privately owned property, used for private purposes, without the consent of the owner. An attempt to do so can be prohibited by the government, through enforcement of trespass laws or otherwise, without infringing on any right protected by the First Amendment. Thus, even if a sit-in on such private property could be considered a form of expression, punishment by the government would not constitute an "abridgment" of expression within the meaning of the First Amendment. In some situations, however, privately owned property may be used in such a way as in effect to be dedicated to public use; or the government may have such a relationship to the property or the owner as to stamp the property with governmental attributes. Such quasi-public property would then be considered the same as public property for purposes of exercising First Amendment rights.[29]

28. In addition to the *Fowler* and *Cox* cases dealing with streets and parks, cited above, see the litigation in *Ellis v. Dixon,* 349 U.S. 458 (1955). Decisions in other courts include the *East Meadow* and *Madole* cases, cited above, and *Bynum v. Schiro,* 219 F. Supp. 204 (E.D. La. 1963), aff'd per curiam 375 U.S. 395 (1964); *Buckley v. Meng,* 35 Misc.2d 467, 230 N.Y.S.2d 924 (Sup. Ct. N.Y. Co. 1962); *Kissinger v. New York City Transit Authority,* 274 F. Supp. 438 (S.D.N.Y.

1967); *Wirta v. Alameda Contra Costa Transit District,* 68 Calif. 2d 61, 64 Calif. Rptr. 430, 434 P.2d 982 (1967). See also *Political and Civil Rights in the United States,* p. 517.

29. Enforcement of the property owner's rights might, under some circumstances, constitute state action supporting a system of segregation, and hence violate the equal protection clause. The Supreme Court's decisions in the sit-in cases revolved about these issues. Only in *Brown*

The decision which first recognized that the propriety of exercising First Amendment rights in any particular place depended upon the function of the property rather than its ownership was *Marsh v. Alabama.* That case involved a company town, Chickasaw, similar in all respects to an ordinary municipality, but wholly owned by a private corporation. Company regulations prohibited any solicitation on the streets of the town. Contrary to these regulations a member of Jehovah's Witnesses distributed religious literature in the business section of the town and was convicted under an Alabama criminal trespass law. The Supreme Court reversed. Justice Black, writing for the majority, held that citizens in the town were entitled to the same First Amendment rights against the town's owners that they would have against the government of a municipality: "Whether a corporation or a municipality owns or possesses the town the public in either case has an identical interest in the functioning of the community in such manner that the channels of communication remain free." [30]

The *Marsh* decision was substantially extended two decades later in *Amalgamated Food Employees Union v. Logan Valley Plaza, Inc.* That case involved the question whether the First Amendment guaranteed the right to picket within the confines of a privately owned shopping center. The Supreme Court held, six to three, that the shopping center was "clearly the functional equivalent to the business district of Chickasaw involved in *Marsh,*" and that "the State may not delegate the power, through the use of its trespass laws, wholly to exclude those members of the public wishing to exercise their First Amendment rights on the premises in a manner and for a purpose generally consonant with the use to which the property is actually put." Justice Marshall, writing for the majority, stressed that the decision rested on the function the property served and the essential requirements of the system of freedom of expression. After pointing out that the "large-scale movement of this country's population from the cities to the suburbs has been accompanied by the advent of the suburban shopping center," and that by 1966 shopping centers accounted for 37 percent of the total retail sales in the United States and Canada, he concluded:

These figures illustrate the substantial consequences for workers seeking to challenge substandard working conditions, consumers protesting

v. Louisiana did the First Amendment play any major role. See discussion *supra.*

30. *Marsh v. Alabama,* 326 U.S. 501, 507 (1946). Justice Frankfurter con-

curred, Justice Reed dissented, and Justice Jackson did not participate. See also *Tucker v. Texas,* 326 U.S. 517 (1946).

shoddy or overpriced merchandise, and minority groups seeking non-discriminatory hiring policies that a contrary decision here would have. Business enterprises located in downtown areas would be subject to on-the-spot public criticism for their practices, but businesses situated in the suburbs could largely immunize themselves from similar criticism by creating a *cordon sanitaire* of parking lots around their stores. Neither precedent nor policy compels a result so at variance with the goal of free expression and communication that is the heart of the First Amendment.[31]

The principle laid down in the *Marsh* and *Logan Valley Plaza* cases has wide implications. The Court in *Logan* expressly reserved decision on the question whether picketing "not thus directly related in its purpose to the use to which the shopping center property was being put" would also be protected. But the logic of the decision would clearly seem to carry that far. The doctrine of the cases would thus apply to various other privately owned areas that function for all practical purposes as public thoroughfares or gathering places. It also furnishes the basis for opening up to canvassers, for exercise of rights of expression, access to quasi-public areas such as corridors in apartment buildings. In these situations, just as in the case of the company town and shopping center, the private owner is exercising control over property of a character that is customarily exercised by government, and the demands of the system of free expression put the owner in the same position as the government.[32]

Private property may also become endowed with public attributes, for purposes of enforcing First Amendment rights, when the government's relation to the property is such as to satisfy the principle that "state action" is involved. These issues have arisen primarily in cases where equal protection rights have been invoked. Whether state action for purposes of equal protection is the same as state action for purposes of the First Amendment has never been decided. But the principle would seem clear that if sufficient state action is present, First Amendment rights must be respected. In *Farmer v. Moses* the principle was applied to the New York World's Fair, operated by a private

31. *Amalgamated Food Employees Union v. Logan Valley Plaza, Inc.*, 391 U.S. 308, 318, 319–320, 324–325 (1968). Justices Black, Harlan and White dissented.

32. 391 U.S. at 320, fn. 9. Decisions of State courts on the apartment house question, reaching various conclusions, are collected in *Political and Civil Rights in the United States*, pp. 552–553. See also *Hall v. Commonwealth*, 188 Va. 72, 49 S.E.2d 369 (1948), app. dis. 335 U.S. 875, 912 (1948). Likewise see *Martin v. Struthers*, 319 U.S. 141 (1943), discussed *infra*.

corporation in close alliance with New York City, and a constitutional right to picket on the Fair's grounds was recognized.[33]

The right to assemble, demonstrate, or canvass in quasi-public places is subject to varying limitations, just as is the exercise of these rights in public places. In fact these restrictions, especially with respect to such areas as apartment houses, might well be extensive. What is significant is that the fundamental constitutional right exists and is the point of departure for consideration of limiting principles.

3. OTHER ASPECTS OF THE BASIC RIGHTS

There are two other noteworthy aspects of the basic rights of assembly and petition. First, the Supreme Court has left it uncertain whether any form of tax, permit fee, or other financial charge can be imposed on exercise of the right of assembly and petition. In *Murdock v. Pennsylvania* and *Jones v. Opelika* the Court invalidated a license tax as applied to Jehovah's Witnesses engaged in door-to-door sales of religious literature. In *Follett v. McCormick* it extended this ruling to invalidate a tax on book agents as applied to a Jehovah's Witness who was a resident of the town making his living from sales of religious books. But in *Cox v. New Hampshire* the Court upheld a parade permit fee that ranged from a nominal sum to $300, depending on the size of the parade and the cost of policing it. Thus the Court would appear to exclude a "tax" but allow a "permit fee." [34]

There is no justification for allowing the government to exact payment of either a tax or a permit fee. In principle both constitute a charge on exercise of a constitutional right, a right chiefly utilized by the individuals and groups least able to bear any financial burden. The cases appear to suggest that a permit fee is justified if limited to an amount necessary to defray the costs of licensing and policing. But this

33. *Farmer v. Moses*, 232 F. Supp. 154 (S.D.N.Y. 1964). See also *Anderson v. Moses*, 185 F. Supp. 727 (S.D.N.Y. 1960), enforcing First Amendment rights against the Tavern-on-the-Green in New York City's Central Park. Other cases which involve in some sense the place issue, but seem more pertinent to questions of limitation, are discussed in Section C, *infra*.

34. *Murdock v. Pennsylvania*, 319 U.S. 105 (1943); *Jones v. Opelika*, 319 U.S. 103 (1943); *Follett v. McCormick*, 321 U.S. 573 (1944); *Cox v. New Hampshire*, 312 U.S. 569 (1941). See also *Busey v. District of Columbia*, 138 F.2d 592 (D.C. Cir. 1943) (fee of $1 per month for canvassing held invalid); *Chester Branch, N.A.A.C.P. v. City of Chester*, 253 F. Supp. 707 (E.D. Pa. 1966) (fee of $25 a day for use of sound truck held unreasonable). The tax cases are discussed in Chapter XII.

might run into enormous sums. Nor would such small amounts as could be collected without nullifying the constitutional right altogether be sufficient to aid the government financially. A fee system therefore serves no legitimate purpose. The right of assembly and petition should be granted in financial as well as in other terms to all citizens.

Second, the Supreme Court has consistently denied First Amendment protection to soliciting, canvassing, or similar conduct that is wholly "commercial" in nature. Thus in *Valentine v. Chrestensen* it upheld a municipal ordinance that prohibited the distribution of commercial handbills or advertising in the street or public places. Such activities fall within the system of commercial enterprise and are outside the system of freedom of expression.[35]

B. Maintaining the Public Peace

Exercise of the right to assemble and petition has generated most concern because of fears that it will lead to physical violence or disorder. Maintenance of the public peace, without destroying the mobility of the society, is a primary requisite of any social order. For the most part this condition must be achieved through laws and institutions that control action. Frequently, however, the community seeks to pursue its goal through restrictions on conduct in the form of expression. Controversies over the extent to which freedom of expression should be limited in the interests of maintaining the public peace have indeed marked the development of the right to assemble and petition from its beginnings.

Legal controls over assembly and petition take various forms, depending upon the point in time at which they are applied. Sometimes the government seeks to punish expression after it has taken place. In such case the sanction is normally a criminal prosecution under laws forbidding incitement to riot, unlawful assembly, breach of the peace, or disorderly conduct. Or the government may attempt to halt the expression while it is still in progress, as when a speaker is ordered to desist or a crowd to disperse. This is generally accomplished by police

35. *Valentine v. Chrestensen*, 316 U.S. 52 (1942). *Cf. Breard v. Alexandria*, 341 U.S. 622 (1951). The problem of excluding the "commercial sector" from the system of freedom of expression is discussed in Chapter XII.

action, such as an arrest or an order enforceable by statutes making it an offense to disobey a police officer. Very often the government seeks to prevent or limit the expression in advance, in order to forestall conduct that it fears may breach the public peace. Such regulation usually takes place through a permit or licensing system administered by executive officials, or through an injunction process commanded by a court.

With respect to each form of governmental control, the issues may arise in two contexts. The threat to public order may come from persons who support the communicator and his views. Or it may emanate from those who are hostile to him and oppose the views being expressed. The two situations are not always clearly distinct. They tend to merge when the speaker engages in provocative communication. Yet different considerations are involved in each and, for purposes of analysis, it is important to keep the distinction in mind.

The various legal devices for controlling the right of assembly and petition had their origins long prior to the adoption of the First Amendment. As with other aspects of free expression it is only in relatively recent times that the task of reconciling these forms of control with the First Amendment has been undertaken. The effort was further delayed by the fact that the controls are enacted and administered by State and local governments, and it was not until the third decade of this century, as we have seen, that the First Amendment was made applicable to the States. The State courts did consider similar questions under State constitutional provisions comparable to the First Amendment, but their decisions prior to the expansion of First Amendment doctrine are of slight significance today. In any event the States must now, of course, conform to the requirements of the Federal Constitution. It is therefore the decisions of the Supreme Court to which we must turn for an understanding of the way in which the basic law on this subject has developed.

1. THE COURSE OF SUPREME COURT DECISION

The first cases to reach the Supreme Court, in the late nineteen-thirties and early nineteen-forties, involved two groups that relied particularly upon public assembly and canvassing to convey their message —labor unions and Jehovah's Witnesses. In *Hague v. C.I.O.* the Court dealt with the possibility of violence arising from union organizational activities. Among the devices employed by Jersey City officials to exclude the C.I.O. from their city was an ordinance that authorized the Director of Safety to refuse a permit for a public meeting when in his opinion such a refusal would prevent "riots, disturbances or disorderly assemblage." The prevailing opinion of Justice Roberts held this ordinance invalid on its face: "It can thus, as the record discloses, be made the instrument of arbitrary suppression of free expression of views on national affairs, for the prohibition of all speaking will undoubtedly 'prevent' such eventualities. But uncontrolled official suppression of the privilege cannot be made a substitute for the duty to maintain order in connection with the exercise of the right." [36]

The more difficult problem of formulating rules to govern the use of expression that might lead to a breach of the peace in the streets came before the Court in two Jehovah's Witnesses cases. In *Cantwell v. Connecticut* a member of the Jehovah's Witnesses stopped two men on the street in New Haven in a Catholic neighborhood and, with their permission, played a phonograph record called "Enemies," which militantly attacked the Catholic religion and church. The two men, who were Catholics, "were incensed by the contents of the record and were tempted to strike Cantwell unless he went away." Cantwell left, but was arrested and convicted of the common law crime of inciting a breach of the peace. The Supreme Court unanimously set aside the conviction. Justice Roberts, again writing for the Court, first observed that the "[d]ecision as to lawfulness of the conviction demands the weighing of two conflicting interests." He then went on to say:

> The offense known as breach of the peace embraces a great variety of conduct destroying or menacing public order and tranquility. It includes not only violent acts but acts and words likely to produce violence in others. No one would have the hardihood to suggest that the principle of freedom of speech sanctions incitement to riot or that religious liberty connotes the privilege to exhort others to physical attack upon those belonging to another sect. When clear and present danger of riot, disorder, interference with traffic upon the public streets, or other immediate threat to public safety, peace, or order, appears, the power of the State to prevent or punish is obvious. Equally obvious is it that a State may not unduly suppress free communication of views, religious or other, under the guise of conserving desirable conditions.

36. *Hague v. C.I.O.*, 307 U.S. 496, 516 (1939), discussed in the preceding section. Justice Roberts spoke for only three members of the Court but Justices Stone and Reed, who concurred in the result, did not express any disagreement with Justice Roberts on this issue.

Here we have a situation analogous to a conviction under a statute sweeping in a great variety of conduct under a general and indefinite characterization, and leaving to the executive and judicial branches too wide a discretion in its application.[37]

Justice Roberts concluded that, although the phonograph record "not unnaturally aroused animosity," in the absence "of a statute narrowly drawn to define and punish specific conduct as constituting a clear and present danger to a substantial interest of the State," Cantwell's communication "raised no such clear and present menace to public peace and order as to render him liable to conviction of the common law offense in question." [38]

Justice Roberts' opinion contains a mixture of a balancing test, an incitement test, a clear and present danger test, and a test of overbreadth, but the clear and present danger element seems to predominate. The Court made another effort to state some of the guiding principles shortly afterwards in *Chaplinsky v. New Hampshire*. Chaplinsky, another Jehovah's Witness, was distributing literature on the streets of Rochester, New Hampshire, and encountered opposition from his listeners. After "a disturbance occurred" Chaplinsky was taken into custody. While on the way to the police station he met the City Marshal and said to him: "You are a God damned racketeer" and "a damned Fascist and the whole government of Rochester are Fascists or agents of Fascists." Chaplinsky was convicted under a statute which made it an offense to address "any offensive, derisive or annoying word to any other person who is lawfully in any street or other public place." This time the Supreme Court unanimously affirmed. Justice Murphy's opinion for the Court held that the statute was not too vague or indefinite and, in words that were to be repeated many times in later years, laid down the applicable doctrine:

Allowing the broadest scope to the language and purpose of the Fourteenth Amendment, it is well understood that the right of free speech is not absolute at all times and under all circumstances. There are certain well-defined and narrowly limited classes of speech, the prevention and punishment of which have never been thought to raise any Constitutional problem. These include the lewd and obscene, the profane, the libelous, and the insulting or "fighting" words—those which by their very utterance inflict injury or tend to incite an immediate breach of the peace. It has been well observed that such utter-

37. *Cantwell v. Connecticut,* 310 U.S.   38. 310 U.S. at 311.
296, 307, 308 (1940).

ances are no essential part of any exposition of ideas, and are of such slight social value as a step to truth that any benefit that may be derived from them is clearly outweighed by the social interest in order and morality.[39]

In between the Jehovah's Witnesses cases the Supreme Court decided the *Meadowmoor Dairies* case, involving labor union activities. The case arose out of a dispute between the Milk Wagon Drivers Union and certain dairies in the Chicago area. The Union represented employees of dairies that distributed milk by door-to-door methods. The dairies involved in the dispute distributed their milk through "vendors" who operated their own trucks and sold to "cut rate" stores. The Union was attempting to persuade these dairies to adhere to union working standards. To this end it began to picket retail stores which handled the products of dairies using the vendor system. The picketing was peaceful but the dispute engendered considerable violence directed against the dairies, vendors and stores. The Illinois courts had upheld an injunction against the Union that prohibited not only the acts of violence but also the peaceful picketing. In a six to three decision the Supreme Court sustained the Illinois courts. Justice Frankfurter, writing for the majority, reaffirmed the doctrine of *Thornhill v. Alabama* that peaceful picketing to publicize the facts of a labor dispute was protected under the First Amendment. Nevertheless he held that "a state can choose to authorize its courts to enjoin acts of picketing in themselves peaceful when they are enmeshed with contemporaneously violent conduct which is concededly outlawed." More specifically he ruled:

> No one will doubt that Illinois can protect its storekeepers from being coerced by fear of window-smashings or burnings or bombings. And acts which in isolation are peaceful may be part of a coercive thrust when entangled with acts of violence. The picketing in this case was set in a background of violence. In such a setting it could justifiably be concluded that the momentum of fear generated by past violence would survive even though future picketing might be wholly peaceful.[40]

Justice Black, with whom Justice Douglas joined, dissented. "There was no evidence," he found, "to connect [the pickets] with any kind or type of violence at any time or place." Nor did he find any evidence that the "dissemination of information by pickets stimulated

---

39. *Chaplinsky v. New Hampshire*, 315 U.S. 568, 571–572 (1942).
40. *Milk Wagon Drivers Local 753 v. Meadowmoor Dairies, Inc.*, 312 U.S. 287, 292, 294 (1941).

anyone else to commit any act of violence." Hence "it is going a long way to say that because of the acts of these few men [who were responsible for the violence] six thousand other members of their Union can be denied the right to express their opinion." [41]

Justice Reed, also dissenting, pressed the issues further. "If the fear engendered by past misconduct coerces storekeepers during peaceful picketing," he said, "the remedy lies in the maintenance of order, not in denial of free speech." As to the outer limits of this principle he declared:

> This nation relies upon public discussion as one of the indispensable means to attain correct solutions of problems of social welfare. Curtailment of free speech limits this open discussion. Our whole history teaches that adjustment of social relations through reason is possible while free speech is maintained. This Court has the solemn duty of determining when acts of legislation or decrees of courts infringe that right guaranteed to all citizens. Free speech may be absolutely prohibited only under the most pressing national emergencies. Those emergencies must be of the kind that justify the suspension of the writ of habeas corpus or the suppression of the right of trial by jury. [42]

The next series of cases arose out of the political crosscurrents of the post–World War II era. In the first of these, *Terminiello v. Chicago,* the issues were sharply presented but carefully avoided. Terminiello, a suspended Catholic priest, delivered an address at a meeting sponsored by the Christian Veterans of America in Chicago. The speech was a flamboyant attack upon "Communistic Zionistic Jews," Negroes, the Roosevelt Administration, and others. It was couched in general terms, however, and did not urge any specific action. A crowd of eight hundred filled the auditorium to capacity and a hostile crowd of a thousand or more gathered outside to protest the meeting. According to Justice Douglas, who described the situation in a low key, the police inside "were not able to prevent several disturbances" and the "crowd outside was angry and turbulent." According to the more vivid description of Justice Jackson, the police were "dealing with a riot and with a speech that provoked a hostile mob and incited a friendly one, and threatened violence between the two." Terminiello was found guilty of disorderly conduct. The Supreme Court, in a five to four decision, reversed on a point that had not previously been raised. Without reaching the basic issues, the Court found error in the trial court's charge to the jury that "breach of the peace" can be com-

41. 312 U.S. at 313, 314, 316.   42. 312 U.S. at 319–320.

mitted by speech that "stirs the public to anger, invites dispute, brings about a condition of unrest, or creates a disturbance." In a passage that became the foundation stone of opinions upholding First Amendment rights in public assembly cases, Justice Douglas said:

> [A] function of free speech under our system of government is to invite dispute. It may indeed best serve its high purpose when it induces a condition of unrest, creates dissatisfaction with conditions as they are, or even stirs people to anger. Speech is often provocative and challenging. It may strike at prejudices and preconceptions and have profound unsettling effects as it presses for acceptance of an idea. That is why freedom of speech, though not absolute, *Chaplinsky v. New Hampshire,* . . . is nevertheless protected against censorship or punishment, unless shown likely to produce a clear and present danger of a serious substantive evil that rises far above public inconvenience, annoyance, or unrest. . . . There is no room under our Constitution for a more restrictive view. For the alternative would lead to standardization of ideas either by legislatures, courts, or dominant political or community groups.[43]

Chief Justice Vinson dissented on the ground that Terminiello's speech constituted "fighting words." Justice Jackson, joined by Justices Frankfurter and Burton, would have upheld the conviction for the reason that the speech created a clear and present danger of "rioting and violence." In a long and eloquent opinion Justice Jackson pointed to the rise of Hitler in Germany and warned against discrediting and paralyzing the authority of local governments to maintain democratic procedures in the face of "rival totalitarian groups" engaged in a "battle for the streets." He ended his opinion by saying:

> The Court has gone far toward accepting the doctrine that civil liberty means the removal of all restraints from these crowds and that all local attempts to maintain order are impairments of the liberty of the citizen. The choice is not between order and liberty. It is between liberty with order and anarchy without either. There is danger that, if the Court does not temper its doctrinaire logic with a little practical wisdom, it will convert the constitutional Bill of Rights into a suicide pact.[44]

The Court moved closer to the Jackson position in the next case, *Feiner v. New York*. This case arose out of an open-air meeting held on a street corner in Syracuse in March 1949. As usual, the facts were viewed differently by different members of the Court. As summarized

---

43. *Terminiello v. Chicago*, 337 U.S.   44. 337 U.S. at 25, 37.
1, 3, 13, 4–5 (1949).

by Chief Justice Vinson in the majority opinion, however, they were in essence as follows: Feiner was addressing a crowd of seventy-five to eighty people, both white and Negro, urging them to attend a meeting to be held that night sponsored by the Young Progressives of America, an affiliate of Henry Wallace's Progressive Party. In the course of his speech Feiner made "derogatory remarks" about President Truman, the American Legion, the Mayor of Syracuse, and other local political figures. "He gave the impression that he was endeavoring to arouse the Negro people against the whites, urging that they rise up in arms and fight for equal rights." These statements "stirred up a little excitement." Some of the onlookers complained to the police and one threatened violence if the police did not act. Others favored the speaker. "Because of the feeling that existed in the crowd both for and against the speaker, the [police] finally 'stepped in to prevent it from resulting in a fight.' " The police several times asked Feiner to cease talking and, when he kept on, arrested him. Feiner was convicted of disorderly conduct. The Supreme Court affirmed, by a vote of six to three.[45]

Chief Justice Vinson's opinion was brief and somewhat imprecise. In substance it held that the New York courts had reached the conclusion that the police officers were justified in taking action to prevent a breach of the peace and there was nothing in the record to compel the Supreme Court to reverse this conclusion. Chief Justice Vinson quoted the passage from the *Cantwell* case embodying the clear and present danger test but did not elaborate further on that doctrine. He summed up his position in the final paragraph as follows:

> We are well aware that the ordinary murmurings and objections of a hostile audience cannot be allowed to silence a speaker, and are also mindful of the possible danger of giving overzealous police officials complete discretion to break up otherwise lawful public meetings. . . . But we are not faced here with such a situation. It is one thing to say that the police cannot be used as an instrument for the suppression of unpopular views, and another to say that, when as here the speaker passes the bounds of argument or persuasion and undertakes incitement to riot, they are powerless to prevent a breach of the peace. Nor in this case can we condemn the considered judgment of three New York courts approving the means which the police, faced with a crisis, used in the exercise of their power and duty to preserve peace and order. The findings of the state courts as to the existing situation and the imminence of greater disorder coupled with petitioner's deliberate

45. *Feiner v. New York,* 340 U.S.
315, 317 (1951).

defiance of the police officers convince us that we should not reverse this conviction in the name of free speech.[46]

Justice Black, dissenting, felt that the majority had failed to follow the rule that "despite findings below, we will examine the evidence for ourselves to ascertain whether federally protected rights have been denied"; as a result, "because the trial judge fully accepted the testimony of the prosecution witnesses on all important points," "we must blind ourselves" to the actual facts. As he viewed the evidence, "it seems far-fetched to suggest that the 'facts' show any imminent threat of riot or uncontrollable disorder." Moreover, he rejected "the implications of the Court's opinion that the police had no obligation to protect petitioner's constitutional right to talk"; "if, in the name of preserving order, they ever can interfere with a lawful public speaker, they first must make all reasonable efforts to protect him." In addition, it was the policeman's duty, "at least where time allows," to explain to the speaker the reason for his order. Justice Black's conclusion was: "The end result of the affirmance here is to approve a simple and readily available technique by which cities and states can with impunity subject all speeches, political or otherwise, on streets or elsewhere, to the supervision and censorship of the local police." Justice Douglas, with whom Justice Minton agreed, also dissented, stressing the failure of police protection.[47]

In two cases decided the same day as *Feiner,* the Supreme Court dealt with the permit system. In one of these, *Kunz v. New York,* a permit had been refused to a religious speaker because on previous occasions his meetings, in which he militantly attacked Catholics and Jews, had created disturbances. The Court's primary holding was that the permit system was invalid because it lacked appropriate standards. But Chief Justice Vinson's opinion touched peripherally and inconclusively on the issue whether a permit can be withheld because of past violence:

> The court below mistakenly derived support for its conclusion from the evidence produced at the trial that appellant's religious meetings had, in the past, caused some disorder. There are appropriate public remedies to protect the peace and order of the community if appellant's speeches should result in disorder or violence. . . . We do not express any opinion on the propriety of punitive remedies which the New York

46. 340 U.S. at 320–321.
47. 340 U.S. at 322, 323, 325, 326, 327.

authorities may utilize. We are here concerned with suppression—not punishment.[48]

The most recent decisions of the Supreme Court on public assemblies and the public peace have grown out of the civil-rights movement. In *Edwards v. South Carolina*, decided in 1963, a group of 187 Negro high school and college students conducted a demonstration on the State House grounds in Columbia, South Carolina. They walked single file or two abreast in an orderly manner carrying signs protesting segregation. A crowd of two hundred to three hundred onlookers collected nearby. There was no evidence of "any threatening remarks, hostile gestures, or offensive language," though one witness testified that some members of the crowd were "possible trouble makers." After the demonstration had gone on for thirty to forty-five minutes, the police told the students that they would be arrested if they did not disperse within fifteen minutes. Instead of dispersing the demonstrators sang patriotic and religious songs, "while stamping their feet and clapping their hands," and one member of the group delivered a "religious harangue." At the end of fifteen minutes the demonstrators were arrested. Their conviction of the common law crime of breach of the peace was set aside by the Supreme Court, Justice Clark alone dissenting.[49]

Justice Stewart, writing for the Court, found there was no violence or threat of violence, and police protection was "ample." The case was therefore a "far cry" from *Feiner*. The demonstrators were convicted, he said, not under a narrowly drawn statute regulating specific conduct but for "an offense so generalized" as to be "not susceptible of exact definition." Moreover, they were "convicted upon evidence which showed no more than that the opinions which they were peaceably expressing were sufficiently opposed to the views of the majority of the community to attract a crowd and necessitate police protection." Quoting *Terminiello*, he concluded that the South Carolina courts had punished them for having only "stirred people to anger, invited dispute, or brought about a condition of unrest."[50]

Justice Clark in dissent painted a different picture: "Here 200 youthful Negro demonstrators were being aroused to 'fever pitch' be-

48. *Kunz v. New York,* 340 U.S. 290, 294–295 (1951). Justice Jackson interpreted the majority opinion to mean that "language such as [that used by Kunz], in the environment of the street meeting, is immune from prior municipal control."

340 U.S. at 298. The other decision was *Niemotko v. Maryland,* 340 U.S. 268 (1951).

49. *Edwards v. South Carolina,* 372 U.S. 229 (1963).

50. 372 U.S. at 236, 237, 238.

fore a crowd of some 300 people who undoubtedly were hostile . . . It is my belief that anyone conversant with the almost spontaneous combustion in some Southern communities in such a situation will agree that the [police] action may well have averted a major catastrophe." Under such circumstances, "to say that the police may not intervene until the riot has occurred is like keeping out the doctor until the patient dies." [51]

A more difficult problem confronted the Court in *Cox v. Louisiana.* Here some two thousand students gathered in downtown Baton Rouge to protest the arrest of a group of their fellows the day before for picketing stores that maintained segregated lunch counters. Despite objections from the police, the students walked two or three abreast several blocks to the courthouse where the arrested students were being held in jail. With the agreement of the police they assembled on the sidewalk across the street from the courthouse, "about five feet deep and spread almost the entire length of the block." A small crowd of one hundred to three hundred "curious white people" gathered on the opposite sidewalk and on the courthouse steps, about a hundred feet away. Some seventy-five to eighty policemen were stationed in the street between the two groups. The demonstrators sang songs, pledged allegiance to the flag, and prayed. The students in their jail cells in the courthouse building, out of sight, joined in the singing. Then Cox, who was the leader of the demonstration, made a speech. At the end of the speech, he told his audience it was lunch time and suggested that they go eat at twelve stores that had segregated lunch counters. At this point the Sheriff, considering the appeal for a sit-in at the lunch counters "inflammatory," ordered the students to break up the demonstration. When they did not do so the police fired several tear gas shells and the crowd dispersed. No demonstrators were arrested at the time but the next day Cox was taken into custody and charged with breach of the peace. His conviction was set aside by the Supreme Court.[52]

Justice Goldberg, writing for the majority, considered the facts of the case "strikingly similar to those present in *Edwards v. South Carolina,*" and held that the State had "infringed appellant's rights of free speech and free assembly" by convicting him under the breach of the

51. 372 U.S. at 244. In the following term the Supreme Court reversed per curiam two other cases where breach of the peace convictions had been obtained in South Carolina under similar circumstances. *Fields v. South Carolina,* 375 U.S. 44 (1963); *Henry v. City of Rock Hill,* 376 U.S. 776 (1964).

52. *Cox v. Louisiana,* 379 U.S. 536 (1965).

peace statute. Brushing aside the call for a sit-in, Justice Goldberg declared that "this part of Cox's speech obviously did not deprive the demonstration of its protected character under the Constitution as free speech and assembly." Reviewing the evidence, including a film of the events, he concluded that the demonstration was "orderly and not riotous." As to the contention of the State that the police feared that "violence was about to erupt," his review of the record convinced him that the police "could have handled the crowd." [53]

Justice Goldberg also put the decision on another ground. The Louisiana breach of the peace statute defined the offense as applying to a person who "with intent to provoke a breach of the peace, or under circumstances such that a breach of the peace may be occasioned thereby . . . congregates with others." The Louisiana Supreme Court had interpreted the term "breach of the peace" as meaning "to agitate, to arouse from a state of repose, to molest, to interrupt, to hinder, to disquiet." The statute as thus interpreted, Justice Goldberg ruled, was subject to the same objection as the judge's charge in *Terminiello:* "it sweeps within its broad scope activities that are constitutionally protected free speech and assembly." [54]

Justice White, with whom Justice Harlan agreed, concurred on the ground that the case was governed by *Edwards v. South Carolina.* Justice Black concurred, but only because he considered the Louisiana statute, on its face and as construed by the Louisiana court, unconstitutionally vague; he viewed *Edwards* as holding no more than this. Justice Clark thought the statute no more vague than the New York law involved in *Feiner,* but concurred because it exempted labor unions and therefore violated equal protection.

During the 1968–1969 Term the Court had two opportunities to clarify its position but chose to avoid the issue. In *Carroll v. President and Commissioners of Princess Anne* a white supremacist organization, the National States Rights Party, had held a rally in Princess Anne, Maryland, that was "aggressively and militantly racist." The speakers had "engaged in deliberately derogatory, insulting, and threatening language, scarcely disguised by protestations of peaceful purposes." A crowd had gathered, including many Negroes, but no disturbance occurred. When the group scheduled another meeting for the following evening the authorities obtained an injunction, *ex parte,* restraining them from holding any meeting "which will tend to disturb

---

53. 379 U.S. at 544–545, 546, 547, 550.   54. 379 U.S. at 551, 552.

and endanger the citizens of the County." The Supreme Court, in an opinion by Justice Fortas, found it unnecessary to "decide the thorny problem of whether, on the facts of this case, an injunction against the announced rally could be justified." It set aside the injunction on the ground that it had been issued *ex parte,* without any effort to give notice to those enjoined, and hence did not meet the strict procedural requirements essential in cases of prior restraint. Justices Black and Douglas concurred.[55]

The other case, *Gregory v. City of Chicago,* also involved violence feared from a hostile opposition. Dick Gregory had led a group of demonstrators, protesting failure to eliminate segregation in the public schools, from downtown Chicago to Mayor Daley's home. There they proceeded to march around the block. A hostile crowd gathered, which began to get unruly. Rocks and eggs were thrown at the marchers. Fearing a riot the police ordered the demonstrators to leave and, when they refused, arrested them for disorderly conduct. The Supreme Court unanimously reversed. Chief Justice Warren, joined by four colleagues, thought it was "a simple case" and disposed of it summarily. He put the decision on the narrow ground that the demonstrators had not been disorderly and therefore could not have violated the disorderly conduct statute under which they were convicted. In addition he held, as in *Terminiello,* that the judge's charge to the jury was too broad. The other members of the Court concurred for similar reasons, Justice Black stressing that the statute was vague and overbroad. Thus none of the Justices dealt with the crucial issue of whether the demonstrators were justified in disobeying the police order to disperse.[56]

Reviewing this course of development in the Supreme Court decisions dealing with the problem of maintaining the public peace, one is struck by the fact that the doctrinal basis for the Supreme Court's position remains curiously obscure. The primary principle to be applied—the rule for determining at what point the First Amendment permits speech to be cut off when it may lead to violence or disorder—has never been made precise. The balancing test, tentatively suggested by

55. *Carroll v. President and Commissioners of Princess Anne,* 393 U.S. 175, 176, 177, 180 (1968). The Court was following *Freedman v. Maryland,* 380 U.S. 51 (1965), discussed in Chapter XIII.

56. *Gregory v. City of Chicago,* 394 U.S. 111 (1969). See also *Turner v. New York,* 386 U.S. 773 (1967). In *Watts v.*

United States, 394 U.S. 705 (1969), the Court held, per curiam, that the statement made by a young man about to be drafted, "If they ever make me carry a rifle the first man I want to get in my sights is L.B.J.," did not constitute a "threat" to the President within the meaning of 18 U.S.C. §871(a).

Justice Roberts in *Cantwell,* has plainly been abandoned. There is frequent reference to an incitement test, and sometimes to a clear and present danger test. Yet neither has been formally accepted as the guiding principle. The "fighting words" doctrine, originally applied in *Chaplinsky,* still retains some force, but, being relevant only in special situations, remains only a supplementary test. The Court relies heavily upon doctrines of vagueness and undue breadth, and in permit cases upon the rule that overmuch discretion cannot be delegated to administrative officials. These principles, however, are by nature secondary; presumably intelligent draftsmen can at some point overcome them. The rules for determining how much discretion will be allowed the police in deciding when to cut off expression fall into a blurred area between *Feiner* on the one hand and *Edwards* and *Cox* on the other. The theory for separating expression and action can hardly be considered settled by the divided decision in *Meadowmoor.*

The balancing test has never been utilized as a basis for determining when the government may curtail speech that seems to threaten the public peace. It is far too crude an instrument to serve this purpose. The test would ask whether the social interest in avoiding violence and disorder outweighs the social interest in allowing freedom of expression, but applied in general terms it supplies no satisfactory answer. If the interest in maintaining the public peace is deemed to outweigh the interest in freedom of speech, then speech would always be sacrificed and no system of free expression could exist. If the balance were struck the other way, and freedom of expression preferred, then the Court would be adopting a full protection theory; but the test would give no answer to such crucial questions as defining expression or separating expression from action, and therefore would supply no rational basis for making an "absolute" system work. Nor is there any sound way to employ the balancing test on a more particularistic basis. For this would immediately plunge the Court into the forbidden role of evaluating the content of particular speech.

The "incitement" test, suggested in *Cantwell* and *Feiner,* seems to come closer to providing a more relevant and refined tool. But its weakness lies in the fact that the word "incite" does not furnish a rational frame of reference within which to make a decision. It supplies a vague word, hence an arbitrary formula, not a method of approaching the problem in light of the critical underlying considerations that must be brought to bear upon its solution.

The Court has placed some reliance upon the clear and present danger test. In *Cantwell* and *Terminiello* that test figured prominently in the Court's thinking. It was mentioned, but not expressly adopted, in *Feiner*. But it played no part in *Edwards* and *Cox*. Why has the Court been so diffident about the clear and present danger test in this situation?

In some ways the clear and present danger test seems to offer a workable solution to the problem of determining the limits of expression that may end in violence. The "substantive evil" feared—breach of the public peace—is sufficiently grave so that the courts customarily strike a balance (usually not explicit) in favor of preserving the peace and against speech. Under such circumstances it is important to have a formula that allows speech to be cut off only at the last possible point. The clear and present danger test tends to perform this function. The term "clear" embodies the idea that the proof of danger must be strong, not speculative; that the danger must be a specific, not a generalized, one; and that there is some presumption in favor of speech and against restriction. The term "present" means immediate, imminent, not remote; the rationale is, not only that the requirement of immediacy of danger arbitrarily protects more speech, but that the more remote the danger the more uncertainty there is about its occurrence and therefore the less justification there is for suppression of the speech. As to "danger," the word has emotional overtones not associated with a weaker word, such as "threat" or "likelihood"; this emotional content works toward greater protection of speech. Thus the formula does tend to focus consideration on important issues.

Nevertheless, the clear and present danger test has numerous deficiencies, many of which have already been pointed out. As applied to the public assembly problem its main disadvantages are these:

(1) The clear and present danger test seeks to ascertain and weigh the degree of the danger. In any communication of this sort there is always likely to be some danger. Whether it is sufficiently clear and present is a wide-open question, depending upon the speculative judgment of a court or jury, which cannot possibly be predicted by the speaker. The variance in the facts as perceived by different justices in the cases just described highlights the difficulty.

(2) The test's inevitable vagueness takes on additional significance when the test is used as a guide for police officers in stopping a meeting or breaking up a demonstration.

(3) The clear and present danger test is totally unsuitable if the threat of violence or disorder comes from persons opposed to the

speaker or demonstrators rather than from the speaker or his supporters. To cut off expression when a hostile group creates a clear and present danger of disorder is to entrust enjoyment of constitutional rights to the opposition, and indeed to encourage violence and disorder in public assemblies. This is not a minor problem. Our experience has been that the likelihood of disorder arises far more frequently from the activities of a hostile opposition than from the conduct of the speaker and his followers. Indeed, of the Supreme Court decisions surveyed above, in all except *Meadowmoor* the threat of violence emanated from the opposition. This undoubtedly is the main reason why the Supreme Court, while it has toyed with the clear and present danger test, has never in this situation embraced it wholeheartedly.

(4) The clear and present danger test is also most unsatisfactory as a standard to be utilized as the basis for granting or denying a permit. The test is vague enough when invoked in the context of an actual assembly. It becomes hopelessly speculative when applied to an assembly that has not yet taken place. In the hands of administrative officials empowered to deny a permit, the test would afford very little protection to the First Amendment right.

The "fighting words" doctrine, enunciated in *Chaplinsky,* seems to have survived very much in its original form. The concept, as pointed out later, is not without value. But the scope of the principle has never been clarified by the Supreme Court. As a matter of fact the *Chaplinsky* case itself reveals considerable confusion over its function and use. To say that "fighting words" are "no essential part of any exposition of ideas" is by no means true. To say that they are of "slight social value as a step to truth" is to inject the Court into value judgments concerned with the content of expression, a role foreclosed to it by the basic theory of the First Amendment. The Court may be on sounder ground in arguing that such words "tend to incite an immediate breach of the peace." But, if so, the *Chaplinsky* decision itself is wide of the mark. For in that case the words were addressed to a police officer, and his obligation is to prevent, not create, a breach of the peace. The "fighting words" doctrine thus requires further clarification.

It should not come as any surprise that the Court has utilized extensively the doctrines of vagueness, overbreadth, and excessive delegation. The common law, statutory and institutional system of controls developed by state and local governments to protect the public peace, arose from an ancient lineage not connected with First Amendment theory. The process of adjusting that system to the requirements of the

First Amendment has naturally been a prolonged one. In any event, the insistence by the Supreme Court that the controls be specifically, narrowly and carefully drawn is of crucial importance to the system of freedom of expression. This will always remain true. It should be noted, however, that the practical effect of the Court's attention to these doctrines, appropriate as they may be, has been to postpone development of more basic constitutional principles.[57]

The Supreme Court seems to be aware, by and large, of the difficult problems of judicial administration that arise when the government seeks to cut off the right of assembly and petition in the interests of the public peace. Perhaps nowhere else in the system of freedom of expression do police officers and local officials play such a direct and crucial role. The decision as to whether communication is to be curtailed or stopped while it is in progress, and the decision as to whether and how it is to be allowed under a permit system, is made initially by these officials. As a practical matter, the initial decision frequently is also the final one. Effective supervision by the courts of these decisions calls not only for substantive principles of law that are as precise as possible, but also for workable rules of judicial review. In *Feiner* the majority seemed willing to afford only a sparse scope of review; in effect it was ready to accept the police judgment as to the need for intervention. Justice Black was rightly disturbed that under such an approach the vital principles of the First Amendment could become only token guarantees. But the Court, in this area as in others, has gradually increased its willingness to make an independent judgment on the record. This trend was plainly reflected in *Edwards* and *Cox*. The Court has not, however, attempted to formulate specific rules on the subject. Its position rests more upon attitude than upon articulated principles.

Finally, the Supreme Court has touched only lightly upon the important problem of separating expression from action in the context of disturbance of the public peace. In *Meadowmoor* a majority of the Court refused to make the separation under circumstances in which it would have seemed imperative to do so. It is doubtful that the problem would be handled in the same manner today.

Generally speaking, the effect of the Supreme Court decisions in this area has been to support the system of freedom of expression. But many issues remain open and many of the principles undeveloped. The

---

57. The problems of vagueness, overbreadth and excessive delegation are discussed in greater detail later in this chapter.

lower Federal courts and the State courts have been left without guidance, and have tended to flounder.

2. APPLICATION OF THE EXPRESSION-ACTION THEORY

The full protection theory of the First Amendment meets one of its severest tests when it is applied to expression uttered in the context of a public assembly which may lead to violence or disorder. Many people instinctively feel that society must draw the line at "incitement to violence" or a "clear and present danger of violence." The inadequacies of those tests, however, make it imperative to explore the exact manner in which the expression-action test would operate.

a. The Basic Rules   First, let us review the main lines of division between conduct classified as expression and conduct classified as action, in connection with exercise of the right to assemble or petition. All ordinary verbal conduct, such as speech, singing and signs, and nonverbal conduct associated with assembly and petition, such as gathering on the street, marching and picketing, are plainly "expression." On the other hand, verbal conduct such as shouted commands to a mob engaged in acts of violence, or nonverbal conduct such as actual violence or preparation for violence clearly fall within the category of "action." We are concerned here with some of the intermediate conduct not so readily classified.

Starting from the "expression" end of the spectrum, academic or philosophic discussion, or sheer exposition not involving any element of urging, though concerned with the use of violence, would fit within all ordinary concepts of "expression." Communication referring to acts of violence in the past, as a matter of history, would also be generally accepted as "expression." Prediction or warning of violence in future contingencies, or justification of the use of violence under designated circumstances, comes closer to the line. Yet as long as such utterances are general in character and relate to the future they would, in our view, remain within the area of "expression." So also would the urging of force in future contingencies, as in the case of self-defense in event of subsequent attack, so long as it is general and refers to future events. On the other hand, the urging of immediate, specific acts of violence would, under circumstances where violence was possible and likely, fall within the category of "action." Such communication would be so interlocked with violent conduct as to constitute for all practical purposes part of the action; it would be in effect the beginning of the action itself. In short the basic effort would be to formulate the definition of "expression" in terms of the difference between ideational preparation for subsequent conduct and actual participation in it.

To carry the analysis beyond this point it becomes necessary to consider some concrete instances in more detail. The distinction lies not so much in the literal content of the communication as in its context; the question is whether functionally the conduct amounts to a command, an instruction or some other form of action. None of the Supreme Court cases surveyed above presented this basic issue of when the communication itself, apart from hostile opposition to it, moves from expression to action. Equally significant, very few decisions from the State or lower Federal courts deal with this matter. Apparently, the government has usually found it sufficient to punish the action that followed after the communication, if any did, rather than attempt to punish the communication itself. Despite the paucity of cases, however, it is possible to find enough examples to throw some further light on where the line between "expression" and "action" would be drawn.[58]

The clearest cases in which communication is not protected under any theory of the First Amendment are those involving utterances that are plainly part of a single course of action. Thus in *State v. Schleifer* the defendant was charged with solicitation to commit crimes "by oral address, in language in substance as follows":

> You will never win the strike with soft methods. You young men ought to go out on the bridge. Don't use eggs; use coal or indelible ink. Break foremens' windows at their homes. Watch the scabs when they come from work, lay for them, especially on pay day. Take them in a dark alley and hit them with a lead pipe. That is the softest thing you can use. Reimburse yourselves for what we have sacrificed for five months. Don't forget to bump off a few now and then, so Mr. Pearson will know that you are not getting cold feet. You car men know how to take a brake shoe off. Take the brake shoe and put it under something that

58. There is one possible exception to the Supreme Court's silence. In *Cox v. Louisiana* Cox urged his listeners to engage in a sit-in. The Court ruled that this communication was protected ex-pression. 379 U.S. at 546. The issue is not clear-cut, however, for the sit-in might not have been unlawful. See also *Watts v. United States, supra* note 56.

will put the cars off the irons. A little sand or emery in the journal boxes will help greatly . . . Don't forget to tie them up with derailments. You boys ought to cut them all up.[59]

There was no allegation that any further illegal action had taken place. The decision did not deal with any constitutional issue of freedom of speech. In terms of First Amendment doctrine, however, one would readily conclude that verbal communication of this nature, in the context of the strike, constituted "action" rather than "expression."

Similar types of speech have been at issue in other cases. Thus in *State v. Quinlan* the defendant was indicted for violation of a statute making it a misdemeanor for any person "by speech, writing, printing or by any other mode or means" to "advocate, encourage, justify, praise or incite the unlawful burning, destruction of public or private property . . . or the killing or injuring of any class or body of persons." The specific violation alleged was that the defendant had said, at a meeting of strikers from the Paterson silk mills, "I make a motion that we go to the silk mills, parade through the streets, and club them out of the mills; no matter how we get them out, we got to get them out." At the trial it was proved that the strikers had in fact entered a mill and "behaved in a riotous manner." The appellate court held this evidence relevant but unnecessary to the conviction. An objection based upon the State constitutional provision guaranteeing freedom of speech was made but abandoned, and the court did not consider that issue. But the treatment of the communication as part of a course of action, whether or not it came to fruition, would seem entirely justified.[60]

The breaking point between "expression" and "action" may be clarified by two instances in which the communication, under the rules here urged, would fall into the category of "expression." In *People v. Most* the defendant, an anarchist, was indicted under a New York statute against unlawful assembly. The charge was based on defendant's speech at a meeting, held in a hall in the rear of a saloon in New York City, on the day after the hanging of the Haymarket anarchists in Chicago. The meeting was attended by eighty to one hundred persons, mostly fellow anarchists. After denunciation of the police for having prevented the meeting scheduled for another hall, Most "went on to

59. *State v. Schleifer*, 99 Conn. 432, 434, 121 A. 805 (1923).

60. *State v. Quinlan*, 86 N.J.L. 120, 91 A. 111 (1914). For a similar situation, see *Commonwealth v. Merrick*, 65 Pa. Super. 482 (1917). See also *Bullock v. U.S.*, 265 F.2d 683 (6th Cir. 1959), cert. denied 360 U.S. 909 (1959); *Brewer v. Hoxie School District*, 238 F.2d 91 (8th Cir. 1956).

extol the bravery of their brethren who had died on the gallows at Chicago," attacked the fairness of their trial, and continued:

> If I had known the executioner who murdered, who strangled our brothers, I would never rest until he had shared their fate.
>
> The day of revolution will soon come. First of all will be Grinnell; then comes Judge Gary; then the Supreme Court of Illinois; then the highest murderers of the land, the Supreme Court of the United States. The most cowardly of all Oglesby, the governor of Illinois. He must not think because he pardoned two of our brethren to a lingering death of life imprisonment, he will be spared.
>
> I again urge you to arm yourself, as the day of revolution is not far off; and when it comes, see that you are ready to resist and kill those hirelings of capitalists.
>
> What do we care for a few soldiers? We have a weapon a hundred-fold worse than theirs. They think they kill five of our brethren, but we will have a hundred or five hundred for every one they have murdered. I am an anarchist, and am willing to die for its cause.[61]

Most was convicted and the New York Court of Appeals affirmed. The decision does not deal with the constitutional issues but considers only whether the language used came within the terms of the statute. The court was not impressed by the argument "that the threats related to acts not presently to be done, but to be performed at some future time, when affairs were ripe for the revolution predicted." Rather it said, "No one can foresee the consequences which may result from language such as was used on this occasion, when addressed to a sympathizing and highly excited audience." In constitutional terms, however, the communication would have to be classified as "expression." It was a general and indefinite call to revolution. The action urged was confined to the future, and directed against persons in Illinois and Washington, not in New York City. Under the circumstances, the language could scarcely be considered an integral part of any specific or immediate acts of violence.[62]

The second instance took place in 1949. A concert featuring Paul Robeson in Peekskill, New York, had been broken up, after two hours of rioting, by persons from the surrounding area. The program was then scheduled for the following week and preparations were made by the sponsors to protect the concert from further violence. At a meeting

61. *People v. Most,* 128 N.Y. 108, 110–111, 27 N.E. 970, 971 (1891).

62. 128 N.Y. at 115–116, 27 N.E. at 972.

in Harlem, prior to the second concert, Benjamin Davis, a member of the Communist Party, was reported to have said: "We warn all the flunkeys on Wall Street, whether they wear white sheets or black robes like Judge Medina, that we are peace-loving people. But we are not pacifists and we are going to stand up toe to toe and slug it out." [63]

No action was taken against Davis. His remarks would appear to fall within the category of "expression." The call to "slug it out" referred to a future contingency—another attack on the concert—and was remote in time from the actual event.

Two additional cases, which may be considered close to the borderline, present the issues most sharply. Both grew out of communications made in the context of racial tension. The first involved the activities of John Kasper, who had taken a leading part in opposing desegregation of the public schools in Clinton and Nashville, Tennessee, in 1956 and 1957. The evidence showed that Kasper had come to Nashville toward the end of July 1957. "At that time there was considerable feeling and unrest among a substantial number of residents of Nashville because of a Federal District Court order requiring the first grades in all City schools to be integrated upon the opening of the September 1957 term of school." Kasper made a number of speeches at which, it was testified, he repeatedly made statements of the following sort:

> Well, he said that people were getting pretty excited about it (the school opening) and he said, we don't want any trouble here but people are getting pretty excited. I remember he said, I had a fellow come up to me and say, "John, why don't you hang the School Board?" He said, "I don't say we should do that" . . . He said, "another fellow came up to me and said, "John, I don't want to have any trouble here but my kids aren't going to school with Negroes, and if I have some dynamite, I know how to use it." [64]

In one speech Kasper also said "he was not advocating any violence but there would be bombings, dynamiting, bloodshed and probably killings but regardless, they were not going to put Negroes in our schools." On the night before the schools were to open, at a meeting in the center of the city attended by some seven hundred people, Kasper

63. James Rorty and Winifred Raushenbush, "The Lessons of the Peekskill Riots," *Commentary*, Vol. 10 (1950), pp. 309, 316.

64. *Kasper v. State*, 206 Tenn. 434, 437–438, 326 S.W.2d 664, 665, 666

(1959), cert. denied 361 U.S. 930 (1960). Other cases involving Kasper are *Kasper v. Brittain*, 245 F.2d 92 (6th Cir. 1957), cert. denied 355 U.S. 834 (1957); *Bullock v. U.S., supra* note 60.

"spoke his usual line of stating what would happen if the integration was proceeded with but was careful, of course, not to make any statements or threats as to what he would do himself personally. He designated pickets to go to some of the schools; he held up a rope with a noose in the end of it and suggested that a lot of people would like to see Z. Alexander Looby hanged (this latter person being a Negro lawyer and a member of the City Government of the City of Nashville). The defendant posed for a picture holding some wooden mallets crossed in his hands, these mallets being of the type used by stonemasons." At this meeting leaflets were passed out, with Kasper's name printed on them, which among other things "stated that these were the last days of peace between the white and Negro races." After the meeting about 150 of the crowd went to one of the schools "where a riot occurred." Later that night another school was dynamited. It was not shown that Kasper was present when these acts of violence took place.[65]

Affirming a conviction for inciting to riot, the Tennessee Supreme Court pointed out, "As for his alleged non violent attitude, it seems to be a case of the voice of Jacob and the hand of Esau." On the First Amendment issue the court simply said:

> There is no doubt in anybody's mind that any citizen has a right to express his opinion about the opinion of the Supreme Court of the United States in the integration cases but the right of free speech is limited just as are all other so-called rights and when one goes beyond a proper expression of opinion and incites to riot, he has gone beyond the area of freedom of speech. The great Justice Oliver Wendell Holmes said that no one has a right to yell "Fire" in a crowded theater when there is no fire.[66]

While the court did not apply even the clear and present danger test, but relied on a standard of "incitement," the result reached is probably correct. Kasper was urging immediate, specific acts of violence in a situation where violence was likely to occur. His speech was definitely an integral feature of a course of action on an extended scale to prevent integration of the schools by force and violence. The communication was thus properly treated as participation in the illegal action that shortly ensued.

The final example is the case of William Epton, chairman of the

---

65. 206 Tenn. at 439, 440–441, 326 S.W.2d at 666, 667.

66. 206 Tenn. at 442, 443, 326 S.W. 2d at 667, 668.

Progressive Labor Movement in Harlem. In the summer of 1964 Epton addressed an open-air meeting in Harlem called to protest police brutality and specifically the killing of a fifteen-year-old Negro youth by an off-duty police lieutenant. About fifty persons were present. In the course of his speech Epton said:

> [W]e'll begin a campaign to organize a mass demonstration against the cops somewhere in this city. As it stands now, many organizations are talking and planning of where this demonstration is going to take place and we're not saying it's going to be a peaceful demonstration . . . They [the cops] declared war on us and we should declare war on them and every time they kill one of us damnit, we'll kill one of them and we should start thinking that way right now . . . because we had better stop talking about violence as a dirty word . . .
>
> If we're going to be free, and we will not be fully free until we smash this state completely and totally. Destroy and set up a new state of our own choosing and of our own liking. And in that process of making this state, we're going to have to kill a lot of these cops, a lot of these judges, and we'll have to go up against their army. We'll organize our own militia and our own army. . . . Think about it because no people in this world have ever achieved independence and freedom through the ballot or having it legislated to them. All people in this world who are free got their freedom through struggle and through revolution. That's the way to gain freedom.
>
> We will take our freedom. We will take it by any means necessary and any means necessary as we know the beast that we are dealing with is that we have to create a revolution in this country and we will create a new government that is run by the people. . . . Those who are ready to come with us and stand with us and join the Harlem Defense Council . . . will go back into their blocks and organize their blocks into defense committees so when the deal goes through they will be able to be in the street tens of thousands strong ready to face that man. And we know how to use weapons just like they know how to use weapons. And when the deal goes down we have to be ready to confront them and beat them.

About an hour after Epton's meeting was over riots broke out in Harlem that lasted several days. There was no evidence of "any direct, causal connection" between Epton's speech and the riots. During the course of the riots, according to the New York Court of Appeals, the Harlem headquarters of the Progressive Labor Movement "became a beehive of activity with the defendant exhorting those in attendance to organize their blocks to combat the police and with defendant and his helpers feverishly getting out leaflets attacking the police." There was testimony that during this period Epton addressed a group of thirty-five to forty persons saying "that there were various means of defeating the police, including 'suckering' the officers off the main avenues into the side streets away from other policemen where they could be killed one by one." There was also testimony that on another occasion Epton told his audience "that their 'block captains' could teach them how to make weapons out of things in the street, informing his audience that when bottles are filled with a 'certain substance' (presumably gasoline) they become 'very effective' (as Molotov cocktails)."

Epton was convicted of advocating criminal anarchy, under the statute involved in *Gitlow,* conspiring to advocate criminal anarchy, and conspiring to commit the crime of riot. His indictment for committing riot was dismissed for lack of evidence. The Court of Appeals affirmed the convictions and the Supreme Court denied certiorari.[67]

The result of applying the expression-action test in this case would seem to be that the initial speech should be construed as expression. Taken as a whole the references to violence were general in character, not directed at specific persons or urging specific acts, and primarily embodying an indefinite call to revolution in the future. Most likely Epton's remarks did operate to prepare the minds of his audience for subsequent violence. But this is not the test. The communication must be so closely associated with violent conduct as to be fairly considered a part of the riot itself. This did not appear. On the other hand, Epton's subsequent conduct, other than preparation or dissemination of the leaflets, would more likely be classified as action. As in the *Kasper* case, it consisted of specific instructions to commit immediate particular acts of violence in the context of a riot then actually in progress.[68]

These illustrations indicate, roughly at least, where the expression-action theory would draw the line between communication protected under the First Amendment and communication not so protected. Not everyone might agree with the actual line of division suggested here.

67. *People v. Epton,* 19 N.Y.2d 496, 281 N.Y.S.2d 9, 227 N.E.2d 829 (1967), cert. denied 390 U.S. 29 (1968).

68. For further discussion of the New York Criminal Anarchy statute see Chapter V. A somewhat similar attempt to draw the line between protected and un-protected communication, dealing with some additional cases, may be found in Paul Harris, "Black Power Advocacy: Criminal Anarchy or Free Speech," *California Law Review,* Vol. 56 (1968), p. 702.

The definition of "expression" and "action" leaves some flexibility in determining what conduct should be put in what category, and hence how far the social interest in maintaining the public peace can be promoted through control of borderline conduct. The test is based, however, upon the fundamental requirements of a system of freedom of expression, which demand that expression be allowed and only action regulated. It therefore rests upon a functional basis that permits rational application. Moreover, it is far more precise than any of the other tests proposed. It therefore satisfies, at least more than other doctrines, the administrative requirements of the system.

Is the expression-action theory, as applied in this way, a sensible one? Or does it, in Justice Jackson's words, convert the First Amendment into a "suicide pact"? Perhaps the strongest argument for believing that it is workable is the scarcity of cases that involve this problem. If violence or public disorder actually occurred as a result of the communication the social interest in public order is usually vindicated through legal sanctions directed against the ensuing action itself. In such event any prior communication is likely to be either clearly part of the unlawful action, or unnecessary to the prosecution. On the other hand, if violence or disorder did not take place any public interest in punishing the communication would usually be slight. It may be objected that the expression-action test does not permit the punishment of leaders who do not directly engage in some ensuing action. This is not wholly true. The expression-action test, as in the cases of Kasper and Epton, would permit prosecution of any conduct that amounted to participation in action, whether or not the participant actually threw the stone or applied the torch. Punishment for anything less than this would, for all practical purposes, amount to punishment because of official or popular antagonism to the ideology or goals of the communicator. It may not be entirely accidental that such few cases as do exist relate to anarchists, labor organizers in the period before World War I, and racial militants. In any event, the lack of reported decisions would indicate that the application of the expression-action test would adequately protect the public interest in maintaining internal order.

b. The Problem of the Hostile Opposition   Much of the public concern over the right to assemble and petition comes from fear of action resulting not from the conduct of those exercising the right, but from the conduct of persons opposed. The overwhelming proportion of court decisions are concerned with this problem of the hostile audience.[69]

The starting proposition is that the existence of a hostile opposition cannot be grounds for cutting off or curtailing expression. Rather it is the constitutional duty of the government to protect the person seeking to exercise the right of expression. The next question is whether any qualification of the principle must be made, or, put another way, are there any circumstances in which the conduct of the speaker toward his audience is such that his communication loses its character as expression and hence can be denied protection?

If the speaker's conduct towards those who hear the communication constitutes action, as when he directs a physical assault upon an opposing group, such conduct is not, of course, protected by the First Amendment. An issue of this kind was present but not decided in *Terminiello*. The problem here is the same as that previously discussed, and it is necessary to draw the same sort of line between expression and action. Under the guidelines set forth above, Terminiello's speech would be considered expression. The problem of the hostile audience, however, seldom arises in this form. Most commonly the question is not one of aggression but of provocation. This element was also present in *Terminiello*.

It is frequently said that speech that is intentionally provocative, and therefore invites physical retaliation, can be punished or suppressed. Yet plainly no such general proposition can be sustained. Quite the contrary, it is clear that expression which leads an opponent to violent counter-action nevertheless remains "expression," and that the ensuing conduct of the opponent is separable "action." This rule applies even where the speaker is deliberately provocative. The provocative nature of the communication does not make it any the less "expression." Indeed, the whole theory of free expression contemplates that expression will in many circumstances be provocative and arouse hostility. The audience, just as the speaker, has the obligation to maintain physical restraint.

Under the expression-action theory, the only point at which the communication could be classified as action is when the communicator in effect participates in an act of violence. This can be said to occur only when the provocation takes the form of a personal insult, delivered face to face. Such "fighting words" can be considered the equiva-

---

69. For a collection of materials on the problem of the hostile audience see *Political and Civil Rights in the United States*, p. 547.

lent of knocking a chip off the shoulder—the traditional symbolic act that puts the parties in the role of physical combatants. It is, in short, the beginning of action. But the classification of provocative or insulting words as "action" is limited to direct encounters. Thus, if such language is used in the course of a speech addressed generally to the audience, even though the speaker refers to specific persons, organizations, or groups, the communication must still be considered "expression." Unless the speaker singles out specific members of his audience, and addresses insulting or fighting words to them personally, the communication cannot be said to constitute part of action. Applied in any other way the "fighting words" doctrine becomes a "bad tendency" test.

It is only in this sense, therefore, that "fighting words" fall outside the protection of the First Amendment. It should be noted that the reason for this is not, as the Supreme Court argued in *Chaplinsky*, because fighting words have "slight social value," but rather because they are "verbal acts." It should be noted also that if the doctrine of "fighting words" is limited, as it should be, to face-to-face encounter with an identified individual, there are relatively few occasions when it will be invoked against the speaker.[70]

The same basic rules apply to heckling the speaker. Up to a point heckling or other interruption of the speaker may be part of the dialogue. But conduct that obstructs or seriously impedes the utterance of another, even though verbal in form, cannot be classified as expression. Rather it is the equivalent of sheer noise. It has the same effect, in preventing or disrupting communication, as acts of physical force. Consequently it must be deemed action and is not covered by the First Amendment. The speaker is entitled to protection from this form of interference as from any other physical obstruction.

The general proposition stands, then, that all persons seeking to engage in meetings, parades, demonstrations or other forms of assembly or petition are entitled to full protection, despite hostile opposition, as long as they confine their conduct to expression and do not participate in unlawful action. This means that they are not subject to subsequent prosecution on account of any expression, even though violent or other unlawful action resulted from activities of hostile opponents. It means also that the expression cannot be interrupted, by arrest of the speaker or orders to disperse, because the police believe in

70. For references to discussion of the "fighting words" doctrine, see *Politi-*   *cal and Civil Rights in the United States*, pp. 522–523.

good faith that violence from the opposition will occur. There should be no such doctrine as protective custody or protective silencing in American law. In this situation it is the duty of the police to preserve order, and the expression should be allowed to continue until the necessary order in fact no longer exists. Finally, no permit should be refused or injunction against expression issued on the ground that a hostile opposition is likely to cause violence. Again, the doctrine of protective silencing has no place in a system of freedom of expression.

These are bold principles, and they involve some risks. They would require that Feiner be allowed to continue his speech. They would also require that Terminiello not be prosecuted for his address and that his meeting be permitted to go on until it was no longer a meeting. They would nullify the injunction in *Princess Anne* and the police order to disperse in *Gregory*. They would allow demonstrators to seek out centers of the opposition—Nazis to march through Jewish areas and blacks through white neighborhoods. They would foreclose an injunction against blackface in the Philadelphia Mummers parade. In every case they would insist that the right of expression could not be denied to any person because of opposition to his exercising it.[71]

The chief justification for these rules is that they are required by any constitutional system that undertakes to guarantee minority or individual rights. This basic principle has been consistently recognized and followed by the Supreme Court. Thus in *Cooper v. Aaron* the Court refused to suspend the rights of Negro children to attend unsegregated schools on the ground that an attempt to grant them that constitutional right had been attended by conditions of "chaos, bedlam, and turmoil"; that there were "repeated incidents of more or less serious violence"; that "a serious financial burden" had been cast on the School District; that the local police department would not be able "to detail enough men to afford the necessary protection"; that there would be continued need of "military assistance or its equivalent"; and that the situation was "intolerable." The Court, in an opinion to which every member subscribed, said:

> The constitutional rights of respondents are not to be sacrificed or yielded to the violence and disorder which have followed upon the actions of the Governor and Legislature. As this Court said some 41 years ago in a unanimous opinion in a case involving another aspect

71. In *Nichols v. Philadelphia Chapter of CORE,* 9 R.R.L.R. 326 (Ct. C.P. Pa. 1964), the court enjoined both mummers and protesters. See also *Jewish War Veterans v. American Nazi Party,* 260 F. Supp. 452 (N.D. Ill. 1966).

of racial segregation: "It is urged that this proposed segregation will promote the public peace by preventing race conflicts. Desirable as this is, and important as is the preservation of the public peace, this aim cannot be accomplished by laws or ordinances which deny rights created or protected by the Federal Constitution." Buchanan v. Warley, 245 U.S. 60, 81. Thus law and order are not here to be preserved by depriving the Negro children of their constitutional rights.[72]

Justice Frankfurter in a supplemental opinion added:

No explanation that may be offered in support of such a request [to defer desegregation] can obscure the inescapable meaning that law should bow to force. To yield to such a claim would be to enthrone official lawlessness, and lawlessness if not checked is the precursor of anarchy. On the few tragic occasions in the history of the nation, North and South, when law was forcibly resisted or systematically evaded, it has signaled the breakdown of constitutional processes of government on which ultimately rest the liberties of all. Violent resistance of law cannot be made a legal reason for its suspension without loosening the fabric of our society.[73]

Objection to the application of these principles is sometimes based on grounds of financial costs. The Supreme Court rejected this position in *Cooper v. Aaron.* The Federal government was quite properly not deterred by the costs of bringing out the armed forces to enforce the right of James Meredith to enter the University of Mississippi in 1962. It may well be that a community would find it cheaper to silence a speaker or prohibit a demonstration than to furnish police or possibly military protection. But the constitutional right cannot be measured in financial terms. Many aspects of democracy, including holding elections and granting due process in criminal trials, are more costly than other modes of procedure. Yet this has never been considered ground for dispensing with the democratic process.

A more compelling objection to the principle of full protection in the face of hostile opposition is that it is likely to result in more violence or disorder than the community can tolerate. But it would be the unusual situation if a determined showing of official force could not

72. *Cooper v. Aaron,* 358 U.S. 1, 13, 16 (1958).

73. 358 U.S. at 22. To the same effect are *Bush v. Orleans Parish School Board,* 188 F. Supp. 916 (E.D. La. 1960), aff'd 365 U.S. 569 (1961); *Wright v. Georgia,* 373 U.S. 284, 293 (1963); *Nesmith v. Alford,* 318 F.2d 110 (5th Cir. 1963), cert. denied 375 U.S. 975 (1964). For a survey of the cases in other areas where the courts have insisted upon enforcement of a constitutional right despite the possibility of violence or disorder, see Jay Murphy, "Free Speech and the Interest in Local Law and Order," *Journal of Public Law,* Vol. 1 (1952), p. 40.

maintain order. If violence occurred despite such protection it would most probably be the result of a willingness on both sides to incur it. Under these conditions violence would probably take place anyway, whether or not it was preceded by a public assembly.

Moreover, when violence becomes unavoidable the community is confronted with a choice of risks. If the community permits one group to shut off the right of expression by others, it may well be inviting more disorder in the end than if it had kept the channels of expression open. Its better hope may lie not in denying the constitutional right, and thereby covering over the underlying problems, but in seriously attempting to restore conditions that make exercise of the right once again possible. At least this is the theory of the First Amendment.

If the situation deteriorates to a point where violence and disorder can in fact no longer be borne, then the remedy open to the community is, as Justice Reed declared in *Meadowmoor,* to invoke the emergency powers of martial law. Once it is clear that the constitutional guarantee of freedom of assembly cannot be extended to every citizen, the only recourse is to substitute temporarily a different kind of system. Under martial law all freedom of assembly would be suspended, or at least all citizens would be treated on the same basis. Such a remedy is, of course, a desperate and a dangerous one. It concedes a breakdown of the democratic process. It shuts off important avenues of communication and works against the forces for adjustment of differences. But there are significant factors that limit the danger. One is that suspension would operate only in a relatively small geographical area. Another is that, with all assembly cut off, pressures would presumably build up from many sources in the community for restoration of the right. It is also possible that judicial guidelines would eventually emerge to control the conditions under which martial law could be invoked, the rights available during its existence, and the criteria for its termination.[74]

One can certainly argue that the alternative of full protection or martial law is a false and unnecessary one; that it is better to impose some limitations on expression and thereby preserve the system of free expression in part than, in seeking an impossible ideal, suspend the system altogether. There is of course much force in this argument. The system has often operated on this basis in the past. Nevertheless there

---

74. For reference to some of the materials dealing with martial law see *Political and Civil Rights in the United States,* pp. 1470–1471. See also Note, "Judicial Control of the Riot Curfew," *Yale Law Journal,* Vol. 77 (1968), p. 1560.

are serious dangers inherent in such a compromise with principle. The dynamics of limitation do not afford a ready stopping place. It becomes too easy for the authorities and too tempting for those seeking an advantage to invoke the specter of disorder and cut off expression. The system then no longer performs its function. In the long run the community is better off to strive for full protection of free expression. At any rate that is the principle it should follow, however much it may fall short in practice.

The Supreme Court has never made its position fully clear on the hostile audience problem. It has repeatedly declared that it is the duty of the government to afford police protection to the exercise of First Amendment rights. But it has left ambiguous what the limits of its rule, if any, should be. In *Feiner,* the majority seemed to be laying down the doctrine that the police could break up an assembly if they had reasonable grounds to believe that violence would occur. But the decision also turns, at least in part, on the position that Feiner had passed "the bounds of argument and persuasion and undertaken incitement to riot." *Edwards* and *Cox,* while resting on the proposition that there was no danger of violence, leave the impression that the Court would no longer follow *Feiner. Gregory* is inconclusive. These crucial issues thus remain unresolved.[75]

c. The Permit System   Certain special problems are involved when the question of maintaining the public peace arises in connection with government regulations that undertake to control the right of assembly or petition, prior to its actual exercise, through a permit system or by court injunction. Most important is the fact that the basic principle of full protection is here reinforced by the doctrine of prior restraint. The underlying rationale of the prior restraint doctrine is particularly applicable when the attempt is made to prevent expression on the ground that it may lead to breach of the public peace. The ease with which the expression may be curtailed, the pressures to play safe, the speculative basis of the restriction, are all abundantly present when the standard of possible violence is used as grounds for denying a permit or granting an injunction.

75. For statements of the duty to furnish protection, see *Hague v. C.I.O.,* 307 U.S. 496, 516 (1939); *Wright v. Georgia,* 373 U.S. 284, 293 (1963); *Cox v. Louisiana,* 379 U.S. 536, 550–551 (1965); *Brown v. Louisiana,* 383 U.S. 131, 133 (1966). Lower Federal court decisions include *Sellers v. Johnson,* 163 F.2d 877 (8th Cir. 1947), cert. denied 332 U.S. 851 (1948); *Downie v. Powers,* 193 F.2d 760 (10th Cir. 1951).

The position of the Supreme Court on this issue has never been developed. In *Meadowmoor* it sanctioned an injunction against picketing because of prior and indeed somewhat unrelated violence. On the other hand in *Kunz* it appeared to exclude any standard for a permit system that was based on the possibility of "disorder or violence." In other permit cases the Court has indicated that the only valid standards are those related to time, place and manner. Then in *Princess Anne,* it left the door open to limitations based on the possibility of violence, although it made a strong statement in support of the prior restraint rule:

> Ordinarily, the State's constitutionally permissible interests are adequately served by criminal penalties imposed after freedom to speak has been so grossly abused that its immunity is breached. The impact and consequences of subsequent punishment for such abuse are materially different from those of prior restraint. Prior restraint upon speech suppresses the precise freedom which the First Amendment sought to protect against abridgment.[76]

The lower Federal courts and the State courts have varied. In most cases they have required that a permit be granted or have refused an injunction to stop expression, despite the possibility of violence; but in some cases they have ruled the other way. There seems to be some tendency to be more restrictive in injunction cases than in review of permit denials. A particularly noteworthy decision, in which the issues were thoroughly discussed, is that of the New York courts in *Rockwell v. Morris.* In 1960 the New York City Commissioner of Parks refused a permit to George Lincoln Rockwell, head of an American Nazi group, to make a speech in Union Square. The New York Supreme Court upheld the Commissioner, saying: "Petitioner Rockwell, in words recorded and concededly accurate, as well as in signed pamphlets circulated freely by him and his followers, has accused more than two million New York City residents of Jewish faith and another half-million or more Negro and Puerto Rican residents of this city of being traitors. He has complimented Adolf Hitler as a great Christian crusader and openly advocates Hitlerian actions in this country. . . . This court cannot agree that the constitutional guarantee of free

76. *Milk Wagon Drivers Local 753 v. Meadowmoor Dairies, Inc.,* 312 U.S. 287, 292, 294 (1941); *Kunz v. New York,* 340 U.S. 290, 294 (1951); *Niemotko v. Maryland,* 340 U.S. 268, 271 (1951); *Poulos v. New Hampshire,* 345 U.S. 395, 404 (1953); *Carroll v. President and Commissioners of Princess Anne,* 393 U.S. 175, 180–181 (1968). For a collection of materials, see *Political and Civil Rights in the United States,* pp. 582–599.

speech encompasses such an invitation to public disorder, violence and even incitement to murder." The Appellate Division reversed, Justice Breitel concluding for the court: "[T]here is no power in government under our Constitution to exercise prior restraint of the expression of views, unless it is demonstrable on a record that such expression will immediately and irreparably create injury to the public weal—not that such expression, without itself being unlawful, will incite criminal acts in others." The New York Court of Appeals affirmed and the United States Supreme Court denied certiorari.[77]

The doctrine of prior restraint, in its pure form, would go further than *Rockwell*. It would preclude denial of a permit or issuance of an injunction to cut off speech before it is uttered, regardless of the possibility of ensuing action. The expression-action theory, which requires maximum separation of controls over action from those over expression, would reach the same conclusion. Up to this point, however, the courts have been unwilling to commit themselves to full protection.

One other kind of problem sometimes arises in connection with control of assembly and petition through a permit system. At the Pentagon demonstration in October 1967 the leaders of the demonstration announced in advance that the meeting at the Lincoln Memorial and the march to the Pentagon would be followed by acts of civil disobedience; those who were committed to such a course would attempt nonviolently to enter the Pentagon grounds and building. The civil disobedience would, of course, constitute action and not expression. Under these circumstances would the government be justified in refusing a permit to hold the meeting and march?

The issue is one of separating expression and action. Again the principle to be applied is that this separation should be made to the maximum degree possible. It would therefore follow that the possibility, or even probability, of ensuing unlawful action should not be grounds for cutting off the expression. As often turns out, it was evident that as a practical matter the granting of the permit would probably lessen rather than increase the possibility of disorder. Whether on grounds of principle or practicality, or both, the government granted

---

77. *Rockwell v. Morris,* 26 Misc.2d 229, 208 N.Y.S.2d 154 (Sup. Ct. N.Y. Co. 1960); rev'd 12 App. Div. 2d 272, 277–278, 211 N.Y.S.2d 25, 32 (App. Div., 1st Dept. 1960); app. dis. 9 N.Y.2d 791, 215 N.Y.S.2d 502, 175 N.E.2d 162 (1961); cert. denied 368 U.S. 913 (1961).

Other cases are collected in *Political and Civil Rights in the United States,* pp. 594–596. See also *Hurwitt v. City of Oakland,* 247 F. Supp. 995 (N.D. Cal. 1965); *Norton v. Ensor,* 269 F. Supp. 533 (D. Md. 1967). For further discussion of prior restraint see Chapter XIII.

the permit. Its action was hardly compelled, however, by the course of Supreme Court decisions.[78]

C. Protecting Other Social Interests

In addition to its interest in maintaining the public peace, the community is concerned with the impact of the right to assemble and petition upon various other social interests. This involves a fundamental distinction. When adjustment of the system of free expression to another social interest requires an allocation of physical facilities, doctrines other than the principle of full protection must be applied. For example, the streets are used for normal traffic purposes as well as for purposes of assembly, and ordinarily cannot be used for both purposes at the same time. The problem is one of dividing limited facilities among competing uses. Clearly such an issue cannot be resolved on the basis of giving full protection to expression (allowing a parade down Main Street at any time) and securing the other social interest by regulation of the ensuing action. Under such circumstances a different principle is necessary and, as we shall see, satisfactory—a principle of fair accommodation. These matters are dealt with in the following section. Here we examine those remaining social interests which, like the interest in maintaining the public peace, can and must be safeguarded by methods other than limitation on the right of assembly and petition.

The major kinds of social interest with which the reported cases have been concerned relate to (1) littering of the streets; (2) prevention of personal harm; and (3) effective operation of government functions.

---

78. For an account of the episode, see *The New York Times,* Oct. 10, 1967, and Oct. 21–23, 1967. See *Resistance v. Commissioners of Fairmount Park,* 298 F. Supp. 961 (E.D. Pa. 1969). Cases dealing with bans on campus speakers alleged to be "subversive" are noted in Chapter XVI. Cases denying the use of public buildings to groups alleged to be "subversive" are collected in *Political and Civil Rights in the United States,* pp. 548–550.

1. LITTERING THE STREETS

A series of early Supreme Court decisions, beginning in the late nineteen-thirties, dealt with the efforts of local authorities to restrict the distribution of leaflets and door-to-door canvassing. Most of these cases involved members of Jehovah's Witnesses, who at the time were one of the principal purveyors of unwanted ideas through this medium. Attempts were made to justify the municipal ordinances, among other reasons, on the ground that they fulfilled the social purpose of preventing littering of the streets.

The first case of this sort was *Lovell v. Griffin*. Here the ordinance prohibited the distribution of "circulars, handbills, advertising, or literature of any kind" without first obtaining written permission from the City Manager. In a unanimous decision the Supreme Court held the ordinance invalid on its face as a prior restraint. While the Court seemed to have no doubt of the result, it evidently had a feeling, as yet inarticulate, that some restriction on the right to distribute literature would have to be allowed. In any event, Chief Justice Hughes, stressing the point that the ordinance in question was a total prohibition, said: "It is not limited to ways which might be regarded as inconsistent with the maintenance of public order or as involving disorderly conduct, the molestation of the inhabitants, or the misuse or littering of the streets." The implication, perhaps not intended, was that ordinances serving those purposes would be valid.[79]

The issue was set at rest, however, at least as far as littering the streets was concerned, in *Schneider v. State*. The following year the Supreme Court had before it ordinances from four cities, three of which prohibited distribution of leaflets on the streets or in similar places. The State courts had upheld the ordinances, and distinguished the *Lovell* case, on the ground that they were intended to prevent littering of the streets. The Supreme Court, with only Justice McReynolds dissenting, reversed in each case. Justice Roberts, writing for the Court, announced as applicable doctrine:

> In every case, therefore, where legislative abridgment of the rights
> [of free speech] is asserted, the courts should be astute to examine the
> effect of the challenged legislation. Mere legislative preferences or be-
> liefs respecting matters of public convenience may well support regu-

79. *Lovell v. Griffin*, 303 U.S. 444, 451 (1938).

lation directed at other personal activities, but be insufficient to justify such as diminishes the exercise of rights so vital to the maintenance of democratic institutions. And so, as cases arise, the delicate and difficult task falls upon the courts to weigh the circumstances and to appraise the substantiality of the reasons advanced in support of the regulation of the free enjoyment of the rights.[80]

Justice Roberts applied the doctrine in the following manner:

> We are of opinion that the purpose to keep the streets clean and of good appearance is insufficient to justify an ordinance which prohibits a person rightfully on a public street from handing literature to one willing to receive it. Any burden imposed upon the city authorities in cleaning and caring for the streets as an indirect consequence of such distribution results from the constitutional protection of the freedom of speech and press. This constitutional protection does not deprive a city of all power to prevent street littering. There are obvious methods of preventing littering. Amongst these is the punishment of those who actually throw papers on the streets.[81]

Justice Roberts' handling of the decision is most interesting. He does not rely upon the clear and present danger test, although that doctrine had by then come into full favor. Actually, that test would have led to the opposite result, for there surely is a clear and present danger that leaflet distribution in the streets will produce littering. What Justice Roberts does is to offer, tentatively, a balancing test, with the balancing weighted by a preference for First Amendment rights. The Roberts formulation of the balancing test in *Schneider v. State* was indeed the precursor of the more fully developed balancing tests which came to flower in the nineteen-fifties and sixties, beginning with the *Douds* case. When he actually comes to decide the issue, however, Justice Roberts in effect moves to a full protection theory. He does not really attempt to balance. Rather he flatly asserts "the constitutional protection of freedom of speech and press" and tells the cities to protect their interest in clean streets by punishing the action of littering. Constitutional doctrine with respect to littering the streets remains at that point today.[82]

80. *Schneider v. State*, 308 U.S. 147, 161 (1939).

81. 308 U.S. at 162.

82. For a recent case in accord with *Lovell* and *Schneider*, see *United Steel-workers of America v. Bagwell*, 383 F.2d 492 (4th Cir. 1967). *Cf. Chicago Park District v. Lyons*, 39 Ill.2d 584, 237 N.E. 2d 519 (1968), cert. denied 393 U.S. 939 (1968).

2. PREVENTION OF PERSONAL HARM

Attempts were also made to justify the ordinances restricting leaflet distribution and canvassing as protecting individuals on the streets or in their homes against various kinds of personal harm. The injuries envisaged included annoyance or molestation; deceit or misrepresentation; criminal acts such as robbery or assault by persons gaining access to homes or being present on the street; obtaining money by fraud; and obscenity and libel. The restrictions usually took the form of requiring a license obtainable only if specified conditions designed to secure the social interest involved were met. In other forms these regulations directly prohibited certain conduct or required disclosure of certain information.

The Supreme Court, while not entirely eliminating the possibility that a narrowly drawn regulation dealing with these problems might be valid, has never in fact upheld such a law. The licensing schemes are likely to run afoul of the prior restraint doctrine, and all forms of regulation are vulnerable to rules against vagueness, overbreadth, and excessive delegation of discretion. Since the Supreme Court decisions have rested, at least in part, on such doctrines it is not possible to say with certainty to what extent carefully drawn restrictions of this kind would be upheld, if at all, or on what theory they would be judged.

In *Schneider v. State* one of the ordinances before the Court required that any person wishing to canvass or distribute circulars must obtain a permit from the Chief of Police; that the applicant must supply certain information, including a photograph and fingerprints; that the Chief of Police must refuse a permit if he found the applicant was "not of good character" or was "canvassing for a project not free from fraud"; that canvassing could be done only between 9 A.M. and 5 P.M.; that the permittee "must be courteous to all persons in canvassing" and "must not importune or annoy the town's inhabitants"; and other conditions of a similar nature. The Court conceded that "commercial soliciting and canvassing" could be subject to such regulation, and that "reasonable hours" for noncommercial canvassing could be fixed. But it struck down the remainder of the ordinance. Justice Roberts' opinion does not make it fully clear whether the fatal defect was that the Chief of Police was given excessive discretion or that the objectives sought by the city could not be achieved through any form of restriction upon freedom of expression. The tone of his remarks supports the latter view:

> Conceding that fraudulent appeals may be made in the name of charity and religion, we hold a municipality cannot, for this reason, require all who wish to disseminate ideas to present them first to police authorities for their consideration and approval, with a discretion in the police to say some ideas may, while others may not, be carried to the homes of citizens; some persons may, while others may not, disseminate information from house to house. Frauds may be denounced as offenses and punished by law. Trespasses may similarly be forbidden. If it is said that these means are less efficient and convenient than bestowal of power on police authorities to decide what information may be disseminated from house to house, and who may impart the information, the answer is that considerations of this sort do not empower a municipality to abridge freedom of speech and press.[83]

A short time later Justice Roberts reiterated this position in *Cantwell v. Connecticut*. There a State law provided that no person "shall solicit money, services, subscriptions, or any valuable thing for any alleged religious, charitable or philanthropic cause . . . unless such cause shall have been approved by the secretary of the public welfare council." The secretary could approve only if he found that the cause "is a religious one or is a bona fide object of charity or philanthropy and conforms to reasonable standards of efficiency and integrity." Justice Roberts stated that "a State may by general and non-discriminatory legislation regulate the times, places, and the manner of solicitation upon its streets, and of holding meetings thereon." He went somewhat beyond *Schneider* in saying that a State "may protect its citizens from fraudulent solicitation by requiring a stranger in the community, before permitting him publicly to solicit funds for any purpose, to establish his identity and his authority to act for the cause which he purports to represent." But he pointed out that "penal laws are available to punish" frauds upon the public. He concluded by saying that to condition a license to solicit upon "a determination by state authority as to what is a religious cause" lays a "forbidden burden upon the exercise of liberty protected by the Constitution." [84]

Martin v. Struthers brought up the validity of an ordinance that made it an offense for any person "distributing handbills, circulars or

83. *Schneider v. State*, 308 U.S. 147, 164 (1939).

84. *Cantwell v. Connecticut*, 310 U.S. 296, 304, 306–307 (1940).

other advertisements to ring the door bell, sound the door knocker, or otherwise summon the inmate." The law was aimed primarily at the protection of householders from annoyance and the decision turned largely on issues of privacy. But another purpose was the prevention of crime by burglars posing as canvassers. The Supreme Court, in a five to four decision, held the ordinance invalid. Justice Black, writing for the majority, cited the *Cantwell* case for the proposition that "the peace, good order, and comfort of the community may imperatively require regulation of the time, place and manner of distribution." He gave as examples the right of a city to forbid "a man with a communicable disease to distribute leaflets on the street or to homes," or to prevent distribution "in a church against the will of the church authorities." Justice Black went on to say that the issue was one of "weighing the conflicting interests." After noting the social interests sought by the regulation and the role of leaflet distribution in the dissemination of ideas, he concluded that, "putting aside reasonable police and health regulations of time and manner of distribution," the freedom to distribute information "must be fully preserved." He added: "The dangers of distribution can so easily be controlled by traditional legal methods, leaving to each householder the full right to decide whether he will receive strangers as visitors, that stringent prohibition can serve no purpose but that forbidden by the Constitution, the naked restriction of the dissemination of ideas." Thus Justice Black commences with a balancing test and ends up in a full protection position.[85]

The next case, *Thomas v. Collins,* was inconclusive because there was no majority opinion. In that case Texas, faced with a major C.I.O. organizing drive, passed a law requiring that any labor organizer, "before soliciting any members for his organization," must file with the Secretary of State an application giving his name and affiliation and "describing his credentials," and obtain an "organizer's card." R. J. Thomas, president of the United Automobile Workers Union and vice-president of the C.I.O., went to Texas with a view to testing the law. He addressed a mass meeting, sponsored by a local C.I.O union, in the course of which he asked all persons present to join the Union and specifically solicited the membership of one individual. Thomas was

---

85. *Martin v. Struthers,* 319 U.S. 141, 143, 147 (1943). Justices Frankfurter, Reed, Roberts and Jackson dissented, primarily on privacy grounds. The privacy aspects of the case are discussed in Chapter XIV. See also *Breard v. Alexandria,* 341 U.S. 622 (1951), holding contrary to *Struthers* where a commercial element was involved. *Breard* is discussed in Chapter XII.

convicted of contempt for violating a restraining order which had been issued against him prior to his address. It was argued that the Texas statute was a valid exercise of the police power taken to safeguard "laborers from imposture when approached by an alleged organizer." The Supreme Court reversed, five to four.[86]

Justice Rutledge, in an opinion with which Justices Black, Douglas and Murphy concurred, wrote the prevailing opinion. He took the position that no restriction on free speech or free assembly would be permitted under the First Amendment except on a showing of clear and present danger. He then argued, "Lawful public assemblies, involving no element of grave and immediate danger to an interest the State is entitled to protect, are not instruments of harm which require previous identification of the speakers." Since what Thomas had done, in essence, was simply to address a meeting the requirement of registration was an invalid restriction. But he added: "Once the speaker goes further, however, and engages in conduct which amounts to more than the right of free discussion comprehends, as when he undertakes the collection of funds or securing subscriptions, he enters a realm where a reasonable registration or identification requirement may be imposed." Justice Jackson concurred, on the theory that "this case falls into the category of a public speech, rather than that of practicing a vocation as a solicitor." Justice Roberts, with whom Chief Justice Stone and Justices Reed and Frankfurter agreed, dissented on the ground that the Texas statute did not interfere with freedom of speech at all, but was simply normal regulation of a business or profession.[87]

Thus Justice Rutledge, starting from a clear and present danger position, ultimately reached a full protection view. Justice Jackson said nothing about clear and present danger; his opinion was couched in full protection language throughout. Both opinions drew a sharp line between speech and non-speech, placing most aspects of the solicitation of funds outside First Amendment protection. The dissenters viewed the restriction as applying exclusively to unprotected conduct.[88]

One final decision, coming somewhat later, touched on the problem of restricting leaflet distribution in the interest of preventing per-

86. *Thomas v. Collins*, 323 U.S. 516 (1945).

87. 323 U.S. at 539, 540, 548.

88. In *Staub v. City of Baxley*, 355 U.S. 313 (1958), the Court held an ordinance requiring a permit to solicit members in an organization collecting dues invalid on grounds of excessive delegation of discretion, without discussing other issues. See also *Adams v. City of Park Ridge*, 293 F.2d 585 (7th Cir. 1961).

sonal harm. In *Talley v. California* a Los Angeles city ordinance prohibited the distribution of handbills that did not have printed on them the name and address of the person who prepared them and of the persons who distributed them. In support of the ordinance it was urged that the law was aimed at prevention of "fraud, deceit, false advertising, negligent use of words, obscenity and libel." The Supreme Court held the ordinance invalid in a six to three decision. Justice Black, writing for five members of the Court, started from a full protection stance. He interpreted the *Schneider* case in this light: "This Court refused to uphold the four ordinances on those grounds [prevention of frauds, disorder, or littering] pointing out that there were other ways to accomplish those legitimate aims without abridging freedom of speech and press. Frauds, street littering and disorderly conduct could be denounced and punished as offenses, the Court said." He then noted that counsel for Los Angeles had argued that the ordinance was "aimed at providing a way to identify those responsible for fraud, false advertising and libel." But the ordinance "is in no manner so limited," he said, and "[t]herefore we do not pass on the validity of an ordinance limited to these or any other supposed evils." He concluded by reverting to the full protection position: "There can be no doubt that such an identification requirement would tend to restrict freedom to distribute information and thereby freedom of expression." Justice Harlan concurred, balancing interests in favor of freedom of expression, and Justices Clark, Frankfurter and White dissented, balancing interests in favor of the regulation.[89]

The actual positions reached in these decisions of the Supreme Court are wholly consistent with the theory that expression should be given full protection under the First Amendment, and that the social interest in safeguarding persons against possible harm from leaflet distribution and canvassing should be achieved through laws dealing directly with the harm and not by laws restricting expression. Moreover,

---

89. *Talley v. California*, 362 U.S. 60, 63, 64 (1960). In *Zwickler v. Koota*, 389 U.S. 241 (1967), and *Golden v. Zwickler*, 394 U.S. 103 (1969), the Supreme Court found it unnecessary to pass on the validity of a New York statute that made it a crime to print or distribute election campaign literature without printing on it the names and addresses of the printer and the persons who ordered the literature. A three-judge court had held the law unconstitutional on First Amendment grounds. *Zwickler v. Koota*, 290 F. Supp. 244 (E.D.N.Y. 1968). For a discussion of restrictions on political campaigning see Chapter XVII. See also *Prince v. Massachusetts*, 321 U.S. 158 (1944), upholding restriction upon distribution of literature by children, an area not within the adult system of freedom of expression.

the language of the decisions, though it often starts from another premise, largely concludes in those terms. Some of the dicta in the Court's opinions, however, raise doubts as to the Court's complete position. Most frequently reiterated is the statement that the government may regulate the "time, place and manner" of assembly and canvassing. What this means is unclear. Presumably it would include restrictions with respect to place and regulations required in the allocation of physical facilities. Presumably it also covers certain general police regulations, not related to control of expression, such as a general curfew or a physical isolation of persons with communicable diseases. This seems to be Justice Black's interpretation. Such restrictions have no bearing upon the maintenance of a system of freedom of expression. If "time, place and manner" is to mean more than this, however, it would probably be inconsistent with the full protection theory.

The other principal dictum is that first stated by Justice Roberts in *Cantwell* and later the subject of dispute in *Thomas v. Collins*—that "solicitation of funds" is subject to regulation. The problem here is one of drawing the line between expression and action. Insofar as solicitation of funds is an integral part of the communication of ideas, either by the individual or through an association formed to express them, it must be considered "expression." Justice Roberts' view, at least in its unqualified form, would therefore be contrary to the full protection theory. But collection of funds for a labor organization, to be used primarily in promoting collective bargaining or other economic interests of the union, would not be considered expression. Thus the position of Justice Rutledge in *Thomas v. Collins* is not necessarily inconsistent with the full protection theory.

The results reached by the Court, it need hardly be added, are fully justified in terms of the primary conditions for operation of an effective system of freedom of expression. Surely one has no hesitation in subordinating the claimed freedom from molestation and annoyance, by being approached on the street or summoned to the door, to the right of free expression. Deceit and misrepresentation in the communication of ideas are problems for the individual citizen to handle, not for the government to supervise. Prevention of criminal acts by persons pretending to engage in expression presents a clear case for direct control of the criminal, not the suppression or restriction of expression. The same is true for any fraudulent obtaining of money, and even more plainly true for the control of obscenity and libel. The falling off in recent years of efforts to regulate leaflet distribution or canvassing indicates that the full protection resolution of these issues has become generally accepted.[90]

3. PROTECTING GOVERNMENT OPERATIONS

A third series of restrictions upon the right of assembly and petition has been designed to protect certain operations of the government. The most common of these forbids assembly or picketing near a courthouse. Other statutes or regulations limit assembly or picketing in the vicinity of the legislature, the office or residence of the Chief Executive, and sometimes public premises generally. There are also laws forbidding such conduct near a schoolhouse and near a foreign embassy. The Supreme Court has passed upon these restrictions only in two instances.

One of the convictions in *Cox v. Louisiana* was based upon a Louisiana statute that provided: "Whoever, with the intent of interfering with, obstructing, or impeding the administration of justice, or with the intent of influencing any judge, juror, witness, or court officer, in the discharge of his duty pickets or parades in or near a building housing a court of the State of Louisiana . . . shall be fined not more than five thousand dollars or imprisoned not more than one year, or both." The Supreme Court held, five to four, that Cox had not violated this statute because the police had in effect given him permission to hold the demonstration near the courthouse; but it was unanimous in ruling that the statute was constitutional.[91]

Justice Goldberg, writing for the Court, first pointed out that the Louisiana statute was modeled on a similar Federal statute enacted in 1950 as a result of the picketing of Federal courthouses during the Communist trials under the Smith Act. He then held the Louisiana statute valid on its face, resting this decision on the ground that picketing was not "speech" but "conduct" and hence "subject to regulation even though intertwined with expression and association." Turning to the application of the statute in the case before him, Justice Goldberg, without conceding the relevancy of the clear and present danger test,

---

90. Cases involving exercise of the right of assembly to exert economic pressures or enforce boycotts are considered in Chapter XII, Section B. Cases on picketing of private residences are dealt with in Chapter XIV as an issue of the right of privacy.

91. *Cox v. Louisiana*, 379 U.S. 559 (1965).

rejected that position, saying it could not be concluded "that crowds, such as this, demonstrating before a courthouse may not be prohibited by a legislative determination based on experience that such conduct inherently threatens the judicial process." Finally, he found that the intent required by the statute had been established even though "the students were not then on trial and had not been arraigned." Justice Goldberg's primary justification for the validity of the statute and its application to Cox was embodied in the following paragraph:

> It is, of course, true that most judges will be influenced only by what they see and hear in court. However, judges are human; and the legislature has the right to recognize the danger that some judges, jurors, and other court officials, will be consciously or unconsciously influenced by demonstrations in or near their courtrooms both prior to and at the time of the trial. A State may also properly protect the judicial process from being misjudged in the minds of the public. Suppose demonstrators paraded and picketed for weeks with signs asking that indictments be dismissed, and that a judge, completely uninfluenced by these demonstrations, dismissed the indictments. A State may protect against the possibility of a conclusion by the public under these circumstances that the judge's action was in part a product of intimidation and did not flow only from the fair and orderly working of the judicial process.[92]

The view that a peaceable assembly is "conduct" (action) rather than "speech" (expression), and hence is not entitled to the normal protection extended by the First Amendment, cannot be reconciled with the theory or function of that constitutional guarantee. As a result of adopting this erroneous premise, Justice Goldberg found it unnecessary to apply even a balancing test to determine the general validity of the Louisiana statute. It was enough that the statute could be considered to "vindicate important interests of society." The decision comes close to writing the right of assembly out of the First Amendment.[93]

Justice Goldberg's reasoning in upholding the application of the statute to the particular facts of the *Cox* case follows from his earlier premise. He accepts as final "the legislative determination based on experience" that a crowd before a courthouse "inherently threatens the judicial process." In other words, having decided that all picketing near a courthouse is "conduct" outside the First Amendment it is no

92. 379 U.S. at 563, 565, 566, 567.   93. 379 U.S. at 564.
The Federal statute is found in 64 Stat.
1018, 18 U.S.C. §1507.

longer necessary to examine the circumstances of the particular case to decide whether the actual conduct did in fact interfere with the administration of justice. He thus scraps the clear and present danger test, and even an ad hoc balancing requirement, and reverts to the *Gitlow* doctrine that the only issue is whether the conduct falls within the terms of the statute. In this way Justice Goldberg upholds the application of the statute to Cox even though "the entire meeting from the beginning until its dispersal by tear gas was orderly and not riotous," the jail as well as the court was housed in the building, no trial was in progress or even scheduled, and the demonstration was not directed at any specific "judicial process" or proceeding but at the general system of law that resulted in the arrests. By its initial legerdemain the Court disregards the whole line of cases, from *De Jonge* onwards, which hold that restrictions on expression must be narrowly drawn to meet the precise evil feared.

Looking at the problem from the viewpoint of the full protection theory, the issue is whether an assembly that takes place near a courthouse, and even is directed at a particular judicial proceeding then taking place there, loses its character as expression so as to be subject to regulation otherwise forbidden. Justice Goldberg's argument on this point is unconvincing. He contends that "some" judges, jurors or court officials "will be consciously or unconsciously influenced." But this is a standard function of expression—to "influence" government officials. No one has seriously suggested that the judicial system be given immunity from public criticism. In fact in the nearest comparable cases— those involving alleged danger to the administration of justice through oral or written publications—the Court has taken the opposite position. Mere "influence" is not enough to change expression into action, or to make a special exception to the general theory of the First Amendment in the case of courts. Nor is Justice Goldberg's Caesar's wife argument any more persuasive. The same objection can be made to any expression directed at government policy. Surely the remedy for public misunderstanding of the motives of government officials does not lie in cutting off the right to advise or criticize them.[94]

The solution to the problem lies in making the appropriate distinction between expression and action. Normally peaceable exercise of the right of assembly in front of a courthouse would be expression. On

94. The cases dealing with influence on the judicial process through oral or written communication are discussed in Chapter XII, Section C.

the other hand physical interference with the operation of the judicial process would be classified as action. Thus an assembly that seriously obstructed egress or ingress, or created noise that hampered the conduct of business, could be prohibited as action. Activity of the assembly that constituted actual intimidation of court officials, such as threats of physical harm, would likewise be punishable as action. Our experience to date with the picketing of courthouses strongly supports the view that no greater restrictions upon public assemblies are necessary to secure the fair administration of justice in our courthouses.

Similar considerations apply to public assemblies in the vicinity of the legislature, Executive Mansion, or public buildings. Assuming the basic right to use open public places for assembly and petitioning, a total prohibition on the ground that all such conduct near a government building is "inherently intimidating" cannot be justified. Most such assemblies are not intimidating, and to prevent all of them in advance on the possibility that some may result in illegal action is contrary to the primary doctrines that govern in all other areas of First Amendment rights. As a matter of fact the rule against discrimination would, in this situation, usually foreclose such total prohibition; for the areas surrounding the capitol and the Executive Mansion are normally the scene of numerous officially sanctioned parades, ceremonies, and other gatherings. In any event the same sort of rules for distinguishing expression and action that were suggested in connection with courthouse picketing would provide a sound basis for adjusting the right of assembly and petition to the conduct of government operations in the legislative and executive branches. Any conduct that amounted to physical interruption of governmental operations, including physical intimidation, would be classified as action and subject to regulation.

The Supreme Court touched on these issues in *Cameron v. Johnson*. The Mississippi Anti-Picketing Law made it unlawful "to engage in picketing or mass demonstrations in such a manner as to obstruct or unreasonably interfere with free ingress or egress to and from any public premises . . . or with the transaction of public business or administration of justice therein . . . or so as to obstruct or unreasonably interfere with the free use of public streets, sidewalks, or other public ways adjacent or contiguous thereto." The Court unanimously held the statute valid on its face. Relying on *Cox* for the proposition that picketing was "subject to regulation even though intertwined with expression and association," Justice Brennan ruled that prohibition of the conduct proscribed by the statute "does not abridge constitutional liberty." [95]

Apart from its reasoning, whether the Court was correct in its result depends upon the interpretation given to "obstruct," "unreasonable interference," and "free." The right of assembly does not of course embrace an unlimited right to "obstruct" or "interfere" with ingress or egress to or from public buildings or the use of adjacent streets. But it does involve, by its very nature, some degree of "interference" with, and in some sense "obstruction" of, other uses of the area in which the assembly takes place. These are questions partly of drawing the line between expression and action, and partly of accommodating different uses of the same physical facilities. Unfortunately the Court, misguided by its premise that conduct in the form of assembly is largely unprotected by the First Amendment, never addressed itself to these crucial issues. [96]

As to the picketing of schools, the same doctrines would seem applicable. In such a situation the court might well find, however, that actual interruption of the school's activities occurred at an earlier point in the demonstration than when the assembly took place on the grounds of the capitol or before the Executive Mansion. The problem of demonstrating against a foreign embassy is somewhat different. In *Frend v. United States* a prohibition on demonstrating within five hundred feet of an embassy was upheld as necessary to protect foreign officials from embarrassing disturbances that might jeopardize foreign relations. The restriction would seem justifiable, but only on the theory that the embassy was in effect foreign territory and hence outside the American system of freedom of expression. [97]

In general the Supreme Court seems readily disposed to sustain restrictions on the right of assembly on or near public premises. It has

---

95. *Cameron v. Johnson*, 390 U.S. 611, 617 (1968).

96. Cases in the lower Federal courts concerned with the power to limit assembly that might affect government operations include *Coppock v. Patterson*, 272 F. Supp. 16 (S.D. Miss. 1967); *Davis v. Francois*, 395 F.2d 730 (5th Cir. 1968); *Committee to End War in Viet Nam v. Gunn*, 289 F. Supp. 469 (W.D. Tex. 1968), on appeal to the Supreme Court; *Jeanette Rankin Brigade v. Chief of Capitol Police*, —— F.2d —— (D.C. Cir. 1969); *United States v. Nicholson* (D.D.C.

1969); *A Quaker Action Group v. Hickel*, —— F.2d —— (D.C. Cir. 1969). See also *Flores v. Denver*, 122 Colo. 71, 220 P.2d 373 (1950).

97. On picketing of schools see *State v. Wiggins*, 272 N.C. 147, 158 S.E.2d 37 (1967), cert. denied 390 U.S. 1028 (1968); *Sprowal v. New York*, 49 Misc. 2d 806, 268 N.Y.S.2d 444 (1966), 17 N.Y.2d 884, 271 N.Y.S.2d 310, 218 N.E.2d 343 (1966), app. dis. 385 U.S. 649 (1967). The *Frend* case is reported in 100 F.2d 691 (D.C. Cir. 1938), cert. denied 306 U.S. 640 (1938).

followed the theory that assembling, marching and picketing are not entitled to the same protection as "pure speech" to uphold broad regulations, not attempting to differentiate between the kinds of conduct that may be involved. The same tendency on the part of the Court was revealed in *Adderley*. The Court's approach is in marked contrast to its position in other First Amendment situations where it has insisted upon refinement and precision. In this area it seems to have departed from principles fundamental to an effective system of free expression.

D. Allocation of Physical Facilities

It has previously been noted that exercise of the right of expression may, in its physical manifestations, come in conflict with use of the same facilities for other purposes, and that issues of this sort must be resolved not by a theory of full protection for expression but by a principle of fair accommodation. The problem of adjusting competing claims for use of the same facilities may arise in a variety of situations; one of the best known occurs in the allocation of a limited number of wave lengths to radio and television stations. But the question is raised particularly in connection with assembly and petition. The large numbers of persons likely to be involved, the use of public places where other persons are present on other business, the attempt to search out an audience, and other characteristics of assembly and petition all combine to create a special problem in this area of expression.

The guiding principle here has never been and cannot be one of automatically allocating the facilities to exercise of the right of expression. No system of freedom of expression contemplates such a resolution of the issue, and adjustment on another basis cannot be considered an "abridgment" of the right of expression. Nor is the question to be settled by application of an incitement test, a clear and present danger test, or even a balancing of interests. Rather the problem is essentially one of traffic control. The governing principle can only be a fair accommodation of opposing interests. This is, of course, a kind of balancing test. But it seeks not to foreclose one interest or the other, but to permit both to function; it does not deal at all with the content of the expression but merely with the time, place and, to some extent the manner, of its utterance; and it is susceptible of resolution in terms of specific factors that reasonable men can usually agree on. If the facilities are very limited, as in the case of radio wave lengths, the problems mount; but when all interests can normally be accommodated, as in the case of assembly and petitioning on the streets, the issues are susceptible of relatively ready solution. They are also within manageable range when they involve a conflict between two persons or groups each wishing to use the same facilities at the same time for purposes of assembly or petitioning.

The issues have arisen most frequently where the right of assembly and petition has been exercised in the streets, parks or other open areas to which the public has general access. The main competing use has been for normal traffic, pedestrian and vehicular; but other uses, such as rest or recreation in the parks, have also been involved. In the leaflet distribution and canvassing cases these problems were present, but the Court found little need to deal with them beyond saying that regulation of "time, place and manner" was permissible. In *Cox v. New Hampshire,* however, the Supreme Court considered the issues more directly. In this case a group of Jehovah's Witnesses had been convicted of parading without a permit. They challenged the permit requirement on the ground that it violated freedom of speech, press and assembly, but their objections were unanimously overruled. Chief Justice Hughes, writing for the Court, carefully pointed out the "limited objective" of the permit statute:

> [T]he state court considered and defined the duty of the licensing authority and the rights of appellants to a license for their parade, with regard only to considerations of time, place and manner so as to conserve the public convenience. The obvious advantage of requiring application for a permit was noted as giving the public authorities notice in advance so as to afford opportunity for proper policing. And the court further observed that, in fixing time and place, the license served "to prevent confusion by overlapping parades or processions, to secure convenient use of the streets by other travelers, and to minimize the risk of disorder." But the court held that the licensing board was not vested with arbitrary power or an unfettered discretion; that its discretion must be exercised with "uniformity of method of treatment upon the facts of each application, free from improper or inappropriate considerations and from unfair discrimination." [98]

The municipality, Chief Justice Hughes concluded, "cannot be denied authority to give consideration, without unfair discrimination, to

98. *Cox v. New Hampshire,* 312 U.S.
569, 575–576 (1941).

time, place and manner in relation to other proper uses of the streets." The Supreme Court reached the same conclusion in *Poulos v. New Hampshire* with respect to another part of the ordinance which required a license to hold an open-air public meeting on any ground abutting on a public street. The New Hampshire court, as in *Cox,* had ruled that the ordinance was limited to a "systematic, consistent and just order of treatment, with reference to the convenience of public use of the highways." The Supreme Court upheld the law as thus construed.[99]

The Supreme Court again considered the problem in *Cox v. Louisiana,* and left the legal doctrine somewhat more unsettled. One of the statutes under which Cox was convicted provided that no person "shall wilfully obstruct the free, convenient and normal use of any public sidewalk, street, highway [etc.] . . . by impeding, hindering, stifling, retarding or restraining traffic or passage thereon or therein." The statute thus violated the principle of fair accommodation by prohibiting all assembling and petitioning which obstructed "normal" use of the streets, rather than attempting to make an adjustment between the use for assembly and the use for other purposes. The majority opinion, however, expressly refused to consider this issue. It reversed the conviction of Cox, but on the ground that the practice in the city had been to allow some meetings and parades and the statute was therefore being discriminatorily applied at the discretion of the city officials. Justice Goldberg's opinion did nevertheless restate the negative elements of the fair accommodation rule. Summarizing prior decisions, he said:

> From these decisions certain clear principles emerge. The rights of free speech and assembly, while fundamental in our democratic society, still do not mean that everyone with opinions or beliefs to express may address a group at any public place and at any time. The constitutional guarantee of liberty implies the existence of an organized society maintaining public order, without which liberty itself would be lost in the excesses of anarchy. The control of travel on the streets is a clear example of governmental responsibility to insure this necessary order. A restriction in that relation, designed to promote the public convenience in the interest of all, and not susceptible to abuses of discriminatory application, cannot be disregarded by the attempted exercise of some civil right which, in other circumstances, would be entitled to protection. One would not be justified in ignoring the familiar red light because this was thought to be a means of social protest. Nor

99. 312 U.S. at 576; *Poulos v. New Hampshire,* 345 U.S. 395, 398 (1953).

could one, contrary to traffic regulations, insist upon a street meeting in the middle of Times Square at the rush hour as a form of freedom of speech or assembly. Governmental authorities have the duty and responsibility to keep their streets open and available for movement.[100]

The problem of accommodating the right of assembly to other uses of public property was also raised, as noted above, in *Cameron v. Johnson*. But the Court did not consider the question there.[101]

The fair accommodation issue can arise in situations in which there is no permit system or obstruction statute that makes express provision for adjustment between competing uses. In such a case the court would have to make its decision in terms of a breach of the peace or other general statutory provision, or in exercise of its equity powers to grant an injunction. The Supreme Court has not dealt directly with the problem in this form. Minor obstruction of traffic occurred in both the *Feiner* and *Edwards* cases. But neither decision turned on the point.

The law thus remains in a state of some uncertainty. About all that is sure is that the government does have authority to regulate assembly and petitioning that takes place in streets, parks and other open places for the purpose of preserving other uses of those facilities. But the theory of such regulation has never been fully articulated and the details of its operation never elaborated. The lower Federal courts and the State courts have been more heavily involved in these issues. They have faced the problems in connection with permit systems, obstruction statutes, and injunctions; and have at times considered detailed formulations for adjustment of competing interests. No clear pattern, however, emerges from their efforts.[102]

100. *Cox v. Louisiana*, 379 U.S. 536, 554–555 (1965). Justice Black, with whom Justice Clark concurred, would have upheld the total prohibition. Justices White and Harlan, without passing on the total prohibition point, believed the demonstration had reached the point where it could validly be stopped under the statute. See the prior discussion of the case in Section A, *supra*.

101. *Cameron v. Johnson*, 390 U.S. 611 (1968). In *Shuttlesworth v. Birmingham*, 382 U.S. 87 (1965), the Court reversed a conviction of the Rev. F. L. Shuttlesworth for violation of a city ordinance which punished loitering that resulted in obstruction of free passage, but

the Court dealt only peripherally with First Amendment issues.

102. See the cases cited in *Political and Civil Rights in the United States*, pp. 580–581; Note, "Regulation of Demonstrations," *Harvard Law Review*, Vol. 80 (1967), pp. 1773, 1775–1776. See also *Hamer v. Musselwhite*, 376 F.2d 479 (5th Cir. 1967); *Robinson v. Coopwood*, 292 F. Supp. 926 (N.D. Miss. 1968). For efforts to spell out the adjustment in great detail see the *Rockwell* and *Hurwitt* cases, *supra* note 77, and *Williams v. Wallace*, 240 F. Supp. 100 (M.D. Ala. 1965) (Selma to Montgomery march). A full account of a case in which the police attempted to make ad hoc adjustments on

Somewhat different problems arise if the attempt is made to exercise the right of assembly or petition in areas not open to general public passage or in areas used for more particular purposes than the streets, parks and similar open places. Examples are the distribution of leaflets in the New York Port Authority bus terminal or a delegation seeking to present a grievance at the office of a public official. Under such circumstances, the principle of fair accommodation would certainly leave less room for exercise of the right of assembly or petition and more room for conduct of the other business. The decision in *Brown v. Louisiana,* in which the Court upheld the right of protesters to remain in a library after being refused service, indicates that the right of petition must receive some recognition even in facilities customarily devoted to a very special use. On the other hand, in some situations the special use would be totally favored. This would certainly be true in a courtroom, a legislative chamber, or the office of the Chief Executive. The principle of fair accommodation ends, in other words, where exercise of the right of expression is out of bounds under the doctrines of place discussed earlier.

Exercise of the right of assembly or petition may involve physical manifestations besides merely occupying space, and thereby interfere with traffic or other pursuits. It frequently, for instance, creates noise, and this may be as physically disruptive of other uses of an area as the blocking of passage. Here also the principle of fair accommodation is applicable. The only consideration of this issue by the Supreme Court seems to be in the sound truck cases. In *Saia v. New York* an ordinance which required a permit from the police to operate sound amplifying devices on the streets, with "no standards prescribed for the exercise" of discretion by the police, was ruled unconstitutional as a prior restraint. In *Kovacs v. Cooper,* however, an ordinance construed by the State court to prohibit only sound amplifiers that emitted "loud and raucous" noises was upheld. The Court was closely divided in both cases, and there was sharp conflict over what might constitute a proper adjustment, but the principle of fair accommodation seems to have been accepted by all but two members of the Court.[103]

---

the scene is given in Kermit Lipez, "The Law of Demonstrations: The Demonstrators, the Police, the Courts," *Denver Law Journal,* Vol. 44 (1967), p. 499.

103. *Saia v. New York,* 334 U.S. 558 (1948); *Kovacs v. Cooper,* 336 U.S. 77 (1949). Justices Frankfurter and Jackson

would have allowed a total prohibition of outdoor sound amplifying devices. For reference to other material dealing with the sound truck issue see *Political and Civil Rights in the United States,* p. 553. See also the *Chester* case, *supra* note 34, the *Gunn* case, *supra* note 96, and *Wol-*

The use of the same facilities by different persons or groups, each seeking to exercise the right of assembly or petition, does not ordinarily present very difficult problems of fair accommodation so long as the available facilities are not seriously limited. Usually a first come, first served rule would settle the matter. Indeed such issues have never come before the Supreme Court and have seldom, if ever, been the subject of reported decisions in other courts.

E. Administration of Controls

Administration of controls over assembly and petition, and over related conduct, poses particularly difficult problems. Yet here, perhaps more than in any other area, the quality of the system of free expression depends upon the manner in which the theoretical rules are carried out in practice. The major questions that have arisen concern (1) the form in which controls are framed, and (2) the remedies for their wrongful administration. The problems vary, of course, depending upon whether the regulation is designed to punish conduct after the event, to authorize control while the assembly or petitioning is in progress, or to ward off an anticipated danger by prohibiting or restricting the conduct in advance.

1. FORM OF THE REGULATION

a. Punishment of Past Conduct In transforming theoretical powers to control assembly and petition into actual laws that punish conduct not conforming to prescribed standards, the major problem has been to satisfy the doctrines of vagueness and overbreadth. The rule against vagueness requires that the regulation be drawn with sufficient specificity so that persons seeking to exercise First Amendment rights, as well as those attempting to enforce the regulation, will know definitely what is being prohibited. The rule against overbreadth demands that the regulation be framed to cover only that conduct which

---

lam v. City of Palm Springs, 59 Calif. 2d 276, 29 Cal. Rptr. 1, 379 P.2d 481 (1963). The sound truck cases can also be considered from the viewpoint of invasions of privacy. See Chapter XIV.

is constitutionally subject to control, and not embrace conduct protected under the First Amendment or conduct that might be protected but which it is not necessary to control in order to achieve the desired objective. Failure to meet either of these requirements means that the regulation is void on its face, regardless of the validity of particular applications. The courts have used these doctrines in part to avoid a direct decision on First Amendment issues. But the doctrines also play a crucial role in maintaining an effective system of freedom of expression. They are essential, as a practical matter, to prevent a partially valid restriction from operating to curb First Amendment rights far beyond its legitimate range.

The Supreme Court has applied the doctrines of vagueness and overbreadth most frequently in connection with laws seeking to preserve the public peace. It has employed them with varying degrees of strictness, its later decisions tending to invoke the rules more stringently. In *Cantwell v. Connecticut,* reversal of a conviction of the common law offense of breach of the peace was based in part upon both doctrines; the Court objected to "the most general and undefined nature" of the crime, and said it was analogous to "a statute sweeping in a great variety of conduct under a general and indefinite characterization, and leaving to the executive and judicial branches too wide a discretion in its application." But in *Chaplinsky v. New Hampshire* a challenge on vagueness grounds was overruled, the Court saying that a statute which punished "any offensive, derisive or annoying word" was "narrowly drawn and limited." In *Feiner v. New York,* a broad but typical disorderly conduct statute was apparently not attacked on vagueness grounds and the Court said nothing about the problem. In *Edwards v. South Carolina,* however, the Court moved back to *Cantwell.* Dealing with a common law crime of breach of the peace again, it reversed the conviction in part on the ground that the offense was "so generalized as to be, in the words of the South Carolina Supreme Court, 'not susceptible of exact definition.'" In *Cox v. Louisiana,* the Court invalidated a Louisiana breach of the peace statute, which prohibited congregating with others "with intent to provoke a breach of the peace, or under circumstances such that a breach of the peace may be occasioned," on the ground that it was "unconstitutionally vague in its overly broad scope." [104]

---

104. *Cantwell v. Connecticut,* 310 U.S. 296, 308 (1940); *Chaplinsky v. New Hampshire,* 315 U.S. 568, 573 (1942); *Feiner v. New York,* 340 U.S. 315 (1951); *Edwards v. South Carolina,* 372 U.S. 229, 237 (1963); *Cox v. Louisiana,*

Sedition or insurrection laws, other than those specifically forbidding advocacy of overthrow of the government by force and violence, would certainly run into similar difficulties. The Federal Riot Act, incorporated in the Civil Rights Act of 1968, also seems vulnerable on grounds of both vagueness and overbreadth.[105]

The task of drafting a statute to punish expression that threatens the public peace would seem to be increasingly complex. So long as the statute is clearly confined to penalizing action the drafting problem appears manageable, although designating the line between action and expression obviously presents some difficulties. But when the draftsman seeks to incorporate some expression within the statutory prohibition, he must make clear what expression is in and what is out, and he cannot go over the constitutional boundary. He may not solve the problem by incorporating the balancing test within the statute, for that certainly would violate the rule against vagueness. Possibly he can couch the prohibition in terms of expression that creates a clear and present danger of some action, or possibly he can utilize a concept of "incitement." Yet neither of these may satisfy the *Yates* requirement, applied to noncriminal controls in *Keyishian,* that only advocacy of action rather than advocacy of ideas can be restricted. The implication of *Cox v. Louisiana* is that most existing breach of the peace, disorderly conduct, general sedition, and similar statutes are unconstitutional. Just how the Supreme Court will resolve the problem remains to be seen. What is clear is that the issue cannot be settled until the Court decides upon its basic test for applying the First Amendment in this area.[106]

Laws that have sought to protect other social interests, such as those intended to prevent littering, personal injury, or interference with government functions, have usually not run afoul of the vagueness or overbreadth doctrines. Many of these have been held invalid on straight First Amendment grounds, but those which have survived that attack have also overcome the vagueness and overbreadth objec-

---

379 U.S. 536, 551 (1965). See also the opinions of Justices Black and Harlan in *Gregory v. City of Chicago,* 394 U.S. 111 (1969). Some of the lower Federal court cases dealing with the problem are cited in *Wright v. City of Montgomery,* 406 F.2d 867 (5th Cir. 1969). The problem is again before the Supreme Court in *Boyle v. Landry* and *Gunn v. University Committee to End the War in Viet Nam,* both set down for reargument in the 1969–1970 Term. 395 U.S. 955, 956 (1969).

105. On the sedition and insurrection laws see Chapter V. The Federal Riot Act, 18 U.S.C. §§2101, 2102, is discussed in Chapter XI.

106. *Yates v. United States,* 354 U.S. 298 (1957); *Keyishian v. Board of Regents,* 385 U.S. 589 (1967).

tions. Thus in *Cox* the prohibition against picketing or parading "near" a courthouse was upheld as "a precise, narrowly drawn regulatory statute." The drafting problem is less troublesome here when no effort is made to measure the effect of the expression, as where all leaflet distribution is cut off, all door-bell ringing stopped, or all picketing of the courthouse prohibited. Yet in *Cameron v. Johnson,* where the statute prohibited only picketing that "unreasonably interfered" with ingress or egress, the Court still found the law neither vague nor overbroad. The principal reason seems to be that this type of regulation, unlike the catchall breach of the peace or disorderly conduct statute, deals with a narrow area of conduct.[107]

Laws regulating the place in which the right of assembly and petitioning can be carried on, usually framed as trespass laws, also have not created problems under the vagueness and overbreadth rules. In *Adderley v. Florida,* Justice Black rejected such a contention for the reason that a trespass statute does not "cover a multitude of types of conduct as does the common law breach of the peace charge," but "is aimed at conduct of one limited kind, that is, for one person or persons to trespass upon the property of another with a malicious and mischievous intent."[108]

On the other hand, attempts to allocate physical facilities by means of a criminal statute are likely to be vulnerable to the vagueness and overbreadth rules. Thus in *Cox* the Louisiana statute, which on its face prohibited all street assemblies but was administered to allow some, was struck down as the "equivalent" of a system of "completely uncontrolled discretion." Similar difficulties are presented by an ordinance such as that of Danville, Virginia, which required that "[m]arching shall be in single file and pickets or demonstrators shall be spaced at a distance of not less than ten feet apart, and not more than six pickets shall picket or demonstrate before any given place of business or public facility." Possibly such restrictions might be necessary to adjust the right of assembly to other use of the streets under one particular set of circumstances; but the general prohibition obviously sweeps too broadly. In *Kovacs v. Cooper* the sound truck ordinance which prohibited "loud and raucous" noise was upheld against a challenge of vagueness. But it is unlikely the Court would sanction such broad and uncertain prohibitions anymore. Application of the fair accommoda-

---

107. *Cox v. Louisiana,* 379 U.S. 559, 562 (1965); *Cameron v. Johnson,* 390 U.S. 611 (1968).

108. *Adderley v. Florida,* 385 U.S. 39, 42 (1966).

tion rule is very difficult to achieve by a general statute designed to punish past conduct. The problem usually must be handled on an individual basis, which normally requires a permit system.[109]

b. Controls Exercised While the Communication Is in Progress
Controls exercised during the period that the assembly or other communication is actually taking place are normally effectuated through the police. The power of the police in the main derives from the right to make an arrest for violation of a law. The problems here are the same as those just discussed. The laws the police are enforcing should be sufficiently definite so that the police as well as the citizen know whether a violation has occurred, and sufficiently narrow so that the police do not have, and do not appear to have, authority to interfere with conduct that is protected by the First Amendment. As often pointed out, the fact that the laws are being given meaning and substance by police officials, on the spot and often under pressure, makes it more imperative that the rules against vagueness and overbreadth be scrupulously applied.

In addition to the usual authority to arrest for violation of an existing law, the police are frequently given the power to create new rules on the scene and to enforce them by arrest. These laws are normally framed in terms of making it an offense to refuse to comply with a police order. Serious questions are immediately raised as to how much authority of this sort can legitimately be given to the police.

The Supreme Court has never fully considered these issues. In *Feiner* the majority put substantial, though indeterminate, weight upon "the refusal of petitioner to obey the police requests" and "petitioner's deliberate defiance of the police officers." There was some implication that, even if Feiner was not otherwise violating the law, his refusal to obey the stop order would by itself have constituted a violation. Justice Black disagreed that the "policeman's unexplained request" justified an arrest or conviction. Not only did the police action violate Feiner's "constitutional right of free speech," he urged, but it was itself a " 'deliberate defiance' of ordinary official duty": "For at

---

109. *Cox v. Louisiana*, 379 U.S. 536, 557, 558 (1965). For the Danville ordinance see *Baines v. City of Danville*, 337 F.2d 579, 585 (4th Cir. 1964). *Kovacs v. Cooper*, 336 U.S. 77 (1949). See also *People v. Katz*, 21 N.Y.2d 132, 286 N.Y.S.2d 839, 233 N.E.2d 845 (1967), holding invalid a New York City ordinance which made it unlawful "to encumber or obstruct any street . . . with any article or thing whatsoever."

least where time allows, courtesy and explanation of commands are basic elements of good official conduct in a democratic society. . . . Petitioner was entitled to know why he should cease doing a lawful act." [110]

Some years later, in *Cox v. Louisiana,* the Court was much more cautious about the power of the police to create law during the course of a demonstration. Justice Goldberg, arguing that the Louisiana statute prohibiting a demonstration "near" a courthouse was not unconstitutionally vague, recognized that the police could be given some such power: "it is clear that the statute, with respect to the determination of how near the courthouse a particular demonstration can be, foresees a degree of on-the-spot administrative interpretation by officials charged with responsibility for administering and enforcing it." Hence permission by the police for the demonstrators to conduct a meeting across the street from the courthouse was not "a waiver of law which is beyond the power of the police," but an exercise of "administrative discretion" to apply the statute. Justice Goldberg was careful, however, to qualify the authority conferred on the police: "This administrative discretion to construe the term 'near' concerns a limited control of the streets and other areas in the immediate vicinity of the courthouse and is the type of narrow discretion which this Court has recognized as the proper role of responsible officials in making determinations concerning the time, place, duration, and manner of demonstrations." Nor indeed did Justice Goldberg say expressly that, in the reverse situation, if the police had forbidden the marchers to approach within 101 feet of the courthouse, the marchers would necessarily have been bound by the ruling.[111]

The Court also considered another facet of the problem in *Cox.* Near the end of the demonstration the sheriff, stating that an appeal by Cox to sit in at lunch counters constituted a violation of law, ordered the meeting to break up. Refusal to obey the order, the Court held, was not ground for upholding the conviction, since the reason given was not a valid one. As to the State's argument that the original interpretation of "near" had been withdrawn, the Court said that no such reason was stated by the sheriff. To the further argument that the time allowed by the police had expired, the Court declared that not only was this not given as a reason but nothing in the statutes "authorize[d]

110. *Feiner v. New York,* 340 U.S. 315, 320–321, 327–328 (1951).

111. *Cox v. Louisiana,* 379 U.S. 559, 568, 569 (1965).

the police to draw the narrow time line, unrelated to any policy of these statutes." [112]

Finally in *Shuttlesworth v. Birmingham* the Court reacted even more strongly against conferring extensive powers upon the police. Here the Court dealt with an ordinance which provided: "It shall . . . be unlawful for any person to stand or loiter upon any street or sidewalk of the city after having been requested by any police officer to move on." With respect to this provision Justice Stewart, speaking for the Court, said:

> Literally read . . . this ordinance says that a person may stand on a public sidewalk in Birmingham only at the whim of any police officer of that city. The constitutional vice of so broad a provision needs no demonstration. It "does not provide for government by clearly defined laws, but rather for government by the moment-to-moment opinions of a policeman on his beat." *Cox v. Louisiana,* 379 U.S. 536, 579 (separate opinion of Mr. Justice Black). Instinct with its ever-present potential for arbitrarily suppressing First Amendment liberties, that kind of law bears the hallmark of a police state.[113]

The Court then went on to say that the Alabama court had interpreted the statute narrowly to apply only in the case of "blocking free passage." "As so construed," it concluded, "we cannot say that the ordinance is unconstitutional, though it requires no great feat of imagination to envisage situations in which such an ordinance might be unconstitutionally applied." [114]

The position of the Supreme Court thus remains somewhat ambiguous and largely undeveloped. It would appear to be a sound conclusion, however, that police authorization to issue orders, violation of which constitutes an offense in itself, must be limited to two narrow situations. One is when the police are implementing the rules for allocation of physical facilities between competing uses. These are on-the-spot regulations of time, place and manner necessary to adjust the use of the facilities for assembly and petitioning to their use for traffic and other purposes. The other is when minor control of the actions of the assemblage or onlookers is necessary to assist the police in maintaining order. Since the police have an affirmative obligation to protect the assembly and prevent disorder, their on-the-spot regulation of such things as confining the demonstrators and the opposition in

112. 379 U.S. at 573.
113. *Shuttlesworth v. Birmingham,* 382 U.S. 87, 90–91 (1965).

114. 382 U.S. at 91. See also *Gregory v. City of Chicago,* 394 U.S. 111 (1969).

separate areas does not constitute an abridgment of freedom of assembly or petition. These are matters within the competence of the police, and the exercise of such powers, if employed in a narrow compass and on a reasonable basis, will facilitate freedom of expression. Beyond these two areas, however, police authority to establish the rules should not extend. Police have discretion to arrest persons violating the law, but they do not have discretion to determine what the law is.[115]

One further qualification of police authority is also important. The police should not only give notice of any order they issue but, when circumstances permit, they should also give the reasons for making it. Justice Black was certainly right in *Feiner* that "courtesy and explanation of commands are basic elements of good official conduct." Justice Goldberg in *Cox* also indicated that a failure to give the reason for an order can be fatal to its validity. In most situations, except when serious violation of law has already occurred, an explanation of the order is feasible, and, given the sound equipment normally available to the police, it is technically possible. The advantages are obvious. It forces the police to consider the justification for their order, encourages cooperation by the assemblage, and establishes a tone that may have an important bearing on whether the outcome will be compliance or conflict.

c. Preventive Controls Controls designed to prohibit or regulate assembly or petitioning in advance are by nature highly flexible. They can be applied on a case-by-case basis, and hence can be tailored to meet the requirements of the individual situation. Most frequently such preventive controls take the form of a permit or license system administered by executive officials.

From the time of *Cox v. New Hampshire* it has been clear that, under some circumstances, the government may demand that a permit be secured in advance of engaging in assembly or petitioning, and that the permit may impose certain conditions upon the exercise of the right. But the Supreme Court has never made it entirely clear under what circumstances a permit may be required and what conditions may be laid down. It has been argued above that a permit system is valid only when employed to accommodate the exercise of the right of assembly or petition to other uses of the same physical facilities, and that the conditions attached to a permit may deal only with matters

115. For an account of regulation by the police of the areas where the demonstrators and the opposition may operate, see Lipez, *op. cit. supra* note 102.

connected with that accommodation, namely, the time, place and manner of exercising the constitutional right. These propositions follow from the full protection theory of the First Amendment. They are not contradicted, though they are not wholly confirmed, in the decisions of the Supreme Court to date.[116]

Within this framework, the major doctrine that bears upon the form of permit systems stems from the rules against vagueness and overbreadth. It holds that the standards by which a permit is to be granted, denied, or shaped must be sufficiently detailed and specific so that the officials administering the system are not given uncontrollable authority. The Supreme Court laid down this rule in *Lovell v. Griffin,* the first case in which it considered a permit system, and has reiterated it on numerous occasions through *Shuttlesworth v. City of Birmingham,* decided in 1969. In these cases the Court has either held invalid permit systems that contained no standards at all or in which the standards were considered vague, or upheld systems that left no discretion with the administering officials to deny a permit. The Court has never had occasion to consider in detail what kinds of time, place and manner conditions could be imposed. As in the case of breach of the peace and disorderly conduct statutes, much existing legislation undoubtedly fails to meet the Supreme Court requirements. In this situation, however, the problem of drafting satisfactory standards, limited to time, place and manner, is by no means insuperable.[117]

Another doctrine that has played a part in the permit system cases is the rule against prior restraint. This doctrine, as noted previously, holds that in general expression cannot be cut off in advance of publication but can only be controlled by subsequent punishment. The doctrine of prior restraint has never been applied, however, to preclude permit systems designed to allocate physical facilities and limited to regulation of time, place and manner, such as were upheld in *Cox* and *Poulos.* The Supreme Court has not explained the reason for this exception, or indeed articulated how far the exception runs. It can be justified, of course, in practical terms as necessary to the process of

---

116. See *Cox v. New Hampshire,* 312 U.S. 569 (1941); *Thomas v. Collins,* 323 U.S. 516 (1945); and discussion above.

117. Cases in which the Court has struck down permit systems include: *Lovell v. Griffin,* 303 U.S. 444 (1938); *Hague v. C.I.O.,* 307 U.S. 496 (1939); *Schneider v. State,* 308 U.S. 147 (1939); *Cantwell v. Connecticut,* 310 U.S. 296 (1940); *Lar-* *gent v. Texas,* 318 U.S. 418 (1943); *Kunz v. New York,* 340 U.S. 290 (1951); *Staub v. City of Baxley,* 355 U.S. 313 (1958); *Shuttlesworth v. City of Birmingham,* 394 U.S. 147 (1969). Cases in which permit systems were upheld are *Cox v. New Hampshire,* 312 U.S. 569 (1941); *Poulos v. New Hampshire,* 345 U.S. 395 (1953).

accommodating competing uses of the same facilities. In doctrinal terms, the exception is fully consistent with the protection given First Amendment rights under the full protection theory.

Curiously, the Supreme Court has often invoked the doctrine of prior restraint in those cases in which it has invalidated the permit system under the rule of uncontrollable discretion. Thus in *Lovell v. Griffin*, after pointing out that the City Manager could grant or withhold permission to distribute literature "in his discretion," the Court declared that the First Amendment was intended to assure "freedom from previous restraint upon publication," citing *Near v. Minnesota*, and concluded: "Legislation of the type of the ordinance in question would restore the system of licensing and censorship in its baldest form." Used in this way the doctrine of prior restraint is merely an appendage of the uncontrollable discretion rule and plays no part of its own.[118]

The same rules that are applicable to permit systems should likewise govern the courts in the issuance of injunctions designed to control the exercise of the right to assemble and petition. Indeed the doctrine of prior restraint was first applied in a case involving a court injunction. Under the prior restraint rule no restrictions would be valid except those dealing with time, place and manner. The same result would follow from the full protection theory. The courts have not always, however, so confined themselves. They have on occasion issued injunctions prohibiting assembly or imposing restrictions going beyond time, place and manner, in most cases designed to forestall violence. The inspiration for such action undoubtedly springs from increased use of the injunction in labor or other economic picketing. In any event use of the injunction in this way fails to separate expression from action. The right to control violence or other action by injunction does not extend to the prevention of expression.[119]

2. REMEDIES FOR WRONGFUL ADMINISTRATION

a. Controls Administered During and After the Assembly or Petitioning Unlawful interference by government authorities with the right to assemble and petition can take many forms. Frequently the

118. *Lovell v. Griffin*, 303 U.S. at 451–452; *Near v. Minnesota*, 283 U.S. 697 (1931), discussed in Chapter XIII.

119. For collection of cases on the use of the injunction against assembly and petition see *Political and Civil Rights in the United States*, pp. 594–596.

harassment consists of plainly illegal action, such as unwarranted arrests, police brutality, or arbitrary refusal to grant to one group privileges extended to others. At other times the harassment may be based upon pseudo-legal techniques, such as use of an invalid statute or misuse of a valid one. Theoretically legal remedies are available to counteract these infringements of First Amendment rights. Constitutional issues may be raised by way of defense to a prosecution, and an affirmative action for damages, injunction or declaratory judgment is usually available. In practice, of course, legal relief may be cumbersome, expensive, uncertain and long-delayed. Here, perhaps more than in any other area of free expression, the promise of the constitutional guarantee is betrayed to the realities of everyday life.

The major development in legal techniques designed to improve the situation was the extension of Federal judicial power over the conduct of State and local authorities. The Federal courts, more responsive to national trends and more remote from local conflicts, have presented a more friendly forum for vindication of minority rights to freedom of expression, as they have to equal protection. This Federal supervision has been available not only through appeal from State court action in which Federal constitutional rights have been invoked, but also by way of initial litigation seeking affirmative relief. Thus a suit for damages lies under the original Federal Civil Rights Acts, now embodied in 42 U.S.C. §1983, against any person who under color of State law deprives any other person of his rights under the First Amendment. Damage suits against government officials are notoriously ineffective, but a considerable potential inheres in this provision. More importantly, Section 1983 also authorizes an injunction for vindication of First Amendment rights in the Federal courts. This provision has been employed with some success against State or local authorities who have flagrantly denied rights of assembly or petition. It is only useful, however, if the harassment represents a pattern of continuing action and injunctive relief is feasible. The criminal provisions of the Federal Civil Rights Acts, embodied in 18 U.S.C. §§241 and 242, authorize Federal prosecution of State officials or private persons who deprive an individual of his constitutional rights. But these provisions have in practice been utilized primarily if the denial of constitutional rights is effectuated through violence of some kind, and have never been directly invoked in a case involving denial of First Amendment rights. Under other Federal statutes, such as those protecting the right to vote, an injunction suit initiated by the Federal government is available to safeguard the right of assembly and petition. Yet such cases have been rare. Habeas corpus and removal of State prosecutions to Federal courts complete the list of legal devices for obtaining Federal review of State action claimed to infringe First Amendment rights.[120]

Section 1983 can also be used to test the constitutionality of a statute that threatens the rights of assembly and petition, and to enjoin prosecutions under an invalid statute or a statute which, though valid, is being wrongfully applied. Litigation of this nature is, of course, subject to the rules of *Dombrowski, Zwickler* and *Cameron,* discussed in Chapter V. An argument can be made that Federal supervision over State prosecutions alleged to interfere with First Amendment rights should be extended on a broader basis than these rules allow. Even under existing formulations, however, the protection afforded by the Federal courts can be of major significance to the right of assembly and petition. Unfortunately in the second *Cameron v. Johnson* decision the Supreme Court decided to apply the rules in a particularly niggardly fashion.[121]

---

120. The availability of the damage suit under Section 1983 was reaffirmed in *Monroe v. Pape,* 365 U.S. 167 (1961), and applied to a denial of First Amendment rights in *Nesmith v. Alford,* 318 F.2d 110 (5th Cir. 1963), cert. denied 375 U.S. 975 (1964). For other cases see *Political and Civil Rights in the United States,* pp. 1452–1453. The injunction suit based on Section 1983 was first used to protect rights of assembly and petition in *Hague v. C.I.O.,* 307 U.S. 496 (1939). For a collection of other cases see *Political and Civil Rights in the United States,* pp. 547–548, 599, 1452–1453; Note, "The Federal Injunction as a Remedy for Unconstitutional Police Conduct," *Yale Law Journal,* Vol. 78 (1968), p. 143. Cases and references on the use of the criminal provisions of the Federal Civil Rights Acts may be found in *Political and Civil Rights in the United States,* pp. 1402–1439. These provisions were strengthened by amendments in 1968, 82 Stat. 73–75. Injunction suits brought by the Federal government to protect First Amendment rights include *United States v. U.S. Klans,* 194 F. Supp. 897 (M.D. Ala. 1961); *United States v. Clark,* 249 F. Supp. 720 (S.D. Ala. 1965); *United States v. Mc-*

Leod, 385 F.2d 734 (5th Cir. 1967). See also *Political and Civil Rights in the United States,* p. 1469. An unsuccessful effort to compel the Federal government to exert its powers to protect the constitutional rights of individual citizens was made in *Moses v. Kennedy,* 219 F. Supp. 762 (D.D.C. 1963). On habeas corpus and removal, see Anthony Amsterdam, "Criminal Prosecution Affecting Federally Guaranteed Civil Rights: Federal Removal and Habeas Corpus Jurisdiction to Abort State Court Trial," *University of Pennsylvania Law Review,* Vol. 113 (1965), p. 793; *Political and Civil Rights in the United States,* pp. 1824–1869; *Georgia v. Rachel,* 384 U.S. 780 (1966); *City of Greenwood v. Peacock,* 384 U.S. 808 (1966).

121. *Cameron v. Johnson,* 390 U.S. 611 (1968): See Chapter V for discussion. For the argument that the Federal courts should take jurisdiction over all State prosecutions in which any First Amendment issue is raised see D'Army Bailey, "Enjoining State Criminal Prosecutions Which Abridge First Amendment Freedoms," *Harvard Civil Rights–Civil Liberties Law Review,* Vol. 3 (1967), p. 67.

In *Cameron,* as noted, the Court unanimously held the Mississippi Anti-Picketing Law valid on its face. The demonstrators also claimed, however, that Mississippi officials were prosecuting them under the statute in bad faith, with no expectation of obtaining convictions, and asked that further harassment be enjoined. Justice Brennan, writing for the majority, did not review the evidence in his opinion but stated his conclusion that "[w]e cannot say from our independent examination of the record that the District Court erred in denying injunctive relief." Bad faith was not shown, he said, by evidence adduced at the hearing that "the pickets' conduct throughout the period would not be sufficient, in the view of appellants, to sustain convictions on a criminal trial":

> The mere possibility of erroneous application of the statute does not amount "to the irreparable injury necessary to justify a disruption of orderly state proceedings." *Dombrowski v. Pfister* . . . The issue of guilt or innocence is for the state court at the criminal trial; the State was not required to prove appellants guilty in the federal proceeding to escape the finding that the State had no expectation of securing valid convictions. Appellants say that the picketing was non-obstructive, but the State claims quite the contrary, and the record is not totally devoid of support for the State's claim.[122]

Justice Fortas, joined by Justice Douglas, dissented. Examining the record in detail he declared that the "evidence in this record that the picketing interfered with or even inconvenienced pedestrians is negligible," and that there was "no evidence that access to the courthouse was actually obstructed." From these and other circumstances he concluded that "the State was not here engaged in policing access to the courthouse or even freedom of the sidewalks, but in a deliberate plan to put an end to the voting-rights demonstration":

> There is powerful evidence in this record that the State cannot possibly anticipate a conviction of the pickets which will withstand the tests this Court has laid down in the First Amendment and Fourteenth Amendment areas; and it requires more indulgence than this Court has permitted in cases involving First Amendment freedoms for us to say that the State has made a tolerable showing to the contrary.[123]

Cameron v. Johnson can only be described as a drastic retreat from the Supreme Court's previous willingness to employ the Federal judicial power to protect First Amendment rights against interference

---

122. 390 U.S. at 619, 621–622.   123. 390 U.S. at 624, 627–628.

by actions of State and local authorities. The attitude of the majority seems distinctly hostile to the view that the Federal courts should scan the local proceedings with a sharp and realistic eye. Moreover, Justice Brennan's position that a record "not totally devoid of support for the State's claim" is sufficient to overcome the weight of evidence, puts a virtually impossible burden upon the person seeking Federal relief. *Cameron v. Johnson* in effect gives the citizen little hope that in prosecutions based on a law not invalid on its face he can secure Federal scrutiny except after a long journey through the State courts.

Thus the exercise of Federal authority to control abuses by State and local officials remains in a state of flux. Substantial power exists, in the form of both civil and criminal proceedings. But it has never been fully utilized. In its latest decisions the Supreme Court appears to be approaching the problems with extreme caution.

b. Controls Exercised Before the Communication Takes Place
When controls on assembly and petitioning operate in advance, through a permit system or a court injunction, the problem of affording a remedy for wrongful restriction becomes particularly acute. Time is almost always of the essence in exercising these rights. Delay is endemic in administrative and judicial procedures. Moreover, a prior restraint is more easily imposed, requires less foundation in provable facts, and is less carefully weighed than subsequent punishment. Even with the best of intentions a system of advance controls is difficult to administer in a way that fully safeguards freedom of expression; with the worst of intentions it can easily be utilized to throttle that constitutional right. These problems will become of increasing importance as States and municipalities learn, as they eventually will, to frame permit systems in a manner that conforms to constitutional requirements.

One development in this area has already begun. As the price for sanctioning prior control of expression the courts will demand improved procedures, including fair consideration, prompt action by administrative officials, and swift judicial review. Requirements of this sort have already been imposed upon movie censorship systems, and the same conditions will be exacted of permit systems that undertake to control the right of assembly and petition. In *Carroll v. President and Commissioners of Princess Anne* the Supreme Court moved sharply in this direction. It invalidated an order restraining the holding of a meeting by the National States Rights Party for the reason that the order had been issued *ex parte,* without formal or informal notice to the Party. Referring to its rules in the movie censorship cases, the Court declared that "a noncriminal process of prior restraints upon expression 'avoids constitutional infirmity only if it takes place under procedural safeguards designed to obviate the dangers of a censorship system.' " Included among these safeguards, the Court made clear, is the right to a prompt decision. Thus, while the Court shied away from applying the prior restraint rule with vigor on the merits, it did give notice that it would attempt to enforce maximum procedural protection to persons subjected to that form of restriction.[124]

It is doubtful, however, that procedural advances will fully solve the underlying problems. A system of granting permits for assembly and petition faces greater difficulties than a movie censorship system. The necessary facts are harder to determine, the issues are more highly charged, and the effects of delay more serious. Hence it is unlikely that abuse of permit systems in this field can ever be entirely eliminated. Under these circumstances it becomes important to develop the rules that apply in cases of self-help. To what extent must the applicant stay within the permit system and pursue his administrative and judicial remedies to their exhausting end? Or may he break out of the system, exercise his claimed right to assembly and petition without advance approval, and then challenge the denial of permission in defense to a criminal prosecution for violating the permit requirement? This may be a risky option for him. But the applicant may feel it is the only way he can avoid being smothered in a maze of procedural restrictions.

It is clear that if an administrative permit system is constitutionally defective, as many of them still are, a person desiring to exercise the right of assembly or petition may proceed to do so without a permit and raise his constitutional objections in an ensuing prosecution. In the first major decisions dealing with the operation of permit systems —*Kunz v. New York* and *Niemotko v. Maryland*—the Supreme Court found the permit system unconstitutional and reversed convictions of persons who had held meetings in violation of the regulations after having been denied permits. In *Staub v. City of Baxley* the Court held that it was not even necessary to apply for a permit under an invalid system. In *Shuttlesworth v. City of Birmingham* the Court reiterated: "[O]ur decisions have made clear that a person faced with such an unconstitutional licensing law may ignore it and engage with impunity in the exercise of the right of free expression for which the

---

124. *Carroll v. President and Commissioners of Princess Anne*, 393 U.S. 175, 181 (1968). On the movie censorship cases see Chapter XIII.

law purports to require a license." The rule seems eminently sound and has not been seriously contested.[125]

A different question arises if the permit system is a valid one but a permit is denied on invalid grounds. The problem came before the Supreme Court in *Poulos v. New Hampshire,* decided in 1953. In that case a Jehovah's Witness applied for a permit to conduct religious meetings in a public park on June 25 and July 2. On May 4 his request was refused. Without seeking judicial redress, the applicant then conducted a meeting anyway. When he was prosecuted for holding the meeting without a permit the applicant was not allowed to raise as a defense the fact that the permit had been improperly denied, though it was agreed that the refusal of the permit was "arbitrary and unreasonable." He was convicted and the Supreme Court, by a seven to two vote, upheld the conviction. Justice Reed, after ruling that the permit system was basically valid, overruled the contention that the refusal to allow the defense of improper denial violated the First Amendment:

It must be admitted that judicial correction of arbitrary refusal by administrators to perform official duties under valid laws is exulcerating and costly. But to allow applicants to proceed without the required permits to run businesses, erect structures, purchase firearms, transport or store explosives or inflammatory products, hold public meetings without prior safety arrangements or take other unauthorized action is apt to cause breaches of the peace or create public dangers. The valid requirements of license are for the good of the applicants and the public. It would be unreal to say that such official failures to act in accordance with state law, redressable by state judicial procedures, are state acts violative of the Federal Constitution. Delay is unfortunate, but the expense and annoyance of litigation is a price citizens must pay for life in an orderly society where the rights of the First Amendment have a real and abiding meaning. Nor can we say that a state's requirement that redress must be sought through appropriate judicial procedure violates due process.[126]

Justices Black and Douglas dissented. They considered the permit system invalid and their opinions do not make any sharp distinction between the rights of an applicant under a valid or an invalid system.

125. *Kunz v. New York,* 340 U.S. 290 (1951); *Niemotko v. Maryland,* 340 U.S. 268 (1951); *Staub v. City of Baxley,* 355 U.S. 313 (1958); *Shuttlesworth v. City of Birmingham,* 394 U.S. 147, 151 (1969). The Court had applied the same rule in earlier decisions striking down permit systems. See, *e.g., Lovell v. Griffin,* 303 U.S. 444 (1938); *Cantwell v. Connecticut,* 310 U.S. 296 (1940); *Thomas v. Collins,* 323 U.S. 516 (1945).

126. *Poulos v. New Hampshire,* 345 U.S. 395, 409 (1953).

It seems clear, however, that both felt the First Amendment required that the applicant be allowed to proceed with the meeting and to raise all questions of validity in any subsequent prosecution. Both agreed that an applicant for a license to run a business or engage in similar conduct would have to pursue his legal remedies if permission were refused, but considered that rights under the First Amendment held a "preferred position" and were entitled to "special protection." Justice Douglas went on to say:

> If a citizen can flout the legislature when it undertakes to tamper with his First Amendment rights, I fail to see why he may not flout the official or agency who administers a licensing law designed to regulate the exercise of the right of free speech. Defiance of a statute is hardly less harmful to an orderly society than defiance of an administrative order. The vice of a statute, which exacts a license for the right to make a speech, is that it adds a burden to the right. The burden is the same when the officials administering the licensing system withhold the license and require the applicant to spend months or years in the courts in order to win a right which the Constitution says no government shall deny.[127]

A similar issue, but arising in the context of an injunction proceeding, was presented to the Supreme Court in *Walker v. City of Birmingham*. A city ordinance made it unlawful to hold or participate in a parade, procession, or other demonstration on the streets of Birmingham unless a permit had been secured from the City Commission. The Commission was required to grant the permit "unless in its judgment the public welfare, peace, safety, health, decency, good order, morals or convenience require that it be refused." In 1963 a group under the sponsorship of the Southern Christian Leadership Conference, headed by Martin Luther King, Jr., and its Alabama affiliate conducted a series of demonstrations in Birmingham protesting racial discrimination. On April 3 and again on April 5 the Negro groups attempted to obtain a permit but were turned down. Demonstrations were held on April 6–7 and April 9–10 and a number of Negroes were arrested for parading without a permit. On the night of April 10 the city obtained an *ex parte* injunction enjoining the two organizations and 139 individuals from participating in parades or processions without a permit, from violating the ordinances of the City of Birmingham, and from engaging in other stated acts. The Negro groups, who had planned to hold parades on Good Friday, April 12, and Easter Sun-

127. 345 U.S. at 422, 423–424.

day, April 14, went ahead with these demonstrations despite the court order. Eight Negro ministers, including Dr. King, were cited for contempt, convicted, and sentenced to five days in jail and $50 fines.

The trial court held that the only issues before it were whether the court had jurisdiction to issue the temporary injunction and whether the defendants had knowingly violated it. The court declined to consider contentions that the ordinance was unconstitutional in that it was vague and overbroad, that it violated the First Amendment, and that it had been discriminatorily administered. It also refused to deal with the contention that the injunction was invalid as vague and overly broad. The Alabama Supreme Court affirmed and, when the case reached the United States Supreme Court in 1967, it also affirmed, by a vote of five to four.[128]

Justice Stewart, writing for the majority, followed the rule laid down in earlier labor injunction cases: "An injunction duly issuing out of a court of general jurisdiction with equity powers upon pleadings properly invoking its action, and served upon persons made parties therein and within the jurisdiction, must be obeyed by them however erroneous the action of the court may be, even if the error be in the assumption of the validity of a seeming but void law going to the merits of the case." Justice Stewart stated the rule without qualification, but in discussing its application to the case before him he suggested three possible circumstances which might have produced a different result: (1) "this is not a case where the injunction was transparently invalid or had only a frivolous pretense to validity"; (2) "it could not be assumed that this ordinance was void on its face"; and (3) "[t]his case would arise in quite a different constitutional posture if the petitioners, before disobeying the injunction, had challenged it in the Alabama courts, and had been met with delay or frustration of their constitutional claims." Then he concluded on another note:

> The rule of law that Alabama followed in this case reflects a belief that in the fair administration of justice no man can be judge in his own case, however exalted his station, however righteous his motives, and irrespective of his race, color, politics, or religion. This Court cannot hold that the petitioners were constitutionally free to ignore all the procedures of the law and carry their battle to the streets. One may sympathize with the petitioners' impatient commitment to their cause. But respect for judicial process is a small price to pay for the civilizing

128. *Walker v. City of Birmingham,*
388 U.S. 307 (1967).

hand of law, which alone can give abiding meaning to constitutional freedom.[129]

Separate dissenting opinions were issued by Chief Justice Warren, Justice Douglas and Justice Brennan, with Justice Fortas concurring in all three. The dissenters stressed that the ordinance and the injunction were patently invalid; that to allow State courts to impose prior restraints on speech through use of the injunctive power would stifle First Amendment rights; and that the right to disobey an invalid law had long been recognized by the courts as essential to preserve freedom of expression. The views of the dissenters are reflected in the two following extracts. Justice Brennan declared:

> Yet by some inscrutable legerdemain these constitutionally secured rights to challenge prior restraints invalid on their face are lost if the State takes the precaution to have some judge append his signature to an *ex parte* order which recites the words of the invalid statute. The State neatly insulates its legislation from challenge by mere incorporation of the identical stifling, overbroad and vague restraints on exercise of the First Amendment freedoms into an even more vague and pervasive injunction obtained invisibly and upon a stage darkened lest it be open to scrutiny by those affected. The *ex parte* order of the judicial officer exercising broad equitable powers is glorified above the presumably carefully considered, even if hopelessly invalid, mandates of the legislative branch. I would expect this tribunal, charged as it is with the ultimate responsibility to safeguard our constitutional freedoms, to regard the *ex parte* injunctive tool to be far more dangerous than statutes to First Amendment freedoms.[130]

Chief Justice Warren, arguing that he did not think that " 'the civilizing hand of law' would be hampered in the slightest by enforcing the First Amendment in this case," said:

> It has never been thought that violation of a statute indicated such a disrespect for the legislature that the violator always must be punished even if the statute was unconstitutional. On the contrary, some cases have required that persons seeking to challenge the constitutionality of a statute first violate it to establish their standing to sue. Indeed, it shows no disrespect for law to violate a statute on the ground that it is unconstitutional and then to submit one's case to the courts with the willingness to accept the penalty if the statute is held to be valid . . .

129. 388 U.S. at 314, 315, 317, 318,   130. 388 U.S. at 346.
320–321.

I do not believe that giving this Court's seal of approval to such a gross misuse of the judicial process is likely to lead to greater respect for the law any more than it is likely to lead to greater protection for First Amendment freedoms. The *ex parte* temporary injunction has a long and odious history in this country, and its susceptibility to misuse is all too apparent from the facts of this case. . . . Respect for the courts and for judicial process was not increased by the history of the labor injunction.[131]

Walker was a particularly strong case for allowing the defendants to raise questions going to the validity of the Birmingham ordinance and the ensuing injunction in proceedings for violation of the court's order. On the basis of all prior decisions the Birmingham ordinance was invalid on its face as vague and overbroad, beyond the possibility of redemption by judicial interpretation. Charges were made, clearly not unfounded, that the ordinance had been administered on a discriminatory basis. The temporary injunction had been issued *ex parte*. Defendants had only one day in which to move for judicial reconsideration before the scheduled demonstration on the strategic day, Good Friday. The injunction served no purpose except to transpose proceedings for violation of the ordinance from criminal to contempt procedures, and to immunize the ordinance from constitutional attack. The entire context of the affair made it plain that the city officials, led by Police Commissioner Eugene (Bull) Connor, were engaged in a determined attempt to prevent the Negro groups from exercising their rights of assembly and petition. If, as the majority conceded, there are some occasions when the respect owed the courts is outweighed by other circumstances, this would seem to be such a case. The majority's refusal to permit this undoubtedly reflected a feeling that reversal of the contempt convictions would create public uncertainty about governmental powers to maintain law and order in a period of mounting tensions.[132]

Assuming this would be a sound disposition of the *Walker* case, more difficult questions arise when the basic statutory framework is valid and the invalidity lies only in the application of the law to a particular case. A distinction could be drawn here between the violation of a court order and the violation of an administrative refusal to

---

131. 388 U.S. at 327, 330–331.
132. The Birmingham ordinance was in fact held invalid on its face two years later in *Shuttlesworth v. City of Birmingham*, 394 U.S. 147 (1969). See also *Thomas v. Collins*, 323 U.S. 516 (1945).

grant a permit. It can be argued that a judicial decision is entitled to a greater presumption of validity and judicial action should be accorded a higher degree of respect. Yet it is doubtful that the distinction is a sound one in this situation. The degree of probability that a mistake will occur is not a very satisfactory criterion for denial of a First Amendment right. A lessened probability does not help the particular individual who has lost his constitutional right because an error has in fact been made. The argument based on preserving an image of the judicial process as essentially infallible is equally dubious. Such a position saves the courts from paying for their own mistakes, but it also transfers the burden to others. In the long run no mystical respect for the courts is likely to persist on the basis of a rule of law that allows the court to punish an individual even when the court itself has been wrong. It is not unreasonable, therefore, to consider the court order and the permit denial as raising essentially the same problem.

The issue is, of course, not whether refusal to comply with a valid judicial or executive order shall go unpunished, but merely whether all available defenses can be raised in a proceeding for punishing violation of an order whose validity has not yet been determined. In order to answer this question it is necessary to consider the requirements of a system of freedom of expression. Two aspects of such a system are of special importance here. First, the rights of assembly and petition are peculiarly subject to the exigencies of time. Most occasions for exercise of these rights come and go quickly. Unless the meeting is held, the demonstration given, the petition signed and presented, the reason for it soon passes. Hence the delay necessarily involved in determining the validity of the restriction in advance is very often the equivalent of denial of the constitutional right. In *Princess Anne* the Supreme Court held that the issue of whether a permit should have been granted or an assembly enjoined did not become moot in law before the legal question could be finally decided. But in most cases, under the *Poulos* and *Walker* rule, the issue would become moot in practice.[133]

Secondly, there must be taken into account all those factors which underlie the rule against prior restraint of expression. The relative ease with which freedom of expression can be curbed by a minor judicial or executive official, with little or no procedure or consideration, creates imminent danger of abuse. As an exception to the prior restraint rule a

---

133. *Carroll v. President and Commissioners of Princess Anne*, 393 U.S. 175, 178–179 (1968).

permit system, whether administratively or judicially enforced, must be confined to the narrowest possible range.

These considerations, given the preference stated in the First Amendment for the right to freedom of expression, should be conclusive. But it may be helpful to examine further whether a ruling allowing challenge to the validity of the prior restraint disregards other public interests to such an extent as to be unsupportable. Such is not the case. In the first place, as the dissents in *Walker* repeatedly pointed out, the power to enforce an invalid law is rarely conferred by our legal system. No such power exists with respect to virtually all statutes enacted by the legislature, virtually all regulations or orders of administrative tribunals, and many orders issued by the courts, including citations for contempt committed in the presence of the court. Secondly, the advantage gained by the *Poulos* and *Walker* rule in maintaining "the rule of law" is minimal. Most persons will obey the law, even when they think it is in error. Thirdly, the argument that disrespect for the law will be encouraged does not carry the weight it has been given in *Poulos* and *Walker*. If the law is right it can be vindicated; if it is wrong it should not be.

Most of these considerations become less decisive if time is available for judicial review or further judicial consideration before the date set for exercise of the right to assembly or petition. It can be argued that the person or group denied the permit or enjoined from assembling has an obligation to pursue further judicial remedies to the extent possible up to the last moment. Such a rule would have the advantage of inducing the courts to act quickly in reviewing the legal issues. Yet a doctrine of this sort might place an undue burden upon those who do not have counsel or cannot afford litigation. While there can be no objection to the courts framing rules to encourage the maximum resort to the judicial process, an unqualified requirement to that effect in all cases would not satisfy the demands of the First Amendment.

Finally, the dimensions of the problem depend a great deal upon the substantive issue of what standards a court or executive official is authorized to employ in determining whether to issue an injunction or grant a permit. If the rules of prior restraint are relaxed to the point that the licensing authority is entitled to consider such factors as the danger of disorder or the costs of police protection, then many more problems arise. If, as urged here, only factors of time, place and manner are considered, under the doctrine of fair accommodation, the problem diminishes. Under such circumstances disagreement is less likely, judicial review more rapid, and the need for resort to self-help in order to vindicate constitutional rights less imperative.[134]

In sum, one must conclude that the legal techniques for achieving the right of assembly and petition in practice have not developed very fast or very far. Undoubtedly there has been progress in public understanding of the principle and in public acceptance of the practice. Likewise, the increase in legal services available—both through private civil liberties organizations and through publicly supported legal aid—have greatly increased the possibility of securing the rights theoretically granted. This is indeed the main hope. But the Supreme Court has unfortunately not been willing, in its more recent decisions, to broaden some of the most promising legal devices for improving the actual operation of the system.

F. Conclusion

The right of assembly and petition has come to be one of the most significant features of our system of freedom of expression. It has proved to be a powerful instrument for social change in the hands of those who seek to oppose official policies and conventional ways but who do not have access to the official or conventional means of communication. Its role as a key factor in the civil-rights movement, the peace movement, the black movements, and the New Left has been one of the most striking developments of the last decade.

At the same time, or rather as a result of these developments, the right of assembly and petition has come under increasing pressure from opposing directions. On the one side those who feel that the traditional forms of assembly and petition have not achieved sufficiently substantial or sufficiently rapid results have pressed for the creation of

134. For other comment on the *Walker* problem see Sheldon Tefft, "Neither Above the Law Nor Below It: A Note on Walker v. Birmingham," *Supreme Court Review*, Vol. 1967 (1967), p. 181; Joel L. Selig, "Regulation of Street Demonstrations by Injunction," *Harvard Civil Rights–Civil Liberties Law Review*, Vol. IV (1968), p. 135; Henry P. Monaghan, "First Amendment 'Due Process,'" *Harvard Law Review*, Vol. 83 (1970), p. 518; Note, "Defiance of Unlawful Authority," *Harvard Law Review*, Vol. 83 (1970), p. 626.

new forms and for utilization of more "direct action." This has produced demands for expansion of the older concepts, based upon expression, into areas formerly considered action. From the other side, pressure has mounted from those who dislike the objectives sought through use of the right to assemble and petition, and those who fear that its use leads to or is indistinguishable from civil disobedience, riots, and violence. This has generated demands for narrowing the scope of assembly and petition and broadening the devices for its restriction. Both tendencies are dangerous.

To ask of the right to assemble and petition more than it can or should deliver, or to stretch the underlying concepts into areas that constitute action, can only obliterate the fundamental premise upon which the First Amendment is based—the distinction between expression and action—and ultimately destroy the system. The other tendency is even more dangerous. It assumes that civil disorders can be eliminated or diminished by curbing freedom of assembly and petition. The opposite is certainly true. Tensions of the times that produce disorder arise from basic economic, social and political problems, which can only be solved by action going to the roots of those problems. Curtailment of the right of assembly or petition increases the likelihood of solution through violence because it removes a main instrument for facilitating the process of change. It is true that a peaceable assembly can conclude in a riot. But this does not mean that the riot can be prevented by stopping the assembly. Such a course of action leads only towards the establishment of a police state and ultimately more violence in the society.

The role of the Supreme Court is to hold the balance between these two opposing tendencies. But it has not always performed that function with understanding. It has not drawn an appropriate line between protected expression and unprotected action in this area. It came close to abandoning the doctrine that there is an "immemorial right" to use the streets, parks and other public places for purposes of assembly and petition. True, the Court has not permitted unsubstantial fears of violence to curtail the constitutional right. Nor has it subordinated the right to other social interests. Yet it has never developed a satisfactory theory for handling such problems. Nor has it articulated a principle for accommodating physical use of facilities for assembly and petition to their use for other purposes. Finally, it has been reluctant to extend the principles of federalism to give adequate protection to the right of assembly and petition at the local level, or to expand devices for safeguarding the right in its actual working. Thus the Court has neither drawn the proper boundaries for those who would push the right of assembly and petition beyond its inherent limits nor held the line firm against those who would curtail the scope of its proper operation.

X

Internal
Order:
Criminal Libel
and
Group Libel

The adjustments that are necessary between a system of freedom of expression and the social interest in internal order are not confined to problems that grow out of the right to assemble and petition. Among other issues which may arise are those concerned with the laws relating to criminal libel and group libel.

A. Criminal Libel

Most states have criminal libel laws, but they are rarely invoked. These statutes are, in part, intended to supplement civil libel laws by providing the additional deterrence of a criminal prosecution for libelous communications directed at private (nongovernmental) persons. As such they are designed to protect the reputation, economic welfare or personal feelings of the individual member of the community. In this respect they stand on the same footing as civil libel laws, a problem considered in Chapter XIV. We are here concerned with criminal libel laws insofar as they are intended to safeguard internal order by punishing utterances critical of the government or eliminating private feuds which might endanger the public peace.

As measures to penalize expression directed against government policies, institutions or officials, criminal libel laws are designed to perform the same function as the early law of seditious libel. Their purpose is to preserve the prestige of government and the effectiveness of its operations by suppressing criticism. Clearly they are in flat contradiction to the First Amendment. The issue is identical with that posed by the Sedition Act of 1798. It is not one to be resolved by an incitement test, the clear and present danger test, or the balancing test. As the Supreme Court said in *New York Times v. Sullivan* the Sedition Act was unconstitutional because it violated "the central meaning of the First Amendment." [1]

The criminal libel laws possess no greater validity as measures to prevent a breach of the peace springing from physical retaliation by those verbally attacked. That social interest can be safeguarded, certainly in this day and age, by measures punishing the ensuing action without suppressing the communication. Moreover, as in any hostile audience situation, enforcement of such a law would have the effect of suppressing the speech because there is opposition to it.

Strangely enough, although the Supreme Court has twice considered the validity of criminal libel laws utilized for the above purposes, it has never gone all the way in finding them unconstitutional. In *Garrison v. Louisiana,* a district attorney was convicted under the Louisiana Criminal Defamation Statute for remarks critical of the judges in his district. The Supreme Court reversed, but on the ground that the Louisiana statute was not limited to the punishment of statements made with "actual malice," that is, with knowledge of their falsity or with reckless disregard of whether they were false or not. Justices Black, Douglas and Goldberg, concurring, would have held all criminal libel statutes unconstitutional as contrary to the First Amendment. [2]

The Supreme Court again considered criminal libel in *Ashton v. Kentucky.* Here the defendant was convicted under the common law crime of criminal libel for defaming the sheriff, the chief of police and a newspaper owner for their conduct in connection with a labor dispute. The trial court defined criminal libel as "any writing calculated

---

1. *New York Times v. Sullivan,* 376 U.S. 254, 273 (1964).

2. *Garrison v. Louisiana,* 379 U.S. 64 (1964), discussed further in Chapter XIV.

to create disturbances of the peace, corrupt the public morals, or lead to any act, which, when done, is indictable." The Supreme Court reversed on the ground that "to make an offense of conduct which is 'calculated to create disturbances of the peace' leaves wide open the standard of responsibility" and hence is void for vagueness. The First Amendment was considered only as requiring especially strict application of the vagueness rule.[3]

The position of the majority of the Supreme Court seems to be that "deliberate or reckless falsehood" is "at odds with the premises of democratic government" and does "not enjoy constitutional protection." The inference is that criminal libel laws are valid to the extent they prohibit statements of this nature. But surely the majority has missed the point. Under the basic principles of the First Amendment expression critical of the government is protected whether it is deemed true or false, and whether it is uttered with malice or with the best of intentions. Indeed the Sedition Act of 1798 applied only to "false" utterances, made with "intent" to defame. In denouncing the constitutionality of that legislation the Supreme Court never suggested it would have been valid had it clearly applied only to "deliberate or reckless falsehood." The fact seems to be that the majority of the Court in *Garrison* and *Ashton* has failed to distinguish between the use of criminal libel laws as seditious libel and their use as a criminal supplement to the law of civil libel. Whatever may be the justification for declining to protect intentional falsehood in the civil libel situation, there is no warrant for refusing to protect it in the criminal libel context and thereby resurrecting the ancient law of seditious libel.[4]

B. Group Libel

Group libel laws are designed to promote internal order by eliminating or reducing friction among racial, religious, national or similar groups. In general they seek to prohibit, through criminal or civil

3. *Ashton v. Kentucky,* 384 U.S. 195, 200 (1966).

4. 379 U.S. at 75; 1 Stat. 596 (1798), discussed in Chapter V. For other materials on criminal libel see Thomas I. Emerson, David Haber and Norman Dor-

sen, *Political and Civil Rights in the United States* (Boston, Little, Brown & Co., 3d ed. 1967), pp. 711–713 (cited hereafter in this chapter as *Political and Civil Rights in the United States*).

process, communications that are abusive, offensive, or derogatory with respect to a group, or that tend to arouse public contempt, prejudice, or hatred toward the group. In language and form the group libel laws appear to be simply an extension to groups, classes and races of the protection against defamation that the libel laws historically gave only to individuals. Actually they serve quite different purposes. They are not concerned so much with protecting the interests of individual members of the group as they are with removing sources of group conflict within the society.[5]

In the United States group libel laws were once looked upon as a major weapon in combating racial and religious intolerance. During the period following World War II, in particular, they were strongly urged as a means of forestalling the growth of racism in this country such as had developed in Germany under Hitler. In more recent years they have received less attention. But calls are still frequently heard for the use of such laws against the continuous stream of hate propaganda that emanates from various sources in America. A number of other countries have experimented with group libel laws in one form or another. Recently Great Britain has turned to this device in hopes of aiding in the solution of its newly acquired race relations problem. In 1963 the United Nations adopted a Declaration in which it called on all nations to "take immediate and positive measures, including legislative and other measures, to prosecute and/or outlaw organizations which promote or incite to racial discrimination." [6]

---

5. A collection of materials on group libel laws may be found in *Political and Civil Rights in the United States,* pp. 671–691. See also Note, "Race Defamation and the First Amendment," *Fordham Law Review,* Vol. 34 (1966), p. 653; "Symposium, Race Defamation," *New York Law Forum,* Vol. 14 (1968), p. 1. We deal in this chapter with group defamation only so far as it pertains to racial, religious, national or similar large groups. Efforts to extend the ordinary libel laws to cover corporations, organizations, or other associations or small groups raise somewhat different problems. Insofar as such laws seek to protect individual reputations, the issues are the same as arise under ordinary libel laws (see Chapter XIV); insofar as they protect property or economic rights, the issues fall into the commercial sector; but insofar as they seek to protect the same sort of interests as in the case of the larger groups, the issues are the same as those here discussed.

6. On the development of group libel laws in other countries see Peter J. Belton, "The Control of Group Defamation: A Comparative Study of Law and Its Limitations," *Tulane Law Review,* Vol. 34 (1960), pp. 299, 469; "Group Defamation Symposium," *Cleveland-Marshall Law Review,* Vol. 13 (1964), p. 1. The British legislation is Race Relations Act of 1965, Public General Acts, 1965, Chapter 73; for discussion see Anthony Dickey, "English Law and Race Defamation," *New York Law Forum,* Vol. 14 (1968), p. 9. The United Nations Declaration on the Elimination of All Forms of Racial Discrimination is General Assembly Resolution 1904 (XVIII), reported in U.N. General Assembly, *Official Records,* Agenda Item 43, 18th Sess. (1963).

Group libel laws in the United States have taken various forms. Occasional efforts have been made to utilize ordinary criminal libel, breach of the peace, or disorderly conduct laws as group libel laws. But this has largely failed. Any serious attempt to control dissemination of hate propaganda clearly demands a specific statute directed to that end. At present such special statutes, some of them very limited in scope, exist in less than a dozen States.[7]

The Supreme Court has dealt with a group libel law on only one occasion, in *Beauharnais v. Illinois,* decided in 1952. The Illinois statute there before the Court made it unlawful for any person to sell or exhibit any publication which "portrays depravity, criminality, unchastity, or lack of virtue of a class of citizens, of any race, color, creed or religion, [or which] exposes the citizens of any race, color, creed or religion to contempt, derision, or obloquy or which is productive of breach of the peace or riots." Beauharnais, president of the White Circle League, distributed a leaflet in Chicago that called upon the Mayor and City Council "to halt the further encroachment, harassment and invasion of white people, their property, neighborhoods and persons, by the Negro." Calling for "[o]ne million self respecting white people to unite," it added: "If persuasion and the need to prevent the white race from becoming mongrelized by the Negro will not unite us, then the aggressions . . . rapes, robberies, knives, guns and marijuana of the Negro, surely will." At the bottom was an application blank for membership in the White Circle League. Beauharnais was convicted of violating the statute and fined $200. The Supreme Court affirmed by vote of five to four.[8]

Justice Frankfurter, speaking for the majority, treated the statute as "a form of criminal libel law." He then noted that all the States had criminal libel laws punishing libel of an individual, and accepted the dictum in *Chaplinsky v. New Hampshire* that the "libelous" was one of those "well-defined and narrowly limited classes of speech, the prevention and punishment of which has never been thought to raise any Constitutional problem." The "precise question" before the Court, he said, was whether the due process clause of the Fourteenth Amendment prevented a State from punishing libels "directed at designated collectivities and flagrantly disseminated." "But if an utterance

7. For a recent survey of group libel laws in the United States see Belton, *op. cit. supra* note 6; James J. Brown and Carl L. Stern, "Group Defamation in the U.S.A.," *Cleveland-Marshall Law Review,* Vol. 13 (1964), p. 7.

8. *Beauharnais v. Illinois,* 343 U.S. 250 (1952).

directed at an individual may be the object of criminal sanctions, we cannot deny to a State power to punish the same utterance directed at a defined group, unless we can say that this is a wilful and purposeless restriction unrelated to the peace and well-being of the State." On this Justice Frankfurter had no doubts:

> Illinois did not have to look beyond her own borders or await the tragic experiences of the last three decades to conclude that wilful purveyors of falsehood concerning racial and religious groups promote strife and tend powerfully to obstruct the manifold adjustments required for free, ordered life in a metropolitan, polyglot community. From the murder of the abolitionist Lovejoy in 1837 to the Cicero riots of 1951, Illinois has been the scene of exacerbated tension between races, often flaring into violence and destruction. In many of these outbreaks, utterances of the character here in question, so the Illinois legislature could conclude, played a significant part.[9]

To the First Amendment Justice Frankfurter devoted only a single paragraph, the next to last in his opinion:

> Libelous utterances not being within the area of constitutionally protected speech, it is unnecessary, either for us or for the State courts, to consider the issues behind the phrase "clear and present danger." Certainly no one would contend that obscene speech, for example, may be punished only upon a showing of such circumstances. Libel, as we have seen, is in the same class.[10]

The four dissenters each wrote separate opinions. Justice Reed, although he assumed "the constitutional power of a state to pass group libel laws to protect the public peace," objected to the statute because it "contains without statutory or judicial definition words of such ambiguous meaning and uncertain connotations as 'virtue,' 'derision,' or 'obloquy'." Because the conviction "may rest upon these vague and undefined words, which permit within their scope the punishment of incidents secured by the guarantee of free speech," he concluded that it should be reversed. Justice Jackson devoted much of his opinion to the proposition that "the Fourteenth Amendment did not 'incorporate' the First, that the powers of Congress and of the States over this subject are not of the same dimensions, and that because Congress probably could not enact this law it does not follow that the States may not." Nevertheless, he felt that the Illinois statute, as applied in the case before him, did not include certain safeguards "essential to our

9. 343 U.S. at 255–256, 258–259. 10. 343 U.S. at 266.

concept of ordered liberty," specifically the defenses of truth, fair comment and privilege, and proof of clear and present danger.[11]

The dissents of Justices Black and Douglas went deeper. Justice Black argued that the majority decision sanctioned infringement upon First Amendment freedoms whenever the Court finds a "rational basis." He objected strongly to the majority's treatment of the statute as a criminal libel law, pointing out that such laws "confined state punishment of speech and expression to the narrowest of areas involving nothing more than purely private feuds," whereas its expansion "to punish discussions of matters of public concern means a corresponding invasion of the area dedicated to free expression by the First Amendment." He observed that under the Illinois statute "it is now very dangerous indeed to say something critical" or "unduly offensive to any race, color, creed or religion." Stressing that "Beauharnais is punished for publicly expressing strong views in favor of segregation," he concluded, "I think the First Amendment, with the Fourteenth, 'absolutely' forbids such laws without any 'ifs' or 'buts' or 'whereases.' Whatever the danger, if any, in such public discussions, it is a danger the Founders deemed outweighed by the danger incident to the stifling of thought and speech." [12]

Justice Douglas took the position that, except for a conspiracy to engage in conduct amounting to "free speech plus," or certain kinds of "inflammatory talk" such as shouting "fire" in a school or theater, public interests cannot "override the plain command of the First Amendment" unless the "peril of speech" is "clear and present, leaving no room for argument, raising no doubts as to the necessity of curbing speech in order to prevent disaster." Agreeing with Justice Black, he thought that "placing in the hands of the legislative branch the right to regulate 'within reasonable limits' the right of free speech" was "an ominous and alarming trend." He drew a different picture of the function of free expression from that which had guided the majority:

> Today a white man stands convicted for protesting in unseemly language against our decisions invalidating restrictive covenants. Tomorrow a Negro will be haled before a court for denouncing lynch law in heated terms. Farm laborers in the West who compete with field hands drifting up from Mexico; whites who feel the pressure of orientals; a minority which finds employment going to members of the dominant religious group—all of these are caught in the mesh of today's decision. Debate and argument even in the courtroom are not always calm and dispas-

11. 343 U.S. at 283, 284, 288, 299.   12. 343 U.S. at 269, 272, 273, 275.

sionate. Emotions sway speakers and audiences alike. Intemperate speech is a distinctive characteristic of man. Hotheads blow off and release destructive energy in the process. They shout and rave, exaggerating weaknesses, magnifying error, viewing with alarm. So it has been from the beginning; and so it will be throughout time. The Framers of the Constitution knew human nature as well as we do.[13]

The *Beauharnais* decision reflected the mood of the Vinson Court as it moved away from an assured reliance upon the virtues of rough and tumble speech and towards greater acquiescence in state regulation of more militant forms of expression. The majority cursorily read the whole area of libel law out of the First Amendment, on the basis of a prior dictum. It then viewed the Illinois statute as a mild extension of traditional libel law, governed only by due process requirements of reasonableness. In this way the majority did not face any of the crucial problems posed by such a statute for a system of freedom of expression. If it had it might have perceived that the decision struck at the heart of the First Amendment. For the Court failed to distinguish between governmental regulation of defamatory statements made about an individual, and governmental regulation of expression that dealt with the basic political issues of the day. Moreover, the Court was but a short step away from sanctioning governmental control over expression that defamed the government, a form of control that likewise derived from the ancient laws of libel, in this case seditious libel. Few decisions of the Supreme Court have been more widely or more justly criticized.[14]

The major premise of *Beauharnais*—that libel laws are not within the coverage of the First Amendment—was overruled by *New York Times v. Sullivan* in 1964. A minor premise—that criminal libel laws are outside the First Amendment—was expressly repudiated a few months later in *Garrison v. Louisiana*. Hence little remains of the doctrinal structure of *Beauharnais*. Nevertheless, the problem of group libel laws still exists. They continue on the statute books of several States and are occasionally invoked. Greater reliance upon them is frequently suggested. How, then, do group libel laws square with our constitutional system? [15]

13. 343 U.S. at 284–285, 286–287.
14. See, *e.g.*, Harry Kalven, Jr., *The Negro and the First Amendment* (Columbus, Ohio State University Press, 1965), ch. I.
15. *New York Times v. Sullivan*, 376 U.S. 254 (1964); *Garrison v. Louisiana*, 379 U.S. 64 (1964), noted above. The Illinois statute was repealed in 1961 and replaced by another which prohibited "criminal defamation" by communication which "tends to provoke a breach of the

Upon any careful examination it is virtually impossible to reconcile group libel laws with constitutional requirements. In the first place, once the blind analogy to individual libel is abandoned, the terms necessarily used in group libel laws are seen as excessively vague. As Justice Reed pointed out in *Beauharnais,* "To say that the mere presence of the word 'virtue' in the individual libel statute makes its meaning clear in the group libel statute is a *non sequitur.*" It is highly doubtful whether any words employed to define "defamation" of a class or race can meet the standards of specificity demanded in the First Amendment area. In the second place, for much the same reasons, a group libel statute would be most likely to fall as overbroad. The prohibition of defamation of a class or race would inevitably include expression that on any theory of the First Amendment would be protected.[16]

Assuming that a group libel statute survived these attacks on its facial validity, the scope of its application would presumably depend upon what test of the First Amendment was employed. A balancing test could lead to any result. However, it is more likely that a court, faced with a statute that potentially covered such a large area of "pure speech," would apply the clear and present danger test. This test also allows great leeway. It is not certain what kind of danger, whether actual breach of the peace or mere influence on attitude, the court would demand be shown. It is doubtful that any immediate danger of the former sort could be proved in most cases, especially as the great bulk of hate propaganda is in the form of written material. An incitement test would probably operate even more narrowly in this situation. All in all, a reasonably strict application of any of the three tests would limit the scope of a group libel law to an area not much broader than that embraced by a breach of the peace statute.

Under the expression-action theory of the First Amendment a group libel law would be clearly invalid. The conduct prohibited by such laws is admittedly expression. Indeed the relation between the proscribed communication and any possible ensuing action is more uncertain and remote here than in any other field of First Amendment law, with the possible exception of obscenity. Except in the special case of "fighting words," the effect of the expression, as in *Beauharnais,* is entirely upon beliefs and attitudes.

peace." Ill. Ann. Stat., ch. 38, §§27–1, 27–2 (1961). See *City of Chicago v. Lambert,* 47 Ill. App.2d 151, 197 N.E.2d 448 (App. Ct., 1st Dist., 1st Div. 1964). 16. 343 U.S. at 282.

The constitutional results reached under the expression-action theory are confirmed by numerous considerations growing out of the nature of our system of free expression. In the first place, group libel laws are premised on the proposition that the government is entitled to determine the social value of expression and to proscribe any expression it decides has insufficient value. In application of the laws this decision is made in particular cases by a judge or a jury. Moreover, since truth must be accepted as a defense, the judge and jury may be called upon to decide the truth of various political and social contentions that are highly complex and controversial. Under the fundamental principles of the First Amendment the government has no business making judgments on any of these matters. In the second place, because of the inherent vagueness of their provisions, group libel laws are likely to have a severe inhibiting effect upon wide areas of expression. The fact that such laws are never made applicable to political groups, though their logic would certainly extend that far, indicates recognition of the potential sweep of their impact and of the potential abuse of their application. Much of the political literature trained on the Communist Party or other left- and right-wing groups would fall under the ban.

Many other problems arise out of the practicalities of administration. The publicity of litigation is likely to have wider repercussions than the original publication. An acquittal or a judgment for the defendant appears to put an official stamp of approval upon the alleged defamation, or might make the defendant a hero or a martyr. Prosecuting attorneys may be inept representatives of the cause of the minority group that has been defamed. Prominent persons will never be prosecuted, the burden of the law falling only upon the less respectable or the less powerful. In civil proceedings the measure of damages is unascertainable and the role of the individual bringing suit ambiguous.

Finally, and most important, the group libel law is an ineffective way of meeting the real problems that lie below the surface. Conflicts between groups will never be settled in litigation over the question whether one group has been defamed. The tactics of arousing racial, religious or class hatred are too subtle to be bound by such controls. The effort to use the judicial process for this purpose merely diverts attention and energies from far more important measures essential to resolve the underlying grievances.

The hope that group libel laws will help rid us of racial, religious or class bigotry, or at least keep conflict on a more benign level, has been shared by many people. Faced with the extravagances of hate propaganda men of goodwill are likely to think at once in terms of legal prohibitions. But our experience indicates that group libel laws are not the answer. In those States where they appear upon the statute books, they have rarely been used. The Illinois statute had, prior to *Beauharnais,* been before the courts only twice in the thirty years of its existence. Yet one cannot doubt that there had been countless violations. In recent years the use of group libel statutes in connection with our racial conflicts would appear inconceivable. As tensions have grown both white and black militants have "defamed" the other race. Much of what has been said is without question in violation of group libel laws. Yet no one would give a second thought to the suggestion that present racial conflicts could be ameliorated through application of group libel laws.

XI

Inchoate Crimes: Solicitation, Attempt, Conspiracy

It is necessary at this point to interrupt the analysis in terms of social interest and to focus on a problem that is common to much of the previous discussion. The question concerns the impact on the system of freedom of expression of those measures which deal with the inchoate elements of the conduct that society ultimately seeks to control. While the problem does not arise only in connection with regulations that relate to national security and internal order, most of the specific issues have appeared in those areas. Nor does regulation of inchoate conduct take the form only of criminal laws; it may also involve noncriminal provisions. In order to simplify the issues, however, we deal here only with criminal offenses.

The underlying objective of social regulation is to protect or advance the interests of society or its members through control of action in some form. Injury to those interests, at least of a nature that calls for social control, does not arise directly from expression. This is, of course, the fundamental premise upon which the system of freedom of expression is based. Social regulations, however, are not always confined to control of action in its ultimate stage. Frequently they range much more broadly and deal with inchoate conduct that has not yet matured into final action.

Social regulation of action may involve inchoate conduct in two ways. In the first place, the regulation may constitute a direct control of the earlier stages of action, with a view to preventing the final action from ever taking place. A clear example can be found in the law of attempts, in which preliminary conduct that never reaches the final stage is nevertheless made a criminal offense. Secondly, in the course of controlling ultimate action, the regulatory mechanisms may rely upon preliminary conduct as proof of the final action that is to be regulated. Thus certain conduct, while itself not punishable, may be used as evidence to establish subsequent action, or as evidence of the intent of subsequent action. Hence, while the law may not be designed to control inchoate conduct as such, it does have an important impact upon it.

Inchoate conduct frequently takes the form of expression. Indeed beliefs, opinions, and communications are almost always the preliminaries of action. Consequently social regulations that reach back into inchoate conduct may raise serious First Amendment problems. In the form of direct regulation of expression the impact is obvious. When the regulatory mechanism relies on expression as evidence of subsequent action, the result may be almost as serious. In such a case the expression becomes in effect subject to regulation, or runs the risk of regulation if a jury or other fact-finder infers a connection between the expression and the ultimate action.

The First Amendment issues are serious whether or not one adopts the full protection theory of the First Amendment. But they become crucial if the expression-action analysis is accepted and the theory applied. In its concrete manifestations the problem has arisen in four major contexts: (1) The government may seek to make an utterance itself an inchoate crime, as in the law of solicitation to crime. (2) The government may seek to use expression as evidence of a crime of action, as could happen in the prosecution of almost any offense. (3) Both kinds of problem are present in a special form in the law of attempts. (4) These issues become particularly acute in the law of conspiracy.

As happened in other areas, the law of inchoate crimes developed independently of the law of the First Amendment. The courts have given little explicit consideration to reconciling one set of doctrines with the other. Nevertheless the issues are gradually beginning to emerge as the increasingly complex controls of modern society range further into inchoate conduct in the effort to punish or prevent ultimate action.[1]

A. Solicitation to Crime

The offense of solicitation to crime includes, broadly speaking, not only the common law crime of solicitation, but various statutory provisions making it an offense to solicit, advise, counsel, aid, abet, or otherwise induce a crime. These laws undertake to punish inchoate conduct directly, though the real concern of society is not with the solicitation as such but with preventing the ultimate action. In the early stages of First Amendment development it was assumed that the traditional law of solicitation was not affected by the constitutional guarantee. The issues, however, are plainly not that simple.

Actually the First Amendment problem in solicitation cases is basically the same as in numerous other situations in which the question is whether, or to what extent, the government can punish a communication that might lead to undesired consequences. The fact that the evil feared is a criminal offense bears upon the nature of the danger to society but does not change the fundamental principles. The Supreme Court has never dealt explicitly with the common law offense of solicitation to crime or with a statute drafted in those precise terms. But it has considered the basic issue in numerous decisions, including the Selective Service cases on advising and counseling, the sedition cases on advocacy of overthrow of government, and the public assembly cases on incitement to violence. A few additional cases in which similar questions have been presented to the Court may be noted here.

In *Musser v. Utah,* a group of Mormons were convicted of conspiring to "advocate, counsel, advise and urge the practice of polygamy and unlawful cohabitation by other persons," but the case went off on issues of vagueness. Similarly *Winters v. New York* involved a statute inter-

---

1. For a general survey of the law of inchoate crimes see Herbert Wechsler, William Kenneth Jones, and Harold L. Korn, "The Treatment of Inchoate Crimes in the Model Penal Code of the American Law Institute: Attempt, Solicitation, and Conspiracy," *Columbia Law Review,* Vol. 61 (1961), pp. 571, 957. It is noteworthy that the authors, draftsmen of the Model Penal Code's provisions on the subject, give only cursory attention to the First Amendment problems.

preted to prohibit publications that "so massed their collection of pictures and stories of bloodshed and of lust 'as to become vehicles for inciting violent and depraved crimes against the person'," but the enactment was struck down as not embodying a sufficiently definite standard of conduct. The Court did reach direct First Amendment issues in *Kingsley International Pictures Corp. v. Regents of the University of the State of New York*. The Regents had denied a license to show the film *Lady Chatterley's Lover* on the ground that the "theme is the presentation of adultery as a desirable, acceptable and proper pattern of behavior." Holding this action violated the First Amendment, Justice Stewart said: "Advocacy of conduct proscribed by law is not, as Mr. Justice Brandeis long ago pointed out, 'a justification for denying free speech where the advocacy falls short of incitement and there is nothing to indicate that the advocacy would be immediately acted on.' " The issue was also raised in *Shuttlesworth v. City of Birmingham*, where Reverend Shuttlesworth, who was organizing a sit-in, was convicted of "inciting, aiding and abetting a violation of the city criminal trespass ordinance." The case was reversed, however, on the theory that the sit-in was not itself a violation of law.[2]

The Supreme Court has never settled upon any single theory for deciding cases, such as the above, in which the communication is charged with having produced or being likely to produce a violation of law. Justice Stewart in *Kingsley* suggests an incitement test, but relies upon Justice Brandeis who favored the clear and present danger test. The recent decisions in the *Bond* and *Brandenburg* cases also suggest that the Court has turned to an incitement test.

The issue should be resolved in terms of the usual rules for determining what is expression and what is action. Under these doctrines solicitation can be constitutionally punished only when the communication is so close, direct, effective, and instantaneous in its impact that it is part of the action. The speaker must, in effect, be an agent in the action.

---

2. *Musser v. Utah,* 333 U.S. 95 (1948); *Winters v. New York,* 333 U.S. 507 (1948); *Kingsley International Pictures Corp. v. Regents of the University of the State of New York,* 360 U.S. 684, 689 (1959); *Shuttlesworth v. City of Birmingham,* 373 U.S. 262 (1963). See also *Watts v. United States,* 394 U.S. 705 (1969) (threatening life of the President). For a collection of materials on the solicitation problem see Thomas I. Emerson, David Haber and Norman Dorsen, *Political and Civil Rights in the United States* (Boston, Little, Brown & Co., 3d ed. 1967), p. 600. See also notes in 35 A.L.R. 961 (1925), and 51 A.L.R. 2d 953 (1957).

With respect specifically to solicitation cases, certain more concrete considerations can be suggested. The more general the communication—the more it relates to general issues, is addressed to a number of persons, urges general action—the more readily it is classified as expression. On the other hand, communication that is specifically concerned with a particular law, aimed at a particular person, and urges particular action, moves closer to action. Communication also tends to become action as the speaker assumes a personal relation to the listener, deals with him on a face-to-face basis, or participates in an agency or partnership arrangement. Other factors may affect the ultimate determination of whether the communication is expression or action. The essential issue is whether the speaker has made himself a participant in a crime or attempted crime of action. Short of this the community must satisfy itself with punishment of the one who committed the violation of law or attempted to do so, not punishment of the person who communicated with him about it.

B. Use of Expression as Evidence of a Crime of Action

The problem here is how far the government, in seeking to punish a crime of action, can push its inquiry back into inchoate stages of the action which consist of expression. The issue arises, as noted above, when the government seeks to use expression either as evidence that the subsequent action took place or as evidence of the state of mind of the person who engaged in the action. Plainly there must be some limits if the system of freedom of expression is to remain intact. For expression may be seriously inhibited when the speaker knows that what he says can be used against him at a later time if some unforeseen action ensues, can be taken into account by a jury in determining his state of mind in performing a subsequent act, or can perhaps be the decisive factor in a jury's general verdict against him.

The Supreme Court has never really addressed itself to these issues. The principle of law that should be applied is difficult to state with precision. It is clear that rules of relevancy, or reasonable relationship, should not be employed in the customary manner. The umbrella effect of the First Amendment demands that the courts utilize these doctrines in a special way. Perhaps the best formulation that can be made, until a body of case law develops, is that there must be an unusually close connection between the expression and the action, that the expression must be an integral part of the action, not remote or unattached. This judgment should be made in any particular case from a functional point of view, with regard to the essential requirements of an uninhibited system of freedom of expression.[3]

The application of the principle would not be difficult in many situations. Thus a conversation between two persons planning a bank robbery would clearly be admissible to prove that those persons were in fact the ones who did rob the bank. Or a speech urging the blocking of traffic on a bridge in protest of the Vietnam war might be introduced in proof of the state of mind of the speaker when his car later stalled on the bridge. On the other hand, a tract criticizing government policies in Vietnam should not be admitted to show the intent of the writer to engage in violence in a subsequent antiwar demonstration. A speech urging the audience to attend a demonstration should not be put before the jury as possible evidence that the speaker planned that the large number of persons participating would result in a riot. In the first two examples the expression is intimately related to, if not a part of, the action. In the latter two instances, the expression is remote from the action, and to allow its use in proof of subsequent action would have a devastating effect upon those who contemplate criticizing government policy or organizing a meeting.

In addition to imposing strict application of the rules of relevance the umbrella effect of the First Amendment might lead to modification of other standard doctrines when attempts are made to use expression as proof of action. Thus special rules as to order of proof might be necessary to protect First Amendment rights: the government might be required to establish the action part of the offense before it would be allowed to prove any elements of expression. The rules with respect to presumptions (a form of inchoacy) might be affected: any use of expression as a presumption of action, rebuttable or not, would be ruled out.

These proposals are put forward in a tentative and inconclusive form. They pose rather than solve the problems. But they suggest the kind of development that must take place if the expression-action anal-

3. The Supreme Court touched on the problem, without exploring its implica- tions, in *Street v. New York,* 394 U.S. 576 (1969), discussed in Chapter IV.

ysis is to be carried forward into full protection of First Amendment rights.

C. Attempts

The crime of attempt punishes conduct that has not yet reached its final stage because of some intervening event, failure, or impossibility. The law has always, of course, recognized some limits on how far back in the chain of events the interrupted conduct can be punished. It is agreed, for instance, that mere thought cannot be made a crime. But there has been very little effort to mesh the law of attempt with the law of the First Amendment.[4]

The starting proposition is clear from the discussion of solicitation. The crime of attempt must be limited to an attempt to engage in conduct which amounts to action. An attempt to engage in expression cannot be punished under the First Amendment. In the case of attempts, however, this principle must be carried one step further. Not only must the ultimate crime, which has been interrupted and hence never committed, be a crime of action; the conduct which demonstrates that the attempt was made, that is, the conduct actually being punished, must go beyond expression and include action. Otherwise expression alone is abridged, a plain violation of the First Amendment.

There is, in other words, a constitutional requirement of an "overt act." The concept of "overt act," developed in conspiracy law and embodied in our law of treason, was designed to serve a similar purpose. Its function was, as Justice Holmes said, to assure that "the conspiracy has passed beyond words and is on foot." As applied in present conspiracy law the requirement of an "overt act" has constituted a very thin line of defense for the alleged conspirators. It has tended to become a fiction or be disregarded in practice by the jury. As a constitutional necessity in the law of attempt, however, the concept of "overt act" would be given much more significance. The overt act

4. For a discussion of the law of criminal attempts, which refers to earlier material on the subject, see Arnold N. Enker, "Impossibility in Criminal At- tempts—Legality and the Legal Process," *Minnesota Law Review,* Vol. 53 (1969), p. 665.

would have to consist of substantial action, not just incidental or trivial. It would also have to be sufficient to give the total conduct for which the punishment is levied the cast of "action." In the absence of such a predominant element of action punishment would be accorded for conduct amounting to no more than expression.[5]

The second proposition developed above is also applicable to the crime of attempt. If evidence consisting of expression is used to prove the offense, as it often would be, strict rules of relevancy would be required by the umbrella effect of the First Amendment. Expression used as evidence could not be remote from the action; nor could the jury be allowed to draw too extended inferences from expression to action. Because proof in an attempt case is likely to carry far back into inchoate conduct the rules are especially significant in this area.

These First Amendment requirements apply to all prosecution for crimes in the nature of attempt. Hence they are applicable to prosecutions brought under statutes which, while not formally labeled such, operate in the same way as attempt statutes. The Federal Anti-Riot Act of 1968, for instance, is legislation of this character. It imposes criminal penalties upon any person who (1) travels in interstate commerce or uses any facility of interstate commerce; (2) with the intent to incite a riot or "to organize, promote, encourage, participate in, or carry on a riot"; and (3) then or thereafter "performs or attempts to perform any other overt act" for the purposes specified. The statute thus contemplates that no final action amounting to incitement, encouragement or participation in a riot is necessary. It is sufficient if the person travels with the requisite intent and then performs any "overt act" to carry out that intent. In every real sense the Federal Anti-Riot Act is an attempt statute, punishing inchoate conduct.

Tested in the light of the First Amendment requirements just outlined, the statute would seem vulnerable. It seeks to punish conduct that never gets beyond the stage of expression. In the first place the intended conduct may consist only of expression. There is no requirement that "organize, promote, [or] encourage" constitute action; or even that it constitute "unprotected expression" within the clear and present danger, incitement, or "advocacy of action" tests. Hence the conduct for which the person is punished could be nothing more than

---

5. The Holmes quotation is from *Hyde v. United States*, 225 U.S. 347, 388 (1912). The discussion above is confined to First Amendment requirements. There would also be substantive due process requirements going to the question of what kind of action could be punished as an attempt. The umbrella effect of the First Amendment would demand that these due process limitations be strictly applied.

an attempt to engage in expression. Secondly, even if the intended conduct consisted of action, nothing in the statute requires that the overt act consist of action, much less action so substantial as to make the total conduct punished predominantly action. Consequently the conduct for which the accused is punished would include intent and expression, but no action whatever.[6]

D. Conspiracy

Criminal conspiracy, speaking roughly, consists in two or more persons entering into an agreement to commit an unlawful act. The essence of the offense is the making of the agreement. Under the common law nothing more was required. Under some statutes an "overt act" in furtherance of the agreement must be established. However, such an "overt act" need not consist of action and tends to be a mere fiction. Under the law of conspiracy, once proof of the original agreement has been established each member of the conspiracy is bound by the statements and actions of every other member. In addition, the use of a conspiracy prosecution relaxes the ordinary rules of evidence, often makes available a higher penalty than the substantive crime, may extend the statute of limitations, and usually affords the prosecuting officials other significant advantages. It can readily be seen that the law of conspiracy reaches far back into inchoate conduct and has serious implications for the system of freedom of expression.[7]

The Supreme Court has dealt with a number of cases in which conspiracy law has affected First Amendment rights. Most of the sedition cases, including *Gitlow, Dennis* and *Yates,* were conspiracy prosecutions. In all these cases, however, the Supreme Court has simply accepted the usual rules of conspiracy law. Indeed the only court

6. The Federal Anti-Riot Act is 18 U.S.C. §2101–2102. The first prosecution under the statute was brought against eight leaders of the New Left charged with promoting riots at the time of the Democratic National Convention in Chicago in August 1968. *United States v. Dellinger et al.* (No. 69 CR 180, N.D. Ill.). The constitutionality of the Act was upheld in *National Mobilization Com-* *mittee to End the War in Viet Nam v. Foran,* 411 F.2d 934 (7th Cir. 1969).

7. Generally on the law of conspiracy see "Developments in the Law—Criminal Conspiracy," *Harvard Law Review,* Vol. 72 (1959), p. 920; Abraham S. Goldstein, "Conspiracy to Defraud the United States," *Yale Law Journal,* Vol. 68 (1959), p. 405.

which has thus far addressed itself squarely to the special problems involved in applying conspiracy law to First Amendment conduct seems to be the Court of Appeals for the First Circuit in the *Spock-Coffin* case. There the majority concluded that First Amendment rights should be protected by imposing strict standards of proof upon the government to show that each person charged with conspiracy had the "specific intent to adhere to the illegal portions" of the agreement. The dissent thought that the government had gone too far in attempting to apply conspiracy doctrine to an "ill-defined, shifting" group operating "in the public domain," but ran into difficulties in saying just where the line should be drawn. It is safe to say that the problems deserve greater attention than they have so far received.[8]

Again, the initial proposition is that the object of the conspiracy must be action. Conspiracy to engage in expression cannot constitutionally be made an offense. And again, as in the case of attempts, this principle carries further implications. Under the traditional law of conspiracy the offense is committed by entering into the agreement. Yet such conduct would normally consist entirely of expression and, if nothing more were shown, the conviction would entail punishment for expression alone. Hence an "overt act" becomes a constitutional necessity under the First Amendment. Moreover, as in the law of attempts, that overt act must be action of a kind that gives a substantial quality of action to the conduct being punished. In addition, the rules stated previously with regard to the relevancy of evidence in the form of expression are fully applicable.

These principles take on added significance in conspiracy law. Without the requirement of an overt act, merely entering into an agreement would be punishable, a stage of conduct even more remote than that punished under the law of criminal attempts. Moreover, the wide sweep of a conspiracy charge, and the multiplicity of participants, make it possible for the prosecution to claim that broad areas of expression are relevant to the case. Most important, the conspiracy law is a technique for making some persons criminally responsible for the expression and action of others. This combination of inchoacy,

8. The *Gitlow, Dennis* and *Yates* cases are discussed in Chapter V; see also the *Scales* case, a Smith Act membership rather than conspiracy case, in which the opinions did touch upon these issues. In dissenting from denial of certiorari in the *Epton* case, discussed in Chapter IX, Justice Douglas thought that the Supreme Court ought to decide the question whether the overt acts in a conspiracy case could consist solely of protected expression. *Epton v. New York*, 390 U.S. 29 (1968). The *Spock-Coffin* case, discussed in Chapter IV, is *United States v. Spock*, 416 F.2d 165, 173, 186 (1st Cir. 1969).

breadth, and vicarious responsibility can be devastating to a system of freedom of expression. Persons loosely engaged in a common endeavor, such as a campaign on a public issue, or even in a more specific enterprise such as a demonstration, can be prosecuted in a single proceeding for conspiracy. All are responsible for the conduct of each. No final action need be shown on the part of any. The penalty on conviction may be substantially more severe. The possibility of serious abridgment of freedom of expression is manifest.

In practice, conspiracy law can be even more harmful to uninhibited expression. A jury, which may be hostile to an unpopular cause, decides who is in the conspiracy, what the intent of the parties was, whether the agreement contemplated some action that occurred later, and similar crucial matters. It thus becomes dangerous for any individual to participate in a campaign or demonstration that in the course of its unfolding may give rise to some violation of law. It is hard to conceive of a more chilling effect upon the system of free expression.

Finally, in some aspects of conspiracy law the umbrella effect of the First Amendment should be given great weight. The claim that a group of persons, seeking to exercise their right of expression in a common enterprise, have entered into a conspiratorial "agreement" should be scrutinized with skepticism. The issue whether any particular person had the required criminal intent to enter such a conspiracy should also be examined with care. The rules attributing the conduct of one member of the conspiracy to the others should be applied with equal caution. The courts should, in short, be fully aware that the whole field of conspiracy law is filled with traps for the unwary and opportunities for the repressor.

E. Conclusions

Generally and tentatively stated, these are some of the principles that should govern the relationship between the system of freedom of expression and the efforts of society to regulate inchoate conduct. Even if one does not accept the full protection theory of the First Amendment, similar issues would be presented and similar doctrines would have to be developed: The actual conduct punished cannot consist of "protected expression." Proof of a crime cannot be evidenced by "protected expression" that is so remote from action, or so subject to risk of penalty, that freedom of expression is curtailed. The conduct which demonstrates that a criminal attempt has been committed must include something more than "protected expression," whether or not it is called an "overt act." A criminal conspiracy cannot embrace a loose coalition of individuals seeking only to engage in "protected expression."

Analysis of the issues in these terms, however, introduces additional complications. When some expression is protected and some is not, the principles become more difficult to state and more complex to apply. The need to work out effective rules of decision in this important area thus provides a further reason for the courts to move to an expression-action analysis and a full protection theory.

XII

Other Social Interests

In addition to national security and internal order, the major problems that have arisen when the system of freedom of expression comes in contact with controls designed to protect particular social interests concern (1) taxation and business regulation; (2) a special aspect of this, economic interests protected against picketing, boycotts, and similar forms of pressure; and (3) fairness in governmental proceedings, especially criminal trials.

A. Taxation and Business Regulation

The system of freedom of expression operates in a world engaged in many other pursuits, including economic activities of various sorts, and subject to governmental controls of many different kinds. The individuals and groups who exercise the right to freedom of expression carry on these other enterprises also. Moreover, even in the process of exercising their rights of expression, they are part of this world of regulation. The publisher of a newspaper, for instance, buys and sells, owns property, makes contracts, employs other people. The adjustment of the system of freedom of expression to this mass of regulatory controls raises some important issues.

The problem may come up in two different, but related, contexts. The government regulation may be directed at a bona fide objective, legitimately subject to control, but may nevertheless have a significant effect upon freedom of expression. Or the regulation may be a pretense, ostensibly aimed at a legitimate objective, but actually seeking to control expression. The two situations are of course not entirely separable. The regulation may involve elements of both, or the intention to control expression may be ambiguous or impossible to prove. In any event the ultimate issue is whether the regulation infringes upon the system of freedom of expression.

In resolving this question the usual concepts of First Amendment theory are relevant. It is necessary to distinguish between expression and action, and it is imperative to separate control of action from control of expression to the greatest extent possible. In this situation, however, the concept of "abridgment" plays a more important role. The user of expression is also a citizen of the regulatory world. He is protected in his expression by various government services, enjoys government facilities, and engages in activities similar to those not protected by the First Amendment. Hence he should share some of the costs and conform to the general controls. Moreover, the non-expression portion of his conduct is subject to regulation and this must inevitably have some effect upon his conduct that does involve expression. The question is therefore whether the government regulation is simply a necessary feature of the social and economic life, or whether it imposes a special burden on, or constitutes a special control of, expression. The issue is reversely analogous to that arising under the clause prohibiting an establishment of religion, in which the problem is to distinguish between services performed for all members of the public and services performed especially in aid of religion.

The issue that frequently arises, then, is whether the government control "abridges" freedom of expression. This must be determined in light of the function and operation of the system of freedom of expression. It is partly a question of community expectations and common sense. It may also, if the regulation is suspected of being a pretense, involve some probing into motives. The doctrine that alternative methods not affecting freedom of expression must be used, if available, to solve a problem occupies a particularly important place in this area.

The rule that communications in the "commercial sector" of our society are outside the system of freedom of expression also requires more detailed attention here. This doctrine, while it has been widely observed, has never been fully explained. For one thing neither the courts nor commentators have made clear just what constitutes the "commercial sector." Roughly it embraces the production and exchange of goods and services for profit, as distinct from the production or exchange of ideas on political, religious, artistic, and similar matters. This is, of course, a very crude definition. Moreover, the reasons for denying First Amendment protection to communication that takes place in the "commercial sector" have not been explicitly stated by the courts or convincingly expounded by the commentators. One might say it speaks well for a society that it accords greater freedom to the exchange of ideas than it gives to the exchange of material things. A less worthy rationale may be that society feels it necessary to give greater protection to its citizens in material affairs than in the affairs of the mind. However all this may be, the doctrine is well established in our constitutional law. Its reach can best be discerned by an examination of concrete applications.[1]

First mention of the doctrine that communications of a commercial character are not protected by the First Amendment appears in *Schneider v. State*. Justice Roberts states in passing, "We are not to be taken as holding that commercial soliciting and canvassing may not be subjected to such regulation as the ordinance [in that case] requires." But the rule was first squarely applied in *Valentine v. Chrestensen*. That case involved the validity of the Sanitary Code of New York City, which prohibited distribution on the streets of "commercial and business advertising matter." Chrestensen was convicted for distributing a handbill advertising the exhibition of a submarine, for which an admission fee was charged. The Supreme Court had previously made it clear that dissemination of religious and political literature on the streets could not constitutionally be forbidden. It was just as certain that commercial literature could be. Justice Roberts, for a unanimous Court, disposed of the problem in one paragraph:

> This court has unequivocally held that the streets are proper places for the exercise of the freedom of communicating information and disseminating opinion and that, though the states and municipalities may appropriately regulate the privilege in the public interest, they may not

---

1. For a general discussion of the "commercial sector," including an attempt to explain the underlying rationale, see Note, "Freedom of Expression in a Commercial Context," *Harvard Law Review*, Vol. 78 (1965), p. 1191. The argument that there is no justification for distinguishing commercial speech from speech on political and religious matters is made in George K. Gardner, "Free Speech in Public Places," *Boston University Law Review*, Vol. 36 (1956), p. 239. See, for further materials, Thomas I. Emerson, David Haber and Norman Dorsen, *Political and Civil Rights in the United States* (Boston, Little, Brown & Co., 3d ed. 1967), pp. 602–624 (cited hereafter in this chapter as *Political and Civil Rights in the United States*); George Cooper, "Taxation of Grass Roots Lobbying," *Columbia Law Review*, Vol. 68 (1968), pp. 801, 831–841.

unduly burden or proscribe its employment in these public thoroughfares. We are equally clear that the Constitution imposes no such restraint on government as respects purely commercial advertising.
Whether, and to what extent, one may promote or pursue a gainful
occupation in the streets, to what extent such activity shall be adjudged
a derogation of the public right of the user, are matters for legislative
judgment.[2]

The rationale and scope of the doctrine was not as clear, however,
as the Court assumed in *Chrestensen*. In *Breard v. City of Alexandria*
the Court dealt with a municipal ordinance that prohibited door-to-
door solicitation for the sale of "goods, wares and merchandise" unless
the householder had given advance permission. The issue was whether
the ordinance could be constitutionally applied to a person soliciting
subscriptions for the *Saturday Evening Post* and similar magazines.
The solicitation was commercial, but the literature was not. Not long
before, the Court had held in *Martin v. Struthers* that door-to-door
canvassing for purposes of disseminating religious literature could not
be forbidden. In *Breard,* however, the Court upheld the ordinance.
Justice Reed, writing for a majority of six, left the "commercial" doctrine in a state of some confusion. He did not apply it to eliminate all
First Amendment rights. "We agree," he said, "that the fact that periodicals are sold does not put them beyond the protection of the First
Amendment." But, he added, the "selling . . . brings into the transaction a commercial feature." He distinguished *Martin v. Struthers* on
the ground that there "no element of the commercial entered." He
then went on to apply the balancing test and found the balance to
support the regulation.[3]

Justice Black, joined by Justice Douglas, dissented. He argued, citing *Chrestensen*, that the ordinance "could constitutionally be applied
to a 'merchant' who goes from door to door 'selling pots'." But the
"constitutional sanctuary for the press must necessarily include liberty
to publish and circulate." He concluded: "In view of our economic
system, it must also include freedom to solicit paying subscribers."[4]

Breard left somewhat up in the air the question whether all or any
of the safeguards of the First Amendment extended to the distribution

2. *Valentine v. Chrestensen*, 316 U.S.
52, 54 (1942). The quotation from
Schneider v. State is from 308 U.S. 147,
165 (1939). See also *Railway Express
Agency v. New York*, 336 U.S. 106
(1949).

3. *Breard v. City of Alexandria*, 341
U.S. 622, 642, 643 (1951); *Martin v.
Struthers*, 319 U.S. 141 (1943).

4. 341 U.S. at 650. Chief Justice Vinson and Justice Douglas also dissented on
other grounds.

of protected expression through commercial channels. The matter was set at rest, however, in *Smith v. California,* an obscenity case, in which the Court explicitly stated with respect to the First Amendment rights of a bookseller, "It is of course no matter that the dissemination takes place under commercial auspices." This was reaffirmed in *New York Times v. Sullivan* in which a newspaper that published a paid advertisement on a political issue was given First Amendment protection.[5]

The doctrine that "commercial" communications are outside the system of freedom of expression has been applied most widely in connection with controls over commercial advertising. Thus the authority of the Federal Trade Commission to prohibit false and misleading advertising has been held not limited by the First Amendment. Even books found to have been used as advertisements to sell commercial products or as part of their labeling have been subject to false advertising or labeling laws. The power of the Post Office to close the mails to fraudulent practices does not violate the First Amendment. Securities and Exchange regulations of truth in the marketing of securities have never even been challenged on First Amendment grounds. The Supreme Court has also upheld laws making it unlawful to use the American flag for commercial purposes.[6]

At times the "commercial sector" theory has been pressed further, but at this point enough has been said to indicate its relevance in the adjustment of various forms of business regulations to the system of freedom of expression.

5. *Smith v. California,* 361 U.S. 147, 150 (1959); *New York Times v. Sullivan,* 376 U.S. 254, 265–266 (1964).

6. On the Federal Trade Commission's power over false advertising see *American Medicinal Products, Inc. v. Federal Trade Commission,* 136 F.2d 426 (9th Cir. 1943); *E. F. Drew & Co. v. Federal Trade Commission,* 235 F.2d 735, 739 (2d Cir. 1956), cert. denied 352 U.S. 969 (1957). Proceedings based on use of books are reported in *In the Matter of the Attorney General of the State of New York,* 10 N.Y.2d 108, 176 N.E.2d 402 (1961), cert. denied 368 U.S. 947 (1961); *United States v. Articles of Drug,*

32 F.R.D. 32 (S.D. Ill. 1963); *Rodale Press, Inc. v. Federal Trade Commission,* 407 F.2d 1252 (D.C. Cir. 1968). But see Commissioner Elman's dissent in the *Rodale* case. 3 Trade Reg. Rep. ¶17,996. With regard to the Post Office, see *Donaldson v. Read Magazine, Inc.,* 333 U.S. 178 (1948). The flag case is *Halter v. Nebraska,* 205 U.S. 34 (1907). See, generally, "Developments in the Law: Deceptive Advertising," *Harvard Law Review,* Vol. 80 (1967), p. 1005, esp. pp. 1027–1038; *Banzhaf v. F.C.C.,* 405 F.2d 1082, 1101–1102 (D.C. Cir. 1968), cert. denied 396 U.S. 842 (1969).

1. TAXATION

The initial, and still leading, case on the power of the government to tax aspects of the system of free expression is *Grosjean v. American Press Co.,* decided in 1936. A Louisiana statute, passed in 1934, provided that all persons or corporations selling advertisements in newspapers or magazines having a circulation of more than twenty thousand copies a week must pay a license tax for the privilege of engaging in such business, amounting to 2 percent of the gross receipts of sales. Nine newspapers in Louisiana brought suit to enjoin enforcement of the law and were successful. The Supreme Court unanimously held the statute invalid. Justice Sutherland, writing for the Court, traced the history of English and early American "taxes on knowledge,"—taxes on newspapers and advertisements, designed "to suppress the publication of comments and criticisms objectionable" to the government and "to prevent, or curtail the opportunity for, the acquisition of knowledge by the people in respect of their governmental affairs." In adopting the First Amendment, he declared, "it was meant to preclude the national government, and by the Fourteenth Amendment to preclude the states, from adopting any form of previous restraint upon printed publications, or their circulation, including that which had theretofore been effected by these two well-known and odious methods [taxes on newspapers and advertisements]." Justice Sutherland made clear that the Court was not suggesting "that the owners of newspapers are immune from any of the ordinary forms of taxation for support of the government." The distinguishing characteristics of the Louisiana tax, which brought it into conflict with the First Amendment, were:

> [T]his is not an ordinary form of tax, but one single in kind, with a long history of hostile misuse against freedom of the press. . . .
> The tax here involved is bad not because it takes money from the pockets of the appellees. If that were all, a wholly different question would be presented. It is bad because in the light of its history and of its present setting, it is seen to be a deliberate and calculated device in the guise of a tax to limit the circulation of information to which the public is entitled in virtue of the constitutional guaranties. . . .
> The form in which the tax is imposed is in itself suspicious. It is not measured or limited by the volume of advertisements. It is measured alone by the extent of the circulation of the publication in which the

advertisements are carried, with the plain purpose of penalizing the publishers and curtailing the circulation of a selected group of newspapers.[7]

The Court in *Grosjean* thus stressed three factors as making the Louisiana tax invalid. First, it was "single in kind," that is, it focused exclusively on a vital element in the system of freedom of expression— newspapers and periodicals. Second, by "curtailing information to which the public is entitled," it imposed a serious burden on the system of freedom of expression. Third, the tax was a pretense, actually intended to penalize a "selected group of newspapers." The Court handled this last point somewhat gingerly. The fact was that the tax was imposed by the Huey Long regime in Louisiana as a method of punishing or crippling the larger newspapers in the State, which, unlike the smaller ones in the rural areas, opposed the Long administration. Nevertheless the Court did definitely probe beneath the surface and undoubtedly was strongly influenced by the underlying motivations of the legislature.[8]

The *Grosjean* decision was followed and extended by the Court of Appeals of Maryland in *Mayor of Baltimore v. A. S. Abell Co.* This case involved two city tax ordinances. One imposed a tax of 4 percent upon the gross sales price paid by purchasers of advertising in newspapers and other publications, on radio and television, and on billboards; and the other laid a tax of 2 percent upon the sellers of such advertisements. One of the three elements of *Grosjean* was missing, for there was no indication that the taxes were designed to favor one group of publishers over another. But the Court struck the taxes down upon the two remaining grounds. They were focused upon the news media, in effect more particularly upon newspapers: "[W]hen the tax is imposed upon a business that enjoys one of the constitutional immunities of the First Amendment, it must be general in its nature and character and affect this business only incidentally as it affects other businesses in their combined duty to support the government." Moreover, the taxes constituted a grave burden on the system of freedom of expression, calculated at about $350,000 a year for the Sunpapers alone. In

---

7. *Grosjean v. American Press Co.*, 297 U.S. 233, 246–247, 249, 250–251 (1936). For a collection of materials on the taxation problem see *Political and Civil Rights in the United States*, pp. 602–604.

8. For the background of the Louisiana tax law, see Zechariah Chafee, Jr., *Free Speech in the United States* (Cambridge, Harvard University Press, 1941), pp. 381–384.

a number of other cases, various general taxes imposed upon all business or on a large segment of business, but including also the news
media, have been upheld.[9]

Two other decisions of the Supreme Court throw further light
upon the problem. In *Murdock v. Pennsylvania,* the city imposed a
license tax upon "all persons canvassing for or soliciting . . . orders
for goods . . . wares, or merchandise of any kind." The tax
amounted to $1.50 a day, $7 a week, $12 for two weeks, and $20 for
three weeks. It was attacked by members of Jehovah's Witnesses who
traveled from town to town selling religious literature. The Supreme
Court, dramatically reversing a contrary decision made only a year
before, struck down the tax by a vote of five to four. The majority, in
an opinion by Justice Douglas, pointed out that the activities of the
Jehovah's Witnesses were religious, not "commercial" in nature. He
went on to say that the tax was not a nominal fee imposed to defray
expenses in policing the licensing system but "a flat license tax levied
and collected as a condition to the pursuit of activities whose
enjoyment is guaranteed by the First Amendment." To Justice Douglas it was the same as if the city had undertaken "to exact a tax . . .
for the privilege of delivering a sermon." He also found that such
taxes were "as severe and telling in their impact on freedom of press
and religion as the 'taxes on knowledge' at which the First Amendment
was partly aimed"; in fact, he argued, the activities of colporteurs
could be "crushed and closed out by the sheer weight of the toll or
tribute which is exacted town by town, village by village." The dissenters took the view that the ordinance, covering all solicitors, amounted
to no more than a general tax and that the Jehovah's Witnesses were
merely being asked to pay a fair share of the costs of government. The
Court reached a similar result in *Follett v. McCormick,* invalidating a
license tax on "business, occupation and professions" insofar as it
applied to a Jehovah's Witness who lived in the town and made his
living from the sale of religious books to persons he called upon in the
course of his preaching. Justice Douglas placed the decision upon the
same grounds as in *Murdock*—that a flat tax "restrains in advance

9. *Mayor of Baltimore v. A. S. Abell
Co.,* 218 Md. 273, 287, 145 A.2d 111,
118 (1958). Cases upholding the taxes
include *City of Corona v. Corona Daily
Independent,* 115 Cal. App.2d 382, 252
P.2d 56 (Ct. App. 1953), cert. denied
346 U.S. 833 (1953), Justices Black and
Douglas dissenting; *Tampa Times Co. v.
City of Tampa,* 158 Fla. 589, 29 So.2d
368 (1947), app. dis. 332 U.S. 749
(1947); *Steinbeck v. Gerosa,* 4 N.Y.2d
302, 175 N.Y.S.2d 1, 151 N.E.2d 170
(1958). See Note, *Columbia Law Review,*
Vol. 59 (1959), pp. 359, 360–361.

. . . constitutional liberties" and "inevitably tends to suppress their exercise." [10]

Murdock and *Follett* introduced a fourth element into the test for the validity of a tax impinging on First Amendment rights. The main emphasis of both decisions was that the government may not impose a tax directly upon exercise of the right itself. A tax on income, property, sales, or some other attribute of a person or firm engaged in protected expression would be acceptable (providing the other three conditions were met); but a levy on the very conduct of expression was not. The doctrine would seem to be a sound one. It is consistent with the theory that expression is entitled to full protection against any kind of governmental restriction; and the flat rule is helpful in preventing administrative abuse. The minority argued strenuously that general and nondiscriminatory taxes were justified, even though falling on the exercise of a First Amendment right, as a part of the common financial burden all citizens should bear. The contention is not persuasive. For the person without resources the tax is oppressive, or at least the burden of proving in each case that it is oppressive is normally beyond his means; moreover, the amount he can contribute to the tax fund is minute. The tax contribution of the person or corporation with resources can be obtained readily by shifting the tax base to some other aspect of its operations. The majority's decision, in other words, protects the underprivileged without depriving the government of tax income.[11]

The *Murdock* and *Follett* decisions also rested on another ground. The majority stressed in *Murdock* that the tax placed a heavy, even crippling, burden on one segment of the system of free expression, namely colporteurs. It took the same position, though there was less factual basis for it, in *Follett*. Thus the tax failed to meet one of the tests laid down in *Grosjean*. Though the minority disagreed on the facts it did accept the general proposition that a tax could not impose "an unjustifiable burden" on a First Amendment right.[12]

Freedom of expression can be affected by other features of the tax

---

10. *Murdock v. Pennsylvania,* 319 U.S. 105, 114, 112, 114–115 (1943); *Follett v. McCormick,* 321 U.S. 573, 575 (1944). The *Follett* decision was six to three. Compare the permit fee cases, discussed in Chapter IX.

11. It may be that the Court is in fact willing to apply the *Murdock* and *Follett* rule only to the underprivileged. In the *Corona* case, cited in a previous note, the Court denied certiorari of a decision upholding a license tax on the privilege of doing business, even as applied to newspapers. Justices Black and Douglas dissented on the *Murdock-Follett* ground, saying: "No government can exact a price for the exercise of a privilege which the Constitution guarantees." 346 U.S. at 834.

12. *Murdock v. Pennsylvania,* 319 U.S. at 139.

laws, such as tax deductions and exemptions. An issue of this sort was presented to the Court in *Cammarano v. United States*. Under the Internal Revenue Code a taxpayer, in computing his Federal income tax, is allowed to deduct from gross income "the ordinary and necessary expenses" incurred in carrying on a business. But Treasury Regulations provide that no such deductions shall be allowed for "sums of money expended for lobbying purposes [or] the promotion or defeat of legislation." Cammarano and his wife were part owners of a wholesale beer business in the State of Washington which contributed money to a campaign to defeat an initiative measure that would put the sale of wine and beer exclusively in the hands of the State. They challenged the refusal of the Treasury to allow the contribution as a business expense, on the ground, inter alia, that it constituted a charge on the exercise of First Amendment rights. The Court unanimously rejected the contention: "Petitioners are not being denied a tax deduction because they engage in constitutionally protected activities," said Justice Harlan for the Court, "but are simply being required to pay for those activities entirely out of their own pockets, as everyone else engaging in similar activities is required to do under the provisions of the Internal Revenue Code." While the Court perhaps too readily distinguished a tax deduction from a tax imposition, there would clearly seem to be no "abridgment" of the right to freedom of expression in such a case. The decision is interesting because Justice Douglas, concurring, undertakes to examine further the exclusion of "commercial" communication from First Amendment protection. He indicates doubts about the soundness of *Valentine v. Chrestensen*, but concludes that the issue was not present in the *Cammarano* case.[13]

The use of the tax laws to control the system of freedom of expression could have become an important and complex problem. This does not appear to have been the case. So far, at least, the *Grosjean* ruling seems in full command.[14]

---

13. *Cammarano v. United States*, 358 U.S. 498, 513 (1959).

14. Cases involving the use of tax exemptions to control the content of expression in the interests of national security are discussed in Chapter VI.

2. BUSINESS REGULATIONS GENERALLY

Business regulations that have an impact upon the system of freedom of expression are governed by much the same rules as were developed in the tax cases. A business enterprise, whether in the form of a corporation or otherwise, has a constitutional right to protection under the First Amendment when it engages in expression. In the case of a business, of course, much of its communication may take place in the "commercial sector" and hence not be covered by the First Amendment. But the fact that it is operating for profit does not place it outside the system of freedom of expression.[15]

General and nondiscriminatory regulations, not covertly designed to control expression, can validly be made applicable to business enterprise engaged in protected expression. Thus newspapers have been held subject to the National Labor Relations Act, the wage and hour laws, and the anti-trust laws. Such effect as these laws may have upon the collection and dissemination of news is plainly not an "abridgment" within the meaning of the First Amendment. But business regulations that operate as direct controls on expression, and thereby do "abridge" such expression, are impermissible. Thus the anti-trust laws cannot be employed to prevent a group of railroads from joining together to lobby for legislation favorable to their interests. Nor can State laws regulating the legal profession prohibit individuals from associating in an organization formed to obtain legal services for its members and to sponsor cases to vindicate their legal rights.[16]

The National Labor Relations Act and other laws establishing the right of employees to organize and bargain collectively have posed questions concerning the right to freedom of expression in various aspects of employment relations. The courts have dealt with innumerable specific issues and there is an extensive literature on the subject.

---

15. See the cases cited above in the discussion of the "commercial sector." For a collection of references on business regulations and freedom of expression generally, see *Political and Civil Rights in the United States*, pp. 602–604.

16. The cases holding general business regulations applicable to newspapers are *Associated Press v. National Labor Relations Board*, 301 U.S. 103 (1937); *Oklahoma Press Publishing Co. v. Walling*, 327 U.S. 186 (1946); *Associated Press v. United States*, 326 U.S. 1 (1945); see also *Lorain Journal Co. v. United States*, 342 U.S. 143 (1951). The lobbying case is *Eastern R.R. Presidents Conference v. Noerr Motor Freight, Inc.*, 365 U.S. 127 (1961); see also *United Mine Workers v. Pennington*, 381 U.S. 657, 669–670 (1965). The cases on the legal profession are discussed in the following section.

But, on the whole, the underlying doctrines have not been in dispute. It seems to be agreed that these communications are not within the "commercial sector." It is also generally accepted that legislation of this character cannot, on any theory of clear and present danger or balancing or otherwise, deprive employers and employees of their rights under the First Amendment to discuss any matter of concern to them. The issue has been one of drawing the distinction between expression and action. Communication by either employer or employee that is physically or economically coercive, or that implies a threat of such coercion, is action and not protected. This was the position taken in the first decision of the Supreme Court to deal with this problem, and it has remained the guiding principle since that time.[17]

Some of the potentially troublesome problems involved in adjusting business regulations to the system of freedom of expression were raised before the California Supreme Court in *Weaver v. Jordan*. At issue was the constitutionality of an initiative measure, adopted by the California electorate in 1964, which prohibited home subscription television in the State The California Supreme Court, with one justice dissenting, ruled the measure unconstitutional as a violation of the First Amendment. Justice Burke, writing for the majority, held that the total prohibition of pay television in the home constituted a restriction on First Amendment freedoms; decided that, because the enactment was "so broad as to impose a complete ban of expression and communication through a specified medium," the balancing test "may be dispensed with"; applied the clear and present danger test, as modified into a probability test in *Dennis;* and concluded that "[a]ny suggestion of the existence of a 'clear and present danger' to be obviated by the Act here involved would be utterly specious." Justice Mosk,

17. *National Labor Relations Board v. Virginia Electric & Power Co.,* 314 U.S. 469 (1941); *National Labor Relations Board v. Gissel Packing Co.,* 395 U.S. 575, 616–620 (1969). The principle was incorporated in the National Labor Relations Act by amendment in 1947 which provided that expression which "contains no threat of reprisal or force or promise of benefit" cannot constitute or be evidence of an unfair labor practice. 61 Stat. 142 (1947), 29 U.S.C. §158 (c). The policy of the National Labor Relations Board in setting aside employee representation elections in which materially false or misleading statements are made without opportunity for rebuttal, or in which inflammatory statements appealing to race prejudice are made, seems of doubtful constitutionality. These issues have not been passed upon directly by the Supreme Court. But see *Linn v. United Plant Guard Workers of America,* 383 U.S. 53 (1966); and Derek C. Bok, "The Regulation of Campaign Tactics in Representation Elections Under the National Labor Relations Act," *Harvard Law Review,* Vol. 78 (1964), p. 38. For reference to the literature on employer and employee free speech see *Political and Civil Rights in the United States,* p. 604.

dissenting, argued that the "target here is not speech" since the enactment did not prohibit television in the home but simply forbade charging for it. In his view the measure was merely an economic regulation of a business in the same way that other businesses were regulated. He also believed that the case was controlled by the doctrine of *Valentine v. Chrestensen,* since the measure was an effort "to control commercial invasion of homes." The decision raises some interesting questions as to when a business regulation constitutes an "abridgment" of expression rather than a mere economic control, a particularly difficult issue in a field as thoroughly controlled by government as radio and television. Nevertheless it seems clear in this case that the legislation imposed a special and severe burden upon the system of freedom of expression—almost equivalent to a law forbidding newspapers to charge for their product—and cut off communication that in no sense could be considered part of the "commercial sector." [18]

On the whole the expanding range of business regulation has not proved difficult to adjust to the system of freedom of expression under full protection doctrines. The problems may grow more complex in the future.

3. ATTACK ON FREEDOM OF ASSOCIATION: THE N.A.A.C.P. CASES

In a group of decisions beginning in 1958 the Supreme Court dealt with an effort by various southern States to use business regulations as a means of harassing or destroying civil-rights organizations operating in the South, particularly the National Association for the Advancement of Colored People. The cases are significant as demonstrating how the courts undertake to handle problems of pretense regulations. They are also important because it was in these cases that the Supreme Court first developed the concept of an independent constitutional "right of association." [19]

The initial decision was in *N.A.A.C.P. v. Alabama ex rel. Patterson.* An Alabama statute, similar to that in many other States, re-

18. *Weaver v. Jordan,* 49 Cal. Rptr. 537, 543, 544, 547, 555, 411 P.2d 289, 295, 296, 299, 307 (1966), cert. denied 385 U.S. 844 (1966).

19. The treatment of these problems is based upon, and in part extracted from, my more detailed analysis in "Freedom of Association and Freedom of Expression," *Yale Law Journal,* Vol. 74 (1964), p. 1. For other material on both the attack on civil-rights organizations and the right of association see *Political and Civil Rights in the United States,* pp. 605–625.

quired a foreign corporation doing business in Alabama to file its charter and to designate a place of business and an agent to receive service
of process. The N.A.A.C.P. was a non-profit corporation organized
under the laws of New York. Affiliates had operated in Alabama since
1918 and the Association opened a regional office there in 1951. Believing itself exempt from the Alabama qualification statute the
N.A.A.C.P. had never complied with that legislation. In 1956 the Attorney General of Alabama brought an equity suit to enjoin the
N.A.A.C.P. from conducting further activities in Alabama and to
oust it from the State. In the course of the proceeding the Attorney
General sought an order from the Alabama court requiring the
N.A.A.C.P. to produce various records and papers including a list of
the names and addresses of all its members, alleged to be necessary for
use in the hearing on the injunction. Upon its refusal to produce the
membership lists the N.A.A.C.P. was held in contempt of court. The
United States Supreme Court unanimously reversed.[20]

Justice Harlan, writing for the Court, first held that the Association was entitled to assert the constitutional rights of its members. He
then proceeded to define the constitutional right involved:

> Effective advocacy of both public and private points of view, par-
> ticularly controversial ones, is undeniably enhanced by group associa-
> tion, as this Court has more than once recognized by remarking upon
> the close nexus between the freedoms of speech and assembly. *De Jonge
> v. Oregon,* 299 U.S. 353, 364; *Thomas v. Collins,* 323 U.S. 516, 530.
> It is beyond debate that freedom to engage in association for the ad-
> vancement of beliefs and ideas is an inseparable aspect of the "liberty"
> assured by the Due Process Clause of the Fourteenth Amendment,
> which embraces freedom of speech. . . . Of course, it is immaterial
> whether the beliefs sought to be advanced by association pertain to
> political, economic, religious or cultural matters, and state action which
> may have the effect of curtailing the freedom to associate is subject to
> the closest scrutiny.[21]

Mr. Justice Harlan thus initially treated freedom of association as
derivative from the First Amendment rights to freedom of speech and
assembly, and as ancillary to them. In the remainder of his opinion,
however, he elevated freedom of association to an independent right,
possessing an equal status with the other rights specifically enumerated

20. *N.A.A.C.P. v. Alabama ex rel.*   21. 357 U.S. at 460–461.
Patterson, 357 U.S. 449 (1958).

in the First Amendment. He repeatedly used the phrase "freedom of association" by itself, and at one point carefully distinguished it by referring to "these indispensable liberties, whether of speech, press, *or* association." In the end he had established, as new doctrine, the "constitutionally protected right of association." [22]

Justice Harlan went on to say that the fact that Alabama "has taken no direct action" to restrict the right of association "does not end inquiry. . . . The governmental action challenged may appear to be totally unrelated to protected liberties," but would nevertheless be struck down, as in *Grosjean* and *Murdock*, "when perceived to have the consequence of unduly curtailing" constitutional liberties. In this case, he pointed out, "compelled disclosure of affiliation with groups engaged in advocacy may constitute as effective a restraint on freedom of association" as the taxes in those cases. The "final question" then was "whether Alabama has demonstrated an interest in obtaining the disclosures it seeks from petitioner which is sufficient to justify the deterrent effect which we have concluded these disclosures may well have on the free exercise by petitioner's members of their constitutionally protected right of association." Applying this balancing test he concluded that Alabama's interest was insufficient. Justice Harlan's opinion was the only one rendered in the case.[23]

Very similar issues were present in the next case, *Bates v. City of Little Rock*. Local ordinances in two Arkansas cities, enacted under authority to impose a licensing tax on organizations operating within the city, required production of membership lists. Officials of the local branch of the N.A.A.C.P. were convicted for refusing to produce the lists. Mr. Justice Stewart, writing for the majority, began by deriving "the right of association" from the right of peaceable assembly, and went on to treat it as an independent constitutional right. Like Justice Harlan, he cited *Grosjean* and *Murdock* for the proposition: "Freedoms such as these are protected not only against heavy-handed frontal attack, but also from being stifled by more subtle governmental interference." Pointing out the damaging effect of disclosing membership lists, he adopted as the controlling principle: "Where there is a significant encroachment upon personal liberty, the State may prevail only upon showing a subordinating interest which is compelling." Finding "no relevant correlation" between the power of the city to

22. 357 U.S. at 461, 463. Italics supplied.   23. 357 U.S. at 461, 462, 463.

impose a licensing tax and the compulsory disclosure of membership, he concluded that "the municipalities have failed to demonstrate a controlling justification for the deterrence of free association." [24]

This time Justices Black and Douglas concurred in a separate opinion. They viewed the ordinances as violating freedom of speech and assembly. With respect to association they observed: "one of those rights, freedom of assembly, includes of course freedom of association." In addition, they declined to apply the balancing test, saying that "First Amendment rights are beyond abridgment either by legislation that directly restrains their exercise or by suppression or impairment through harassment, humiliation, or exposure by government." [25]

The two following cases have already been discussed in other connections. *Shelton v. Tucker* did not, strictly speaking, involve a business regulation, but a statute requiring all teachers to list every organization to which they had belonged over the past five years. Justice Stewart, again writing for the majority, thought that the case was "not of a pattern" with the *Patterson* and *Bates* cases: "In those cases the Court held that there was no substantially relevant correlation between the government interest asserted and the State's effort to compel disclosure of the membership lists involved. Here, by contrast, there can be no question of the relevance of a State's inquiry into the fitness and competence of its teachers." Nevertheless he concluded that "the right of association" was violated in this case because the statute was too broadly drawn: "The statute's comprehensive interference with associational freedom goes far beyond what might be justified in the exercise of the State's legitimate inquiry into the fitness and competency of its teachers." [26]

In *Louisiana ex rel. Gremillion v. N.A.A.C.P.*, one of the two Louisiana statutes involved required the principal officers of various types of "benevolent" associations operating in Louisiana to file lists of the names and addresses of all officers and members. Justice Douglas, writing the majority opinion, did not apply any kind of balancing test but simply asserted that "where it is shown . . . that disclosure of membership lists results in reprisals against and hostility to the members, disclosure is not required." He also, citing *Shelton*, found the statute too broadly drawn.[27]

24. *Bates v. City of Little Rock*, 361 U.S. 516, 523, 524, 527 (1960).

25. 361 U.S. at 528.

26. *Shelton v. Tucker*, 364 U.S. 479, 485, 490 (1960). Four Justices dissented.

For further discussion see Chapter VII.

27. *Louisiana ex rel. Gremillion v. N.A.A.C.P.*, 366 U.S. 293, 296 (1961). The four Justices who dissented in *Shelton v. Tucker* concurred in the result but

N.A.A.C.P. v. Button involved a Virginia statute which, as interpreted by a majority of the Court, would have prohibited the N.A.A.C.P. from urging Negroes to seek legal redress for violations of their civil rights by instituting litigation through members of the Association's legal staff. On this occasion Mr. Justice Brennan wrote the opinion for the majority. He first addressed himself to the question whether the activities prohibited by the statute fell within the area of freedoms protected by the First Amendment, and found that they did. Justice Brennan's opinion is notable as extending the concept of expression to a point that no decision of the Court had previously reached:

> We meet at the outset the contention that "solicitation" is wholly outside the area of freedoms protected by the First Amendment. To this contention there are two answers. The first is that a State cannot foreclose the exercise of constitutional rights by mere labels. The second is that abstract discussion is not the only species of communication which the Constitution protects; the First Amendment also protects vigorous advocacy, certainly of lawful ends, against governmental intrusion. . . . In the context of NAACP objectives, litigation is not a technique of resolving private differences; it is a means for achieving the lawful objectives of equality of treatment by all government, federal, state and local, for the members of the Negro community in this country. It is thus a form of political expression. . . . And under the conditions of modern government, litigation may well be the sole practicable avenue open to a minority to petition for redress of grievances.

> We need not, in order to find constitutional protection for the kind of cooperative, organizational activity disclosed by this record, whereby Negroes seek through lawful means to achieve legitimate political ends, subsume such activity under a narrow, literal conception of freedom of speech, petition or assembly. For there is no longer any doubt that the First and Fourteenth Amendments protect certain forms of orderly group activity. Thus we have affirmed the right "to engage in association for the advancement of beliefs and ideas. *NAACP v. Alabama*." [28]

Justice Brennan then went on to hold that the Virginia statute violated petitioners' constitutional rights on two grounds: the statute was too vague and too broad; and the interest of the State in regulating the kind of activity involved was not sufficiently compelling to justify invasion of First Amendment rights.

---

not in the opinion. For further discussion see Chapter V.

28. *N.A.A.C.P. v. Button*, 371 U.S. 415, 429–430 (1963).

Justice Harlan, dissenting with Justices Clark and Stewart, argued
that, while "the basic rights in issue are those of the petitioner's members to associate, to discuss, and to advocate," nevertheless "litigation
. . . is *conduct;* it is speech *plus.*" In such a situation, he contended,
the standard for determining whether there has been an infringement
of the individual's right is whether "the regulation has a reasonable
relationship to a proper governmental objective and does not unduly
interfere with such individual rights." He continued:

> Although the State surely may not broadly prohibit individuals with
> a common interest from joining together to petition a court for redress
> of their grievances, it is equally certain that the State may impose
> reasonable regulations limiting the permissible form of litigation and the
> manner of legal representation within its borders. . . . [Such] regula-
> tions are undeniably matters of legitimate concern to the State and their
> possible impact on the rights of expression and association is far too re-
> mote to cause any doubt as to their validity.[29]

Finally, the *Patterson* case came back to the Court in *N.A.A.C.P.
v. Alabama ex rel. Flowers.* After various intermediate proceedings,
the Alabama courts enjoined the N.A.A.C.P. from doing business in
Alabama and from attempting to qualify to do business there. The
grounds for exclusion consisted of eleven charges made against the
organization. The Court, in a unanimous opinion delivered by Justice
Harlan, dealt with the issues in terms of the "right of association."
Some of the grounds for exclusion, such as the efforts of the
N.A.A.C.P. to enroll Negro students in the University of Alabama,
involved conduct protected by the First Amendment. With respect to
these grounds the Court, without elaboration, ruled that "such a
challenge cannot stand." The remaining grounds, such as "organizing,
supporting and financing an illegal boycott" against a Montgomery
bus line, involved conduct that the Alabama court had found to be in
violation of State law. Assuming the invalidity of this conduct, the Supreme Court nevertheless held that such activities did not justify the
exclusion: "[A] governmental purpose to control or prevent activities

29. 371 U.S. at 454–455. The practice
of a labor union in arranging for legal
services for its members was upheld in
*Brotherhood of R.R. Trainmen v. Vir-
ginia,* 377 U.S. 1 (1964). Justice Black,
writing the opinion, did not mention the
right of association but held that "the
First Amendment's guarantees of free
speech, petition and assembly give railroad workers the right to gather together
for the lawful purpose of helping and
advising one another in asserting the
rights Congress gave them." 377 U.S. at
5. Accord is *United Mine Workers of
America v. Illinois State Bar Association,*
389 U.S. 217 (1967).

constitutionally subject to state regulation may not be achieved by means which sweep unnecessarily broadly and thereby invade the area of protected freedoms." The Court declared that the penalty of exclusion "unduly" infringed the constitutional right and that the objective sought by Alabama could be "more narrowly achieved." In short, the charges "suggest no legitimate governmental objective which requires such restraint." In the end, evidently exasperated, the Court cast aside the whole fiction: "This case, in truth, involves not the privilege of a corporation to do business in a State, but rather the freedom of individuals to associate for the collective advocacy of ideas." [30]

The Supreme Court was thus successful, apart from the long delays involved, in preventing the N.A.A.C.P. from being destroyed or crippled through the use of ordinary business regulations. The Court did not formally, until the very end, look below the surface of what was taking place, though there is no doubt it was fully aware of, and strongly influenced by, the realities of the situation. Basically it relied upon the balancing test, with help from the overbreadth rule. One may well doubt whether this doctrinal basis is adequate to meet the needs of the situation, at least in less obvious cases. The balancing test here, as Justice Stewart indicated in *Shelton*, is not much more than a test of relevance, or at most of reasonableness. The overbreadth rule is also a weak prop to rely on, as the close division in *Shelton* showed, and one that can often be overcome by careful redrafting.

The Supreme Court's creation of an independent constitutional "right of association" is an important development. It has received a great deal of attention and has been widely hailed as a significant addition to the arsenal of constitutional guarantees. But its value as constitutional doctrine is highly questionable. There can be no doubt that freedom of association, as a basic element in the democratic process, must receive constitutional protection. But the freedom to be safeguarded is so inclusive, appears in so many different forms, and is subject to such varied restrictions, that the rules for its protection cannot be capsuled into a single doctrine called the "right of association." To do so would require that that constitutional term be stretched to cover so many things, and be limited by so many qualifications, as to be meaningless. Claims to different kinds of associational rights give rise to different kinds of constitutional problems. They may be matters of

30. *N.A.A.C.P. v. Alabama ex rel. Flowers*, 377 U.S. 288, 307, 308, 309 (1964).

due process, freedom of religion, freedom of expression, equal protection, bill of attainder, or others. But they can hardly be effectively safeguarded under the single rubric "right of association." [31]

The conduct involved in the N.A.A.C.P. cases constituted expression rather than action. This was conceded in all the cases except *Button*, and there Justice Brennan's reasoning is persuasive. The cases, therefore, could have been more appropriately handled through the application of the basic doctrines here urged as governing other First Amendment issues.

The expression here at stake, it is true, was associational rather than individual expression. But it is clear from the functions served by association in a democratic society that associational expression should be entitled to the same complete protection as individual expression. Organization primarily supplies the mechanism for reaching a wider audience. It does not change the character of expression as the communication of beliefs, opinions, information and ideas, or its content. Thus associational expression is simply an extension of the individual right of expression and, for the same reasons and to the same extent, should be free of governmental abridgment.

The same conclusion follows from the whole theory of free expression. The purpose of a system of freedom of expression—to allow individuals to realize their potentialities and to facilitate social change through reason and agreement rather than force and violence—cannot be effectively achieved in modern society unless free rein is given to association designed to enhance the scope and influence of communication. Such hostility as the state may have had for association when the government was weak is hardly justified when the government is powerful and pervasive. Moreover, the government still retains the power to deal with action. It may not only apply its controls against force and violence or other overt acts, but it may and must take steps to assure those basic economic and social conditions in the nation that are essential to the survival of the democratic process. Further, the controls and apparatus necessary for the restriction of associational expression—investigations, files, informers, constant surveillance— are incompatible with a free society. Restriction of associational expression is likely to become, in practice, an effort to suppress a whole social or political movement. History and experience warn us that such

31. For a fuller development of this position, see Emerson, *op. cit. supra* note 19.

attempts are usually futile and merely tend to obscure the real grievances which a society must, if it is to survive, face squarely and solve.
Finally, it is clear from the very language of the First Amendment that
it was designed to safeguard associational expression. Both "the right
of the people peaceably to assemble" and the right "to petition the
Government for a redress of grievances" plainly were intended to
bring associational expression within the ambit of the constitutional
protection extended to individual expression.

The question therefore becomes whether in the N.A.A.C.P. cases
freedom of expression was "abridged" by the various State regulations, ostensibly enacted as business controls but impinging upon associational expression. On this issue the rules adopted in the tax cases
become applicable. Here the result could not be in doubt. In each case
the government action was intended to and did impose a serious and
special burden upon a particular group seeking to exercise its rights to
freedom of expression. The regulation, without resort to balancing,
overbreadth, or the "right of association" must fall. This, in substance,
was the position of Justices Black and Douglas.[32]

B. Economic Pressures: Picketing and Boycotts

One special aspect of the adjustment necessary between a system
of freedom of expression and the social interests protected by business
regulation concerns the use of various forms of communication to
exert economic pressure. Generally, the economic pressure consists in
withholding an economic relationship, or persuading or coercing
others to do so, in order to induce or force a business enterprise to take
certain action. Pressure is brought to bear in many ways, by action as
well as expression, but we are concerned primarily with the role in the
process of those methods associated with picketing and boycotts.

Economic pressures are routinely employed in the relations of
business enterprises with each other. They are also a common feature
of labor-management relations. But their use is not confined to these
fields. Picketing and boycotts as means of exerting economic pressure

---

32. Other aspects of freedom of association, as it relates to freedom of expression, are considered in Chapter V. See
also *Williams v. Rhodes,* 393 U.S. 23
(1968); *Pollard v. Roberts,* 283 F. Supp.
248 (E.D. Ark. 1968), aff'd 393 U.S. 14
(1968).

are not infrequently utilized, by all shades of opinion, in various kinds of controversy. The civil-rights movement in the South commenced with a boycott of the Montgomery buses in December 1955. Negro leadership, both national and local, has since invoked the boycott technique on many occasions. The boycott is perhaps the chief tactical weapon of the consumer and has recently been adopted by tenants in the form of the rent strike. It has been used by religious groups in protesting the showing of moving pictures considered objectionable, and by right-wing groups in opposing the employment in private corporations of persons considered subversive. On the whole, outside the business and labor areas, economic pressures of this sort have been employed only spasmodically and without marked success. But, in our highly organized and vulnerable society, they could become tactics of immense power and significance.[33]

The development of legal doctrine in this area has been strongly influenced by two factors. In the first place, most of the cases have arisen in the business and labor fields. There is very little law dealing with the use of economic pressures, through picketing and boycotts, in other areas. The tendency has been, however, to apply the rules that have evolved from the business and labor cases, without full consideration of differing factors, to the race, consumer and other types of cases. Secondly, the business and labor cases have themselves been greatly affected by earlier theories of property and contract rights, as well as by anti-labor bias. The impact of these factors still persists and is likewise transferred to the nonbusiness and non-labor cases. It should be noted also that, as in so many other areas, the earlier law took shape prior to the development of First Amendment doctrine, and the two have never been merged into a single consistent whole.

33. On the Montgomery bus boycott see Martin Luther King, Jr., *Stride Toward Freedom* (New York, Harper & Co., 1958). For other materials on the use of economic pressure in racial controversies see Mulford Q. Sibley, "Direct Action and the Struggle for Integration," *Hastings Law Journal*, Vol. 16 (1965), p. 351; Hannah Lees, "Boycott in Philadelphia," in Alan F. Westin (ed.), *Freedom Now* (New York, Basic Books, 1964), p. 231; Arthur I. Waskow, *From Race Riot to* *Sit-In* (Garden City, N.Y., Doubleday & Co., 1966); J. J. Seldin, "The Dixie Boycott," *The Nation*, April 28, 1956, p. 360; *Political and Civil Rights in the United States*, p. 1606. With respect to the use of economic sanctions in the censorship area, see *ibid.*, pp. 849–868; in nongovernment loyalty programs *ibid.*, pp. 424–426, 898. For earlier material, see Note, "Non-Labor Picketing and the Thornhill Case," *Columbia Law Review*, Vol. 41 (1941), p. 89.

I. THE EXISTING LAW OF PICKETING AND BOYCOTTS

Controls over the use of economic pressures through picketing and boycotts derive from three main sources—tort law, statutory law, and the equity powers of a court to grant an injunction. In tort law the principal doctrines applicable are defamation, trade libel, interference with contractual relationships or prospective advantage, and prima facie tort. In areas outside the commercial sector the most important of these causes of action is interference with contractual relationships or prospective advantage. Speaking very roughly, the tort is committed by persons who cause harm to another by a concerted refusal to enter into or continue business relations with him, or who induce other persons to do so, without sufficient justification under the circumstances. The central issue—whether the conduct is justified under the circumstances—turns upon various factors going to the objective of the action and the means used. Again very roughly, if the objective is illegal or contrary to public policy, then the conduct is tortious; if not, the question of justification is determined by balancing the injury to the persons affected against the interests of the persons applying the economic pressures. Concerning means, the most relevant considerations are whether they involve persuasion or coercion, whether communications are true or false, and whether neutral parties are brought into the controversy. Outside the business and labor fields, there are very few cases in the State courts dealing with tort actions against those exerting economic pressures. The United States Supreme Court has never decided a case of this nature. The First Amendment issues, however, are the same as those that arise in the context of a statute or an injunction, on which there is some Supreme Court authority.[34]

34. The best discussions of tort liability, in areas other than business and labor, are Note, "Legal Responsibility for Extralegal Censure," *Columbia Law Review*, Vol. 62 (1962), p. 475; Note, "The Common-Law and Constitutional Status of Anti-Discrimination Boycotts," *Yale Law Journal*, Vol. 66 (1957), p. 397; Harold W. Horowitz, "Legal Aspects of Political Blacklisting in the Entertainment Industry," *Southern California Law Review*, Vol. 29 (1956), pp. 263, 292–305; Note, "Tort Liability of Organizations for Intentionally Impairing Economic Relations," *Indiana Law Journal*, Vol. 28 (1953), p. 467. See also Note, "Group Action: Civil Rights and Freedom of Association," *Northwestern University Law Review*, Vol. 54 (1959), pp. 390, 399–404; Note, "Extralegal Censorship of Literature," *New York University Law Review*, Vol. 33 (1958), pp. 989, 1003–1007. For discussion of earlier cases see Note, *Columbia Law Review*, *supra* note 33. Generally on tort liability see Fowler V. Harper and Fleming James, Jr., *The Law of Torts* (Boston, Little, Brown & Co., 1956), §§6.11–6.13; American Law

In a series of early cases, prior to the main development of First Amendment doctrine, the Supreme Court held that boycotts by labor unions against employers were both unlawful under the Sherman Act and could be enjoined as an illegal conspiracy apart from that statute. In *Gompers v. Bucks Stove and Range Co.* the boycott was carried on in part through publication in the American Federation of Labor's periodical, the *American Federationist,* of the employer's name on the "Unfair" and "We don't patronize" lists. To the contention that this conduct was protected by the First Amendment the Court replied: "In the case of an unlawful conspiracy, the agreement to act in concert when the signal is published, gives the words 'Unfair,' 'We don't patronize,' or similar expressions, a force not adhering in the words themselves, and therefore exceeding any possible right of speech which a single individual might have. Under such circumstances they become what have been called 'verbal acts,' and as much subject to injunction as the use of any other force whereby property is unlawfully damaged." Subsequently labor organizations were exempted from the anti-trust laws and the Court never dealt further with labor boycotts of this nature. Beginning in 1940, however, the question of what protection the First Amendment afforded to labor picketing was constantly before the Court.[35]

The first case, *Thornhill v. Alabama,* involved an Alabama statute which provided that any persons "who, without a just cause or legal excuse therefor, go near to or loiter about the premises" of a business "with the intent of influencing, or inducing other persons not to trade with, buy from, sell to, have business dealings with, or be employed" by such business, or "who picket the works or place of business . . . for the purpose of hindering, delaying, or interfering with or injuring" such business, "shall be guilty of a misdemeanor." In the course of a strike against the Brown Wood Preserving Company the union maintained a picket line at the plant, with two picket posts manned by six to eight pickets. There was no violence or threat of violence, but the pickets did persuade at least one employee not to enter the plant for work. Thornhill, president of the union, was convicted under the statute and sentenced to fifty-nine days and a fine of one hundred dol-

---

Institute, *Restatement of Torts* (St. Paul, American Law Institute Publishers, 1939), §§765–774.

35. *Gompers v. Bucks Stove and Range Co.,* 221 U.S. 418, 439 (1911). Other boycott cases were *Loewe v. Law-*lor, 208 U.S. 274 (1908) (Danbury Hatters case); *Duplex Printing Press Co. v. Deering,* 254 U.S. 443 (1921); *Bedford Cut Stone Co. v. Journeymen Stone Cutters' Association,* 274 U.S. 37 (1927).

lars. The Supreme Court reversed, with Justice McReynolds alone dissenting.[36]

Justice Murphy, writing for the Court, first observed that when First Amendment rights were claimed to be abridged, "the courts should 'weigh the circumstances' and 'appraise the substantiality of the reasons advanced' in support of the challenged regulations," quoting *Schneider v. State*. He next held that the statute "must be judged upon its face" because, like those in *Lovell* and *Hague,* it "does not aim specifically at evils within the allowable area of state control but, on the contrary, sweeps within its ambit other activities that in ordinary circumstances constitute an exercise of freedom of speech or of the press." Justice Murphy then pointed out the precise conduct for which Thornhill had been convicted: "[The statute] has been applied by the state courts so as to prohibit a single individual from walking slowly and peacefully back and forth on the public sidewalk in front of the premises of an employer, without speaking to anyone, carrying a sign or placard on a staff above his head stating only the fact that the employer did not employ union men affiliated with the American Federation of Labor." He noted that the statute as thus applied "leaves room for no exceptions based upon either the number of persons engaged in the proscribed activity, the peaceful character of their demeanor, the nature of their dispute with an employer, or the restrained character and the accurateness of the terminology used in notifying the public of the facts of the dispute." Justice Murphy concluded that the statute was invalid on its face:

> In the circumstances of our times the dissemination of information concerning the facts of a labor dispute must be regarded as within that area of free discussion that is guaranteed by the Constitution. . . .
>
> It may be that effective exercise of the means of advancing public knowledge may persuade some of those reached to refrain from entering into advantageous relations with the business establishment which is the scene of the dispute. Every expression of opinion on matters that are important has the potentiality of inducing action in the interests of one rather than another group in society. But the group in power at any moment may not impose penal sanctions on peaceful and truthful discussion of matters of public interest merely on a showing that others may thereby be persuaded to take action inconsistent with its interests. Abridgment of the liberty of such discussion can be justified only where the clear danger of substantive evils arises under circumstances afford-

36. *Thornhill v. Alabama,* 310 U.S. 88 (1940).

ing no opportunity to test the merits of ideas by competition for acceptance in the market of public opinion. We hold that the danger of
injury to an industrial concern is neither so serious nor so imminent as
to justify the sweeping proscription of freedom of discussion embodied
in [the Alabama statute].[37]

Justice Murphy's opinion was cautious and inconclusive. He carefully narrowed the decision to the exact facts of *Thornhill's* case—an
instance of mild picketing which induced a few employees not to report for work. He indicated there were other situations in which the
First Amendment might not afford protection to picketing, but did not
attempt to delineate them in detail. Nor did he expound a theory that
would adequately mark the boundary in future cases. Significantly, he
accepted picketing as an obvious exercise of First Amendment rights.
But then, after flirting with the balancing test and overbreadth, he
found the controlling principle to be the clear and present danger test.
Applying that test he conceded that the picketing did result in economic injury to the employer but found such injury "neither so serious
nor so imminent" as to justify restriction of the First Amendment right.
There was no future in this approach. For it implied that only ineffective or superfluous picketing would be protected. As soon as picketing
operated to force an employer to take significant action to his detriment, it would create a "serious" and "imminent" "danger of injury"
and therefore could be prohibited. Plainly *Thornhill* was not to be the
final word.

The following year in *Milk Wagon Drivers Union v. Meadowmoor*
the Court held that picketing could be enjoined when it is "enmeshed
with contemporaneously violent conduct which is concededly outlawed." There was dissent over the relation between the violence and
the picketing in that case but the underlying proposition that picketing
which constituted violence was subject to prohibition was not in dispute. Beyond this point, however, *Meadowmoor* did not throw any
light.[38]

That the problem remained in a state of flux was apparent from the
decision of the Supreme Court a year later in *Bakery and Pastry Drivers v. Wohl.* The picketing in that case was carried on by members of
the Teamsters Union who had organized the drivers of trucks distribut-

37. 310 U.S. at 96, 97, 98–99, 102,
104–105. In accord with *Thornhill* is
Carlson v. California, 310 U.S. 106
(1940).

38. *Milk Wagon Drivers Local 753 v.
Meadowmoor Dairies, Inc.*, 312 U.S. 287,
292 (1941), discussed in Chapter IX.

ing baked goods from bakeries to retail stores. In competition with them, but not conforming to union standards, was a group of "peddlers" who bought goods from the bakeries and sold them to the retailers. The number of peddlers had increased substantially because many of the bakeries, in an effort to avoid the New York social security and unemployment compensation laws, were attempting to convert their former drivers into "independent contractors" exempted from the provisions of those laws. The Union picketed the bakeries from which the peddlers obtained their goods and the retail stores to which they sold them. There were no more than two pickets at any one place, carrying placards stating the Union's position; the picketing was entirely peaceful; and it was not proved that the two peddlers who brought suit to enjoin the picketing had sustained any monetary loss. An injunction was granted by the State court and the Supreme Court unanimously reversed.[39]

Justice Jackson, writing for the majority, made no mention of *Thornhill v. Alabama*. Nor did he undertake to formulate any alternative theory. He made clear that some picketing could be controlled: "A state is not required to tolerate in all places and all circumstances even peaceful picketing by an individual." But he made no effort to go beyond this stark dictum. As to the case before him he simply said: "We . . . can perceive no substantive evil of such magnitude as to mark a limit to the right of free speech which the petitioners sought to exercise." Justice Douglas, concurring with Justices Black and Murphy, reiterated the main points of *Thornhill*. In doing so, however, Justice Douglas introduced a new principle of limitation upon picketing, one that was destined to become dominant in subsequent cases:

> Picketing by an organized group is more than free speech, since it involves patrol of a particular locality and since the very presence of a picket line may induce action of one kind or another, quite irrespective of the nature of the ideas which are being disseminated. Hence those aspects of picketing make it the subject of restrictive regulation.[40]

The suggestion of Justice Douglas was brought to fruition in *Giboney v. Empire Storage and Ice Co.*, decided in 1949. Members of a union that included retail ice peddlers picketed the plant of Empire Storage and Ice Co., a wholesale ice distributor, in an effort to persuade the Company not to sell ice to nonunion peddlers. Most of the

---

39. *Bakery and Pastry Drivers v. Wohl,* 315 U.S. 769 (1942).

40. 315 U.S. at 775, 776–777.

Empire's truck drivers were members of other unions and they refused
to cross the picket lines. Indeed they were subject to fine or suspension
by their union if they did so. As a result Empire's business was immediately cut by 85 percent. On the other hand, had Empire refused to
sell to nonunion peddlers it would have been guilty of violating the
Missouri anti-trust law. The Company, claiming that the activities of
the Union constituted a violation of the State anti-trust law, obtained
an injunction against further picketing by the peddler's union. The Supreme Court unanimously affirmed.[41]

Justice Black, who wrote the Court's opinion, took the basic position that picketing involved more than speech and hence could be regulated: "A concurring opinion in the *Wohl* case," he noted, "pointed
out that picketing may include conduct other than speech, conduct
which can be made the subject of restrictive legislation." The union
pickets here, he said, were doing more than "attempting peacefully to
publicize truthful facts about a labor dispute": "Thus all of appellants'
activities—their powerful transportation combination, their patrolling, their formation of a picket line warning union men not to cross
at peril of their union membership, their publicizing—constituted a
single and integrated course of conduct, which was in violation of Missouri's valid law." Justice Black did not make entirely clear wherein
the picketers' conduct went beyond speech. He relied in part upon the
fact that the conduct involved more than simply displaying placards, in
part that the picketing evoked immediate economic pressure, and in
part that the objective constituted a violation of law. This ambiguity
was to be the cause of many later difficulties. But he seemed to place
main emphasis upon the last two factors, saying, with a glance at the
clear and present danger test:

> There was clear danger, imminent and immediate, that unless restrained,
> appellants would succeed in making [the State's anti-trust policy] a dead
> letter insofar as purchases by nonunion men were concerned. Appel-
> lants' power with that of their allies was irresistible. And it is clear that
> appellants were doing more than exercising a right of free speech or
> press [citing *Wohl*]. They were exercising their economic power to-
> gether with that of their allies to compel Empire to abide by union
> rather than by state regulation of trade.[42]

As a result of *Giboney* the Supreme Court soon reached the position that any labor picketing could be enjoined if it was designed to

41. *Giboney v. Empire Storage and*   42. 336 U.S. at 501, 498, 503.
Ice Co., 336 U.S. 490 (1949).

secure an objective that was contrary to "public policy." The rationale developed by *Wohl* and *Giboney*—that picketing was more than speech—was not further explored. But the rule of decision was reasonably clear. As stated by Justice Frankfurter in *International Brotherhood of Teamsters v. Vogt* it was as follows:

> This series of cases, then, established a broad field in which a State, in enforcing some public policy, whether of its criminal or its civil law, and whether announced by its legislature or its courts, could constitutionally enjoin peaceful picketing aimed at preventing effectuation of that policy.[43]

By the time of *Vogt* it was being said that nothing remained of *Thornhill*. On the basis of the Court's reasoning in *Giboney* and *Vogt* this appeared to be true. In 1964, however, the Court's decision in *N.L.R.B. v. Fruit and Vegetable Packers* hinted at some refinement of the *Wohl-Giboney* doctrine, and a reprieve for *Thornhill*. The immediate issue before the Court concerned the interpretation of Section 8(b)(4) of the National Labor Relations Act, designed to outlaw secondary boycotts. This provision made it an unfair labor practice for a union to "threaten, coerce or restrain any person" with the object of "forcing or requiring any person to cease using, selling, handling, transporting, or otherwise dealing in the products of any other producer . . . or to cease doing business with any other person." The Union, engaged in a strike against fruit packers and warehousemen in Washington, had instituted a consumer boycott against apples sold by companies involved in the strike. Some of the apples were being marketed through the Safeway chain of retail stores. The Union placed pickets before forty-six Safeway stores in Seattle, normally two at each store, who wore placards and distributed handbills appealing to Safeway customers and to the public generally to refrain from buying Washington apples. The Union made clear, on the handbills and otherwise, that the picket line was not directed at Safeway, not intended to interfere with Safeway employees, and not designed to obstruct deliveries and pickups at Safeway stores. Nor, in fact, was there any such effect. The Supreme Court, reversing the National Labor Relations Board, held that Section 8(b)(4) was not intended to outlaw the kind

---

43. *International Brotherhood of Teamsters v. Vogt,* 354 U.S. 284, 293 (1957). Chief Justice Warren and Justices Black and Douglas dissented. For a discussion of the cases, see Francis E. Jones, Jr., "Free Speech: Pickets on the Grass, Alas! Amidst Confusion, A Consistent Principle," *Southern California Law Review,* Vol. 29 (1956), p. 137, and other materials collected in *Political and Civil Rights in the United States,* p. 569.

of picketing involved, and indicated strongly that it reached this conclusion because of "concern that a broad ban against peaceful picketing might collide with the guarantees of the First Amendment." [44]

Justice Brennan, writing for the majority, did not elaborate further on the constitutional issue. But in construing the statutory terms—"threaten, coerce or restrain"—he developed a distinction between union picketing designed to apply the customary economic pressures to an employer and picketing which merely asked the consuming public not to buy the struck product:

> When consumer picketing is employed only to persuade customers not to buy the struck product, the union's appeal is closely confined to the primary dispute. The site of the appeal is expanded to include the premises of the secondary employer, but if the appeal succeeds, the secondary employer's purchases from the struck firms are decreased only because the public has diminished its purchases of the struck product. On the other hand, when consumer picketing is employed to persuade customers not to trade at all with the secondary employer, the latter stops buying the struck product, not because of a falling demand, but in response to pressure designed to inflict injury on his business generally. In such case, the union does more than merely follow the struck product; it creates a separate dispute with the secondary employer. [45]

Justice Black, concurring, construed the statute as intended to outlaw all consumer picketing of secondary establishments, and hence reached the constitutional questions. Elaborating on his views in *Giboney*, he divided picketing into two parts: " 'Picketing' . . . includes at least two concepts: (1) patrolling, that is, standing or marching back and forth or round and round on the streets, sidewalks, private property, or elsewhere, generally adjacent to someone else's premises; (2) speech, that is, arguments, usually on a placard, made to persuade other people to take the picketers' side of a controversy." He set forth the constitutional doctrine he would apply in the following terms: "[W]hen conduct not constitutionally protected, like patrolling, is intertwined, as in picketing, with constitutionally protected free speech and press, regulation of the non-protected conduct may at the same time encroach on freedom of speech and press. In such cases it is established that it is the duty of courts, before upholding regulations of patrolling, 'to weigh the circumstances and to appraise the substantiality

---

44. *N.L.R.B. v. Fruit and Vegetable Packers*, 377 U.S. 58, 63 (1964).

45. 377 U.S. at 72.

of the reasons advanced in support of the regulation of the free enjoyment of the rights' of speech and press" (citing *Schneider v. State,* 308
U.S. at 161). In the case before him, however, Justice Black
concluded that, since the statute did not undertake to bar all patrolling, it was aimed at the speech aspects of the picketing. Moreover, the
picketing was not directed at an unlawful objective. For these reasons
the provision, as applied in this case, constituted a violation of the
First Amendment. Justice Harlan, with whom Justice Stewart concurred, also reached the constitutional issues. He would have upheld
the decision of Congress "to effect an accommodation between the
rights of unions to publicize their position and the social desirability of
limiting a form of communication likely to have effects caused by
something apart from the message communicated." [46]

Meanwhile, shortly after *Giboney,* the Supreme Court rendered a
decision, of far-reaching importance, applying in routine fashion the
rules for labor picketing to racial and consumer picketing. In *Hughes
v. Superior Court* the Progressive Citizens of America requested a
retail grocery chain to hire Negroes at one of its stores, as white clerks
quit or were transferred, until the proportion of Negro clerks to white
clerks approximated the proportion of Negro to white customers,
about 50 percent. Upon refusal the P.C.A. began to picket the store,
carrying placards stating that the store refused to hire Negro clerks in
proportion to Negro customers. The California courts granted an injunction against the picketing. Their position was that, although there
was no statute which prevented the store from hiring Negroes on a
quota basis, the purpose of the picketing to accomplish that end was
nevertheless contrary to the public policy of the State. The Supreme
Court unanimously affirmed.[47]

The opinion of the Court, written by Justice Frankfurter, followed
closely the reasoning of *Wohl* and *Giboney.* It declared that "industrial picketing" is "more than free speech," quoting *Wohl;* that picketing "is not beyond the control of the State if the manner in which
picketing is conducted or the purpose which it seeks to effectuate gives
ground for its disallowance"; and the fact "that California's policy is
expressed by the judicial organ of the State rather than by the legislature" is "immaterial." In elaborating the reasons for finding that picketing is "more than free speech," Justice Frankfurter said:

46. 377 U.S. at 77–78, 93.
47. *Hughes v. Superior Court,* 339
U.S. 460 (1950).

Publication in a newspaper, or by distribution of circulars, may convey the same information or make the same charge as do those patrolling a picket line. But the very purpose of a picket line is to exert influences, and it produces consequences, different from other modes of communication. The loyalties and responses evoked and exacted by picket lines are unlike those flowing from appeals by printed word.[48]

The Supreme Court has also decided a number of cases under the anti-trust laws involving the boycotting of a business enterprise by other business enterprises. There appear to be no cases of one business picketing another. Whatever the means used, such conduct has been deemed to fall within the "commercial sector" and not to raise First Amendment problems. It is possible that the Federal anti-trust laws would apply to non-labor boycotting or picketing, but they do not appear to have been thus invoked up to now. The lower Federal courts and the State courts have followed the Supreme Court closely in labor picketing cases. They have also decided some cases concerned with racial and consumer picketing, reaching varying results and not settling on any coherent pattern.[49]

2. APPLICATION OF FIRST AMENDMENT DOCTRINE TO ECONOMIC PICKETING AND BOYCOTTS

In applying the First Amendment to the exertion of economic pressure through picketing and boycotts the first, and in many respects the most crucial, issue is to decide whether the conduct involved constitutes "expression" or "action." This determination must be made regardless of what theory concerning the degree of protection afforded conduct covered by the First Amendment is adopted. It is here that the courts largely have gone wrong.

48. 339 U.S. at 464, 465, 466. Justice Black, with whom Justice Minton agreed, concurred, saying simply that the case was "controlled by the principles announced" in *Giboney*. Justice Reed also concurred separately. Justice Douglas did not participate. See also *New Negro Alliance v. Sanitary Grocery Co.*, 303 U.S. 552 (1938); *N.A.A.C.P. v. Overstreet*, 384 U.S. 118 (1966).

49. The anti-trust cases are analyzed in Note, "Use of Economic Sanctions by Private Groups: Illegality Under the Sher-

man Act," *University of Chicago Law Review*, Vol. 30 (1962), p. 171. Lower Federal and State cases are collected in Note, "Legal Responsibility for Extra-legal Censure," *Columbia Law Review*, Vol. 62 (1962), p. 475; Note, "Prior Restraint of Racial Picketing," *University of Florida Law Review*, Vol. 17 (1964), p. 453; Note, "Regulation of Demonstrations," *Harvard Law Review*, Vol. 80 (1967), p. 1773. See also *1621, Inc. v. Wilson*, 402 Pa. 94, 166 A.2d 271 (1960); *Smith v. Grady*, 411 F.2d 181 (5th Cir. 1969).

We may start with the question of picketing. The first thing to note is that there is a fundamental difference between most labor picketing and most non-labor picketing. Labor picketing normally has a special kind of economic impact, derived from its institutional setting. An employer who is picketed is usually sealed off from many economic contacts by the tradition that union labor will not cross the picket line. This form of pressure is applied by closely knit, powerful organizations, with membership in the thousands or hundreds of thousands and a nationwide network of affiliates. It is supported by a system of power based upon common economic interests, loyalties, social pressures, economic sanctions, and bureaucratic force. A labor picket line is thus not so much a rational appeal to persuasion as a signal for the application of immediate and enormous economic leverage, based upon an already prepared position. As such it must, under ordinary circumstances, be classified as action, rather than expression.[50]

Most non-labor picketing is of a substantially different character. It is usually undertaken by relatively small groups, with relatively limited resources, as compared with labor organizations. Such groups are not highly organized around a major economic interest, but ordinarily are more loosely put together, with a narrower claim on the loyalties of their members. They do not have at their command the apparatus for applying economic pressures that the labor organizations do. Nor do they occupy such a strategic position of power vis-à-vis the object of their pressure. Their appeal is, in fact, usually directed much more to the general public than to their own members. Picketing under such circumstances is a call to reason, not the application of economic coercion, and as such must be classified as expression.[51]

Not all labor picketing can be described as action. It may, as in the *Fruit and Vegetable Packers* case, be similar in its impact to non-labor picketing and classified as expression. Similarly, not all non-labor picketing is necessarily to be classified as expression. Some non-labor groups may already have, and others may in time come to have, economic power of the sort exerted by the labor unions, available for immediate application upon a signal conveyed by picketing. In such a

50. For discussion of the impact of labor picketing see Edgar A. Jones, Jr., "Picketing and Coercion: A Jurisprudence of Epithets," *Virginia Law Review*, Vol. 39 (1953), p. 1023, and supplemental articles immediately following; Donald H. Wollett, "The Weapons of Conflict: Picketing and Boycotts," in Joseph Shister, Benjamin Aaron, and Clyde W. Summers (eds.), *Public Policy and Collective Bargaining* (New York, Harper & Row, 1962), p. 121.

51. For discussion of these matters see Horowitz, *op. cit. supra* note 34.

case their conduct would have to be judged in the same way. Moreover, other factors must be taken into account. Picketing that involves violence or undue physical obstruction must also be classified as action rather than expression. The problems here are much the same as those discussed in connection with the right of assembly and petition. In general the decision has to be made on the facts of each case. The significant point is that the issue of whether the conduct in question is covered by the First Amendment, and entitled to its protection, must be judged by these criteria.

The Supreme Court has not totally ignored these considerations. In *Giboney* it put some stress on them, and in *Fruit and Vegetable Packers* it made the same sort of distinction as that developed above, though not in constitutional terms. On the whole, however, the Court has given only glancing attention to these factors and has put its major emphasis upon two other lines of reasoning. It has constantly stressed that picketing is not protected by the First Amendment if the objective sought is contrary to public policy, either as embodied in a statute or merely in the view of a court. This position, in effect, eliminates all constitutional protection for picketing, since the government can always make the objective of picketing contrary to public policy by enacting a law or by merely saying so. More important, the objective of the picketing is irrelevant to the question whether the conduct involved is of such a nature as to fall within the coverage of the First Amendment, although it might bear upon the extent of protection granted by that guarantee. The other line of approach invokes the "two-level" theory of the First Amendment. Advanced particularly by Justice Black, this view divides all picketing into two parts—speech and patrolling—and gives the conduct as a whole only a due process (reasonable) type of protection. The "two-level" theory of political picketing has already been discussed in connection with the right of assembly and petition. As applied to economic picketing, its effect is to exclude such conduct totally from the shelter of the First Amendment.

In terms of results reached the Supreme Court has not always pressed these two lines of reasoning to their logical conclusion. But as long as they remain part of the Court's doctrinal equipment the Court's position remains confused and unsatisfactory. Thus it becomes impossible to reconcile *Thornhill* with *Giboney* in terms of these doctrines. They leave no room for the protection of any picketing that the government wants to outlaw. Furthermore, this kind of reasoning, together with the failure to distinguish labor from non-labor picketing, has led the Court to *Hughes v. Superior Court*. Under the doctrine of that case all racial, consumer and other non-labor picketing can be eliminated by legislative or even judicial action. Fortunately, Justice Brennan's opinion in *Fruit and Vegetable Packers* indicates that the Court may be coming around to a sounder position based on a more realistic analysis of the actual effect of picketing in terms of a system of freedom of expression.[52]

The problem of drawing the line between expression and action may arise not only in connection with picketing but in relation to other techniques for exerting economic pressures as well. In general, appeals for a boycott communicated through speeches, pamphlets, press, radio and television, correspondence, and the like would clearly constitute "expression." Of course, such communication that falls within the "commercial sector"—that is, is carried on by a business enterprise and directed against another business enterprise—would not be protected under the First Amendment. Communication of this sort that is part of a boycott organized by a labor union against an employer, however, would not be in the "commercial sector." Some forms of economic pressure would certainly constitute "action." Thus mass lining up at a bank window to obtain change for a dollar bill, or trying on clothes with no intention of buying, or similar efforts to cause economic disruption of a business enterprise would not appear to come within the category of "expression." The problems here are not very different from those already discussed in connection with the right of assembly and petition.

Having decided that particular conduct constitutes "expression," and therefore is entitled to the protection of the First Amendment, the next question is to determine what degree of protection should be afforded. In *Thornhill* the Court relied upon the clear and present danger test. But that formula has more than its usual drawbacks here. It would protect communication that had no material effect upon the economic position of the business affected. This, however, would not be of any moment. If the economic pressure is effective, the conduct will by hypothesis create a clear and present danger of economic injury, a possible "substantive evil." The issue thus shifts to the question whether the "substantive evil" is such that the government has a right to prevent it at the cost of restricting expression. But this is really the

---

52. Some courts have recognized the distinction between labor and non-labor picketing and have protected the latter type under the First Amendment. See the opinion of Judge Bazelon in the *Fruit and Vegetable Packers* case, 308 F.2d 311 (D.C. Cir. 1962); *1621, Inc. v. Wilson*, 402 Pa. 94, 166 A.2d 271 (1960).

balancing test, and indeed the balancing test might open a wider and more relevant range of inquiry. The clear and present danger test is therefore inappropriate. It is not surprising that the Supreme Court abandoned the test soon after *Thornhill*.[53]

A First Amendment balancing test, curiously, has seldom been applied in this area. Other kinds of balancing have, however, been utilized. Thus in the tort cases, where the key question has been whether the boycott is "justified," the courts have normally balanced a variety of factors considered relevant to that issue. The boycott cases arising under the anti-trust laws have also involved some balancing. But these balances have not taken into account First Amendment interests; they have been balances primarily of the economic interests of the two parties. Moreover, in most cases the Supreme Court has not balanced at all. It has resolved the First Amendment issue, as in the picketing cases, by simply excluding the conduct from First Amendment protection. In a way this has amounted to application of an "absolute" test. The Court may have sensed that judicial striking of a balance between the social and individual interest in freedom of expression, and the social and individual interest in the economic welfare of a business enterprise, is a haphazard operation. The elements on each side of the scale have even less in common than usual, and there is little that the Court can do except to adopt the legislative or State court judgment. In any event balancing has never taken hold here and would seem to have a dubious future.

There remains, then, application of the full protection rule. Under this doctrine most labor picketing, being considered action, would not be protected by the First Amendment. Nor would picketing that took the form of violence or undue physical obstruction; nor other forms of exerting economic pressure that could not be classified as expression. All communication in the "commercial sector" would also be excluded. But most racial, consumer and other non-labor picketing would receive full protection. So would expression used in promoting boycotts or other forms of economic pressure, such as speaking, pamphleteering, radio and television announcements, and similar forms of persuasion. The issue would be determined on a rational basis founded in the fundamental requirements of a system of freedom of expression.

---

53. Other courts have, however, used it. See, *e.g.*, Judge Bazelon's opinion in *Fruit and Vegetable Packers, supra* note 52, which applies the *Dennis* probability version of the clear and present danger test. 308 F.2d at 317.

The full protection theory would, of course, run counter to some of the traditional features of picketing and boycott law. Truthfulness in the communication, or even the absence of "actual malice" under the *New York Times* rule, would not be a prerequisite to protection under the First Amendment. Nor would the degree of remoteness or secondary effect of the economic pressure be controlling. Thus expression designed to persuade customers, to put pressure on automobile dealers, to convince General Motors, to refuse to advertise on a radio station that discriminated in its employment policies, would be protected in the same way as other expression. Likewise, the fact that the objective of the economic pressure was contrary to "public policy," or even that the purpose of the pressure was to persuade a business to engage in conduct that would violate existing law, would not be grounds for restriction. Thus a group attempting to induce a corporation to engage in preferential hiring, favoring white or black, would still be protected. At some point advocacy of law violation, as discussed in previous chapters, would become action. But so long as the communication remained expression it would be permissible under the First Amendment.

Some of these consequences of the full protection theory might at first glance arouse doubts. But the position sketched above simply makes applicable in this area the basic rules that apply to any form of expression. Limitations of truth, relevance, directness, or adherence to official policy cannot be made conditions of exercising the right to freedom of expression. Social interests can be advanced by control of action, but not expression. The full protection rule brings with it the usual risks, but that is the price society must pay for a viable system of free expression.

C. Administration of Justice

Freedom of expression may come into opposition, at various points, with individual and social interests in the proper administration of justice. It is generally accepted that the system of freedom of expression has no application to the actual conduct of a judicial proceeding itself. The judge presiding over a trial may enforce many kinds of limitation upon the right of persons in the courtroom to express themselves. He may do this in the interests of orderly procedure, decorum, respect for the court, or any other purpose relevant to the effective management of the proceeding. The judge's actions are limited by certain constitutional requirements, primarily that he accord due process. But it has never been considered that restrictions upon the right of communication under these circumstances constitute an "abridgment" of freedom of expression within the meaning of the First Amendment. Questions under the First Amendment do arise, however, when the expression takes place at a point further removed from the immediate conduct of the judicial proceeding.

In practice the issues of free press and fair trial have been presented in two major forms. One is the out-of-court communication that constitutes a direct criticism of, or some other kind of attack upon, the court itself or its operation. The other, which is far more common, arises when out-of-court publications concerning a pending matter tend to create hostilities or prejudice toward one of the parties. This occurs primarily in connection with press coverage of dramatic criminal cases. The principal difference between the two situations is that, in the first, the judicial institution or the judge himself is primarily affected by the communication. In the second, the impact falls principally upon the jurors, witnesses, or the community generally. The two situations obviously are not sharply distinguishable, but the applicable considerations are sufficiently different to justify separate treatment.

There are a number of methods for enforcing restrictions upon expression that is felt to impair the proper administration of justice. Such restrictions can be imposed through regular criminal sanctions or other ordinary court process. But historically and currently the principal device used has been the citation for contempt of court. A Federal court is limited in this respect, having power to punish for contempt only for misbehavior "in its presence or so near thereto as to obstruct the administration of justice." The State courts are not necessarily so restricted. Because the contempt power can be exercised through summary procedures, without jury trial or other safeguards, it poses a special threat to a system of freedom of expression. This is an important consideration in any effort to resolve possible conflict between rights under the First Amendment and the interest in proper administration of justice.[54]

54. The Federal contempt statute is 18 U.S.C. §401, interpreted in *Nye v. United States,* 313 U.S. 33 (1941). On the contempt power, see Ronald L. Goldfarb, *The Contempt Power* (New York, Columbia University Press, 1963), and

I. CRITICISM OF THE COURT

Communications aimed directly at the court or its manner of operation may create concern on two grounds. They may be thought to bring the court into disrepute in the community, to undermine its prestige, or in similar ways to impair its effective functioning. In this respect the impact of the communication is not very different from that of any hostile utterance addressed to the legislative or executive branch of government. In addition the communication may be felt, more specifically, to bring strong pressure against one of the parties to the proceeding and thereby to interfere with his right to an impartial and otherwise fair determination of the issues, or at least to give the appearance of doing so. Such an effect flowing from expression raises somewhat different questions.

The Supreme Court has addressed itself to these issues in a series of cases beginning in 1941. The first of these, *Bridges v. California,* involved contempt citations by two California courts for statements made by the *Los Angeles Times* and by labor leader Harry Bridges in connection with pending judicial proceedings. The *Times* had published three editorials vigorously denouncing two members of a labor union who had been found guilty of assaulting nonunion truck drivers, and calling upon the trial judge to give them severe sentences. The strongest statement was: "Judge A. A. Scott will make a serious mistake if he grants probation to Matthew Shannon and Kennan Holmes. This community needs the example of their assignment to the

---

other material cited in *Political and Civil Rights in the United States,* pp. 669–670.

For material dealing with the general problem of First Amendment rights and the administration of justice, see *Political and Civil Rights in the United States,* p. 670. Subsequent material includes: American Bar Association, Advisory Committee on Fair Trial and Free Press, *Standards Relating to Fair Trial and Free Press* (1966) (the Reardon Report); Association of the Bar of the City of New York, Special Committee on Radio, Television, and the Administration of Justice, *Final Report with Recommendations, Freedom of the Press and Fair Trial* (1967) (the Medina report); American Newspaper Publishers Association, Special Committee on Free Press and Fair Trial, *Free Press and Fair Trial* (New York, 1967); Judicial Conference of the United States, Committee on the Operation of the Jury System, *Report on the "Free Press–Fair Trial" Issue* (1968), 4 F.R.D. 391, recommendations adopted by the Judicial Conference, September 19, 1968, reported in *The New York Times* of September 20, 1968; Alfred Friendly and Ronald L. Goldfarb, *Crime and Publicity* (New York, Twentieth Century Fund, 1967); Jeffrey A. Barist, "The First Amendment and Regulation of Prejudicial Publicity," *Fordham Law Review,* Vol. 36 (1968), p. 425; Telford Taylor, *Two Studies in Constitutional Interpretation* (Columbus, Ohio State University Press, 1969), Pt. II.

jute mill." Bridges had made public a telegram to the Secretary of Labor at a time when a motion for a new trial was pending in a case involving a representation dispute between his C.I.O. union and a rival A.F. of L. union. The telegram said that the judge's decision was "outrageous"; that attempted enforcement of it would "tie up the Port of Los Angeles and involve the entire Pacific Coast" (by a strike of longshoremen); and that the C.I.O. union "does not intend to allow state courts to override the majority vote of members in choosing its officers and representatives." The Supreme Court, after hearing argument twice and dividing five to four, held that both contempt citations violated the First Amendment.[55]

Justice Black, writing for the majority, accepted as the controlling principle the clear and present danger test, although he did not consider that test "to mark the furthermost constitutional boundaries of protected expression." Applying that doctrine he began by emphasizing "how much, as a practical matter, [the judgments below] would affect liberty of expression." He then went on to define more precisely the interest of the State, noting that the "substantive evil here sought to be averted . . . appears to be double: disrespect for the judiciary; and disorderly and unfair administration of justice." The "disrespect" aspect of the case Justice Black disposed of summarily:

> The assumption that respect for the judiciary can be won by shielding judges from published criticism wrongly appraises the character of American public opinion. For it is a prized American privilege to speak one's mind, although not always with perfect good taste, on all public institutions. And an enforced silence, however limited, solely in the name of preserving the dignity of the bench, would probably engender resentment, suspicion, and contempt much more than it would enhance respect.[56]

The other evil feared, "disorderly and unfair administration," Justice Black thought "is more plausibly associated with restricting publications which touch upon pending litigation." Upon analysis of the particular utterances involved, however, he concluded that the "degree of likelihood" of unfair administration of justice was not "sufficient to justify summary punishment." The *Times* editorial "did no more than threaten future adverse criticism which was reasonably to be expected anyway in the event of a lenient disposition of the pending case. To regard it, therefore, as in itself of substantial influence upon the course

55. *Bridges v. California*, 314 U.S. 252, 272, 276 (1941).

56. 314 U.S. at 263, 268, 270, 270–271.

of justice would be to impute to judges a lack of firmness, wisdom, or honor—which we cannot accept as a major premise." As to the Bridges telegram, Justice Black pointed out that the judge was undoubtedly aware of the possibility of a strike as a consequence of his decision, that such a strike would not be illegal, and that if the judge "was not intimidated by the facts themselves, we do not believe that the most explicit statement of them could have sidetracked the course of justice." [57]

Justice Frankfurter, with whom Chief Justice Stone and Justices Roberts and Byrnes agreed, vigorously dissented. He accepted, in form, the clear and present danger test, but interpreted it as meaning no more than the "reasonable tendency" test which the State court had applied. He agreed, also, that "[j]udges as persons, or courts as institutions, are entitled to no greater immunity from criticism than other persons or institutions." But he emphasized that "administration of justice by an impartial judiciary has been basic to our conception of freedom ever since Magna Carta." And, while "[c]omment however forthright is one thing . . . [i]ntimidation with respect to specific matters still in judicial suspense [is] quite another." A State therefore has power "to protect immediate litigants and the public from the mischievous danger of an unfree or coerced tribunal." Moreover, he felt that judges were more susceptible to "coercive interference with their work" than other government officials. Finally, he concluded that the California courts were justified in treating the publications "as a threat to impartial adjudication." [58]

In the following case, *Pennekamp v. Florida,* the Supreme Court was unanimous in striking down the contempt citation. A Florida newspaper had published two editorials and a cartoon strongly attacking the local court and its judges for delays, undue technicalities, and general softness in dealing with criminal cases. Actions taken in specific cases were criticized, including one situation in which indictments had been dismissed on technical grounds and the defendants reindicted. Justice Reed, writing for all but one member of the Court, accepted the clear and present danger test, but treated it as the equivalent of a general balancing test. He considered the issue to be only whether the publication constituted a "threat to the impartial and orderly administration of justice," and concluded that the danger of this

57. 314 U.S. at 271, 273, 278.
58. 314 U.S. at 282, 289, 291, 292, 295, 299.

revealed by the record "has not the clearness and immediacy necessary to close the door of permissible public comment." Justice Frankfurter concurred, saying that the issue was not whether the publication operated "to bring the courts of a State into disrepute and generally to impair their efficiency" but that the "decisive consideration is whether the judge or jury is, or presently will be, pondering a decision that comment seeks to affect." [59]

The Court again split in the next case, *Craig v. Harney*. Here three Texas newspapers had printed a series of articles and an editorial concerning the trial of a civil case in which the judge had directed a verdict for one of the parties and a motion for a new trial was pending. The article gave an inaccurate and unfair report of the trial and the editorial attacked the decision vigorously, calling it "arbitrary action," a "travesty on justice," and asserting that the judge's behavior had properly brought down "the wrath of public opinion upon his head." Justice Douglas, writing for the majority, adopted the clear and present danger test. As to the article he found that "it takes more imagination than we possess to find in this rather sketchy and one-sided report of a case any imminent or serious threat to a judge of reasonable fortitude." As to the editorial, he concluded: "Giving the editorial all the vehemence which the court below found in it we fail to see how it could in any realistic sense create an imminent and serious threat to the ability of the court to give fair consideration to the motion for rehearing." Justice Frankfurter, joined by Chief Justice Vinson, dissented, saying: "We cannot say that the Texas Court could not properly find that these newspapers asked of the judge, and instigated powerful sections of the community to ask of the judge, that which no one has any business to ask of a judge, except the parties and their counsel in open court, namely, that he should decide one way rather than another." Both Justice Frankfurter and Justice Jackson, who also dissented, vigorously criticized the majority for assuming that judges were relatively immune to the effects of hostile publicity. Said Justice Jackson:

> I do not know whether it is the view of the Court that a judge must be thickskinned or just thickheaded, but nothing in my experience or observation confirms the idea that he is insensitive to publicity. Who does not prefer good to ill report of his work? And if fame—a good public

<hr/>

59. *Pennekamp v. Florida,* 328 U.S.   Murphy and Rutledge also wrote separate
331, 336, 350, 368–369 (1946). Justices   opinions.

name—is, as Milton said, the "last infirmity of noble mind," it is frequently the first infirmity of a mediocre one.[60]

Not until fifteen years later, in 1962, did the Supreme Court return to the problem. In *Wood v. Georgia,* three judges of a county court made public a charge to a grand jury in which they gave it special instructions to investigate "bloc voting" by Negroes in prior elections, charges of purchasing votes, and other "practices which, while not technically in violation of law, are yet so immoral or corrupt as to be destructive of the purposes of our system of elections." The charge was issued in the midst of a primary election campaign. Wood, the county sheriff, had announced his candidacy for office and was to run in the following general election against the winner of the primary. The following day Wood issued a public statement in which he said that the judges' action in ordering the grand jury investigation was "one of the most deplorable examples of race agitation to come out of Middle Georgia in recent years"; that "this action appears either as a crude attempt at judicial intimidation of Negro voters and leaders, or, at best, as agitation for a 'Negro vote' issue in local politics"; and that it "is hoped that the present Grand Jury will not let its high office be a party to any political attempt to intimidate the Negro people in this community." Wood's conviction for contempt was reversed by the Supreme Court in a six to two decision.[61]

Chief Justice Warren, delivering the opinion of the Court, relied upon the *Bridges, Pennekamp,* and *Craig* cases as requiring application of the clear and present danger test. As noted earlier, the clear and present danger test had by this date fallen into disuse; this was the first time it had been invoked by the Court since its transformation into a "probable danger" test in the *Dennis* case eleven years before. In any event there was no proof in the record that the publication had had any actual effect upon the grand jury and Chief Justice Warren readily concluded that no showing had been made of "a substantive evil actually designed to impede the course of justice." The opinion does not make clear exactly what kinds of impediments to the "course of justice" would justify the use of the contempt power. Chief Justice Warren plainly considered the context of the controversy to be more a

---

60. *Craig v. Harney,* 331 U.S. 367, 375, 378, 390, 396 (1947). Justice Murphy concurred with the majority in a separate opinion.

61. *Wood v. Georgia,* 370 U.S. 375 (1962). Justices Harlan and Clark dissented; Justice Frankfurter did not participate.

political than a judicial one. But he did say that the fact that the publication was directed to a grand jury rather than a judge did not, "[i]n the circumstances of this case," distinguish the issue from that in the *Bridges* case. He also took care to point out that "this case does not represent a situation where an individual is on trial; there was no 'judicial proceeding pending' in the sense that prejudice might result to one litigant or the other"; and that it was not necessary "to consider the variant factors that would be present in a case involving a petit jury." [62]

Justice Harlan, taking up the torch for Justice Frankfurter, dissented. His view, with which Justice Clark concurred, was summarized in a concluding sentence: "I do not understand how it can be denied that a grand juror, reading in the course of this investigation the sheriff's statement that the judges who instructed the grand jury to undertake it were racial bigots making discriminatory use of the laws for purposes of political repression, and that the charges themselves were incredibly false, might well be influenced in his deliberations." [63]

Perhaps the chief conclusion that emerges from this series of cases is that the Supreme Court has never upheld a contempt citation for expression critical of a court or its operations. There is some indication in the opinions that this result is due in part to the summary nature of the contempt proceeding itself and to its considerable potential for abuse. It is conceivable, therefore, that if prosecution was brought under a criminal statute, such as a criminal libel statute, the Court would react differently. Yet a careful reading of the decisions indicates that the outcome would not have been otherwise had the restriction been imposed in another form. The Court seems clearly determined to extend a high degree of protection to discussion of the administration of justice.

In reaching this result the Supreme Court has made consistent use of the clear and present danger test. Indeed this is the only area in which that test still seems to remain acceptable to the Court. But it will

62. 370 U.S. at 389.

63. 370 U.S. at 402. In *In re Sawyer*, 360 U.S. 622 (1959), the Supreme Court reversed, by a vote of five to four, the action of the Hawaiian courts in suspending for one year a lawyer who, at the time she was participating as defense counsel in a Smith Act trial, made a public speech alleged to have impugned the integrity of the presiding judge and to have reflected upon his impartiality and fairness in conducting the trial. The majority decision was based upon the ground that the record was insufficient to support the findings, and did not pass on the First Amendment issues. The special problems involved in the rights of lawyers, as "officers of the court," to discuss out-of-court matters relating to the administration of justice are considered in the next subsection.

be noted that the Court has carefully limited the application of the clear and present danger test through the device of narrowly defining the "substantive evil" which the government has a right to prevent. Justice Black made clear in the *Bridges* case that "substantive evil" does not include the likelihood that the court will suffer damage to its reputation or standing in the community. Even the dissenters agreed with this view. In subsequent cases the Court did not expressly attempt to refine further the concept of "substantive evil." But both majority and minority, in essence, took the position that the only "substantive evil" of concern was prejudice to a litigant in a pending proceeding.[64]

Moreover, the majority applied the "clear and present" element of the test in a highly restrictive way. It came near to holding that a judge was expected to be a person of fortitude and never seriously affected by anything that might be said. At the very least it would have found no danger accruing unless the expression amounted to "coercion" or "intimidation." It was on this point that the dissenters ultimately took issue. While Justice Frankfurter started from a "coercion" or "intimidation" position in *Bridges,* the minority eventually reached the view that a clear and present danger of "influence" was sufficient. Whatever the exact labels, however, the prevailing rule has come to be that the expression cannot be restricted unless its impact goes substantially beyond "persuasion" or "influence."

The approach taken by the Supreme Court thus comes very close to the full protection rule. Under that doctrine a communication critical of the court could be punished or suppressed only if it amounted to "action" rather than "expression." Threats of physical violence would be classified as "action." So might utterances embodying other direct pressures of the sort, for example, that an employer can bring to bear upon his employee. The communications with which we are here concerned, of course, are seldom of this nature. Most of them, like the ones involved in the cases considered above, would clearly be classified as "expression" and hence protected under the First Amendment.

The application of the full protection doctrine here seems fully justified. So far as the impact of the expression involves the prestige of the court or judges, there would appear to be no convincing reason for treating it in any way different from similar criticism addressed to other parts of the government. It is true that judges do not operate in the rough political environment that some other government officials

---

64. Justice Harlan, in *Wood v. Georgia,* included in this category the interest of the government as litigant in bringing a prosecution. 370 U.S. at 398.

do. But it is just as important to maintain open and "robust" discussion of judicial administration as of other public issues. It is also true that judges themselves feel reluctant to engage in public controversy. But there is rarely a lack of spokesmen to defend the judiciary and public debate is thus not shut off. Hence the right of expression should remain as free here as elsewhere. There is no reason to believe that judges cannot live under such a regime. They have full authority to control the actual management of the judicial proceeding. But they cannot, consistently with a system of freedom of expression, extend that control into the remoter areas of public debate and discussion. Seditious libel or criminal libel laws are no more justified here than elsewhere.

A more appealing argument for control of expression can be made if the criticism leveled at the court tends to impair the right of a litigant to an impartial determination of the issues. In this situation, somewhat different considerations prevail. A litigant is entitled to have the proceeding conducted according to judicial, not political, rules. But the question remains whether suppression of expression is the proper solution of this problem.

Most of the communications with which we are here concerned are directed to judges or to prosecutors, rather than to juries, witnesses or other functionaries. No one has suggested that the prosecutor be shielded from criticism or attack. As to the judges the dilemma is immediately presented that the judge himself must find that he will not perform, or is not capable of performing, his obligation to give impartial justice. There are some situations in the law in which a finding or presumption of this sort is made. Thus a judge who has a financial interest in the outcome of a case is presumably prejudiced. But these are normally specific situations that can be governed by a flat rule. When a judge is subjected to out-of-court pressures from the community no cut-and-dried rule is available. Every judge cannot be presumed incapable of doing justice. Each case must be viewed on its own facts, and indeed involves a personal assessment of the judge. Under these circumstances it is no accident that the minority justices of the Supreme Court, who tended to favor the litigant, were forced to the position of saying that expression which "influenced" the judge could be punished. The majority, placing greater emphasis upon freedom of expression, reached a "full protection" result. The nature of the issue tends to compel such a choice. But the minority remedy is inevitably too sweeping; it virtually eliminates public discussion of pending judicial matters. Such an outcome cannot be reconciled with the purposes of the First Amendment.

If the impact of the communication falls on the jury, witness, or other functionary, and threatens to prevent an impartial decision, additional factors come into play. Criticisms addressed to the court rarely have this effect. Prejudice at this level is far more likely to arise from press publicity about the case. To these matters we now turn.

2. PREJUDICIAL PUBLICITY

Most of the controversy over the impact of the system of freedom of expression upon the administration of justice has been concerned with prejudicial publicity. News reports of events that will later come before the courts for adjudication, or are already there, can exercise a great influence upon the course of the proceedings. This is particularly likely to be true in notorious criminal cases. Publication of the circumstances surrounding the crime and the arrest, reports of confessions, stories about prospective witnesses and evidence, accounts of prior arrests and convictions of the accused, often create an atmosphere of hostility throughout the community, disclose facts or claims which would not be admissible in a criminal trial, and affect prosecutors, juries, and witnesses in other ways that make a fair trial difficult or impossible. Press handling of such cases as the Hall-Mills murders, the Lindbergh kidnapping, the trial of Dr. Sheppard in Cleveland, the assassination of President Kennedy, to take only a few extreme examples from the past, readily illustrate the nature of the difficulty.

There is some controversy over the extent of the problem. Certainly the issues arise in only a small proportion of the cases handled by the courts. Nevertheless, few will contest that the occasions of possible unfairness are sufficiently common to arouse deep concern, and that even a single instance of prejudice demands a remedy. Actually, there has been a greater volume of discussion of the subject than in almost any other area of freedom of expression. Books, articles, speeches, studies, reports, and proposed codes are voluminous. In general the press and the legal profession have tended to move in opposite directions.

Three main forms of control are available for dealing with prejudicial publicity. The first is direct sanction against the press or others,

either through contempt or more ordinary judicial proceedings, to prohibit publication of material likely to be prejudicial. The second is control over the sources of the publicity, utilizing the government's power
to direct prosecuting, police and other officials, and attorneys as officers of the court, to refrain from release of information or public discussion of the issues. The third is control over the judicial proceeding
itself, through such devices as change of venue, continuance, selection
of the jury, management of the courtroom, and the like, to eliminate
or mitigate the effects of the publicity. The principal First Amendment
issues arise over proposals to institute direct sanctions against publication.

The Supreme Court has never passed upon the constitutionality of
imposing a direct prohibition upon the press for the purpose of eliminating possible prejudicial publicity. It has had the chance to do so but
has not taken advantage of the opportunity. In *Maryland v. Baltimore
Radio Show* a court in Baltimore found three radio stations and a
broadcaster guilty of contempt and imposed fines because of broadcasts dealing with the arrest of a man charged with murder of a child.
In addition to announcing the arrest, the broadcaster had said that the
accused had confessed, that he had a long criminal record, that he had
gone to the scene with police officers and reenacted the crime, and that
he had there recovered the knife which he had used in the murder. The
broadcasts, according to the court, were "devastating," had "an indel-
ible effect upon the public mind," and forced counsel for the accused
to waive jury trial. The Court of Appeals of Maryland, relying upon
the *Bridges, Pennekamp,* and *Craig* cases, reversed the convictions on
First Amendment grounds. The Supreme Court denied certiorari. Justice Frankfurter, however, took occasion to point out that a denial of
certiorari "carries with it no implication whatever regarding the
Court's views on the merits of a case," and that "the power of States to
safeguard the fair administration of criminal justice by jury trial from
mutilation and distortion by extraneous influences" had not been adjudicated. It has also been suggested that the language of Chief Justice
Warren in *Wood v. Georgia,* distinguishing the situation in which a
judicial proceeding was pending before a petit jury, demonstrates that
the issue is still open in the Supreme Court.[65]

65. *Maryland v. Baltimore Radio
Show,* 338 U.S. 912, 919, 920 (1950);
Wood v. Georgia, 370 U.S. at 389–390.
See also *United States v. Tijerina,* 412
F.2d 661 (10th Cir. 1969), cert. denied
396 U.S. —— (1969). In *Baltimore Ra-
dio Show* Justice Frankfurter set forth in
an appendix to his opinion a collection of

Opinion about the constitutionality of direct restrictions on the press for publication of prejudicial material is divided. The present trend of State court decision is to consider such limitations invalid. The Special Committee on Radio, Television, and the Administration of Justice of the Association of the Bar of the City of New York agreed: "After exhaustive study . . . we have concluded that direct controls on the radio and television industries and on the press by a governmental scheme of regulation are untenable in light of the First Amendment's guarantee of free speech and free press." On the other hand, the American Bar Association report recommended a limited use of the contempt power against persons who, during the course of a trial, disseminate matter that is "wilfully designed . . . to affect the outcome of the trial, and that seriously threatens to have such an effect." Commentators reflect the same disagreements.[66]

Presumably the Supreme Court, in determining the validity of direct sanctions upon the publication of prejudicial material, would apply the clear and present danger test as it did in *Bridges, Pennekamp, Craig,* and *Wood.* It is at once apparent, however, that a test of whether a particular publication created a clear and present danger of "prejudice" would be even more vague, and outlaw far more expression, than the test of whether a publication creates a clear and present danger of "coercion" or "intimidation." "Prejudice" is a much more illusive term, and the likelihood of its occurring much greater. A publisher would have small chance of knowing in advance what the effect of his publication might turn out to be, and whether a prosecutor or court might consider it violated the law. Inevitably there would be

English decisions dealing with the problem. For other discussion of the English rules, which impose severe limitations upon publication of material relating to matters *sub judice,* see Zelman Cowen, "Prejudicial Publicity and the Fair Trial: A Comparative Examination of American, English and Commonwealth Law," *Indiana Law Journal,* Vol. 41 (1965), p. 69; Friendly and Goldfarb, *op. cit. supra* note 54, ch. 9; *Political and Civil Rights in the United States,* p. 670.

66. As to the State court decisions see, in addition to *Baltimore Radio Show, Phoenix Newspapers v. Superior Court,* 101 Ariz. 257, 418 P.2d 594 (1966). But compare cases cited in Thomas L. Shaffer,

"Direct Restraint on the Press," *Notre Dame Lawyer,* Vol. 42 (1967), pp. 865, 876, fn. 83; *Edmundson v. Tennessee* (Tenn. Cr. App. 1968), cert. denied, 396 U.S. 844 (1969). The quotation from the Association of the Bar Committee appears in its report on page 1. The American Bar Association recommendations are set forth in *American Bar Association Journal,* Vol. 54 (1968), pp. 347, 351, and its Code of Professional Responsibility (1969); its argument for their constitutionality may be found in its *Report,* pp. 150–154. Reference to the position of various commentators appears in Shaffer, *supra.*

only sporadic and perhaps discriminatory enforcement of the requirement, or the mere existence of the prohibition would effect a sweeping repression of the news media, or more likely both.

Alternatively, direct restrictions could be framed in more specific terms. They could prohibit the publication of certain kinds of information, such as accounts of confessions, prior arrests and the like, or permit the publication of only certain items, such as the name of the accused and the charge. This would eliminate application of the clear and present danger test "in each case" and substitute a general rule applicable to all cases whether or not prejudice did in fact occur. Such a rule would tend to solve the vagueness problem, but would necessarily cut off a great deal of expression from which no prejudice would have ensued. It could be validated only on a general balancing theory. It would furthermore constitute a major curtailment of rights that the news media have historically exercised.

Moreover, the administrative problems created by direct controls would be serious. If the controls were of the first, more general, variety they would tend to interfere with the firm application of remedies available in the judicial proceeding itself. Both forms of control would be based on the same factual conclusion, namely, that prejudice was likely to occur. Thus a court would not grant a motion for change of venue unless it determined that prejudicial publicity had interfered with the prospect of a fair trial; in that event it would feel compelled to prosecute the news media responsible for the situation. The result would be pressures for more prosecutions of the press or less rigorous administration of other judicial remedies. In addition, any form of direct control would tend to involve the courts and the news media in a series of unseemly conflicts, the result of which would neither add to public respect for the courts nor create an atmosphere favorable to a free press.

Application of the full protection theory would avert all these difficulties. Conceivably the communication might be of such a nature as to be classifiable as "action." Such would be a threat of physical violence to a juror. But ordinarily the utterance would clearly be expression and would be protected against any form of direct sanction. The remedy for prejudicial publicity then would have to be found in other forms of control. Indeed there is substantial evidence that controls over sources of information and controls over the immediate judicial process are or can be made sufficient to meet the problem. This was the conclusion of the Special Committee of the Association of the Bar of the City of New York. The American Bar Association largely agreed:

> The experience in Newark, together with other factors more fully discussed below, suggest that enhancement of remedies available to defendants, combined with reasonable restrictions on release of information by lawyers and official sources, ought in large measure to be adequate to cope with the problem. Surely, they should be fully exhausted before more drastic measures are considered.[67]

Controls over the sources of information themselves raise certain questions under the First Amendment. Most of these, however, are readily resolved. Strict prohibition upon the release of information by prosecutors, police, court officials, or other government employees would not seem to impair any constitutional right of those persons. Restriction on communication by government employees that is essential to performance of the job for which they are employed cannot be considered an "abridgment" of freedom of expression. It has been argued that controls over sources improperly curtail access by the news media and others to information and thereby infringe First Amendment rights. However, the temporary withholding of information that might prejudice the fairness of a judicial proceeding cannot be considered invasion of any constitutional right of access to information.

More troublesome is the question whether similar rigid restrictions can be placed upon the right of attorneys to discuss pending judicial matters in public or disclose information about them. Attorneys are in a halfway position. They are not government employees. But they are "officers of the court" for certain purposes and members of a profession that can require adherence to certain ethical and professional standards. On the other hand in their capacity as private citizens attorneys perform a crucial function as critics of the judicial process. They are, of course, experts on the judicial system. Moreover, they are often leaders and spokesmen of other individuals and groups. Frequently the attorney engaged in an unpopular cause is alone in a position to alert

67. American Bar Association *Report*, p. 72; Association of the Bar of the City of New York *Report*, p. 1. See also Robert B. McKay, in Symposium, "A Free Press and a Fair Trial," *Villanova Law Review*, Vol. 11 (1966), p. 726; Note, " 'Free Press–Fair Trial' Revisited: Defendant-Centered Remedies as a Publicity Policy," *University of Chicago Law Review*, Vol. 33 (1966), p. 512; Note, "The Impartial Jury—Twentieth Century Dilemma: Some Solutions to the Conflict Between Free Press and Fair Trial," *Cornell Law Quarterly*, Vol. 51 (1966), pp. 306, 322–327; Taylor, *op. cit. supra* note 54. My own views on this issue have changed since publication of *Toward a General Theory of the First Amendment* (New York, Random House, 1966), pp. 72–74.

the public to abuse or mobilize the support necessary to prevent a perversion of justice. To limit unduly the role of attorneys in discussing the administration of justice, including pending matters, would thus encroach seriously upon the system of freedom of expression.[68]

It follows that any restriction upon the right of an attorney to discuss the administration of justice generally, or to talk about a particular case, must be limited to what is narrowly essential to his performance as a partial "officer of the court" engaged in the judicial process. This would rule out any blanket prohibition of discussion of a pending matter or any rigid limitation to a narrow area. Communications by an attorney engaged in a judicial proceeding which prejudiced the right of any party to fair treatment in that proceeding could be made the subject of sanctions. But few such cases are likely to arise. In criminal prosecutions, statements by a private attorney do not ordinarily affect the accused adversely. In civil proceedings, which do not usually involve the emotional atmosphere of a criminal trial, prejudice from such sources is again unlikely. As to the possibility that a private attorney would seriously prejudice the government's case, in either a criminal or civil proceeding, there would appear to be little practical danger in most instances. These rules would, of course, put prosecuting officials under more stringent restrictions than those applied to private attorneys. But this seems inevitable in the nature of the situation. It is primarily government officials who are in the position to create prejudice by releasing information, and for them a broad rule of thumb is essential. Moreover, it should be remembered that protection of expression by private citizens, not expression by the government, is the main function of the First Amendment. Thus any limitation imposed upon private attorneys that goes beyond sanctions directed to utterances creating specific prejudice to private parties in a particular case would constitute an abridgment of freedom of expression.[69]

Controls over the immediate judicial proceeding, designed to re-

68. See the opinion of Justice Brennan in *In re Sawyer*, 360 U.S. 622 (1959). For discussion of the lawyer's role in alerting the public to possible miscarriages of justice, see Note, *University of Chicago Law Review, supra* note 67, p. 521; Louis L. Jaffe, "Trial By Newspaper," *New York University Law Review*, Vol. 40 (1965), pp. 504, 512.

69. Broader restrictions upon attorneys, going beyond the limits suggested here, have been recommended in the American Bar Association *Report*, pp. 80–97; in the Association of the Bar of the City of New York *Report*, pp. 14–26; and by the Judicial Conference, 45 F.R.D. at 404–407. In *Sheppard v. Maxwell*, 384 U.S. 333, 361 (1966), the Supreme Court said by way of dictum that "the trial Court might well have prescribed extra judicial statements by any lawyer." See also *State v. Van Duyne*, 43 N.J. 369, 204 A.2d 841 (1964), cert. denied 380 U.S. 987 (1965).

move the impact of prejudicial publicity, have been employed more widely and more intensively over the past several decades. Thus, in *Irvin v. Dowd,* decided in 1961, the Supreme Court for the first time set aside a State court conviction because newspaper publicity had prevented a fair trial. Since then the Court has reversed other convictions, including that of Dr. Samuel H. Sheppard in Ohio, on similar grounds. Other methods of protecting the right to an impartial trial have also been utilized on a growing scale. In *Estes v. Texas* the Supreme Court, holding that televising of courtroom proceedings deprived Billie Sol Estes of due process, reaffirmed the power of the courts to control the immediate conduct of the proceedings to the extent necessary to assure fairness. No difficult First Amendment problems are presented by these controls. The "right to know" cannot be justifiably invoked in such situations, and the authority of the court to maintain an atmosphere of impartiality and calm in the courtroom itself is scarcely open to question.[70]

All in all, the task of protecting the judicial process from this kind of bias or distortion remains a serious one. The solution can be found, however, in tightening the controls over sources of information and in refining the techniques for eliminating or neutralizing prejudice in the actual conduct of judicial proceedings. This is the solution demanded by the First Amendment. Expression itself cannot be abridged. But it is possible to perfect other ways by which prejudice emanating from the necessary operation of the system of free expression in the community can be overcome.

70. *Irvin v. Dowd,* 366 U.S. 717 (1961); *Rideau v. Louisiana,* 373 U.S. 723 (1963); *Sheppard v. Maxwell,* 384 U.S. 333 (1966). See also *Marshall v. United States,* 360 U.S. 310 (1959). For further discussion see Note, *Cornell Law Quarterly, supra* note 67; Friendly and Goldfarb, *op. cit. supra* note 54, pp. 298–311. *Estes v. Texas,* 381 U.S. 532 (1965). On control in the courtroom see also *Sheppard v. Maxwell, supra,* at pp. 358–359.

XIII

Obscenity

The most striking thing about the law of obscenity is that it is *sui generis,* not following most of the rules developed in other areas of the First Amendment. This state of affairs is probably due in large part to the intense and emotional pressures on the courts from the conventional wisdom which views obscenity, at least when available to others, as highly corrupting of the mind and spirit. Hence, although obscenity usually appears in the form of expression, the courts dare not treat it in the same way as other kinds of expression. The troubles of the courts are compounded because, while the effect of the expression is ordinarily a key factor in their rules for its treatment under the First Amendment, there is a serious lack of evidence as to what the effects of obscenity, if any, actually are. All this results in considerable uncertainty about what social interests need to be protected by obscenity laws and how far that protection should be extended.

The principal legal device for treating obscenity according to its own special rules is the doctrine that obscenity is "outside" the protection of the First Amendment. This formulation leaves many problems unresolved because there is still need to define "obscenity" in constitutional terms. But such an approach does result in posing the constitutional issues in a wholly different way.

The special rules developed for obscenity have been confined rather carefully to the domain of the sexual. Kindred areas have not been brought within the concept of obscenity. Thus expression portraying violence not directly connected with sex has been treated under the regular rules rather than the obscenity rules. Obscenity doctrine has likewise not been extended to the sacrilegious. Blasphemy seems not to raise any serious current problems. At times, scatological expression has been subsumed under the rubric of obscenity. With this possible exception, however, the concept of obscenity has been limited strictly to the sexual.[1]

1. See *Winters v. New York,* 333 U.S. 507 (1948) (portrayal of violence);

The constitutional problems involved in the law of obscenity fall into two main categories. The first relates to the standards developed by the courts for defining obscenity or determining to what extent allegedly obscene expression is protected by the First Amendment. The other comprises a series of collateral issues, of crucial importance but less directly related to the basic First Amendment question, involving such matters as the rule against vagueness, the requirement of scienter, searches and seizures, and the procedures for enforcing restrictions.[2]

A. Standards

Legislative restrictions on obscenity were slow to develop. There is no convincing evidence that obscenity in the current sense was a common law crime in England, and the offense does not appear to have been clearly established there until the enactment of Lord Campbell's Act in 1857. The first reported case in America, interestingly enough involving *Memoirs of a Woman of Pleasure,* occurred in 1821. But the problem of obscenity did not receive legislative attention in this country until after the Civil War when, prodded by Anthony Comstock, the State and Federal governments began to enact obscenity statutes. Thus

Burstyn v. Wilson, 343 U.S. 495 (1952) (sacrilege); *Hannegan v. Esquire,* 327 U.S. 146 (1946) (vulgarity); *United States v. Klaw,* 350 F.2d 155, 163 (2d Cir. 1965); and the comment in Harry Kalven, Jr., "The Metaphysics of the Law of Obscenity," *Supreme Court Review,* Vol. 1960 (1960), pp. 1, 34. See also William B. Lockhart and Robert C. McClure, "Literature, the Law of Obscenity, and the Constitution." *Minnesota Law Review,* Vol. 38 (1954), pp. 295, 320–324.

2. For a collection of materials and references on the law of obscenity see Thomas I. Emerson, David Haber and Norman Dorsen, *Political and Civil Rights in the United States* (Boston, Little, Brown & Co., 3d ed. 1967), ch. VII, especially the bibliography on p. 804 (cited hereafter in this chapter as *Political and Civil Rights in the United States*). Later material includes: Note, "More Ado About Dirty Books," *Yale Law Journal,* Vol. 75 (1966), p. 1364; Henry P. Monaghan, "Obscenity, 1966: The Marriage of Obscenity Per Se and Obscenity Per Quod," *Yale Law Journal,* Vol. 76 (1966), p. 127; C. Peter Magrath, "The Obscenity Cases: Grapes of Roth," *Supreme Court Review,* Vol. 1966 (1966), p. 7; Richard H. Kuh, *Foolish Figleaves?* (New York, Macmillan, 1967); Charles Rembar, *The End of Obscenity* (New York, Random House, 1968); Richard S. Randall, *Censorship of the Movies* (Madison, University of Wisconsin Press, 1968); O. John Rogge, "[T]he High Court of Obscenity," *Colorado Law Review,* Vol. 41 (1969), pp. 1, 201; Harry M. Clor, *Obscenity and Public Morality* (Chicago, Chicago University Press, 1969); and Notes in *Stanford Law Review,* Vol. 19 (1966), p. 167, and *University of Chicago Law Review,* Vol. 34 (1967), p. 367.

it was well into the nineteenth century, under the impact of the Victorian era, before obscenity laws played any significant part in the system of freedom of expression.[3]

The leading test for determining what material was obscene soon came to be that first enunciated by Lord Cockburn in the famous case of *Regina v. Hicklin,* decided in 1868:

> . . . I think the test of obscenity is this, whether the tendency of the matter charged as obscenity is to deprave and corrupt those whose minds are open to such immoral influences, and into whose hands a publication of this sort may fall.[4]

The *Hicklin* test, which brought within the ban of the obscenity statutes any publication containing isolated passages that the courts felt would tend to exert an immoral influence on susceptible persons, was widely accepted in the American courts well into the twentieth century. Application of the rule, to note its impact only in Massachusetts, resulted in the banning of Theodore Dreiser's *An American Tragedy* in 1930; and its effects were still felt in decisions holding obscene Lillian Smith's *Strange Fruit* in 1945, and Erskine Caldwell's *God's Little Acre* in 1950. *Forever Amber,* however, passed the Massachusetts courts. Other States were sometimes less restrictive, but in general censorship under the *Hicklin* rule was severe.[5]

Opposition to the strictness of the *Hicklin* rule did appear in some quarters. As early as 1913 in *United States v. Kennerley* Judge Learned Hand, while feeling obliged to follow the rule, protested, "I hope it is not improper for me to say that the rule as laid down, however consonant it may be with mid-Victorian morals, does not seem to me to answer to the understanding and morality of the present time."

3. On the English background see Leo M. Alpert, "Judicial Censorship of Obscene Literature," *Harvard Law Review,* Vol. 52 (1938), p. 40; Norman St. John-Stevas, *Obscenity and the Law* (London, Secker and Warburg, 1956); M. C. Slough and P. D. McAnany, "Obscenity and Constitutional Freedom," *St. Louis University Law Journal,* Vol. 8 (1964), pp. 279, 449. Lord Campbell's Act is 20 and 21 Vict., c. 83 (1857). On the American background see Alpert, *supra;* Slough and McAnany, *supra;* James C. N. Paul and Murray L. Schwartz, *Federal Censorship: Obscenity in the Mail* (New York, Free Press of Glencoe, 1961), ch. I.

4. *Regina v. Hicklin,* [1868] L.R. 3 Q.B. 360, 371.

5. *Commonwealth v. Friede,* 271 Mass. 318, 171 N.E. 472 (1930) (*American Tragedy*); *Commonwealth v. Isenstadt,* 318 Mass. 543, 62 N.E.2d 840 (1945) (*Strange Fruit*); *Attorney General v. Book Named "God's Little Acre,"* 326 Mass. 281, 93 N.E.2d 819 (1950); *Attorney General v. Book Named "Forever Amber,"* 323 Mass. 302, 81 N.E.2d 663 (1948). For discussion of the *Hicklin* test in the American courts, see Alpert, *op. cit. supra* note 3, pp. 62–63, 68–69; Lockhart and McClure, *op. cit. supra* note 1, pp. 325–329.

By the nineteen-thirties American courts were beginning to reject the *Hicklin* test and the tide turned decisively against it in 1933 with the celebrated decision of Judge Woolsey in *United States v. One Book Entitled "Ulysses."* Judge Woolsey held that the test should not be whether the publication might tend to deprave morals, but whether it would tend "to stir the sex impulses or to lead to sexually impure and lustful thoughts." More important, he ruled that the book must be judged "in its entirety," not by isolated excerpts, and that the issue was not its effect upon a susceptible person but upon a normal person, "a person with average sex instincts." The Court of Appeals, in an opinion by Judge Augustus Hand, affirmed Judge Woolsey and expressly repudiated the *Hicklin* test. In its place the Court substituted:

> While any construction of the statute that will fit all cases is difficult, we believe that the proper test of whether a given book is obscene is its dominant effect. In applying this test, relevancy of the objectionable parts to the theme, the established reputation of the work in the estimation of approved critics, if the book is modern, and the verdict of the past, if it is ancient, are persuasive pieces of evidence; for works of art are not likely to sustain a high position with no better warrant for their existence than their obscene content.[6]

Meanwhile the issues had not been resolved by the Supreme Court. In 1947 the New York Court of Appeals, unanimously and without opinion, held Edmund Wilson's *Memoirs of Hecate County* obscene. The case was taken to the Supreme Court and it was hoped that a decision from that Court would clarify a confused situation. But Justice Frankfurter, a friend of Wilson's, disqualified himself and the Court ended in a four to four deadlock, without opinion, leaving New York Court's decision standing.[7]

6. *United States v. Kennerley,* 209 F. 119, 120 (S.D.N.Y. 1913); *United States v. One Book Entitled "Ulysses,"* 5 F. Supp. 182, 184, 185 (S.D.N.Y. 1933), aff'd 72 F.2d 705, 708 (2d Cir. 1934). For discussion of these cases and others of the period, see Alpert, *op. cit. supra* note 3, pp. 65–70; Lockhart and McClure, *op. cit. supra* note 1, pp. 326 *et seq.* Other decisions dealing with the obscenity issue prior to its reaching the Supreme Court include Judge Curtis Bok's opinion in *Commonwealth v. Gordon,* 66 Pa. D.&C. 101 (1949), aff'd sub nom. *Commonwealth v. Feigenbaum,* 166 Pa. Super. 120, 70 A.2d 389 (1950); and Judge Jerome Frank's concurring opinion in *United States v. Roth,* 237 F.2d 796, 801 (2d Cir. 1956). Both are classic discussions of the problem.

7. *Doubleday and Co. v. New York,* 335 U.S. 848 (1948). For an account of the case see Lockhart and McClure, *op. cit. supra* note 1, pp. 295–301.

1. THE SUPREME COURT'S DECISIONS

It was not until 1957, therefore, that the Supreme Court came to grips with the obscenity issue. The decision was on a subsidiary, but significant, point. *Butler v. Michigan* involved a Michigan law that prohibited the distribution to the general reading public of material "containing obscene, immoral, lewd or lascivious language, or . . . prints, pictures, [etc.] . . . tending to incite minors to violent or depraved or immoral acts, manifestly tending to the corruption of the morals of youth." The Supreme Court unanimously struck down the statute. Justice Frankfurter, writing for the Court, characterized the legislation as "quarantining the general reading public against books not too rugged for grown men and women in order to shield juvenile innocence." The result, he went on, "is to reduce the adult population of Michigan to reading only what is fit for children." The *Butler* decision did not throw any light upon what kinds of material could or could not be outlawed under obscenity laws. But it did establish at the outset the basic proposition that the rights of the general population could not be curtailed in an effort to protect children, or any other limited segment of the population, against the evils of obscenity.[8]

Later in 1957 came the decisions in *Roth v. United States* and *Alberts v. California,* marking the real beginning of the Supreme Court's struggle with obscenity legislation. The *Roth* case involved a Federal statute that made it a crime to mail material that was "obscene, lewd, lascivious, or filthy" or "other publication of an indecent character." The *Alberts* case raised the constitutionality of a California law that prohibited the publication, sale or distribution of "any obscene or indecent" material or the advertising of it. The Supreme Court in both cases proceeded on the assumption that the materials in question were "obscene," and hence the constitutional issue was considered as an abstract question of whether "obscene" expression was protected by the First Amendment. The two cases were decided together and the Court upheld both statutes, with Justices Black and

8. *Butler v. Michigan,* 352 U.S. 380, 383 (1957). For discussion see William B. Lockhart and Robert C. McClure, "Censorship of Obscenity: The Developing Constitutional Standards," *Minnesota Law Review,* Vol. 45 (1960), pp. 5, 13–18; Kalven, *op. cit. supra* note 1, pp. 5–7.

Douglas dissenting altogether and Justice Harlan dissenting with respect to the Federal statute.[9]

The majority opinion, representing the views of five members of the Court, was written by Justice Brennan. It enunciated two major principles. The first was that "obscenity is not within the area of constitutionally protected speech or press." Justice Brennan based this conclusion upon scattered dicta in prior cases; upon the contention that the First Amendment was not intended to outlaw libel, blasphemy and profanity laws in existence at the time of its adoption; and upon the following rationale:

> All ideas having even the slightest redeeming social importance—unorthodox ideas, controversial ideas, even ideas hateful to the prevailing climate of opinion—have the full protection of the [First Amendment] guaranties, unless excludable because they encroach upon the limited area of more important interests. But implicit in the history of the First Amendment is the rejection of obscenity as utterly without redeeming social importance.[10]

Having thus excluded "obscenity" from the coverage of the First Amendment, Justice Brennan found it unnecessary to pass upon the question whether "obscene material will perceptibly create a clear and present danger of antisocial conduct," or upon any other questions relating to possible effects of obscene expression. It was necessary, however, to define "obscenity," and in such a way as not to be "unconstitutionally restrictive of the freedoms of speech and press." Expressly rejecting the *Hicklin* test, Justice Brennan laid down, as the second major principle of the case, the rule for determining whether particular material was obscene. It was: ". . . whether to the average person, applying contemporary community standards, the dominant theme of the material taken as a whole appeals to prurient interest." [11]

Justice Brennan had earlier defined "prurient interest" as "having a tendency to excite lustful thoughts." It was not necessary to apply this test in the cases before him, however, because the materials involved were admittedly "obscene." Nothing further remained, therefore, except to rule that the statutes were not unconstitutionally vague and to affirm the convictions.[12]

Chief Justice Warren, concurring, introduced the first note of disagreement. He thought that the decision should be limited "to the facts

9. *Roth v. United States, Alberts v. California*, 354 U.S. 476 (1957).

10. 354 U.S. at 485, 484.

11. 354 U.S. at 486, 489.

12. 354 U.S. at 487.

before us and to the validity of the statutes in question as applied"; that while the nature of the materials and their effect upon recipients were relevant, "[t]he conduct of the defendant is the central issue"; that the defendants of these cases "were plainly engaged in the commercial exploitation of the morbid and shameful cravings for materials with a prurient effect"; and that "such conduct" could constitutionally be punished.[13]

Justice Harlan, concurring in *Alberts* and dissenting in *Roth,* took an entirely different position. He believed that the State should have greater leeway under the Fourteenth Amendment to deal with erotic publications than the Federal Government has under the First Amendment. As to the States, he would "inquire only whether the state action so subverts the fundamental liberties implicit in the Due Process Clause that it cannot be sustained as a rational exercise of power." With respect to the Federal Government he would limit its power to the prohibition of "hard-core" pornography.[14]

Justice Douglas, with whom Justice Black agreed, dissented in both *Roth* and *Alberts.* He objected that, under the standards used by the majority, "punishment is inflicted for thoughts provoked, not for overt acts nor antisocial conduct." He pointed out that the majority test required "only the arousing of sexual thoughts," yet that "happens every day in normal life in dozens of ways." He warned that the "test of obscenity the Court endorses today gives the censor free range over a vast domain." The essence of the Douglas-Black position was stated in the concluding paragraphs:

> Freedom of expression can be suppressed if, and to the extent that, it is so closely brigaded with illegal action as to be an inseparable part of it. . . . As a people, we cannot afford to relax that standard. For the test that suppresses a cheap tract today can suppress a literary gem tomorrow. All it need do is to incite a lascivious thought or arouse a lustful desire. The list of books that judges or juries can place in that category is endless.
>
> I would give the broad sweep of the First Amendment full support. I have the same confidence in the ability of our people to reject noxious literature as I have in their capacity to sort out the true from the false in theology, economics, politics, or any other field.[15]

13. 354 U.S. at 494, 495, 496.
14. 354 U.S. at 501, 507.
15. 354 U.S. at 509, 514. For discussion of *Roth* and *Alberts* see Kalven, *op. cit. supra* note 1, pp. 7–28; Lockhart and McClure, *op. cit. supra* note 8, pp. 18–29; Magrath, *op. cit. supra* note 2, pp. 9–25.

The *Roth* case made clear that, in general, obscenity laws were constitutional. But it did not cast much light on what kind of material the Supreme Court was likely to hold obscene. That question was answered in part by three decisions the following year, in none of which the Supreme Court wrote an opinion, but which marked out some of the boundaries. In these cases the Supreme Court reversed, per curiam, lower court rulings that a nudist magazine, the motion picture *Game of Love,* and a magazine for homosexuals were obscene. The Court seemed to be moving to the position that only "hard-core pornography" would be included within the definition of "obscenity." [16]

The next case in which the Supreme Court wrote an opinion on the standards for determining obscenity was *Kingsley International Pictures Corp. v. Regents,* decided in 1959. Like *Butler, Kingsley Pictures* ruled on a collateral but significant issue. The New York Board of Regents had denied a license for showing the motion picture *Lady Chatterley's Lover,* on the ground that "the whole theme of this motion picture is immoral [under the New York statute], for that theme is the presentation of adultery as a desirable, acceptable and proper pattern of behavior." The New York Court of Appeals affirmed the action of the Board of Regents. The United States Supreme Court reversed unanimously, although the justices did not agree on the reasons. Justice Stewart, in an opinion that received the support of five justices, interpreted the decision of the New York Court of Appeals as resting on the proposition, not that the film was "obscene," but that it "alluringly portrays adultery as proper behavior." This violated the First Amendment:

> What New York has done, therefore, is to prevent the exhibition of a motion picture because that picture advocates an idea—that adultery under certain circumstances may be proper behavior. Yet the First Amendment's basic guarantee is of freedom to advocate ideas. The State, quite simply, has thus struck at the very heart of constitutionally protected liberty.[17]

16. *Sunshine Book Co. v. Summerfield,* 355 U.S. 372 (1958); *Times Film Corp. v. Chicago,* 355 U.S. 35 (1957); *One Inc. v. Olesen,* 355 U.S. 371 (1958). For details see Lockhart and McClure, *op. cit. supra* note 8, pp. 32–39. Other cases decided without opinion between 1957 and 1964 are cited in Note, *Yale Law Journal, supra* note 2, p. 1373.

17. *Kingsley International Pictures Corp. v. Regents of the University of the State of New York,* 360 U.S. 684, 685, 687, 688 (1959). Justices Black and Douglas concurred, but added that any licensing system involved prior restraint and was contrary to the First Amendment. Justices Frankfurter, Harlan, Whittaker and Clark concurred in the result on other grounds, without expressly rejecting the Stewart thesis.

The Court in *Kingsley Pictures* thus excluded from the concept of "obscenity" expression that did not in itself arouse lustful thoughts, even though it might persuade or induce the recipient to engage in "obscene" conduct. Such expression was to be governed by the regular First Amendment rules. This treatment of so-called thematic obscenity or ideological obscenity operated, consistently with other decisions of the Court, to narrow substantially the area controlled by obscenity doctrines. Although the Stewart opinion was endorsed by only five justices, the position there taken has not been subsequently challenged.[18]

Not until five years after *Kingsley Pictures*—in 1964—did the Supreme Court render a further opinion on the standards for judging obscenity. Then, in *Jacobellis v. Ohio,* the Court split six ways. The case involved a conviction under an Ohio law of the manager of a motion picture theater for showing the French film *Les Amants*. The Supreme Court reversed, three justices dissenting, but no more than two justices agreed on any single position. Justice Brennan, speaking for himself and Justice Goldberg, expanded the *Roth* test for separating "obscenity from constitutionally protected expression." First he made explicit what he had only implied in *Roth,* that "a work cannot be proscribed unless it is 'utterly' without social importance." Secondly, he added that the *Roth* test required a finding that the material "goes substantially beyond customary limits of candor in description or representation." Finally he interpreted the "contemporary community standards" of the *Roth* test to refer to national rather than local standards. Applying the revised test, Justice Brennan found the film not obscene.[19]

Justices Black and Douglas, concurring, adhered to their position in *Roth,* saying only that "the conviction of appellant or anyone else for exhibiting a motion picture abridges freedom of the press as safeguarded by the First Amendment." Justice Stewart, also concurring, took the position that the obscenity laws must be "constitutionally limited to hard-core pornography." As to the definition of that term he said:

I shall not today attempt further to define the kinds of material I understand to be embraced within that shorthand description; and perhaps

18. For discussion of *Kingsley Pictures* see Kalven, *op. cit. supra* note 1, pp. 28–34; Lockhart and McClure, *op. cit. supra* note 8, pp. 39–43.

19. *Jacobellis v. Ohio,* 378 U.S. 184, 187, 191 (1964). Justice Goldberg also wrote a separate concurring opinion. In a prior case, *Manual Enterprises v. Day,* 370 U.S. 478 (1962), Justice Harlan alone (Justice Stewart concurring) dealt with the standards problem.

I could never succeed in intelligibly doing so. But I know it when I see it, and the motion picture involved in this case is not that.[20]

Justice White concurred in the reversal but wrote no opinion. Chief Justice Warren, with Justice Clark agreeing, thought that "we should try to live" with the original *Roth* test, but that the "community standards" applied should be local, not national, ones. Chief Justice Warren would have added to the *Roth* test the view he previously expressed in *Roth*, that "the use to which various materials are put—not just the words and pictures themselves—must be considered in determining whether or not the materials are obscene." He then went on to say that the Supreme Court should not make "an independent *de novo* judgment on the question of obscenity," but should simply apply a "sufficient evidence" standard of review. On that basis he would affirm the State court. Justice Harlan, also dissenting, applied his prior standard for review of cases arising under State laws, a test of "rationality": "I would not prohibit [the States] from banning any material which, taken as a whole, has been reasonably found in state judicial proceedings to treat with sex in a fundamentally offensive manner, under rationally established criteria for judging such material." [21]

Following *Jacobellis* the Supreme Court returned to its practice of deciding obscenity cases per curiam, without opinion. Thus on the same day it decided *Jacobellis* it reversed rulings of the Florida courts that had found *Pleasure Was My Business* and Henry Miller's *Tropic of Cancer* obscene. Meanwhile the lower courts were having difficulty in applying the Supreme Court's rules, coming to different conclusions on *Tropic of Cancer* and *Fanny Hill*. In 1966 the Supreme Court handed down three major decisions, covering various aspects of the obscenity problem. These were *A Book Named "John Cleland's Memoirs of a Woman of Pleasure" v. Attorney General of Massachusetts*, involving *Fanny Hill; Ginzburg v. United States;* and *Mishkin v. New York.* By this time the fragmentation of the Court was nearly complete: there were fourteen opinions in the three cases.[22]

20. 378 U.S. at 196, 197.

21. 378 U.S. at 200–201, 202–203, 204. For a summary of the theories developed by the different justices through *Jacobellis*, see Note, *Yale Law Journal, supra* note 2, pp. 1364–1377.

22. *Tralins v. Gerstein*, 378 U.S. 576 (1964) (*Pleasure Was My Business*, described as "containing numerous descriptions of abnormal sex acts and indecent conversations supposed to have taken place in a Florida brothel"); *Grove Press v. Gerstein*, 378 U.S. 577 (1964) (*Tropic of Cancer*). For reference to the lower court decisions, see *Political and Civil Rights in the United States*, p. 765. The 1966 obscenity decisions are *A Book Named "John Cleland's Memoirs of a Woman of Pleasure" v. Attorney General of Massachusetts*, 383 U.S. 413 (1966);

In *Fanny Hill* a holding of the Massachusetts Court that the book was obscene was reversed by a vote of six to three. Justice Brennan, writing for himself, Chief Justice Warren and Justice Fortas (who had replaced Justice Goldberg), applied the revised *Roth* test. In their view a book could not be obscene unless "[e]ach of the three federal constitutional criteria" were independently met, namely (1) prurient appeal; (2) patent offensiveness; and (3) material *"utterly* without redeeming social value." The Massachusetts Court had ruled that, while "the testimony may indicate this book has some minimal literary value," such fact "does not mean it is of any social importance." This, Justice Brennan held, was error and required reversal. Justice Brennan then went on to adopt the view that Chief Justice Warren had urged in *Roth* and *Jacobellis,* saying that "the circumstances of production, sale, and publicity are relevant in determining whether or not the publication or distribution of the book is constitutionally protected." "Evidence that the book was commercially exploited for the sake of prurient appeal" might thus make a critical difference. However, since the Massachusetts Court had only passed upon the book in the abstract, and without reference to its method of distribution, this factor was not present in the case. The net effect of the Brennan opinion seems to be that *Fanny Hill* is not obscene unless "exploited by panderers." [23]

Justices Black, Douglas and Stewart concurred in the reversal on theories they had previously expounded. The two former felt that "the First Amendment does not permit the censorship of expression not brigaded with illegal action." Justice Douglas also thought that *Fanny Hill* met the *Roth* test, it not being shown that the book was "utterly without redeeming social importance," and rejected the position that a "book that concededly has social worth can nonetheless be banned because of the manner in which it is advertised and sold." Justice Stewart adhered to his position that only "hard core pornography" could be suppressed. Implied in his concurrence is the view that *Fanny Hill* is not "hard core pornography." [24]

Justices Clark, White, and Harlan dissented. Justice Clark took the view that the social importance element "does not constitute a separate and distinct constitutional test," but should only be considered along with appeal to prurient interest and patent offensiveness, which are the

---

Ginzburg v. United States, 383 U.S. 463 (1966); *Mishkin v. New York,* 383 U.S. 502 (1966).

23. 383 U.S. at 419, 420, 421.
24. 383 U.S. at 426, 426–427.

basic and sufficient criteria for determining obscenity. After vividly
describing the contents of *Fanny Hill,* he concluded that "the book's
repeated and unrelieved appeals to the prurient interest of the average person leave it utterly without redeeming social importance." Justice White agreed with Justice Clark that " 'social importance' is not
an independent test of obscenity but is relevant only to determining
the predominant prurient interest of the material." Justice Harlan reiterated his previous positions, which he believed "represent the sound-
est constitutional solution of this intractable problem." The *Roth* tests
"offer only an illusion of certainty and risk confusion and prejudice."
In his view *Fanny Hill* was not "hard-core pornography" and could
not be barred from the Federal mails. But "the Fourteenth Amendment requires of a State only that it apply criteria rationally related to
the accepted notion of obscenity and that it reach results not wholly
out of step with current American standards." [25]

In *Ginzburg* five members of the Court accepted and applied the
Warren principle that the manner in which the material was disseminated could be a controlling factor in a determination of obscenity.
Ralph Ginzburg, editor of *Eros* magazine, was convicted of violating
the Federal obscenity statute in using the mails to advertise and circulate three publications: *Eros,* a hard-cover magazine of expensive
format, devoted to "literary pornography"; *Liaison,* a biweekly news-
letter containing articles on sex; and a book entitled *The Housewife's
Handbook on Selective Promiscuity,* a detailed autobiography of the
author's sex life and philosophy. The Supreme Court affirmed the conviction, which carried a five-year prison sentence for Ginzburg, by a
vote of five to four.

Justice Brennan wrote the majority opinion, speaking for himself,
Chief Justice Warren, and Justices Clark, White and Fortas. He assumed, without deciding, that the material in the abstract could not
have been ruled obscene, but found a violation of the statute when the
publications were viewed "against a background of commercial exploitation of erotica solely for the sake of their prurient appeal." As
evidence of this background he pointed to the fact that *Eros* had first
sought mailing privileges from the post offices in Intercourse and Blue
Ball, Pennsylvania, and had later obtained them from the postmaster
in Middlesex, New Jersey. He noted further, "The 'leer of the sensual-
ist' also permeates the advertising for the three publications." This evi-

25. 383 U.S. at 445, 450, 462, 456,
458–459, 457, 458.

dence, he said, "was relevant in determining the ultimate question of obscenity and, in the context of this record, serves to resolve all ambiguity and doubt." He concluded:

> It is important to stress that this analysis simply elaborates the test by which obscenity vel non of the material must be judged. Where an exploitation of interests in titillation by pornography is shown with respect to material lending itself to such exploitation through pervasive treatment or description of sexual matters, such evidence may support the determination that the material is obscene even though in other contexts the material would escape such condemnation.[26]

Justices Black, Douglas, Harlan and Stewart dissented, each on the basis of positions marked out in prior cases. They also objected strongly to the pandering test, arguing that Ginzburg had had no warning the statute would be applied to him on any such theory; that the mode of disseminating material had no logical relation to whether the material was obscene; and that the standard of obscenity had been rendered even more vague and meaningless. In addition Justice Stewart undertook to define "hard core pornography." He quoted "a description, borrowed from the Solicitor General's brief, of the kind of thing to which I have reference":

> Such materials include photographs, both still and motion picture, with no pretense of artistic value, graphically depicting acts of sexual intercourse, including various acts of sodomy and sadism, and sometimes involving several participants in scenes of orgy-like character. They also include strips of drawings in comic-book format grossly depicting similar activities in an exaggerated fashion. There are, in addition, pamphlets and booklets, sometimes with photographic illustrations, verbally describing such activities in a bizarre manner with no attempt whatsoever to afford portrayals of character or situation and with no pretense to literary value. All of this material . . . cannot conceivably be characterized as embodying communication of ideas or artistic values inviolate under the First Amendment. . . .[27]

In *Mishkin* the defendant was convicted under a New York obscenity statute for producing and selling some fifty books of the "pulp" variety, depicting not only "relatively normal heterosexual relations" but also "such deviations as sado-masochism, fetishism, and homosexuality." The Supreme Court affirmed, with Justices Black, Douglas and

---

26. 383 U.S. at 466, 468, 470, 475– 476.   27. 383 U.S. at 499.

Stewart dissenting. Justice Brennan, writing for the same group of justices as in *Ginzburg,* held that the New York courts, which had interpreted the New York statute "to cover only so-called 'hard-core pornography,'" had properly found the books obscene within the *Roth* test. Indeed Mishkin did not challenge this conclusion except with respect to the so-called bondage books, those that portrayed "various deviant sexual practices, such as flagellation, fetishism, and lesbianism." These, Mishkin argued, did not satisfy the prurient appeal test for the reason that they did not appeal to the prurient interest of the "'average' person in sex," that "instead of stimulating the erotic, they disgust and sicken." Justice Brennan quickly rejected the argument:

> Where the material is designed for and primarily disseminated to a clearly defined deviant sexual group, rather than the public at large, the prurient-appeal requirement of the *Roth* test is satisfied if the dominant theme of the material taken as a whole appeals to the prurient interest in sex of the members of that group. . . . We adjust the prurient-appeal requirement to social realities by permitting the appeal of this type of material to be assessed in terms of the sexual interests of its intended and probable recipient group; and since our holding requires that the recipient group be defined with more specificity than in terms of sexually immature persons, it also avoids the inadequacy of the most-susceptible-person facet of the *Hicklin* test.[28]

Justice Harlan concurred, on the basis of his "rationality" test for reviewing convictions under State laws. Justice Stewart's dissent was on the ground that the publication did not meet his test of "hard core pornography." Justices Black and Douglas reiterated their basic opposition to all obscenity laws.

The 1966 obscenity cases leave the reader with some sympathy for Justice Black's complaint in his *Ginzburg* dissent:

> My conclusion is that certainly after the fourteen separate opinions handed down in these three cases today no person, not even the most learned judge much less a layman, is capable of knowing in advance of an ultimate decision in his particular case by this Court whether certain material comes within the area of "obscenity" as that term is confused by the Court today.[29]

28. 383 U.S. at 505, 508–509.

29. 383 U.S. at 480–481. For discussion of the 1966 cases see Monaghan, *op. cit. supra* note 2, pp. 141–150; Ma-

grath, *op. cit. supra* note 2, pp. 25–56; Note, *Yale Law Journal, supra* note 2, pp. 1377–1398.

After the 1966 obscenity cases the Supreme Court went back once more to the device of deciding cases per curiam. No further elaboration of the multiple viewpoints was therefore forthcoming. The actual decisions made did of course give some content to the various theories and outlined vaguely the common element in the positions of a controlling majority. Thus the *Redrup* case in 1967 made clear that at least seven justices on the Court did not think that paperback books entitled *Lust Pool* and *Shame Agent,* or "girlie" magazines, were obscene.[30]

In 1968, however, the Supreme Court did address itself at length to the difficult problem of restrictions on the sale of obscene materials to children. *Ginsberg v. New York* involved a New York statute that made it unlawful for any person to sell to minors under seventeen years of age any picture or similar representation "which depicts nudity, sexual conduct or sado-masochistic abuse and which is harmful to minors," or any book or other printed matter which contains similar material "or explicit or detailed verbal descriptions or narrative accounts of sexual excitement, sexual conduct or sado-masochistic abuse and which, taken as a whole is harmful to minors." The phrases "nudity," "sexual conduct," "sexual excitement," and "sado-masochistic abuse" were defined in comparatively specific terms. Thus "nudity" meant "the showing of the human male or female genitals, pubic area or buttocks with less than a full opaque covering, or the showing of the female breast with less than a fully opaque covering of any portion thereof below the top of the nipple, or the depiction of covered male genitals in a discernibly turgid state." The words "harmful to minors" were defined as meaning representations of any of the foregoing which "(i) predominantly appeals to the prurient, shameful or morbid interest of minors, and (ii) is patently offensive to prevailing standards in the adult community as a whole with respect to what is suitable material for minors, and (iii) is utterly without redeeming social importance for minors."

Ginsberg, who with his wife operated a stationery store and luncheonette in Bellmore, Long Island, was convicted under this statute of selling a sixteen-year-old boy two "girlie" magazines containing pictures of female nudes that fell within the statutory definition of "nu-

---

30. *Redrup v. New York,* 386 U.S. 767 (1967). The opinion contains a summary of the different views of the seven justices making up the majority. For a list of the cases disposed of without opinion, see *Ginsberg v. New York,* 390 U.S. 629, 634 fn. 3 (1968).

dity." The Supreme Court, in a six to three decision, upheld the statute and affirmed the conviction.[31]

Justice Brennan, writing for five members of the majority, noted that the magazines were "not obscene for adults" within prior decisions of the Court, and reaffirmed *Butler*. He also pointed out that Ginsberg had made no argument that the materials were not "harmful to minors" within the definition of the statute, and hence the only issue he presented to the Court was "the broad proposition that the scope of the constitutional freedom of expression secured to a citizen to read or see material concerned with sex cannot be made to depend upon whether the citizen is an adult or a minor." To this contention Justice Brennan answered flatly: "we cannot say that the statute invades the area of freedom of expression constitutionally secured to minors." The test was whether "it was rational for the legislature to find that the minors' exposure to such material might be harmful." The legislature had found that the material condemned by the statute was "a basic factor in impairing the ethical and moral development of our youth and a clear and present danger to the people of the state." Justice Brennan thought it "very doubtful that this finding expresses an accepted scientific fact." "But," he said, "obscenity is not protected expression and may be suppressed without a showing of the circumstances which lie behind the phrase 'clear and present danger,' " citing *Roth*. Therefore it was only necessary that "we be able to say that it was not irrational for the legislature to find that exposure to material condemned by the statute is harmful to minors." While the finding made by the State could not be proved it "has not been disproved either." Hence no showing of irrationality was made. Finally, Justice Brennan upheld the statute against the charge that the term "harmful to minors" was unconstitutionally vague, pointing out that the term was defined in the words of the *Roth* test.[32]

Justice Stewart, concurring in the result, spelled out more carefully the application of the First Amendment to freedom of expression for children:

31. *Ginsberg v. New York*, 390 U.S. 629 (1968).

32. 390 U.S. at 634, 636, 637, 639, 641, 642, 643. In Appendix B to his opinion Justice Brennan cites the statutes of 35 other States which include provisions relating to obscenity for minors. It notes that none is "a precise counterpart" of the New York statute and "we imply no view whatever on questions of their constitutionality." 390 U.S. at 637. See also *Bantam Books, Inc. v. Sullivan*, 372 U.S. 58 (1963).

The First Amendment guarantees liberty of human expression in order to preserve in our Nation what Mr. Justice Holmes called a "free trade in ideas." To that end, the Constitution protects more than just a man's freedom to say or write or publish what he wants. It secures as well the liberty of each man to decide for himself what he will read and to what he will listen. The Constitution guarantees, in short, a society of free choice. Such a society presupposes the capacity of its members to choose. . . .

I think a State may permissibly determine that, at least in some precisely delineated areas, a child—like someone in a captive audience —is not possessed of that full capacity for individual choice which is the presupposition of First Amendment guarantees. It is only upon such a premise, I should suppose, that a State may deprive children of other rights—the right to marry, for example, or the right to vote— deprivations that would be constitutionally intolerable for adults.[33]

Justice Fortas dissented. He agreed "that the State in the exercise of its police power—even in the First Amendment domain—may make proper and careful differentiation between adults and children." But he thought the Court had an obligation, before letting Ginsberg's conviction stand, to define what would be "obscene" for children but not for adults. Justices Douglas and Black stuck to their position. They objected to the application of due process doctrine to First Amendment issues and felt that the guarantee of that constitutional provision prohibited restriction on the right of anyone to speak or hear.[34]

Finally, in 1969 the Supreme Court went out of its way to decide a

33. 390 U.S. at 649–650.
34. 390 U.S. at 673. For discussion of the case see Samuel Krislov, "From Ginzburg to Ginsberg: The Unhurried Children's Hour in Obscenity Legislation," *Supreme Court Review*, Vol. 1968 (1968), p. 153. In a case decided the same day the Court struck down a Dallas ordinance providing for the classification of films as suitable or not suitable for minors. *Interstate Circuit, Inc. v. City of Dallas*, 390 U.S. 676 (1968). The decision rested on grounds of vagueness but implied that a specific classification system for minors would be valid. The case is considered in the next section. Another portion of the New York statute, already repealed, was also stricken for vagueness in *Rabeck v. New York*, 391 U.S. 462 (1968). See also Note, "Exclusion of Children From Violent Movies," *Columbia Law Review*, Vol. 67 (1967), p. 1149.

Justice Harlan's opinion in *Interstate Circuit* undertakes a summary of the varying positions taken by the different members of the Court in obscenity cases beginning with *Roth*, and lists all obscenity cases decided by the Court, with and without opinion, from *Roth* onwards. 390 U.S. at 704. For surveys by lower Federal courts of the development of obscenity law see *United States v. Klaw*, 350 F.2d 155 (2d Cir. 1965); *Luros v. United States*, 389 F.2d 200 (8th Cir. 1968). A table showing all Supreme Court actions in obscenity matters through 1968 may be found in Rogge, *op. cit. supra* note 2, pp. 54–59.

case that raised a new aspect of obscenity law. In *Stanley v. Georgia* Federal and State officials obtained a warrant to search Stanley's home for evidence of bookmaking activity. They did not find that kind of evidence but in a desk drawer in an upstairs bedroom they did find three reels of eight-millimeter film which was admittedly obscene. Stanley was convicted under a Georgia obscenity law that included in the offense a prohibition against "knowingly hav[ing] possession of obscene matter." The Supreme Court unanimously reversed. Justices Stewart, Brennan and White, in an opinion by the former, avoided the First Amendment issues altogether, finding it unnecessary "to move on to newer constitutional frontiers." They would have held that the warrant did not authorize the searching officials to seize the films. But the other members of the Court based the decision on First Amendment grounds.[35]

Justice Marshall, writing for five members of the Court, first faced the problem of distinguishing the *Roth* two-level theory that obscenity is outside the protection of the First Amendment. He accomplished this awkward task by declaring that *Roth* and succeeding cases dealt with "regulation of commercial distribution of obscene material" and did not "foreclose an examination of the constitutional implications of a statute forbidding mere private possession of such material." Justice Marshall then proceeded to assert that the First Amendment protects the "right to receive information and ideas, regardless of their social worth." He observed that this First Amendment right "takes on an added dimension" in the context of "unwanted governmental intrusions into one's privacy." He concluded his affirmative case by saying:

> Whatever may be the justifications for other statutes regulating obscenity, we do not think they reach into the privacy of one's own home. If the First Amendment means anything, it means that a State has no business telling a man, sitting alone in his own house, what books he may read or what films he may watch. Our whole constitutional heritage rebels at the thought of giving government the power to control men's minds.[36]

Justice Marshall went on to examine the claim made by the State of Georgia that various social interests justified its regulation of the private possession of obscene materials. The first argument he characterized as amounting only to "the assertion that the State has the right

35. *Stanley v. Georgia*, 394 U.S. 557,   36. 394 U.S. at 563–564, 564, 565.
569 (1969).

to control the moral content of a person's thoughts." This he dismissed as "wholly inconsistent with the philosophy of the First Amendment." Georgia's second claim of interest was that "exposure to obscenity may lead to deviant sexual behavior or crimes of sexual violence." Concerning this Justice Marshall said "there appears to be little empirical basis for that assertion" and, more importantly, "in the context of private consumption of ideas and information we should adhere to the view that '[a]mong free men, the deterrents ordinarily to be applied to prevent crime are education and punishment for violations of the law,' " quoting Justice Brandeis in *Whitney v. California*. Finally, Justice Marshall rejected the argument that control of the possession of obscenity was "a necessary incident to statutory schemes prohibiting distribution." He thought that "the individual's right to read or observe what he pleases . . . is so fundamental to our scheme of individual liberty, its restriction may not be justified by the need to ease the administration of otherwise valid criminal laws." [37]

It is not at all clear what the effect of the *Stanley* decision will be on the Supreme Court's handling of obscenity laws. On its face *Stanley* seems to undermine much of the theoretical structure built up in prior decisions. Yet the Court appeared to consider the case as wholly exceptional, quite outside the mainstream of obscenity law. Until further evidence is forthcoming, therefore, we must treat the *Stanley* decision in this light, and assume it was not meant to alter the basic course of Supreme Court doctrine in the obscenity field.

Taken as a whole, the Court's decisions have resulted in some notable gains for the system of freedom of expression. The Court has adopted a relatively narrow concept of obscenity, limiting it to sexual (including scatological) matters. It has made clear that the rights of the ordinary adult reader cannot be curtailed through restrictions designed to protect children or "specially susceptible" persons, or to prohibit possession of obscenity in the home. It has not permitted relaxation of the protection normally extended by the First Amendment to "thematic" or "ideological" support for obscenity, that is, advocacy of conduct that might be considered obscene. The results of its decisions have been broadly permissive, certainly as compared with the situation prevailing before 1957. Roughly speaking, no serious or artistic work

37. 394 U.S. at 565, 566, 566–567, 568. Justice Black concurred on his usual ground that the First Amendment protected all speech, "whether labeled obscene or not." See also *Stein v. Batchelor*, 300 F. Supp. 602 (N.D. Tex. 1969), prob. juris. noted by Supreme Court, Dec. 8, 1969.

is likely to be outlawed under its rules. The standard for banning expression that seems to be applied in practice (apart from materials presented on radio or television) is rather close to the so-called hard-core pornography rule.[38]

Nevertheless, it is safe to say that few people are satisfied. Those who strongly object to censorship can hardly feel comfortable with the constitutional principle that obscenity, or what the government says is obscenity, is totally outside the protection of the First Amendment. Nor are they happy with the uncertainty that surrounds the Court's decisions and opinions—the vagueness of its doctrine, the discretion allowed to the prosecutor, and the possibility that the liberal results can readily be reversed. Supporters of the Court are distressed at its many disagreements, its inability to reach a stable position, its failure to come to grips with some of the real issues. Advocates of obscenity controls are not reassured either. To them it appears that the Court, while ostensibly banning "obscenity," actually permits more and more of it to circulate. The reasons for the Court's distinctions are not apparent to them. A closer examination of the various theories propounded by the Court may throw some light upon the reasons for this background of concern and hostility.

The doctrine that has claimed most adherents on the Court has been the *Roth* test revised. This position starts with the proposition that "obscenity" is outside the coverage of the First Amendment—the two-level theory. It then proceeds to define "obscenity." Initially, in the *Roth* case, the test of obscenity appeared to be simply whether to the average person, applying contemporary community standards, the material taken as a whole appeals to prurient interest—the prurient appeal element. Later, in the *Jacobellis* elaboration, there was made explicit the requirement that the material must go substantially beyond the customary limits of candor in the description or representation of sexual matters—the patently offensive element. Also made express by *Jacobellis* was a third requirement that the material be utterly without redeeming social importance—the social importance element. These three elements are independent and each must be present in order for the material to be obscene. A fourth and final factor, taken over from Chief Justice Warren and adopted by a majority in *Mishkin*, is that in close cases commercial exploitation may show that the material does

---

38. For accounts of the impact of the Supreme Court decisions upon the kinds of materials available to the reading and viewing public see *Political and Civil* *Rights in the United States*, pp. 782–787; Magrath, *op. cit. supra* note 2, pp. 24–25; *United States v. Klaw*, 350 F.2d 155 (2d Cir. 1965).

not have sufficient social importance and thereby renders obscene what would not otherwise have been so—the pandering element.

The "two-level" approach to obscenity is a disastrous beginning. In one sense the two-level theory is an unreal exercise in semantics: it does not solve the problem because the Court must still define obscenity. But in another sense the objections go deeper. In excluding "obscenity" from the coverage of the First Amendment, the Court is led to define what is excluded in terms that are not related to the reasons for excluding it. Thus the Court uses the two-level approach to cut off consideration of what interests society is attempting to protect by obscenity laws, what the actual effects of obscenity may be, how these problems bear on a system of freedom of expression, what the limits on restricting obscenity for children may be, and other real problems of a similar nature. Furthermore, the two-level theory abandons all First Amendment doctrine in an important area of expression and leaves that expression with only due process protection. Finally, the two-level approach misleads the public. It gives the impression that "obscenity" is beyond the pale of constitutional protection and then it upholds *Fanny Hill* on constitutional grounds. The two-level theory of libel was abandoned in *New York Times v. Sullivan*. The theory should also be given up in the field of obscenity.[39]

The "prurient appeal" element of the *Roth* test contains three sub-elements: (1) the prurient appeal of the material, (2) taken as a whole, (3) to the average person. The most significant of these is the first; it establishes the kind of material that will qualify as obscenity whereas the other two merely limit the initial classification. But the phrase "prurient appeal," which the courts cannot define further than as meaning "to arouse lustful thoughts," is patently overbroad. It would embrace just about everything that has to do with sex, including advertising and other materials in which the sexual appeal is subconscious. Moreover, the test is highly subjective, for the same material appeals to different individuals, in different ways, under different circumstances. As used in the original *Roth* case, the prurient interest test is fantastically absurd. Actually it did not survive for long. Inevitably it was supplemented by the "patently offensive" and "social importance" elements. Even in combination with other factors, however, the prurient appeal test does no more than indicate the general area with which obscenity laws attempt to deal.

39. *New York Times v. Sullivan*, 376 U.S. 254 (1964). See Chapter XIV.

The requirement that the material be "taken as a whole" makes little sense in terms of the assumptions upon which obscenity laws are based. To someone looking for material with a "prurient interest," there is not much difference whether he finds it on one page or on every page. The effects, whatever they are, most likely are the same. This portion of the test is primarily useful for cutting down, essentially on an arbitrary basis, the volume of material that would otherwise be classified as obscene. To the extent that its operation is rational, the requirement probably tends to save material of a more artistic or literary quality. If obscenity laws continue to be enforced, however, the requirement is bound to be modified. Censorship of motion pictures is usually accomplished by cutting out particular scenes, and only four of the fifteen articles in *Eros* were challenged as obscene.

The requirement that the prurient appeal be to the "average person" is likewise a somewhat arbitrary, but necessary, device for reducing the amount of material that would otherwise be banned by the prurient interest test. From the viewpoint of the proponents of obscenity laws the requirement, at least in the broad form used in *Roth,* seriously undermines the effectiveness of those laws. If suppression of obscenity serves any public purpose the statutes should be geared exactly to those who are most "susceptible" to obscenity and whose exposure to it will bring about the most social harm. To measure obscenity by the average person test makes as much sense as measuring the danger of advocacy of violent overthrow of the government by its appeal to members of the Century Club. It is hardly surprising therefore, as *Mishkin* shows, that the average person portion of the *Roth* test is beginning to break down.

All this is not to imply that, in the context of the *Roth* test, the "taken as a whole" and the "average person" tests are wrong or worthless. In that context they are essential. But it does seem clear that these requirements run so counter to the objectives of obscenity laws that they will be constantly subjected to great pressure, and are therefore likely to be whittled away, as long as the *Roth* test remains the measure of obscenity.

The "patently offensive" element in the *Roth* test, by which the right of the individual to express himself or hear the expression of others is suppressed on the basis of the majority taste, is diametrically opposed to all concepts of freedom of expression. Virtually every theory of the First Amendment holds that the individual cannot be tied down to the average, least of all with respect to matters of form, acceptability, or convention. Furthermore, if enforced, the requirement could only lead to complete stagnation of art and literature. There are other difficulties with this part of the *Roth* test. Proof of community standards of offensiveness is difficult and uncertain, thereby leaving vast discretion in the enforcement authorities. If local community standards are used as the test, the right of expression will vary in each locality. On the other hand there are probably no national standards. Altogether the "patently offensive" element, once again, can be justified only as imposing some degree of limitation upon the basic prurient appeal criterion.

The "social importance" element in the *Roth* test also runs counter to the ideas underlying a system of freedom of expression. The judgment of whether any particular expression possesses social value or no social value is not for the government to make. If freedom of expression is to mean anything that judgment must be made by the individual who speaks or wishes to hear. Sponsors of the *Roth* test never explain why the social utility of expression should be decisive only in obscenity cases. Hiding behind the two-level theory—that obscenity is outside the First Amendment—they do not reach the question.

It should be noted, however, that in utilizing the social importance element the *Roth* test comes as close as it ever gets to considering the problem of what the effects of obscenity actually are. If it is correct that "obscenity" is utterly without *redeeming* social importance, that must be because obscenity has a harmful effect of some kind upon the community. But the proponents of the *Roth* test never seriously face this question. They assume that some such harmful effect flows from obscenity, but never venture to state what it is. Actually the assumption is that expression having artistic or literary merit according to conventional standards, despite an appeal to prurient interest, should be saved from the obscenity laws. The question at once arises, however, as to why the constitutional protection should stop there. Essentially the "social importance" element brings into the *Roth* test distinctions based upon class, educational attainments, and intellectual preferences.

The "pandering" element in the *Roth* test classifies material that would not otherwise be so labeled as obscene by virtue of the way in which the material is marketed. On one level this makes very little sense, as Justice Douglas pointed out in *Mishkin*. An "obscene" book remains an "obscene" book regardless of the method of its distribution. It is true that the effects of reading or seeing prurient material may depend substantially upon the context in which the reading or seeing takes place. But dissemination by "commercial exploitation" is surely only a minor factor in creating conditions that affect the result. In any event obscenity laws are not directed at controlling the circumstances in which obscene material is seen or read, an obviously impossible task.

At another level the pandering test appears to be more logical. It is designed to prevent the dissemination of prurient material by certain kinds of publishers, through certain kinds of retail outlets, using certain kinds of advertising. It is directed, in short, at the "offensive" sectors of the publishing business. Here it serves much the same purpose as the social importance test. It limits the impact of obscenity laws to prurient materials which have little or no claim to artistic or literary merit, or are inelegantly packaged or advertised. The conviction of Ralph Ginzburg for circulating high- or middle-class pornography is not really an exception to this point; he was caught by surprise when the *Roth* test was expanded.

There are two other major objections to the pandering element of the *Roth* test. First, it ignores the constitutional rights of the reader. It makes the rights of the individual to see or hear expression dependent, not upon the material, but upon the motives or methods of the publisher or distributor. This is so even though such motives and methods are not by themselves illegal or objectionable. Second, the requirement is hopelessly vague and incapable of objective administration. This arises largely out of the fact that most publication and distribution of literature is conducted for profit, and the attempt to distinguish legitimate from non-legitimate motives and methods in terms of "commercial exploitation" is virtually impossible. The result is that the pandering test adds an additional level of vagueness to the already vague complex of tests for obscenity and necessarily produces a far greater repressive effect.

To this analysis of the *Roth* doctrine there must be added the serious problems that arise in the administration of the test. The various parts of the test, and the test as a whole, convey very little meaning apart from the results reached in particular cases. But the results could easily change without the test being changed. In consequence, not only are all parties unsure of what the law means, but official and unofficial attempts to ban material under the obscenity laws are never stilled. The uncertainties, costs, delays, and other harassments to publisher, distributor, and retailer can gravely impede the system of free expression. The vagueness of the *Roth* test also creates difficulties in judicial administration. The Supreme Court is forced to deal with the obscenity problem on a case-by-case basis, each Justice examining the material in every case in order to determine whether it violates the *Roth* standards. This places an immoderate and dubious burden on the Supreme Court and renders vindication of First Amendment rights a costly, cumbersome and possibly rare achievement.[40]

The "hard-core pornography" test, applied by Justice Stewart in all cases and by Justice Harlan in Federal cases, has certain advantages over the *Roth* test. In the first place, it can be less vague. It does not deal with the materials in subjective terms of an appeal to inward thoughts and emotions but in more objective and descriptive terms. Thus it can define obscene material as that which portrays certain specific conduct, such as sexual intercourse, or depicts certain parts of the human body, such as the genital organs. Justices Stewart and Harlan have not carried the test to this point, but the New York statute considered in *Ginsberg* indicates the possibilities. Moreover, the hard-core pornography test proscribes a narrower range of expression. It attempts to concentrate the statutory prohibition only upon what is considered the most "objectionable" material, the kind of material against which public pressures are strongest. It thus may satisfy public demands for control without interfering as much with the system of freedom of expression.

Yet serious problems remain. Vagueness and uncertainty are by no means eliminated. Even if the hard-core pornography test allows more specific description of the materials proscribed, the court must still decide by what standards certain types of material are to be included or excluded. Furthermore, the terms used are not so precise as they may seem on first impression. Like the *Roth* test, the hard-core pornography test does not really intend to exclude all the material which satisfies the description. Ancient pottery, or a picture by a famous artist, are not meant to be covered. The failure to achieve precision is well illustrated by the *Mishkin* case, in which the New York Court of Appeals found material to be hard-core pornography but Justice Stewart, patron saint of the hard-core pornography test, judged it otherwise.

40. For discussion of some of the practical consequences of the *Roth* test, see Leon Friedman, "The Ginzburg Decision and the Law," *American Scholar,* Vol. 36 (Winter 1966–1967), pp. 71, 79–86; Magrath, *op. cit. supra* note 2, pp. 68–69; American Civil Liberties Union, "Ginzburg: The Fallout," *Civil Liberties* (Oct. 1966), p. 3.

Actually, while it may not be possible to define hard-core pornography, it is possible to say what the major elements in the hard-core pornography test are. Essentially the test undertakes to ban material on the basis of three factors: (1) the explicitness of the representation of sexual activities; (2) the lack of artistic merit; and (3) the degree of pandering. The first element—explicitness—gives the test its greater precision, though it does not solve the vagueness problem. The explicitness element is also more relevant to the effect of the material in causing social harm, though the test does not turn on any such effect and is not defended on that ground. The second element—lack of artistry—tends to reintroduce the vagueness problem. More importantly, it runs squarely counter to the principles of the First Amendment. Like the social importance element of the *Roth* test it involves a governmental judgment on the value of certain kinds of expression that the government has no right to make. The pandering element is subject to the objections already made. Taking the requirement of artistic merit and the absence of commercial exploitation together, the hard-core pornography test is, like the *Roth* test, a way of allowing high-class, elegantly packaged pornography, while denying pornography to the less affluent, educated, or supposedly intelligent. Also like the *Roth* test, it does not rest on any demonstrable relation to the effect of the material in causing social harm or on any serious effort to conform to the requirements of a system of freedom of expression.[41]

Justice Harlan's test for State cases—that the State need only apply some "rational" standard and reach a result "not wholly out of step"—constitutes virtual abdication of Federal judicial review over the operation of State obscenity laws. Indeed, this is its main appeal to Justice Harlan. Believing the *Roth* test unmanageable and the hard-core pornography test too severe, he sees the only feasible alternative as withdrawal from the arena. If accepted by a majority of the Supreme Court the Harlan solution would unquestionably result in widespread suppression of allegedly obscene materials at State and municipal levels. Without the aid of a more vigorous constitutional principle publishers and distributors would have a difficult time fending off, in

41. A strong case for the hard-core pornography test is made out in Magrath, *op. cit. supra* note 2, pp. 69–77. Other proponents of the hard-core pornography test include former Judge Thurman Arnold, who also believed that judges should not try to write opinions explaining what obscenity is, and Lockhart and McClure, who would modify the test in terms of their variable obscenity concept. See Kalven, *op. cit. supra* note 1, pp. 43–45, quoting Judge Arnold; Lockhart and McClure, *op. cit. supra* note 8, pp. 49–88.

Justice Douglas' words, the forces of the Philistines. As it is, no other member of the Court has supported the Harlan view.

Justices Black and Douglas take a full protection position, opposed to obscenity laws of any kind. Yet their approach is an extremely rigid one. They are unwilling to make any concessions, even in the case of children. While they talk at times of protecting only expression not "so closely brigaded with illegal action as to be an inseparable part of it," they make no effort to consider further where this line should be drawn in the obscenity area. Similarly, although they have objected elsewhere to imposing expression upon a "captive audience," they have not attempted to explore that concept further as it may apply in the obscenity field. As a result of this hard-line position, the Black-Douglas solution has been attacked, with some justification, as being callous of public concern with obscenity and hence wholly impractical.[42]

Apart from the various tests employed by members of the Supreme Court, the other principal formula proposed for measuring the extent of governmental control over obscenity is the clear and present danger test. The chief proponent of this approach has been the American Civil Liberties Union. Under this formulation the government would have to show, in each case, that the material sought to be suppressed created a clear and present danger that the normal adult would be induced to engage in illegal behavior. The clear and present danger test has the outstanding virtue of focusing attention upon a real problem: what is the actual effect of reading or seeing obscene material upon future conduct? With the exception of an inconclusive exchange between Justices Clark and Douglas in *Mishkin* the Supreme Court opinions have never attempted to deal with this issue. The clear and present danger test would force the Court to face the effect problem, and thereby bring the law of obscenity back into the mainstream of First Amendment doctrine.

On the other hand, application of the clear and present danger test in obscenity cases has severe drawbacks. Most important is the fact that at the present state of knowledge it is impossible to say one way or another what the effects of obscenity, if any, really are. Furthermore, under any foreseeable circumstances it is unlikely that proof of the effects of obscenity in any particular case could ever be made. The

---

42. The quotation from Justice Douglas appears in *Roth,* 354 U.S. at 514. For criticism of the Black-Douglas position on these grounds see Magrath, *op. cit. supra* note 2, pp. 57–59.

impact of the clear and present danger formula, therefore, turns on a burden of proof issue. Since the burden of proof is put on the government the results of applying the test would be that there could never be a successful prosecution for obscenity. This is fully recognized by most proponents of the test. The outcome under the clear and present danger test thus becomes highly artificial, not related in any way to the merits of the original proposition.

There are other disadvantages in the clear and present danger test. When used in obscenity cases the formula does not lose its vague and indefinite character; in fact in this area speakers and enforcement officials would be even less likely to be able to calculate in advance when a communication would run afoul of the test. Again, the clear and present danger test would have to be applied on a case-by-case basis, thus creating a serious problem of judicial administration. Finally, even this test does not pose the issue in proper form. Assuming obscene material could be proved to create a clear and present danger of illegal behavior, it would not follow that the expression should be suppressed. Rather the basic principles of a system of freedom of expression would require that society deal directly with the subsequent action and leave the expression alone.

Other approaches for dealing with the obscenity problem have been suggested. It is noteworthy, however, that use of the balancing test has never been seriously urged. This is undoubtedly due in part to the fact that the two-level theory eliminated the need for any balance. But it may also be attributable to the fact that the balancing test is particularly unworkable because the interests of the state in prohibiting obscenity rest upon such unascertainable foundations.[43]

The Supreme Court's efforts to deal with laws designed to prevent obscene materials from reaching children have been little more successful, from a doctrinal point of view, than its performance in the adult area. In *Ginsberg* the Court summarily holds that the standards of obscenity for children may be different from those applicable when adults are concerned. But it offers no rationale to explain why or to what extent this is true. Justice Brennan simply resorts to a children's two-level theory and concludes that materials that are "obscene" vis-à-

---

43. The American Civil Liberties Union position on obscenity is stated in *Policy Guide of the A.C.L.U.*, Policy No. 4 (June 1966). Albert B. Gerber in "A Suggested Solution to the Riddle of Ob-scenity," *University of Pennsylvania Law Review*, Vol. 112 (1964), p. 834, suggests a form of balancing, but makes clear in advance how he thinks the balancing should come out.

vis children, even though not "obscene" for adults, are outside the coverage of the First Amendment. He then reduces all further questions, including the problem of defining "children's obscenity," to the due process issue of whether the legislative judgment can be said to be irrational. The result is that all the difficult issues are bypassed, at least for the time being, and no reasoned basis for development of future doctrine is suggested.[44]

2. A PROPOSED THEORY OF OBSCENITY CONTROLS

There remains, then, the task of analyzing the obscenity problem in terms of the expression-action theory of the First Amendment here being proposed. Clearly most communication alleged to be obscene constitutes "expression." It appears in oral, written or pictorial form, as speech, a book, picture, film, play, or the like. There are, however, some areas in which the conduct alleged to be obscene, or to contain obscenity, would be classified as "action." Thus most of what may be called "live conduct" falls into the category of action. For example adultery or fornication, even though done as a protest against the current moral code, would be considered as essentially action. Likewise swimming in the nude or other public nudity, unless done with an intention to communicate, would be treated as action. On the other hand portrayal of such conduct in books, films, or as part of a dramatic presentation in the theater would be considered expression. Essentially the issues in such cases are whether the action element in the conduct predominates; and whether the person is trying to *tell* something or *do* something, whether his conduct is representation or actuality. Admittedly these are difficult lines to draw at times. The result reached may on the surface sometimes appear arbitrary or nonsensical. But the distinctions embody a concept absolutely fundamental to the maintenance of a system of freedom of expression. The court must do the best it can. If it seriously undertakes to apply the principle there is no great danger that in close cases a judgment falling on one side of

44. For material dealing with obscenity laws designed to protect children, published before *Ginsberg,* see *Political and Civil Rights in the United States,* pp. 772–774. The Supreme Court has also dealt with the rights of minors to freedom of expression in *Tinker v. Des Moines Independent Community School District,* 393 U.S. 503 (1969), discussed in Chapter XVI. See also *Prince v. Massachusetts,* 321 U.S. 158 (1944).

the line rather than the other will gravely damage the system of free expression or severely harm society by leaving illegal action unpunished.[45]

Another aspect of the distinction between "expression" and "action" in the obscenity field is crucial. If an obscene communication is forced upon another person against his will it can have a "shock effect" and such a communication can properly be described as "action." An obscene telephone call is an obvious example. But the problem is not confined to that form of communication. Generally speaking, as already noted, the effects of erotic material upon the recipient are presently unknown. But the available evidence does seem to establish that exposure to such material is for some persons an intense emotional experience. A communication of this nature, imposed upon a person contrary to his wishes, has all the characteristics of a physical assault. The harm is direct, immediate, and not controllable by regulating subsequent action. Such communications can therefore realistically be classified as action. Moreover, from a slightly different point of view, forcing obscenity upon another person constitutes an invasion of his privacy, and for that reason also falls outside the system of freedom of expression. The distinction between this area of conduct and the expression protected by the First Amendment touches a limited but central feature of the obscenity problem.[46]

In addition to drawing the line between expression and action, it is necessary to deal with one other major issue posed by the obscenity laws. This is the place of children in a system of freedom of expression. As previously indicated, that system cannot and does not treat children on the same basis as adults. The world of children is not the same as the world of adults, so far as a guarantee of untrammeled freedom of the mind is concerned. The reason for this is, as Justice Stewart said in *Ginsberg,* that a child "is not possessed of that full capacity for individual choice which is the presupposition of the First Amendment guarantees." He is not permitted that measure of independence, or able to exercise that maturity of judgment, which a system of free ex-

45. For a discussion of this problem, rare in judicial decisions, see Judge Burke's opinion in *Trans-Lux Distributing Corp. v. Board of Regents,* 14 N.Y.2d 88, 248 N.Y.S.2d 857 (1964), reversed on other grounds, 380 U.S. 259 (1965).

46. For evidence supporting the proposition that forced obscenity has a "shock effect" see Robert B. Cairns, James C. N. Paul, and Julius Wishner, "Sex Censorship: The Assumptions of Anti-Obscenity Laws and the Empirical Evidence," *Minnesota Law Review,* Vol. 46 (1962), p. 1009. On the relation between the system of freedom of expression and the system of privacy in our society, see Chapter XIV.

pression rests upon. This does not mean that the First Amendment extends no protection to children; it does mean that children are governed by different rules. This differentiation concerns one of the most delicate aspects of the obscenity problem and embodies a key concept for dealing with that problem.

Upon the basis of these considerations the guiding principles emerge. Any communication that can be classified as "expression," whether or not containing erotic material, is protected against any kind of abridgment by the government. In terms of the obscenity laws this means primarily that restrictions upon alleged obscenity are permissible only if a communication having a shock effect is forced upon a person against his will, or if the restriction operates only to limit dissemination of erotic materials to children. These general principles require some further elaboration and a testing against the realities of the current obscenity problem.

Appraisal of the full protection approach is best made through an examination of its impact upon the various social interests that obscenity laws are thought to foster. Proponents of such laws have never been very precise in defining these interests. Nor has the Supreme Court, thanks to the two-level theory, done much to clarify the situation. Commentators have been more fruitful, but not always agreed. If an attempt is made, however, to classify the possible social interests in terms most relevant to the problem of adjusting obscenity controls to the system of freedom of expression, the issues resolve into the protection of society against (1) immediate harmful actions resulting from exposure to erotic materials; (2) longer-range, more remote, harmful actions; and (3) internal reactions of the individual, not necessarily reflected in overt action. The third category in turn breaks down into (a) the fantasy effect and (b) the shock effect. At another level are (4) the possible harmful results, of any of the types mentioned, from the exposure of children to erotic materials.[47]

(1) The possibility of immediate harmful action following from exposure to erotic material would seem to supply the strongest reason for prohibiting access to such materials. Nevertheless this likelihood, or even certainty, would not justify restriction of expression under the

47. For other classifications of the social interests sought to be protected by obscenity laws see Kalven, *op. cit. supra* note 1, pp. 3–4; Paul and Schwartz, *op. cit. supra* note 3, pp. 191–202; Friedman, *op. cit. supra* note 40, pp. 86–87, quoting classifications suggested in the Government's brief in *Ginzburg;* Lockhart and McClure, *op. cit. supra* note 1, pp. 329–342, 373–387. See also Justice Marshall's discussion in the *Stanley* case, *supra*.

theory of the First Amendment here advocated. The government is expected to direct its restrictions to action and the possible advantage of preventing the action from occurring in some cases by a prior suppression of expression in all cases would not warrant the damage done to expression. Only if the communication is so closely linked to action as to be considered a part of it could the government punish or restrict the earlier stage. If this position is sound when expression consists of direct advocacy of violence or other violation of law it would appear equally sound in the case of obscenity.

Indeed, the argument for suppression of erotic materials, on the ground they may induce illegal action, would seem substantially weaker than the argument for suppressing direct advocacy of illegal action. In the latter case the connection between the expression and the action, while often uncertain and remote, is generally thought to exist. In the former case there is no conclusive proof that any connection exists. Moreover, while the scientific case has not been demonstrated either way, there is substantial evidence that the relationship between erotic material and illegal action is at most tenuous and sporadic. Thus the leading study of sex crimes, by members of the Institute for Sex Research, reports: "It would appear that the possession of pornography does not differentiate sex offenders from nonsex offenders. Even the combination of ownership plus strong sexual arousal from the material does not segregate the sex offender from other men of comparable social level." There is also evidence that the reading of erotic material may, by acting as a catharsis, in some cases diminish illegal acts. In addition, there is no reason to suppose that only the "objectionable" erotic materials would have the feared effect, and hence there is no ground for singling out the particular kind of eroticism the obscenity laws seek to reach. Under such circumstances the presumptions in favor of First Amendment rights would plainly call for no departure from the principles applied to other forms of expression.[48]

48. The quotation is from Paul H. Gebhard et al., Sex Offenders (New York, Harper & Row, 1965), p. 678. For a summary of the social science material dealing with the effects of obscenity see Cairns, Paul and Wishner, op. cit. supra note 46; Magrath, op. cit. supra note 2, pp. 49–56; John H. Gagnon and William Simon, "Pornography—Raging Menace or Paper Tiger?" Transaction (July– August 1967), p. 41; Rogge, op. cit. supra note 2, pp. 220–229; Political and Civil Rights in the United States, pp. 788–792. Ned Polsky, in a sociological analysis of pornography, views it as a functional alternative to prostitution, pornography being the fantasy (expression) and prostitution action. Hustlers, Beats, and Others (Chicago, Aldine Publishing Co., 1967), pp. 186–202.

(2) The social interest in the longer-range, more remote, effects of exposure to obscenity affords even less support for obscenity laws. Again there is no conclusive scientific basis for asserting that erotic materials shape attitudes or character in a manner that is harmful to society in the long run. It is most likely, of course, that reading does change attitudes and character; at least most people, especially writers, certainly assume so. Erotic reading may be injurious in its long-term effects. But no one contends that expression in any other area can be suppressed on such grounds. To do so would destroy the system of freedom of expression. Censorship of expression relating to sexual matters on any such basis is equally contrary to the fundamental premises of a system of freedom of expression and equally destructive.

(3) (a) The original purpose of the obscenity laws was undoubtedly far less concerned with the impact of erotic materials on overt behavior than with their impact on internal moral standards. The arousing of lustful thoughts was held to be morally corrupting and it was felt necessary that society protect its members from such dangers. These moral considerations undoubtedly remain the chief driving force behind obscenity laws in the present day; otherwise it is hard to account for the emotional fervor that still surrounds the enforcement of such laws. There can be little doubt that erotic materials are designed to, and do, result in "heightened sexual arousal" in many persons under proper circumstances, ranging from mild sexual excitement to orgasm. The question is whether the government may constitutionally attempt to prevent its citizens from voluntarily seeking such sexual fantasies by a system of censorship. The state may, of course, enact legislation to promote and protect the morals of its citizens. But under the First Amendment it may not pursue that goal by means of restricting expression. No one disputes that the government cannot suppress speech or writing for the purpose of shielding its citizens from nonsexual thoughts or fantasies, regardless of their effect upon moral character. There is no basis in the First Amendment, or in the concepts underlying our system of freedom of expression, for applying a different rule in the case of sexual thoughts.[49]

It should be added that not only is the prohibition of erotic materials, voluntarily sought by adults, incompatible with a system of freedom of expression, but such censorship is futile and discriminatory as

49. For an analysis of the obscenity laws in terms of the effort to achieve moral goals see Louis Henkin, "Morals and the Constitution: The Sin of Obscenity," *Columbia Law Review,* Vol. 63 (1963), p. 391.

well. Our society is crammed full of sexually stimulating reading matter, sights and events. It is literally impossible for the government to
suppress all stimuli that may arouse sexual excitement, any more than
it can eliminate sex. Nor can it suppress even the most erotic without
eliminating much of the world's literature and art. The consequence is,
as already noted, that the impact of obscenity laws falls primarily, or
would if the laws could be enforced, upon particular groups in our
society who happen not to prefer or be able to afford elite pornography.

(b) When erotic materials are not voluntarily acquired or perused,
but are thrust upon an individual or the general public, a different question is presented. If such a communication entails a shock
effect it may be classified as "action" and subjected to appropriate regulation. The treatment of erotic communications in this manner raises
some troublesome questions. Ordinarily an individual seeking to exercise the right of expression is allowed considerable leeway in obtaining
access to other persons, whether or not such persons have indicated a
desire to receive the communication. The emotional response to a
communication, even if agonizing, is normally not ground for curtailing expression. A system of freedom of expression is supposed to "invite dispute" and encourage "robust and wide-open" controversy.
Under such a system even the law of libel should not authorize restriction upon communication short of an invasion of privacy. Why, then,
should erotic communication be considered to pose any different problem? The answer lies in the intensity of the psychological forces that
pervade our society in the area of sex. This is what creates the en-
gulfing popular demand for obscenity laws. In our concept of privacy
the sexual realm occupies an important, not to say the central, part.
The notion of a "captive audience," compelled to see or hear erotic
communications, is intolerable to us. It seems reasonable, therefore, to
give the ordinary person and the public at large greater protection
against unwanted intrusion from the presentation of erotic material
than is afforded in other areas of expression.

If one accepts this approach many further issues remain. The first
question is how to define the erotic material that would be subject to
restriction under this "shock effect" concept. Most likely the phrase
"patently offensive because it affronts contemporary community
standards" provides the best answer. Such a formula, while vague as
all formulae in this area are vague, embodies the elements that must be
taken into account. Other questions concern the kinds of regulation

that would be permissible. These would seem to fall into two categories. The first would relate to public displays of erotic material. Thus an advertisement on a billboard or on a theater marquee might be prohibited whereas the same advertisement in a book could not. Public nudity is subject to regulation but pictures of nudes in a magazine are not. The other category involves erotic material forced into the home. It is important not to proscribe a legitimate right of access. But if a householder affirmatively makes his views known, with sufficient specificity, the government would be entitled to enforce his wishes. The difficult question here concerns radio and television. In view of the fact that radio and television signals are broadcast publicly, and enter the household without much opportunity for selection in advance, the shock effect concept would probably apply in this area also.[50]

The Supreme Court, it should be noted, has given some indication that it is prepared to accept the "shock effect" doctrine. Thus in the course of its per curiam opinion in *Redrup* the Court observed that in none of the three cases before it "was there any suggestion of an assault upon individual privacy by publication in a manner so obtrusive as to make it impossible for an unwilling individual to avoid exposure to it." The following term, in *Fort v. City of Miami,* the Court let stand a conviction for public display of allegedly obscene sculptures in the defendant's backyard. The Court has not, of course, followed the proposal made here that the shock effect principle constitute the only ground for restriction of erotic communication to adults.[51]

(4) Acceptance of the principle that children are not part of the adult system of freedom of expression still leaves some unresolved problems. First of all it is necessary to define what materials are to be judged "obscene" for children, or otherwise proscribed for them. Such

---

50. The formula is taken from the *Ginzburg* case, 383 U.S. at 479. In 1967 Congress passed a law providing that any person who "mails or causes to be mailed any pandering advertisement which offers for sale matter which the addressee in his sole discretion believes to be erotically arousing or sexually provocative shall be subject to an order of the Postmaster General to refrain from further mailings of such materials to designated addressees thereof." 39 U.S.C.A. §4009. The statute was upheld by a three-judge District Court, against vagueness and other objections, in *Rowan v. Post Office Department,* 300 F. Supp. 1036 (C.D. Calif.

1969), prob. juris. noted 396 U.S. 885 (1969). On the treatment of obscenity on radio and television see the Federal Communications Commission decisions in *Palmetto,* 33 F.C.C. 250 (1962), aff'd in *Robinson v. F.C.C.,* 334 F.2d 534 (D.C. Cir. 1964), cert. denied 379 U.S. 843 (1964); *Pacifica Foundation,* 36 F.C.C. 147 (1964). A Federal statute, enacted in 1968, prohibits obscene telephone calls interstate. 47 U.S.C. §223.

51. *Redrup v. New York,* 386 U.S. 767, 769 (1967); *Fort v. City of Miami,* 389 U.S. 918 (1967), Justices Black, Douglas and Stewart dissenting.

a task takes us beyond the limits of this book, and no real answer to the question will be attempted. By hypothesis the full protection theory of the First Amendment cannot be applied. Nor, in view of the present lack of knowledge about the subject, can the clear and present danger test be employed, or any test based on the effect of obscenity on children. Even a balancing test would not be feasible. We are left then, at least for the time being, with little more than a due process test—that the restriction be a reasonable one. Such a test can be supplemented by the principle that a presumption exists in favor of First Amendment rights, and can be narrowed by use of the void for vagueness rule and similar procedural devices. Over the course of time sufficient knowledge may be gained to refine and elaborate the test. But presently the courts can probably do little more than accept the legislative standard if it comes within the broad contours of reasonableness.

While the legislature may have considerable leeway in the choice of standards, it is severely circumscribed by the need to fit the restrictions pertaining to children into the system of freedom for adults. Under the *Butler* doctrine the rights of adults cannot be curtailed by regulations designed to protect children. In the case of motion pictures or the theater, this problem is easily solved. A classification system can be established and children refused admission to those performances designated obscene under it. Otherwise, the problem of drafting regulations that will be effective for children and not interfere with adults is almost insuperable. A classification scheme in a bookstore, by which certain shelves are marked "For Adults Only," presents obvious difficulties. Any exceptionally tight system for preventing sales to minors that resulted in retailers not stocking books banned for children would run afoul of the *Butler* rule. In any event, as long as material is available to adults it is hopeless to try to keep it out of the hands of adolescents.

In short, while *Butler* stands, laws attempting to restrict the availability of erotic materials for minors are likely to be ineffective. Controls over such matters will have to remain, as they undoubtedly should, with parents, schools, churches and similar institutions. Legislation can partially reinforce those controls and it can give the public a feeling that "something is being done." Beyond this it is likely to have little practical significance.

To conclude, it is possible to bring obscenity laws into line with the basic principles of a system of freedom of expression. Dissemination of erotic materials to those who voluntarily choose to read or see them would be protected under the First Amendment. Forcing such material upon individuals who did not want them, or did not want their children to have them, or upon the public at large, would be prohibitable. Special rules could be made for children so long as they did not infringe upon adult rights.

A system of this sort appears entirely feasible. Denmark and Sweden seem to have found it workable. Furthermore, the public demands for obscenity laws, which have led the courts to abandon all ordinary First Amendment doctrine in dealing with obscenity, might well be satisfied with such a system. Public morality would be upheld; those who did not voluntarily choose to read or see erotic materials would be protected; and parental control over material available to children would be supported. To go beyond this and try to keep erotic materials away from adults who want to see them is rather hard to justify in this day and age. A majority of the Supreme Court in effect conceded this in the *Stanley* case. Finally, a system of this kind would be honest. It would not ban "hard-core" pornography and allow elite pornography. Nor would it remain largely unenforced. The most likely consequence would be, as the Danish experience has shown, that, pornography no longer being unlawful and therefore tempting, the volume in circulation would diminish.[52]

B. Prior Restraint

Apart from the question of standards, the courts have dealt with a variety of other issues in obscenity cases. Of these, one of the most important, and the one most closely related to First Amendment theory, is the doctrine of prior restraint. Though this doctrine plays a part in other areas of freedom of expression it is of most significance today in connection with obscenity laws.

The doctrine of prior restraint is a principle of great potential significance in the operation of obscenity laws. Speaking very generally,

52. For accounts of the Danish and Swedish experience see *The New York Times,* Nov. 5, 1967, p. 27, col. 1; *Washington Post,* Apr. 11, 1968, p. D 17; *The New York Times,* Nov. 6, 1968; *Time* Magazine, June 6, 1969, p. 47. In January, 1968 President Johnson, pursuant to legislation passed by Congress in 1967 (P.L. 90–100, 81 Stat. 253), appointed a Commission on Obscenity and Pornography, headed by Dean William B. Lockhart of Minnesota Law School, to investigate the whole problem. The Commission was to report by July 30, 1970.

the doctrine holds that governmental restrictions cannot be imposed upon speech or other kind of expression in advance of publication. It does not touch on the question of what, if any, subsequent punishment can be administered for engaging in expression. The doctrine thus is solely concerned with limitations on the form of governmental control over expression. Even if the communication is subject to later punishment or can otherwise be restricted, it cannot be proscribed in advance through a system of prior restraint. Inasmuch as obscenity controls can often be applied most effectively through a censorship board or similar kind of preventive regulation, the doctrine of prior restraint has a major effect upon the form that obscenity laws are permitted to take.

The doctrine of prior restraint has its roots in the English system of censorship that began to develop shortly after the introduction of printing into England in the fifteenth century. Under that system all printing presses and printers were licensed and nothing could be published except with prior approval of the state or church authorities. The licensing laws expired in 1695 and were not extended. Thereafter freedom of the press from licensing came to be recognized in England as a common law or natural right. The law was summarized by Blackstone in a famous passage:

> The liberty of the press is indeed essential to the nature of a free state; but this consists in laying no *previous* restraint upon publications, and not in freedom from censure for criminal matter when published. Every freeman has an undoubted right to lay what sentiments he pleases before the public; to forbid this, is to destroy the freedom of the press; but if he publishes what is improper, mischievous, or illegal, he must take the consequence of his own temerity.[53]

When the First Amendment was adopted in 1791 it was clearly meant to outlaw any system of prior restraint similar to the English licensing system. There were indeed some who argued that this was all the First Amendment was intended to do. That position was, of course, ultimately rejected. But no one ever challenged the basic prohibition against prior restraint. Not until 1931 in *Near v. Minnesota*, however, did the Supreme Court undertake to clarify the broad concept and reduce it to a working principle of constitutional law.[54]

Near v. Minnesota involved the so-called Minnesota Gag Law, an

53. *Blackstone's Commentaries on the Laws of England,* Vol. 4, pp. 151–152.

54. For a summary of the background of the doctrine of prior restraint see

Thomas I. Emerson, "The Doctrine of Prior Restraint," *Law and Contemporary Problems,* Vol. 20 (1955), p. 648.

experiment in control of the press that had aroused the concern of the newspaper world. The statute provided that any person "engaged in the business" of regularly publishing or circulating an "obscene, lewd and lascivious" or a "malicious, scandalous and defamatory" newspaper or periodical "is guilty of a nuisance"; and that suit could be brought by the State "to enjoin perpetually the persons committing or maintaining any such nuisance." Such a suit had been commenced against the publishers of a weekly Minneapolis newspaper which had printed a series of articles that "charged in substance that a Jewish gangster was in control of gambling, bootlegging and racketeering in Minneapolis, and that law enforcing officers and agencies were not energetically performing their duties." No allegation was made that the publication was obscene. The State court perpetually enjoined the publishers from issuing "any publication whatsoever which is a malicious, scandalous or defamatory newspaper, as defined by law." The United States Supreme Court in a five to four decision reversed.[55]

Chief Justice Hughes, writing for the majority, held the statute invalid as a prior restraint. He reviewed the English licensing laws and the adoption of the First Amendment, stated that the principle of "immunity from previous restraint" is subject to limitation "only in exceptional cases," and laid down the basic rule:

> The exceptional nature of its limitations places in a strong light the general conception that liberty of the press, historically considered and taken up by the Federal Constitution, has meant, principally although not exclusively, immunity from previous restraints or censorship.[56]

With specific reference to the case before him he concluded:

> The fact that the liberty of the press may be abused by miscreant purveyors of scandal does not make any the less necessary the immunity of the press from previous restraint in dealing with official misconduct. Subsequent punishment for such abuses as may exist is the appropriate remedy . . .[57]

The decision in *Near v. Minnesota,* while a major breakthrough in First Amendment doctrine, left important matters unexplained and unexplored. First of all it did not clearly indicate the kinds of restrictive measures to which the term "prior restraint" would be applied. The classic form of prior restraint involved a system that prohibited publication without advance approval of an executive official. The sit-

55. *Near v. Minnesota,* 283 U.S. 697, 702–703, 704–706 (1931).

56. 283 U.S. at 715–716.
57. 283 U.S. at 720.

uation in *Near v. Minnesota* was somewhat different. At issue there
was a court injunction against further publication of "malicious, scandalous and defamatory" matter, enforced by a subsequent contempt
proceeding. Justice Butler, on behalf of the minority, argued that this
form of restriction did not fall within the Blackstone concept of a prior
restraint. The majority had some justification for holding that it did;
the practical effect of the injunction was that the publishers, in order to
avoid risk of summary punishment for contempt, had to clear material
in advance with the judge. But the majority did not explain adequately
the basis for expanding the scope of the prior restraint concept or explore just how far the concept would carry.

Again, the Court left in considerable confusion the question of
what exceptions, if any, should be permitted to the prior restraint doctrine. Chief Justice Hughes' opinion asserted that the doctrine would
not be applicable in "exceptional cases." He gave as examples certain
obstructions to the conduct of war, obscenity, and incitement to violence. But the reasons for making these exceptions are unclear—some
of them do not even involve expression—and the whole matter
remains obscure.

Finally, the Court never undertook to explain the functional basis
of the prior restraint doctrine. Its decision rested primarily upon historical grounds. A rational basis for the concept does exist. A system
of prior restraint is in many ways more inhibiting than a system of
subsequent punishment: It is likely to bring under government scrutiny a far wider range of expression; it shuts off communication before
it takes place; suppression by a stroke of the pen is more likely to be
applied than suppression through a criminal process; the procedures
do not require attention to the safeguards of the criminal process; the
system allows less opportunity for public appraisal and criticism; the
dynamics of the system drive toward excesses, as the history of all censorship shows. It is true that in some situations subsequent punishment
may be more restrictive. But this does not negate the fact that a system
of prior restraint presents inherent dangers that make it highly disfa-
vored as a form of regulation. In any event consideration of these
factors is essential to a rational application of the ancient concept to
current problems.[58]

The failure of the Supreme Court in *Near* and later cases to pull
together some of these loose ends in the prior restraint doctrine, and

58. For discussion of the rational
basis for the doctrine of prior restraint
see Emerson, *op. cit. supra* note 54, pp.
655–660.

thereby to give it some content and precision, has resulted in greatly diminishing the usefulness of the doctrine as an instrument for protection of freedom of expression. The doctrine was employed loosely to strike down taxes on newspapers and taxes on the right to disseminate religious literature. It was used to invalidate blanket licensing requirements for the distribution of leaflets or door-to-door canvassing, but the Supreme Court did not make clear whether the doctrine would allow licensing systems of a more limited nature. The doctrine was also invoked to void permit systems for meetings and parades that incorporated overly broad standards, but the Court upheld permit systems more narrowly drawn. In none of these cases did the Court succeed in formulating a cohesive doctrine. The lack of precision is highlighted by Justice Black's argument in *Dennis* that conviction of a conspiracy to advocate overthrow of the government constituted a prior restraint.[59]

Under these circumstances it is not surprising that the prior restraint doctrine has never attained full growth in the obscenity area. Its application there started out, of course, with the initial handicap that Chief Justice Hughes had said in *Near* that obscenity was an exception to the general rule. This has not proved to be the case. No flat exception has been granted in obscenity cases. But the doctrine has received only limited application and in the case of motion picture censorship has been sharply altered in form.

The first test of the prior restraint doctrine in the obscenity field came in *Kingsley Books v. Brown,* decided in 1957 on the same day as *Roth.* In that case a New York statute authorized local authorities to bring an injunction suit against any person selling or intending to sell obscene materials, and to obtain a court order enjoining sale or distribution of the material and directing its destruction. The Supreme Court upheld the statute, as applied to the sale of paperbacks found to be "obscene," in a five to four decision. Justice Frankfurter, writing for the majority, accepted the argument that the doctrine of prior restraint applied in obscenity cases and that it would "preclude what may fairly be deemed licensing or censorship." But he held that the New York statute had no greater, and perhaps less, restraining effect than the ordinary criminal statute. In both cases the law applied only after publication, and the seller had an opportunity to contest the charge of obscenity before any penalty attached. The provision for de-

---

59. The tax cases are discussed in Chapter XII; licensing and permit cases in Chapter IX; and the *Dennis* case in Chapter V.

struction, he said, was a traditional sanction for dealing with "the instruments of ascertained wrongdoing." Chief Justice Warren, following his views in *Roth*, dissented on the ground that the proceeding
should be brought against a person, not a book: "To do otherwise is to
impose a prior restraint." Justice Douglas, joined by Justice Black,
thought "every publication is a separate offense which entitles the accused to a separate trial." Justice Brennan also dissented because the
seller should have a right to a jury determination of the issue of "obscenity." [60]

The *Kingsley Books* case established that, contrary to *Near*, obscenity cases were not "exceptions" to the general rule against prior
restraint. But the decision did not throw much light upon prior restraint theory. It dealt with a complex type of regulation, falling somewhere between a system of advance clearance for publication or dissemination and straight subsequent punishment by criminal process.
Since the regulation did not impose any requirement for obtaining
prior approval in order to distribute the publication, and provided for
a judicial proceeding before the prohibition became effective, the
Court could well have concluded that there was no prior restraint involved without seriously jeopardizing the significance of that principle.
But the casual treatment of prior restraint, both by the majority and
the dissenters, indicated no serious interest in any real development of
the doctrine.[61]

The application of the prior restraint doctrine to movie censorship
was squarely presented to the Supreme Court in *Times Film Corp. v.
City of Chicago*, decided in 1961. In that case a Chicago ordinance
required submission of all motion pictures, prior to their public exhibition, for examination by a designated city official who was empowered
to refuse permission if the film was "obscene" or did not meet other
specified standards. The Times Film Corporation sought to test the
ordinance by refusing to submit the film *Don Juan* for examination
and brought suit to enjoin the City from requiring advance permission.

60. *Kingsley Books v. Brown*, 354
U.S. 436, 441, 444, 446, 447 (1957).

61. It should be noted that the New
York statute did authorize an injunction
pendente lite, though it provided that the
trial must begin within one day after
joinder of issue and decision rendered by
the court within two days of the conclusion of the trial. Justice Douglas specifically objected to this provision as a "prior
restraint and censorship at its worst," and
there is considerable justification for his
position. But in the case before the Court
the sellers had consented to the issuance
of an injunction *pendente lite* and this
provision, which was not central to the
statutory scheme, did not figure prominently in the decision. 354 U.S. at 446.

The Court held, five to four, that the ordinance was valid. Justice Clark, who wrote for the majority, noted that the issue was posed in its baldest form: "Admittedly, the challenged section of the ordinance imposes a previous restraint, and the broad justiciable issue is therefore present as to whether the ambit of constitutional protection includes complete and absolute freedom to exhibit, at least once, any and every kind of motion picture." He emphasized that the exhibitor was claiming that "even if this film contains the basest type of pornography, or incitement to riot, or forceful overthrow of orderly government, it may nonetheless be shown without prior submission for examination." Pointing out that it had never been held that "all previous restraints on speech are invalid," and recognizing Chicago's "duty to protect its people against the dangers of obscenity," Justice Clark rejected "the claim of absolute privilege against prior restraint under the First Amendment." He added the caution, however, that the Court was saying no more than that "we are dealing only with motion pictures and, even as to them, only in the context of the broadside attack presented on this record." [62]

Chief Justice Warren, writing for the four dissenters, conceded that the Court "has stated that the protection afforded First Amendment liberties from previous restraint is not absolutely unlimited." But the "exceptional cases," he contended, did not include "licensing or censorship"; and the Chicago ordinance was such a system. The majority, he said, "thus gives formal sanction to censorship in its purest and most far-reaching form, to a classical plan of licensing that, in our country, most closely approaches the English licensing laws of the seventeenth century which were commonly used to suppress dissent in the mother country and in the colonies." In a long opinion Chief Justice Warren not only analyzed the prior restraint cases but dealt at length with the manner in which a system of prior restraint operates and examined the actual workings of movie censorship in the United States. Justice Douglas, in a separate opinion, further expanded on the "evils of 'prior restraint.'" Thus the dissenters in *Times Film* finally came to grips with some of the basic considerations underlying the doctrine of prior restraint. But it was too late. At least as far as movie censorship was concerned, the doctrine in its original form was abandoned. [63]

At this point the Supreme Court undertook to repair some of the

62. *Times Film Corp. v. City of Chicago,* 365 U.S. 43, 46, 47, 49, 50 (1961).

63. 365 U.S. at 53, 55–56, 82.

damage by requiring that the censorship system conform to strictly procedural norms. In *Freedman v. Maryland* a theater owner challenged the constitutionality of a Maryland movie censorship statute. The law provided that all films must be submitted to the Maryland State Board of Censors before exhibition; that if the film was disapproved or cuts ordered the applicant had a right of appeal to two or more members of the Board; and that he could appeal from there to the City Court and eventually to the Maryland Court of Appeals. During this process, which in the only prior case took six months, the film could not be exhibited. The Supreme Court unanimously struck down the statute on the ground that the "Maryland scheme fails to provide adequate safeguards against undue inhibition of protected expression, and this renders the . . . requirement of prior submission of films to the Board an invalid previous restraint." Justice Brennan, delivering the opinion for seven members of the Court, reaffirmed *Times Film* but held that "a noncriminal process which requires the prior submission of a film to a censor avoids constitutional infirmity only if it takes place under procedural safeguards designed to obviate the dangers of a censorship system." He then stated the requirements to be (1) "the burden of proving that the film is unprotected expression must rest on the censor"; (2) since only "a judicial determination suffices to impose a valid final restraint" the censor must "either issue a license or go to court to restrain showing the film"; and (3) the procedure must "assure a prompt final judicial decision." Justice Brennan added his reasons:

> Without these safeguards, it may prove too burdensome to seek review of the censor's determination. Particularly in the case of motion pictures, it may take very little to deter exhibition in a given locality. The exhibitor's stake in any one picture may be insufficient to warrant a protracted and onerous course of litigation. The distributor, on the other hand, may be equally unwilling to accept the burdens and delays of litigation in a particular area when, without such difficulties, he can freely exhibit his film in most of the rest of the country; for we are told that only four States and a handful of municipalities have active censorship laws.[64]

Justice Douglas, with Justice Black joining, concurred. He reiterated his view that "movies are entitled to the same degree and kind of

64. *Freedman v. Maryland,* 380 U.S.
51, 60, 58–59 (1965).

protection under the First Amendment as other forms of expression."
He adhered to his previous position on prior restraint: "I would put an
end to all forms and types of censorship and give full literal meaning to
the command of the First Amendment." [65]

The Supreme Court has insisted upon strict conformity with the
conditions laid down in *Freedman*. In *Teitel Film Corp. v. Cusack* it
invalidated, per curiam, the Chicago Motion Picture Ordinance, altered somewhat from the period of *Times Film*, because it contemplated fifty to fifty-seven days to complete administrative proceedings
before initiation of judicial proceedings and contained no provision
for a prompt judicial decision.[66]

In sum, it is hard to say how much vitality the doctrine of prior
restraint retains at the present time. Starting out in *Near* as a hard and
fast rule, though with "exceptions," it has been applied loosely to areas
beyond its original scope and limited drastically in some areas central
to its original purpose. Thus use of the doctrine in the tax cases is
possible only by giving it a meaning that would make it applicable to
virtually all types of regulation which have an inhibiting effect upon
First Amendment freedom. When employed in this way the concept
becomes so broad as to be worthless as a legal rule. In leaflet distribution, canvassing, and assembly permit cases, the doctrine has likewise
not been utilized with precision, being applied primarily to strike down
regulations that were considered too broad. In movie censorship systems, a "classic" form of prior restraint, the doctrine has been limited
to procedural requirements. The result of all this is that, to a substantial extent, a "prior restraint" now merely signifies a type of restriction
that the courts will scrutinize with special care.

Yet the doctrine surely has more blood in it than this summary
would indicate. It is hard to believe that the courts would allow prior
restraint of book and magazine publishing to be carried beyond that
permitted in *Kingsley Books*. The doctrine would probably be revital-
ized to strike down even that much censorship of the press. The doc-

---

65. 380 U.S. at 61–62.

66. *Teitel Film Corp. v. Cusack,* 390
U.S. 139 (1968). Accord is *Trans-Lux
Distributing Corp. v. Board of Regents,*
380 U.S. 259 (1965). For an earlier case
in which the Court found procedurally
inadequate an informal system of censorship, see *Bantam Books, Inc. v. Sullivan,*
372 U.S. 58 (1963), discussed *infra*. In
Interstate Circuit Inc. v. City of Dallas,
390 U.S. 676 (1968), the Court indicated
approval of the procedural provisions in
a Dallas ordinance. See also the *Marcus*
and *Quantity of Books* cases, discussed
in the next section. For further discussion
see Henry P. Monaghan, "First Amendment 'Due Process,'" *Harvard Law Review,* Vol. 83 (1970) p. 518.

trine of prior restraint should not therefore be written off as obsolete or impractical of application. It showed considerable promise in *Near* and that promise may yet be realized.

C. Other Aspects of Obscenity

From the viewpoint of pure First Amendment theory, the central problems of obscenity laws lie in the definition of standards of obscenity and in the doctrine of prior restraint. From a broader perspective, looking at the actual impact of obscenity laws upon our system of freedom of expression, many other factors play a crucial role. Thus the courts have dealt with a great variety of collateral issues, mostly procedural in nature, that bear upon the manner in which the obscenity laws are in practice applied. In addition, the exertion of official pressures on an informal basis, and particularly the efforts by the mass media and private groups to impose nonlegal controls, are important features of the total picture.

After drastically limiting the prior restraint doctrine in movie censorship cases, the Supreme Court undertook to impose severe procedural restrictions upon the operation of censorship systems. This tactic is characteristic of the position taken by the Court throughout the whole area of obscenity. Having adopted more relaxed rules for obscenity controls than for any other restrictions on expression the Court, as if to compensate for the inadequacy of its basic standards, has developed peripheral protections for alleged obscene expression more intensively than in any other sphere.

The rule against vagueness has been used extensively, and not entirely consistently, to strike down legislation that attempts to restrict expression beyond the area of "obscenity." In *Winters v. New York,* the Court invalidated on vagueness grounds a New York statute that prohibited the publication of material "devoted to . . . and principally made up of criminal news, police reports, or accounts of criminal deeds of bloodshed, lust or crime." In *Burstyn v. Wilson,* it ruled unconstitutional the denial of a license to a film, *The Miracle,* under the standard of "sacrilegious." The Court has also rejected such standards as: "of such character as to be prejudicial to the best interests of the people of said city"; "moral, educational or amusing and harmless";

"immoral" and "tend to corrupt morals"; and "approve such films . . . which are moral and proper . . . [and] disapprove such as are cruel, obscene, indecent, or immoral, or such as tend to debase or corrupt morals." On the other hand, in *Winters v. New York* the Court said that terms like "obscene," "lewd," "lascivious," "filthy," and "indecent," all of which are construed to carry the same meaning, have that "permissible uncertainty . . . caused by describing crimes by words well understood through long use in the criminal law." In *Roth* the Court expressly upheld the same terms, quoting an earlier statement that "the Constitution does not require impossible standards." In *Mishkin* Justice Brennan refused to consider the merits of the contention that the terms "sadistic" and "masochistic" were unduly vague because the State court had interpreted them as synonymous with "obscene." [67]

The Supreme Court has also used the vagueness doctrine to impose some limits on the regulation of children's "obscenity," otherwise largely unlimited under the "irrational" test. It upheld the statute in *Ginsberg* against a vagueness challenge. But in *Interstate Circuit, Inc. v. City of Dallas* it found too vague such standards as "describing or portraying . . . sexual promiscuity or extra-marital or abnormal sexual relations in such a manner as to be, in the judgment of the Board, likely to incite or encourage delinquency or sexual promiscuity on the part of young persons or to appeal to their prurient interest." In *Rabeck v. New York* it struck down an earlier New York statute that prohibited sale of any magazines "which would appeal to the lust of persons under the age of eighteen years or to their curiosity as to sex or to the anatomical differences between the sexes." [68]

The Supreme Court has also called into service other doctrines to soften the impact of obscenity legislation. In *Smith v. California* it insisted that obscenity laws incorporate a strict scienter requirement, invalidating a statute which imposed criminal liability upon a bookseller for possessing or selling an obscene book when there was no proof of his knowledge of its content. In *Marcus v. Search Warrant* and in *A Quantity of Copies of Books v. Kansas*, the Court imposed rigid re-

67. *Winters v. New York,* 333 U.S. 507, 518 (1948); *Burstyn v. Wilson,* 343 U.S. 495 (1952); *Gelling v. Texas,* 343 U.S. 960 (1952); *Superior Films, Inc. v. Department of Education,* 346 U.S. 587 (1954); *Commercial Pictures Corp. v. Regents,* 346 U.S. 587 (1954); *Holmby Productions, Inc. v. Vaughn,* 350 U.S. 870 (1955); *Roth v. United States,* 354 U.S. 476 (1957); *Mishkin v. New York,* 383 U.S. 502, 506 (1966).

68. *Interstate Circuit, Inc. v. City of Dallas,* 390 U.S. 676, 681 (1968); *Rabeck v. New York,* 391 U.S. 462 (1968).

quirements for search and seizure of obscene materials, holding that there must be specific description of the publications to be seized and a prior judicial determination that the materials were obscene. Some of the justices of the Court, in *Manual Enterprises, Inc. v. Day,* have questioned the procedures of the Post Office in excluding obscene material from the mails. Many other collateral issues, including questions of evidence, expert testimony, burden of proof, role of the judge and jury, and the scope of judicial review, have a significant bearing on the operation of obscenity laws and will in due time receive Supreme Court attention.[69]

Extralegal controls, as noted above, may take the form of informal pressures by police or prosecuting officials to discourage dissemination of material thought by portions of the community to be obscene. Or they may be entirely unofficial in nature. Thus some sections of the mass media have adopted industry codes, such as the Motion Picture Production Code, or other schemes of self-regulation. In addition, religious or other private groups undertake to enforce their own standards through publicity, boycotts, and similar measures. For many reasons, including the emotional content of the obscenity issue and the vulnerability of various commercial enterprises, all these pressures can play a major role in the system of freedom of expression. Their general effect, running counter to the procedural protections which the Supreme Court has thrown up around formal obscenity controls, is to increase the degree of restriction within the system.

The Supreme Court has had little occasion thus far to pass upon issues growing out of the complex of informal obscenity controls. But it has dealt with some aspects of the problem in one important case. In *Bantam Books, Inc. v. Sullivan* the Court considered a Rhode Island statute which created a Commission "to educate the public concerning any book . . . or other thing containing obscene, indecent or impure language, or manifestly tending to the corruption of youth as defined [in other sections] and to investigate and recommend the prosecution

69. *Smith v. California,* 361 U.S. 147 (1959); *Marcus v. Search Warrant,* 367 U.S. 717 (1961); *A Quantity of Copies of Books v. Kansas,* 378 U.S. 205 (1964), with which *Lee Art Theater, Inc. v. Virginia,* 392 U.S. 636 (1968), is in accord; *Manual Enterprises, Inc. v. Day,* 370 U.S. 478 (1962). See also John P. Frank, "Obscenity: Some Problems of Values and the Use of Experts," *Washington Law* *Review,* Vol. 41 (1966), p. 631; Monaghan, *op. cit. supra* note 2, pp. 150–154; *Political and Civil Rights in the United States,* pp. 798–802, 820–823, 792–794. With reference to judicial controls over Post Office and Customs laws and regulations on obscenity see Paul and Schwartz, *op. cit. supra* note 3; *Political and Civil Rights in the United States,* pp. 824–831.

of all violations of said sections." In practice the Commission sent notices to booksellers informing them that certain books were objectionable for minors, indicating that copies of the notices had been sent to the local police, reminding the distributor that the Commission had power to recommend prosecution, and asking them to cooperate. Out-of-state publishers sought an injunction and declaratory judgment. The Supreme Court held the law and its administration unconstitutional, saying: "We are not the first court to look through forms to the substance and recognize that informal censorship may sufficiently inhibit the circulation of publications to warrant injunctive relief." The underlying philosophy of the Court is well expressed in the following paragraph:

> Thus, the Fourteenth Amendment requires that regulation by the States of obscenity conform to procedures that will ensure against the curtailment of constitutionally protected expression, which is often separated from obscenity only by a dim and uncertain line. It is characteristic of the freedoms of expression in general that they are vulnerable to gravely damaging yet barely visible encroachments. Our insistence that regulations of obscenity scrupulously embody the most rigorous procedural safeguards . . . is therefore but a special instance of the larger principle that the freedoms of expression must be ringed about with adequate bulwarks. . . . "[T]he line between speech unconditionally guaranteed and speech which may legitimately be regulated . . . is finely drawn. . . . The separation of legitimate from illegitimate speech calls for . . . sensitive tools. . . ." *Speiser v. Randall,* 357 U.S. 513, 525.[70]

The Supreme Court's concern with developing "sensitive tools" to separate obscenity from non-obscenity is fully justified. Such devices would be necessary under any kind of obscenity controls. But they cannot be considered a satisfactory substitute for bringing the basic standards for obscenity regulation more fully into line with the requirements of a system of freedom of expression.

---

70. *Bantam Books, Inc. v. Sullivan,* 372 U.S. 58, 67, 66 (1963). For a collection of materials on extralegal controls of obscenity, see *Political and Civil Rights in the United States,* pp. 831–838.

XIV

Libel and Privacy

Generally speaking, the law of libel seeks to protect various individual interests against injury resulting from false and defamatory communication. It thus runs squarely into the right to freedom of expression. The law of privacy attempts to secure a segment of the private life of an individual against invasion by outsiders. Insofar as that invasion takes the form of communication, whether true or false, privacy law may also oppose the right to freedom of expression. Until recently it was assumed that the law of libel and the law of privacy simply constituted exceptions to the law of the First Amendment. But it is now fully recognized that the problems cannot be resolved that easily. They remain among the most complex and troublesome in the whole field of First Amendment doctrine.

Libel law and privacy law have in common the fact that both deal with interests that are more individual and private in character than social or public. In both the injury is peculiar to the individual, rather than shared with others, and may concern the most intimate aspects of the person's life. It is to be noted, however, that the long-range trend of the law has been different in the two situations. The law of libel has been subject to restrictive forces that push in the direction of allowing more and more controversies over alleged defamation to be settled in the marketplace. The law of privacy, on the other hand, has tended to expand, and thus to withdraw greater areas from the collective arena. These trends are not inconsistent. The fact seems to be that the two areas of law are tending to merge.[1]

1. This chapter deals only with civil libel, designed to protect individual interests, and criminal libel to the extent that it serves the same purpose. Criminal libel, insofar as it seeks to protect social interests, and group libel are considered in Chapter X.

A. Libel

The modern law of libel has its roots in criminal and civil forms of action that were designed primarily to protect the government against criticism or to prevent breach of the peace by persons resorting to self-help in defense of their honor. In its present form the action for libel no longer serves these functions. Rather it is intended to protect the individual against unfair damage to his reputation. Roughly speaking, it applies to a communication that subjects a person to ridicule, hatred or contempt in his community or lowers him in the estimation of his fellows. The precise interests jeopardized by such damage to reputation have never been fully agreed upon. But they may be said to include:

(1) Injury in one's trade, profession or other economic pursuits.

(2) Injury to prestige or standing in the community, which affects one's position as decision maker or participant in the community.

(3) Injury to feelings, arising out of an affront to one's dignity, distortion of one's identity, reflection on one's honor, or lessening of the approval of one's peers.

Protection of these interests is afforded through a civil action for damages brought by the person claiming to be defamed. In such suit the truth of the statement made constitutes a defense. Thus, while the burden of proving truth may be on the defendant, recovery is allowed only if the statement is found to be false. In some states the rights of the person defamed may also be enforced through criminal prosecution.[2]

The law of libel, as summarized thus far, would seem to open up vast opportunities for trying out the merits of numerous controversies in the forum supplied by the courts. But this has not been the case. One main reason is that the courts have increasingly interposed various qualifications stringently limiting the scope of the action for libel. These limitations include the exclusion of organizations and groups from access to the libel suit; the absolute immunity granted to judges,

2. In a few jurisdictions truth alone is not a defense but has to be accompanied by a showing that the statement was published with good motives and for justifi- able ends. See Fowler V. Harper and Fleming James, Jr., *The Law of Torts* (Boston, Little, Brown & Co., 1956), Vol. I, §5.20.

legislators and, recently, executive officials with respect to matters connected by even the thinnest thread to the performance of their functions; the right to report official documents and official proceedings; the privilege of fair comment; and other similar rules. As Professor Leon Green has said, "No other formula of the law promises so much and delivers so little." [3]

The impact of libel laws on the system of free expression has also been limited by the practical obstacles to maintaining a successful suit. Litigation is likely to be protracted. Delay is sure. Results are uncertain. Damages are speculative. Attitudes of judges, lawyers and the public all tend to be unfavorable.

The result is that public and private controversies have normally been carried on without recourse to libel litigation. The law of libel may well have affected the style of controversy. It undoubtedly has had an impact upon the press, both in supplying pressure for accuracy and in limiting material that is published. But on the whole the role of libel law in the system of freedom of expression has been relatively minor and essentially erratic. [4]

The increasing limitations imposed on the action for libel reflected the change in function served by the libel law as it moved from protection of social to protection of individual interests. The restrictions likewise reflected, an aspect of the same tendency, the recognition that the system of freedom of expression demanded greater space for freewheeling controversy than the original libel law technically allowed. But these factors were seldom explicitly articulated as problems of reconciling the law of libel with the law of the First Amendment. The Supreme Court was not called upon to decide the issue directly. In several dicta, however, the Court had accepted the proposition that the libel laws were simply not affected by the First Amendment. The state-

3. Leon Green, "The Right to Communicate," *New York University Law Review*, Vol. 35 (1960), pp. 903, 907.

4. Generally on the law of libel see, Harper and James, *op. cit. supra* note 2, ch. 5; William L. Prosser, *Handbook of the Law of Torts* (St. Paul, West Publishing Co., 3d ed. 1964), ch. 21; Van Vechten Veeder, "The History and Theory of the Law of Defamation," *Columbia Law Review*, Vol. 3 (1903), p. 546, and Vol. 4 (1904), p. 33; David Riesman, "Democracy and Defamation," *Columbia Law Review*, Vol. 42 (1942), pp. 1085, 1282; Richard C. Donnelly, "History of Defamation," *Wisconsin Law Review*, Vol. 1949 (1949), p. 99; Note, "Developments in the Law—Defamation," *Harvard Law Review*, Vol. 69 (1956), p. 875. Other material is cited in Thomas I. Emerson, David Haber and Norman Dorsen, *Political and Civil Rights in the United States* (Boston, Little, Brown & Co., 3d ed. 1967), pp. 722–732 (cited hereafter in this chapter as *Political and Civil Rights in the United States*).

ment of Justice Murphy in *Chaplinsky v. New Hampshire,* mentioned
earlier, expressed the accepted view:

> Allowing the broadest scope to the language and purpose of the Four-
> teenth Amendment [as it incorporated the First Amendment], it is well
> understood that the right of free speech is not absolute at all times and
> under all circumstances. There are certain well-defined and narrowly
> limited classes of speech, the prevention and punishment of which have
> never been thought to raise any Constitutional problem. These include
> the lewd and obscene, the profane, the libelous, and the insulting or
> "fighting" words—those which by their very utterance inflict injury or
> tend to incite an immediate breach of the peace. It has been well ob-
> served that such utterances are no essential part of any exposition of
> ideas, and are of such slight social value as a step to truth that any
> benefit that may be derived from them is clearly outweighed by the
> social interest in order and morality.[5]

Only Justice Black took another position. He found the law of libel
incompatible with the First Amendment and would have held all libel
laws, State and Federal, unconstitutional.[6]

Such was the situation when the issues were precipitated by way of
a formidable attack on freedom of expression growing out of the civil-
rights struggle. In 1964, in *New York Times v. Sullivan,* the Supreme
Court was forced to face the problem squarely. In that case, and in
decisions immediately following, the Court at last undertook to bring
the law of libel into harmony with the First Amendment.

1. *NEW YORK TIMES* AND PROGENY

In *New York Times* the action was brought by L. B. Sullivan, Commissioner of Public Affairs in Montgomery, Alabama. He alleged that
he had been libeled by an advertisement published in *The New York*

5. *Chaplinsky v. New Hampshire,* 315
U.S. 568, 571–572 (1942). Similar dicta
appear in *Near v. Minnesota,* 283 U.S.
697, 707–708 (1931); *Beauharnais v.
Illinois,* 343 U.S. 250, 254–261 (1952);
Roth v. United States, 354 U.S. 476, 482–
483 (1957). The *Beauharnais* case, upholding the Illinois group libel law, could
be considered a direct holding. See Chapter X.

6. Edmond Cahn, "Justice Black and

First Amendment 'Absolutes': A Public
Interview," *New York University Law
Review,* Vol. 37 (1962), pp. 549, 557–
558. There was very little discussion of
the problem by commentators. But see
Harry Kalven, Jr., "The Law of Defamation and the First Amendment," in University of Chicago Law School, *Conference on the Arts, Publishing and the Law*
(1952), p. 3.

Times by the Committee to Defend Martin Luther King and the Struggle for Freedom in the South. The charge was based on two paragraphs of the advertisement, which read:

> In Montgomery, Alabama, after students sang "My Country, 'Tis of Thee" on the State Capitol steps, their leaders were expelled from school, and truckloads of police armed with shotguns and tear-gas ringed the Alabama State College Campus. When the entire student body protested to state authorities by refusing to re-register, their dining hall was padlocked in an attempt to starve them into submission.
>
> Again and again the Southern violators have answered Dr. King's peaceful protests with intimidation and violence. They have bombed his home almost killing his wife and child. They have assaulted his person. They have arrested him seven times—for "speeding," "loitering" and similar "offenses." And now they have charged him with "perjury"—a *felony* under which they could imprison him for *ten years* . . .[7]

Some of the statements made in these paragraphs were not correct. The students sang the National Anthem, not "My Country, 'Tis of Thee." The students were expelled for demanding service at a lunch counter, not for leading a demonstration on the Capitol steps. Most, but not all, of the students protested the expulsion; and the protest took the form of boycotting classes for a day, not refusing to register. No students were barred from eating except those without meal tickets. Police were deployed near the campus in large numbers, but did not "ring" it. King was arrested four times, not seven.

The suit was tried in accordance with Alabama libel law and a jury awarded Sullivan $500,000 in damages. The Supreme Court of Alabama affirmed. Similar suits had been brought by other plaintiffs in Alabama against *The New York Times* claiming damages of $5,600,-000; and suits against Columbia Broadcasting System totaled $1,700,-000.

Faced with these circumstances the United States Supreme Court unanimously reversed, holding that the Alabama libel law applied in the case did not meet the requirements of the First Amendment. Justice Brennan, writing for six members of the Court, first disposed of the earlier dicta that had placed the libel laws outside the First Amendment. None of those statements, he said, "sustained the use of libel laws to impose sanctions upon expression critical of the official conduct of public officials." He went on more broadly: "[L]ibel can claim

7. *New York Times v. Sullivan,* 376 U.S. 254, 257–258 (1964).

no talismanic immunity from constitutional limitations. It must be measured by standards that satisfy the First Amendment." Thus, in a single paragraph, the wall of separation between libel and the First Amendment came tumbling down.[8]

Justice Brennan then turned his attention to applying the First Amendment in the libel area. Summarizing previous statements of the Court on the underlying purposes of the First Amendment he concluded: "Thus we consider this case against the background of a profound national commitment to the principle that debate on public issues should be uninhibited, robust, and wide-open, and that it may well include vehement, caustic, and sometimes unpleasantly sharp attacks on governmental and public officials." The advertisement involved, he pointed out, was "an expression of grievance and protest on one of the major public issues of our time," and "would seem clearly to qualify for the constitutional protection." The issue resolved itself, then, into the question whether the communication "forfeits that protection by the falsity of some of its factual statements and by its alleged defamation of respondent." [9]

Having thus framed the issues, Justice Brennan held that neither factual error nor injury to official reputation, nor the combination of both, afforded "warrant for repressing speech which would otherwise be free." As to the injury to official reputation, a law punishing criticism of public officials would constitute a return to the old law of seditious libel, typified by the Sedition Act of 1798, and would violate "the central meaning of the First Amendment. . . . The right of free public discussion of the stewardship of public officials," he paraphrased Madison, is "a fundamental principle of the American form of government." On the issue of falsity, Justice Brennan rested his conclusion on two grounds. The first was that "erroneous statement is inevitable in free debate and . . . must be protected if the freedoms of expression are to have the 'breathing space' that they 'need . . . to survive.' " The second ground was:

> A rule compelling the critic of official conduct to guarantee the truth of all his factual assertions—and to do so on pain of libel judgments virtually unlimited in amount—leads to . . . "self-censorship." Allowance of the defense of truth, with the burden of proving it on the defendant, does not mean that only false speech will be deterred. . . .

8. 376 U.S. at 268, 269. Compare Justice Brennan on obscenity, *supra* Chapter XIII.

9. 376 U.S. at 270, 271.

Under such a rule, would-be critics of official conduct may be deterred from voicing their criticism, even though it is believed to be true and even though it is in fact true, because of doubt whether it can be proved in court or fear of the expense of having to do so. They tend to make only statements which "steer far wider of the unlawful zone." . . . The rule thus dampens the vigor and limits the variety of public debate.[10]

Reaching the final step in his argument, Justice Brennan stated the rule of libel law that would satisfy the demands of the First Amendment:

The constitutional guarantees require, we think, a federal rule that prohibits a public official from recovering damages for a defamatory falsehood relating to his official conduct unless he proves that the statement was made with "actual malice"—that is, with knowledge that it was false or with reckless disregard of whether it was false or not.[11]

Justice Brennan did not explain further why he cut off the right to speak at this point. He did note that the rule "is appropriately analogous to the protection accorded a public official when *he* is sued by a private citizen." A similar privilege should be given "the citizen-critic of government": "It is as much his duty to criticize as it is the official's duty to administer." [12]

Applying the rule of actual malice to the case before him, Justice Brennan held that it was impossible to tell from the record whether the principle had been followed, and remanded the case. Significantly, the Court did not stop there. It felt that, since Sullivan might seek a new trial, "considerations of effective judicial administration require us to review the evidence in the present record to determine whether it could constitutionally support a judgment for respondent." The Court thereupon made "an independent examination of the whole record" and concluded that (1) "the proof presented to show actual malice lacks the convincing clarity which the constitutional standard demands, and hence . . . would not constitutionally sustain the judgment for respondent under the proper rule of law"; (2) the evidence was "constitutionally defective in another respect: it was incapable of supporting the jury's finding that the allegedly libelous statements were made 'of and concerning' respondent." Finally the Court indicated that, if necessary, it would also consider whether the "dis-

10. 376 U.S. at 272, 273, 275, 271–272, 279.

11. 376 U.S. at 279–280.

12. 376 U.S. at 282.

crepancies between what was true and what was asserted were sufficient to injure respondent's reputation." [13]

Three members of the Court concurred but thought that the majority had not gone far enough. Justice Black, joined by Justice Douglas, took the position that an "unconditional right to say what one pleases about public affairs is . . . the minimum guarantee of the First Amendment." He felt that malice is "an elusive, abstract concept, hard to prove and hard to disprove"; that it "provides at best an evanescent protection"; and that the record "certainly does not indicate that any different verdict would have been rendered here whatever the Court had charged the jury about 'malice' . . . or any other legal formulas which in theory would protect the press." [14]

Justice Goldberg, with Justice Douglas agreeing, felt that the First Amendment afforded "to the citizen and to the press an absolute, unconditional privilege to criticize official conduct despite the harm which may flow from excesses and abuses." The right to speak out about "public officials and affairs," he said, "should not depend upon a probing by the jury of the motivation of the citizen or press." [15]

New York Times v. Sullivan, without any doubt, is a landmark decision. The Court unanimously agreed that libel laws would have to be brought into conformity with the system of freedom of expression. It based its conclusion on fundamental principles underlying the First Amendment, applied in a functional and realistic manner. There was disagreement, however, as to how far the First Amendment protection extended. Many other questions, of doctrine and application, remained open. As subsequent cases unfolded the Court became more and more fragmented.

The next case, *Garrison v. Louisiana,* involved criminal rather than civil libel. Garrison, the District Attorney in New Orleans, had issued a statement at a press conference charging that the large backlog of pending criminal cases was due to the inefficiency, laziness and excessive vacations of the judges, and that, by refusing to authorize disbursements for investigation of vice, the judges had hampered his efforts to enforce the vice laws. "This raises interesting questions about the racketeer influences on our vacation-minded judges," he added. Garrison was prosecuted and convicted under the Louisiana criminal libel law.[16]

---

13. 376 U.S. at 284–289.
14. 376 U.S. at 297, 293, 295.
15. 376 U.S. at 298.

16. *Garrison v. Louisiana,* 379 U.S. 64 (1964), also discussed in Chapter X.

The Supreme Court's opinion reversing the conviction was again written by Justice Brennan. Like *New York Times,* the case involved criticism of public officials for official conduct. In this situation, Justice Brennan ruled, criminal libel laws serve the same interests as civil libel laws and for the same reasons must conform to the rule of actual malice. Justice Brennan then went on to explain why the line should be drawn at actual malice rather than at full immunity. "Calculated falsehood," he said, is "no essential part of any exposition of ideas" and hence should enjoy no constitutional protection.[17]

Justice Brennan took up one additional point—the line between criticism of public officials and "private defamation." Even though Garrison's statement affected the private reputation of the judges, nevertheless it was relevant to their fitness for office and hence fell within the "public official" rule. The Court did not find it necessary to examine the evidence further, since the Louisiana statute itself was invalid in not allowing for the actual malice defense.[18]

Justices Black and Douglas concurred, each writing a separate opinion. They reiterated their view that the actual malice rule was inadequate and would have held all criminal libel laws invalid. Justice Goldberg also concurred, holding to his position that there should be an "unconditional freedom to criticize official conduct." [19]

In *Rosenblatt v. Baer* the Supreme Court began to explore the question of how far the First Amendment protection extended into public officialdom. A newspaper columnist had criticized the operation of a State recreation center and ski resort of which Baer had been Supervisor. The column in question asked, "What happened to all the money last year? and every other year?" Baer brought suit for libel, alleging the column had imputed mismanagement and peculation to him. The Court reversed a judgment for Baer and remanded for a new trial.[20]

Justice Brennan, this time writing for only three members of the Court, put the decision on two grounds. First, examining the evidence and instructions to the jury, he saw error in the failure to require the jury to find that Rosenblatt's statement had specifically referred to Baer rather than merely to a group of officials of which Baer was one. Second, Justice Brennan found that Baer was a "public official" under

17. 379 U.S. at 75.
18. 379 U.S. at 76, 77.
19. 379 U.S. at 88. In a subsequent criminal libel case, also involving criticism of a public official, the Court reversed per curiam. *Henry v. Collins,* 380 U.S. 356 (1965).

20. *Rosenblatt v. Baer,* 383 U.S. 75 (1966).

the *New York Times* doctrine and that the trial court erred in not applying the actual malice rule. He considered it unnecessary to draw "precise lines" for purposes of determining who was a "public official." But he did say that "the 'public official' designation applies at the very least to those among the hierarchy of government employees who have, or appear to the public to have, substantial responsibility for or control over the conduct of governmental affairs." [21]

Justice Douglas concurred but thought that the question should be "whether a public *issue,* not a public official, is involved." Justice Black, with Justice Douglas joining, concurred in the reversal but not in the remanding. Justice Fortas, who had taken Justice Goldberg's place, dissented on the ground that the trial had occurred before the Supreme Court decision in *New York Times,* that the issues were not shaped in accordance with that decision, and that therefore the writ of certiorari was improvidently granted. Justice Clark concurred in the result without opinion. Justice Stewart concurred in the Brennan opinion but stressed that the *New York Times* rule should be applied only "where a State's law of defamation has been unconstitutionally converted into a law of seditious libel." Justice Harlan concurred but dissented from part of the Brennan reasoning with regard to application of the statements made in the column to Baer.[22]

The disagreement foreshadowed in *Rosenblatt* came to full flower in the 1967 decisions in *Curtis Publishing Co. v. Butts* and *Associated Press v. Walker.* In the first case the *Saturday Evening Post* had published an article asserting that, prior to a football game between the University of Georgia and the University of Alabama in 1962, Wallace Butts, athletic director at Georgia, had given to Paul Bryant, Alabama coach, "Georgia's plays, defensive patterns, all the significant secrets Georgia's football team possessed." Butts filed a libel action and the jury returned a verdict for $60,000 general damages and $3,000,000 punitive damages, which were reduced to a total of $460,-000 by the trial judge. The second case was brought by General Edwin A. Walker, a well-known and outspoken retired army officer. He alleged that he had been libeled by an Associated Press report which said that, during the riot at the University of Mississippi over the admission

21. 383 U.S. at 85.

22. 383 U.S. at 91, 93. In a case decided the same day as *Rosenblatt v. Baer* the Court held in a five to four decision that a libel suit growing out of a National Labor Relations Board election was not preempted by the Federal legislation and could be maintained in the State courts. *Linn v. Plant Guard Workers,* 383 U.S. 53 (1966). Justice Fortas, dissenting, took occasion to note the subjectivity of the actual malice rule.

of James Meredith, General Walker "had taken command of the violent crowd and had personally led a charge against the federal marshals." Walker obtained a verdict of $500,000 compensatory damages and $300,000 punitive damages.[23]

The Supreme Court unanimously reversed the *Walker* case, but affirmed the *Butts* case by a vote of five to four. The justices split into four groups:

(1) Justice Harlan, joined by Justices Clark, Stewart and Fortas, took the position that the *New York Times* rule of actual malice should not be extended to "public figures" who were not "public officials." Actions for libel brought by "public officials" were analogous to seditious libel and hence had to be allowed with "extreme caution." But criticism of "public figures" was better governed by "the rules of liability which prevail in our society with respect to compensation of persons injured by the improper performance of a legitimate activity by another." Allowing for the free speech interest, the rule in such cases should be that damages could be obtained "on a showing of highly unreasonable conduct constituting an extreme departure from the standards of investigation and reporting ordinarily adhered to by responsible publishers." Examining the evidence and findings in the two cases, these justices concluded that their standard was satisfied in the *Butts* case but not in the *Walker* case. Hence they voted to affirm in *Butts* and reverse in *Walker*.[24]

(2) Chief Justice Warren voted to apply the *New York Times* standard of actual malice to "public figures" as well as "public officials." In his view, "differentiation between 'public figures' and 'public officials' and adoption of separate standards of proof for each has no basis in law, logic, or First Amendment policy." Chief Justice Warren then reviewed the trial judge's instructions to the jury and the evidence adduced in each case. He concluded the standard had not been met in the *Walker* case but that it had been in the *Butts* case. He thus cast the fifth vote for Butts, resulting in the affirmance of that case.[25]

(3) Justices Brennan and White agreed with Chief Justice Warren that the rule of actual malice should apply to the public figures involved in the two cases, and agreed with him that this required reversal in the *Walker* case. They also agreed that the evidence would support the verdict for Butts under the doctrine of actual malice. But they

---

23. *Curtis Publishing Co. v. Butts* and *Associated Press v. Walker*, 388 U.S. 130 (1967). Both cases were dealt with in the same opinion.

24. 388 U.S. at 153, 154, 155.
25. 388 U.S. at 163.

voted to reverse in *Butts* because the trial judge's charge to the jury did not conform to that standard.

(4) Justices Black and Douglas held to their view that libel laws should not be used to limit discussion of public issues. Their vote was to reverse in both cases.[26]

The Supreme Court's attempt to harmonize the law of libel and the law of the First Amendment has thus produced some measure of agreement. The position that libel laws are simply outside the First Amendment no longer prevails; it is agreed that such laws do raise issues under that provision. It is also agreed that, so far as libel laws operate to limit criticism of public officials and thereby function as seditious libel laws, they must conform at least to the rule of actual malice. Beyond this there are serious differences of opinion within the Court. There is no agreement on (1) the general doctrine that should be employed in considering the application of the First Amendment in the libel field; (2) the degree of protection that the First Amendment should afford; or (3) the area to which that protection should be extended.[27]

2. THE GENERAL THEORY

In reading the Supreme Court decisions in the libel cases one is struck by the fact that the Court does not appear to have invoked the traditional formulae for deciding First Amendment cases. As already noted, the Court quickly abandons the original facile solution of arbitrarily exempting certain areas of speech from First Amendment pro-

26. Many of the same issues involved in the libel cases were discussed also in *Time v. Hill*, 385 U.S. 374 (1967), a privacy case decided a few months before *Butts* and *Walker*. *Time v. Hill* is considered in the next section. In *St. Amant v. Thompson*, 390 U.S. 727 (1968), decided the next year, the Court again reversed a State court libel judgment, applying the actual malice rule with strictness. Only Justice Fortas dissented. See also *Beckley Newspapers Corp. v. Hanks*, 389 U.S. 81 (1967).

27. For discussion of *New York Times* and its progeny see Harry Kalven, Jr., "The New York Times Case: A Note on 'The Central Meaning of the First Amendment,'" *Supreme Court Review*, Vol. 1964 (1964), p. 191 and "The Reasonable Man and the First Amendment: Hill, Butts, and Walker," *Supreme Court Review*, Vol. 1967 (1967), p. 267; Melville B. Nimmer, "The Right to Speak from *Times* to *Time*," *California Law Review*, Vol. 56 (1968), p. 935; and other materials cited in *Political and Civil Rights in the United States*, pp. 722–723. See also William J. Brennan, Jr., "The Supreme Court and the Meiklejohn Interpretation of the First Amendment," *Harvard Law Review*, Vol. 79 (1965), p. 1; J. Skelly Wright, "Defamation, Privacy and the Public's Right to Know," *Texas Law Review*, Vol. 46 (1968), p. 630.

tection—what Harry Kalven calls the two-level theory. Nor does it talk in terms of the clear and present danger test. This would not be surprising except for the fact that the closest analogy to libel of public officials is found in contempt of court by publication, and that is the one area in which the Court has utilized the clear and present danger test since the *Dennis* case. Furthermore the Court does not invoke the ad hoc balancing test, at least in its usual form. The opinions go beyond a simple weighing of the interest in reputation against the interest in free speech.

The approach the Court has taken is more an attempt to ascertain what is necessary or appropriate for maintaining in operation an effective system of freedom of expression. Thus Justice Brennan starts with an analysis of the functions performed by freedom of expression in a democratic society; considers the part played by derogatory criticism of public officials and by inaccurate or false statements; and looks at the consequences of applying various tests of truth, negligence, or malice. Justice Harlan follows a similar path, at least part of the way. Justice Stewart frames his position in terms of the extent to which libel laws operate as sedition laws. Justices Black and Douglas, not surprisingly, devote much of their opinions to the practical operation of the rules proposed.

The libel cases thus represent a significant advance in the treatment of First Amendment issues. One can quarrel with the particular views of the justices as to the functions of freedom of speech, or with their particular judgments concerning the impact of the various rules on the system. But the fact that the opinions are addressed to the fundamental purposes of a system of freedom of expression and the dynamics of that system in operation brings the Court closer to an effective theory of the First Amendment than it has been at any other point in the evolution of First Amendment doctrine.

However, the Court has by no means gone the full distance. Three major objections to its doctrinal analysis must be made. In the first place, the Court fails to accept the fundamental premise of the First Amendment that other social interests cannot be advanced through abridging freedom of expression. Rather, the Court seeks to accommodate interests and give effect to its preferences in resolving conflicts. Thus it is not enough for the Court that the punishment of intentionally false statements through the medium of the libel laws will substantially interfere with the operation of an effective system of freedom of expression. The Court decides that at some point this injury to the system is to be disregarded in favor of the government's interest in not being subject to attack by the citizen-critic. The resulting compromise, in effect, takes the Court back to the balancing test, although the balancing is now done at a more rewarding level. Only Justices Black and Douglas reject this approach.

Secondly, the majority, through Justice Brennan, reverts to earlier modes of thought at a critical point. When Justice Brennan faces the issue of whether "calculated falsehood" should be protected from libel action, he rules it is not entitled to protection on the ground that it is "no essential part of any exposition of ideas." This is a relapse to the two-level theory. More important, it is inconsistent with basic First Amendment theory. It fails to take into account that false statements, whether intentional or not, perform a significant function in a system of freedom of expression by forcing citizens to defend, justify and rethink their positions. Moreover, Justice Brennan's view disregards another tenet of First Amendment theory—that it is no part of the government's business to decide for the citizen-critic what is of social value in communication and what is not. Thus, at a key place in the doctrinal analysis the Court loses its way.

Thirdly, while the Court made some attempt to formulate rules in light of the dynamics of a system of freedom of expression, it seems to have ventured in this direction half-heartedly. Thus, except for Justice Black, it made no real effort to work out rules that were susceptible of effective administration. These aspects of First Amendment theory have not been fully accepted.

In general the majority of the Court fails to appreciate how inconsistent are the concepts underlying libel law with those underlying a system of freedom of expression. In its original form, as a method of preventing criticism of government or breach of the peace, libel law was in flat contradiction with the objectives of the First Amendment. This the Court recognizes in its concern over reinstating the law of seditious libel. The incompatibility persists, however, when libel law in its revised version seeks to protect individual interests in economic ventures, standing in the community, or general good feelings. The notion of encouraging "uninhibited, robust, and wide-open" expression, and "vehement, caustic, and sometimes unpleasantly sharp attacks"—an atmosphere of rough give-and-take—is scarcely in harmony with efforts to foster these interests. Resolution of intellectual controversies by judicial decision, or any form of government decision, is out of line with ideas of subjecting truth and near-truth, falsity and near-falsity, to the process of the marketplace. The superrefined attempts to separate statements of fact from opinions, to winnow truth out of a mass of conflicting evidence (but only a part of the total relevant material), to probe into intents, motives and purposes—all these do not easily fit into the dynamics of a system of freedom of expression.

In short, if one takes into account the fundamental purposes of free expression, looks carefully at the dynamics of its operation, and gives full weight to the initial balance struck against limiting its use, one would expect to find small room remaining for the law of libel. Just how large that area may be depends upon resolution of the specific issues next to be considered.

3. THE DEGREE OF PROTECTION AFFORDED BY THE FIRST AMENDMENT

It is difficult to discuss the degree of protection that should be afforded in the libel field by the First Amendment before having considered the question of coverage—what the First Amendment is being applied to. However, it would be equally or more difficult to discuss these issues in reverse order. In any event we start with the degree of protection issues and assume, for present purposes, that First Amendment coverage extends at least to communications dealing with "public issues" or "matters of public concern." The question is what rules of law should govern the application of the First Amendment in this area.

There is a substantial measure of agreement. It is accepted that all truthful statements are fully protected by the First Amendment, even though they may be defamatory and cause serious injury of the type the libel laws are presently designed to prevent. It is also accepted that not all false statements can be penalized by the libel laws. All the members of the Supreme Court agree that, as to false and defamatory statements made about "public officials" in their "official capacity," the First Amendment requires at least that "actual malice" be proved.[28]

At this point disagreement begins. One group takes the position that, not only as to "public officials" but also as to "public figures"

28. We are concerned at this point with liability in a libel action for false and defamatory statements of fact. The question of liability for defamatory comment or opinion is considered at the end of this subsection.

(and apparently as to all "public issues"), a showing of actual malice is necessary (and sufficient) to sustain a libel action. A second group believes that, outside the area of "public official," proof of "highly unreasonable conduct" should be grounds for recovery. The third group would grant full protection to all discussion of public issues, regardless of truth or falsity and without regard to tests of motive or care. A combination of the first and third groups among the justices in the *Butts* and *Walker* cases results in the "actual malice" rule controlling throughout the whole area of "public issues."

It would not seem necessary to add anything to what has already been said in support of the area of agreement—application of at least an actual malice rule to statements made about public officials in their official capacity. As Justice Brennan made clear in *New York Times,* a central function of the First Amendment is to guarantee the right of the citizen to criticize public officials, which means in effect frequently to defame them. To bind the citizen to a standard of truthfulness, as determined by a jury in a libel action, would so confine and hamper that right as largely to destroy it. Experience has clearly confirmed this judgment. Prior to the civil-rights controversy, the libel action had been used only sporadically, and on the whole ineffectively, as an instrument to silence attacks on public officials. But once the conditions arose in which the libel action came to be so used, and its potential became manifest, the Court could hardly refrain from taking action to protect the First Amendment right. A requirement that the plaintiff show actual malice—knowledge that the statement was false or reckless disregard of whether it was false or not—would seem to be the minimum degree of protection necessary to achieve that end.

The question whether the actual malice rule should be applied in all cases involving statements relating to public issues, or whether the "highly unreasonable conduct" rule should govern outside the public official area requires fuller consideration. In light of what has been said up to this point it seems fair to pose the issue by asking, Why should the First Amendment afford lesser protection to statements made in discussion of public issues generally than to statements made concerning public officials?

One thing seems clear at the outset. As far as an effective system of free expression depends upon affording protection for the speaker against retaliation for his speech, there is no reason for invoking a different rule in the two situations. No one disputes that the function of the First Amendment is to protect all communication dealing with public issues, not just that involving public officials. Indeed there is little doubt that, for purposes of decision making, what goes on in the nongovernment sector is as important as what takes place in the government sector. As Chief Justice Warren said in the *Butts* case, "Increasingly, in this country, the distinctions between governmental and private sectors are blurred." Hence the role of the First Amendment is the same in both areas. Likewise the needs of the system, in terms of practical operation, are the same. There is equal likelihood that errors will be made and that the risk of proving truth or reasonable care will lead to self-censorship. On the basis of all the factors underlying the actual malice rule as applied to public officials, therefore, the system of free expression would suffer serious damage if speakers were not given the same protection in discussing all kinds of public issues.[29]

From the viewpoint of an effective system of free expression, then, the only reason for not preferring the actual malice rule would be if operation of that rule would so discourage persons from entering into discussion of public issues that the system on balance would be adversely affected. It is possible that some persons who might otherwise participate in public discussion would refrain from doing so unless they were assured that the libel laws would effectively protect them against defamatory criticism. However, injury to the system of free expression from this source, at least on any significant scale, seems highly unlikely. In the absence of empirical evidence it certainly cannot be assumed. Under any circumstances it is inconceivable that the difference between the "highly unreasonable conduct" rule and the "actual malice" rule would be decisive.

This being so, the full protection theory of the First Amendment requires acceptance of the actual malice rule in preference to one affording less protection to the system. The basic principle—that expression cannot be suppressed or restricted for the purpose of achieving other interests—compels a decision to protect expression. Only by balancing the right of free expression against the interest in individual reputation can an argument be made for the "unreasonable conduct" rule.

Justice Harlan, in his opinion in *Butts* proposing the "unreasonable conduct" rule, does attempt such a weighing of interests. Unfortunately, like all such attempts, it is an exercise in futility. There is no satisfactory judicial technique for weighing the interest in free expression against the interest of the individual in preserving his reputation.

29. 388 U.S. at 163.

Justice Harlan can do no more than say there are important considerations on each side and conclude: "The fact that dissemination of information and opinion on questions of public concern is ordinarily a legitimate, protected and indeed cherished activity does not mean, however, that one may in all respects carry on that activity exempt from sanctions designed to safeguard the legitimate interests of others." On this approach the First Amendment stands wide open to any interpretation or application the current majority of justices cares to put on it.[30]

Actually, Justice Harlan elects to give minimal weight to First Amendment factors. His primary guide is taken from sources wholly outside the First Amendment context. It is the traditional law of tort— "the rules of liability which prevail in our society with respect to compensation of persons injured by the improper performance of a legitimate activity by another." Adding some First Amendment considerations to this base he reaches the rule of "highly unreasonable conduct." [31]

Finally, the specific reasons given for distinguishing the treatment of false statements made about public officials and similar statements made about public figures are not persuasive. Justice Harlan argues that the first comes close to seditious libel while the second does not. This is perhaps true. But it is irrelevant unless one also takes the position that the function of the First Amendment is confined to protection of expression addressed to the conduct of public officials. Of course no one urges that view. Justice Harlan also notes that a public official has complete immunity against libel action for statements made by him, whereas a private citizen enjoys no such privilege. This again is true, but hardly a forceful ground for distinction. The immunity of a public official to being a defendant in a libel suit has very little to do with the impact he makes on freedom of expression as a plaintiff.

This last point, however, requires further comment. The argument derived from official immunity is one aspect of the broader argument that public officials are in a better position to protect themselves against false statements and in any event have elected to make a career in an arena they know is open to sharp attack. This feeling probably lies at the root of the reluctance to treat private citizens in the same way as public officials. It carries some weight, but can scarcely be decisive. In the first place the ability to defend one's reputation in the

30. 388 U.S. at 150.   31. 388 U.S. at 154.

marketplace varies with the individual and the circumstances. Some private persons have greater opportunity for communication than some government officials. One cannot base a general rule upon this shifting factor. More important, the whole system of free expression in a democracy presupposes a citizenry that is geared to the rough and tumble of public controversy, in which the individual operating in the public arena is not essentially different from a government official. In a sense he is a government official, criticizing his public servants and participating in decisions of policy. To the extent he does this he should be subject to the same rules. This brings us back to the general proposition, stated earlier, that the fundamental assumptions underlying the law of libel are inconsistent with the fundamental assumptions of a system of free expression.

We come, then, to the final question, whether the actual malice rule affords sufficient protection to freedom of expression, or whether an unconditional privilege should be accorded the discussion of public issues. Again one conclusion stands out clearly: the actual malice rule is inadequate, on the Court's own rationale as well as for other reasons, to protect a system of freedom of expression.

In the first place, if the actual malice rule is right as far as it goes, then it does not go far enough. The test of actual malice is subject to the very same defects that led the majority of the Court to reject broader tests of liability. The dissenters are certainly right when they argue that malice is an elusive concept. Proof of "knowledge" that a statement is false involves proof of a mental state, and so in essence does proof of "reckless disregard" of whether a statement is true or false. Seldom are specific facts available to establish such matters on any objective basis. Rather, all the surrounding circumstances are put before the jury and it is asked to draw an inference from the total situation. In the end the requirement that malice be proved adds little or nothing to the requirement that mere falsity be shown, a test the Court rejects. The formula is not saved by the rule that the burden of proof is on the plaintiff and that actual malice must be established with "convincing clarity." Ultimately the case goes to the jury and the subtleties of burden of proof are not likely to be reflected in the final verdict.[32]

32. The argument that the actual malice rule is in practice small protection to the defendant is made in the opinions of Justices Black and Goldberg in *New York* *Times v. Sullivan,* 376 U.S. 254, 293, 297–298 (1964); of Justice Douglas in *Garrison v. Louisiana,* 379 U.S. 64, 81 (1964); of Justice Black in *Rosenblatt*

In fact the Court tacitly concedes that the malice rule cannot actually control the outcome of a libel suit. In *New York Times* itself the Court was unwilling merely to announce the rule and send the case back for retrial in accordance with the new principle. It carefully reviewed the evidence and itself drew the conclusions which the jury would be bound to reach. The Court followed the same procedure in the *Butts* and *Walker* cases. In short, the actual malice rule leaves the speaker with roughly the same degree of risk as the earlier rules of negligence and engenders approximately the same amount of self-censorship. If the system of free expression cannot function under one it cannot under the other.

Secondly, the rationale offered by the majority of the Court for drawing the line at actual malice is unconvincing. In *Garrison* it was explained:

> Calculated falsehood falls into that class of utterances which "are no essential part of any exposition of ideas, and are of such slight social value as a step to truth that any benefit that may be derived from them is clearly outweighed by the social interest in order and morality." . . . Hence the knowingly false statement and the false statement made with reckless disregard of the truth, do not enjoy constitutional protection.

Exactly the same could be said of negligent false statements, which the Court does protect. Moreover, the explanation ignores the whole point of the *New York Times* case, that the practical impact upon truthful speech is the decisive factor. In addition, as observed above, the refusal to give any value to false communication is contrary to the basic theory of the First Amendment; and it is not for the government to decide such questions in any event.[33]

Thirdly, the actual malice rule imposes on the Supreme Court an impossible problem of judicial administration. The application of the formula in the State courts can only be supervised through review in the Supreme Court on an individual case basis. In every libel case considered by the Supreme Court, except *Garrison*, which invalidated the entire statute, the Supreme Court has found it necessary to review the evidence, instructions and findings in complete detail. The very nature

---

v. Baer, 383 U.S. 75, 95 (1966); of Justice Fortas in *Linn v. Plant Guard Workers*, 383 U.S. 53, 70–71 (1966); and of Justice Douglas in *Time v. Hill*, 385 U.S. 374, 402 (1967).

33. 379 U.S. at 75. See also Justice Brennan's opinion in *Time v. Hill*, 385 U.S. 374, 389–390 (1967).

of the problem—to avoid unfair verdicts that dampen the exercise of free expression—makes this inevitable. Thus the constitutional protection is available only if the Supreme Court itself gives the matter individual attention. As Justice Black observes, this is the same dilemma that forced the Court in right of counsel cases to abandon earlier rules that could only be made effective through a case-to-case review.[34]

Finally, serious doubts must arise about a rule of law that requires a government agency to determine the truth or falsity of propositions advanced in debate over issues of public concern. This is certainly true if the matter is one of opinion, comment or judgment. But it is also true of statements of fact, which cannot really be isolated from the other aspects of the controversy. Nor is a jury the most suitable instrument for passing on such questions. One may well doubt, therefore, whether a libel suit ultimately produces the correct answer, or whether participants and observers believe it does. In any event it is the marketplace, not the government, which is supposed to resolve these matters under a system of freedom of expression. Once again we come back to the incompatibility of the libel laws and the First Amendment.[35]

If, then, we conclude that the actual malice rule is inadequate to protect a system of free expression and is indeed inconsistent with the whole theory of the First Amendment, we are left with the rule of unconditional privilege—that full protection be extended to all discussions of public issues. There seems to be no intermediate point. Such a rule is clearly compelled by the view of the First Amendment advanced in this book.

We could stop at this point except for the fact that some students of the subject consider it "unthinkable" that deliberately false statements should go unrestricted. They are concerned not only with the injury to the individual, but with the danger to society from "the great lie" and with the loss of integrity and possible ultimate breakdown of our system of expression itself. These are serious concerns.[36]

With regard to the latter problem—"the great lie" and disintegra-

---

34. See his opinions in *Rosenblatt v. Baer*, 383 U.S. at 94, and in the *Butts* and *Walker* cases, 388 U.S. at 170.

35. On the separation of fact and opinion see Herbert W. Titus, "Statement of Fact Versus Statement of Opinion—A Spurious Dispute in Fair Comment," *Vanderbilt Law Review*, Vol. 15 (1962), p. 1203.

36. For expressions of this point of view see, *e.g.*, Riesman, *op. cit. supra* note 4; Willard H. Pedrick, "Freedom of the Press and the Law of Libel: The Modern Revised Translation," *Cornell Law Quarterly*, Vol. 49 (1964), pp. 581, 596. See also Justice Brennan in *Garrison v. Louisiana*, 379 U.S. at 74–75; and Justice Harlan in the *Butts* and *Walker* cases, 388 U.S. at 153–154.

tion of the system—it seems doubtful that the rule of actual malice would have any substantial effect in preventing such disasters. The big lie generally relates to matters of opinion, historical judgments, or political conclusions, not to statements of fact about particular living persons. It is more likely to defame groups than individuals. It is normally utilized by government, which is immune from libel, or by powerful political factions. One cannot look to the rules of libel in civil proceedings to control forces of this nature and magnitude. Our major experience of this sort—with McCarthyism—confirms this. The same is true of the concern over a general disruption of communication. Other kinds of factors govern. The health and vitality of the system depend more upon untrammeled freedom of discussion, in which all citizens contend vigorously, than in judicial attempts to establish the motives of the participants.

Concern over injury to the individual is less readily answered. We must remember, however, that we are dealing at this point with the discussion of public issues. Citizens have an obligation to enter the public arena, but they also have some obligation to understand how the system works and why it is not possible to assure them immunity from criticism, fair and unfair. Moreover, there are factors other than libel suits that keep public controversy within bounds. Traditions, attitudes, and general rules of political conduct are far more important controls. The fear of opening a credibility gap, and thereby lessening one's influence, holds some participants in check. Institutional pressures in large organizations, including some of the press, have a similar effect; it is difficult for an organization to have an open policy of making intentionally false accusations. The libel laws are thus not the only force at work.

Furthermore, the argument assumes that the libel laws are an effective technique for restraining deliberately false, defamatory statements about individuals during the course of public controversy. They probably have a deterrent effect on the press. Beyond that, however, it is by no means clear that libel laws serve to improve the level of public debate. Recourse to libel litigation, over the course of many years, has been only occasional and the achievements inconclusive. The libel action is an ungainly form of relief; it is neither quick, certain nor cheap. Moreover, a judicial proceeding is a highly inappropriate way of resolving the truth of public issues. Often its results are not accepted by the interested public, anyway.

All this leads to the crucial point. There are other devices for protecting the individual that are not only consistent with a system of freedom of expression but that would strengthen and vitalize it. The most significant is a right of reply. The advantages of this way of dealing with alleged defamatory statements have been set forth by others and will not be considered in detail here. It is sufficient to note that a right of reply could be made available in most situations in which an individual claims that false assertions (and other forms of attack on him) have been made. It is particularly applicable in the case of the press, where abandonment of the libel action would be felt the most. Such a procedure is the most appropriate and probably the most effective way to deal with the problem. The person attacked would have an opportunity to get his position and his evidence quickly before the public. He would have a forum in which to continue the dialogue, rather than being forced to withdraw to the artificial arena of the courtroom. The discussion would thus be kept going in the marketplace, and the issues left up to the public, which must make the final decision anyway.[37]

It is true that the procedure for allowing a right of reply would probably have to be established by legislation rather than judicial decision. But the courts would not be without influence in working towards this solution. For the adoption by the Supreme Court of a rule of full protection in the discussion of public issues—thereby eliminating use of the libel action as a method of relief—would undoubtedly spur the reform.[38]

One further issue remains to be considered. Besides imposing liability for damages in libel because of false defamatory statements of fact, the traditional law of libel imposed liability for defamatory comment or opinion. In most jurisdictions, however, the defense of fair comment was allowed. Under this rule an expression of opinion on a public issue was protected if it was based upon the facts, was fair, and was not malicious in the ordinary (not *New York Times*) sense. The line between a statement of "fact" and an expression of "opinion" is, of course, frequently difficult or impossible to draw. The rules for deal-

---

37. For collection of material on the right of reply and other methods of protecting the individual see *Political and Civil Rights in the United States*, pp. 731–732. See also Note, "Vindication of the Reputation of a Public Official," *Harvard Law Review*, Vol. 80 (1967), pp. 1730, 1734–1749; George E. Frasier, "An Alternative to the General-Damage Award for Defamation," *Stanford Law Review*, Vol. 20 (1968), p. 504. For discussion of

the constitutional issues see Chapter XVII.

38. The argument that the courts would have some powers to require a right of reply is made in Jerome A. Barron, "Access to the Press—A New First Amendment Right," *Harvard Law Review*, Vol. 80 (1967), p. 1641; and "An Emerging First Amendment Right of Access to the Media?", *George Washington Law Review*, Vol. 37 (1969), p. 487.

ing with the two situations were not always sharply separated. Nevertheless in most jurisdictions the right to express defamatory opinions was protected only to the extent that the statement fell within the fair comment rule.

In *New York Times* the Court made clear that the defense of fair comment henceforth had to be permitted even if the opinion were based upon facts that were false (unless false in the sense of actual malice). It said nothing about the other aspects of the fair comment rule—that the opinion had to be "fair" and not "malicious." Nevertheless the rationale of *New York Times* would seem to preclude the imposition of any liability for expression of opinion on a matter of public concern. The risk of incurring liability for an opinion considered by a jury to be "unfair" or "malicious" would surely create much greater and more widespread self-censorship than that found decisive in *New York Times*. The same conclusion, of course, follows from other First Amendment considerations. The basic design of the First Amendment is that all citizens express their views on public issues, regardless of whether other citizens think the opinion fair or unfair, true or false, malevolent or benign. The government may not concern itself with the value judgments of citizens or their motivations. Anything in the law of libel to the contrary is irreconcilable with the First Amendment.[39]

4. COVERAGE OF THE FIRST AMENDMENT

The final question is, What kinds of communication does First Amendment protection against the libel laws embrace? We assume, for purposes of this discussion, that the protection accorded by the First Amendment is complete or, to put it in terms of libel law, the communication is entitled to an unconditional privilege.

There appears to be general agreement that the First Amendment covers at least all discussion of "public issues" or "matters of public concern." Even those members of the Supreme Court who make a distinction between "public officials" and "public issues" do not assert that the latter category should be accorded no First Amendment protection; their position is only that it should receive less protection than the "public official" category. It becomes necessary, therefore, to examine the concept of "public issue" or "matter of public concern."

39. The discussion of fair comment   at 292, fn. 30.
in *New York Times* appears in 376 U.S.

Alexander Meiklejohn, in his development of First Amendment theory, argued that the First Amendment constituted a limitation upon governmental power only with respect to "public speech." Unfortunately, there has never been a satisfactory definition of what is meant by "public speech." If the term is used in the narrow sense, somewhat comparable to "political," it clearly excludes too much. On that view vast areas of communication relating to art, literature, music, science and recreation, to name only some of the major ones, would not be entitled to First Amendment protection. On the other hand, if the term is used expansively, to cover anything of concern to society, then it would seem to have no limits, or at least no easily definable limits. It is hard to conceive of anything, in this day and age, that cannot be said to have some relation to social issues. Presumably some cutoff point is intended, but none is apparent and none has been designated.[40]

Efforts to define the concept "public issue" in the field of libel law have been equally fruitless. One suggestion has been that the term be construed to mean "statements about political and economic activities which materially affect the public welfare." But the limitation to "political and economic activities" is obviously too narrow. Another proposal is that the formula cover "any issue with an important relevance to the public's decision-making process as a self-governing body politic." This sounds as if it were limited to political decision making. But the author interprets it as covering communication dealing with art, literature, sports and the rest, thereby rendering it open-ended. A third proposal—that the test be "public decisionability"—raises the same questions. Unless some further test of relevance is introduced, just about all communication is valuable for purposes of "public decisionability." Concepts borrowed from tort law, which would impose different rules for communication relating to "private character," as distinct from "public affairs," may come closer. But again, as the *Garrison* case illustrates, some statements about "private character" may also have "public" importance. In the end one is reduced to some vague formulation such as that used by Dean Prosser in connection with the fair comment rule: "Those matters which are of legitimate concern to

40. Alexander Meiklejohn's views are set forth in his *Political Freedom* (New York, Harper & Bros., 1960), and in his article "The First Amendment Is an Absolute," *Supreme Court Review,* Vol. 1961 (1961), p. 245. See also Donald Meiklejohn, "Public Speech and the First Amendment," *Georgetown Law Journal,* Vol. 55 (1966), p. 234. For Professor Chafee's criticism of the limitation of the First Amendment to "public speech" see his book review in *Harvard Law Review,* Vol. 62 (1949), p. 891.

the community . . . because they materially affect the interests of all of the community." [41]

The attempt to analyze the problem in terms of defining "public issue" thus inevitably reaches a dead end. An alternative is to look at the issues from the standpoint of what functions the First Amendment is designed to perform and what interests the law of libel undertakes to protect. Insofar as the purpose of a system of free expression is to provide for participation in social decision making and to promote a healthy balance between stability and change, one might be inclined to look for limits that would allow the attainment of these goals without permitting incursions into other areas. Even here, however, the same problem as with a test of "public decisionability" is raised. In the end what can be said to be irrelevant, or at least what standard of relevance can be formulated? These questions become acute especially when one takes into account the other functions of freedom of expression. A system of free expression also serves the goal of advancing knowledge and discovering truth, and for this purpose there can be no restriction to any area, or if there were, it would not be the province of the government to designate or enforce it. Even more clearly, the function of free expression as a means of individual self-fulfillment would admit of no limitation imposed by government. In terms of basic First Amendment theory, therefore, no area of communication should be abridged by libel laws. The interests those laws are intended to achieve must be pursued by other methods.

It is instructive also to consider the problem in terms of the functions served by the libel laws. Indeed if, as a matter of constitutional doctrine, one reopened the balancing process it would be imperative to do this. In part the libel laws are designed to protect against injury to reputation which causes damage of an economic or material nature. Substantial protection against communication affecting economic interests is given in the commercial realm, outside the system of freedom of expression. Within the free speech system, however, one does not

---

41. The definitions, in the order set forth, are from Note, "First Amendment Requires Qualified Privilege to Publish Defamatory Misstatements About Public Officials," *University of Pennsylvania Law Review,* Vol. 113 (1964), pp. 284, 290; Note, "The Limits of Political Speech: *New York Times v. Sullivan* Revisited," *UCLA Law Review,* Vol. 14 (1967), pp. 631, 642; Note, "Free Speech and Defamation of Public Persons: The Expanding Doctrine of *New York Times Co. v. Sullivan," Cornell Law Quarterly,* Vol. 52 (1967), pp. 419, 425; Prosser, *op. cit.* note 4, p. 812. See also Note, "The Scope of First Amendment Protection for Good-Faith Defamatory Error," *Yale Law Journal,* Vol. 75 (1966), pp. 642, 648–649; Pedrick, *op. cit. supra* note 36, pp. 589–601.

have great hesitation in protecting expression at the expense of economic gain or loss. The balance struck in the formulation of the First Amendment does not appear vulnerable at this point.[42]

To the extent the libel laws afford damages for injury to reputation that affects one's standing in the community and hence one's role as decision maker, the problem is somewhat different. But here too the original balance in favor of expression would seem entirely proper. The very essence of a system of free expression is that the participants are the ones who judge standing, prestige, the weight to be accorded a particular speaker, and all similar matters. These issues are to be fought out in the public forum, not decided by government authorities. The attempt to inject the government into such issues through the libel laws should be struck down as opposed to the fundamental nature of the system.

This brings us to the third function of the libel laws, which is to protect against injury to a person's feelings. A serious question can be raised here as to whether communication having this effect should be classified as "expression" at all. In one sense it is the equivalent of "action," similar to a physical assault. The harm done tends to be direct and instantaneous, and not remediable by longer-range social processes that can prevent subsequent damage. In other words, the injury, at least in substantial part, does not flow from action resulting from the communication—action which can be intercepted or repaired before the harm occurs—but directly from the communication itself. Moreover, a civil action for damages in this situation would have a minimal effect upon the operation of a system of free expression. The government's role is primarily that of umpire, with no interest of its own at stake. One could, therefore, within the framework of a system of free expression allow recovery in a libel action when only this kind of injury to individual feelings is involved. It is unnecessary to pursue this approach, however, as other principles now come into play.

We have reached the point where the coverage of the First Amendment extends up to the area of purely personal matters. This issue can be considered also in terms of privacy law. In other words, it may be that the limits on the First Amendment in the libel sphere are controlled by principles underlying the constitutional right of privacy.

42. For discussion of the exclusion of the commercial sector from the system of freedom of expression see Chapter XII.

B. Privacy

The development of the law of privacy has been, in some respects, the reverse of that of the law of libel. Whereas libel law has an ancient lineage, legal protection of a specific right to privacy has been established only in relatively recent times. Moreover, the law of privacy is now in an expanding, rather than contracting, stage. As in the case of libel law, however, recognition of the latent conflict with the First Amendment was slow to surface. It was not until the decision in *Time v. Hill,* rendered in 1967, that the Supreme Court addressed itself directly to the problem.

1. SCOPE OF THE RIGHT TO PRIVACY AND ITS RELATION TO THE FIRST AMENDMENT

There has been much difference of opinion over what the concept of "privacy" embraces or what functions it performs. Warren and Brandeis, in their classic article that initiated development of the tort law of privacy, dealt specifically with unwanted publicity in private affairs. But they viewed the underlying principle more broadly, as that of a right to "inviolate personality" and, adopting Cooley's words, "the right 'to be let alone.'" Subsequently Justice Brandeis, in a situation involving government rather than private interference with privacy, expanded his views:

> The makers of our Constitution undertook to secure conditions favorable to the pursuit of happiness. They recognized the significance of man's spiritual nature, of his feeling and of his intellect. . . . They sought to protect Americans in their beliefs, their thoughts, their emotions and their sensations. They conferred, as against the Government, the right to be let alone—the most comprehensive of rights and the right most valued by civilized men.[43]

Professor Bloustein holds a similar broad view of privacy as involving the "interest in preserving human dignity and individuality,"

43. Samuel D. Warren and Louis D. Brandeis, "The Right of Privacy," *Harvard Law Review,* Vol. 4 (1890), pp. 193, 205, 195; *Olmstead v. United States,* 277 U.S. 438, 478 (1928).

and as needing protection against conduct which "would destroy individual dignity and integrity and emasculate individual freedom and independence." Likewise Professor Konvitz writes of privacy:

> Its essence is the claim that there is a sphere of space that has not been dedicated to public use or control. It is a kind of space that a man may carry with him, into his bedroom or into the street. Even when public, it is a part of the inner man; it is part of his "property," as Locke would say, the kind of "property" with respect to which its owner has delegated no power to the state.[44]

Others define the concept of privacy more narrowly. Thus Professor Westin, in his comprehensive treatment of the subject, adopts as his definition: "Privacy is the claim of individuals, groups, or institutions to determine for themselves when, how, and to what extent information about them is communicated to others." A similar definition is given in the report of the Office of Science and Technology, *Privacy and Behavioral Research:* "The right to privacy is the right of the individual to decide for himself how much he will share with others his thoughts, his feelings, and the facts of his personal life." For our purposes, however, the broader if somewhat looser view of privacy seems preferable as a starting point.[45]

Generally speaking, the concept of a right to privacy attempts to draw a line between the individual and the collective, between self and society. It seeks to assure the individual a zone in which to be an individual, not a member of the community. In that zone he can think his own thoughts, have his own secrets, live his own life, reveal only what he wants to the outside world. The right of privacy, in short, establishes an area excluded from the collective life, not governed by the rules of collective living. It is based upon premises of individualism, that the society exists to promote the worth and the dignity of the individual. It is contrary to theories of total commitment to the state, to society, or to any part thereof.

44. Edward J. Bloustein, "Privacy as an Aspect of Human Dignity: An Answer to Dean Prosser," *New York University Law Review,* Vol. 39 (1964), pp. 962, 1005, 971; Milton R. Konvitz, "Privacy and the Law: A Philosophical Prelude," *Law and Contemporary Problems,* Vol. 31 (1966), pp. 272, 279-280.

45. Alan F. Westin, *Privacy and Freedom* (New York, Atheneum, 1967), p. 7; Executive Office of the President, Office of Science and Technology, *Privacy and Behavioral Research* (Washington, D.C., G.P.O., 1967), p. 2. See also Hyman Gross, "The Concept of Privacy," *New York University Law Review,* Vol. 42 (1967), pp. 34, 35-36; and Frederick Davis, "What Do We Mean by 'Right to Privacy'?", *South Dakota Law Review,* Vol. 4 (1959), p. 1.

In order to maintain this preserve of privacy, it is necessary that there be some degree of protection to the individual against physical intrusion into the zone, against surveillance from the outside, against unwanted communication to others of what goes on inside. There must be some restriction on conduct from the outside that would destroy identity, individuality or autonomy. The form these regulations must take depends on the nature of the individual and the nature of the society; they will vary from time to time, and from place to place.

The purpose of a system of privacy is, in the broader sense, simply to maintain the oneness of the individual despite the demands of the collective. In more specific terms the right of privacy fulfills certain pressing individual needs and supports certain important social objectives. Alan Westin has summarized the functions privacy performs for the individual as including (1) protection of personal autonomy—the avoidance of being manipulated or dominated by others; (2) permitting emotional release—relief from the pressure of playing social roles, from the emotional stimulations of daily life, from the need of strict compliance with social norms, and the like; (3) opportunity for self-evaluation—a chance to integrate one's experience into a meaningful pattern and exert one's individuality on events; and (4) allowance of limited and partial communication—permitting one to share confidences and to set boundaries of mental distance.[46]

In its social impact a system of privacy is vital to the working of the democratic process. Democracy assumes that the individual citizen will actively and independently participate in making decisions and in operating the institutions of the society. An individual is capable of such a role only if he can at some points separate himself from the pressures and conformities of collective life. Professor Bloustein has made the point most eloquently:

> The man who is compelled to live every minute of his life among others and whose every need, thought, desire, fancy or gratification is subject to public scrutiny, has been deprived of his individuality and human dignity. Such an individual merges with the mass. His opinions, being public, tend never to be different; his aspirations, being known, tend always to be conventionally accepted ones; his feelings, being openly exhibited, tend to lose their quality of unique personal warmth and to become the feelings of every man. Such a being, although sentient, is fungible; he is not an individual.[47]

46. Westin, *op. cit. supra* note 45, pp. 32–39.

47. Bloustein, *op. cit. supra* note 44, p. 1003.

Maintenance of privacy has been constantly growing more difficult as our country becomes more populated, our society more technical, our mode of living more intensive. It is small wonder that pressures have been mounting for the development of legal rules to formulate more precisely and enforce more effectively the right of privacy. It is in this context that we must consider the relation of the First Amendment to the development of the law of privacy.[48]

Legal protection for the right of privacy has progressed at two levels. At one level is the body of law dealing with interference by government with the right to privacy. This law is largely based on constitutional provisions that restrict governmental conduct in particular areas and thereby protect some aspect of privacy. The First Amendment itself, in preventing the government from prohibiting the free exercise of religion or abridging freedom of expression, safeguards privacy in holding beliefs and expressing or not expressing opinions. The Third Amendment's prohibition on quartering of troops in homes, the Fourth Amendment's regulation of searches, seizures and arrests, and the Fifth Amendment's privilege against self-incrimination, as well as its due process clause, are important features of the constitutional structure for maintaining a right of privacy. Furthermore, in *Griswold v. Connecticut* the Supreme Court found an independent right of privacy, emanating from these amendments plus the Ninth. The scope of this new constitutional right of privacy is as yet untested but its very existence is a force of major consequence. Finally, there are many statutes on the books which limit government action in ways that protect the right of privacy.[49]

In all this area of the law there is no conflict between the First Amendment and the right of privacy. On the contrary, legal protection of privacy against government intrusion supports the system of freedom of expression.

At the other level the law of privacy is directed not against government interference with privacy but against invasion of privacy by private individuals and groups. This body of law is common law or statute. It includes much of our property and tort law. At this level, also,

48. For a collection of materials on the right of privacy see *Political and Civil Rights in the United States*, pp. 1258–1261. A subsequent study that also collects the prior material is Westin, *op. cit. supra* note 45. See also M. C. Slough, *Privacy, Freedom and Responsibility* (Springfield, Ill., Charles C. Thomas, 1969).

49. *Griswold v. Connecticut,* 381 U.S. 479 (1965). See also *Stanley v. Georgia,* 394 U.S. 557 (1969), discussed in Chapter XIII.

most of the law of privacy does not come into any sort of conflict with the First Amendment. It protects privacy through regulating forms of conduct that constitute "action" rather than "expression." Thus the law of trespass, a major bulwark in the protection of privacy, deals primarily with physical intrusions on property. Other parts of the law are largely designed to prevent outside persons from obtaining information about individuals seeking privacy, rather than to prevent the dissemination of information. This must be the main thrust of any realistic system for the protection of privacy. Attempts to safeguard privacy by bottling up expression are bound to be largely futile and probably self-defeating.

At some places, however, legal protection for privacy does run into possible opposition from the First Amendment. Some of the problems arise out of the tort law of privacy. Others are involved in those forms of government control that deal with some of the physical aspects of expression, such as door-bell ringing, the use of sound trucks, and the picketing of homes. The area of potential conflict is small in relation to the whole system for protection of privacy. But it has given rise to some much-debated issues.

The specific points of controversy may be divided into three categories: (1) public disclosure of embarrassing facts about a person or publicity that places him in a false light in the public eye; (2) intrusion upon a person's solitude or seclusion; and (3) appropriation of a person's name, likeness or personality. Before proceeding to consider specific issues, however, it is necessary to discuss briefly some general issues of theory and approach.[50]

2. FORMULATION OF DOCTRINE

The theoretical problem involved in reconciling the law of the First Amendment with the law of privacy would seem to center around delineating the boundaries of two sectors of our life that fall outside the area in which freedom of expression must be maintained. One is the sector of commercial communication, to which the normal rules for protecting freedom of expression do not apply. Most of the issues arising in the appropriation cases—the third category mentioned

50. The categories are based upon those formulated by Dean Prosser in the article which, next to that of Warren and Brandeis, has been the most influential in the development of the law of privacy. William L. Prosser, "Privacy," *California Law Review*, Vol. 48 (1960), p. 383.

above—require a determination whether the conduct involved falls within the system of commercial communication. The theoretical questions here do not need further discussion at this point. The other sector is the privacy system itself. The relationship of that sector to the system of freedom of expression does require some consideration.

The right of privacy, as we have seen, is essentially the right not to participate in the collective life—the right to shut out the community. A system of privacy is designed to isolate this area of individual life from various kinds of interference by the collective. The rules necessary for such a system must, therefore, cut across—or block the application of—all rules of the collective at the point essential to maintain the privacy system. For example, the rules of the society designed to enforce its criminal laws might well function more effectively if no limits were placed on police rights of search and arrest; but the requirements of a system of privacy cut off those powers at a certain point, established in our Constitution by the Fourth Amendment. Similarly the society might find it advisable to record all available data about all citizens, from birth to death, on computers for ready reference; but the right of privacy would presumably at some point call a halt. All this is equally true with respect to the rules establishing a system of freedom of expression. They, too, are simply outside the privacy system.

The problem of reconciling First Amendment rights and privacy rights, where they conflict, is therefore one of defining the constitutional boundaries of the privacy system. It is necessary to look at the requirements of such a system and to determine what is essential to maintain it. At that point the rules of the system of free expression, like the rules governing other aspects of the life of the collective, are cut off. This process of reasoning is different from the normal balancing of interests within the general social system. Clearly trespass into another's home for purposes of expressing one's opinion to the occupant is not permitted. Why? The law does not balance the interest in freedom of expression against the interest in privacy. It simply concludes that a system of privacy must have such a rule if it is to exist at all. This was the kind of approach taken by Justice Brennan in the *New York Times* case (up to a point) in determining the kind of rule necessary to maintain a system of freedom of expression.

It is true that in this process one does not look exclusively at the system of privacy. It is necessary to take into consideration also those aspects of the collective life, and the rules governing them, that are involved. But one does this from the viewpoint of adjusting the system of privacy to the society in which it operates. The problem is approached as one of exploring the nature of the privacy interest, attempting to understand its function, and judging what relationship to the rules of the collective world is necessary to give it effective operation. The focus is still on the essential requirements of preserving such a system, not on attempting to balance one kind of interest against another.

One might be concerned that from this approach the legal protection of privacy could be carried to the point where the interests of the collective were endangered. As a practical matter such an outcome seems unlikely. Most of the forces at work press the other way. The determination of the boundaries of the right of privacy is itself made by the official representatives of the collective. The possibility that the right of privacy will overwhelm the rights of society is so remote that it is hardly a cause for alarm.

3. PUBLIC DISCLOSURE OF PERSONAL MATTERS AND PUTTING A PERSON IN A FALSE LIGHT

One part of the tort law of privacy deals with claims of invasion of privacy by publication of personal matters that, while true, are embarrassing to the person involved or cause him some other form of mental distress. Typical of such cases are those involving publicity concerning a private debt, publication of distressing matters out of the past, and disclosure of intimate details about the body, sexual practices, or the like. Prior to *Time v. Hill* the courts usually applied to these cases the test of "newsworthiness." If the matter was considered "newsworthy" it was permitted; if not, and it was something that would be offensive to a man of ordinary sensibilities, a cause of action for invasion of privacy was allowed.

Another series of cases in the tort law of privacy are concerned with publication of matters that are false and, while not defamatory, place the individual in a false light in the public eye. Such cases include the use of a photograph in a misleading way or an inaccurate or fictitious account of a person's life or character. The rule of law governing these cases prior to *Time v. Hill* was never very clearly articulated. The issue was whether the falsity or fictionalization defeated the privilege to report newsworthy events and the result turned upon how serious was the divergence from the truth and how negligent the reporter.

Theoretically these areas of privacy law could be distinguished from libel law. The facts in the public disclosure cases were true, and the falsity in the other cases was not defamatory. Moreover, the interest protected was "mental distress" due to invasion of privacy, not "reputation." Actually, the privacy cases were very similar to those libel cases which in effect protect injury to feelings. In practice the two areas of law tended more and more to run together.[51]

The presence of First Amendment issues in this area of the law of privacy is not difficult to discern. The Supreme Court did not reach the question, however, until 1967, in *Time v. Hill*.[52]

Time v. Hill grew out of an incident in 1952 in which three escaped convicts held James Hill and his wife, son, and daughter hostages in their home for nineteen hours. The family was not molested. The story was widely reported at the time but Hill attempted to avoid the publicity and moved his family to another state. The following year a novel appeared, *The Desperate Hours*, based on the Hill incident but varying from it in depicting the father and son as having been beaten and the daughter subjected to a verbal sexual assault. The novel did not mention the Hill family. In 1955 a play, also called *The Desperate Hours* and by the same author, was produced on Broadway. The litigation arose out of an article in *Life* magazine about the play. The article referred to the original episode, naming the Hills, and to the subsequent novel "inspired by the family's experience." It went on to say, "Now they [Americans] can see the story re-enacted in Hayes' Broadway play based on the book." Accompanying the written material were pictures of scenes from the play taken at the former Hill home. They included a picture of the son being "roughed up" by one of the convicts, and a picture of the daughter biting the hand of a convict to make him drop a gun.

Hill sued for damages alleging that the *Life* article had revived a painful episode, causing a serious emotional and nervous illness on the part of his wife; that the *Life* article was false or "fictionalized" in that it gave the impression that the play mirrored the family's actual expe-

---

51. Generally, on this phase of privacy law see Prosser, *op. cit. supra* note 50, pp. 392–401; John W. Wade, "Defamation and the Right of Privacy," *Vanderbilt Law Review,* Vol. 15 (1962), p. 1093; Bloustein, *op. cit. supra* note 44, pp. 977–984, 991–993; Harry Kalven, Jr., "Privacy in Tort Law—Were Warren and Brandeis Wrong?", *Law and Contemporary Problems,* Vol. 31 (1966), p. 326.

52. *Time v. Hill,* 385 U.S. 374 (1967).

rience; and that *Life* magazine knew the article was "false and untrue." The suit was brought under a New York statute that allowed damages for publication of "the name, portrait or picture of any living person without having first obtained the written consent of such person" for advertising or trade purposes. The New York courts construed the statute as not applying to "factual reporting of newsworthy persons and events" but allowing a right of action for material and substantial falsification or "fictionalization." The jury awarded Hill $50,000 compensatory and $25,000 punitive damages, later reduced to $30,000 compensatory damages without punitive damages.

The Supreme Court reversed and sent the case back for a new trial. There were five opinions. Justice Brennan, writing also for Justices Stewart and White, held that the New York statute could be applied to allow redress for false reports on matters of public interest only if there was proof of actual malice in the *New York Times* sense, that is, the defendant published the report with knowledge of its falsity or in reckless disregard of its truth; that the evidence in the case could be construed either as showing innocent or mere negligent mistake, or as showing actual malice; and that the instructions to the jury did not make clear that actual malice was required. Justices Black and Douglas concurred in the decision, in order to make up a majority agreement to a single disposition of the case, but expressed the view that, as in libel cases, the First Amendment prohibited any restriction on communication relating to matters in the public domain. Justice Harlan dissented on the ground that the proper standard of liability should be merely negligent rather than knowing or reckless misstatement. Justice Fortas, joined by Chief Justice Warren and Justice Clark, agreed with the Brennan opinion as to the principles to be applied but thought there was no reason for a new trial since the instructions and evidence met the required standard of actual malice.

The decision in *Time v. Hill* focused on the requirement of actual malice when falsity or fictionalization is involved and, except for Justices Black and Douglas, the justices did not attempt to spell out in detail their views on other aspects of the privacy problem. Nevertheless, by taking advantage of implication and hint, together with other reading between the lines, it is possible to piece out the probable views of the Court upon the major issues in the public disclosure and false light area of privacy. Six members of the Court seemed to agree that (1) truthful accounts of "newsworthy" persons and events were protected by the First Amendment against the claim of invasion of privacy; (2) if the publication was not "newsworthy" a privacy action would be permissible if the revelations were "so intimate and so unwarranted in view of the victim's position as to outrage the community's notions of decency"; (3) if the publication was "newsworthy" but not true (that is, false or fictitious) a privacy action would be permissible if actual malice was shown. Justice Harlan would appear to agree with these principles except that he would substitute the standard of negligence for that of actual malice. Justices Black and Douglas held that, at least as to matters in the public domain, the First Amendment prohibited any action for invasion of privacy.[53]

Looking first at the proposition that truthful accounts of newsworthy matters are protected by the First Amendment, it is possible to make two further assumptions concerning the majority position. One is that a person is newsworthy "whether he be such by choice or involuntarily." The other is that a communication is newsworthy if it relates not only to matters that inform but also to matters that entertain, in other words to "matters of public interest." Thus the Court would clearly give a broad definition to "newsworthy." [54]

Whatever the Court's definition, however, use of the concept of "newsworthiness" to mark the constitutional line between freedom of expression and the right of privacy creates some very serious difficulties. The term "newsworthy" has no generally accepted meaning, nor one that can readily be poured into it. The courts have tended to conclude that anything actually published is "newsworthy." This gives the concept no meaning at all in the context of a right to privacy. The term could be said to mean anything which "ought" to be published, or anything published by the established or responsible press. But this is hardly a satisfactory solution. The concept is not saved by broadening it to mean "matters of public interest." This formulation is even more vague than the original term, and it hides the same problem: does it refer to what is or what ought to be a matter of public interest? If the former, then it is no limitation; if the latter, the Court is plunging into uncertain and dangerous waters.[55]

53. 385 U.S. at 383, fn. 7, quoting from *Sidis v. F-R Publishing Co.*, 113 F.2d 806, 809 (2d Cir. 1940), cert. denied 311 U.S. 711 (1940). For discussion of *Time v. Hill* see Kalven, "The Reasonable Man and the First Amendment," *supra* note 27; Nimmer, *op. cit. supra* note 27.

54. 385 U.S. at 384, quoting the New York Court of Appeals in *Spahn v. Julian Messner, Inc.*, 18 N.Y.2d 324, 328, 221 N.E.2d 543, 545 (1966); 385 U.S. at 388.

55. For discussion of the term "newsworthy" see Note, "The Right of Privacy: Normative-Descriptive Confusion in the Defense of Newsworthiness," *University of Chicago Law Review*, Vol. 30 (1963), p. 722.

Nor can it be said that the concept of "newsworthiness" is acceptable from a First Amendment point of view. If it is construed in the sense of matter suitable for use by the press, then the government is given the power to curtail speech on the vague ground that it does not consider the material fit for publication. In fact, no matter how the term is construed, a classification that bases the right to First Amendment protection on some estimate of how much general interest there is in the communication is surely in conflict with the whole idea of the First Amendment.

As a criterion for establishing limits to the right of privacy the concept likewise fails. From a privacy point of view, the more newsworthy, the greater the invasion of privacy.

The second proposition implied in the view of the majority is that, if the publication is not "newsworthy," a cause of action for invasion of privacy may arise. This requires some further definition of when a non-newsworthy communication will be deemed to violate the right of privacy. Apparently the rule is that this occurs when "revelations" are "so intimate and so unwarranted . . . as to outrage the community's notions of decency." Other courts have suggested the test of whether the communication is "offensive to ordinary sensibilities." These formulae are, of course, extremely vague. On the Court's theory, however, it would not be necessary for constitutional purposes to define the rule further. The position seems to be that, if the publication is not "newsworthy," then the First Amendment protection drops off and the only remaining issue is whether the publication falls within the common law or statutory definition of an invasion of privacy. On the other hand, if one accepts the theory that the First Amendment is applicable to all expression, up to the point where it is cut off by a constitutional right of privacy, then it would be necessary to consider the issues further in light of the demands of a system of privacy.

The third proposition deals with the situation in which the publication is "newsworthy" but not truthful. This aspect of the case received the major emphasis in the Brennan opinion. The line of reasoning parallels that of the *New York Times* case. After establishing that the publication in question falls within the scope of the First Amendment as relating to a matter of public interest, Justice Brennan goes on to say that it would "create a grave risk of serious impairment" of freedom of expression if "we saddle the press with the impossible burden of verifying to a certainty the facts associated in news articles with a person's name, picture or portrait, particularly as related to nondefamatory matter"; that "[e]ven negligence would be a most elusive standard"; but that "calculated falsehood," being "no essential part of any exposition of ideas" and of "slight social value as a step to truth," does not "enjoy constitutional protection." He therefore adopts the actual malice rule.[56]

The three dissenters agreed with these principles but felt that Justice Brennan was applying them too reluctantly, with insufficient regard for the right of privacy. Justice Black, who had dissented in the *Griswold* case against the establishment of any constitutional right of privacy, felt that there was no way of reconciling the right of privacy with the First Amendment except by balancing interests. This he was unwilling to do. Justice Douglas, who has written more often in support of privacy than any other justice, saw no substantial issue of privacy involved in the case: "Such privacy as a person normally has ceases when his life has ceased to be private." The publication was "in the public domain as fully as the matters at issue in *New York Times v. Sullivan*," and to make an "elusive exception" for knowing or reckless falsity would in effect destroy First Amendment protection.[57]

The views of the prevailing justices on this phase of the privacy issue likewise do not appear to offer a satisfactory solution. So far as the matter of falsity is concerned, the same questions are raised as in the libel cases. If liability for negligent untruth has a chilling effect upon the free exercise of expression, so would the imposing of sanctions for what the jury found to be intentional or reckless untruth. The rule of actual malice requires that in *Time v. Hill,* as in the libel cases, the Supreme Court make a detailed review of the evidence, instructions and findings in the particular case. In addition, it is anomalous to have the issue in privacy cases turn upon falsity at all. The injury is not to reputation but to feelings. The true could be just as damaging as the false. Hence the approach of the majority in *Time v. Hill* seems wrong as to the First Amendment and wide of the mark as to privacy.

Furthermore, the other half of the Court's position, involving a determination whether the communication was "newsworthy" or concerned with a "public issue," is likewise unhelpful. That approach is uncertain in result and unfocused as a technique.

The question is whether it is possible to create legal doctrine for accommodating the two rights without simply leaving it up to the court in each case to "balance" the injury to privacy against the damage to freedom of expression. The approach suggested here rests on two

56. 385 U.S. at 389, 390.   57. 385 U.S. at 401.

propositions. The first is that the First Amendment interest be held as a constant, that is, without attempting fine distinctions as to whether the communication has great or small social value or is important or unimportant to the exposition of ideas. The second is that the right of privacy be viewed as protected by rules which cut across any opposing rules of the collectivity. These privacy rules should be designed to establish a "sphere of space that has not been dedicated to public use or control," and would be determined by what is necessary to achieve that objective. They would be derived from an examination of the purposes, functions and dynamics of a system of privacy.

Viewed from this point it would seem that the constitutional cutoff would be drawn at a point which would leave only a very narrow area in which disclosure of embarrassing facts about a person or fictionalization of matter concerning him would fall within the protection of the privacy system. The psychological needs of the individual served by privacy, as outlined by Professor Westin, would not seem to require any broader protection. Nor would the social functions performed by the privacy system. Any individual living among others is, by the very nature of society, subject to an enormous amount of comment, gossip, criticism and the like. His right to be left alone does not include any general right not to be talked about. The law cannot do much to solace hurt feelings from this source or repair a distorted public image. At most it can protect only the most inner core of the personality, involving the kind of intimate details of personal life that were the Court's concern in *Griswold v. Connecticut,* where the constitutional right to privacy was born. In the main the right of privacy depends upon guaranteeing an individual freedom from intrusion and freedom to think and believe, not freedom from discussion of his opinions, actions or affairs.

Where, then, would a focus on rules of this sort bring us out? The plaintiff in *Time v. Hill* would certainly lose. An individual caught up in a public event, even though through no fault of his own, cannot expect to keep it private, either at the time or later. The injury to his feelings, like any other accident he meets with, is part of his life in society. Prohibition on discussion of matters such as those depicted in the play or in the magazine article is not compelled by either the psychological needs of the individual or the social needs for independent citizens underlying the privacy system.

The same would be true of Warren Spahn, the famous baseball pitcher, about whom a "fictionalized" biography was published containing "a host, a preponderant percentage, of factual errors, distortions and fanciful passages." Insofar as the biography put him in a false light he was in the same boat as thousands of others who attract public attention. He could not expect a system of privacy to protect him from such comments. Nor would the law of privacy permit recovery in cases such as those involving publicity given to private debts. Statutes prohibiting publication of the name of the victim in rape cases, at least when formulated in general terms, would likewise not be justified by the rules of privacy.[58]

The narrow area of protection would reach only to communication that touched the inner core of intimacy. The case of *York v. Story* furnishes an example. In that case a woman who came to the police complaining of an assault was asked by a police officer to undress and pictures were taken of her in the nude. The officer who took the pictures and other officers who circulated them later were made defendants in a suit brought under the Federal Civil Rights Act. The court upheld the claim as an infringement of the constitutional right of privacy. Descriptions or photographs of a woman in childbirth, of sexual intercourse, of similar personal and intimate details of one's life would receive similar protection. Beyond this point, however, disclosure of embarrassing facts or fictionalization would not be embraced by the legal system of privacy.[59]

4. INTRUSION ON SECLUSION

Protection of privacy through preventing intrusion on solitude or seclusion is a major feature of any system of privacy. This protection may take legal form as a constitutional limitation on governmental conduct or as statutory regulation of intrusion from nongovernmental sources. In the former case no conflict with the First Amendment would normally be involved; indeed protection to privacy may actu-

58. *Spahn v. Julian Messner, Inc.*, 18 N.Y.2d 324, 329, 221 N.E.2d 543, 545 (1966), judgment for Spahn vacated, 387 U.S. 239 (1967); judgment for Spahn affirmed on remand 21 N.Y.2d 124, 233 N.E.2d 840 (1967), appeal dismissed by agreement of the parties 393 U.S. 1046 (1969). For discussion of the statutes prohibiting publication of the names of rape victims see Marc A. Franklin, "A Constitutional Problem in Privacy Protection: Legal Inhibitions on Reporting of Fact," *Stanford Law Review*, Vol. 16 (1963), p. 107, and other materials cited in *Political and Civil Rights in the United States*, p. 1260.

59. *York v. Story*, 324 F.2d 450 (9th Cir. 1963), cert. denied 376 U.S. 939 (1964).

ally be based on that constitutional provision. If the government seeks to prevent invasion of privacy from private sources, however, conflict with First Amendment rights is possible. Again it should be noted that most of these intrusions, such as trespass or wiretapping, are clearly classifiable as "action." Invasion by "expression" is a minor part of the problem. It may be for this reason that the Supreme Court, while it has several times touched upon the issues arising from this kind of intrusion, has never formulated any clear-cut doctrine.

The question was first presented, so far as it involved statutory protection of privacy from nongovernmental intrusion, in *Martin v. Struthers*. A municipal ordinance forbade any person "to ring the door bell, sound the door knocker, or otherwise summon the inmate or inmates of any residence to the door" for the purpose of receiving handbills, circulars or similar literature. The ordinance was justified partly as a crime prevention measure, but mainly as a protection for the privacy of the residents, some of whom worked on night shifts and slept during the day. The Supreme Court, by a five to four vote, held the ordinance invalid as an infringement upon the First Amendment. Justice Black, writing for the majority, posed the question as one of balancing the interest in crime prevention and privacy against the interest in freedom of speech. He acknowledged that the government could impose reasonable health and police regulations on the time and manner of distributing literature but found that, under the circumstances and in view of the alternatives available, the ordinance violated the First Amendment. The dissenters would have upheld the ordinance as a reasonable regulation for the protection of important social interests. The case would probably not be handled in quite the same way today, but a majority would undoubtedly treat the problem as a First Amendment issue and resolve it by balancing interests. Viewed in terms of the requirements of a system of privacy, however, the case is not a difficult one. Surely the right of privacy does not, in theory or practice, require a blanket prohibition against seeking access to houses for purposes of communication.[60]

Similar issues came before the Court in the sound truck cases. In *Saia v. New York* a municipal ordinance prohibited the use of outdoor sound amplification without permission of the Chief of Police. The Supreme Court, in another five to four decision, invalidated the ordi-

60. *Martin v. Struthers,* 319 U.S. 141 (1943). It would appear that Justice Black in the sixties would adhere to his 1943 views and also balance interests, viewing the ordinance as an "indirect" limitation on speech. See his dissent in *Konigsberg v. State Bar of California,* 366 U.S. 36, 56 (1961).

nance as constituting a prior restraint with unlimited discretion vested in a police official to decide whether to allow speech. A year later, in *Kovacs v. Cooper,* the Court upheld, also five to four, a municipal ordinance that imposed a criminal penalty upon persons using sound amplification which "emits therefrom loud and raucous noises." There were five opinions and no majority view. In spite of the general confusion left by the two decisions, there appears to have been substantial agreement on principle. Only two members of the Court seemed to feel that a complete prohibition upon sound amplification would be constitutional. The remainder took the view that there must be an accommodation between the two interests that would allow reasonable regulation of volume, time and place. One may reach the same conclusion by looking simply at the needs of a system of privacy. Such a system does not require that all sound amplification be shut off. It does demand that sound trucks ranging through a residential area in the middle of the night be silenced.[61]

More difficult questions are presented by situations involving the picketing of private homes. Strong claims to privacy can be presented here. Some accommodation of the interests of free expression and privacy is possible, as in limiting such picketing to daylight or normal working hours. But a serious question is still raised as to whether residential picketing should be allowed at all. The Supreme Court has not passed on the issue. Other courts have permitted the picketing, but there is an increasing tendency to recognize the right of privacy as controlling. It would be hard to say that a narrowly drawn statute or carefully structured judicial policy limiting this kind of picketing is not justified as necessary to a system of privacy, and therefore not invalid under the First Amendment.[62]

Difficult questions are also raised by captive audience situations. To some extent a captive audience problem was involved in the sound truck decisions, but the issue was submerged by the noise aspects of those cases. The issue has come before the Supreme Court, but in a case where the government itself was charged with holding the audience captive and hence the First Amendment and privacy interests

61. *Saia v. New York,* 334 U.S. 558 (1948); *Kovacs v. Cooper,* 336 U.S. 77 (1949). See generally on the problem of noise George A. Spater, "Noise and the Law," *Michigan Law Review,* Vol. 63 (1965), p. 1373.

62. See Note, "Picketing the Homes of Public Officials," *University of Chicago Law Review,* Vol. 34 (1966), p. 106; Alfred Kamin, "Residential Picketing and the First Amendment," *Northwestern University Law Review,* Vol. 61 (1966), p. 177.

coincided rather than conflicted. In *Public Utilities Commission v. Pollak,* suit was brought against the Public Utilities Commission of the District of Columbia to prevent it from permitting the local transit company to broadcast music, news and advertising on its streetcars and buses. The Court rejected both First Amendment and privacy claims. There was no violation of the First Amendment, said the majority, because the broadcasts did not interfere with ordinary conversation and they did not involve objectionable propaganda. There was no violation of the Fifth Amendment because the right of privacy outside the home was not the equivalent of that in the home, and the regulation here was a reasonable one. Justice Black, concurring, made clear he would find a violation of the First Amendment if propaganda were being broadcast. Justice Douglas, dissenting, made a strong plea for recognition of the right of privacy as protecting the integrity and independence of citizens in their capacity as decision makers:

> If liberty is to flourish, government should never be allowed to force people to listen to any radio program. The right of privacy should include the right to pick and choose from competing entertainments, competing propaganda, competing political philosophies. If people are let alone in those choices, the right of privacy will pay dividends in character and integrity. The strength of our system is in the dignity, the resourcefulness, and the independence of our people. Our confidence is in their ability as individuals to make the wisest choice. That system cannot flourish if regimentation takes hold. The right of privacy, today violated, is a powerful deterrent to any one who would control men's minds.[63]

The captive audience issue can arise, of course, where the government undertakes to prohibit an individual or organization from communicating to an audience bound for some reason to listen. If the Public Utilities Commission, for instance, had prohibited the transit company from broadcasting, such an issue would be presented. Here the right of privacy and the First Amendment are in opposition. It seems unlikely that the Supreme Court would adhere to the *Pollak* case in refusing to give any substantial recognition to a right of privacy outside the home. It would most likely acknowledge the interest and attempt to solve the problem by balancing. Obvious difficulties are presented in trying to assess the weight to be given to freedom of expression in these circumstances. A more rational approach would be to

63. *Public Utilities Commission v. Pollak,* 343 U.S. 451, 469 (1952).

make the decision in terms of what is necessary to maintain an effective system of privacy.

5. APPROPRIATION

A large proportion of the tort law of privacy is concerned with the situation in which a person claims that his name, likeness or personality has been appropriated by another for the latter's advantage. The issues are akin to those arising in property law. It is questionable whether the interests at stake here are properly classified as interests in privacy. In any event there are good reasons for not considering such expropriation of property as being protected under a system of privacy. But it is not necessary to pursue the point. We are concerned here with the scope of the constitutional protection for freedom of expression. It is clear, as the Supreme Court recognized in *Time v. Hill*, that the First Amendment issues raised by expropriation statutes are quite different from those just considered.[64]

The problem in expropriation cases is to define the area of commercial speech, which falls outside the boundaries of the system of freedom of expression. At some points the answer is clear. Prohibition of the use of a photograph for advertising the sale of goods, without the owner's consent, would surely raise no more question under the First Amendment than does the copyright law. But a biography of a public figure, even though it exploits the experience and personality of another, is just as clearly protected. As is usual in commercial speech situations, the theoretical line is hard to draw. For present purposes it is enough to say that First Amendment issues in this area of privacy law must be resolved on the principle that the system of free expression does not extend to commercial speech.[65]

64. For discussion of the appropriation issue see Prosser, *op. cit. supra* note 50, pp. 401–407; Wade, *op. cit. supra* note 51, pp. 1096–1101; and, for a different view, Bloustein, *op. cit. supra* note 44, pp. 985–991. The reference in *Time*

v. Hill is 385 U.S. at 381. For an attempt to enjoin publication of a biography see *Frick v. Stevens,* 43 Pa. D. & C.2d 6 (1967).

65. On the commercial sector see Chapter XII.

C. Conclusion

We are now in a position to bring together the law of libel and the law of privacy insofar as they relate to the law of the First Amendment. Communication that invades the inner core of the personality, assaulting the dignity of the individual by depicting matters of a wholly personal and intimate nature, may be subject to government control. Under existing legal doctrine, if such a communication contained matter that was false and defamatory, it would be governed by the law of libel. If the matter was not false, it would be subject to a privacy action. Or either kind of communication might be regulated by some other form of governmental sanction. Outside this narrow area the First Amendment would afford full protection.

Under this approach, it would no longer be necessary to distinguish the libel action from the privacy action. In fact the stricter rules applicable in defamation actions, such as those imposing heavier burdens of proof on the plaintiff, would not make sense. There would be no reason to create greater safeguards for the defendant when the communication was false than when it was true. Thus the incipient tendency to merge the two forms of action would be brought to fruition.

However that may be, from the First Amendment point of view the problem would be resolved by establishing a constitutional right of privacy. The scope of that right would be determined by what was necessary to maintain an effective system of privacy, a guarantee of that "sphere of space" essential to the integrity and freedom of the individual. The rules safeguarding the right of privacy would block out the rules governing the system of free expression, as they would block out all other rules of the collectivity.

XV

Government
Employees

The right of government employees to freedom of expression has become a matter of growing importance over the last several decades. One reason is the sheer increase in the number of persons employed by government and thereby directly affected. At the close of the nineteen-sixties there were some three million employees of the Federal government and about nine million employees of State and local governments. This represents approximately 15 percent of the total working force and, together with family and dependents indirectly affected, a correspondingly high proportion of the total population. Obviously it is a matter of grave concern whether such large numbers of persons in the nation are to be seriously restricted in their expression on controversial public issues, in their political activities, or otherwise in their normal role as citizens.[1]

There are also qualitative aspects to the question. Government employees are often a significant source of information, when information is hard to come by. They frequently possess valuable expertise, when issues are growing too complex for the ordinary citizen to handle. Government employees may thus make important contributions to the discussion of public issues, and those contributions may become the more vital as the viewpoint of the speaker diverges from

1. U.S. Bureau of the Census, *Statistical Abstract of the United States: 1968* (89th ed.) (Washington, D.C., G.P.O., 1968), pp. 429, 215. These figures do not include members of the armed forces. For reasons already explained the right to freedom of expression by persons in military service raises somewhat different problems. See Chapter IV. Those issues are not considered here. For discussion of the problem see Detlev F. Vagts, "Free Speech in the Armed Forces," *Columbia Law Review*, Vol. 57 (1957), p. 187; John G. Kester, "Soldiers Who Insult the President: An Uneasy Look at Article 88 of the Uniform Code of Military Justice," *Harvard Law Review*, Vol. 81 (1968), p. 1697.

official policy. Furthermore, freedom of expression on the part of government employees can play an important role in counteracting those stultifying forces which customarily pervade bureaucracy. Organizational pressures toward dullness and conformity in the public service can perhaps be partly overcome by establishing firm principles that encourage, or at least protect, diversity in opinion and discussion. Modern First Amendment doctrine, therefore, should safeguard and promote the rights of government employees to participate as fully as possible in the system of free expression.[2]

Only in recent times, however, has First Amendment theory moved in this direction. The original concept of the status of a government employee was that, by accepting government employment, the employee waived all constitutional rights that could be considered as conflicting in any way with his strict obligation as a "servant" of the government. In effect public employees were put in the same position, with the same absence of rights, as employees of private enterprise. This basic view was formulated in the familiar epigram of Justice Holmes in *McAuliffe v. Mayor of New Bedford*. Rejecting the claim of a policeman that his constitutional rights had been violated by his discharge for engaging in political activities, Justice Holmes said: "The petitioner may have a constitutional right to talk politics, but he has no constitutional right to be a policeman." [3]

Justice Holmes went on to explain: "There are few employments for hire in which the servant does not agree to suspend his constitutional right of free speech, as well as of idleness, by the implied terms of his contract. The servant cannot complain, as he takes the employment on the terms which are offered him." [4]

The Holmes view that government employment was a privilege, to which no constitutional rights attached, was widely accepted by the courts for many years, and still echoes in some of their decisions. As a result the government employee had few substantive or procedural protections, other than those accorded him by grace of the government in the civil service laws. Even as to those rights the courts exercised an exceedingly narrow scope of review over executive action. Moreover, far from according First Amendment rights to government employees,

2. The converse problem—limitation upon participation in the system of freedom of expression by government officials who may use their position to impair the free working of the system—is considered in Chapter XIX.

3. *McAuliffe v. Mayor of New Bedford*, 155 Mass. 216, 220, 29 N.E. 517 (1892).

4. 155 Mass. at 220, 29 N.E. at 517–518.

the thrust of the civil service regulations was to take away such rights as a means of protecting government employees from the spoils system. That policy was embodied in legislation in the Hatch Act, enacted in 1939, which prohibited Federal employees from taking "any active part in political management or political campaigns." This provision of the Hatch Act was upheld against First Amendment challenge in *United Public Workers v. Mitchell* on the ground that "[f]or regulation of employees it is not necessary that the act regulated be anything more than an act reasonably deemed by Congress to interfere with the efficiency of the public service." [5]

The basic doctrines relating to the rights of government employees have now, however, changed substantially. Even in the *United Public Workers* case the Supreme Court acknowledged that there were "limitations on congressional power" to restrict the conduct of Federal employees. It would not be constitutional, the Court said, to "enact a regulation providing that no Republican, Jew or Negro shall be appointed to federal office, or that no federal employee shall attend Mass or take any active part in missionary work." The Court's decisions in the State loyalty cases further undermined the Holmes position. By 1967, in *Keyishian v. Board of Regents,* the Court was saying: "[T]he theory that public employment which may be denied altogether may be subjected to any conditions, regardless of how unreasonable, has been uniformly rejected." The following year, in *Pickering v. Board of Education,* the Court made clear that the First Amendment extended a substantial measure of protection to government employees and that the status of the *United Public Workers* case was in considerable doubt. The current issue, therefore, is not whether government employment is an unprotected "privilege" but rather, taking the First Amendment as broadly applicable, what limitations will be carved out of it with respect to government employees.[6]

5. *United Public Workers v. Mitchell,* 330 U.S. 75, 101 (1947). Typical of the attitude of the courts toward the rights of government employees, even as late as 1950, is *Bailey v. Richardson,* 182 F.2d 46 (D.C. Cir. 1950), aff'd by an equally divided Court, 341 U.S. 918 (1951), discussed in Chapter VII. For other material see Note, "Dismissal of Federal Employees—The Emerging Judicial Role," *Columbia Law Review,* Vol. 66 (1966), p. 719; M. N. Chaturvedi, "Legal Protection Available to Federal Employees Against Wrongful Dismissal," *Northwestern University Law Review,* Vol. 63 (1968), p. 287; Thomas I. Emerson, David Haber and Norman Dorsen, *Political and Civil Rights in the United States* (Boston, Little, Brown & Co., 3d ed. 1967), pp. 363–364, 635–636 (cited hereafter in this chapter as *Political and Civil Rights in the United States*).

6. *United Public Workers v. Mitchell,* 330 U.S. at 100 (1947); *Keyishian v. Board of Regents of the University of the State of New York,* 385 U.S. 589, 605–

On this basis the controlling principles can be briefly sketched. The conduct with which we are here concerned is that which falls within the definition of "expression"; all other conduct would be "action" and not protected by the First Amendment in any event. In the context of government employment, the "expression" in question would include various forms of outside political activities, discussion of issues in a public forum, and other communications addressed to persons outside the employing agency or outside the government. The term would also include communications made in the regular course of agency business, even a conversation between two employees of the agency on some minor matter pending for agency consideration. In other words, if the communication satisfies the other requirements for classification as "expression," the fact that it takes place within the employment relation does not take it out of the category of "expression." Any other view would, of course, render the First Amendment inapplicable except as to utterances made outside the course of agency business. But there is no reason to draw the line at such a point. Effective functioning of a system of freedom of expression requires, certainly so far as the government employee is concerned, protection for statements made within the employment relation as well as outside it.

The main issues, therefore, center around the question of "abridgment." We may start with the proposition that in general the government employee is entitled to the same right of expression as the ordinary citizen. There are some points, however, where the expectation of the employee in assuming the job and the common understanding of the obligation necessarily imposed on him to maintain an effective government service allow for exceptions to the general rule that would not be considered "abridgments" of the basic right. These points are determined by the fact that the individual has entered into an "employment relation" with the government. The question is what features of that employment relation demand different rules for the government employee than for others. The problem is not answered by open-ended formulations that the government may do whatever is necessary "to promote the efficiency of the service," or that employees may be disciplined or discharged "for good cause," or for conduct "detrimen-

---

606 (1967); *Pickering v. Board of Education*, 391 U.S. 563 (1968). For an account of this development see William W. Van Alstyne, "The Demise of the Right-Privilege Distinction in Constitutional Law," *Harvard Law Review*, Vol. 81 (1968), p. 1439.

tal to the best interests of the service." The governing rules must be more precisely framed.

Upon analysis the crucial factors seem to be that (1) the individual is employed to do a particular job in a particular way, as determined by his superiors; and (2) he is a member of an organization, also with a particular job to do. The first feature requires that the employee be competent and render obedience to orders. The second implies a relationship to supervisors, fellow workers, and inferiors that will permit effective operation of the organization as a whole. It is only upon the basis of factors relevant to these considerations that limitations upon the expression of government employees can be justified as not amounting to an "abridgment." To this should be added one other element, particularly important in this context. The rules should be formulated with a view to the administrative requirements for effective functioning of a system of freedom of expression, subject to the limitations indicated, within the government bureaucracy.

The problems have arisen in two principal forms. One set of issues has concerned the general right of government employees to express their views, particularly when such expression involves criticism of the government, its officials, or its policies. The other relates to the right of government employees to engage more specifically in political activities, as raised by the Hatch Act and similar legislation.

A. The General Right of Expression

Exercise of the general right of expression by a government employee may involve two different kinds of communication. The utterance may relate to the job the employee is performing, that is, the subject matter of the communication may be connected with his immediate work or with the agency to which he is attached. Or the utterance may be unrelated to performance of the employee's work and the functions of his agency. Different considerations govern in the two situations.

1. EXPRESSION NOT CONNECTED WITH THE JOB

When the expression is not connected with the employee's job few difficulties arise. The starting proposition, that a government employee is in the same position as an ordinary citizen, is applicable without substantial qualification. Those factors which might lead to the conclusion that no "abridgment" would occur from limitation of expression are almost wholly absent. Normally no issue of competence to do the job is raised and no failure to obey orders is involved. Nor would the expression create any problem in the relations of the employee with his agency or fellow employees. The employee, therefore, is ordinarily entitled to the same protection as a person who has not entered the employment relationship.

It is possible to envisage some conditions under which expression not connected with the job might have a bearing upon competency. Usually what an employee has said upon a subject unrelated to his employment has little relevance to his ability to perform his work. Nevertheless, certain kinds of communication, such as deliberately false statements, might under certain circumstances reflect upon character and hence upon competency. Thus it is impossible to rule out all qualifications of the general rule. Yet the exceptions would certainly be limited and minor.

What this means, in essence, is that government employment does not in itself prevent an employee from engaging in expression critical of the government or that tends to defeat governmental policies. Our system of government service does not require, and our system of freedom of expression does not permit, that a government employee remain silent on issues of public concern. Quite the contrary, they demand that he be free to exercise the right of expression even in opposition to the government, so long as it does not affect his employment relation. All the considerations previously mentioned—the high proportion of our population involved, the nature of the contribution government employees can make, the need for overcoming the stultifying effect of bureaucracy—support this conclusion. Nor does our modern concept of government employment point in any different direction. We have grown beyond the notion that a government position constitutes a favor and binds the recipient to total, unquestioning "loyalty" to every policy of government. In fact, we are slowly beginning to realize that modern democracy must incorporate the principle that public privileges and benefits, including money and position, should be extended to those who will use them in competition with, and to some extent in opposition to, official policy.

Issues of this nature have not frequently arisen, and there appears to be no judicial decision dealing specifically with them. The problem has, however, at times been presented. In the spring of 1968, for instance, over 2500 Federal employees signed a statement, which was published as an advertisement in the *Washington Evening Star*, expressing strong disagreement with "our nation's policy in Southeast Asia," indicating their "daily, personal anguish [with] the actions taken in Vietnam by the government for which we ourselves work," and calling "for the war's end." Congressman Edwin E. Willis, Chairman of the House Committee on Un-American Activities, responded by ordering the staff of his Committee "to make a preliminary inquiry into the origin, character, and objectives" of the sponsors. He also introduced a bill that would permit the President, in time of war or armed conflict, to remove from office any employee who organized or participated in "any demonstration, program or activity involving the dissemination among two or more employees of the Federal Government of any written or printed statement, or other propaganda or agitational material, for the purpose of . . . impairing the morale, loyalty, or efficiency of employees of the executive branch" with respect to their duties in connection with the war. No formal action was taken.[7]

It would seem clear that expression of this nature is protected under the First Amendment. Indeed that view seems to be generally accepted. The President's Commission on Political Activity of Government Personnel, reporting at the end of 1967, recognized unequivocally: "Public employees should be permitted to express their opinions freely in private and in public on any political subject or candidate." The *Pickering* case, decided in June 1968, in substance also took the view that expression unconnected with the job should be accorded the usual protection of the First Amendment.[8]

7. The statement was printed in the *Washington Evening Star*, April 1, 1968. Congressman Willis' statement and bill may be found in 114 *Cong. Rec.* 6792–6793. Signing of the statement by employees of the Department of Defense, the State Department or a few other agencies might raise the problem, discussed below, of expression connected with the job.

8. Commission on Political Activity of Government Personnel, *Findings and Recommendations* (Washington, D.C., G.P.O., 1968), Vol. I, p. 4; *Pickering v. Board of Education*, 391 U.S. 563 (1968), both discussed *infra*.

2. EXPRESSION CONNECTED WITH THE JOB

Expression connected with the job poses more troublesome questions. Such expression may be divided into two categories: first, that disseminated entirely within the limits of the government agency or agencies involved; and second, that directed to persons outside the agencies immediately concerned. The distinction is not always easy to maintain. But in general it focuses on the differences between communications confined to the relevant organizational framework of the executive branch and communications that reach the outside public. Communications addressed to the legislative branch or to individual legislators, which are very likely to come to public attention and which in effect constitute an appeal to the public, combine characteristics of both categories.

Job-related communications taking place within the organizational context must, as already noted, be classified as "expression" and hence fall within the coverage of the First Amendment. Problems of control over such communications, however, are more likely to involve the internal operations of a government bureaucracy than the maintenance of a system of freedom of expression. Thus, in this area the relationship between the communication of the employee and his competence in the job is usually strong and immediate. Similarly there is a direct connection between such communications and obedience to orders, since official policy is usually carried out through some form of communication. Furthermore communications of this nature are closely bound up with the problem of maintaining harmonious relations inside the organization. Hence the controlling factors are primarily matters of internal management, and the issues must largely be resolved in those terms rather than on free speech considerations. Essentially management controls of this kind do not constitute an "abridgment" of expression.

On the other hand, there remains room within the governmental bureaucracy for the operation, at least on a limited scale, of the system of freedom of expression. Not only do the fundamental objectives of the First Amendment require this, but the vitality and ultimate effectiveness of the government service depend upon it. Except where the necessities of the employment relation demand otherwise, freedom of expression within the bureaucracy should be encouraged and protected. What this means, in more specific terms, is that First Amendment rights should be enforced where control over expression is not predicated upon considerations essential to maintenance of the employment relation or where reliance upon such considerations is simply a pretense for repression of expression. It would mean, also, that the question whether certain expression is subject to sanction would be only part of a broader judgment concerned with the competence, insubordination, or disruptive conduct of the employee concerned. The hazards involved in a court's making determinations of this nature are admittedly formidable. But such a judgment is not totally beyond the reach of judicial capacity.

It should be noted that the authority of the First Amendment within the government bureaucracy is substantially strengthened by the specific clause in that provision guaranteeing the right "to petition the Government for a redress of grievances." There is no authoritative ruling that the First Amendment right of petition applies to the individual grievances of workers in government agencies. But there is nothing in the background or purpose of the First Amendment which precludes this, and there are good reasons for extending such protection to the large and growing mass of government employees. In addition, the Lloyd-LaFollette Act of 1912, as now incorporated in 5 U.S.C. §7102, expressly provides:

> The right of employees, individually or collectively, to petition Congress or a Member of Congress, or to furnish information to either House of Congress, or to a Committee Member thereof, may not be interfered with or denied.

This constitutional and statutory right of petition applies only to certain kinds of expression, those which are couched in the form of a request for redress of a grievance. The legal effect of the right of petition is by no means clear. It certainly safeguards the bare right to petition Congress or executive officials. This might be important, particularly in the case of an employee who seeks to register a protest with a higher official, over the head of his immediate superior. But the right of petition does not eliminate all controls over communication based upon the requirements of the employment relation. Under some circumstances, therefore, the content of the petition might still subject the employee to discipline. Thus the ultimate impact of the right of petition cannot be readily stated. The most that can be said, perhaps, is that where the provision is applicable, the employee stands in a somewhat better position to maintain his claim to freedom of expression.[9]

Thus far the courts have given small recognition to claims of First Amendment protection for job-connected expression occurring within the organizational context. The Supreme Court has never addressed itself to the question and, except in isolated cases involving the right of petition, the lower Federal courts have never ruled in favor of the employee. Some of the decisions, relying upon earlier doctrine, have allowed only the narrowest scope of review, refusing in effect to probe into the agency ruling on dismissal or discipline. The others have applied loose and indeterminate criteria for justification of agency action, such as that the employee's statement was "untrue," "irresponsible," "intemperate," "defamatory," or "disloyal." The courts have failed to come to grips with the critical issue—whether the sanction applied by the agency was demanded by the necessities of the employment relation. In addition the courts have at times upheld the imposition of difficult procedural requirements, such as that the employee prove the truth of his factual assertions.[10]

Typical of the reaction of the courts to these issues is the decision in *Turner v. Kennedy*. Turner, employed as an F.B.I. agent for ten years, was placed on indefinite probation and suspended by J. Edgar Hoover, Director of the Bureau, for "apparently . . . placing . . . personal preferences and conveniences [with respect to assignments and transfers] above the welfare and needs of the F.B.I." Turner then wrote letters to Senator Kefauver and Representative Celler undertaking to refute these charges, and asking action by Congress to compel his reinstatement and to reform F.B.I. personnel practices. In these letters Turner alleged that: "(1) retaliation had been taken because of his re-

9. No court has expressly ruled that the First Amendment right of petition does not extend to the personal grievances of government employees. Two judges have held that it does. *Turner v. Kennedy,* 332 F.2d 304 (D.C. Cir. 1964), Judge Fahy dissenting; *Swaaley v. United States,* 376 F.2d 857 (Ct. Cl. 1967). For further discussion, as well as a survey of the background of §7102, formerly §652(d), see Note, "Dismissals of Public Employees for Petitioning Congress: Administrative Discipline and 5 U.S.C. Section 652(d)," *Yale Law Journal,* Vol. 74 (1965), p. 1156. See also *Steck v. Connally,* cited below.

10. See *Levine v. Farley,* 107 F.2d

186 (D.C. Cir. 1939), cert. denied 308 U.S. 622 (1940); *Keyton v. Anderson,* 229 F.2d 519 (D.C. Cir. 1956); *Houston v. United States,* 297 F.2d 838 (Ct. Cl. 1962), cert. denied, 371 U.S. 815 (1962); *Kennrich v. United States,* 340 F.2d 653 (Ct. Cl. 1965); *Turner v. Kennedy, supra* note 9; *Jenson v. Olson,* 353 F.2d 825 (8th Cir. 1965); *Veatch v. Resor,* 266 F. Supp. 893 (D. Colo. 1967). Other cases are discussed in *Swaaley v. United States, supra* note 9. See Note, *supra* note 9; Note, *George Washington Law Review,* Vol. 36 (1967), p. 447. See also *Leonard v. Douglas,* 321 F.2d 749 (D.C. Cir. 1963); *Ruderer v. United States,* 412 F.2d 1285 (Ct. Cl. 1969).

quest for a transfer; (2) the Bureau had failed to make use of his technical qualifications in assigning him to a 'permanent road trip'; (3) an inspector had been sent to discredit him rather than to conduct an impartial investigation into his claims; (4) a memorandum relating to his work performance was missing from the files; (5) his supervisor was absent from work; and (6) morale in the F.B.I. [was] at an all-time low." The F.B.I. charged that certain statements in Turner's letters were "false, untrue or made irresponsibly." The Bureau also charged that Turner had displayed a "poor attitude toward the F.B.I. and its Director." This ground for dismissal was based on a sentence in Turner's letter to Senator Kefauver declaring: "It would appear that any statement not serving to perpetuate the Hoover myth is therefore an 'unfounded allegation.'" The Civil Service Commission approved Turner's dismissal on both grounds, though the basis for its decision was not entirely clear. The District Court, ruling on cross motions for summary judgment, upheld the discharge without opinion. The Court of Appeals affirmed per curiam, also without discussion of the issues. Judge Fahy dissented on the ground that the Lloyd-LaFollette provision, read in the light of the First Amendment, required that Turner's letters be protected unless it was shown that he had made false statements with "actual malice, that is with knowledge that they were false or with reckless disregard of whether false or not." [11]

The problems raised by the *Turner* case are difficult ones. And the failure of the courts to develop the facts leaves the specific questions there involved obscure. Yet it would seem clear that Turner was raising significant issues, both with respect to his personal treatment and with respect to broader policies of the agency; and it is by no means certain that the demands of the employment relation justified dismissal rather than rational discussion. One can sympathize with the reluctance of the courts to review in depth the decisions of government agencies concerning matters of competence, insubordination and disruption. Moreover, one can imagine that Agent Turner's life in the F.B.I., after reinstatement by the courts, would not be a happy one. Nevertheless it is unfortunate that the courts have not yet begun the

11. *Turner v. Kennedy,* 332 F.2d 304, 307 (D.C. Cir. 1964), cert. denied 379 U.S. 901 (1964). The quotations in the statement of the case are taken from Note, *supra* note 9, which suggests that the Supreme Court may have denied certiorari because the petition was filed late. In *Swaaley v. United States, supra* note 9, dismissal of a Navy Department employee was held improper on grounds similar to those urged by Judge Fahy in *Turner.* See also *Steck v. Connally,* 199 F. Supp. 104 (D.D.C. 1961), holding invalid the dismissal of an employee for circulating a petition to a member of Congress.

task of delineating the reach of the First Amendment within the government bureaucracy and of formulating judicial techniques for assuring its realization in this troublesome but significant sector.

Substantially more progress has been made in the area of job-connected expression that is addressed to the public at large. Here some different considerations are present. Expression of this sort, taking place in the public arena, falls more clearly within the main currents of the system of freedom of expression. It involves an effort to alert the public to problems buried in the depths of the bureaucracy, or at least to participate in open discussion of public affairs. It thus serves one of the basic purposes of the First Amendment in aiding the citizenry to check upon the operations of government. This function is enhanced when the particular employee has a special knowledge of the facts, a particularly relevant experience, or other forms of expertise.

Moreover, the problems presented to the judiciary in this situation are likely to be somewhat more manageable than in the case of expression occurring entirely within the organizational structure. The constitutional issue presented to the court is the same—whether the expression is incompatible with the essential demands of the employment relation. Here, again, the general impact of the expression upon the government's position, even when detrimental, is not ground for suppression. There must be specific proof that the expression has demonstrated incompetence to perform the job, violation of legitimate orders, or creation of serious organizational disruption. In this situation, however, the court is in a better position to weigh the impact of the expression and to judge its effect upon the agency. The court may also feel more ready to prescribe rules that afford greater protection to the employee, such as requiring the government to show the specific results of the expression with respect to the job performance. All this follows from the fact that the expression originates outside the agency and the controversy takes place mostly in the public view. The issues are fought in an open and familiar setting rather than behind the curtain of bureaucratic confidences and secrecy.

There is one further potential difference. The employee may have had the opportunity to express his views inside the government agency before taking them outside to the public. Should he be required to exhaust the possibilities for expression within the agency? In most cases the employee would certainly have done so. His failure to take advantage of such an opportunity might conceivably have a bearing upon the issue of job performance. Yet plainly no rigid requirement of this nature should be exacted. The question is one for the employee to decide for himself. The constitutional right to freedom of expression cannot be made to turn upon an ex post facto judgment that the expression was premature.

The attitude of the courts toward review of agency action in disciplining an employee who engages in public expression on agency affairs was originally much the same as that displayed by the majority in the *Turner* case.[12] Two recent cases, however, have inaugurated a new and more meaningful approach.

In *Meehan v. Macy* the government employee involved, Meehan, was a private on the police force in the Panama Canal Zone and president of the policemen's union. Following rioting by Panamanians in the Canal Zone in 1964 the Governor of the Canal Zone proposed, as a means of improving the situation, to enlist Panamanians to serve on the police force. The union, including Meehan, strongly opposed this proposal. Among other activities, Meehan arranged for the printing of five thousand copies of an anonymous letter and two enclosures, consisting of a poem written by another person and an excerpt from the *Congressional Record*. Copies were circulated and later printed in the *Congressional Record*. The poem attacked the Governor as one who "Recruits the foreign nationals,/ Rejects the native sons." Its strongest verse charged that the Governor "Refutes the wish of Congress/ By subterfuge and lies,/ Twists knives of propaganda/ While factual heartbeat dies." The letter urged the reader to write his Congressman and protest the Governor's plan, its most "offensive" paragraph being: "We do not intend to perpetrate a personal attack upon the Honorable Governor of the Canal Zone, for we are aware that he is only a Major General and in reality only an instrument of the boys in the black strip [sic] pants in the State Department, whose major goal since the time of Alger Hiss has been to implement the policy of New Americanism and erase all opinions opposed to their policies." No issue was raised concerning the excerpt from the *Congressional Record*.

Meehan was discharged for "conduct unbecoming a Police Officer of the Canal Zone Government," as well as on two other grounds not connected with distribution of the letter and poem. The District Court granted the Government's motion for summary judgment. The Court

12. See, *e.g., Eustace v. Day*, 198 F. Supp. 233 (D.D.C. 1961), aff'd per cu- riam 314 F.2d 247 (D.C. Cir. 1962).

of Appeals, after a careful sifting of the evidence, found the two other charges not sustained but held that the first was justified.[13]

Judge Leventhal, writing for the majority, noted, "As Government services multiply, the liberties of Government employees come to be the liberties of an increasing and substantial portion of the citizenry and are accordingly given increased recognition." He rejected the "apparent premise" of the Civil Service Commission that "an employee of the Government cannot claim the right to both a Government job and freedom of speech," observing that the "constitutional climate of today is different from that of 1892 when Justice Holmes struck off his oft quoted phrase." He refused, however, to accept Meehan's contention that "an employee may, without fear of discipline, say anything and anywhere whatever a private person may say without fear of a libel action, under the doctrine of *New York Times,*" pointing out that the "added interests of the sovereign as employer are factors to be considered in adjusting and balancing constitutional concerns." Judge Leventhal then enumerated the legal principles he considered applicable

> Free and open discussion within an agency of Government is different from heated debate flowing into the public arena. While a free society values robust, vigorous and essentially uninhibited public speech by citizens, when such uninhibited public speech by Government employees produces intolerable disharmony, inefficiency, dissension and even chaos, it may be subject to reasonable limitations, at least concerning matters relating to the duties, discretion, and judgment entrusted to the employee involved. There is a reasonable difference between the kind of discipline and limitation on speech the Government may impose on its employees and the kind it may impose on the public at large. To ensure a basic efficiency in public service a limitation may be imposed as a condition of Government employment that is broader than the standard that defines the wrongdoing that subjects a private citizen to penalty or damage action.[14]

Finally Judge Leventhal applied the doctrine to the case before him:

> In our view appellant's conduct in printing and beginning distribution of the letter and poem was a legitimate basis for discharge to promote the efficiency of the service. These documents, especially the poem

13. *Meehan v. Macy,* 392 F.2d 822 (D.C. Cir. 1968). One judge, dissenting in part, would have upheld all three charges on the ground that there was a "rational basis" for the agency's conclusions. 392 F.2d at 840. The decision was affirmed on rehearing *en banc,* May 12, 1969.

14. 392 F.2d at 832, 833.

were intemperate and sarcastic, a contemptuous and defamatory lampoon of the Governor and his policies. This invective by a policeman, charged under the circumstances with special responsibility and requirements of discipline, against the official ranking as chief of the force, is such a flouting of elemental loyalty to his employer and their common enterprise as to provide cause for discharge, except as the employee's acts may be necessary to preserve his own protected rights. Loyalty to the Government employer cannot be held to compel servility of thought and expression, but it does set a limit on channels and methods available to indicate disagreement with a superior official.[15]

Judge Leventhal's opinion marked a distinct advance. It recognized that the First Amendment gave a significant measure of protection to the government employee. It also accepted an obligation on the part of the court to scrutinize agency limitations in detail and with awareness of the difficulties to be faced in assuring employees the protection to which they are entitled. Nevertheless, both in the statement of the governing constitutional principle and in the application of that doctrine to the case before it, the decision did not carry through to an effective conclusion.

The rule of law adopted by the court properly recognized that the "interests of the sovereign as employer" authorize some restriction. But the court did not develop the specific nature of those interests or attempt to formulate the extent of allowable restrictions. In the end it did not go much further than to say that the government employee was subject to "broader" restrictions than the private citizen and that "reasonable limitations" were acceptable. This is hardly an adequate standard.

Similar deficiencies appear in the specific consideration of Meehan's case. The court found that the letter and poem were "intemperate and sarcastic, a contemptuous and defamatory lampoon of the Governor and his policies." The decision thus places primary emphasis upon the form or style of the communication, a doubtful criterion for measuring the limits of free expression even in the case of a government employee. It also gives substantial weight to the presumed effect upon the "policies" that the government was attempting to carry out. Yet, as we have seen, the general impact of the expression upon government policy is not in itself a proper criterion for limiting expression. To hold otherwise would virtually nullify all rights of the employee to effective expression.

15. 392 F.2d at 833–834.

Most important, the decision does not genuinely explore in any concrete way the crucial question whether in actual fact Meehan's expression was incompatible with the employment relation. There was nothing in the situation to compel a conclusion that Meehan was incompetent to do his job, or had refused to obey orders. The court assumed that circulation of the letter created an "intolerable disharmony." But it demanded no proof of this. Actually, the language used was by no means unusual for a rank and file employee, president of his union, to address to the top boss. The polemic style of a policeman is not necessarily that of a diplomat in the State Department. The court did not, however, examine these matters closely.

Undoubtedly a major element in the decision was the fact that the government employee was a policeman, considered to have "special responsibility and requirements of discipline," and that his utterances were made in a "tense and sensitive situation." The case may therefore be viewed as involving somewhat unusual circumstances. In any event, despite the disappointing failure to follow through on an admirable beginning, the decision opened up a promising approach.

The changing attitude of the courts was confirmed a few weeks later by the decision of the Supreme Court in *Pickering v. Board of Education*. Pickering, a high school teacher in Illinois, was dismissed by the Board of Education for writing a letter sharply critical of the administration of the school system to a local newspaper. The letter was written after several proposals made by the Board to raise additional funds through bond issues had been defeated by the voters of the town, and after various letters supporting the bond issues had been published in the newspaper by other teachers and by the Superintendent of Schools. Pickering's letter constituted a detailed attack upon various actions of the Board, particularly its allocation of funds to the school's athletic as opposed to its educational program. It also charged that the Superintendent of Schools had stated that "any teacher that opposes the referendum should be prepared for the consequences" and described the atmosphere at the school as "totalitarianism." The Board charged that there were eight statements in the letter which were false, but the Supreme Court's review of the record reduced these to four. The most important of the factual errors was a statement by Pickering that the Board was spending fifty thousand dollars a year on transportation for athletes, whereas the correct figure was ten thousand dollars. The Board, after hearing, dismissed Pickering on the ground that publication of his letter was "detrimental to the efficient operation and administration of the schools of the district." The Supreme Court, with Justice White dissenting in part, held that the dismissal violated Pickering's First Amendment rights.[16]

Justice Marshall, writing for the Court, formulated the issue in the following terms:

> To the extent that the Illinois Supreme Court's opinion may be read to suggest that teachers may constitutionally be compelled to relinquish the First Amendment rights they would otherwise enjoy as citizens to comment on matters of public interest in connection with the operation of the public schools in which they work, it proceeds on a premise that has been unequivocally rejected in numerous prior decisions of this Court. . . . At the same time it cannot be gainsaid that the State has interests as an employer in regulating the speech of its employees that differ significantly from those it possesses in connection with regulation of the speech of the citizenry in general. The problem in any case is to arrive at a balance between the interests of the teacher, as a citizen, in commenting upon matters of public concern and the interest of the State, as an employer, in promoting the efficiency of the public services it performs through its employees.[17]

Justice Marshall did not "deem it either appropriate or feasible to attempt to lay down a general standard against which all [expression by government employees] may be judged," but proceeded to "indicate some of the general lines along which an analysis of the controlling interests should run." He pointed out, first, that the statements in the letter "are in no way directed towards any person with whom the appellant would normally be in contact in the course of his daily work as a teacher," and thus there was "no question of maintaining either discipline by immediate superiors or harmony among coworkers." Nor were Pickering's "employment relationships" with the Board, or even the Superintendent, "the kind of close working relationships for which it can persuasively be claimed that personal loyalty and confidence are necessary to their proper functioning." Accordingly, "to the extent that the Board's position here can be taken to suggest that even comments on matters of public concern that are substantially correct . . . may furnish grounds for dismissal if they are sufficiently critical in tone, we unequivocally reject it." [18]

Secondly, with respect to the statements found to be false, Justice Marshall made a further, and more elaborate, analysis of the factors to

---

16. *Pickering v. Board of Education,* 391 U.S. 563 (1968).

17. 391 U.S. at 568.

18. 391 U.S. at 569–570.

be considered in the balance. He pointed out that no evidence had been introduced to support the Board's charges that publication of the letter had damaged the professional reputations of the Board and the Superintendent, or would foment controversy among the Board, teachers, administrators and residents; that it could not be presumed that the statements were "detrimental to the interests of the schools"; "more importantly," that teachers were "the members of a community most likely to have informed and definite opinions" as to how school funds should be allotted, and that "it is essential that they be able to speak out freely"; that "the Board could easily have rebutted appellant's errors by publishing the accurate figures itself"; and, in a footnote, that Pickering's statements were not "so without foundation as to call into question his fitness to perform his duties in the classroom." He summed up:

> What we do have before us is a case in which a teacher has made erroneous public statements upon issues then currently the subject of public attention, which are critical of his ultimate employer but which are neither shown nor can be presumed to have in any way either impeded the teacher's proper performance of his daily duties in the classroom or to have interfered with the regular operation of the schools generally. In these circumstances we conclude that the interest of the school administration in limiting teachers' opportunities to contribute to public debate is not significantly greater than its interest in limiting a similar contribution by any member of the general public.[19]

Having equated Pickering's position with that of the ordinary citizen, Justice Marshall applied the rule developed in cases involving libel of public officials—the actual malice test of *New York Times v. Sullivan*.[20]

The Supreme Court's decision in *Pickering* is a major contribution to solution of the problem. As in *Meehan*, the Court makes clear that there is a large, though indefinite, area of free expression granted to the government employee. Again, as in *Meehan*, it enlarges the re-

19. 391 U.S. at 570–573.

20. 391 U.S. at 573–575. Justices Black and Douglas concurred, citing their views in the *New York Times* and other libel cases. See Chapter XIV. For an analogous situation, in which the Court held expression by a government employee protected under the First Amendment when it did not interfere "with the performance of his duties," see *Wood v. Georgia*, 370 U.S. 375, 393–394 (1962), discussed in Chapter XII. See also *Watts v. Seward School Board*, 391 U.S. 592 (1968); *In re Gioglio*, 104 N.J. Super. 88, 248 A.2d 570 (1968); *Puentes v. Board of Education*, 24 N.Y.2d 996, 302 N.Y.S.2d 824, 250 N.E.2d 232 (1969); *Murray v. Vaughn*, 300 F. Supp. 688 (D.R.I. 1969).

sponsibility of the courts to review with care both the findings and judgments of the employing agency. Moreover, going beyond *Meehan*, the Court in *Pickering* holds that, at least as to "comments on matters of public concern that are substantially correct," a government employee may not be dismissed merely on the ground that his statements are "sufficiently critical in tone."

The Court's adoption of a broad balancing test as the controlling constitutional doctrine, however, leads to unfortunate results. At once it becomes impossible, as Justice Marshall himself acknowledged, to formulate any workable standard of judgment. Thus a government employee cannot conceivably know in advance how much weight should be given to the circumstance that he may have a specially "informed and definite opinion" about the issue, or that the agency could "easily have rebutted" his errors. Moreover, the open-ended balancing takes the Court into dangerous and irrelevant territory. Thus the Court finds it necessary to "presume," probably contrary to fact, that Pickering's letter had not "in any way . . . interfered with the regular operation of the schools generally." Here the Court is in the position of suggesting that only innocuous expression is entitled to protection, a view inconsistent with the whole theory of the First Amendment and its own prior emphasis on the need for teachers to be "able to speak out freely." Once again the balancing test proves an ineffectual tool.

It is interesting to note that the *Pickering* opinion, if read carefully, ultimately seems to rest upon those considerations relevant to the question whether the publication of Pickering's letter was incompatible with his commitments as an employee in the school system. Concerning the statements that were "substantially correct," the Court determined that no issue of insubordination or disruption was raised and then "unequivocally rejects" the attempt at discipline. As to the false statements, the Court further notes that no issue of competence is raised, and treats the question as if Pickering were an outside citizen, that is, finds no impairment of the employment relation. It would seem preferable for the Court to have accepted this approach forthrightly, without entangling itself in general balancing. Actually, on the facts of the case, *Pickering* was not a very difficult decision. More troublesome factual situations, which are bound to arise, may produce a sharper analysis.

B. Controls Over Political Activities

Special problems have arisen out of efforts by Federal, State, and local governments to impose broad restrictive measures upon the right of their employees to engage in political activities of the more partisan kind. Most of these activities, including active participation in election contests and in the management of political parties, plainly constitute "expression" and, were ordinary citizens involved, would obviously be protected by the First Amendment. The question is whether, for government employees, such regulations are an essential part of the employment relation and therefore do not abridge freedom of expression.

Controls over the political conduct of government employees have always been closely associated with civil service reform, the attempt to eliminate the "spoils system," and the maintenance of the government service on a merit basis. The Civil Service Act of 1883 and the rules promulgated thereunder by the Civil Service Commission forbid employees in the civil service to use their official authority or influence to coerce the political action of any person or to interfere with elections. In 1907 President Theodore Roosevelt extended the range of controls by an Executive Order, incorporated into the civil service rules, which provided that employees in the classified service, "while retaining the right to vote as they please and to express privately their opinions on all political subjects, shall take no part in political management or in political campaigns." The regulations remained in this form until passage of the Hatch Act in 1939.[21]

The Hatch Act, which is the principal legislation in the field, applies to all employees in the executive branch of the Federal Government, with limited exceptions such as the President's staff and high officials subject to Senate confirmation. Section 9(a), the key provision, reads as follows:

21. The Civil Service Act of 1883 appears in 22 Stat. 403, and the rules in *First Report of the Civil Service Commission* (1884), p. 45. President Roosevelt's order is Executive Order No. 642 (June 3, 1907). The current version of the Civil Service Act may be found in 5 U.S.C. §§1101 et seq., and of the Civil Service Rule in 5 C.F.R. §4.1. For a collection of material on the development of controls over political activities of government employees, see *Political and Civil Rights in the United States,* pp. 635–636. See also the study by Louis S. Loeb, prepared for the National Civil Service League, "Public Employees and Political Activity," printed in *Report of the President's Commission on Political Activity of Government Personnel, supra* note 8, vol. III, pp. 209–222.

It shall be unlawful for any person employed in the executive branch of the Federal Government or any agency or department thereof, to use his official authority or influence for the purpose of interfering with an election or affecting the result thereof. No officer or employee in the executive branch of the Federal Government, or any agency or department thereof, shall take any active part in political management or in political campaigns. All such persons shall retain the right to vote as they may choose and to express their opinions on all political subjects and candidates.[22]

The first sentence of Section 9(a), designed to prevent the use of official authority to interfere with the political rights of Federal employees or others, raises no problems under the First Amendment. Similar to other Federal legislation protecting the political process against intimidation or coercion, it deals not with expression but with action. The second sentence, however, is intended broadly to effect the neutralization of government employees so far as active politics at any level is concerned. Rigorously applied by the Civil Service Commission, the provision "is designed to prevent those subject to it from assuming general political leadership or from becoming prominently identified with any political movement, party, or faction, or with the success or failure of any candidate for election to public office." More specifically an employee is prohibited from running for public office, distributing campaign literature, organizing or speaking at a political meeting, circulating nominating petitions, attending a convention except as a spectator, soliciting or handling political funds, publishing a letter or article soliciting votes, holding office or committee membership in a political party or club, participating in a party caucus, and all similar activity connected with an election campaign or the operation of a political organization. He is allowed to vote, join a political organization, attend meetings, contribute to campaign funds, sign nominating petitions, and wear campaign buttons. Beyond this he cannot go. He is even accountable for political activity by other persons, such as his wife, if he is found to be using her as his agent. The prohibitions are enforced by suspension or removal from office.[23]

22. The Hatch Act as originally passed appears in 53 Stat. 1147 (1939). It was amended in 1940, 54 Stat. 767 (1940), and in 1950, 64 Stat. 475 (1950). The principal provisions of the legislation were embodied in 5 U.S.C. §§118i–n, reenacted in 1966 as parts of 5 U.S.C. §§1302, 1308, 7324–7327, and 1501–

1508. Section 9(a) is now 5 U.S.C. §7324.

23. The quotation and the examples are taken from U.S. Civil Service Commission, *Political Activity of Federal Officers and Employees* (Pamphlet 20) (Washington, D.C., G.P.O., May 1966). The earlier decisions are collected in

By an amendment in 1940 the restrictions of the Hatch Act were extended to employees of a State or local government "whose principal employment is in connection with any activity which is financed in whole or in part by loans or grants made by the United States." In addition many States and some local governments have similar legislation applicable to their own employees, usually known as "little Hatch Acts." The total number of employees covered by this legislation is not precisely known. It was estimated in 1966, however, that some eight million employees and members of their families were affected. The number is, moreover, constantly increasing.[24]

It will readily be seen that legislation of the Hatch Act type presents the constitutional issues in somewhat different form from those involved in the *Pickering* and other cases concerned with the basic right of government employees to freedom of expression. The Hatch Act constitutes a blanket regulation, applicable to virtually all government employees. It operates as a broad prior control, cutting off beforehand "political" conduct of almost every description except voting, without regard to the specific impact in any particular case. It is designed to secure very general goals, the principal ones being to prevent the political exploitation of government employees, to improve efficiency of the service through maintenance of a "merit" system, and to promote impartiality in government administration. All of these objectives are open to attainment by other measures, the control of expression being a supplementary shortcut.

The leading decision of the Supreme Court, *United Public Workers v. Mitchell*, was rendered in 1947. The issues were raised in that case by a suit for injunction and declaratory judgment brought by a group of Federal employees and their union to prevent the Civil Service Commission from enforcing the Hatch Act. The individual employees alleged that they wished to engage in various specified acts of political management and political campaigning. None of the employees, with one exception, had as yet done anything that violated the Act or been threatened with any disciplinary action. Concerning them the Supreme Court held that the issues were hypothetical and that no justiciable issue was presented: "It would not accord with judicial re-

---

Hatch Act Decisions of the U.S. Civil Service Commission, prepared by James W. Irwin, Chief Hearing Examiner, U.S. Civil Service Commission (Washington, D.C., G.P.O., 1949).

24. The 1940 amendments are incorporated in 5 U.S.C. §§1501–1508. The estimate of eight million is taken from Loeb, *op. cit. supra* note 21, p. 209.

sponsibility to adjudge, in a matter involving constitutionality, between the freedom of the individual and the requirement of public order except when definite rights appear upon the one side and definite prejudicial interferences upon the other." The one employee who had already engaged in conduct that violated the Hatch Act was a roller in the United States Mint in Philadelphia. He had served for some time as a ward executive committeeman of his party and was active on election day as a worker at the polls and as a paymaster for the services of other party workers. Reaching the merits in his case the Court held, four to three, that the Hatch Act as applied to him did not violate the First, Fifth, Ninth or Tenth Amendments.[25]

Justice Reed, writing the majority opinion, acknowledged that there were "limitations on congressional power" to regulate the conduct of government employees. Nevertheless, treating the objections raised under the First, Fifth, Ninth and Tenth Amendments as "basically the same," he made clear that the principle of limitation was simply that the conduct regulated be "reasonably deemed by Congress to interfere with the efficiency of the public service." Applying this doctrine to the Hatch Act, Justice Reed had no difficulty in finding that Congress could reasonably decide that "efficiency may be best obtained by prohibiting active participation by classified employees in politics." Moreover, Justice Reed expressly rejected more limited approaches. "The argument that political neutrality is not indispensable to a merit system for federal employees may be accepted," he said. "But because it is not indispensable does not mean that it is not desirable or permissible. . . . Congress may reasonably desire to limit party activity of federal employees so as to avoid a tendency toward a one-party system." Again, to the contention that the Hatch Act applied overbroadly, to industrial as well as administrative employees, he replied that these are "matters of detail for Congress." [26]

Justice Black, dissenting, called attention to the stifling effects of the Hatch Act as it applied to both Federal and State employees: "all these citizens who engage in public work can take no really effective part in campaigns that may bring about changes in their lives, their

25. *United Public Workers of America v. Mitchell,* 330 U.S. 75, 90 (1947). The Court did not reach the question whether the union could sue as representative of its members. 330 U.S. at 82. In a decision handed down the same day the Court sustained the application of the Hatch Act to State and local employees financed through Federal funds. *Oklahoma v. United States Civil Service Commission,* 330 U.S. 127 (1947).

26. 330 U.S. at 100, 95, 101, 99, 100, 102.

fortunes, and their happiness." He then declared that "laws which restrict the liberties guaranteed by the First Amendment should be narrowly drawn to meet the evil aimed at and to affect only the minimum number of people imperatively necessary to prevent a grave and imminent danger to the public," and added that "the provision here attacked is too broad, ambiguous, and uncertain in its consequences" to meet constitutional requirements. Justice Black then proceeded to more absolute grounds. "There is nothing about federal and state employees as a class which justifies depriving them or society of the benefits of their participation in public affairs," he said, and "the Constitution guarantees to them the same right that other groups of good citizens have to engage in activities which decide who their elected representatives shall be." Addressing himself to the purposes Congress sought to obtain through the legislation, he analyzed the contentions that government employees engaged in politics might "corrupt the political process," might "coerce their subordinates or . . . other citizens," or might discharge or promote employees "on a political rather than a merit basis." As to all he concluded that "the law could punish those public officials who engage in the practice," observing: "To punish millions of employees and to deprive the nation of their contribution to public affairs, in order to remove temptation from a proportionately small number of public officials, seems at the least to be a novel method of suppressing what is thought to be an evil practice." He ended by again emphasizing the overwhelming effect of the legislation upon the system of freedom of expression:

> The section of the Act here held valid reduces the constitutionally protected liberty of several million citizens to less than a shadow of its substance. It relegates millions of federal, state, and municipal employees to the role of mere spectators of events upon which hinge the safety and welfare of all the people, including public employees. It removes a sizable proportion of our electorate from full participation in affairs destined to mould the fortunes of the nation. It makes honest participation in essential political activities an offense punishable by proscription from public employment. It endows a governmental board with the awesome power to censor the thoughts, expressions, and activities of law-abiding citizens in the field of free expression, from which no person should be barred by a government which boasts that it is a government of, for, and by the people—all the people. Laudable as its purpose may be it seems to me to hack at the roots of a Govern-

ment by the people themselves; and consequently I cannot agree to sustain its validity.[27]

Justice Douglas, also dissenting, would have made a distinction between industrial and administrative workers in the government service. As to the latter, he argued that "there would be much to support the view of the Court" that the restrictions of the Hatch Act are justified. As to industrial workers, however, which was the case before him, he invoked the rule that "the restrictions should be narrowly and selectively drawn to define and punish the specific conduct which constitutes a clear and present danger to the operations of government." Applying this doctrine, he concluded: "To sacrifice the political rights of the industrial workers goes far beyond any demonstrated or demonstrable need." Both Justice Black and Justice Douglas also believed that the Court should decide the constitutional questions raised by all the individual employees who joined in the suit.[28]

The treatment of First Amendment problems by the majority in *United Public Workers* leaves much to be desired. In the first place, the rule that rights under the Hatch Act can be tested in a judicial proceeding only after the employee has violated the Act and run the risk of discharge has a seriously inhibiting effect. Many employees undoubtedly elect to stay clear of trouble and thus the actual scope of the restriction runs wider than even the *United Public Workers* majority would sanction. More important, the majority of the Court gives freedom of expression no more protection under the First Amendment than it would have under the due process clause. According to the Reed opinion, any reasonable regulation meets the requirements of the First Amendment. Finally, in making Congress the primary judge of what is reasonable, the Court sees its function as simply accepting the judgment of the legislature except under the most unusual circumstances. Yet it is clear, as the Black and Douglas opinions demonstrate, that such sweeping restrictions as the Hatch Act imposes call for far deeper probing and far more sharpening of the issues than the majority undertook to do. The failure of the Court, as late as 1947, to give greater substance to the First Amendment is startling. It is a safe assumption that *United Public Workers* retains little vitality today.

There are, indeed, many signs that a fundamental reappraisal of

27. 330 U.S. at 107, 110, 111–112, 113, 114, 115. Justice Rutledge concurred with Justice Black.

28. 330 U.S. at 122, 126.

Hatch Act legislation is well under way. In 1964 the Supreme Court of California held invalid a county charter provision which forbade a county employee to "take any part in political management or affairs in any political campaign or election . . . other than to cast his vote or to privately express his opinion." Construing the provision as even broader than the Hatch Act, the Court distinguished the *United Public Workers* case. It ruled that the regulation failed to meet the requirement that only a "compelling state purpose" can justify limitations on the political rights of government employees and that such restrictions may not be "broader than are required to preserve the efficiency and integrity of [the] public service." Two years later the same court struck down a State law which provided that no employee of a local agency "shall take an active part in any campaign for or against any candidate, except himself, for an office of such local agency, or for or against any ballot measure relating to the recall of any elected official of the local agency." Expanding its previous ruling the court held that the government "must demonstrate: (1) that the political restraints rationally relate to the enhancement of the public service, (2) that the benefits which the public gains by the restraints outweigh the resulting impairment of constitutional rights, and (3) that no alternatives less subversive of constitutional rights are available." The statute was found not to meet this test. Likewise the Oregon Supreme Court found unconstitutional a State law which forbade a civil service employee to be a "candidate for popular election to any office," unless he first resigned. The Court ruled that the State "must show it has a compelling interest warranting a restriction of a First Amendment right," and that the statute was invalid as overbroad. It is apparent, then, that the courts are not accepting the relaxed standards of *United Public Workers* but are requiring that legislation be far more narrowly directed and more specifically justified.[29]

Demands for reconsideration of Hatch Act legislation have also

29. *Fort v. Civil Service Commission of County of Alameda,* 61 Cal.2d 331, 337–338, 38 Cal. Rptr. 625, 629, 392 P.2d 385, 389 (1964); *Bagley v. Washington Township Hospital District,* 55 Cal. Rptr. 401, 421 P.2d 409 (1966); *Minielly v. Oregon,* 242 Ore. 490, 411 P.2d 69 (1966). For an earlier limiting decision by a Federal District Court see *Wilson v. United States Civil Service Commission,* 136 F. Supp. 104 (D.D.C. 1955). But see *Democratic State Central Committee v. Andolsek,* 249 F. Supp. 1009 (D. Md. 1966); *Wisconsin State Employees Association v. Wisconsin Natural Resources Board,* 298 F. Supp. 339 (W.D. Wis. 1969); *Kearney v. Macy,* 409 F.2d 847 (9th Cir. 1969). For a collection of the cases, see Note, 28 ALR 3rd 717 (1969).

come from other sources. In 1966 Congress created a Commission on Political Activity of Government Personnel, which conducted an extensive inquiry and made its report in the fall of 1967. The Commission recommended drastic changes in the Hatch Act. It proposed that the law be reframed so as to "specify in readily understandable terms those political activities which are prohibited, and specifically permit all others." It would allow Federal employees to "join a political party or other party organization and actively participate in its affairs," except to serve as an officer; to "become a candidate for and serve in a local office" that was part time, paid not more than a nominal compensation, and involved no conflict of interest; and "serve as a delegate to a political or constitutional convention." Half the Commission would also allow Federal employees to hold the office of ward or precinct committeeman. Specifically prohibited would be partisan political fund raising at any level; becoming a candidate for or holding any office other than a "local" one; managing a campaign for a candidate seeking a non-local office; acting as recorder or watcher at the polls; serving as an officer in a political organization. The Commission also proposed clarifying and improving enforcement of statutes directly protecting Federal employees from corrupt political pressures, such as coercion, solicitation of funds, and the like. It suggested further study of a proposal for creating an ombudsman to protect government employees from improper political pressures.[30]

Other proposals for change go beyond those recommended by the President's Commission. Thus the AFL-CIO has endorsed the suggestion that only "policy-affecting" employees be subject to any restriction and that even these "should be free to engage in political activities involving governments other than those in which they are employed." The American Civil Liberties Union urges complete repeal of Hatch Act provisions, "accompanied by machinery to make effective the sanctions now available to deter abuses in the public service." [31]

The outcome of these demands for reappraisal of the Hatch Act will depend in large part upon what view is taken concerning the limi-

---

30. *Report of the President's Commission on Political Activity of Government Personnel, supra* note 8, vol. I, pp. 3–6, 39–60.

31. *Report of the President's Commission on Political Activity of Government Personnel, supra* note 8, p. 122; *Statement of the American Civil Liberties Union on the Hatch Act to the President's Commission* (Sept. 28, 1967). On the British system, see the materials collected in *Political and Civil Rights in the United States,* p. 636.

tations imposed by the First Amendment. Plainly the approach of the Court in the *United Public Workers* case is outdated and must be abandoned. What doctrine, then, should the courts apply?

The right of government employees to engage in political activities is only one aspect of their broader right to freedom of expression. The controlling principle that governs the Hatch Act problem is therefore the same as that set forth previously as the guide to participation by government employees in the system of freedom of expression generally. Restriction on the political conduct of government employees does not abridge their freedom of expression to the extent that it is indispensably required as part of the employment relation; that is to say, is essential to the government's power to carry out its functions through engaging the services of its citizens. Controls are permissible at the point where the expression can be shown to relate to job performance, either by way of indicating the employee's competence, interfering with his capacity to carry out orders, or impairing his relations with the rest of the organization. Hence regulations concerned with the making of deliberately false statements that may reflect upon competence, carrying on political activities during working hours, campaigning against or running for office against an immediate superior, would be justified. So also would controls aimed at eliminating a direct conflict of interest between an employee's political activity and his government position. In addition, needless to say, prohibition of political activities that are not expression at all, such as using official authority for partisan political purposes, political coercion of subordinates, or refusal to comply with the merit system in promotion, would raise no First Amendment problems.

Legislation which broadly curtails the political conduct of government employees, as already noted, is not directly and specifically aimed at protecting these aspects of the employment relation. Rather it is designed to supplement other legislation that seeks to achieve more general goals by direct control of the abuses to be eliminated. Hence we are back to the fundamental proposition that the government cannot undertake to achieve general social interests through curtailment of expression. An analysis of Hatch Act legislation in terms of its stated objectives is necessary to reveal how far, if at all, it is essential to control conduct incompatible with the employment relation.

Political neutrality of government employees was originally conceived as a method of preventing them from being subject to political exploitation. The spoils system operated to enable higher government officials, or party officials, to force government employees into a partisan political machine. One of the elemental provisions of a civil service system is, of course, that political coercion of this sort is prohibited and that employees shall be dealt with on the basis of merit. But it was felt that these direct controls would work more effectively if government employees were removed from the political arena altogether, and this was the purpose of President Theodore Roosevelt's 1907 Executive Order. The result was that government employees were protected from interference with their political rights by having their rights taken away. The solution is much as if an unpopular minority were protected from hostile violence by being forbidden to meet in public. The demonstration that such draconian methods are necessary to prevent political coercion in the government service has never been made and, if made, would scarcely be relevant under accepted First Amendment theory.

A second justification for the political neutrality of government employees has been that it aids in maintaining the merit system and thereby promotes the efficiency of the service. It is urged that employees are more likely to be hired, assigned, promoted and disciplined on a merit basis, and to feel free of political influence about such matters, if they are forbidden to engage in political activity. Again, the operation is performed with a meat axe. Whatever support an emerging civil service may have required in the eighteen-eighties, not many would contend now that it can be maintained only at the price of curtailing freedom of expression throughout the government service. Even Justice Reed in *United Public Workers* agreed that "political neutrality is not indispensable to a merit system." Unless one accepts the doctrine that any "reasonable relation" to the efficiency of the service is enough to cut off First Amendment rights, the argument based on maintaining the merit system must fail.

Finally, it is contended that restrictions upon political activities are important in establishing the impartiality of the government service. The argument is that employees who are active in partisan political affairs may not respond loyally to the demands of their employment, may perform their duties with a partisan bias, or may give the appearance of doing so. Here the justification comes closer to the mark; it deals more directly with indispensable requirements of the employment relation. But it cannot support general legislation. Incompatibility with the employment relation does not arise from the conduct of every employee, holding any kind of job, and engaging in every kind of expression. Quite the contrary, the problems are more limited and more specific. Insofar as the political activity of an employee results in failure to perform his duties, or a conflict of interest, or even an appearance of conflict, his conduct is subject to control without abridgment of the First Amendment. To some extent these controls can be imposed by advance rule rather than merely by subsequent sanction. Such forms of regulation come within the principle already suggested. Considerations of this sort, however, do not justify sweeping legislation of the Hatch Act variety.

Reappraisal of the Hatch Act, therefore, will require elimination of such legislation in its present form. Changes in the civil service system, in the structure of political parties, in the operations of government, in the expansion of government services have made it obsolete, as well as incompatible with First Amendment doctrine. Attention should be given to improving the direct controls that undertake to eliminate coercion, corruption and political influence from our civil service system. Protection for government employees can be advanced through adoption of an ombudsman system or other administrative arrangements. But the effort to achieve these goals through political sterilization of public employees should be abandoned.

XVI

Academic Freedom

Within the last several decades academic freedom has emerged as an elaborate system of claims, principles, procedures and supporting interests. Ultimate inspiration for the system goes back to the concept of the medieval university as a community of scholars dedicated to the pursuit of knowledge. More immediate influences were ideas derived from the nineteenth-century German university, brought back to the United States by American students who did graduate study abroad. The German notions of academic freedom—essentially freedom of the teacher within the university but not outside, and freedom of the student from administrative coercion in the form of a required curriculum —underwent substantial changes as they developed in the United States. The rights claimed as academic freedom in this country during the latter part of the nineteenth century and the early part of the twentieth century primarily involved freedom of the faculty member as teacher and scholar within the university and as a citizen of the outside community. Assertion of these principles took more concrete shape with the formation of the American Association of University Professors (A.A.U.P.) in 1915 and its adoption that year of a formal "Declaration of Principles." The 1915 Declaration was succeeded in 1940 by a more elaborate "Statement of Principles on Academic Freedom and Tenure," adopted jointly by the A.A.U.P. and the Association of American Colleges. Since 1940 the growth of the system has been rapid, not to say phenomenal.[1]

1. The most complete history of academic freedom in this country is Richard Hofstadter and Walter P. Metzger, *The Development of Academic Freedom in the United States* (New York, Columbia University Press, 1955). An extensive collection of materials and references may be found in Thomas I. Emerson, David Haber and Norman Dorsen, *Political and Civil Rights in the United States* (Boston,

The underlying philosophy of the existing system of academic freedom, as applied to colleges and universities, is set forth in the 1940 Statement in the following terms:

> Institutions of higher education are conducted for the common good and not to further the interest of either the individual teacher or the institution as a whole. The common good depends upon the free search for truth and its free exposition.[2]

The heart of the system consists in the right of the individual faculty member to teach, carry on research, and publish without interference from the government, the community, the university administration, or his fellow faculty members. The faculty member also has rights, outside the classroom and the laboratory, as a member of the university community and as a citizen of the outside community. These rights are summarized in the 1940 Statement as follows:

> The college or university teacher is a citizen, a member of a learned profession, and an officer of an educational institution. When he speaks or writes as a citizen, he should be free from institutional censorship or discipline, but his special position in the community imposes special obligations. As a man of learning and an educational officer, he should remember that the public may judge his profession and his institution by his utterances. Hence he should at all times be accurate, should exercise appropriate restraint, should show respect for the opinions of others, and should make every effort to indicate that he is not an institutional spokesman.[3]

The chief device for assuring the faculty member freedom as a teacher, scholar and citizen is his right to tenure. Under this principle

---

Little, Brown & Co., 3d ed. 1967), ch. IX (cited hereafter in this chapter as *Political and Civil Rights in the United States*). More recent material includes Note, "Developments in the Law: Academic Freedom," *Harvard Law Review,* Vol. 81 (1968), p. 1045; Charles Alan Wright, "The Constitution on the Campus," *Vanderbilt Law Review,* Vol. 22 (1969), p. 1027; Stephen R. Goldstein, "The Scope and Sources of School Board Authority to Regulate Student Conduct and Status," *University of Pennsylvania Law Review,* Vol. 117 (1969), p. 373.

2. The 1940 "Statement of Principles on Academic Freedom and Tenure" is printed annually in the *Bulletin* of the American Association of University Professors. See, *e.g.,* Vol. 54 (1968), p. 384. The Statement and others are reprinted in *Political and Civil Rights in the United States,* pp. 915–959, and in Louis Joughin (ed.), *Academic Freedom and Tenure: A Handbook of the American Association of University Professors* (Madison, University of Wisconsin Press, 1967), ch. III and IV.

3. For discussion of the rights of the faculty member as citizen see Thomas I. Emerson and David Haber, "Academic Freedom of the Faculty Member as Citizen," *Law and Contemporary Problems,* Vol. 28 (1963), p. 525.

the faculty member, if he shows academic competence during a probationary period normally not to exceed seven years, is entitled to receive tenure status, which means that thereafter his services can be terminated only for "adequate cause." The term "adequate cause" has not been precisely defined, and probably cannot be, but in general it means that a faculty member is assured of his position except for mental or physical incapacity, serious neglect of duty, conviction of a crime of moral turpitude, lack of university funds to pay him, or attainment of the retirement age. The institution of tenure is designed to guard the faculty member against dismissal for political or other inadmissible reasons, a fact often hard for him to prove, and to assure him economic security in which he can carry on his search for truth in his teaching and research. Other protective devices are embodied in the concept of "academic due process." The principles of academic due process, still in the stage of growth, entitle the faculty member to certain procedural rights in dismissal or disciplinary proceedings, including a determination of the issues, at least in the first instance, by a tribunal of his peers.[4]

Beyond this point the principles embodied in the system of academic freedom are less fully developed and less well accepted. Efforts have been made recently to define more specifically the particular functions that various segments of a university should perform. Thus in 1966 the A.A.U.P., jointly with the American Council on Education and the Association of Governing Boards of Universities and Colleges, issued a "Statement on Government of Colleges and Universities." This document undertook to describe the proper roles of the governing board (trustees), the administration (president and staff), faculty, and students in a university community. To the faculty it gave "primary responsibility for such fundamental areas as curriculum, subject matter and methods of instruction, research, faculty status, and those aspects of student life which relate to the educational process."[5]

4. With respect to tenure see Clark Byse and Louis Joughin, *Tenure in American Higher Education* (Ithaca, N.Y., Cornell University Press, 1959); Fritz Machlup, "In Defense of Academic Tenure," A.A.U.P. *Bulletin*, Vol. 50 (1964), p. 112, reprinted in Joughin, *op. cit. supra* note 2, pp. 306–338. On academic due process see A.A.U.P., 1958 Statement on Procedural Standards in Faculty Dismissal Proceedings, reprinted in Joughin, *op. cit. supra* note 2, pp. 40–45; American

Civil Liberties Union, *Academic Freedom, Academic Responsibility, Academic Due Process* (New York, rev. ed. Sept. 1966); Louis Joughin, "Academic Due Process," *Law and Contemporary Problems*, Vol. 28 (1963), p. 573, reprinted in Joughin, *op. cit. supra* note 2, pp. 264–305.

5. The 1966 "Statement on Government of Colleges and Universities" is reprinted in Joughin, *op. cit. supra* note 2, pp. 90–101. The American Civil Liber-

Other significant aspects of the system concern the relationship of the university as a whole to the outside community. This involves such matters as the power of the State legislature to prescribe the curriculum, the function of the local police in connection with activities taking place on the campus, and the impact of large Federal grants upon the kinds of questions the university attempts to explore and the manner in which it approaches them. Furthermore there are various refinements in the basic principles that make up the system of academic freedom. Thus special rules are necessary for church-controlled colleges and universities.[6]

A further development of recent years has been the extension of the original system of academic freedom into new areas. The most important of these advances has been in the formulation of principles of academic freedom for students. In 1961 the American Civil Liberties Union published, and has since frequently revised, a statement on "Academic Freedom and Civil Liberties of Students in Colleges and Universities." The A.A.U.P., which had issued a similar statement in 1965, joined the National Student Association, the Association of American Colleges, and a number of other organizations in 1967 in promulgating a "Joint Statement on Rights and Freedoms of Students." Declaring that "[f]reedom to teach and freedom to learn are inseparable facets of academic freedom," the Joint Statement dealt with such subjects as admission policies, freedom of expression and inquiry in the classroom, protection against improper disclosure of student views, student organizations and publications, outside speakers, participation in university government, off-campus activities, and procedure in disciplinary proceedings. Demands for "student power" and the greatly increased pace of student activity on and off the campus are forcing a rapid development in the principles and practices of academic freedom for students.[7]

A slower but consistent movement is also taking place in the development of principles of academic freedom applicable to secondary and

---

ties Union statement, cited in the previous note, also deals with this problem.

6. On academic freedom in church-related institutions, see A.A.U.P., "Report of Special Committee on Academic Freedom in Church-Related Colleges and Universities," A.A.U.P. *Bulletin*, Vol. 53 (1967), p. 369.

7. American Civil Liberties Union, "Academic Freedom and Civil Liberties of Students in Colleges and Universities" (New York, rev. ed. Mar. 1965). The A.A.U.P. 1965 statement is printed in A.A.U.P. *Bulletin*, Vol. 51 (1965), p. 447, and the 1967 statement in Vol. 54 (1968), p. 258.

elementary schools. After many years of labor the American Civil Liberties Union in 1968 produced a detailed statement of proposed principles for this area, entitled "Academic Freedom in the Secondary Schools." The issues here vary in important ways from those arising in colleges and universities. The lesser maturity of the students and the need for greater emphasis upon transmitting rather than discovering knowledge pose difficult problems. The principles ultimately found to govern are likely to differ somewhat from those applicable to the realm of higher education.[8]

The institutional structure supporting the system of academic freedom has not kept pace with the expansion of claims and the development of principles. To some degree tenure rights have been written into legislation, but most of this relates to secondary and elementary school teachers. The courts are beginning to take a more active part, particularly in the application of procedural due process requirements. But their role so far has been a limited one. In the main, enforcement of claims to academic freedom in higher education has rested upon persuasion, accompanied by a certain amount of professional pressure. Most of this persuasion and pressure has come from the American Association of University Professors. Since that organization initiated the first formal statement of principles in 1915 it has continued to expand, refine and publicize the basic ideas underlying the system. It has also undertaken to apply those principles in concrete cases of alleged infraction, utilizing a detailed procedure for investigation, report and negotiation of settlement. Other professional organizations and civil-liberties organizations, particularly the Academic Freedom Committee of the American Civil Liberties Union, have joined in the efforts at education and persuasion. On the whole, however, the pressures exerted by the supporters of academic freedom have been relatively mild. The A.A.U.P. employs a procedure for censuring institutions that offend the rules and teachers are asked not to take positions with institutions on the censured list. But the A.A.U.P. has insisted upon remaining a "professional" organization and has steadfastly refused to operate as a labor union. No other organization with strength in colleges and universities wields significant power. The result is that the pressures to conform to the principles of academic freedom have

8. American Civil Liberties Union, "Academic Freedom in the Secondary Schools" (New York, Sept. 1968). See also the material cited in *Political and Civil Rights in the United States,* p. 959.

never attained the force that traditional methods of collective bargaining have been able to generate. Student power, on the other hand, has come in recent years to exert a growing volume of pressure.[9]

It need hardly be added that the importance of the system of academic freedom in the operation of a democratic society can scarcely be overstated. The function of the university in transmitting knowledge to the coming generations might possibly be performed, in some degree at least, in a context of academic repression. But the role of the university in advancing knowledge and in providing the major source of criticism of other institutions in our society would be wholly impossible without the structure of academic freedom. Education of students to play an independent and creative role in society could not conceivably be achieved in the absence of such a system.

The problem to be considered is the extent to which legal doctrine, particularly that emanating from the First Amendment, can be used to support the system of academic freedom.

A. The Court Decisions

Two early decisions of the Supreme Court laid down principles of major importance to a system of academic freedom. *Meyer v. Nebraska,* decided in 1923, involved the validity of a Nebraska statute passed in the aftermath of World War I, which provided that no person "shall, in any private, denominational, parochial or public school, teach any subject to any person in any language other than the English language," and that languages other than English "may be taught as languages only after a pupil shall have attained and successfully passed the eighth grade." An instructor in Zion Parochial School was convicted under the statute for having taught reading in the German language to a pupil who had not yet passed the eighth grade. The Supreme Court held that the statute violated the due process clause of the

9. For an account of the A.A.U.P. procedure for dealing with complaints of violation of academic freedom see Joughin, *op. cit. supra* note 2, ch. II. An analysis of A.A.U.P. cases involving the rights of faculty members as citizens may be found in Emerson and Haber, *op. cit. supra* note 3, pp. 534–543. With respect to the general status of student academic freedom in the middle 1960's see E. G. Williamson and John L. Cowan, *The American Student's Freedom of Expression: A Research Appraisal* (Minneapolis, University of Minnesota Press, 1966).

Fourteenth Amendment because it attempted unreasonably "to interfere with the calling of modern language teachers, with the opportunities of pupils to acquire knowledge, and with the power of parents to
control the education of their own [children]." Justice McReynolds,
writing for the majority, acknowledged the "power of the State to
compel attendance at some school and to make reasonable regulations
for all schools, including a requirement that they shall give instructions
in English." He also did not challenge "the state's power to prescribe a
curriculum for institutions which it supports." He found it "easy to
appreciate" the "desire of the legislature to foster a homogeneous
people with American ideals prepared readily to understand current
discussions of civic matters." But he found that "[n]o emergency has
arisen which renders knowledge by a child of some language other
than English so clearly harmful as to justify its inhibition with the consequent infringement of rights long freely enjoyed," and concluded
that the statute was "arbitrary, and without reasonable relation to
any end within the competency of the State." Justices Holmes and
Sutherland dissented, believing that the statute presented "a question
upon which men reasonably might differ" and hence could not be
banned as arbitrary under the Fourteenth Amendment.[10]

Two years later, in *Pierce v. Society of Sisters,* the Supreme Court
unanimously held invalid, also as a violation of the due process clause
of the Fourteenth Amendment, an Oregon statute that sought to eliminate the private and parochial school systems by compelling all children between the ages of eight and sixteen to attend the public schools.
Justice McReynolds, again stressing the power of the State to provide
that "certain studies plainly essential to good citizenship must be
taught, and that nothing be taught which is manifestly inimical to the
public welfare," nevertheless declared:

> . . . we think it entirely plain that the Act of 1922 unreasonably in-
> terferes with the liberty of parents and guardians to direct the upbring-
> ing and education of children under their control. As often heretofore
> pointed out, rights guaranteed by the Constitution may not be abridged
> by legislation which has no reasonable relation to some purpose within
> the competency of the State. The fundamental theory of liberty upon
> which all governments in this Union repose excludes any general power
> of the State to standardize its children by forcing them to accept in-

10. *Meyer v. Nebraska,* 262 U.S. 390,
401, 402, 403 (1923). The Holmes dissent
appears in a companion case, *Bartels v.
Iowa,* 262 U.S. 404 (1923). For comment and later decisions involving similar
issues see *Political and Civil Rights in
the United States,* p. 983.

struction from public teachers only. The child is not the mere creature of the State; those who nurture him and direct his destiny have the right, coupled with the high duty, to recognize and prepare him for additional obligations.[11]

The *Meyer* and *Pierce* decisions did not mention the First Amendment, which indeed had not yet been held applicable to State legislation. Both rested upon substantive due process, in fact upon the McReynolds variety of that doctrine. Despite the subsequent demise of substantive due process, it is highly probable that the Supreme Court would reach the same results today. It might do this by making a distinction, in the application of substantive due process, between legislation that infringed upon individual or personal rights and legislation that regulated economic or property rights. Or it might invoke the First Amendment. In any event the limitations imposed by *Meyer* and *Pierce* upon government regulation of education are generally accepted as currently effective.[12]

More recently the Supreme Court has dealt with matters touching on academic freedom in cases of loyalty regulations involving educational institutions. These decisions have been discussed in prior chapters, and only their particular relevance to academic freedom will be considered here.

The first case in which the Supreme Court had occasion to consider the impact of a loyalty program upon the schools was *Adler v. Board of Education,* when it upheld the New York Feinberg Law and other loyalty regulations for teachers. Justice Minton's majority opinion took the view that teachers were in no better position than other government employees, so far as a loyalty program was concerned. In fact he indicated there were reasons for applying more stringent loyalty requirements to teachers than to others:

A teacher works in a sensitive area in a schoolroom. There he shapes the attitude of young minds towards the society in which they live. In this, the state has a vital concern. It must preserve the integrity of the schools. That the school authorities have the right and the duty to screen the officials, teachers, and employees as to their fitness to maintain the

11. *Pierce v. Society of Sisters,* 268 U.S. 510, 534–535 (1925).

12. For the argument that substantive due process should be construed differently in cases involving personal rights than in cases involving economic rights see Thomas I. Emerson, "Nine Justices in Search of a Doctrine," *Michigan Law Review,* Vol. 64 (1965), p. 219. The Supreme Court in effect reaffirmed *Meyer* and *Pierce* in *Epperson v. Arkansas,* discussed below.

integrity of the schools as a part of ordered society, cannot be doubted.[13]

Justice Douglas in dissent, joined by Justice Black, expressed a wholly different concept of the educational process. Invoking the principles of academic freedom he urged that loyalty regulations were particularly repressive in an academic setting:

What happens under this law is typical of what happens in a police state. Teachers are under constant surveillance; their pasts are combed for signs of disloyalty; their utterances are watched for clues to dangerous thoughts. A pall is cast over the classrooms. There can be no real academic freedom in that environment. Where suspicion fills the air and holds scholars in line for fear of their jobs, there can be no exercise of the free intellect. Supineness and dogmatism take the place of inquiry. A "party line"—as dangerous as the "party line" of the Communists—lays hold. It is the "party line" of the orthodox view, of the conventional thought, of the accepted approach. A problem can no longer be pursued with impunity to its edges. Fear stalks the classroom. The teacher is no longer a stimulant to adventurous thinking; she becomes instead a pipe line for safe and sound information. A deadening dogma takes the place of free inquiry. Instruction tends to become sterile; pursuit of knowledge is discouraged; discussion often leaves off where it should begin.[14]

Shortly afterwards, in *Wieman v. Updegraff*, the Supreme Court held invalid an Oklahoma loyalty oath that had been challenged by faculty members of Oklahoma A. & M. College. The majority opinion, finding the oath violated due process in penalizing "innocent" as well as "knowing" membership in an organization, placed no emphasis upon the fact that an educational institution was involved. But Justice Frankfurter, in a concurring opinion which Justice Douglas joined, gave express recognition to the principles of academic freedom. After declaring that "inhibition of freedom of thought . . . in the case of teachers brings the safeguards [of the First Amendment] vividly into operation," he went on:

To regard teachers—in our entire educational system, from the primary grades to the university—as the priests of our democracy is therefore not to indulge in hyperbole. It is the special task of teachers to foster

13. *Adler v. Board of Education*, 342 U.S. 485, 493 (1952), discussed in Chapter VII.

14. 342 U.S. at 510.

those habits of open-mindedness and critical inquiry which alone make for responsible citizens, who, in turn, make possible an enlightened and effective public opinion. Teachers must fulfill their function by precept and practice, by the very atmosphere which they generate; they must be exemplars of open-mindedness and free inquiry. They cannot carry out their noble task if the conditions for the practice of a responsible and critical mind are denied to them. They must have the freedom of responsible inquiry, by thought and action, into the meaning of social and economic ideas, into the checkered history of social and economic dogma. They must be free to sift evanescent doctrine, qualified by time and circumstance, from that restless, enduring process of extending the bounds of understanding and wisdom, to assure which the freedoms of thought, of speech, of inquiry, of worship are guaranteed by the Constitution of the United States against infraction by National or State government.[15]

The case in which the theme of academic freedom was most prominent is *Sweezy v. New Hampshire,* decided in 1957. The Attorney General of New Hampshire, acting as a legislative investigating committee, had questioned Paul M. Sweezy about the contents of a lecture on socialism that he had given at the University of New Hampshire. Sweezy refused to answer and was cited for contempt. The Supreme Court reversed the conviction by a vote of six to two. Chief Justice Warren, writing also for Justices Black, Douglas and Brennan, stressed the significance of academic freedom:

> The essentiality of freedom in the community of American universities is almost self-evident. No one should underestimate the vital role in a democracy that is played by those who guide and train our youth. To impose any strait jacket upon the intellectual leaders in our colleges and universities would imperil the future of our Nation. No field of education is so thoroughly comprehended by man that new discoveries cannot yet be made. Particularly is that true in the social sciences, where few, if any, principles are accepted as absolutes. Scholarship cannot flourish in an atmosphere of suspicion and distrust. Teachers and students must always remain free to inquire, to study and to evaluate, to gain new maturity and understanding; otherwise our civilization will stagnate and die.[16]

Chief Justice Warren concluded, however, that he did not need to reach "fundamental questions of state power to decide this case."

15. *Wieman v. Updegraff,* 344 U.S. 183, 195, 196–197 (1952).
16. *Sweezy v. New Hampshire,* 354 U.S. 234, 250 (1957), discussed in Chapter VIII.

He ended by holding that the authority of the Attorney General to propound the questions had not been sufficiently established.[17]

Justice Frankfurter, joined by Justice Harlan, concurred in the result upon First Amendment grounds. Applying the balancing test he gave predominant weight to "the grave harm resulting from governmental intrusion into the intellectual life of a university." He continued:

> Progress in the natural sciences is not remotely confined to findings made in the laboratory. Insights into the mysteries of nature are born of hypothesis and speculation. The more so is this true in the pursuit of understanding in the groping endeavors of what are called the social sciences, the concern of which is man and society. The problems that are the respective preoccupations of anthropology, economics, law, psychology, sociology and related areas of scholarship are merely departmentalized dealing, by way of manageable division of analysis, with interpenetrating aspects of holistic perplexities. For society's good—if understanding be an essential need of society—inquiries into these problems, speculations about them, stimulation in others of reflection upon them, must be left as unfettered as possible. Political power must abstain from intrusion into this activity of freedom, pursued in the interest of wise government and the people's well-being, except for reasons that are exigent and obviously compelling.[18]

The potential of *Sweezy,* however, was not extended further in the *Barenblatt* case, decided two years later. Barenblatt had been a graduate student and teaching fellow at the University of Michigan, and an instructor in psychology at Vassar until shortly before his appearance before the House Committee on Un-American Activities. His refusal to answer questions about Communist Party membership resulted in a conviction for contempt. On appeal to the Supreme Court both Barenblatt and the American Association of University Professors as amicus curiae relied heavily upon academic freedom arguments. They were, however, unsuccessful, the Supreme Court upholding the conviction five to four. Justice Harlan, writing the majority opinion, applied the balancing test. He recognized the academic freedom element in the case: "Of course, broadly viewed, inquiries cannot be made into the teaching that is pursued in any of our educational institutions. When academic teaching-freedom and its corollary learning-freedom, so essential to the well-being of the Nation, are claimed, this Court will always be on the alert against intrusion by Congress into this constitu-

17. 354 U.S. at 251.　　　　18. 354 U.S. at 261–262.

tionally protected domain." But he proceeded: "We think that investigatory power in this domain [Communist activities] is not to be denied Congress solely because the field of education is involved." Concluding that the investigation was not "directed at controlling what is being taught at our universities rather than at overthrow" of government, he resolved the balance against Barenblatt.[19]

The dissenting opinion of Justice Black, joined by Chief Justice Warren and Justice Douglas, proceeded upon straight First Amendment grounds, with little reference to academic freedom. Justice Brennan's dissenting opinion likewise did not rely upon academic freedom.

A majority of the Court returned to the emphasis upon academic freedom some years later in *Keyishian v. Board of Regents*. Reviewing again the New York loyalty requirements for teachers, this time in a case brought by a group of faculty members at the State University of New York in Buffalo, the Court overruled *Adler* and struck down the key provisions of the loyalty program as vague and overbroad. Justice Brennan, writing for the majority of five, supported his position with another strong statement on academic freedom:

> Our Nation is deeply committed to safeguarding academic freedom, which is of transcendent value to all of us and not merely to the teachers concerned. That freedom is therefore a special concern of the First Amendment, which does not tolerate laws that cast a pall of orthodoxy over the classroom. . . . The classroom is peculiarly the "marketplace of ideas." The Nation's future depends upon leaders trained through wide exposure to that robust exchange of ideas which discovers truth "out of a multitude of tongues, [rather] than through any kind of authoritative selection." *United States v. Associated Press*, 52 F. Supp. 362, 372.[20]

Academic freedom also figured in the decision in *Shelton v. Tucker*, a case very similar to the loyalty cases though not strictly in

19. *Barenblatt v. United States*, 360 U.S. 109, 112, 129, 130 (1959), discussed in Chapter VIII.

20. *Keyishian v. Board of Regents of the University of the State of New York*, 385 U.S. 589, 603 (1967). See also *Whitehill v. Elkins*, 389 U.S. 54, 59–60, 62 (1967). In other loyalty cases involving educational institutions the Court did not make any express reference to the academic freedom theme. See *Slochower v. Board of Higher Education of New York City*, 350 U.S. 551 (1956); *Beilan v. Board of Public Education*, 357 U.S.

399 (1958); *Baggett v. Bullitt*, 377 U.S. 360 (1964); *Elfbrandt v. Russell*, 384 U.S. 11 (1966); all considered in Chapter VII. Discussion of the Court's treatment of academic freedom in the loyalty cases may be found in William P. Murphy, "Academic Freedom—An Emerging Constitutional Right," *Law and Contemporary Problems*, Vol. 28 (1963), p. 447; Arval A. Morris, "Academic Freedom and Loyalty Oaths," *Law and Contemporary Problems*, Vol. 28 (1963), p. 487; Note, "Loyalty Oaths," *Yale Law Journal*, Vol. 77 (1968), p. 739.

that category. Here the academic freedom element was used to buttress a holding that the Arkansas statute requiring teachers to list all organizational affiliations was overbroad and invalid. "The vigilant protection of constitutional freedoms," said Justice Stewart for the majority, "is nowhere more vital than in the community of American schools." Justice Frankfurter in dissent was careful to note, "If I dissent from the Court's disposition in these cases, it is not that I put a low value on academic freedom." [21]

Questions of a different kind were involved in *Pickering v. Board of Education.* The issue there was whether and to what extent a high school teacher could publicly criticize the school administration and the board of education. The Supreme Court upheld the teacher on First Amendment grounds but did not make any reference to academic freedom. Rather it dealt with the problem wholly in terms of the teacher as government employee. [22]

Even more profound and more difficult questions of academic freedom were presented to the Supreme Court in *Epperson v. Arkansas.* This time the Court took notice of them and a majority hinted that the principles of academic freedom might put important limits on State power. But in the end all members of the Court shied away from resting the decision upon such grounds. The case involved the validity of an Arkansas statute that made it unlawful "for any teacher in any University, College, Normal, Public School, or other institution of the State, which is supported in whole or in part from public funds . . . to teach the theory or doctrine that mankind ascended or descended from a lower order of animals." The lower court in Arkansas had held the statute unconstitutional under the First Amendment, speaking squarely in academic freedom terms, because it "tends to hinder the quest for knowledge, restrict the freedom to learn, and restrain the freedom to teach." The Supreme Court of Arkansas, however, reversed the lower court and sustained the statute as "a valid exercise of the state's power to specify the curriculum in the public schools." The United States Supreme Court unanimously struck down the statute. All but two of the justices found that the statute violated the establishment of religion clause of the First Amendment; the remaining two believed the law was unconstitutionally vague. [23]

Justice Fortas, writing for the majority of six, made a short

21. *Shelton v. Tucker,* 364 U.S. 479, 487, 495 (1960), discussed in Chapter VII.

22. *Pickering v. Board of Education,* 391 U.S. 563 (1968), discussed in Chapter XV.

23. *Epperson v. Arkansas,* 393 U.S. 97 (1968).

excursion into the area of academic freedom before reaching establishment of religion territory:

> Judicial interposition in the operation of the public school system of the Nation raises problems requiring care and restraint. Our courts, however, have not failed to apply the First Amendment's mandate in our educational system where essential to safeguard the fundamental values of freedom of speech and inquiry and of belief. By and large, public education in our Nation is committed to the control of state and local authorities. Courts do not and cannot intervene in the resolution of conflicts which arise in the daily operation of school systems and which do not directly and sharply implicate basic constitutional values. On the other hand, "[t]he vigilant protection of constitutional freedoms is nowhere more vital than in the community of American schools," *Shelton v. Tucker,* 364 U.S. 479, 487 (1960). As this Court said in *Keyishian v. Board of Regents,* the First Amendment "does not tolerate laws that cast a pall of orthodoxy over the classroom." 385 U.S. 589, 603 (1967).[24]

Justice Fortas then discussed the decision in *Meyer v. Nebraska,* and finally dropped the subject:

> For purposes of the present case, we need not re-enter the difficult terrain which the Court, in 1923, traversed without apparent misgivings. We need not take advantage of the broad premise which the Court's decision in *Meyer* furnishes, nor need we explore the implications of that decision in terms of the justiciability of the multitude of controversies that beset our campuses today. Today's problem is capable of resolution in the narrower terms of the First Amendment's prohibition of laws respecting an establishment of religion or prohibiting the free exercise thereof.[25]

Justice Black, concurring on vagueness grounds, objected strenuously because the Court "leaps headlong into the middle of the very broad problems involved in federal intrusion into state powers to decide what subjects and schoolbooks it may wish to use in teaching state pupils." Thus "[i]t would be difficult to make a First Amendment case out of a state law eliminating the subject of higher mathematics, or astronomy, or biology from its curriculum." He questioned "whether it is absolutely certain, as the Court's opinion indicates, that 'academic freedom' permits a teacher to breach his contractual agreement to teach only the subjects designated by the school

24. 393 U.S. at 104–105.   25. 393 U.S. at 105–106.

authorities who hired him." Justice Harlan, concurring on establishment of religion grounds, sought to "dissociate" himself from the "implications" of the majority opinion on other issues. Justice Stewart, like Justice Black, thought the decision should rest upon vagueness, but he was willing to speculate upon some of the academic freedom issues:

It is one thing for a State to determine that "the subject of higher mathematics, or astronomy, or biology" shall or shall not be included in its public school curriculum. It is quite another thing for a State to make it a criminal offense for a public school teacher so much as to mention the very existence of an entire system of respected human thought. That kind of criminal law, I think, would clearly impinge upon the guarantees of free communication contained in the First Amendment, and made applicable to the States by the Fourteenth.[26]

Shortly after *Epperson* the Supreme Court ventured gingerly into the unexplored territory of academic freedom for high school students in *Tinker v. Des Moines Independent Community School District*. In 1965 a group of adults and students in Des Moines had met at the home of one of their number and decided to publicize their objections to the hostilities in Vietnam and their support of a truce by wearing black armbands. When the school authorities heard of the plan they adopted a regulation forbidding students to wear the armbands in school. Seven students nevertheless wore them and were suspended. The Supreme Court, by a vote of seven to two, held that the action of the school officials violated First Amendment rights.[27]

Justice Fortas, again writing for the majority, dealt with the issue in straight First Amendment terms, making no express reference to "academic freedom." He began by outlining the polar limits of the problem: "First Amendment rights, applied in light of the special characteristics of the school environment, are available to teachers and students." "On the other hand, the Court has repeatedly emphasized the need for affirming the comprehensive authority of the States and of school officials, consistent with fundamental constitutional safeguards, to prescribe and control conduct in the schools." Justice Fortas then sharpened the line of division: "In order for the State in the person of school officials to justify prohibition of a particular expression of opinion, it must be able to show that its action was caused by something

26. 393 U.S. at 110, 111, 114, 116.
27. *Tinker v. Des Moines Independ-* *ent Community School District*, 393 U.S. 503 (1969).

more than a mere desire to avoid the discomfort and unpleasantness that always accompany an unpopular viewpoint." "But conduct by the student, in class or out of it, which for any reason—whether it stems from time, place, or type of behavior—materially disrupts classwork or involves substantial disorder or invasion of the rights of others is, of course, not immunized by the constitutional guaranty of freedom of speech." In the case before him Justice Fortas found that there was "no evidence whatever of petitioners' interference, actual or nascent, with the school's work or of collision with the rights of other students to be secure and to be let alone." [28]

The significance of the *Tinker* decision lay not only in the Court's delineation of the scope of student First Amendment rights but in the Court's willingness to second-guess the school authorities. The District Court had concluded that the action of the school officials "was reasonable because it was based upon their fear of a disturbance from the wearing of the armbands." Justice Fortas rejected the position, saying that "in our system, undifferentiated fear or apprehension of disturbance is not enough to overcome the right to freedom of expression." He went on: "our independent examination of the record fails to yield evidence that the school authorities had reason to anticipate that the wearing of armbands would substantially interfere with the work of the school or impinge upon the rights of other students." [29]

Justice Fortas' opinion also included some broad language on student rights:

> In our system, state-operated schools may not be enclaves of totalitarianism. School officials do not possess absolute authority over their students. Students in school as well as out of school are "persons" under our Constitution. They are possessed of fundamental rights which the State must respect, just as they themselves must respect their obligations to the State. In our system, students may not be regarded as closed-circuit recipients of only that which the State chooses to communicate. They may not be confined to the expression of those sentiments that are officially approved. In the absence of a specific showing of constitutionally valid reasons to regulate their speech, students are entitled to freedom of expression of their views.[30]

Justice White joined the Court's opinion, with only minor reservations. Justice Stewart, also concurring, agreed with the opinion except that he did not "share the Court's uncritical assumption that, school

28. 393 U.S. at 506, 507, 509, 513, 508.

29. 393 U.S. at 508, 509.
30. 393 U.S. at 511.

discipline aside, the First Amendment rights of children are co-extensive with those of adults." Justice Black vigorously dissented. In his view the schools were not appropriate places for the exercise of First Amendment rights and the courts should not take away from the school authorities the right to decide what disciplinary regulations were reasonable. Justice Harlan also dissented. While he agreed that the school authorities were "not wholly exempt" from the requirements of the First Amendment, he felt that "school officials should be accorded the widest authority in maintaining discipline and good order"; that the burden should be "cast upon those complaining" to show that "a particular school measure was motivated by other than legitimate school concerns"; and that there was "nothing in this record which impugns the good faith of respondents in promulgating the armband regulation." [31]

The *Tinker* case is important in that the Supreme Court for the first time expressly held that the conduct of students in elementary and secondary schools was protected by the First Amendment against interference from the school authorities. And the Court went some distance to assure that these rights would be granted in practice as well as in theory, holding it to be the obligation of the courts to look behind the action of the school authorities in taking restrictive measures. Nevertheless the student rights were closely hedged. Freedom of student expression could not be restricted to avoid "discomfort and unpleasantness," but it was plainly subordinate to the power of school officials to control conduct that "would substantially interfere with the work of the school." Moreover, in dealing with students in the secondary schools, the decision did not throw much light upon the rights of students in colleges and universities.

From this survey of the Supreme Court's decisions in which academic freedom has played a role, two major conclusions emerge. The first is that the Supreme Court has touched upon only a small fraction of the total area of academic freedom. It dealt with some basic problems in *Meyer* and *Pierce*, but without mentioning academic freedom and without being aware of its implications. In *Epperson* it declined to venture back into this field of government control over the curriculum except along the clearly marked path furnished by the establishment clause. *Tinker* recognized the general right of students to invoke First Amendment protection against school authorities, but otherwise barely scratched the surface of student academic freedom. The other

31. 393 U.S. at 515, 526.

cases have largely concerned loyalty programs or similar restrictive measures imposed by government. None of them considers the rights of individual faculty members vis-à-vis the administration of their own institutions or vis-à-vis their colleagues. Many other aspects of academic freedom, including the tenure system, faculty participation in the government of the institution, and student power, have never been the subject of Supreme Court attention. As a consequence, the direct impact of Supreme Court decisions upon development of the system of academic freedom has up to now been relatively small.

The second conclusion is that the Supreme Court has never undertaken to establish academic freedom as an independent constitutional right, in the same way, for example, as it created the constitutional right of privacy. The Court has simply used the principles of academic freedom for support in the application of traditional legal doctrine. It has resolved issues in terms of freedom of expression, establishment of religion, due process, the rule against vagueness, or similar constitutional principles. Thus academic freedom factors weigh in the balance in determining First Amendment rights under the balancing theory. Their presence calls for stricter adherence to the rule that the regulation must be specific and narrowly drawn. But it is by no means clear that the results reached in any of the cases would have been different had the academic freedom element been missing. All that the Court has done is to say that academic freedom considerations are relevant in the application of standard doctrine; it has not held that they possess any constitutional dimension of their own.

Many decisions important to the system of academic freedom have issued from the State and lower Federal courts. Some of these deal with matters that have not yet been the subject of Supreme Court decision, such as the extramural utterances of faculty members, speaker bans, student demonstrations, and the like. An increasing number have been concerned with claims to due process in dismissal or disciplinary proceedings, for both faculty members and students. Others relate to statutory or contract rights under tenure provisions. These cases, however, do not change the picture so far as the constitutional status of academic freedom is concerned. While more extensive in scope than the Supreme Court decisions, they leave many areas of academic freedom untouched. Moreover they fall far short of constituting a unified body of theory establishing academic freedom as a protected constitutional right.[32]

32. For a collection of State and   lower Federal court decisions bearing on

The questions remaining for consideration, then, are first, whether it would be feasible to give academic freedom an independent constitutional status; and, second, in the absence of such a development, how the First Amendment should be construed so as to give maximum support to the system of academic freedom.

B. Academic Freedom as an Independent Constitutional Right

In *N.A.A.C.P. v. Alabama ex rel. Patterson*, the Supreme Court created a new constitutional right that did not as such exist before—the right of association. In *Griswold v. Connecticut*, it established the right of privacy as a newly discovered constitutional right. Would it be feasible or wise to recognize academic freedom as such an independent right, guaranteed by the Constitution against invasion? There is much to be said in support of such a proposition.[33]

The general feasibility of elevating academic freedom into a constitutionally protected right is apparent from a number of considera-

---

academic freedom, see *Political and Civil Rights in the United States,* pp. 959–974, 978–979, 983–984, 1001–1002, 1036–1042, 1049–1065; Charles Alan Wright and Note, "Developments in the Law," both cited *supra* note 1; William W. Van Alstyne, "Judicial Trend Toward Student Academic Freedom," *University of Florida Law Review,* Vol. 20 (1968), p. 290; Note, "Reasonable Rules, Reasonably Enforced—Guidelines for University Disciplinary Proceedings," *Minnesota Law Review,* Vol. 53 (1968), p. 301. See also *Grossner v. Trustees of Columbia University,* 287 F. Supp. 535 (S.D.N.Y. 1968); *Powe v. Miles,* 407 F.2d 73 (2d Cir. 1968); *Soglin v. Kauffman,* 295 F. Supp. 978 (W.D. Wis. 1968), aff'd 418 F.2d 163 (7th Cir. 1969); *Zucker v. Panitz,* 299 F. Supp. 102 (S.D.N.Y. 1969); *Jones v. State Board of Education,* 407 F.2d 834 (6th Cir. 1969), cert. granted as to one petitioner, 396 U.S. 817 (1969). University bans on allegedly subversive campus speakers were held invalid in *Dickson v. Sitterson,* 280 F. Supp.

486 (M.D.N.C. 1968); *Snyder v. Board of Trustees of the University of Illinois,* 286 F. Supp. 927 (N.D. Ill. 1968); *Smith v. University of Tennessee,* 300 F. Supp. 777 (E.D. Tenn. 1969); *Brooks v. Auburn University,* 412 F.2d 1171 (5th Cir. 1969).

33. *N.A.A.C.P. v. Alabama ex rel. Patterson,* 357 U.S. 449 (1958); *Griswold v. Connecticut,* 381 U.S. 479 (1965). For discussion of the right of association, see Thomas I. Emerson, "Freedom of Association and Freedom of Expression," *Yale Law Journal,* Vol. 74 (1964), p. 1. On the right of privacy, see "Symposium on the Griswold Case and the Right of Privacy," *Michigan Law Review,* Vol. 64 (1965), p. 197. See also Chapters XII and XIV. The argument that the Supreme Court has already "opened up the possibility of a substantial degree of judicial protection of academic freedom as a right recognized and guaranteed by the United States Constitution" is made in Murphy, *op. cit. supra* note 20, p. 449.

tions. In the first place there is now in existence a coherent body of principles, built around the operations of a major institution in our society—the system of education. Those principles are derived from the functions served by educational institutions and the methods needed to carry on those functions. Both the functions and methods are broadly accepted in the society, or at least seem to have the minimum degree of acquiescence necessary to support a major constitutional development. There is thus available for use by the courts a specific collection of rules, not loosely based upon vague generalities, but closely tied to the concrete operation of an on-going system.

In the second place, there has already developed a significant volume of case law, applying the general principles in concrete cases. This has been the work of nongovernmental organizations—mainly the American Association of University Professors—but it establishes the practicality of utilizing the basic principles of academic freedom in building a common law of academic freedom.

Thirdly, the fundamental principles of a system of academic freedom are readily reducible to judicial rules, administrable by the courts. They can be stated in terms of judicial doctrine and are capable of being enforced by the techniques of judicial review. Thus the courts would not be called upon to exercise affirmative legislative powers, such as creating or financing an educational institution. On the contrary they would be utilizing their negative powers of judicial supervision to block action that controverted constitutional principles and to compel government, educational institutions, or others to comply with those principles. Consequently, in making academic freedom a constitutional right the courts would still be performing their classic function of requiring adherence to fundamental substantive and procedural rights of the individual.

The test of feasibility is posed if we were to imagine a constitution being drafted today and including the provision: "Academic freedom, being essential to the welfare and progress of the nation, shall be respected." One cannot doubt that such a clause would be no more difficult to construe or administer than the Supreme Court has found the provision that "Congress shall make no law . . . abridging freedom of speech, or of the press, or the right of the people peaceably to assemble, and to petition the Government for a redress of grievances." Certainly it is far more precise, and concerns a far narrower area, than the due process clause. Likewise, it is far more closely tied to concrete institutions, functions, and procedures than our latest constitutional addition—the right of privacy. In these broad terms, then, a constitutional right of academic freedom is quite within the realm of plausibility.

The task of finding a constitutional right to academic freedom within the confines of the existing Constitution is likewise not insuperable. Such a right could be discovered in the "liberty" of the due process clause, as has the right to freedom of movement, the right of association, and other fundamental rights. Or conceivably it could be held to be one of the rights reserved to the people by the Ninth Amendment. More properly, however, the right of academic freedom could be derived, like the right of privacy, from the "emanations" of a series of constitutional provisions. These would consist mainly of the free expression provisions of the First Amendment and the due process clause, but would also include the freedom of religion clause of the First Amendment, equal protection, self-incrimination, and perhaps others.

The basic concepts of freedom of expression embodied in the First Amendment are readily applicable to many aspects of academic freedom. Those principles can easily be extended to protect the faculty member in his academic rights to direct expression, that is, in his right to be free of interference in his teaching, research and publication. They would also cover most of the rights accorded him by the principles of academic freedom in his capacity as citizen, both of the university community and the outside community. Freedom of expression concepts would also apply to such problems as improper legislative proscription of the curriculum, and to many features of student academic freedom, including the student's right to form campus organizations, hear outside speakers, demonstrate on the campus, and the like. Moreover, in relation to academic freedom the First Amendment could be given a broadened meaning, stressing some of its affirmative implications. Ultimately any system of freedom of expression depends upon the existence of an educated, independent, mature citizenry. Consequently realization of the objectives of the First Amendment requires educational institutions that produce graduates who are trained in handling ideas, judging facts and argument, thinking independently, and generally participating effectively in the marketplace of ideas. Hence the First Amendment could be said to require the kind of educational institutions that are capable of producing such results. The First Amendment could also be said to guarantee, in addition to a right to speak, a right to know. As applied to academic freedom these latent powers in the First Amendment could be construed to extend constitutional protection to additional areas, such as the right of tenure, the right of faculty autonomy, student participation, and the like.[34]

The "emanations" of the due process clause would likewise afford the constitutional basis for protecting many aspects of academic freedom. On its substantive side the due process clause, as *Meyer* and *Pierce* indicate, could provide the constitutional foundation for the entire system of private schools as well as for protection against interference with the curriculum. On its procedural side, the kind of due process necessary to achieve an effective system of academic freedom would call not only for normally fair procedure in dismissal and disciplinary proceedings, but the utilization of such special devices as a hearing for a faculty member before a tribunal of his peers. It is also not inconceivable to imagine "academic due process," whether substantive or procedural or both, extending to the basic principles which should govern the respective roles of trustees, administrators, faculty, and students in the operation of a university community. It might even be said to embrace the fundamental premises of a tenure system.

Other constitutional provisions contain similar implications for academic freedom. Thus, equal protection principles would clearly govern in such areas as that of admissions policies. The privilege against self-incrimination, in an academic setting, might be considered to extend to students an absolute protection against disclosure of views expressed in a classroom. The Fourth Amendment's guarantee against unreasonable searches and seizures might serve as the intellectual foundation for development of the law governing the activities of police on the campus. The extent to which the constitutional protection applied to nonpublic institutions would, of course, depend upon developments in the law of "state action."

Granted that the creation of a constitutional structure of academic freedom would be generally feasible, and that it could be worked out in legal theory, would it be wise to press in that direction? There are certain serious drawbacks to be considered. Most important, perhaps, is the fact that the gap between the claims made on behalf of academic freedom and the claims the courts are presently likely to recognize is apparently a wide one. As the *Epperson* case indicates, the Supreme

34. For further discussion of the affirmative implications of the First Amendment see Chapter XVII.

Court is hesitant to approach the difficult problems at all in terms of the principles of academic freedom, and would hardly be willing to give as much force and depth to those principles as the proponents of academic freedom believe necessary. This would be particularly true of such unformed areas as faculty participation in university administration and the rights of students. It might be, therefore, that the system of academic freedom would gain more if its supporters concentrated on expanding and consolidating its present concepts and institutional framework before the issues are crystalized in constitutional terms.

A second major objection to the extension of legal controls in support of academic freedom has been that the governmental presence in the academic world would be repressive and destructive rather than liberating. This would not appear to be a serious problem so long as the courts, as they largely have until now, confined their role to one of protecting educational institutions against restrictive measures imposed by the government or the outside community. But it would become more significant insofar as the courts undertook to protect the rights of individual faculty members against the university administration or the students, or both, or otherwise became involved with the internal affairs of an educational institution. The fears expressed on this score are probably overstated, just as were the fears that Federal judicial supervision over State criminal proceedings would destroy the Federal-State relationship. The role of the courts would be simply to enforce "the fundamental principles of academic order." They would leave the actual implementation of such principles to those charged with that function. There is grave doubt that the courts would find it possible as an administrative matter to do anything else. Nevertheless, the problem remains a bothersome one.[35]

In some ways constitutional development tends to be irreversible, at least as far as accretions of jurisdiction are concerned. Once the courts undertook to make academic freedom a constitutional right they would not be likely to withdraw from that position. Moreover, the dangers inherent in such a development are more serious now than they would be when the principles and institutions of academic freedom have become more stabilized. It may be the more prudent

---

35. For a discussion of the dangers of judicial protection of academic freedom see James A. Perkins, "The University and Due Process," *American Library Association Bulletin*, Vol. 62 (1968), p. 977; Clark Byse, "The University and Due Process: A Somewhat Different View," A.A.U.P. *Bulletin*, Vol. 54 (1968), p. 143.

course, therefore, for the courts to continue along the present lines of applying traditional constitutional doctrine in connection with academic freedom issues, rather than to strike out now on new and radical lines. The elevation of academic freedom to an independent constitutional right clearly is, and perhaps should be, some decades away.

C. Application of the First Amendment in the Academic Freedom Area

For the time being then, it can be assumed, the structure of academic freedom will be supported by the courts, to the extent that it is supported at all, through application of disparate constitutional provisions, interpreted in traditional fashion, so far as each seems relevant to an issue arising in the academic freedom area. This development has thus far been carried furthest in the use of the due process clause. We are interested here, however, in the application of the First Amendment to academic freedom problems.

The decisions of the Supreme Court until now, as noted above, have not utilized the First Amendment in any unique way in the academic freedom area. Apart from *Tinker,* the decisions have been concerned largely with governmental restrictions of the loyalty variety. Their approach has been a simple, not to say a superficial, one. The Court has confined itself to eloquent but isolated statements on the significance of academic freedom, considering the academic freedom element of the case as one factor in a balancing test (*Sweezy, Barenblatt*), or as a reason for stricter application of peripheral rules such as vagueness or overbreadth (*Shelton, Keyishian*). The potentialities of such an approach seem limited.

If one undertakes to apply the First Amendment to a broader area, on a deeper and more sophisticated level, more complex problems emerge. This is particularly true if the First Amendment is given fuller meaning through use of the full protection theory. It is not possible here to do more than to suggest some of the problems and a possible approach to them. The discussion will be confined to academic freedom in higher education, passing over the more difficult issues in secondary and elementary education, and will not attempt to deal with the special question of sectarian religious institutions. It will also ignore the distinction between public and private institutions, assuming that state action is present in all situations.[36]

It is necessary at the outset to keep in mind the nature of the problem. The issues are not confined to the simple question of whether a government regulation impinges upon the right to expression of an ordinary individual or private group. Nor are they comparable to those arising in connection with government controls over expression by government employees. Rather they deal with the complex situation of a university functioning as an autonomous institution and composed of the different groups, having different rights and obligations, that make up the university community.

The basic characteristics of a university, which condition the application of the First Amendment to the system of academic freedom, cannot be examined in detail here. Very briefly, the university performs two main functions in a democratic society. One is the transmission of existing knowledge and values to the coming generation. The other is the critical reexamination of existing, and a search for new, knowledge and values, with a view to facilitating orderly change in the society. These two functions carry somewhat different implications so far as concerns the right to freedom of expression of the faculty member and other participants in the university community. Moreover, the university, like a government agency, is an operating organism. As such it must have rules governing the performance of different jobs in the organization and the relationships of the various members to one another. Finally, the university is a community within the general community. It provides space, meals, lodging and other facilities for its members and encloses within its walls a fixed group of people sharing ideas, interests, activities, and a major portion of their lives.[37]

In addition, as just noted, a university community is composed of different kinds of persons. The governing board (trustees), the administration, the faculty, and the students are all distinct groups, performing different functions. Many of the issues of academic freedom that arise concern the relationships among these groups. Thus the right to freedom of expression of a faculty member may depend much more on

36. On the state action problem see Note, *op. cit. supra* note 1, pp. 1056–1064. See also *Political and Civil Rights in the United States*, pp. 1659–1662.

37. For a more elaborate description of the nature of the university, from which the above discussion is taken, see Emerson and Haber, *op. cit. supra* note 3, pp. 547–552.

the controls which the governing board or the administration seek to exercise over him than those imposed by the government itself. In such a context the normal rules of the First Amendment may require substantial adaptation.

Our analysis starts out with the basic proposition that conduct classifiable as expression is fully protected under the First Amendment, and that the government or groups within the university operating under ultimate government authority can control only action. The problem of defining "expression" and "action" is the same here as elsewhere. Obviously much of the conduct taking place within a university is "expression." It is clear, however, that the nature of a university and the relations among the various groups within the university have a bearing on the issue of what constitutes "abridgment" under the First Amendment. In this respect the problem is somewhat like that of determining the right to expression of persons serving in a government agency. Certain controls by the government and by the agency are accepted as essential in performing the particular job within the agency; the problem is to ascertain in what respects the restrictions on expression endemic in a government institution may not be considered an "abridgment" of freedom of expression. There are, however, vast differences between a government agency and a university. Most important, the university deals primarily with matters that form the essence of a system of freedom of expression. It is concerned with imparting knowledge, adding to knowledge, and criticizing society. Hence questions of "abridgment" take on quite a different form.

It is helpful to divide the problems into two parts. One deals with regulation of expression imposed from within the university itself. The other concerns regulation imposed from outside by the government.

I. UNIVERSITY REGULATION

University controls can emanate from the governing board, the administration, faculty groups, or other sources. They do not, of course, bear any criminal sanction but are enforceable through dismissal, denial of promotion, reprimand, and similar forms of university discipline. In terms of academic freedom the major issues arising from these controls relate to the faculty member as teacher and scholar, the faculty member as citizen, students in the classroom, and students outside the classroom.

The faculty member as teacher and scholar is constantly engaged in expression in various forms. The extent to which university regulation of this expression does not constitute an "abridgment" within the meaning of the First Amendment depends largely upon the nature of the university function that the faculty member is performing. So far as his duties involve transmission of knowledge and values to students the permissible university controls would be substantial. They would include the assignment to courses, assignment of textbooks, the coverage of subject matter, and other requirements necessary for carrying on the university function. Unless the demands made upon the faculty member were wholly outside the limits of scholarly acceptance, as judged by the existing state of knowledge at the time, the faculty member could not object to such controls. The point at which university regulation of this sort would infringe the faculty member's rights, under principles of academic freedom and hence under the First Amendment, comes when the university regulation attempts to prescribe in detail the manner in which the faculty member must present the material. This is a difficult line to draw. It would certainly be only in the most extreme situation that claim of violation of a First Amendment right of this nature would receive recognition by the courts.

Where the faculty member is fulfilling the university role as critic of society, discoverer of new knowledge, and facilitator of social change, the university's right of regulation would be at a minimum. Clearly this function calls for the broadest protection of expression. The university could insist on adherence to scholarly standards. Likewise nondiscriminatory controls over funds, housekeeping regulations, and similar organizational arrangements would be permissible. Beyond that, a university restriction would most likely constitute an abridgment of freedom of expression.

A faculty member operates not only as a teacher and scholar in classroom, laboratory and study but as a citizen of the university community and as a citizen of the outside world. Indeed most of the controversies over academic freedom have pertained to the faculty member in his capacity as citizen. Again we start with the proposition that all forms of conduct constituting expression should be fully protected under the First Amendment against interference of any kind by the university or its agents. This follows from the fact that the faculty member is entitled to the same rights as other citizens. In fact, as the Supreme Court has frequently declared, freedom of expression is particularly necessary in the academic context if the university is to perform its function. This consideration applies to the faculty member as citizen as well as to the faculty member as teacher and scholar. He cannot be restricted in one capacity without destroying his freedom in the other.

The question is then presented whether there are any factors operating in the academic context that qualify the basic right in the sense that university regulation would not constitute an abridgment of freedom of expression. Upon analysis each of the major characteristics of a university would seem to imply certain limited restrictions upon the faculty member as citizen, thereby setting him off from the ordinary citizen so far as the right of the university to control his expression is concerned.

(1) The university in performing its various functions, particularly as disseminator of knowledge and social critic, represents to its students and to the outside world that the members of its faculty are competent to speak in their fields of expertise. In one sense the university is certifying to the community that the faculty member is entitled to special attention in the marketplace of ideas, that as one possessing knowledge and training in certain fields his findings and opinions should carry more than ordinary weight. This certifying action of the university is important in facilitating the operation of a democratic society, particularly when the issues are technical and complex. But it entails some responsibility on the part of the university to those who may rely upon its representation. Hence the university is entitled to require that the content of the faculty member's presentation of matters within his field should meet certain professional standards. Such standards cannot be precisely defined; nor would the faculty member be limited to communications of a scholarly nature. But in general the faculty member should be prepared to support his facts, hypotheses and conclusions by a full professional presentation if called upon to do so. Furthermore, for obvious reasons, the university is entitled to require the faculty member, whether speaking in his own field or not, to make clear to his audience that the views expressed are his own and not those of the university.

(2) The fact that the university is an administrative organization, of which the faculty member is a part, also imposes certain conditions upon the faculty member's right of expression. In this context the faculty member's position resembles somewhat that of the government employee, although the atmosphere of a university is likely to be more open and relaxed. In any event the university as an institution is enti-

tled to maintain its own rules and to insist upon relations between its members that do not produce unlivable disruption. This would not, of course, permit the university to stifle ordinary dissent or criticism. But the university would be justified in insisting that a faculty member not advocate violation of its rules or make false statements, deliberately or through gross negligence, about other members of the university community.

(3) The position of the university as a community within a community likewise carries certain implications for freedom of expression as practiced and protected within its walls. For one thing the university has at least a limited custodianship over the students and a resulting obligation that no harm come to them while they are on the campus. There are not many situations in which harm would arise out of exercise of the right of expression. But there is one. The relation of the university to its students would imply that the faculty member should not communicate to students on the campus, when they had not been forewarned, material in such critical areas as sex, race or religion, which is likely to have an immediate traumatic shock effect. Such a restriction, however, should not apply if the communication is necessary to the presentation of information, hypotheses, or conclusions that can be corroborated by a full scholarly presentation. In addition, as an autonomous community the university would have authority to assure minimum conditions of order and safety within its borders. Normally problems of this nature relating to freedom of expression, such as "traffic rules" of time and place of communication or rules on noise, would not be governed by any principle different from equivalent regulations issued by authorities off the campus. But certain differences might appear. Thus, if facilities for communication were limited in any respect, the university would be justified in allocating such scarce facilities upon the basis of needs closer to the educational pattern of the university. The interest of the university in keeping the police off its campus might possibly modify the rules with respect to the holding of meetings in the context of violence.

Apart from these qualifications growing out of the nature of the university, there is no reason for different application of the First Amendment to regulations of the university affecting the faculty member as citizen. Thus loyalty oaths, unless narrowly drawn to cover only conduct classified as "action," are devices for controlling expression, or probing into areas of expression, and cannot be imposed by the university. Membership in the Communist Party or similar organizations, whether on the right or the left of the political spectrum, may not be made the basis for dismissal or other sanction; mere association in a political organization, even though some members of the organization may engage in illegal conduct, is protected as an exercise of the right of expression. Nor would the university be justified in making inquiry of its faculty members into areas of expression, or penalizing a faculty member for refusing to answer government inquiries into expression. These and other interferences with expression all fall within the protection of the First Amendment extended to all citizens.[38]

The First Amendment rights of students in the classroom are, like those of the faculty member, limited to some degree by the nature of the university. Particularly the function of the university in transmitting knowledge would imply certain restrictions. Assignments of study, requirements of tests or examinations, judgment of performance, promulgation and administration of rules for the effective conduct of the class, and similar regulations are all matters within the jurisdiction of the faculty member or the administration. Beyond that, however, students would have similar rights to those of the faculty member, namely complete freedom to speak, within a scholarly framework, subject to traffic regulations. Indeed the *Tinker* case indicates that the student would also bring into the classroom other rights of expression, so long as there was no disruption of the class. Very likely it would be an unusual situation in which student rights in the classroom would be enforced through the judicial process. But, as *Tinker* demonstrates, there would be occasions when vindication in the courts would be feasible.

Moreover, a strong argument can be made that the First Amendment protects students against any nonacademic sanctions emanating from their expression in the classroom. Under standard First Amendment theory, of course, the student could not be subject to any form of legislative punishment for such expression. An affirmative concept of the First Amendment would extend this protection to forbid the use of classroom expression to the detriment of the student in any way, such as by disclosure to government investigators, prospective employers, or otherwise. In practice, such a right could normally be made effective only by university regulation forbidding such disclosure or by individual action of the faculty member.

38. These matters are discussed, outside the academic context, in Chapters V–VIII. For further elaboration of the rights of the faculty member as citizen see Emerson and Haber, *op. cit. supra* note 3.

Outside the classroom the student's right of expression would, for the most part, be governed by the ordinary First Amendment rules applicable to all citizens. As to the exercise of expression on the campus, however, the nature of the university as an administrative organization and as a community would warrant certain forms of regulation that, in this context, could not be considered an abridgment of the student's freedom of expression. These restrictions would be minor. They would include such requirements as that the officers of a student organization be registered with the university, that notification be given the university of invitations to outside speakers, and that the time, place and manner of expression not materially disrupt other university functions. Apart from such controls, students in all their activities—meetings, demonstrations, publications, invitations to outside speakers, political organizing, and the like—would be entitled to full protection so long as their conduct consisted of expression. Action would be governed by other rules.

Off the campus, regulations derived from the character of the university would not be applicable. Students would be subject to the rules of the outside community.[39]

2. GOVERNMENT REGULATION

Government regulations that impinge upon the area of academic freedom fall into two categories. The first embraces those controls relating to matters of curriculum, teaching and research. The second deals with activities in the university that take place outside the classroom and the laboratory. The most difficult problems surround the first kind of regulation. It was such an issue that the Supreme Court sidestepped in the *Epperson* case.

When the government undertakes to regulate the curriculum, teaching or research in a state-financed university we are confronted with a special kind of First Amendment problem. The government is not imposing restrictions upon the free play of private (nongovernmental) expression—the usual situation with which we have been concerned up to now. It is operating a government enterprise and, since a university is involved, taking an affirmative part in the system of free-

39. For attempts to codify the kinds of regulations which the university would be entitled to impose upon student ex- pression on the campus see the A.A.U.P. and the A.C.L.U. statements, *supra* note 7.

dom of expression. The fact that the government is not regulating a laissez-faire system but actively engaging in expression itself, through creation and control of a university, presents new and puzzling First Amendment problems. By what rules is the government obliged to control itself when it participates in the system of freedom of expression?

Two major considerations are fundamental in an approach to this problem. One is that the government is not just an ordinary participant in the system of freedom of expression or in the sector of higher education. The government possesses overwhelming resources, operates a substantial proportion of the existing institutions, controls much of the remainder through grants, and is generally the dominant figure. Access to education is for the great proportion of the population dependent upon government institutions and funds. Thus this sector of the community has many of the elements of a closed system. It is not entirely different from radio and television communication, in which physical limitations upon the number of wave lengths reduce the opportunity of equal participation and preclude an open, free-for-all system. The second consideration is that the government is dealing with a university. The function a university is called upon to perform in our society, as the whole theory of academic freedom stresses, cannot be carried out unless the university remains an autonomous institution, independent of the other institutions of our society that it must criticize.

The principles of the First Amendment, in broader form, must be made applicable to this situation. It is just as vital to the system of freedom of expression that the government take no action "abridging" expression when it operates a closed sector of the community or is the dominant figure there as when it is attempting to regulate private expression in an open system. The formulation of such principles, however, has hardly begun and poses stupendous problems.

Two principles, however, may be suggested. The first is that, as a general proposition, the government may, with respect to State universities, concern itself with educational policy, but not with academic policy. This means that the government can prescribe the board character of the curriculum for a particular institution, provide what general areas are to be emphasized or omitted, even require the offering of certain courses. But it may not prescribe the more immediate details of course content, methods of presentation, techniques of research, and similar matters that involve questions of academic competence. Secondly, to the extent that the government undertakes to lay down educational policy, it must conform to the concept of balanced presentation. This means that it must provide a fairly balanced exposition of various relevant theories and points of view, and of alternatives open to action. The first principle grows out of the nature of the university; the second out of the obligation of the government in a closed or substantially closed system.

If these principles had been applied in the *Epperson* case, the Arkansas statute would have been struck down on First Amendment (freedom of expression) grounds. The proscription upon the teaching of a particular theory of man's development invades the area of academic policy. The requirement of balanced presentation is not met when the teaching of a theory that falls within the area of recognized academic or scientific standards is forbidden. Other kinds of government regulation would undoubtedly pose more complex problems. But the development of some principles for solving these important issues could begin.[40]

In the case of private educational institutions the government's control over general educational policy would be reduced to a minimum. It would not extend beyond controls such as were necessary to assure the general integrity of the enterprise as an educational institution, or to maintain standards essential for the preferred training in a profession or occupation. This would remain true despite the fact that a private university might be sufficiently involved in "state action" so that it was required to administer its own operations in accord with the dictates of the First Amendment. The presence of such "state action" does not give the government power to run the private institution as a government operation. The theory of the *Pierce* case would seem to demand this result. More difficult problems would arise over the controls exercised by the government in the administration of its contract and grant programs. Here the governing principles would be the same as those relating to the denial of benefits or privileges, discussed in Chapter VI.

Attempts by the government to regulate expression outside the classroom and the laboratory, at either State or private universities, should be governed by the same rules that apply to the outside community. There is no valid reason for allowing the government any greater

40. For further discussion see Thomas I. Emerson and David Haber, "The *Scopes* Case in Modern Dress," *University of Chicago Law Review,* Vol. 27 (1960), pp. 522, 526–528.

authority on the campus than off. This means, further, that those qualifications which the university is authorized to place upon First Amendment rights, as discussed above, are not available to the government. Such qualifications are justified in terms of the nature of the university and must be administered by the university itself. There is no need for additional punishment or control imposed by the government. To allow such regulation by the government would destroy the autonomy of the university.

The principles suggested here for applying the First Amendment in the area of academic freedom require refinement and elaboration. But an approach somewhat along these lines would seem to be essential if the First Amendment is to give any effective support to the development of academic freedom.

XVII

*Affirmative
Promotion of
Freedom of
Expression*

The most challenging problems in First Amendment theory today lie in the prospect of using law affirmatively to promote more effective functioning of the system of freedom of expression. The traditional premises of the system are essentially laissez-faire in character. They envisage an open marketplace of ideas, with all persons and points of view having equal access to the means of communication. In supporting this system the First Amendment has played a largely negative role: it has operated to protect the system against interference from the government. Thus the issues have turned for the most part upon reconciling freedom of expression with other social interests that the government seeks to safeguard. The development of legal doctrine has been primarily in the evolution of a series of negative commands. A realistic view of the system of freedom of expression in this country today, however, discloses serious deficiencies that call for a different kind of First Amendment approach.

There are numerous reasons for the failures now threatening the existence of the system. Probably the most significant is the overpowering monopoly over the means of communication acquired by the mass media. Two international news services, Associated Press and United Press International, furnish most of the international news. In 1967, out of 1,547 cities with daily newspapers, there were competing dailies in only 64. Three gigantic networks, ABC, CBS, and NBC, determine most of what is seen in American homes on television. In 1966, thirty-five advertisers supplied over 50 percent of television's total advertising income. In 1967, newspapers held interests in a third of the VHF stations and in 22 percent of the UHF stations. In the same year some twenty-five Congressmen or their families owned interests in radio and television properties, and about a half of the members of Congress were members of law firms that represented broadcasters. The economics of radio and television press inevitably in the direction of programs that appeal to the lowest common denominator of a mass audience. The consequence of all this is that the expression emanating from the mass media tends to represent a single, generally bland, point of view.[1]

Other factors are less overwhelming, but still important. Modern government, by virtue of its size, resources, control of information, and links to the mass media, plays a more dominant and narrowing role in the system. The issues in a technical age grow constantly more complex, and there is at the same time a bewildering mass of information on some subjects and a frustrating paucity of information on others. Costs of all methods of communication steadily rise, beyond the means of the individual or the ordinary group. The growth of voluntary associations on a mass scale, while solving some problems, adds to the disadvantage of the non-belonging person or the less powerful organization.

The result is that the system is choked with communications based upon the conventional wisdom and becomes incapable of performing its basic function. Search for the truth is handicapped because much of the argument is never heard or heard only weakly. Political decisions are distorted because the views of some citizens never reach other citizens, and feedback to the government is feeble. The possibility of orderly social change is greatly diminished because those persons with the most urgent grievances come to believe the system is unworkable and merely shields the existing order. Under these circumstances it

---

1. The figures are taken from Bryce W. Rucker, *The First Freedom* (Carbondale, Southern Illinois University Press, 1968). See also Dan Lacy, *Freedom and Communications* (Urbana, University of Illinois Press, 2d ed. 1965); James R. Wiggins, *Freedom or Secrecy* (New York, Oxford University Press, rev. ed. 1964); Charles A. Reich, "Making Free Speech Audible," *The Nation*, Feb. 8, 1965, p. 138; and other materials cited in Thomas I. Emerson, David Haber and Norman Dorsen, *Political and Civil Rights in the United States* (Boston, Little, Brown & Co., 3d ed. 1967), pp. 900–901 (cited hereafter in this chapter as *Political and Civil Rights in the United States*).

becomes essential, if the system is to survive, that a search be made for ways to use the law and legal institutions in an affirmative program to restore the system to effective working order.

In general, the government must affirmatively make available the opportunity for expression as well as protect it from encroachment. This means that positive measures must be taken to assure the ability to speak despite economic or other barriers. It also means that greater attention must be given to the right of the citizen to hear varying points of view and the right to have access to information upon which such points of view can be intelligently based. Thus, equally with the right and ability to speak, such an approach would stress the right to hear and the right to know.

In terms of First Amendment theory the issues fall into two categories. In the first situation the government relies upon some existing power as the basis for regulation designed to improve operation of the system of freedom of expression. Thus the Federal Government may seek, through use of the commerce power, to require broadcasting stations to give equal time to all political candidates; or a State may, under its general police powers, require disclosure of the sources of campaign contributions. The question is whether, since such a regulation impinges upon freedom of expression, it is permissible under the First Amendment. This issue, however, is not like the question that arises when the government places restrictions upon expression in order to protect or advance some other kind of social interest outside the system of freedom of expression. As an affirmative measure the regulation has its impact entirely within the system; it is designed to make the system work better, not to limit expression in order to promote a conflicting interest. Hence the ordinary First Amendment tests —bad tendency, incitement, clear and present danger, balancing of opposing interests, and full protection—are not applicable. The problem must be resolved in terms of whether there has been an "abridgment" of freedom of expression, and the tests must be framed in terms of accommodation of interests within the system, nondiscrimination, promotion rather than deterrence of expression, and the like.[2]

A second kind of problem arises when governmental power to facilitate operation of the system is sought in the First Amendment itself. Such affirmative power of the First Amendment may be invoked in

2. The issues are much the same as those that arise in maintaining traffic controls over the right of expression, discussed in Chapter IX.

two forms. In one it is self-executing and enforceable by the courts as a constitutional mandate. Thus the claim that a local board of education must make a school building available for public meetings would rest upon the principle that the First Amendment of its own force requires such action. In its other form the affirmative power of the First Amendment manifests itself as the basis for legislation. This might be Federal legislation enacted directly by virtue of the First Amendment, or Federal legislation enacted under Section 5 of the Fourteenth Amendment, which makes the First Amendment applicable to the States. Such uses of the First Amendment as an affirmative power are, of course, rare. But some development of the law has begun in this direction. Here again the applicable tests are quite different from those employed in traditional situations in which the First Amendment is invoked purely as a negative right against government interference.

Apart from the task of developing suitable First Amendment doctrine, grave administrative and procedural problems are posed by any effort to employ governmental authority to facilitate operation of the system of freedom of expression. The attempt to use governmental power to achieve some limited objective, while at the same time keeping the power under control, is always a risky enterprise. Nowhere is this truer than in the area of freedom of expression. Nevertheless there is no alternative. The weaknesses of the existing system are so profound that failure to act is the more dangerous course. Moreover, the government is already deeply involved at many points, some of great importance, as in its regulation of radio and television. The same kind of movement may be found in other areas of individual rights today, such as the development of the affirmative aspects of the equal protection clause. The only prudent course, then, is to formulate principles and devise techniques that use social power to facilitate freedom of expression while holding the instrument of that power in check.[3]

---

3. The first comprehensive effort to consider the question of affirmative promotion of a system of freedom of expression was made in Zechariah Chafee, Jr., *Government and Mass Communications* (Chicago, University of Chicago Press, 1947; reprinted Hamden, Conn., Archon Books, 1965). A recent discussion that has aroused a good deal of interest is Jerome A. Barron, "Access to the Press—A New First Amendment Right," *Harvard Law Review*, Vol. 80 (1967), p. 1641, and "An Emerging First Amendment Right of Access to the Me-

dia?" *George Washington Law Review*, Vol. 37 (1969), p. 487. Materials and references dealing with many of the problems discussed in this chapter may be found in Donald M. Gillmor and Jerome A. Barron, *Mass Communication Law: Cases and Comment* (St. Paul, Minn., West Publishing Co., 1969). See also Charles A. Reich, "The Law of the Planned Society," *Yale Law Journal*, Vol. 75 (1966), p. 1227; Louis H. Mayo, "The Limited Forum," *George Washington Law Review*, Vol. 22 (1954), p. 261.

A. Establishing the Basic Conditions

The initial responsibility of the government is to maintain the basic conditions that a system of freedom of expression requires in order, not just to exist, but to flourish. This obligation is, of course, one that the state owes to all institutions, inside and outside the government, that seek to further the goals of the individual within the society. The government must establish fundamental law and order, must provide essential community services, and must create the underlying economic, social and political circumstances in which systems not based on the use of official force may successfully operate. Even in the case of religious institutions, for which the Constitution specifically prescribes firm separation, the government nevertheless supplies police protection, fire protection, and other services generally made available to the community. Clearly the obligation of the government to support a system of freedom of expression is vastly more extensive and compelling.

Most of the measures designed to achieve these ends operate from outside the system and do not raise any serious First Amendment problems. Ordinarily protection of expression against interference by private persons through force or violence is an accepted role for the police. Similarly other standard governmental aids, such as the right of a group to incorporate, are available to associations engaged in expression in the same manner as to other noncommercial associations. Even devices specifically enacted to promote the system of free expression, such as exempting news reporters from the normal obligation to give testimony in order to protect the confidentiality of news sources, do not pose any First Amendment difficulties. Likewise, measures taken by the Federal Government to eliminate interference with First Amendment rights by a State or its agents, such as the Federal Civil Rights Acts or the laws allowing removal of State prosecutions to Federal courts, are not restricted in any way by First Amendment limitations. Only occasionally in the administration of these provisions, as in the case of the hostile audience or the heckler, do First Amendment issues emerge.[4]

4. With respect to measures designed to protect news sources see Talbot D'Alemberte, "Journalists Under the Axe: Protection of Confidential Sources of In- formation," *Harvard Journal of Legislation*, Vol. 6 (1969), p. 307, and material there cited; James A. Quest and Alan L. Stanzler, "The Constitutional Argument

In one area of police protection, however, difficult questions arise. To what extent is it the responsibility of the government to protect expression against interference from private (nongovernmental) sources other than when such interference takes the form of force or violence? Clearly there are limits. The system of freedom of expression contemplates that many kinds of private pressures—economic, social and personal—will be at work as the community attempts to reach social decisions. The government cannot and should not undertake to prevent or regulate these forms of interchange. On the other hand sometimes such pressures go beyond the bounds of what can be tolerated by a system of expression that can be called "free." This occurs primarily in the case of economic pressure. The economic power of an employer over an employee, a landlord over a tenant, or a highly organized group of union members over a business enterprise may result in coercion upon expression which has all the effect of physical force or violence. The issue resolves itself into one of drawing the line between expression and action. Pressures that can be classified as action are subject to state control, whenever such control is deemed necessary or appropriate, without raising any issue under the First Amendment. Pressure in the nature of expression cannot be abridged in any way.[5]

Some of the measures taken by government to maintain the basic conditions for the functioning of freedom of expression operate wholly within the system itself. The main examples of these are traffic controls, whose regulation of the time, place and manner of expression is essential to prevent conflict. The First Amendment issues arising out of such provisions have been discussed in connection with the right of assembly. If the circumstances require more intensive methods of control, owing to scarcity of facilities for expression or similar factors, government regulation moves beyond mere traffic controls into problems of allocation, accessibility, and diversity.

In general then, with the exceptions noted, the problems in this area do not involve want of power, or concern over the limitations imposed by the First Amendment, but issues of performance. The crucial need is that the society act with vigor and imagination to give

---

for Newsmen Concealing Their Sources," *Northwestern University Law Review,* Vol. 64 (1969), p. 18. On the hostile audience and heckler problems see Chapter IX.

5. See the discussion of boycotts and economic pressures in Chapter XII. The question of when interference emanates from private sources and when from governmental sources presents a question of state action, varying aspects of which are discussed throughout this book.

affirmative support to the system of freedom of expression. This is especially important in the very broadest areas of affirmative action—the maintenance of fundamental economic, political and social conditions necessary for a system of freedom of expression to survive at all.

B. Purification of the System

Freedom of speech, Justice Douglas has said, may "best serve its high purpose when it induces a condition of unrest, creates dissatisfaction with conditions as they are, or even stirs people to anger." Justice Brennan has emphasized that in a democratic society speech should be "uninhibited, robust, and wide-open." A healthy system of freedom of expression embraces all this and more. It contains much that is deliberately false, and much more that is misleading or deceptive. The personal motives of the speaker, financial or otherwise, are usually not revealed, and the listener must make his own discount for bias or ulterior purpose. Often the communication is anonymous or emanates from a source that is concealed. The system is crammed with expression that appeals far more to passion than to reason. In short, participants in the system are likely to violate all the rules for communication between gentlemen.[6]

The temptation to clean up the system is naturally strong and persistent. Very often, as we have seen, efforts to improve the content of the system are undertaken in an attempt to curtail expression that is thought to harm other social interests. But sometimes efforts are made simply to refine the system as a system. Controls are imposed solely to promote the goals of the system—to introduce honesty, decency and openness into it—and thereby to improve the quality and meaningfulness of expression. In this situation, as just noted, different rules for the application of the First Amendment must apply.

The essential consideration is that, while certain limited forms of control may improve the performance of the system, such controls cannot be imposed on any broad scale without destroying the system altogether. This is true not only because the government has no au-

6. The quotations are from *Terminiello v. City of Chicago,* 337 U.S. 1, 4 (1949), and *New York Times v. Sullivan,* 376 U.S. 254, 270 (1964).

thority to determine the content or value of particular expression. Even if the regulation does not touch on such matters, the mere presence of the government, with its apparatus for investigating, deciding and enforcing, is repressive and likely to inhibit the system. Moreover, it is always difficult for a court to determine the motive or effect of a given form of control and the regulation may thus in fact operate to limit rather than to expand the system. In addition the regulations are likely to be vague and uncertain in their impact and almost invariably operate to curtail unorthodox, unpopular or minority expression. In these respects the purification controls are different from those designed to regulate the physical ordering of expression, such as traffic controls. Hence any regulation of this nature presents a danger to the system and can be tolerated in the system only under the most exceptional circumstances.

On the basis of these considerations the controlling principles can be stated:

(1) In general, purification controls constitute an "abridgment" of expression and hence are invalid. They may not be an "abridgment," however, in exceptional situations in which the regulation, in light of its impact on the whole system, operates to expand rather than contract freedom of expression.

(2) In applying this rule the burden of proof is on the proponents of the regulation to establish (a) that the control is clearly necessary to correct a grave abuse in the operation of the system and is narrowly limited to that end, and that this objective cannot be achieved by other means; (b) that the regulation does not limit the content of expression; (c) that the regulation operates equitably and with no undue advantage to any group or point of view; (d) that the control is in the nature of a regulation, not a prohibition, and does not substantially impair the area of expression controlled; and (e) that the regulation can be specifically formulated in objective terms and is reasonably free of the possibility of administrative abuse.

The principal areas in which purification controls have been attempted are (1) corrupt practices legislation and similar controls dealing with the electoral process; (2) lobbying legislation; and (3) various other types of disclosure requirements. Libel and group libel laws are partly intended to purify the system but are mainly directed against the harm thought to accrue to other social interests.

I. CORRUPT PRACTICES LEGISLATION AND
SIMILAR CONTROLS OVER THE ELECTION PROCESS

Federal and State legislation regulating "corrupt practices" in election campaigns and similar legislation dealing with other aspects of the election process is widespread and varied. In general it takes the form of (a) requiring disclosure of the sources of campaign funds and an accounting of expenditures; (b) limiting the amounts contributed or spent for campaign purposes; (c) prohibiting certain groups from contributing or spending in campaigns; (d) requiring disclosure of the authorship or sponsorship of campaign literature; and (e) other regulations designed to improve the conduct of elections. All of these regulations, of course, impinge upon freedom of expression; the issue is whether they "abridge" it. The Supreme Court decisions on the subject are scattered and, while they mark out some of the boundaries, do not throw much light upon the principles involved.[7]

The first direct decision of the Supreme Court in this area came in *Burroughs and Cannon v. United States,* decided in 1934. In that case the Court upheld the validity of the Federal Corrupt Practices Act of 1925, which required all political organizations to render a detailed accounting of contributions received and expenditures made for the purpose of influencing the election of presidential electors or candidates in two or more States. The main constitutional issue discussed by the Court was whether the Federal Government, or only the States, possessed the power to enact such legislation. No issue under the First Amendment was raised by the parties or considered by the Court. Nor has the First Amendment question been decided by the Court in any subsequent case. Hence, while the result is known, the Court's reasoning is not.[8]

The second type of corrupt practices legislation places a ceiling upon the amount of contributions and expenditures in political campaigns. The main provisions of this nature in the present Federal law were enacted in the Hatch Act of 1939. While this kind of regulation has never been the subject of Supreme Court decision, its constitution-

7. For a collection of materials and references upon corrupt practices and similar legislation see *Political and Civil Rights in the United States,* pp. 624–628, 641–645.

8. *Burroughs and Cannon v. United States,* 290 U.S. 534 (1934). See also *Hadnott v. Amos,* 394 U.S. 358 (1969).

ality seems to have been taken for granted by virtue of the *Burroughs* case.[9]

The third type, prohibiting certain groups from giving or spending funds in political campaigns, has received more judicial attention. These issues were presented to the Supreme Court in two cases involving Section 304 of the Taft-Hartley Act of 1947. That provision makes it unlawful for any corporation or labor organization "to make a contribution or expenditure in connection with any election" for Federal office, or "in connection with any primary election or political convention or caucus held to select candidates" for such an office. Shortly after passage of the legislation, the Congress of Industrial Organizations moved to test its constitutionality. The "C.I.O. News," a weekly periodical published by the C.I.O., carried a statement by C.I.O. President Philip Murray urging all C.I.O. members to vote for Judge Ed Garmatz for Congress in a special election in Maryland. Murray and the C.I.O. were indicted for violation of Section 304. The District Court dismissed the indictment on the ground that the statute was invalid under the First Amendment, saying "no clear and present danger to the public interest can be found in the circumstances surrounding the enactment of this legislation." In *United States v. Congress of Industrial Organizations* the Supreme Court unanimously affirmed the District Court. The majority did not reach the constitutional issue, however, as they construed Section 304 not to prohibit publication of the article. Justices Rutledge, Black, Douglas, and Murphy, disagreeing on the interpretation of the statute, would have decided the constitutional question and held the statute invalid as a violation of the First Amendment. Justice Rutledge, writing for this minority, explored the issues at length. His conclusion was that, although some form of regulation might be permissible, a complete prohibition was overbroad and invalid. He also expressed objections on the grounds of vagueness.[10]

The question again reached the Supreme Court in *United States v. International Union United Automobile Workers* in 1957. Here the indictment alleged that during the 1954 elections the U.A.W. had spent some six thousand dollars for a series of television broadcasts in which it had urged the election of certain candidates to Congress. The District Court dismissed the indictment on the ground that "Congress

9. The Hatch Act provisions are 18 U.S.C. §§608 and 609. The history of Federal corrupt practices legislation is traced in Justice Frankfurter's opinion in *United States v. International Union*

United Automobile Workers, 352 U.S. 567 (1957).

10. 18 U.S.C. §610; *United States v. C.I.O.,* 335 U.S. 106 (1948).

did not intend to write an unconstitutional law" and that the expenditures were "not prohibited by the Act." This time the Supreme Court reversed, holding that the expenditures were covered by the Act, and remanded the case to the District Court for trial. Again the majority declined to pass on First Amendment issues, preferring to postpone those questions until a complete record had been made at the trial. Justice Douglas, in an opinion with which Chief Justice Warren and Justice Black joined, dissented. He conceded that "[i]f Congress is of the opinion that large contributions by labor unions to candidates for office and to political parties have had an undue influence upon the conduct of elections, it can prohibit such contributions," and that "in expressing their views on the issues and candidates, labor unions can be required to acknowledge their authorship and support of those expressions." But he declared that Section 304 was not "narrowly drawn" and "abolishes First Amendment rights on a wholesale basis." [11]

The U.A.W., on going to trial, obtained an acquittal and thus the case never got back to the Supreme Court. Nor has any other case under Section 304 come before the Court. At present both unions and corporations have found sufficient loopholes in the law to make it unnecessary for them to press close to the line of violating the statute. Consequently we have no expression of opinion by a majority of the Court on the First Amendment issues, although its eagerness to put off decision would seem to indicate it had serious doubts that the legislation would survive constitutional scrutiny. Justices Rutledge and Douglas, proceeding on theories of overbreadth and vagueness, did not find it necessary to carry the argument beyond that point.

The fourth type of corrupt practices law, prohibiting the distribution of anonymous campaign literature, is found in most of the States and in the Federal legislation. The New York statute was attacked in *Golden v. Zwickler* and held invalid by a Federal three-judge court on First Amendment grounds. The Supreme Court reversed the case for reasons of mootness. Hence the status of such legislation remains uncertain.[12]

11. *United States v. International Union United Automobile Workers*, 138 F. Supp. 53, 59 (E.D. Mich. 1956), 352 U.S. 567, 598, 597 (1957). For materials discussing Section 304 and the cases arising under it, as well as similar State legislation, see *Political and Civil Rights in the United States*, p. 627.

12. *Golden v. Zwickler*, 290 F. Supp. 244 (E.D.N.Y. 1968), 394 U.S. 103 (1969). The case was previously before the Court, on the question of whether the Federal courts should take jurisdiction at that stage, in *Zwickler v. Koota*, 389 U.S. 241 (1967). The Federal statute, 18 U.S.C. §612, was upheld in *United States*

Another form of corrupt practices legislation came before the Supreme Court in *Mills v. Alabama*. That case involved an Alabama statute which made it a crime "to do any electioneering or to solicit any votes . . . in support of or in opposition to any proposition that is being voted on on the day on which the election affecting such candidates or propositions is being held." The statute had been applied to convict the editor of the *Birmingham Post Herald* for publishing an editorial, supporting a mayor-council form of government, on the day an election was being held to decide between a city commissioner and a mayor-council plan. The Supreme Court unanimously reversed, Justice Black writing for all members of the Court except Justice Harlan. After describing the role of the press in a system of freedom of expression, Justice Black simply concluded: "It is difficult to conceive of a more obvious and flagrant abridgment of the constitutionally guaranteed freedom of the press." He then took note of Alabama's justification for the statute—that it "protects the public from confusive last-minute charges and countercharges" when there is no time to answer. To this he replied that the argument, "even if it were relevant to the constitutionality of the law," had a "fatal flaw" because the statute merely moved the time at which no reply was possible one day ahead. Justice Black then ended: "We hold that no test of reasonableness can save a state law from invalidation as a violation of the First Amendment when that law makes it a crime for a newspaper editor to do no more than urge people to vote one way or another in a publicly held election." [13]

The Supreme Court's decisions in the corrupt practices cases, admittedly incomplete, leave unresolved a host of questions. In *Mills* Justice Black appears to be applying his absolute test, though he makes a slight bow in the direction of a "reasonableness" doctrine. The other justices, apart from Justice Harlan, apparently acquiesce. It is hard to see how the absolute test can be applied here without overruling *Burroughs* and invalidating other types of corrupt practices legislation. Yet no effort is made to draw a line between the two or to suggest a theory upon which a distinction should be based.

Moreover, the cases raise questions that go beyond the corrupt

---

v. Scott, 195 F. Supp. 440 (D.N.D. 1961). For other material on the matter see *Political and Civil Rights in the United States*, p. 628.

13. *Mills v. Alabama*, 384 U.S. 214, 219–220 (1966). Justice Harlan concurred on the ground that the statute did not give fair warning that "publication of an editorial of this kind was reached" by the provision under which the defendant was convicted. 384 U.S. at 223.

practices area. If a candidate in an election can be required to disclose his income and expenditures for expression, why cannot all other persons be required to make similar disclosures in connection with other expression? If the government can equalize the amount of speech uttered in a campaign, by controlling the volume of expenditure for expression, why cannot it equalize the amount of speech uttered on any subject? Is it the implication of the *Burroughs* decision that the government has almost unlimited power to allocate resources available for expression, or to regulate access to the marketplace of ideas? The Supreme Court has advanced no theory upon which to base an answer to these questions.

If one undertakes to apply the five criteria suggested above as limiting governmental attempts to purify the system of freedom of expression, progress toward a solution is possible. By a liberal application of the suggested criteria one might conceivably sustain all forms of corrupt practices legislation, except the total prohibition on expression embodied in Section 304 of the Taft-Hartley Act, as well as many regulations for disclosure and equalization in other areas. But if the criteria are applied strictly, as they should be, it is likely one would come out with the proposition that such forms of regulation must be limited to restrictions (1) on the candidate himself, (2) in an election campaign.

For example, the main abuse at which disclosure legislation is directed is the possible influence of large contributions upon the candidate himself, and the primary concern of the equalization provision is the potential monopoly control over expression conferred upon the candidate. Funds expended for expression by the electorate at large do not generate equivalent dangers. Hence a control narrowly limited to correct a grave abuse would not reach beyond restrictions upon the candidate himself, and would not be justified outside the election process. Again, the impact of disclosure upon a candidate who is openly running for office is quite different from that upon a member of the general public who has not officially exposed himself to the public eye. Hence regulation of the candidate would not normally limit the content of expression in the way that disclosure regulation applicable to others would. Measures to assure equality of access to the marketplace by candidates could be drawn equitably, since each candidate has an equal interest. But the same would not be true of the many diverse interests represented in the public at large. Of course, controls that amounted to total prohibition, rather than regulation, would be outlawed whether applied to candidates or to others. Finally, regulations confined to candidates and election campaigns are directed to a limited end and deal with a limited situation. Hence they can be formulated with some objectivity and avoid the dangers of abuse in administration. This cannot be done with regulations, particularly equalization regulations, addressed to the innumerable different kinds of people seeking to express themselves for different purposes throughout the whole system of free expression.

The results derived from such an analysis would not differ markedly from the position the courts seem to have reached in this field. Disclosure and equalization legislation would be limited to candidates, and to that extent *Burroughs* would be modified. Section 304 of the Taft-Hartley Act would be invalid, except to the extent that corporations could be controlled on the theory they were part of the commercial sector and thus outside the regular system of freedom of expression. Zwickler would prevail in his attack on the New York statute, although the rule against anonymous campaign literature could be enforced against candidates. The statute considered in *Mills* would fall. Possibly application of the criteria here suggested as controlling would lead some to other conclusions. But at least this kind of approach would be based upon the functions and requirements of the system of freedom of expression.

2. LOBBYING LEGISLATION

Virtually all States and the Federal Government have enacted legislation to regulate lobbying. Most of this legislation is of the disclosure type, requiring the registration of persons engaged in lobbying and a public accounting of the sources of funds and expenditures. As in the case of election legislation, it is clear that controls of this nature impinge upon freedom of expression. No general requirement of registration prior to exercising the right to freedom of speech or to petition the government, and no general demand for an accounting of funds used, would conceivably be sustained under the First Amendment.

The Supreme Court addressed itself to these issues, as they related to the Federal Regulation of Lobbying Act, in *United States v. Harriss,* decided in 1954. The provisions of the Act were complex, loosely phrased, and extremely broad. Roughly they required detailed reports to Congress from any person "receiving any contribution or expending any money" for the purpose of "influen[cing], directly or indirectly, the passage or defeat of any legislation" before Congress. An information charging an organization and two individuals with failure to report was dismissed by the District Court on the ground that the Act was unconstitutional. The Supreme Court, construing the statute narrowly, reversed. Chief Justice Warren, writing for the majority, interpreted the Act as applying only to persons who received contributions for lobbying purposes or were paid lobbyists and who attempted to influence legislation "through direct communication with members of Congress." This excluded all amateur lobbying and all use of expression to influence Congress other than by "direct communication" with a Congressman. As thus construed, Chief Justice Warren held, the statute did not violate the First Amendment. After pointing out that the purpose of the legislation was to allow members of Congress to "properly evaluate" the "myriad pressures to which they are regularly subjected" and that otherwise "the voice of the people may all too easily be drowned out by the voice of special interest groups seeking favored treatment while masquerading as proponents of the public weal," he went on:

> Toward that end, Congress has not sought to prohibit these pressures. It has merely provided for a modicum of information from those who for hire attempt to influence legislation or who collect or spend funds for that purpose. It wants only to know who is being hired, who is putting up the money, and how much. It acted in the same spirit and for a similar purpose in passing the Federal Corrupt Practices Act—to maintain the integrity of a basic governmental process. See *Burroughs and Cannon v. United States,* 290 U.S. 534, 545.
>
> Under these circumstances, we believe that Congress, at least within the bounds of the Act as we have construed it, is not constitutionally forbidden to require the disclosure of lobbying activities. To do so would be to deny Congress in large measure the power of self-protection. And here Congress has used that power in a manner restricted to its appropriate end.[14]

Justice Douglas, with whom Justice Black concurred, dissented on grounds of overbreadth and vagueness. He conceded, however, that narrowly drawn lobbying legislation would be valid, saying: "I do not mean to intimate that Congress is without power to require disclosure

14. *United States v. Harriss,* 347 U.S.   612, 623, 625–626 (1954).

of the real principals behind those who come to Congress (or get others to do so) and speak as though they represent the public interest, when in fact they are undisclosed agents of special groups." [15]

Chief Justice Warren, while referring to a number of relevant factors, did not spell out any precise theory as the basis for his decision. Nor did Justices Douglas and Black indicate how narrowly drawn lobbying legislation could be reconciled with their absolute theory. In actuality, except by facile use of the ad hoc balancing test, lobbying legislation is difficult to reconcile with the principles of the First Amendment.

In some ways lobbying legislation is similar to corrupt practices legislation. It is designed to improve the system of freedom of expression by allowing the legislator to weigh expression addressed to him through having knowledge of its source. It is also an attempt to equalize access to the legislator by discouraging an excessive volume of communication from a few sources. But it is doubtful whether, in the context of the legislature, these possible distortions of the system are sufficiently grave to warrant interference by the government. Indeed, lobbying legislation really has other objectives. It is primarily intended to curtail bribery or expose the political motivations of the legislator to the electorate, interests that cannot constitutionally be advanced by curtailing expression. Hence lobbying legislation may not satisfy the first criterion listed above for regulation intended to purify the system. On the other hand such legislation may meet the other four criteria about as well as corrupt practices legislation does. In any event, if lobbying legislation is sustainable it would be so only on the theory that it is narrowly confined to the special problem of the legislature and, as declared in *Harriss*, to direct communication with the legislator by a paid lobbyist. Thus far lobbying legislation has proved notoriously unsuccessful in practice.

---

15. 347 U.S. at 632. The Supreme Court had previously drawn a similar line, at the point of direct communication with members of Congress, in *United States v. Rumely*, 345 U.S. 41 (1953), a legislative committee case. See Chapter VIII. For reference to material on lobbying legislation see *Political and Civil Rights in the United States*, p. 641. Other cases concerned with lobbying and the First Amendment are *Cammarano v. United States*, 358 U.S. 498 (1959), and *Eastern R.R. Presidents Conference v. Noerr Motor Freight, Inc.*, 365 U.S. 127 (1961), discussed in Chapter XII. On state lobbying laws see Edgar Lane, *Lobbying and the Law* (Berkeley, University of California Press, 1964).

3. OTHER DISCLOSURE LEGISLATION

Apart from the disclosure requirements found in corrupt practices and lobbying legislation, other forms of disclosure regulation have from time to time been enacted or proposed. Much of this has been designed to promote interests outside the system of freedom of expression, and does not concern us here. But some has been directed at improving the system itself, or at least has been justified in part on that ground. Thus for many years a Post Office regulation has required that newspapers and other publications wishing to avail themselves of second class mailing privileges must file with the Post Office and make public information concerning stockholders and ownership. Similarly the Foreign Agents Registration Act provides for registration of "any person who acts or agrees to act . . . as . . . a public-relations counsel, publicity agent, information-service employee, servant, agent, representative or attorney for a foreign principal." In the period following World War II interest in disclosure legislation increased. Thus President Truman's Committee on Civil Rights recommended in its 1947 Report the "enactment by Congress and the state legislatures of legislation requiring all groups, which attempt to influence public opinion, to disclose the pertinent facts about themselves through systematic registration procedures." Such proposals were aimed primarily at the Communist Party and other groups thought to be associated with it, and formed the original basis for legislation that ultimately emerged as the Internal Security Act of 1950. With the enactment of that statute, however, it became apparent that disclosure requirements could in practice operate as a serious deterrent to freedom of expression, virtually the equivalent of a criminal sanction. Moreover, about this time some of the Southern States began to utilize disclosure requirements as a method of attacking the N.A.A.C.P. and other civil-rights organizations. As a result of these developments suggestions for purification of the system of freedom of expression through disclosure regulation went out of fashion and the issues have remained of only minor importance.[16]

16. 39 U.S.C. §4369 (Post Office regulation); 22 U.S.C. §611–621 (Foreign Agents Registration Act); President Truman's Committee on Civil Rights, *To Secure These Rights* (Washington, D.C., G.P.O., 1947), pp. 164, 51–53. On the Internal Security Act see Chapter V, and on disclosure requirements applied to civil-rights organizations see Chapter XII. For a collection of materials and references on disclosure see *Political and Civil Rights in the United States,* pp. 188–189, 559–560.

The Supreme Court's decisions on the subject have been scattered and inconclusive. The Post Office regulation was upheld in *Lewis Publishing Co. v. Morgan,* but that was in 1913 and there was little discussion of the First Amendment. The validity of the Foreign Agents Registration Act has never been seriously challenged and in fact has been assumed, but that legislation deals with the special problem of foreign control over the speaker. The registration provisions of the Internal Security Act were upheld in *Communist Party v. Subversive Activities Control Board,* but again the decision ultimately rested upon the foreign control element. The closest approach to the problem made by the Supreme Court was in *Talley v. California.* The Los Angeles ordinance involved in that case prohibited the distribution of handbills that did not identify the author or producer and the distributor. Justice Black, writing for a majority of five, applied his absolute test, saying only: "There can be no doubt that such an identification requirement would tend to restrict freedom to distribute information and thereby freedom of expression." Justice Black did not distinguish between the case of the disclosure requirement designed to protect another social interest and that of the one intended to improve the system of free expression. Nor did he attempt to reconcile his position with any of the previous disclosure cases.[17]

If one undertakes to probe more deeply into the issues, it is apparent that, as a general proposition, disclosure requirements will in fact seriously impair the system of freedom of expression. As Justice Black observed in *Talley:*

> Anonymous pamphlets, leaflets, brochures and even books have played an important role in the progress of mankind. Persecuted groups and sects from time to time throughout history have been able to criticize oppressive practices and laws either anonymously or not at all. The obnoxious press licensing law of England, which was also enforced on the Colonies was due in part to the knowledge that exposure of the names of printers, writers and distributors would lessen the circulation of literature critical of the government. The old seditious libel cases in England show the lengths to which government had to go to find

17. *Lewis Publishing Co. v. Morgan,* 229 U.S. 288 (1913) (Post Office regulation); *Viereck v. United States,* 318 U.S. 236 (1943), and *Rabinowitz v. Kennedy,* 376 U.S. 605 (1964) (Foreign Agents Registration Act); *Communist Party v. Subversive Activities Control Board,* 367 U.S. 1 (1961); *Talley v. California,* 362 U.S. 60, 64 (1960). In *Talley* Justice Harlan concurred and Justices Clark, Frankfurter, and Whittaker dissented. See Chapter IX for discussion. The validity of the Foreign Agents Registration Act was also assumed in the *Communist Party* case. 367 U.S. at 99–101.

out who was responsible for books that were obnoxious to the rulers. John Lilburne was whipped, pilloried and fined for refusing to answer questions designed to get evidence to convict him or someone else for the secret distribution of books in England. Two Puritan Ministers, John Penry and John Udal, were sentenced to death on charges that they were responsible for writing, printing or publishing books. Before the Revolutionary War colonial patriots frequently had to conceal their authorship or distribution of literature that easily could have brought down on them prosecutions by English-controlled courts. Along about that time the Letters of Junius were written and the identity of their author is unknown to this day. Even the Federalist Papers, written in favor of the adoption of our Constitution, were published under fictitious names. It is plain that anonymity has sometimes been assumed for the most constructive purposes.[18]

It is true of modern society, also, that there are many occasions on which individuals or groups may wish to exercise the right of expression without revealing their identity. The civil-rights organizations are only the most recent example. Disclosure requirements are thus bound to curtail expression, often from those whom it is most critical for society to hear. Moreover, the administration of such restrictions always entails the risk of violation and prosecution, arising from ignorance, mistake or harassment. This, too, is a major repressive factor.

It will be a rare situation, therefore, when a disclosure requirement enhances the system of freedom of expression, rather than doing it serious damage. Even the Post Office regulation could be inhibiting. Nor can any crucial need for eliminating abuses from the system through disclosure methods usually be shown. Perhaps subliminal communication might create such a need. Ordinarily, however, the harm to the system, or the possibility of harm, precludes the use of disclosure devices.

C. Furnishing Facilities

One important way in which the government can affirmatively promote a system of freedom of expression is by making available to individuals and groups the facilities for engaging in expression. A the-

18. 362 U.S. at 64–65.

oretical right of expression is of no use to a person who does not possess the physical facilities or economic resources enabling him in fact to exercise that right. The government can perform this function in two ways: it can furnish the facilities itself, or it can compel private organizations or individuals who own or control media of communication to allow other persons access to such facilities. The latter problem, which involves reconciliation of the negative and positive features of the First Amendment, is discussed in the next two sections. Here we are concerned with the power and obligation of the government to make the means of expression available on a wider scale by itself supplying the physical or economic facilities.

The major development in this area has occurred in the law concerning the right to use the streets, parks and public open places for purposes of assembly. There is no doubt, of course, that the government has power to make such facilities available if it chooses to do so. If it does, the First Amendment imposes certain limits upon the exercise of that power: the government may not discriminate between users, or differentiate on the basis of the content of the expression, or impose conditions other than time, place and manner. More important, despite the doubt at times expressed by the Supreme Court, there is strong support for the proposition that the government has a constitutional duty to make these facilities available for assembly purposes. That obligation flows from the nature of the right of assembly, which contemplates a public gathering that entails the use of space, and the inadequacy of other areas where a public assembly can be held. The right to use the streets, parks and open places in this way constitutes a clear-cut example of the affirmative impact of the First Amendment.

The law with respect to public buildings and other closed public spaces is less well established. The power of the government to allow these facilities to be used for purposes of expression is, again, not open to doubt. The limitations upon the government if it does so are similar to those applicable to open spaces, with appropriate modifications relating to the nature of the government's own use. That there is an affirmative obligation on the government to make such facilities available for public assembly has not yet been fully recognized by the courts, although the *Port of New York Authority* case carries some distance in that direction. Nevertheless the implications from the law of open spaces would seem to compel acceptance of a similar duty by the government in the case of closed spaces. The notion of assembly embraces the idea of indoor as well as outdoor gatherings that require space; a distinction between facilities with or without a roof seems specious. It is true that privately owned halls and meeting places are more likely to be available, in which case the obligation of the government would certainly diminish. Moreover, it would seem unlikely that a court would, or as an administrative matter could, order the government to build a facility where none was already in existence. It would not appear beyond the bounds of reason to say, however, that where a suitable government facility exists and there is no other space available, the government has a constitutional obligation to permit the public to use the facilities for purposes of expression.[19]

From these instances, then, it would appear that a positive obligation falls upon the government under the First Amendment to furnish facilities for expression if (1) the form of the expression implies the use of certain means for its realization; (2) government facilities exist that would afford such means; and (3) the government possesses a monopoly or near monopoly of such facilities, that is to say no private facilities are available. How would these principles apply in other areas?

One of the main government facilities relevant to a system of freedom of expression is the Post Office. It plays a major role in the communications process. In fact the Post Office does make its services available to all who wish to use them, services subject to the same kind of negative protection as the use of the streets, parks and open places. In a sense, therefore, the issue of affirmative rights is academic. Nevertheless, a strong case can be made for the position that the government has not only the power but the duty to make this facility available; that the individual has a constitutional right to have postal service provided. Freedom of speech and the press imply more than a right of simple expression; they include a right to communicate the expression to those willing to hear. The leaflet distribution cases, from *Lovell v. Griffin* on, are predicated upon this right of dissemination. It is a fundamental feature of a system of freedom of expression. The postal service, already in existence, has a virtual monopoly over the distribution of certain types of printed material. In such circumstances the government has an affirmative obligation under the First Amendment to furnish postal facilities.[20]

19. *Wolin v. Port of New York Authority*, 392 F.2d 83 (2d Cir. 1968), cert. denied 393 U.S. 940 (1968). See also *Kissinger v. New York City Transit Authority*, 274 F. Supp. 438 (S.D.N.Y. 1967). Both cases are noted in Chapter IX.

20. On the negative protections afforded by the First Amendment against denial by the government of the postal

The case of the Government Printing Office is somewhat different. The availability of printing presses and other duplicating devices is essential to the operation of a system of freedom of expression. But in this situation there is no monopoly or near monopoly by the government; private facilities are abundant. Hence no duty falls on the government to provide such services. The government of course does have the power to make printing facilities available, and under some circumstances it might promote freedom of expression to do so.

Radio and television facilities pose some special issues. A modern system of free expression rests in major part upon the means of communication afforded by these facilities. Indeed, effective expression today depends more on these media than it does upon the use of streets, buildings, postal services, printing presses, or any other method of communication. The problem arises out of the fact that the monopoly position of the government is ambiguous in this area. If it be assumed that the government, representing the people as a whole, "owns the airways," in the same manner as the streets and parks, it would seem to follow that there is a corresponding obligation to make those facilities available for purposes of expression. In practice, however, the government has not taken possession of the airways, but allocates them to private broadcasting stations. One can hardly say that the First Amendment precludes this form of control. In any event, the government does not own or operate the actual facilities for broadcasting, and the power of the courts to compel it to do so is at best dubious. The issue is posed, therefore, in terms of allowing access to facilities maintained by private groups, a question discussed in the next section.

Constitutional claims to the use of government facilities for purposes of expression have been made only infrequently in the courts. One such contention was presented in the case of *Avins v. Rutgers*. An author had brought suit against Rutgers University, a State institution, because the *Rutgers Law Review* declined to publish an article submitted by him on the Civil Rights Act of 1875. The article concluded that, in light of the legislative history of the Act, the Supreme Court had erred in *Brown v. Board of Education* in holding that the historical background of the Fourteenth Amendment was "inconclusive" on

---

service see *Hannegan v. Esquire*, 327 U.S. 146 (1946); Chafee, *op. cit. supra* note 3, ch. 13; Jay A. Sigler, "Freedom of the Mails: A Developing Right," *Georgetown Law Journal*, Vol. 54 (1965), p. 30. Other materials and references are collected in *Political and Civil Rights*, pp. 201–206, 824–826.

the subject of school desegregation. The editors of the *Law Review* rejected the article on the ground that "approaching the problem from the point of view of legislative history alone is insufficient." The author contended that the *Law Review* was discriminating against his conservative ideas. The Court of Appeals for the Third Circuit affirmed a summary judgment for Rutgers University. Pointing out that there were other law reviews and other printing facilities the Court held that the author "does not have the right, constitutional or otherwise, to commandeer the press and columns of the Rutgers Law Review for the publication of his article . . . to the exclusion of other articles deemed by the editors to be more suitable for publication." The result seems entirely correct. Apart from the fact that the charge of discrimination was found not proved, the *Rutgers Law Review* was not a neutral facility of the government open to use by anyone. It was operated for specific university purposes, in a field where there was no government monopoly, and the university was entitled to reserve it for its own purposes. It may well be that the university, as a governmental academic institution, had an obligation to present a balance of viewpoints. But it did not have to make the pages of its *Law Review* available for publication by outsiders of material having no relation to the functions of the *Review*.[21]

The argument that the affirmative power of the First Amendment may require the government to furnish facilities for communication is, however, supported by developments in the law which recognize that the First Amendment embraces a right to hear. This feature of the First Amendment has always been accepted but recent decisions have given it new prominence. Thus in *Lamont v. Postmaster General* the Supreme Court held invalid a Federal statute that placed inhibiting restrictions upon the right of persons to receive "communist political propaganda" from abroad. Justice Brennan, concurring, noted the significance of the ruling:

> It is true that the First Amendment contains no specific guarantee of access to publications. However, the protection of the Bill of Rights goes beyond the specific guarantees to protect from congressional abridgment those equally fundamental personal rights necessary to make the express guarantees fully meaningful. . . . I think the right to receive publications is such a fundamental right. The dissemination

21. *Avins v. Rutgers, The State University of New Jersey*, 385 F.2d 151, 153 (3d Cir. 1967), cert. denied 390 U.S. 920 (1968).

of ideas can accomplish nothing if otherwise willing addressees are not free to receive and consider them. It would be a barren marketplace of ideas that had only sellers and no buyers.[22]

Likewise in *Stanley v. Georgia* Justice Marshall stressed that "[i]t is now well established that the Constitution protects the right to receive information and ideas." These decisions make it clear that the right to hear must be considered in First Amendment cases on equal terms with the right to speak. This expanding role of the right to hear was carried further in the *United Church of Christ* case in 1966. In it the Court of Appeals for the District of Columbia Circuit held that listeners to a broadcasting station had the right to a hearing before the Federal Communications Commission on the question of whether the station's license should be renewed. The clear implication of the case is that the government has an affirmative obligation to maintain such control of the broadcasting media as will provide for the listening needs of different groups in the community. This can be accomplished, in radio and television, by assuring access to different points of view or otherwise encouraging diversity. But it also can be done, and the cases emphasizing the right-to-hear element of the First Amendment point also in that direction, through supplying government facilities for communication by individuals or groups who would not otherwise be able to use them.[23]

In addition to furnishing physical facilities the government can promote the system of freedom of expression by supplying financial resources. Government funds that enable private individuals or groups to engage in expression are being made available in many fields at the present time, probably in greater volume than is generally realized. Government grants for education and research undoubtedly make up the largest amount. There are also government subsidies for the promotion of art and entertainment projects, for legal assistance in protecting First Amendment rights, for various types of community organizations and activities under the poverty program, and for many other purposes. The most direct form of government spending in aid of expression is the allowance of tax deductions for political contributions or the free printing of position leaflets in political campaigns. In

22. *Lamont v. Postmaster General*, 381 U.S. 301, 308 (1965), discussed in Chapter V.

23. *Stanley v. Georgia*, 394 U.S. 557, 564 (1969), discussed in Chapter XIII; see also *Marsh v. Alabama*, 326 U.S. 501

(1946). *Office of Communication of the United Church of Christ v. F.C.C.*, 359 F.2d 994 (D.C. Cir. 1966), noted in *Harvard Law Review*, Vol. 80 (1967), p. 670.

1967 Congress established the Corporation for Public Broadcasting, under the control of private directors, to which public funds are appropriated for development of noncommercial radio and television.[24]

Government subsidization of private expression cannot be compelled by any affirmative reading of the First Amendment. Even if the First Amendment were to be construed as imposing such a constitutional duty the courts would certainly lack the capacity to enforce or administer an obligation of that nature. Nor is the First Amendment needed as a source of power for subsidies in aid of expression. The spending power of the Federal Government and the general powers of the States are fully adequate. Moreover, there is nothing in the negative force of the First Amendment, as a general matter, that would prevent the government from using public funds to support various features of the system of freedom of expression. On the other hand the negative features of the First Amendment do impose some restrictions upon the way government funds are expended. In general these limitations would be the same as in the case of the government furnishing physical facilities: there could be no discrimination between users and no regulation of content.[25]

In the case of government subsidies, however, difficult questions arise in the practical application of these limitations. Until recently it was not clear that anyone had standing in the Federal courts to raise the First Amendment issue. Under the doctrine of *Frothingham v. Mellon* neither a taxpayer, a business enterprise suffering economic injury, nor perhaps any other potential litigant, was permitted to challenge Federal spending. This rigid rule was modified in *Flast v. Cohen,* which allowed a taxpayer to raise the question whether Federal funds were being spent in violation of the religious freedom provisions of the First Amendment. The members of the Court could not agree on a single rule, but a majority followed the principle that Federal spending can be challenged if the claim is made that the use of Federal funds

---

24. On government aid in financing political campaigns see Martin Lobel, "Federal Control of Campaign Contributions," *Minnesota Law Review,* Vol. 51 (1966), pp. 1, 50–60. In 1966 Congress passed a Presidential Election Campaign Fund Act, which would have allowed every taxpayer to designate that $1 of his tax be paid into a Presidential Election Campaign Fund, to be distributed to major political parties. 80 Stat. 1587 (1966), 26 U.S.C. §6096. Operation of the Act was later suspended. The legislation creating the Corporation for Public Broadcasting is 81 Stat. 368 (1967), 47 U.S.C. §396.

25. It should be noted that Justice Douglas, concurring in *Cammarano v. United States,* 358 U.S. 498, 513 (1959), suggests that State subsidies for the exercise of First Amendment rights would be invalid. There seems to be no other authority for this position.

contravened a specific constitutional limitation. On this theory a challenge would lie on First Amendment freedom of expression grounds. Most spending by States, and virtually all spending by municipalities, can be attacked in a taxpayer's suit. Hence the standing problem may now be disappearing.[26]

Even were this to happen, however, more serious problems persist. The rule against discrimination between different users becomes difficult to apply when potential recipients are almost unlimited in number; broad discretion must be allowed administrators, and definite proof of discrimination is beyond reach. Moreover, no precise standards are available. The Federal legislation of 1966 allowing deductions for contributions that went only to major political parties was almost certainly unconstitutional. But there still remains a question of defining "political party." And the broader issue of proportional representation in the allocation of funds to groups or individauls with minority points of view, or even individual points of view, is especially complex. Finally, the rule against regulation of content tends to break down in the case of subsidies. The government must designate the purposes for which the funds are granted, and this power inevitably brings government authority into the realm of content. As compared with the furnishing of physical facilities, which can be administered more objectively, judicial supervision over subsidies is tenuous at best.

Nevertheless it seems inevitable that government subsidizing of private expression will grow as the public sector of our national life expands and the private sector contracts. Increased government subsidization of political campaigns appears not far off. The supplying of government funds to enable various groups to utilize radio and television is likely to expand. Even government subsidies of newspapers are being seriously proposed. These developments bring obvious dangers. But they also carry enormous potential. They could lead to spectacular results: an enormous increase in the diversity of the content of the mass media, a significant growth of popular participation at the community level, and a general invigoration of the system of freedom of expression. The crucial question is whether adequate controls can be devised to make such a system work.

Such a set of controls would have to be based on the concept that the government has a political, if not constitutional, obligation to

26. *Frothingham v. Mellon,* 262 U.S. 447 (1923); *Flast v. Cohen,* 392 U.S. 83 (1968).

finance opposition to itself. Such a notion would have been inconceivable a generation ago. But it is gradually beginning to emerge. Its deepest roots are perhaps in the public defender and legal aid programs, which have existed for many years. The recent extension of legal assistance to the community level, through projects by which government finances many forms of litigation against itself, is a notable advance. Other features of the poverty legislation, operating despite intense hostile pressures from many quarters, have resulted in the formation of community groups that have been a major source of expression in opposition to official welfare, city planning, highway and other programs. The movement toward decentralized or community schools is also proceeding in this direction. Thus new public expectations and changed governmental attitudes are beginning to form. New institutions, such as councils of outstanding citizens comparable to the English University Grants Committee, community government at the local level, and ombudsmen, will have to be devised. New judicial doctrines to make more realistic the constitutional protections against discrimination and censorship are also necessary.

All this can be done. But in the end one must return to the proposition that great dangers inhere in this development, and that government-supported expression can never be an acceptable substitute for independently financed expression.

D. Regulation of Privately Owned Media: Radio and Television

The government can also promote the system of freedom of expression through regulation of the privately owned media of communication, with a view to expanding and enriching their output. As noted above, the greatest distortions in our system of free expression have developed in the mass media, and the efforts to eliminate these distortions have created many of the most difficult and controversial questions. The principal goals of regulation are (1) to create a greater diversity in the expression communicated by the media, and (2) to give a greater number of individuals and groups access to the media. The two objectives are of course closely related.

Government regulation along these lines has advanced furthest in radio and television. These two offer special problems. In the first place radio and television are probably the most influential media of communication in our society today. They present, on a selective basis as all communications do, not only information but ideas, attitudes, impressions and fantasies. They pervade the home, the automobile, and many public places. Secondly, radio and television are, by almost unanimous agreement, a "wasteland." The economic, political and social factors that make them so are sufficiently entrenched to discourage expectation of change on the initiative of the industry itself. Thirdly, government involvement in radio and television has always, and necessarily, been extensive. Because they are limited access media, and in any event require elaborate engineering coordination by the government, official controls have permeated the field from the beginning.

A solution of the radio and television problem might have been attempted through government ownership and control of all broadcasting facilities. This has been the approach in most other parts of the world. To the extent that a physical scarcity of facilities is involved, the First Amendment would probably not have prevented this arrangement. But serious First Amendment problems would be posed over the right of access to the media by private individuals and groups, and by the government's use of the monopoly in itself participating in the system of freedom of expression. These issues are not wholly different from those which actually have arisen and are discussed below.

In any event the United States chose, rather than government ownership and control, a different method of regulation. When the unregulated transmission of radio signals had brought about a state of chaos in the nineteen-twenties, Congress passed the Federal Radio Act of 1927 establishing a system of licensing to be administered by the Federal Radio Commission. The statutory scheme was revised and expanded by the Federal Communications Act of 1934, which still remains the basic legislation. Under the Federal Communications Act in its present form the Federal Communications Commission, successor to the earlier Commission, is empowered to grant licenses, for not more than three years but renewable, to applicants for broadcasting facilities on the basis that such grant will serve the "public interest, convenience, or necessity." Section 3(h) expressly provides that licensees shall not become "common carriers." There are specific prohibitions against obscenity, profanity and lotteries. Section 315 makes provision for "equal time" for political candidates and, as amended in 1959, requires broadcasters to "operate in the public interest and to afford reasonable opportunity for the discussion of conflicting views on issues of public importance." Section 326 declares that the Federal Communications Commission has no "power of censorship," nor power to interfere with "the right of free speech." These provisions are the only ones that deal directly with programs or access.[27]

The licensing system that has developed under the Federal Communications Act has several significant features. It is predicated upon the fact that there is a scarcity of physical facilities, that is, wavelengths, and that allocation of those facilities is therefore necessary. The franchise to operate a broadcasting station, often worth millions, is awarded free of charge to enterprises selected under the standard of "public interest, convenience, or necessity." Although licenses must be renewed every three years, renewals are given in all but isolated cases. The commercial sector of broadcasting, which is the dominant sector, obtains its income largely not from the listener, but from advertisers. All of this adds up to the fact that, although the broadcasting industry bears some resemblance to a traditional laissez-faire system, it has basic features that are quite different.

The main First Amendment issues grow out of the attempts by the government to regulate the media in three principal ways:

(1) Some of the controls are directed toward the character of the ownership and control of broadcasting facilities, principally with the aim of assuring independence and diversity among those who own and operate the facilities. These regulations deal with multiple ownership of stations, ownership by newspapers or other media, relation of the station to the networks, and the like. Some are concerned with the financial resources of the licensee, his relation to the community, and similar matters.

(2) Other controls are designed to achieve variety and relevance in programming. Such regulations attempt to obtain balance between different types of programs, inclusion of diverse and controversial subjects in the programs, and the presentation of varying points of view. They are incorporated in the program balance policies of the Federal Communications Commission and in the fairness doctrine.

(3) The third type of control is concerned with access to broad-

27. Federal Radio Act of 1927, 44 Stat. 1162 (1927); Federal Communications Act of 1934, 48 Stat. 1064, 47 U.S.C. §151 ff. The provisions forbidding obscenity, profanity and lotteries are 18 U.S.C. §§1464 and 1304. For the background of the legislation see Justice Frankfurter's opinion in *National Broadcasting Co. v. United States,* 319 U.S. 190 (1943), Justice White's opinion in *Red Lion Broadcasting Co. v. F.C.C.,* 395 U.S. 367 (1969), and materials referred to below.

casting facilities by individuals and groups wishing to use the medium. The main regulations of this kind are the equal time rule and the fairness doctrine.

The constitutional basis for these various controls has been a matter of high dispute. The Federal Communications Commission and the broadcasting industry have been at loggerheads, commentators have disagreed, and the courts were slow to clarify the situation. Finally, in the *Red Lion* decision in 1969 the Supreme Court came forth with a comprehensive theory.[28]

1. DEVELOPMENT OF FIRST AMENDMENT
THEORY IN COURT DECISIONS

The Supreme Court had dealt with the Federal Communications Act in a significant number of cases, but until *Red Lion* it had addressed itself directly to First Amendment issues in only one—*National Broadcasting Co. v. United States*. That decision, rendered in 1943, constituted the landmark case for over twenty-five years. The specific issue involved was the validity of the F.C.C.'s Chain Broadcasting Regulations, which undertook to regulate the relations of individual broadcasting stations to the networks with a view to lessening the dependence of the single station upon the chain. The regulations were attacked upon a number of fronts, including that they constituted a violation of the First Amendment. The Supreme Court, voting five to two, upheld them. Justice Frankfurter, who wrote for the majority,

28. A collection of materials and references on the problem may be found in *Political and Civil Rights in the United States*, ch. VIII. Later material includes Jerome A. Barron, *op. cit. supra* note 3; Harry Kalven, Jr., "Broadcasting, Public Policy and the First Amendment," *Journal of Law and Economics*, Vol. 10 (1967), p. 15; Glen O. Robinson, "The FCC and the First Amendment: Observations on 40 Years of Radio and Television Regulation," *Minnesota Law Review*, Vol. 52 (1967), p. 67; Fred W. Friendly, *Due to Circumstances Beyond Our Control* (New York, Random House, 1967); Roscoe L. Barrow, "The Equal Opportunities and Fairness Doctrines in Broadcasting: Pillars in the Forum of

Democracy," *Cincinnati Law Review*, Vol. 37 (1968), p. 447; Louis L. Jaffe, "The Fairness Doctrine, Equal Time, Reply to Personal Attacks, and the Local Service Obligation: Implications of Technological Change," *Cincinnati Law Review*, Vol. 37 (1968), p. 550.

We are not concerned here with the validity under the First Amendment of restrictions imposed on radio and television for the purpose of protecting social interests outside the system of freedom of expression. These matters have been discussed previously in connection with libel, privacy, obscenity and the like. See also the discussion in Robinson, *op. cit. supra*, pp. 98–111.

dealt with the First Amendment at the end of a long opinion, saying only:

> Freedom of utterance is abridged to many who wish to use the limited facilities of radio. Unlike other modes of expression, radio inherently is not available to all. That is its unique characteristic, and that is why, unlike other modes of expression, it is subject to governmental regulation. Because it cannot be used by all, some who wish to use it must be denied. But Congress did not authorize the Commission to choose among applicants upon the basis of their political, economic or social views, or upon any other capricious basis. If it did, or if the Commission by these Regulations proposed a choice among applicants upon some such basis, the issue before us would be wholly different. The question here is simply whether the Commission, by announcing that it will refuse licenses to persons who engage in specified network practices (a basis for choice which we hold is comprehended within the statutory criterion of "public interest"), is thereby denying such persons the constitutional right of free speech. The right of free speech does not include, however, the right to use the facilities of radio without a license. The licensing system established by Congress in the Communications Act of 1934 was a proper exercise of its power over commerce. The standard it provided for the licensing of stations was the "public interest, convenience, or necessity." Denial of a station license on that ground, if valid under the Act, is not a denial of free speech.[29]

Justice Frankfurter thus made clear that radio broadcasting can be regulated without infringing the First Amendment because, unlike "other modes of expression," the facilities are limited. He concluded that any regulation which met the standard of "public interest, convenience, or necessity" was "not a denial of free speech." There was, however, an exception: the Commission could not choose among applicants "on the basis of their political, economic or social views, or upon any other capricious basis." Justice Frankfurter's opinion was, to say the least, unsatisfactory. It did not explain why the scarcity factor eliminated First Amendment issues, on what theory the exception was made, why the exception was limited to applicants, or numerous other questions that lurked in the problem. Following the *National Broadcasting* case there were scattered lower Federal court opinions, up-

---

29. *National Broadcasting Co. v. United States,* 319 U.S. 190, 226–227 (1943). Justices Murphy and Roberts dissented, without mentioning First Amendment issues. Justices Black and Rutledge did not participate.

holding various actions of the Commission against First Amendment challenges, but they did little to elucidate the issue.[30]

Under these conditions wide differences of opinion on the subject persisted. The broadcasting industry clung to its position that radio broadcasting was similar to newspaper publishing and entitled to the same First Amendment protection. The F.C.C. adopted the broad view that the licensee was in effect a public trustee bound to operate its station in accordance with the public interest. It recognized First Amendment limitations, but never made very plain how or why they applied. Commentators argued for these and various other positions.[31]

The *Red Lion* decision involved two cases, each challenging aspects of the F.C.C. fairness doctrine. The fairness doctrine, in the words of Justice White's opinion, required that the "broadcaster must give adequate coverage to public issues . . . and coverage must be fair in that it accurately reflects the opposing views." Originally a policy of the F.C.C. in applying the "public interest, convenience, or necessity" standard, the rule was written into the statute by Congress in its 1959 amendment of Section 315. One special feature of the fairness doctrine was that when a personal attack had been made in a broadcast upon a person involved in a public issue, the broadcaster must give that person an opportunity to respond. There was also a rule requiring any broadcaster who endorsed one candidate in a political editorial to offer the other candidates time to reply. The Court of Appeals for the District of Columbia had upheld the personal attack rule, but the Court of Appeals for the Seventh Circuit had invalidated regulations embodying both the personal attack rule and the political editorial rule. The Supreme Court unanimously upheld both rules.[32]

Justice White began his analysis of the First Amendment issues, as had Justice Frankfurter, with the scarcity of physical facilities for broadcasting: "only a tiny fraction of those with resources and intelli-

---

30. The lower Federal court cases are summarized in the Kalven and Robinson articles, *op. cit. supra* note 28, and in Roscoe L. Barrow, "The Attainment of Balanced Program Service in Television," *Virginia Law Review*, Vol. 52 (1966), pp. 633, 644–652. See also the lower court decisions in *Red Lion*, and *Banzhaf v. F.C.C.*, 405 F.2d 1082 (D.C. Cir. 1968), cert. denied 396 U.S. 842 (1969).

31. The broadcasting industry's view may be found in W. Theodore Pierson, "The Need for Modification of Section

326," *Federal Communications Bar Journal*, Vol. 18 (1963), p. 15. The F.C.C.'s theories are discussed in Robinson, *op. cit. supra* note 28, pp. 142–144; Barron, *op. cit. supra* note 3, pp. 1664–1665. For Commissioner Loevinger's dissent from the F.C.C. view see Kalven, *op. cit. supra* note 28, pp. 18–19. See also the briefs in the *Red Lion* case in the Supreme Court.

32. *Red Lion Broadcasting Co. v. F.C.C.*, 395 U.S. 367, 377 (1969). Justice Douglas did not participate.

gence can hope to communicate by radio at the same time if intelligible communication is to be had, even if the entire radio spectrum is utilized in the present state of commercially acceptable technology." For this reason the government must allocate frequencies, and therefore "it is idle to posit an unabridgeable First Amendment right to broadcast comparable to the right of every individual to speak, write, or publish." "No one has a First Amendment right to a license," he went on, "or to monopolize a radio frequency." He then explained the constitutional status of the broadcaster in the following terms:

> By the same token, as far as the First Amendment is concerned those who are licensed stand no better than those to whom licenses are refused. A license permits broadcasting, but the licensee has no constitutional right to be the one who holds the license or to monopolize a radio frequency to the exclusion of his fellow citizens. There is nothing in the First Amendment which prevents the Government from requiring a licensee to share his frequency with others and to conduct himself as a proxy or fiduciary with obligations to present those views and voices which are representative of his community and which would otherwise, by necessity, be barred from the airwaves.[33]

In extending the protection of the First Amendment to the broadcast situation, Justice White continued, "[i]t is the right of the viewers and listeners, not the right of the broadcasters, which is paramount." He repeated: "It is the right of the public to receive suitable access to social, political, aesthetic, moral, and other ideas and experiences which is crucial here." The fairness doctrine, he concluded, gives effect to this First Amendment right of the public. It simply forces the licensee to share a scarce resource with "those who have a different view." Justice White completed the constitutional picture by adding that the provisions of Section 315 requiring equal time for candidates were valid on the same grounds and, reaffirming *National Broadcasting,* declared that the F.C.C. "neither exceeded its powers under the statute nor transgressed the First Amendment in interesting itself in general program format and the kinds of programs broadcast by licensees." [34]

Justice White's answers to two contentions advanced by the broadcasters throw additional light on the Supreme Court's position. It had been "strenuously argued" that "if political editorials or personal attacks will trigger an obligation in broadcasters to afford the opportunity for expression to speakers who need not pay for time and whose

33. 395 U.S. at 388, 389.   34. 395 U.S. at 390, 391, 395.

views are unpalatable to the licensees, then broadcasters will be irresistibly forced to self-censorship and their coverage of controversial public issues will be eliminated or at least rendered wholly ineffective." To this Justice White replied that such a possibility "is at best speculative," that the "fairness doctrine in the past has had no such overall effect," and that "if the present licensees should suddenly prove timorous, the Commission is not powerless to insist that they give adequate and fair attention to public issues." Justice White also examined the contention that a scarcity of broadcast facilities no longer existed. Relying mainly on the increasing demand for competing uses of the frequency spectrum, from marine, aviation, amateur, military and common carrier users, he concluded: "Nothing in this record, or in our own researches, convinces us that the resource is no longer one for which there are more immediate and potential uses than can be accommodated, and for which wise planning is essential." [35]

The *Red Lion* decision marked an important advance in First Amendment theory concerned with affirmative promotion of the system of freedom of expression. Certain implications of the decision, and some wider perspectives on the problem, require further consideration.

2. THE THEORY OF RADIO AND TELEVISION CONTROL

In attempting to formulate a satisfactory theory of the First Amendment in its application to the regulation of radio and television two initial concepts must be given brief attention. First, it has sometimes been argued that the public as a whole "owns" the airways and the government may therefore allocate their use on such terms as are in the general interest, subject only to constitutional prohibitions against discriminatory or arbitrary action. This theory, much like the Frankfurter opinion in *National Broadcasting,* fails to come to grips with the real issues. It could equally well be said that the public "owns" the streets and parks, and that consequently individuals have no right to use them for purposes of expression except on the government's own terms. Moreover, the problem is not solved simply by bringing into the picture the doctrine of unconstitutional conditions—that if the government extends the privilege of using the airways to private individuals or groups it cannot attach conditions that violate the First Amendment. Surely the affirmative power of the First Amendment de-

35. 395 U.S. at 392–393, 399.

mands that the government make available for general use, as a constitutional right, the most significant medium in our whole system of freedom of expression. The government cannot maintain a monopoly of the airways any more than it can maintain a monopoly of the streets, or of printing presses. Starting from this point, then, the First Amendment issues begin to grow far more complex than the "public ownership" theory envisages.

The second concept that needs initial clarification is the doctrine of prior restraint. On the face of it the requirement that any person obtain a license before engaging in communication by broadcasting is the baldest kind of prior restraint. The conditions for obtaining a license, moreover, go far beyond the time, place and manner regulations that have been upheld in other permit systems. Even if it is conceded, under *Times Film,* that the doctrine of prior restraint is subject to some exceptions, the Supreme Court has in *Freedman v. Maryland* insisted upon procedural safeguards that are totally lacking in the Federal Communications Commission licensing system. How, then, does one reconcile radio and televison licensing with the doctrine of prior restraint? The Supreme Court has ignored this problem. There would seem to be two possible answers. One is that the factor of limited facilities necessitates a modification of the prior restraint rule. The other is that public "ownership" of the airwaves justifies or requires this kind of prior restraint and that First Amendment rights are protected through other methods. These suggested answers bring us to the major issues.

There can be no doubt that the scarcity of facilities is a major consideration in the application of the First Amendment to radio and television regulation. The essential point is that the scarcity is physical, rather than economic. This condition takes radio and television out of the traditional laissez-faire system that is the basis of the First Amendment's application to the press, publishing, and other types of media. The open marketplace may control access to such media in a distorted way, but it is the traditional means of control and, while the government may attempt to expand the marketplace, it cannot totally usurp its function. In radio and television, however, the open market condition brings only physical chaos. Not everybody can be accommodated. The government, therefore, has a different function, and that function is to bring initial order into the system by regulating access to limited facilities.

When broadcasting controls were first initiated there was no question whatever that the physical facilities were in fact limited. Since that time there has been a significant expansion in available facilities, owing to the development of FM in radio, UHF in television, and CATV. Indeed, the number of radio and television stations in operation came to exceed by far the number of daily newspapers. In 1966, for example, there were 5,881 radio and 721 television stations, compared with 1,751 newspapers. Moreover, there were some frequencies, particularly UHF television channels in the lesser market areas, still unallocated. It is contended that the major factor now limiting the number of radio and television stations is not physical but economic. On the basis of these considerations the broadcasters urged in *Red Lion* that the scarcity factor can no longer serve as justification for radio and television controls different from those applicable to the press and other media.[36]

The developments just recounted, however, would not appear to change the basic scarcity factor. As Justice White argued in *Red Lion* there are growing demands from industrial, military, and other users for available frequencies. Moreover, the total number of radio and television stations operating in the country does not signify there is no longer a shortage of facilities in specific areas, particularly centers of dense population. Nor does reliance upon the total number of stations take into account the possibility of an untapped demand for diversity. Furthermore, to the extent that economic considerations restrict the number of stations now, those factors could easily change. More important than all of these considerations, however, is the fact that the scarcity of facilities should not be measured by the number of *stations* allowed to broadcast but by the number of *individuals or groups* who wish to use the facilities, or would use them if they were more readily available. The real problem is whether there is a scarcity as to potential users, not as to stations operating at a profit under present conditions. In this sense a more significant comparison would be not with the number of newspapers, but with the number of printing presses. In these terms there remains a serious scarcity and one that is likely to persist.[37]

36. Materials dealing with the problem of scarcity in available frequencies are cited in *Red Lion*, 395 U.S. at 397. The figures on the number of radio and television stations and newspapers are from U.S. Bureau of the Census, *Statistical Abstract of the United States* (Washington, D.C., G.P.O., 87th ed. 1966), p. 523.

37. For the argument that no scarcity of facilities now exists see John Paul Sullivan, "Editorials and Controversy: The Broadcaster's Dilemma," *George Washington Law Review*, Vol. 32 (1964), pp.

Once it is assumed that a scarcity of broadcasting facilities exists the next question becomes, what follows from that? The question can be answered on two levels. In purely common-sense terms it would seem to follow that, if the government must choose among applicants for the same facilities, it should choose on some sensible basis. The only sensible basis is the one that best promotes the system of freedom of expression. Since a laissez-faire system does not select the users, and the government is forced to do so, it would be intolerable, and actually inconsistent with the First Amendment, for the government to choose in another way. Consequently all three kinds of regulations listed above would be valid under the First Amendment if they in fact promoted the system of freedom of expression.

The question can also be answered on a deeper level, which leads into a public agency or trustee theory. If broadcasting facilities are physically limited, then the government is obliged by the First Amendment to permit citizens to use the facilities without discrimination. This would be true whether the affirmative power of the First Amendment compelled the government to make them available, or whether the government just did so as a matter of policy. The obligation flows both from the First Amendment's right to communicate and its right to hear. Under either concept it would be a violation of the constitutional guarantee for the government to give a monopoly to any person or group. The licensee therefore can only be considered as the agent of the government, or trustee of the public, in a process of further allocation. Hence the licensee would have no direct First Amendment rights of his own, except as to his own expression. The First Amendment right would run from the individual or group seeking to engage in expression, or seeking to listen, to the government; not from the licensee (except as to his own expression) to the government. This would mean that there could be no censorship of the actual user of the facilities, but there could be controls over the licensee to assure that he made a fair allocation of the limited facilities both to users and to listeners. Only through such a system, indeed, would the requirements of the First Amendment be met.

This is essentially the position the Supreme Court reached in *Red*

719, 759; Robinson, *op. cit. supra* note 28, pp. 157–161. For the counter argument see Jerome A. Barron, "In Defense of 'Fairness': A First Amendment Rationale for Broadcasting's 'Fairness Doctrine,'" *University of Colorado Law Review*, Vol.

37 (1964), pp. 31, 39–41. Professor Kalven seems to accept the scarcity theory. See Kalven, *op. cit. supra* note 28, pp. 34, 37. The issue is of course, at least temporarily, disposed of by *Red Lion*.

Lion. Justice White found the force of the First Amendment to lie in the right of the public to hear, and he ignored the right of the ordinary citizen to use broadcasting facilities to speak. But he did conclude that the broadcaster had only the First Amendment rights of a "proxy or fiduciary," with an obligation "to present those views and voices which are representative of his community." [38]

Along either path from the physical scarcity factor, it is necessary to proceed further and to outline, at least in a general way, the kinds of limitation which the First Amendment would impose upon government operation of such a licensing system. The *Red Lion* decision did not move very far in this direction. It found the fairness doctrine a reasonable method of sharing a scarce resource, and it brushed off as "speculative" the broadcasters' contention that the fairness doctrine would result in reduced coverage of controversial issues. But it did not pursue the questions further.

The basic issue would be whether the government control "abridged" freedom of expression. It might do so in at least two ways:

(1) The regulations might, as a substantive matter, diminish rather than expand the amount of expression, lessen rather than increase diversity, or in similar respects harm rather than promote the system of freedom of expression. The broadcasters made this claim in *Red Lion.* Such a judgment would at times be difficult to make, or for a court to document. But it should be noted that the issue is not the broad one of whether in an abstract way the product of the system is "better" on some particular scale of values. The government cannot control the content of individual expression, or normally try to purify the system, or favor one person over another. Its powers are limited to removing obstructions in the system. It therefore must confine itself to increasing the number of participants in the system, enlarging the diversity of the expression, or removing obstacles to effective working of the system. All this must be carried out, of course, in light of the basic functions of the system.

(2) The regulations might, as an administrative matter, operate to smother freedom of expression through the power of surveillance, threats of informal sanction, or other form of harassment available to government officials because of the regulatory mechanism. This kind

---

38. The Court's position was not greatly different from that taken by the F.C.C., but the Commission had never spelled it out or accepted its implications. See also Barron, *op. cit. supra* note 37, pp. 43–45, and *op. cit. supra* note 3, pp. 1663–1665.

of limitation is likewise hard to measure. The government presence is always inhibiting. The courts would probably find it unduly repressive only in exceptional circumstances. It remains a meaningful limitation, however, and in the course of time might be given more specific content. In general, like the doctrine of *Freedman v. Maryland,* it would give the courts supervisory power over the practical details of administering the controls.[39]

Quite apart from the scarcity factor in radio and television facilities, it is possible to fashion a theory of control out of affirmative concepts of the First Amendment. The regulations we are here concerned with are not those designed to restrict expression on behalf of other social interests. They are intended to promote the system of free expression through encouraging wider participation by those who wish to communicate and greater diversity for those who wish to hear. In general the affirmative features of the First Amendment would permit this. The ordinary negative limits of the First Amendment, as applied to government restrictions seeking to safeguard other social interests, would not be relevant. Rather, in this context the negative limitations —the measure of "abridge"—would be those just set forth as controlling when the government power was based on the scarcity theory.

Such a doctrine of First Amendment power and limitation is far-reaching and entails obvious dangers. Applied to the press, for example, it might authorize controls over newspaper coverage that would be highly questionable. In the area of radio and television, however, the government is already heavily involved with the task of preventing electrical interference and solving similar engineering problems. Thus the regulations have a different substantive and administrative impact and would not necessarily constitute an abridgment of free expression in the same way as comparable regulations in other areas not already heavily weighted by government controls.

The application of these principles, whether derived from the scarcity factor theory or the pure affirmative theory, would involve detailed and complex factual judgments. Regulations in the first category—those directed towards the character of ownership and control by licensees—would probably have the least difficulty in passing First Amendment muster. A regulation limiting the number of stations one enterprise may own, or forbidding ownership of a broadcasting station by a newspaper, or forbidding a network to compel an affiliate station to carry all network programs, is appropriate to assure the

39. *Freedman v. Maryland,* 380 U.S. 51 (1965), discussed in Chapter XIII.

independence of the licensee and thereby promote diversity. In most respects these forms of control are not different from those exercised through the anti-trust laws, whose application to the mass media was upheld in *Associated Press v. United States*. Likewise, the financial resources of the licensee, his support by various groups in the community, and his personal character are relevant to his function as public agent or trustee, though not relevant to the exercise of his own right of expression through the use of radio and television facilities. Unless it appeared that some substantive impact of the regulation or some feature of its administration burdened rather than enlarged the system of freedom of expression the regulation would be immune to attack under the First Amendment.[40]

Regulations of the Federal Communications Commission designed to assure program balance would also, as a general proposition, not violate any mandate of the First Amendment. Such regulations require that a licensee present programs falling into different categories, such as news, education, politics, local talent, entertainment and the like. They are essential to assure that the licensee is carrying out his obligation as public trustee to secure the First Amendment rights of the listening public to hear. The distinction the Federal Communications Commission makes between a requirement that the licensee broadcast programs within its general categories, and control over the contents of a particular program, conforms exactly to the theory that the government can take measures to expand the variety of expression but may not censor the actual expression itself. There may be a close question as to whether any given action by the F.C.C. does in fact promote diversity, or whether in the context of a particular situation specialization on the part of one station might not serve the purpose better. Within such limitations, however, the F.C.C. is not abridging freedom of speech.

The most difficult problems arise when the government attempts to introduce greater diversity, particularly by compelling a licensee to present varied points of view on controversial issues, or by forcing him to grant access to persons whose interests are affected by a broadcast. These efforts are presently confined to the fairness doctrine and the equal time provision, but they could be greatly expanded. In general regulations of this nature add to the number of participants, increase

---

40. *Associated Press v. United States,* 326 U.S. 1 (1945). The chain broadcasting regulations were, of course, upheld in *National Broadcasting Co. v. United States,* discussed *supra*.

diversity, and eliminate discrimination in the use of broadcast facilities, without controlling the content of the expression. They are therefore prima facie justified under the First Amendment. Serious questions may arise, however, when the limiting conditions prescribed by the First Amendment are applied in this area. The controls may in fact operate to reduce the amount of controversial discussion, at least as the broadcasting industry is now structured, and they provide the basis for intensive informal influence of government officials on private expression. Particularly difficult issues arise in according fair representation to minority or even individual points of view. But they cannot be avoided; ignoring them is a greater violation of the First Amendment than a rough but practical solution. On all such matters the judicial judgment under the First Amendment must turn largely on the circumstances of the particular case.

All in all, the fundamental principles that govern the control of radio and television are not too hard to formulate. *Red Lion* has laid a firm foundation. If the possibilities now opened up are exploited the implementation of those principles will pose more difficult problems. Nevertheless the guiding doctrines are available. Whether as a practical matter broadcasting facilities will ever be available on a wide scale to minority groups and people without funds is, of course, another question.

E. Regulation of Privately Owned Media: The Press

Government regulation designed to promote the system of freedom of expression takes on quite a different cast when it is applied to media of communication other than radio and television. Of the other principal mass media, the motion picture industry has received little attention. The anti-trust laws are applicable to motion picture production, distribution, and exhibition, but beyond this there has been no significant regulation and no obvious need for controls. We are therefore concerned here primarily with the press, consisting of newspapers, magazines, books, and other forms of publishing.

It is at once apparent that the basic conditions surrounding the press are unlike those prevailing in radio and television. There are no technical attributes of the press that require engineering coordination and no scarcity of physical facilities that demands allocation among potential users. Traditionally the press has operated in the classic laissez-faire pattern. In some areas, particularly newspaper publishing, economic factors have seriously curtailed the number of participants. Even so, there are no characteristics inherent in the medium that imperatively demand government regulation. Moreover, the fact that the government is by necessity so heavily involved in radio and television, with all the dangers implicit in that situation, makes it important for the balance of the total system of expression that the press remain relatively free of government controls. Hence, in the case of the press, the doctrines limiting governmental efforts to promote the system apply with much greater force. In terms of substantive impact, the government regulation is much less likely to promote the system. In terms of administrative impact, the government regulation is much more likely to be repressive.

There is one type of government control that has long been applied to the press and has raised little question under the First Amendment. This is anti-trust legislation, designed to eliminate monopoly and increase diversity in the medium. The validity of anti-trust controls was sharply challenged in *Associated Press v. United States*, decided in 1945. In that case the government suit attacked practices of the Associated Press which imposed serious restrictions upon a newspaper wishing to use its services if the newspaper competed with other papers that were already members of Associated Press. In reply to the argument that the First Amendment prohibited the application of anti-trust legislation to the press, Justice Black made what, at least until *Red Lion,* has been the leading statement from the Court in support of the affirmative aspects of the First Amendment:

It would be strange indeed, however, if the grave concern for freedom of the press which prompted adoption of the First Amendment should be read as a command that the government was without power to protect that freedom. The First Amendment, far from providing an argument against application of the Sherman Act, here provides powerful reasons to the contrary. That Amendment rests on the assumption that the widest possible dissemination of information from diverse and antagonistic sources is essential to the welfare of the public, that a free press is a condition of a free society. Surely a command that the government itself shall not impede the free flow of ideas does not afford non-governmental combinations a refuge if they impose restraints upon that constitutionally guaranteed freedom. Freedom to publish means freedom for all and not for some. Freedom to publish is guaranteed by the Constitution, but freedom to combine to keep others from publishing is not. Freedom of the press from governmental interference under the First Amendment does not sanction repression of that freedom by private interests. The First Amendment affords not the slightest support for the contention that a combination to restrain trade in news and views has any constitutional immunity.[41]

The anti-trust laws have, as a practical matter, had little effect in preventing a drastic decline in the number of newspapers, or in otherwise promoting diversification in the press. Recently legislative proposals have tended to take a different tack. The Failing Newspaper Bill, advanced as a partial solution to the problem of a declining press, would allow some consolidation of economic resources where necessary to keep at least one newspaper alive. There would seem to be no serious First Amendment objection to this form of legislation either. As long as the government regulation in fact promoted diversity in the press, and did not choke the press under a mass of administrative regulation, the First Amendment would not proscribe such an attempt to encourage a more vital role for that medium.

Much more far-reaching proposals have recently been made for regulation of the press, aimed at compelling newspapers to give space in their columns for a right of reply, at airing of controversial issues now ignored, and for expression of viewpoints rarely represented. In an article in 1967 that has received wide attention Professor Jerome Barron argued that "at some point the newspaper must be viewed as impressed with a public service stamp and hence under an obligation to provide space on a nondiscriminatory basis to representative groups in the community." Such a right of access, he suggested, could be imposed either by judicial action or by legislative provision, and would extend to all material ordinarily "suppressed and underrepresented by the newspaper." The following year, at its biennial convention, the American Civil Liberties Union voted to move cautiously in the direction proposed by Professor Barron.[42]

In analyzing the First Amendment issues involved in such propositions it is first necessary to define more carefully the type of matter

---

41. *Associated Press v. United States,* 326 U.S. 1, 20 (1945). See also *Lorain Journal Co. v. United States,* 342 U.S. 143 (1951).

42. Barron, *op. cit. supra* note 3, p. 1666. Professor Barron summarizes the case law on the subject and notes that there are no decisions thus far which require a newspaper to grant a right of access. *Ibid.* pp. 1667–1671. The A.C.L.U. National Board later declined to implement the convention resolution.

the newspaper might be required to publish and the manner in which the regulation would be administered. Various categories of material can be envisaged. First the newspaper might be required to accept paid noncommercial advertisements, on roughly the same basis as it accepts commercial advertisements, in which controversial issues could be discussed or minority views expressed. Secondly, the newspaper might be compelled to grant roughly equal space in its columns to any person who has been libeled or personally attacked in order that he may make a reply. Thirdly, the newspaper might be made to open its letters-to-the-editor columns or make other space available for statements by individuals or groups on issues not reported or on viewpoints not represented by the paper. Finally, a kind of "fairness doctrine," similar to that employed in radio and television, could be imposed on newspapers, requiring them to provide on their own motion for coverage of all "newsworthy" subject matter and expression of all "responsible" viewpoints. There are other possibilities, of course, but these seem to present the main issues.

The right of reply to libelous matter, and perhaps the right to buy noncommercial advertising space, could be imposed by judicial action, were a court disposed to do so. The other rights of access would almost certainly have to be established in the first instance by legislative action. More important for First Amendment purposes, however, would be the nature of the administrative machinery necessary to enforce the various kinds of controls effectively. The first two categories —the noncommercial advertisements and the reply to libel or personal attack—could be phrased in precise terms and readily administered through the usual forms of judicial process, *i.e.*, by injunction or criminal process. The obligation to print statements, on the other hand, would raise intricate problems of whether certain issues had been properly covered, whether all points of view had been presented, whether a particular person or group was representative, whether a specific viewpoint was responsible, "crackpot," or irrelevant, and many like issues. The "fairness doctrine" would be even more complex to administer. It is likely that these two latter categories could be enforced, if at all, only through some form of administrative tribunal.

If we apply to this situation the two tests set forth above, which limit the power of government to promote the system of freedom of expression by control of the mass media, the first two forms of regulation might be found valid and the second two invalid under the First Amendment. In their substantive impact the first two regulations would increase the number of participants in the system and produce greater diversity; they would not seem to entail any serious adverse effect upon the newspaper. The latter two forms of regulation would also add to the number of participants and provide more diversity, but they would reduce by an equal amount the volume and kind of expression the newspaper itself sought to promulgate. These substantive factors might not point clearly in any one direction. But the administrative impact would appear persuasive. The first two forms of regulation are narrow, objective, and readily enforced. The two latter would require an immense administrative apparatus that would seriously threaten the independence of the medium.[43]

We conclude, then, that the kinds of regulation acceptable, indeed unavoidable, in radio and television are unacceptable, indeed unconstitutional, as applied to the press. A limited right of access to the press can be safely enforced. But any effort to solve the broader problems of a monopoly press by forcing newspapers to cover all "newsworthy" events and print all viewpoints, under the watchful eyes of petty public officials, is likely to undermine such independence as the press now shows without achieving any real diversity. Government measures to encourage a multiplicity of outlets, rather than compelling a few outlets to represent everybody, seems a far preferable course of action. Such a goal cannot be reached by mere enforcement of the antitrust laws. It will undoubtedly be necessary to go to the economic roots of the problem and either by government subsidies or other devices create an open market with a new form of economic base.

F. Supplying the Raw Materials and Improving the Skills Necessary for Achieving an Effective System

An effective system of freedom of expression depends upon an abundance of raw materials feeding into the system, in the form of information, ideas, and alternative solutions; and upon the development of skills for utilizing those raw materials, in the form of ability to understand, appraise, and create. This is especially true of the system's function as a mechanism for the solution of political and social prob-

43. See the discussion of these problems in Chafee, *op. cit. supra* note 3, pp. 624–650.

lems. The government can probably do more to vitalize the system by supplying raw materials and improving the skills with which they are employed than by any other form of promotion. At one time it may have been thought sufficient for the government to furnish an occasional public library and a one-room schoolhouse. But that degree of involvement is inadequate for a modern technological society. It is necessary that conscious attention be given to the role of the government in supporting the system at these critical points.

To some extent, of course, the input of raw materials in the system has expanded in modern times. New media of communication and improvements in the old have made more information more readily and rapidly available. The development of television has added a new dimension. Likewise the scholarly production of educational and research institutions has grown rapidly, as has the supply of information and opinion from other sources. Nevertheless, there have been countervailing forces at work. The growing complexity of the issues has meant that more information must be made available if the citizen is to have some rational basis for judgment. The growth of the government bureaucracy has resulted in the concentration of more critical information in the control of institutions that inherently tend to operate within their own framework and to shut the public out.

Not very much has been done to meet these problems. The government has increased its own participation in the system, but that is not an unmitigated advantage. The single most promising development has probably been the enactment of right-to-know laws. These, including the Moss Act passed by Congress in 1966, require government agencies to make certain types of information about their operations public. Thus far the laws have been weak and easily evaded. Furthermore, neither the communication media nor private citizens have pressed very hard to take advantage of them. The right-to-know laws nevertheless stand as an example of the kind of measure that can be devised to enlarge and enrich the flow of material into the system.[44]

---

44. The Moss Act is 80 Stat. 250 (1966), codified by 81 Stat. 54 (1967), 5 U.S.C. §552. On the right-to-know problem, see Harold L. Cross, *The People's Right to Know* (New York, Columbia University Press, 1953, Supp. 1959); Wiggins, *op. cit. supra* note 1; Note, "Open Meeting Statutes: The Press Fights for the 'Right to Know,'" *Harvard Law Review*, Vol. 75 (1962), p. 1199; Note, "Freedom of Information: The Statute and the Regulations," *Georgetown Law Journal*, Vol. 56 (1967), p. 18; Kenneth C. Davis, "The Information Act: A Preliminary Analysis," *University of Chicago Law Review*, Vol. 34 (1967), p. 761; Note, "The Freedom of Information Act: Access to Law," *Fordham Law Review*, Vol. 36 (1968), p. 765.

With respect to the improvement of the skills needed to assimilate and use the raw materials provided by the system, there have also been some advances. Thus the illiteracy rate is low and the number of students in our institutions of higher learning is at an all-time high. It is here, however, that the glaring defects in our educational system are most disturbing. The incredibly low standards of education in many of our elementary and secondary schools, and the bland and conformist character of much of our higher education, hardly equip our citizens with the interest, understanding, independence and maturity that are essential to a healthy system of freedom of expression.

No First Amendment problems would arise from the use of legislative power to enrich the flow of materials into the system or to sharpen the skills with which the material is used. Adequate power resides in government for these purposes and the negative limitations of the First Amendment could easily be satisfied. More intriguing questions emerge, however, if one speculates about the power of the courts to employ the First Amendment affirmatively to achieve certain immediate objectives along the lines suggested. It might well be argued, for instance, that the positive demands of the First Amendment would require the government to make public certain types of information necessary for public decision making. It might even be that certain practices of the public school or university, most obviously detrimental to achieving the objectives of the First Amendment, could be remedied by judicial decree. The courts would, of course, be faced with all the difficulties stemming from lack of power, money and administrative techniques that are presented by attempts to administer an economic and social bill of rights through the judicial process. Furthermore, they would have to operate within the principles of academic freedom. It is not inconceivable, however, that First Amendment doctrine may begin to move in this direction.

XVIII

Protection for Freedom of Expression within Private Centers of Power

Voluntary associations in American society wield enormous influence over many phases of our national life. We have already discussed the controls exercised by government over the external activities of such groups. Other important issues grow out of the internal operations of these private centers of power. One such issue is whether, and to what extent, members of voluntary associations should be legally protected in their right of expression against infringement by the organization itself or its officials. In other words, to what degree should the official system of freedom of expression be transferred to the internal workings of private centers of power? [1]

1. On the problems of this chapter see Zechariah Chafee, Jr., "The Internal Affairs of Associations Not for Profit," *Harvard Law Review*, Vol. 43 (1930), p. 993, rightly considered the seminal article; Note, "Judicial Control of Action of Private Associations," *Harvard Law Review*, Vol. 76 (1963), p. 983; Robert J. Affeldt and Henry W. Seney, "Group Sanctions and Personal Rights—Professions, Occupations and Labor Law," *Saint Louis University Law Journal*, Vol. 11 (1967), p. 382, Vol. 12 (1968), p. 179; and other material and references contained in Thomas I. Emerson, David Haber and Norman Dorsen, *Political and*

The conditions that give rise to the problem are familiar. Voluntary associations exist in virtually every area of public and private life, as business corporations, labor unions, farm organizations, professional associations, political parties, religious sects, educational institutions, recreational and cultural groups, and in many other forms. Frequently they are entrusted with special privileges or official powers by the government. Often economic or social pressures make membership in them almost or fully mandatory. Under any circumstances they are likely to play a prominent role in the life of individual members, sometimes a more dominant one than the government itself. In fact, and this is the core of the problem, voluntary associations in our society tend to become, for all practical purposes, private governments. They grow into large, impersonal, bureaucratic machines, possessing an identity and life of their own. When this happens, the single member has no power by himself, and can exercise his influence only in common with others through the elaborate organizational machinery. In this situation the members of a voluntary association have the same need for freedom of expression as they do vis-à-vis the formal government. The function of a system of freedom of expression within such a private center of power is much the same as it is in the broader society.

The First Amendment, of course, is a limitation only upon the Federal Government and, since *Gitlow*, upon State governments. It does not, strictly speaking, bind private persons or groups. Hence on the face of things legal power to control voluntary associations might seem to be lacking, thus leaving the system of freedom of expression within private centers of power to laissez-faire forces. In point of fact, however, the possibility of extensive legal control exists. Many private centers of power are so related to the formal government that the requirement of "state action" can be found to bring the First Amendment into play. There are also various common law doctrines which give the courts authority to supervise the affairs of voluntary associations. In addition Federal and State legislatures can utilize their normal complement of powers to enact laws, within the framework of the First Amendment and other constitutional limitations, designed to assure freedom of expression to members of private organizations. The main problem is not so much searching for authority by which to regulate as it is determining the character and extent of the controls.

Civil Rights in the United States (Boston, Little, Brown & Co., 3d ed. 1967), ch. XI (cited hereafter in this chapter as *Political and Civil Rights in the United States*).

These issues are difficult ones. Voluntary associations, by nature and function, must in a democratic society be guaranteed basic autonomy. Government regulation in this area presents the usual paradox of imposing governmental controls in order to maintain a system that is intended to control the government. The dangers may be somewhat reduced because private centers of power have more resources to resist abuse of authority than private individuals. Nevertheless the dangers are real. On the other hand the stakes are high. A system of freedom of expression that allowed private bureaucracies to throttle all internal discussion of their affairs would be seriously deficient. There seems to be general agreement that at some points the government must step in. In any event the law is moving steadily in that direction.

Efforts to extend the legal system of free expression to private centers of power also pose some doctrinal problems. The standards by which the government is restrained from curtailing the expression of citizens are not necessarily those by which a voluntary association should be governed in dealing with the expression of its members. Moreover, complexity is introduced by the addition of a third party to the regulatory process. The model of control is not the simple one of the regulation impinging directly upon the person or group seeking to exercise a right of expression. In this instance the government is forcing the association to recognize the rights of its members; yet the association itself is engaging in expression, as well as other legitimate activities, which may be jeopardized by the very fact of control. Thus two participants in the system must be accommodated.

The actual problems arise in two forms. One concerns the right of individual members to express themselves in ways that the association, its officials, or some of its other members disagree with and seek to curb. The other involves the right of the association to express itself, and particularly to use the contributions of a member for that purpose, in ways that the individual member disagrees with. These two aspects of the question raise somewhat different issues.

A. The Right of Expression by Individual Members

When an individual member of an association, or a prospective member, engages in expression that is opposed to the association, its officers, or policies, the usual sanctions available to the association are refusal of membership, expulsion, or some kind of organizational discipline. Governmental controls over this process may take the form of judicial application of the First Amendment in order to protect the individual right of expression, or legislative enactment guaranteeing the individual right. In the latter case the legislative power is derived from non–First Amendment sources but is limited in its impact upon the association by the requirements of the First Amendment.

I. JUDICIAL APPLICATION OF THE FIRST AMENDMENT

In considering the judicial application of the First Amendment to private centers of power, the first question is essentially one of jurisdiction. Does the First Amendment, invoked in a judicial proceeding by a member of a private association, operate at all to limit the conduct of the association? In its most common form up to now this has been framed as an issue of "state action." In First Amendment terms, the problem posed in this way is whether the conduct of the association constitutes "law."

The concept of "state action" has, of course, become an exceedingly complex one. State action doctrine has developed primarily in the equal protection area. And it is by no means certain that what constitutes "state action" for equal protection purposes should constitute "state action" for First Amendment purposes (or Fourteenth Amendment as incorporating the First Amendment). There are not many Supreme Court decisions dealing with state action in a First Amendment context. But those that exist seem to indicate that the doctrine will be liberally extended to the activities of private associations. Thus the Supreme Court held in *Marsh v. Alabama* that residents of a company town could invoke First Amendment rights against the corporation owning the town, and in *Amalgamated Food Employees Union v. Logan Valley Plaza* that pickets could invoke it against owners of a shopping center. In *Railway Employees' Department v.*

Hanson and *International Association of Machinists v. Street* the Court ruled that a labor organization authorized by Federal statute to enter into a union shop contract with an employer was bound to respect the First Amendment rights of its members. In *Lathrop v. Donohue* it extended First Amendment protection to members of an integrated bar. Beyond these decisions it is necessary to proceed by way of analogy and theory.[2]

It is clear that there are many circumstances in which voluntary associations would meet the requirements of state action for First Amendment purposes. One principal indication of state action is the degree of government involvement in the organization. This test would bring within the First Amendment a wide variety of private centers of power. Under the *Hanson* and *Street* decisions a labor organization permitted by law to contract for a union shop or a closed shop would be bound to afford its members rights under the First Amendment. The same would seem to be true, under *Steele v. Louisville and Nashville R.R.*, of any labor union authorized by statute to act as exclusive representative of the employees for purposes of collective bargaining. Under *Lathrop* the relation of an integrated bar association to its members would be governed by the First Amendment. By the same token any bar association to which the government had delegated powers, such as the processing of grievances against attorneys, would be likewise bound. Similarly most medical associations and other professional associations would be in the same position. It would not be difficult to find the requisite government involvement in farm organizations, political parties, private universities, and many other private centers of power.[3]

The other main test for "state action" is the public nature of the function performed by the private association. This concept, also, would embrace many private centers of power. A company town according to *Marsh*, and a shopping center according to *Logan Valley*, must extend First Amendment rights to its public. Under *Terry v. Adams* a political party is engaged in such a vital public function that it takes on the character of government. The *Girard College* case indi-

---

2. *Marsh v. Alabama,* 326 U.S. 501 (1946); *Amalgamated Food Employees Union v. Logan Valley Plaza, Inc.,* 391 U.S. 308 (1968); *Railway Employees' Department v. Hanson,* 351 U.S. 225 (1956); *International Association of Machinists v. Street,* 367 U.S. 740 (1961); *Lathrop v. Donohue,* 367 U.S. 820 (1961). The *Hanson, Street* and *Lathrop* cases are discussed in the following section. See also *Public Utilities Commission v. Pollak,* 343 U.S. 451 (1952).

3. *Steele v. Louisville and Nashville R.R.,* 323 U.S. 192 (1944).

cates that the same may be true of "private" educational institutions. It can be argued that labor unions, professional associations, and even major sports associations fit the category. In the end the concept of "state action" leads all the way to the purely private sector of associational activity. Only the private club, the social or recreational organization that does not participate in public affairs, and similar associations operate beyond the widening boundaries of "state action." [4]

There is another path whereby the courts may afford First Amendment protection to members of private centers of power. The courts have always exercised jurisdiction over the internal affairs of private associations through common law doctrines of contract, trust, tort and property. In the application of such doctrines the rights guaranteed by the First Amendment are logical standards for measuring the obligation of the association to its members. Thus, if a court holds that the relations between an association and its members are governed by an implied contract, then it is eminently reasonable to say that one of the conditions of such a contract is recognition of the right of expression. Likewise it might violate the fiduciary relationship or constitute a tort for the association to deny a member First Amendment rights. Even property theory could be applied in a similar fashion. Indeed, under the theory of *Shelley v. Kraemer* a court enforcing such common law rights would be bound to conform to the requirements of the First Amendment. The utilization of common law doctrines in this manner would extend the scope of the First Amendment to all voluntary associations, public or private. [5]

The law has not yet, of course, developed to this point. But its trend is in this direction. There is no reason why ultimately the courts should not go all the way. If this occurred any member in any private center of power could look to judicial protection of the right to freedom of expression in accordance with the principles of the First Amendment.

The more difficult questions concern the rules for application of the First Amendment to private centers of power. Court decisions are of very little help here. The Supreme Court has never dealt directly with the problem. In the *Street* and *Lathrop* cases Justices Frankfurter

4. *Terry v. Adams*, 345 U.S. 461 (1953), and see also *Ray v. Blair*, 343 U.S. 214 (1952); *Pennsylvania v. Brown*, 270 F. Supp. 782 (E.D. Pa. 1967), aff'd 392 F.2d 120 (3d Cir. 1968), cert. denied 391 U.S. 921 (1968) (Girard College case). For a collection of materials and references on "state action," see *Political and Civil Rights in the United States*, pp. 2111–2116. Later material includes Charles L. Black, " 'State Action,' Equal Protection, and California's Proposition 14," *Harvard Law Review*, Vol. 81 (1967), p. 69.

5. *Shelley v. Kraemer*, 334 U.S. 1 (1948).

and Harlan, who took the strictest view of the limitations imposed by the First Amendment upon private associations, assumed that individual members of labor unions and bar associations would have the right to express themselves in opposition to the organization and to participate in the decision-making process. Justice Douglas clearly shared that view, and it is unlikely any of the justices disagreed. But the extent of protection afforded by the First Amendment was not considered. Lower Federal courts and State courts have touched on the issue only in isolated cases and do not provide any significant guidance. The applicable principles must be found, therefore, without much assistance from precedent, upon the basis of the requirements of the system of freedom of expression.[6]

At the outset it should be noted that there are important differences between guaranteeing freedom of expression within the confines of a private association and within the body politic at large. By its very nature a private association performs a specialized function and puts particular reliance upon its members to carry out that function. We have seen in connection with academic freedom that the peculiar character of a university community imposes a special type of limitation upon the faculty member's normal right of expression. The relation of the government employee to the organization with which he is connected also requires special modification of his general right of expression. Moreover, it is commonly understood and expected that a person participating in a private association commits himself to some obligation, in contrast to nonmembers, to pursue the broad objects of the organization. These considerations are less compelling, of course, when an individual joins an association because of economic pressure or is forced into it by government edict. Nevertheless, assuming the pressures and the command are constitutionally justified, these basic elements in the situation remain the same.

Other factors are also involved. The capacity of a private association of limited powers to effectuate its policies through control of "action" alone is substantially less than that of government. Also, the relations between members of a private association are likely to be more intimate, and the arena in which the association's activities are carried on less suitable for open conflict, than in the general polity composed of all citizens. Again, the private center of power itself plays a vital role in the system of freedom of expression, and that function

6. See 367 U.S. at 806, 808, 856, 776–777.

can be impaired by overintensive regulation of its internal affairs. The very nature of pluralism demands that the private association, even if its members are compelled to participate, retain a major area of autonomy and independent action.

All these characteristics differ, of course, among different kinds of associations. The broader the goals of the association, the larger its membership, the more impersonal the relations of its members to each other, the more compulsion there is to join, then the more similar the private government becomes to public government. Conversely, the closer the association approaches to a purely private affair, the less is government protection of the right of expression for its members necessary or appropriate.

The foregoing considerations shape the application of the First Amendment to private associations. The distinction between "expression" and "action" remains the same. The issue of "abridgment," however, is somewhat different. One starts with the presumption that the expression of the individual member is protected against infringement by the association. But restrictions imposed by the association that are essential to allow it to perform its special task and to maintain itself as an organization would not constitute an "abridgment."

These principles would operate differently in different kinds of situations. In a bar association freedom to criticize association policy and officials would be virtually unlimited, but advocacy of violation of law or of disregard for professional obligations might be ground for discipline. A labor union might be justified in expelling or disciplining a member who campaigned for a rival union in a labor election. Presumably a political party could demand adherence to the basic tenets of the party as a condition of membership. The member of a university faculty would be restricted by the peculiar features of the university community. A country club, if the First Amendment applied at all, would have considerable leeway to determine what kind of expression it wanted to hear from its members. But residents of a company town would have rights equivalent to those of citizens.

At this stage in the progress of the law only the general principles can be stated. A more significant and deeper understanding of those principles will have to await case-by-case development.

2. LEGISLATIVE PROTECTION OF EXPRESSION

Protection to freedom of expression by members of private centers of power may be extended through legislative enactment. The major example of this is found in the so-called Bill of Rights of the Labor-Management Reporting and Disclosure Act of 1959. On freedom of expression and assembly that statute provides:

(a)(1) Equal rights.

Every member of a labor organization shall have equal rights and privileges within such organization to nominate candidates, to vote in elections or referendums of the labor organization, to attend membership meetings, and to participate in the deliberations and voting upon the business of such meetings, subject to reasonable rules and regulations in such organization's constitution and bylaws.

(2) Freedom of speech and assembly.

Every member of any labor organization shall have the right to meet and assemble freely with other members; and to express any views, arguments, or opinions; and to express at meetings of the labor organization his views, upon candidates in an election of the labor organization or upon any business properly before the meeting, subject to the organization's established and reasonable rules pertaining to the conduct of meetings: *Provided,* That nothing herein shall be construed to impair the right of a labor organization to adopt and enforce reasonable rules as to the responsibility of every member toward the organization as an institution and to his refraining from conduct that would interfere with its performance of its legal or contractual obligations.[7]

Whether legislative action of this kind is appropriate or wise depends upon a number of factors. For reasons already mentioned, government control over the internal affairs of private associations, especially in the form of legislation administered by a bureaucracy, always poses a threat to the independence of the association. The First Amendment problems involved, however, would not appear to be serious. Power to enact such legislation derives from the general police power of the State or from some delegated power of the Federal Gov-

7. 29 U.S.C. §§411–413. For material discussing the Labor-Management Reporting and Disclosure Act and the cases under it see *Political and Civil Rights in the United States,* pp. 1216–1218. Later material includes James B. Atleson, "A Union Member's Right of Free Speech and Assembly: Institutional Interests and Individual Rights," *Minnesota Law Review,* Vol. 51 (1967), p. 403; *Kelsey v. Philadelphia Local 8,* 294 F. Supp. 1368 (E.D. Pa. 1968).

ernment—the commerce power in the case of the Labor-Management Reporting and Disclosure Act. The First Amendment comes into play only by way of limitation upon the legislative enactment, as it affects the right of expression either of the members or of the association itself.

It would be unlikely that a statute designed to protect the rights of members would attempt to reduce those rights or would be interpreted by the courts to do so. In any event, legislation could clearly not take away rights to which members are entitled under the self-executing force of the First Amendment. As to the right of expression by the association, that would scarcely be put in jeopardy by legislation protecting the rights of members. To the slight degree that it might be affected, the validity of the statute would be judged by the principles applicable when the government is regulating expression not to protect other social interests outside the system, but to expand the system of expression itself. These principles are that the regulation must in fact expand rather than contract the system of expression, and that the administrative impact of the regulation must not smother the free expression of those regulated.

The Labor-Management Reporting and Disclosure Act would not appear to violate these principles. Nor would most legislation of this kind be likely to do so. On the other hand, if the effect of legislation directed at associations operating within the private sector was to curtail the right of association without expanding the right of expression, the legislation would fail to meet the requirements of the First Amendment.

B. Right of Expression by the Association

The operations of private centers of power have also produced problems concerning the right of the association itself to engage in expression. The basic question has been whether the association may express or support positions that are opposed to the views of some of its members. The issue arises primarily when the association is using funds contributed in part by members who object to the expression, and becomes particularly acute when membership in the association is the result of economic pressures or governmental requirement.

The Supreme Court has considered these matters in three related cases. In its first decision—*Railway Employees' Department v. Hanson*—the Court dealt with threshold problems. Under the Railway Labor Act a railroad and a labor organization representing a majority of the employees in an appropriate collective bargaining unit were authorized to enter into a contract requiring all employees to become members of the union and providing for a check-off by the employer of all dues, initiation fees, and assessments. A group of employees challenged the statute on the ground that it infringed their First Amendment rights because it compelled them to join and pay dues to an organization that advocated political ideas, supported political candidates, and advanced national economic concepts with which they might disagree. The Supreme Court unanimously upheld the union shop provision as a general proposition, saying it "does not violate either the First or the Fifth Amendments." Since the record did not show whether the union was in fact spending funds for political purposes the Court found it unnecessary to pass on those issues.[8]

The Supreme Court was faced with that problem in the next case —*International Association of Machinists v. Street*—decided in 1961. Here the employees specifically alleged that "the money each was thus compelled to pay to hold his job was in substantial part used to finance the campaigns of candidates for federal and state offices whom he opposed, and to promote the propagation of political and economic doctrines, concepts and ideologies with which he disagreed." The Georgia courts, in which the suit was filed, found the allegations proved and enjoined enforcement of the union shop agreement on the ground that it violated, among other constitutional provisions, the First Amendment. The United States Supreme Court, in a six to three decision with five opinions, reversed.[9]

Justice Brennan, in the prevailing opinion to which three other members of the Court subscribed, found it unnecessary to pass on the constitutional questions. Construing the statute "to avoid serious doubt of [its] constitutionality," he held that its primary purpose was "to force employees to share the costs of negotiating and administering collective agreements, and the costs of the adjustment and settlement of disputes"; and that it was not intended "to provide the unions with a means for forcing employees, over their objection, to support political

8. *Railway Employees' Department v. Hanson*, 351 U.S. 225, 238 (1956).
9. *International Association of Ma-*

chinists v. Street, 367 U.S. 740, 744 (1961).

causes which they oppose." He did not consider it necessary to decide what the statute intended as to expenditures to which individual employees might object in the intermediate area between meeting collective bargaining costs and supporting "union political activities." Having established the basic principles, Justice Brennan turned to the practical problems of administration. He held that the remedy was not to enjoin enforcement of the union shop agreement as a whole, but only to prevent the use of funds contributed by employees "who have made known to the union officials that they do not desire their funds to be used for political causes to which they object." This could be accomplished, he suggested, either by enjoining expenditure of that proportion of the funds to be spent for political purposes which was exacted from the complaining employees, or refunding that proportion to such employees. Under either remedy funds would be withheld only for those employees who specifically notified the union of their opposition to the expenditure. Justice Brennan also ruled that, since affirmative objection by each employee was necessary, the proceeding could not be brought as a class suit. On this latter point there was no dissent.[10]

Justice Whittaker concurred in the Brennan opinion except with respect to the remedy. He felt that it was impossible to separate out the funds being illegally used and concluded that the whole union shop agreement should be enjoined. The other four justices reached the constitutional issues:

Justice Douglas started with the proposition that, if membership in an association is compelled, the individual cannot be forced to relinquish to the group any of his rights to freedom of expression. This position he stated unequivocally:

> Once an association with others is compelled by the facts of life, special safeguards are necessary lest the spirit of the First, Fourth, and Fifth Amendments be lost and we all succumb to regimentation. I expressed this concern in *Public Utilities Comm'n v. Pollak,* 343 U.S. 451, 467 (dissenting opinion), where a "captive audience" was forced to listen to special radio broadcasts. If an association is compelled, the individual should not be forced to surrender any matters of conscience, belief, or expression. He should be allowed to enter the group with his own flag flying, whether it be religious, political, or philosophical; nothing that the group does should deprive him of the privilege of preserving and expressing his agreement, disagreement, or dissent, whether it coincides with the view of the group, or conflicts with it in minor or

10. 367 U.S. at 749, 764, 770, 774.

major ways; and he should not be required to finance the promotion of causes with which he disagrees.[11]

Justice Douglas conceded that the government could authorize the union shop and he agreed with the decision in *Hanson* "that it was permissible for the legislature to require all who gain from collective bargaining to contribute to its cost." But he concluded that "since the funds here in issue are used for causes other than defraying the costs of collective bargaining," they were being spent in violation of the rights of employees who protested such use.[12]

Justice Black went beyond Justice Douglas, believing that the government could not make an employee become a member of an association against his will, but could only assess him for the costs of collective bargaining. He saw "no constitutional reason why a union or other private group may not spend its funds for political or ideological causes if its members voluntarily join it and can voluntarily get out of it." But a different situation arises "when a federal law steps in and authorizes such a group to carry on activities at the expense of persons who do not choose to be members of the group as well as those who do." Such a law "cannot be used in a way that abridges the specifically defined freedoms of the First Amendment." Therefore, he concluded,

> In my view, [the statute] can constitutionally authorize no more than to make a worker pay dues to a union for the sole purpose of defraying the cost of acting as his bargaining agent. Our Government has no more power to compel individuals to support union programs or union publications than it has to compel the support of political programs, employer programs or church programs. And the First Amendment, fairly construed, deprives the Government of all power to make any person pay out one single penny against his will to be used in any way to advocate doctrines or views he is against, whether economic, scientific, political, religious or any other.[13]

Justice Frankfurter, with whom Justice Harlan joined, also dissented, but in total disagreement with Justices Douglas and Black on the First Amendment issues. He pointed out that the rights of the individual to express his own views had in no way been "checked or

11. 367 U.S. at 776.

12. 367 U.S. at 776, 778. Justice Douglas expressed doubts about Justice Brennan's proposals for "proportional" relief but ultimately concurred in order to obtain the five votes needed for a judgment.

13. 367 U.S. at 788, 789, 791. Justice Black, by way of remedy, would enjoin the union from barring employment to the protesting employees and require a refund of all the dues they had paid. He would not attempt a "proportional" remedy.

curbed": "The individual member may express his views in any public or private forum as freely as he could before the union collected his dues." Moreover, he may "participate in determining union policies" and "assert [his] weight in defining the purposes for which union dues may be expended." Justice Frankfurter also noted that the statute did not compel the railroad and the unions to enter into a union shop agreement but only authorized it, arguing that there was a "vital distinction between authorization and compulsion." But most of all Justice Frankfurter stressed that "[i]t is a commonplace of all organizations that a minority of a legally recognized group may at times see an organization's funds used for the promotion of ideas opposed by the minority." Even the Federal Government "expends revenue collected from individual taxpayers to propagandize ideas which many taxpayers oppose." The unions have traditionally spent their funds for political purposes, and indeed it is impossible to insulate their political interests from their economic interests. To uphold the position of the minority employees, therefore, "would be to mutilate a scheme designed by Congress for the purpose of equitably sharing the cost of securing the benefits of union exertions," would "greatly embarrass if not frustrate conventional labor activities which have become institutionalized through time," and would "grant a miniscule claim constitutional recognition." [14]

On the same day it decided the *Street* case the Supreme Court handed down its decision in *Lathrop v. Donohue*. At issue was the constitutionality of the institution known as the "integrated bar." Acting under a statute passed by the Wisconsin legislature the Supreme Court of Wisconsin promulgated rules and bylaws creating "The State Bar of Wisconsin." Under this arrangement all lawyers practicing in Wisconsin were required to be members of the State Bar and to pay annual dues of fifteen dollars. The State Bar functioned as an ordinary bar association. A Wisconsin lawyer brought suit for refund of his dues claiming that he could not constitutionally be compelled "to be a member of and financially support an association of attorneys . . . which . . . among other things, uses its property, funds and employees for the purpose of influencing a broad range of legislation and public opinion." The Wisconsin Supreme Court affirmed a dismissal of the complaint. It held squarely that there was no violation of the First Amendment, even though part of plaintiff's dues were "used to

14. 367 U.S. at 806, 808, 807, 818.

advocate causes to which he is opposed," because the public interest in an integrated bar "outweighs the slight inconvenience to the plaintiff resulting from his required payment of the annual dues." The United States Supreme Court affirmed, again without majority agreement and expressing its points of view in five opinions.[15]

Justice Brennan, in an opinion which Chief Justice Warren and Justices Clark and Stewart joined, first addressed himself to the question whether a lawyer could be required to join an association such as the State Bar. He pointed out, quoting the Wisconsin Court, that the lawyer was not compelled "to associate with anyone"; that he was "free to attend or not attend [the association's] meetings or vote in its elections as he chooses"; and that the "only compulsion" was the payment of annual dues. Justice Brennan conceded that the State Bar dealt not only with "the internal affairs of the profession," such as legal aid and the unauthorized practice of law, but also to some extent with broader issues including legislative proposals for court reform and public debates on world peace through law. But he stressed that the bulk of its activities were "wholly outside the political process" and "without apparent political coloration." He concluded on this point: "We think that the Supreme Court of Wisconsin, in order to further the State's legitimate interests in raising the quality of professional services, may constitutionally require that the costs of improving the profession in this fashion should be shared by the subjects and beneficiaries of the regulatory program, the lawyers, even though the organization created to attain the objective also engages in some legislative activity." [16]

Justice Brennan, declining to go further, refused to decide on the record before him "whether [plaintiff's] constitutional rights of free speech are infringed if his dues money is used to support the political activities of the State Bar." Decision on those matters was unnecessary, he asserted, because "[n]owhere are we clearly apprised as to the views of the [plaintiff] on any particular legislative issues on which the State Bar has taken a position, or as to the way in which and the degree to which funds compulsorily exacted from its members are used to support the organization's political activities." [17]

Justices Harlan and Frankfurter concurred in the result, their views expressed this time by Justice Harlan. He thought it "unfortu-

15. *Lathrop v. Donohue,* 367 U.S. 820, 827, 844–845 (1961).

16. 367 U.S. at 828, 834, 839, 843.
17. 367 U.S. at 844, 845–846.

nate" that the integrated bar association—which exists in twenty-five
States in addition to Wisconsin—"should be left in such disquieting
Constitutional uncertainty," and that it was necessary to face the constitutional issues that Justice Brennan had avoided. Like Justice
Frankfurter in *Street* he could not find in the integrated bar arrangement any significant injury to freedom of expression; indeed he felt
that the claims of infringement of First Amendment rights "border on
the chimerical." The taking of the member's dues, thereby reducing
the funds available to the member for his own expression, Justice
Harlan thought no different from ordinary government taxation.
While he agreed that the government could not use the integrated bar
to favor "particular candidates for judicial or legal office or particular
types of legislation," he thought that the Wisconsin arrangement
clearly did not do this. To the objection that the dues payer was being
made to finance views which he opposed, Justice Harlan answered that
the member retained his right of dissent and his right to participate in
the association's decision, and that there was "little basis for a right
not to have one's opposition heard." Besides, he observed, it is commonplace "in the everyday operation of our society" to be required to
contribute to groups that spend money contrary to the wishes of the
contributor, as in the case of labor unions and ordinary taxes. Finally,
he rejected the argument that membership in the integrated bar
amounted to compulsion to express a belief, it being well understood
that an organization did not necessarily speak for every member. On
the other hand he found important social interests being served by the
requirement of an integrated bar. He concluded: "In this instance it
can hardly be doubted that it was Constitutionally permissible for Wisconsin to regard the functions of an Integrated Bar as sufficiently important to justify whatever incursions on these individual freedoms
may be thought to arise from the operations of the organization." [18]

Justice Whittaker thought that the practice of law was a "special
privilege" and the requirement of an annual fee of fifteen dollars for
engaging in practice did not violate the Constitution.

Justice Black dissented on the grounds expressed in his opinion in
Street. Again, he drew a line between compulsory payments to finance
"non-political and non-controversial activities" and payments to support a "controlling group [that] is trying to pass laws or advance political causes that he is against." Justice Black specifically objected to

18. 367 U.S. at 848, 852, 853, 857,
861.

Justice Harlan's balancing test and Justice Whittaker's privilege theory.[19]

Justice Douglas also dissented, carrying his views beyond those expressed in *Street*. His principal objection went to the power of the government to force individuals into any form of association, unless "exceptional circumstances" were shown. The *Hanson* case, he thought, represented "a narrow exception to be closely confined." Otherwise "we practically give *carte blanche* to any legislature to put at least professional people into goose-stepping brigades." [20]

This bewildering array of positions and opinions in *Hanson, Street* and *Lathrop* leaves the reader with a feeling of something less than satisfaction. Not only has the Court been unable to agree on a single theory, but the various viewpoints never seem to come in contact with one another. Nor, upon further analysis, does any appear to meet the underlying problem adequately.

Justice Brennan, joined by three colleagues, takes the position that compulsion to join and pay dues to an association is not in itself unconstitutional and that therefore the institution of the union shop or the integrated bar is as a general proposition valid. Such an association, he further contends, can use the contributions of all members, protesting or not, for certain kinds of expression, but he draws the line at "political" expression. Expenditure of association funds for "political" expression would, he indicates, be unconstitutional. Justice Brennan does not find it necessary to define carefully the boundary between "political" and "non-political" expression, and probably never will, because that issue becomes submerged in the administration of his remedies for illegal use of associational funds. The association can operate as usual unless a member officially objects. Then the member can enjoin the association from using a proportion of his contribution for unconstitutional purposes, or can obtain a refund of that much. No class suit for this purpose, however, is permissible. Since the amount involved is very small, and the dissenting member cannot bring down the whole institution, no individual or group has any incentive to pursue the matter further. It is hardly surprising that the issues Justice Brennan tortuously dodged have not come back to haunt the Court.

The objection to the Brennan view goes deeper, however, than his solution of the problem in terms of procedures. The distinction made between associational expression that is "political" and associational expression that is "not political" appears inadequate. Expenditures by

19. 367 U.S. at 877.　　　　　　20. 367 U.S. at 882, 884.

a labor union to support a political candidate may be less objectionable to an individual member, and less significant to the system of expression, than expenditures to defeat right-to-work laws or to improve the social security program. The distinction focuses on dramatic expenditures but is essentially superficial. Hence the Brennan theory fails to supply a full answer.

Justices Frankfurter and Harlan, while they talk in quite different terms, are essentially in accord with the Brennan position. They also would allow an association based on compulsory membership to function but would not validate certain types of associational expression, that supporting "particular candidates for judicial or legal office or particular types of legislation." The distinction is drawn at a slightly different point but is subject to the same objections.

Justice Douglas is in the middle on the subject of compulsory membership. He considers it valid for a labor union but not for a professional association. The basis for the distinction is not made clear. Insofar as he accepts the validity of compulsory membership Justice Douglas finds himself in the same dilemma as Justice Brennan. Any form of activity by the association is likely to involve expression and protesting members may have as serious objection to the associational view on one subject as another. To the extent that Justice Douglas objects to compulsory membership he is in the Black camp.

Justice Black takes a firm position in opposition to any expenditure for purposes of expression from funds contributed by a compulsory member. But he does not define "compulsion." He treats the statutory permission to enter into a union shop agreement as identical with a statutory mandate to join the bar association. Justice Black's position would therefore curtail large areas of associational expression. For example, it would seem doubtful that any union with a closed shop agreement sanctioned under the National Labor Relations Act could use union funds for expression, except perhaps on matters directly related to its collective bargaining. This position is difficult to reconcile with Justice Black's view in *United States v. C.I.O.* that the Taft-Hartley prohibition against expenditures in election campaigns is unconstitutional. In any event it would have far-reaching repercussions on the present system of freedom of expression.[21]

If we examine the problem more closely it begins to appear that the key issue is not so much the nature of the associational expression as the character and degree of governmental involvement in the com-

21. *United States v. C.I.O.*, 335 U.S. 106 (1948), discussed in Chapter XVII.

pulsory membership. This was not explored in the Supreme Court opinions, apart from a brief reference by Justice Frankfurter in *Street.* Indeed all members of the Court treated *Street* and *Lathrop* as raising identical issues.

When the association is the creature of the government, because of compulsory membership or otherwise, then Justice Black is clearly right. To take a member's forced contribution and use it for expression of views to which the member objects is plainly an infringement of his constitutional rights. It is not too distant from the forced expression of belief struck down in *West Virginia State Board of Education v. Barnette.* In any event it is a regimentation of expression that is wholly foreign to the postulates of the First Amendment. This is true of expression on any subject, whether in support of a political candidate or in opposition to cigarette smoking. The Frankfurter-Harlan argument that this is done all the time by the government with funds extracted from taxpayers is not persuasive. It assumes that the position of the citizen in the general body politic is the same as the position of the individual member in an association. There are, as we have seen, important differences in the two situations as far as the system of freedom of expression is concerned. While the individual may have somewhat less freedom to express himself as a member of an association than as a general citizen, he has correspondingly greater rights concerning the disposal of his contributions. Furthermore, it is not to be assumed, as Justices Frankfurter and Harlan do, that there are no restrictions upon expression by the government.[22]

On the other hand the problem is different with respect to associations operating in the nongovernmental sphere. Clearly this is true when membership in an association is purely voluntary, so that a member can move in and out with few regrets or hesitations. Here no problem of associational expression is considered to exist. Ordinarily majority rule, or even authoritarian rule, determines the nature of the associational expression. Indeed, an effort by the government to prohibit or limit associational expression on any subject would clearly violate the First Amendment. Associations in this category would probably include all those involving no economic or governmental pressure to become a member.

The issues are not as clear if there are serious economic pressures

22. *West Virginia State Board of Education v. Barnette,* 319 U.S. 624 (1943), discussed in Chapter II. On participation by the government in the system of freedom of expression, see the next chapter.

to join the association, and even less clear if those pressures are supported by governmental measures. Nevertheless such an association is still operating outside the sphere of government. In terms of the system of free expression it is part of the pluralistic forces that bring to the marketplace views different from the official one promulgated by government. An opposing view would, or at least could, persist despite government support. Such an organization, as long as it retains its essential character as a private association, should not be restricted in the form of its expression by reason of minority viewpoints existing within its ranks. Quite the contrary, such a restriction would itself violate the First Amendment.

Here the Frankfurter-Harlan arguments are applicable. Individual members have the right to express their own views within the organization and to participate in the making of associational decisions. These rights are constitutionally guaranteed. They should be held sufficient to make applicable in the field of expression the usual rules for determining associational action by majority decision. This conclusion is buttressed by other considerations. As Justices Frankfurter and Harlan point out, it is generally understood that a member of an association is not personally committed to the views of the association; "guilt by association" is not ordinarily carried to that point. Moreover, there are many forces for self-correction within the association, especially where dues and assessments are concerned, and these may at least preserve majority rule. Besides, there is no satisfactory alternative to allowing full freedom of associational expression. As the Brennan position indicates, any judicial remedy that does not invalidate the whole organization is in practice worthless. Finally, for reasons already stated, it is hard to draw a meaningful line between the kind of expression to be allowed and that to be suppressed. Attempts to curb associational expression under these conditions would seriously damage the system of free expression.

There are, of course, difficulties in drawing a line between associations that are creatures of the government, whose expression is outlawed under the Black position, and associations that are merely supported by the government but retain their private character, whose expression is sanctioned under the Frankfurter-Harlan rationale. One rule of thumb may be ventured. If membership in an association is directly compelled by the government, such an association would fall into the category of government creature and could not use membership dues for associational expression. The dangers of regimentation that alarm Justice Douglas are readily apparent in such a situation. Beyond that point, however, a judgment would have to be made in each case as to whether the government penetration was sufficiently extensive to remove the association from the private sector of the system of freedom of expression.

Under these principles the union in *Street* would be allowed full freedom of expression. But the integrated bar in *Lathrop* would not.

It will be conceded that serious objections can be raised to this disposition of the problem. To the individual member it might make little difference whether membership in the association was compelled by economic pressure or government edict. The distinction between the governmental sphere and the nongovernmental sphere is in many ways a shadowy one. Most of the Frankfurter-Harlan arguments would apply also to the association in which membership is compelled by the government. The use of membership funds to support particular candidates in political campaigns can be distinguished from other forms of political expression. New procedural remedies might be devised. All these considerations carry weight. Whether or not they compel rejection of the thesis urged here, they do emphasize that analysis of the basic issues has barely begun.

C. Conclusions

It will be seen that the problem involved in assuring freedom of expression to individuals within private centers of power is a most puzzling one. The right of individual members to express themselves in opposition to the association is probably the less difficult half of the problem. Here there are strong resemblances to the right of individuals to speak in opposition to the government establishment, which is the main substance of First Amendment law. Yet the analogy cannot be pressed too far. For the rights and obligations of the individual as member of a private association, committed in some measure to achieve the limited objectives of the organization, are not the same as the rights and obligations of the individual as member of the community as a whole. The reasons for and the extent of these differences are crucial to an analysis of the whole problem. Unfortunately these matters have been little explored, and the significance of the associational factor is hard to measure. Some assistance can be derived from consideration of the rights of government employees, or the rights of members of an academic community in relation to the university. But few guidelines are thus far available.

The other half of the problem—the right of the association to express itself contrary to the views of some of its members, using funds taxed from those members—is even more intractable. The answer would not seem to lie in the kind of expression uttered by the association, although presumably no organization would be justified in engaging in expression not related to its functions. If the solution is sought in the degree of compulsion upon the individual to join, it becomes difficult to draw a line that would not seriously curtail associational expression. An analysis in terms of government involvement seems more consistent with the premises of the system of free expression. Here again the differences in the relation of the individual to the all-encompassing unit of organization, the government, and his relation to the smaller, partial unit, the private association, becomes crucial and demands further exploration.

XIX

Government Participation in the System of Freedom of Expression

The system of freedom of expression is normally viewed from the laissez-faire perspective. Attention is focused upon the rights of the private participants in the system and upon the obligation of the government to refrain from interference with, to protect, to eliminate distortions in, and to affirmatively promote the system. The reality is, of course, that the government itself participates in the system, both as communicator and listener. This government participation is active, varied and extensive. It takes the form of oral communications, such as speeches, statements, press conferences, and fireside chats, as well as written communications, such as pamphlets, books, periodicals, and other publications. It utilizes all available media, including printing presses, radio and television, motion pictures, and still pictures, and it achieves its dramatic effects through confrontations in hearings, investigations, and debates. The government has developed special organizations to assist it as communicator, such as public relations departments, the wartime Office of War Information, and the current United States Information Agency; and techniques to assist it as listener, such as intelligence services and public opinion polls. It also operates certain opinion-forming institutions, of which the most prominent is in public education. The government is indeed not just another voice in the system. Government expression is a dominant characteristic of the system.

Participation by the government in the system of freedom of expression is an essential feature of any democratic society. It enables the government to inform, explain, and persuade—measures especially crucial in a society that attempts to govern itself with a minimum use of force. Government participation also greatly enriches the system; it provides the facts, ideas, and expertise not available from other sources. In short, government expression is a necessary and healthy part of the system.

Yet government participation in the system also brings with it serious dangers. Emanating from a source of great authority in the society government expression carries extra psychological weight for many citizens. It comes from officials who often wield enormous actual power over those they address, thereby evoking concern in the listener lest he offend the powers that be by appearing to oppose. The government controls many of the sources of information in the society. It also possesses almost unlimited capacity to reach all members of the community, seldom having problems of access to an audience. The tendency of government expression to be uniform and repetitive in its message gives it a more concentrated impact than other expression. Above all there are no independent institutions in the society that can guard individuals or the society against abuse from government expression. The only direct controls are those administered by the government itself.

Despite the fact that the government is endowed with such a powerful voice, a system of free expression remains viable as long as the government voice is not overpowering and other voices are free to reply and criticize. At some times or in some areas, however, the functions or powers of government may give it a monopoly or near-monopoly over expression and other voices are closed off. This state of affairs is obviously the antithesis of a system of free expression. The control of government expression in such a situation presents particular difficulties.

Though government participation in a system of freedom of expression is of great and growing significance very little attention has been paid to it. No comprehensive effort to appraise the government role or to formulate principles of control has been undertaken.[1]

1. Virtually the only material dealing with the problem is Zechariah Chafee,

We can approach these tasks with the initial proposition that the government has a broad right to engage in expression as part of its regular functions. This statement implies a general limitation. The government's right of expression does not extend to any sphere that is outside the governmental function. This might not seem to be much of a limitation; the governmental function certainly covers an extensive area. Nevertheless the principle does impose some limits. Thus the government would not be empowered to engage in expression in direct support of a particular candidate for office. It is not the function of the government to get itself reelected. Government expression must therefore operate within these general boundaries.

Beyond this, various other problems concerned with government expression are beginning to emerge. There presently appear to be four areas that require consideration: government expression used as a sanction against exercise of the right to expression by private persons and groups; government expression that causes injury to individual and social interests outside the system of freedom of expression; government expression addressed to a captive audience; and government expression that monopolizes or otherwise distorts the system of freedom of expression.

A. Use of Government Expression as a Sanction Against Private Expression

As a starting proposition it may be assumed that the government should have the same right of expression as a private citizen. Under some circumstances, however, government expression has a special impact on the system, substantially different from that of private expression. A major example of this is the effect of government expression used to deter or suppress private expression. This may happen in various ways. Most commonly it takes place when the government expression hints at or threatens official reprisals against persons or groups holding views in conflict with official policy; or when the gov-

---

Jr., *Government and Mass Communications* (Chicago, University of Chicago Press, 1947, reprinted Hamden, Conn., Archon Books, 1965), Vol. II; Ted Fin- man and Stewart Macaulay, "Freedom to Dissent: The Vietnam Protests and the Words of Public Officials," *Wisconsin Law Review*, Vol. 1966 (1966), p. 632.

ernment expression arouses hostility in the community against certain opinions and thereby brings private economic and social pressures to bear on those who espouse the unpopular position. These effects may be deliberately created by government officials engaged in expression or may be an unintended by-product of their expression, or a combination of both. The Vietnam war has occasioned several illustrations of the problem. They include statements by high government officials hinting that criminal prosecutions might be brought against dissenters, charging that Communist Party influence was a major factor in anti-war demonstrations, and suggesting that opposition to the war gave aid and comfort to the enemy.[2]

Communications of a similar character emanating from private persons or groups would ordinarily be acceptable, in fact a routine feature of the system. Coming from the government, however, such expression takes on a different character. It becomes for all practical purposes an informal sanction against private dissenting expression, often equivalent in its effect to a formal sanction. This anomalous situation presents a new and difficult problem.[3]

In theory the government's use of expression to curb private expression would clearly constitute a violation of the First Amendment. The government is surely under a constitutional obligation not to use its power of expression, any more than any other power, to abridge freedom of expression. Moreover, there is no real paradox involved in invoking the First Amendment to restrict government expression. The purpose of the First Amendment is to protect private expression and nothing in the guarantee precludes the government from controlling its own expression or that of its agents.[4]

Furthermore, some statutory basis presently exists by which a pri-

2. See Chapter IV. An extensive account of government expression which attempted to counter opposition to the Vietnam war, through February 1966, may be found in Finman and Macaulay, *op. cit. supra* note 1.

3. There is a question as to whether communication emanating from the government that operates as a sanction upon private expression should not be termed "action," just as a threat of economic reprisal by an employer against an employee would be considered action. Nevertheless the word "expression" is used here to refer to government conduct of the same general nature as conduct that would be considered expression if emanating from a nongovernment source. As set forth below, the government can control its own conduct, whether "expression" or "action," so the distinction between them is of no real consequence in this context.

4. The right of the government to control the *private* expression of its agents or employees is a different matter. See Chapter XV. See also the discussion in Chapter XII of the control of police, prosecutors and other government officials in connection with assuring an accused a fair trial.

vate person or group might obtain judicial relief against government expression that curtails the right of private expression. The Federal Civil Rights Acts provide both criminal and civil sanctions against persons acting under color of State law who infringe First Amendment rights. The Federal courts would also seem to have general jurisdiction to grant injunctive relief to persons whose constitutional rights are being abridged by Federal or State officials. State libel and privacy laws are another source of statutory authority. Existing statutory gaps could readily be filled.[5]

Nevertheless the courts have ordinarily refused to afford a judicial remedy. Main reliance for this result has been placed on doctrines of official immunity. In the case of Federal legislators the immunity rule is based upon Article I, Section 6 of the Federal Constitution, which provides that "for any Speech or Debate in either House, [members] shall not be questioned in any other Place." Most State constitutions contain similar provisions, though they would not necessarily grant immunity for violations of Federal constitutional rights. Judicial and executive immunity arises from judge-made law. Closely tied to immunity doctrine, but not necessarily coextensive, is the principle of separation of powers. The cases in which the courts have applied these rules to deny redress for claimed invasion of First Amendment rights by government expression require brief attention.

Legislative immunity for members of Congress was first upheld by the Supreme Court in *Kilbourn v. Thompson,* decided in 1881. In that case—a suit for false imprisonment brought by a witness who had been held in jail for refusing to answer questions before a House committee—the Court granted immunity to members of the House but denied it to the Sergeant-at-Arms. The Court did not consider legislative immunity again for seventy years. But the next case, *Tenney v. Brandhove,* raised more nearly the question with which we are here concerned.[6]

The *Tenney* case involved a suit by Brandhove against the members of the California Senate Factfinding Committee on Un-American Activities, known as the Tenney Committee. Brandhove sued under

---

5. The main provisions of the Federal Civil Rights Acts are 18 U.S.C. §241 and 242, and 42 U.S.C. §1983. Jurisdiction of the Federal courts to enjoin Federal or State officials from conduct that violates individual rights guaranteed by the Federal constitution is conferred by 28 U.S.C. §1343. These provisions have frequently been utilized to prevent government interference with First Amendment rights where such interference takes the form of "action."

6. *Kilbourn v. Thompson,* 103 U.S. 168 (1881); *Tenney v. Brandhove,* 341 U.S. 367 (1951).

the Federal Civil Rights Acts, alleging that the Committee had violated his constitutional rights, including his right to freedom of speech
and petition, by asking local prosecuting officials to institute criminal
proceedings against him, by summoning him before the Committee, by
reading into the record a statement concerning his alleged criminal
record, and by having him prosecuted for refusing to answer questions. The Supreme Court, with Justice Douglas alone dissenting, held
that the complaint should be dismissed. Without reaching the constitutional questions directly, Justice Frankfurter ruled that the Federal
Civil Rights Acts could not be interpreted as applying to a situation in
which the traditional principles of legislative privilege would have
granted immunity. Those principles would protect members of the legislature, he said, as long as they "were acting in the sphere of legitimate legislative activity." They were designed to assure that "the legislature must be free to speak and act without fear of criminal or civil
liability." He went on to elaborate:

> Legislators are immune from deterrents to the uninhibited discharge of
> their legislative duty, not for their private indulgence but for the public
> good. One must not expect uncommon courage even in legislators. The
> privilege would be of little value if they could be subjected to the cost
> and inconvenience and distractions of a trial upon a conclusion of the
> pleader, or to the hazard of a judgment against them based upon a
> jury's speculation as to motives.[7]

Justice Frankfurter also touched on the separation of powers element in the situation:

> Legislative committees have been charged with losing sight of their duty
> of disinterestedness. In times of political passion, dishonest or vindictive
> motives are readily attributed to legislative conduct and as readily be-
> lieved. Courts are not the place for such controversies. Self-discipline
> and the voters must be the ultimate reliance for discouraging or cor-
> recting such abuses. The courts should not go beyond the narrow con-
> fines of determining that a committee's inquiry may fairly be deemed
> within its province.[8]

A later case, which never reached the Supreme Court, raised even
more acutely the question of abridgment of First Amendment rights

---

7. 341 U.S. at 376, 375, 377.

8. 341 U.S. at 377–378. Justice Douglas in his dissent stated that, while he
agreed with the opinion of the Court "as
a statement of general principles governing the liability of legislative committees
and members of the legislatures," he did
"not agree that all abuses of legislative
committees are solely for the legislative
body to police." 341 U.S. at 381–382.

through legislative expression. In 1955 the Subcommittee on Internal Security of the Senate Judiciary Committee issued a pamphlet entitled "The Communist Party of the United States—What It Is—How It Works—A Handbook for Americans." In this pamphlet the Subcommittee stated, inter alia, that "the Communists have formed religious fronts such as the Methodist Federation for Social Action"; and at another point that sometimes "fronts" will "assume a name similar to some well-known and respectable organization," giving as an example the Methodist Federation for Social Action. A few months later, when Congress voted to print 75,000 additional copies of the pamphlet, the Federation sued the members of the Subcommittee, the Public Printer, and the Superintendent of Documents of the Government Printing Office, to enjoin printing and distribution of the pamphlet. A three-judge District Court in the District of Columbia dismissed the complaint against the members of the Subcommittee on legislative immunity grounds and against the Public Printer and the Superintendent of Documents on separation of powers grounds. Judge Edgerton, with whom Judge Prettyman agreed, stated flatly:

> Nothing in the Constitution authorizes anyone to prevent the President of the United States from publishing any statement. This is equally true whether the statement is correct or not, whether it is defamatory or not, and whether it is or is not made after a fair hearing. Similarly, nothing in the Constitution authorizes anyone to prevent the Supreme Court from publishing any statement. We think it equally clear that nothing authorizes anyone to prevent Congress from publishing any statement.[9]

Legislative immunity for conduct involving expression, though the expression was not claimed to have abridged a First Amendment right, was likewise considered by the Supreme Court in *United States v. Johnson*. Here a Congressman was convicted of conspiracy to defraud the United States by attempting to procure the dismissal of certain indictments in return for money payments. A material portion of the government's case rested on a speech that the Congressman had made in the House. The Court reversed the conviction, holding that

9. *Methodist Federation for Social Action v. Eastland*, 141 F. Supp. 729, 731 (D.D.C. 1956). Judge Wilkin dissented. Questions of legislative immunity were also raised in the District of Columbia courts in three defamation suits against members of Congress: *Cochran v. Couzens*, 42 F.2d 783 (D.C. Cir. 1930); *Long v. Ansell*, 69 F.2d 386 (D.C. Cir. 1934), aff'd 293 U.S. 76 (1934); *McGovern v. Martz*, 182 F. Supp. 343 (D.D.C. 1960). None of the suits was successful, but dicta in the latter two indicate that legislative immunity would not apply to republication of Congressional statements for redistribution to constituents.

the speech was privileged and could not be used in proof of the conspiracy. Justice Harlan, for the majority, observed:

> There is little doubt that the instigation of criminal charges against critical or disfavored legislators by the executive in a judicial forum was the chief fear prompting the long struggle for parliamentary privilege in England and, in the context of the American system of separation of powers, is the predominate thrust of the Speech or Debate clause.[10]

The law pertaining to executive immunity rests primarily upon the case of *Barr v. Matteo*, decided in 1959. In that case the Acting Director of the Office of Rent Stabilization had issued a press release charging that two employees of the agency had been responsible for making financial arrangements concerning annual leave, which were under severe criticism in Congress, and that when he assumed office in the next few days "the suspension of these employees will be his first act of duty." The employees sued for libel. In a five to four decision the Supreme Court held that the statement of the Acting Director was entitled to an absolute privilege as long as it was "within the outer perimeter of [his] line of duty." Justice Harlan, writing the majority opinion, stated that the immunity applied in "civil damage suits for defamation and kindred torts," and indicated that the privilege would be extended to "officers of lower rank in the executive hierarchy." The rationale for the absolute privilege he explained in the following terms:

10. *United States v. Johnson*, 383 U.S. 169, 182 (1966). The Supreme Court also dealt with legislative immunity problems in *Wheeldin v. Wheeler*, 373 U.S. 647 (1963), holding that no Federal cause of action existed where an investigator for the House Committee on Un-American Activities had allegedly served a subpoena upon the plaintiff without authority and had caused him to lose his job; *Dombrowski v. Eastland*, 387 U.S. 82 (1967), dismissing a damage suit against Senator Eastland but remanding Committee Counsel J. G. Sourwine to trial, the charges being that the two had unlawfully seized the files of the Southern Conference Educational Fund; *Powell v. McCormack*, 395 U.S. 486 (1969), dismissing injunction and declaratory judgment action brought by Adam Clayton Powell for wrongful exclusion from the House against five members of the House and Speaker McCormack, but sustaining the action against the Clerk, the Sergeant-at-Arms and the Doorkeeper. None of these cases involved legislative conduct in the nature of expression. See also *Stamler and Hall v. Willis*, 415 F.2d 1365 (7th Cir. 1969).

For general discussion of legislative immunity see Leon R. Yankwich, "The Immunity of Congressional Speech—Its Origin, Meaning and Scope," *University of Pennsylvania Law Review*, Vol. 99 (1951), p. 960; Note, "Absolute Privilege as Applied to Investigators for Congressional Committees," *Columbia Law Review*, Vol. 63 (1963), p. 326; Note, "The Scope of Immunity for Legislators and Their Employees," *Yale Law Journal*, Vol. 77 (1967), p. 366.

The reasons for the recognition of the privilege have been often stated. It has been thought important that officials of government should be free to exercise their duties unembarrassed by the fear of damage suits in respect of acts done in the course of those duties—suits which would consume time and energies which would otherwise be devoted to governmental service and the threat of which might appreciably inhibit the fearless, vigorous, and effective administration of policies of government.[11]

It is likewise well established, and has been for some time, that judges of courts of superior or general authority are absolutely privileged in civil suits based on actions taken by them in the exercise of judicial functions. This judicial immunity also extends to other officers of the government whose duties are related to the judicial process.[12]

It is clear that immunity doctrines impose serious obstacles to judicial protection against government expression used as a sanction to abridge private expression. Yet, with the possible exception of the express constitutional protection afforded members of the Federal legislature, the existence of immunity rules cannot be considered dispositive of the issue. The absolute privilege granted to members of the legislature has not been extended to legislative employees. Executive privilege does not have any express constitutional mandate, received only the narrowest of majorities in the *Barr* case, is still the subject of extensive debate, and contains potential loopholes in terms of the extent to which it will be applied to the lower echelons and the kind of conduct that may be considered within the "line of duty." Moreover, executive immunity is applicable only in suits for damages for defamation and "kindred torts"; it does not prevent other forms of relief, such as injunction or declaratory judgment. State legislators are not liable to suit under the present interpretation of the Federal Civil Rights Acts, but have no constitutional immunity for conduct abridging Fed-

11. *Barr v. Matteo*, 360 U.S. 564, 569, 573, 571 (1959). Chief Justice Warren and Justices Douglas, Brennan and Stewart dissented. See also *Howard v. Lyons*, 360 U.S. 593 (1959). Decisions of lower courts following *Barr v. Matteo* and granting absolute privilege to lower Federal officials are collected in Note, *Yale Law Journal, supra* note 10, pp. 374–375. See also *Heine v. Raus*, 399 F.2d 785 (4th Cir. 1968) (absolute privilege extended to C.I.A. agent). For general discussion of executive immunity see Joel F. Handler and William A. Klein, "The Defense of Privilege in Defamation Suits Against Government Executive Officials," *Harvard Law Review*, Vol. 74 (1960), p. 44; Arno C. Becht, "The Absolute Privilege of the Executive in Defamation," *Vanderbilt Law Review*, Vol. 15 (1962), p. 1127.

12. *Bradley v. Fisher*, 80 U.S. 335 (1871); *Barr v. Matteo*, 360 U.S. at 569.

eral First Amendment rights. State executive officials are not even exempted from the Federal Civil Rights Acts.

In addition, it should be noted that there are some cases of judicial relief being granted when the government conduct seems to resemble that involved in the decisions just discussed. Thus in *Joint Anti-Fascist Refugee Committee v. McGrath,* organizations which the Attorney General labeled as "Communist" and put on his list of "subversive organizations" were successful in raising the constitutionality of the Attorney General's action. In *Bantam Books, Inc. v. Sullivan,* book publishers obtained declaratory relief and injunction against the Rhode Island commission that was sending communications to distributors informing them of books considered objectionable to the commission. In general, as the Steel Seizure case demonstrates, executive officials engaged in an unconstitutional course of conduct are routinely held accountable by the courts in forms of litigation that do not make them personally liable for money damages.[13]

Nevertheless, the granting of judicial relief against government expression that interferes with private expression raises especially difficult problems. In the first place the considerations underlying immunity doctrines apply with particular force here. The argument that government officials "must be free to speak . . . without fear of criminal or civil liability," and that their right of expression "would be of little value if they could be subjected to the cost and inconvenience and distractions of a trial," are the same arguments that justify the full protection doctrine for private expression. The relations between the judicial and other branches of the government, especially the legislature and top executive officials, are particularly delicate if expression rather than action is the subject of controversy. Equally important, no certain or adequate standards are available for the courts to use in deciding when government expression has passed the bounds of persuasion and become an abridgment of private expression.

Professors Finman and Macaulay, in a path-breaking article on government expression directed against opponents of the Vietnam war, suggested a series of principles to govern the statements of public officials that might impair the right of private expression. The first rule, they propose, is that "statements issued for the purpose of provoking

---

13. *Joint Anti-Fascist Refugee Committee v. McGrath,* 341 U.S. 123 (1951); *Bantam Books, Inc. v. Sullivan,* 372 U.S. 58 (1963); *Youngstown Sheet & Tube Co. v. Sawyer,* 343 U.S. 579 (1952).

resort to private sanctions are improper." Their second principle is that if the indirect effect of government expression is to encourage the use of private sanctions, its constitutional justification depends on a balance of the interests and values at stake. In determining such a balance, they would consider whether "the official has taken care to avoid misstatements," whether he has "restrict[ed] his comments to those that are justified by reliable data and sound reasoning," and whether he has "couple[d] his criticism of dissent with a reminder that protest and dissent are a vital part of the American tradition." Having taken into account these factors the final balance would be struck as to whether "the risks of suppressing dissent or inciting violence may be too great, when weighed against the purpose the statement might serve, to justify its issuance." Professors Finman and Macaulay do not argue that these principles should be applied as "legal" obligations, through judicial restraint or legislative or administrative rules, but only as "moral" or "ethical" obligations based upon the values embodied in the First Amendment and the due process clause. The rules they propose serve, however, to illustrate the nature of the doctrines the courts would have to devise if they did undertake to impose judicial restrictions upon government expression. That the application of such rules would have a "chilling effect" upon government expression is hardly open to doubt.[14]

Other difficulties are presented by the nature of the relief available to the courts in restricting government expression that operates as a sanction on private expression. Use of a criminal sanction would be highly destructive of the freedom with which government officials participate in the system of expression. It would also be entirely impracticable. The government seldom prosecutes its own officials, even for the most heinous crimes, much less for mere expression of views. Obviously members of the legislature, the President, and high executive officials would never be subjected to a criminal sanction. Suits for money damages are open to most of the same objections. Moreover, it would be difficult to calculate any measure of damages. Injunction proceedings and declaratory judgment suits are generally not an appropriate form of relief. While the doctrine of prior restraint would presumably not apply to government control of its own utterances, government expression often does not involve a pattern that could be effectively enjoined or ruled to be unconstitutional. Publication of

14. Finman and Macaulay, *op. cit. supra* note 1, pp. 695, 696, 697, 677–678.

written or audio-visual materials might be an exception to this, however, and there may be other situations in which an injunction or declaratory judgment is capable of affording adequate relief.

Despite this last possibility, taking all the above considerations into account it is plain that judicial restriction can hardly be considered a viable device for the protection of private expression against abridgment by government expression. Safeguards will have to be found mainly, as Professors Finman and Macaulay suggest, in the development of "moral" and "ethical" principles among government officials and citizens alike. It should be added, however, that the factors precluding effective relief against government expression do not apply with such force to conduct falling clearly into the category of government action. This may be the explanation of *Joint Anti-Fascist* and *Bantam Books,* in both of which the conduct of the government would probably have to be classified as action rather than expression. Even the immunity rules, as the Supreme Court's decision in *Dombrowski v. Eastland* hints, might be applied less rigorously to government action. Developments along this line, therefore, may solve some of the problem.[15]

B. Government Expression That Causes Injury to Individual or Social Interests Outside the System of Freedom of Expression

Government expression, like private expression, at times must be reconciled with individual or social interests outside the system of freedom of expression. Thus government expression may injure a person's reputation, invade his privacy, or deny him the right to a fair trial. It might also incite to violence or breach obscenity laws. Likewise it could violate the constitutional provision against establishment of religion. Regulation or prohibition of government expression having these effects would not appear to raise any problems under the First Amendment. As already noted, the government can restrict its own expression, or that of its agents (aside from their own private expression), without invading any First Amendment right. The only constitutional limitations, therefore, would be those derived from immunity and separation of powers doctrines. Thus members of the legislature would have an absolute privilege for speech or debate, *i.e.* expression, in the performance of their functions; judicial officials might have a similar immunity; and executive officials might have an absolute immunity against damage claims based in tort. Very likely executive immunity, though not legislative immunity and probably not judicial immunity, could be waived if the government wished.

As far as concerns government expression affecting individual interests, the results reached under immunity doctrines are in general the same as those that would obtain under the principles previously advocated for the governance of private expression. Thus the refusal to grant relief against government officials for alleged defamation conforms to the proposal that recovery in libel suits growing out of private expression be severely limited. This is not true, however, of claims based on invasion of the right to privacy. In this area, as far as the Constitution permits, it would seem appropriate to allow relief against government officials. The impact of such a rule on freedom of expression would seem to be minimal.

Concerning government expression that injures social interests, *i.e.* constitutes a criminal offense, under immunity doctrines only executive officials would appear to be liable to prosecution. In practice, of course, such proceedings are seldom instituted. Thus the practical outcome is also consistent with the principle of affording full protection for private expression.

It is important to note, however, that the government has other forms of control, at least over executive officials, apart from traditional criminal or civil proceedings. On the basis of the employment relation, the government can instruct its officials on matters of expression and discipline them for failure to comply. This is the chief method for protecting an accused against government expression that may impair his right to a fair trial. Such controls are less effective in other areas of government expression, such as defamation or invasion of privacy, where detailed, specific rules cannot be promulgated in advance. Nevertheless they remain an important form of restriction upon government expression.

C. Government Expression and the Captive Audience

The government, like a private person or group, has some rights to seek out an audience. On the other hand it is a cardinal principle of the system of freedom of expression that no person can be compelled to listen against his will. The line between gaining access to an audience and forcing the audience to hear is sometimes difficult to draw. In the case of private communication the line is established at the point where the communication invades an individual's right of privacy or trespasses upon his property. But in the case of government communications special considerations prevail. The government is in a far more commanding position to force its communication upon unwilling or indifferent ears. The government exercises general control over the streets, parks and other places where people congregate. It has unlimited resources. The listener is not able to defend himself or retaliate by exercising economic or social pressures against the government. Factors inherent in the system of expression, therefore, demand that additional limitations be placed upon the government's right to communicate to a captive audience.

The Supreme Court has dealt with this issue only in *Public Utilities Commission v. Pollak,* previously considered in connection with the right of privacy. The issue in that case, it will be remembered, was whether the Commission could authorize the Capital Transit Company to broadcast music, news and commercials in its streetcars, buses and waiting rooms. Upon the First Amendment issue Justice Burton, speaking for six members of the Court, simply said:

> The Commission . . . did not find, and the testimony does not compel a finding, that the programs interfered substantially with the conversation of passengers or with rights of communication constitutionally protected in public places. It is suggested also that the First Amendment guarantees a freedom to listen only to such points of view as the listener wishes to hear. There is no substantial claim that the programs have been used for objectionable propaganda. There is no issue of that kind before us.[16]

16. *Public Utilities Commission v. Pollak,* 343 U.S. 451, 463 (1952), discussed also in Chapter XIV.

Justice Douglas, dissenting, relied primarily upon the right to privacy. But he also stressed that the First Amendment prohibited the government from taking advantage of a captive audience:

> Freedom of religion and freedom of speech guaranteed by the First Amendment give more than the privilege to worship, to write, to speak as one chooses; they give freedom not to do nor to act as the government chooses. . . .
>
> When we force people to listen to another's ideas, we give the propagandist a powerful weapon. Today it is a business enterprise working out a radio program under the auspices of government. Tomorrow it may be a dominant political or religious group. Today the purpose is benign; there is no invidious cast to the programs. But the vice is inherent in the system.[17]

It should be noted that the *Pollak* case did not present a clear-cut issue of government expression. "State action" was involved, to some degree, because the Public Utilities Commission had power to permit or prohibit the communication. But the government of the District of Columbia was not actually doing the broadcasting. Indeed, as far as the First Amendment was concerned, the District of Columbia government could not have forbidden the Company to broadcast or regulated its content, except possibly on the ground that the expression fell into the commercial sector. Hence only a private communication was involved, and the real issue was one of the right to privacy.

Had the Capital Transit Company been a governmentally operated enterprise, however, surely broadcasts to the captive audience would have violated the First Amendment. Government communication of that kind, at least on any substantial scale, would quickly destroy freedom of expression. The resulting system would be closer to that depicted in George Orwell's *1984* than to any envisaged by the First Amendment. It has fortunately not been necessary to define the exact contours of the principle that the government may not engage in expression directed at a captive audience, or otherwise force its citizens to listen. There can be no doubt, however, that the principle is central to any system of freedom of expression.

One further matter is closely related to the question of the captive audience. On some occasions in our history the government has se-

---

17. 343 U.S. at 467–468, 469. Justice Black, dissenting partially, thought that the broadcasting of music would not violate the First Amendment but the broadcasting of "news, public speeches, views, or propaganda of any kind" would.

cretly subsidized the publication or distribution of materials that supported its official policies. Thus in 1967 the United States Information Agency acknowledged that it had contributed over $25,000 for publication of three books on Vietnam and China without revealing the source of the funds. Similarly, the Central Intelligence Agency has secretly subsidized student and other organizations actively engaged in expression. The reasons that ordinarily make it an infringement upon First Amendment rights to compel disclosure in the case of private communication have no application to the government. Full disclosure of government authorship or assistance in expression would not in any way inhibit the government in its right to communicate. On the other hand, failure to reveal the part played in the system of expression by the government, with its immense resources, jeopardizes the health of the whole system. Judicial remedies for nondisclosure by the government of its participation are difficult to devise or administer. But the violation of the constitutional guarantee embodied in the First Amendment is plain.[18]

D. Government Expression That Distorts the System

In all the situations considered above, the government has been just another participant in the system of freedom of expression. The government's communication can be challenged on its facts, tested, criticized, countered, or refuted by private expression. In short, it is offered for acceptance in the marketplace of ideas. It is true that the government's expression often carries unusual weight in the marketplace. But that is true also of other communications and no system of freedom of expression can ever eliminate all inequalities.

On the other hand it is very easy to visualize situations in which the government's voice may overwhelm or displace all others and thus seriously distort the system of free expression. This occurs mainly when the government has a monopoly or near-monopoly over the media or institutions of communication. When a private group achieves such a dominating position in any sector of the system the government is

18. On the U.S.I.A. see *The New York Times*, Feb. 24, 1967, and Mar. 22, 1967; on the C.I.A. see *Ramparts Magazine* (Mar. 1967); *The New York Times*, Feb. 14 to 27, Mar. 5 to 7, and Mar. 30, 1967; Christopher Lasch, *The Agony of the American Left* (New York, Alfred A. Knopf, 1969), ch. 3.

available to restore diversity and balance. Not only is there nothing in the First Amendment that forbids such control, but the government has an affirmative obligation to eliminate these obstructions in the system. When the distortion arises from the government's own dominance of the system, however, what is the remedy if the government is unwilling to yield voluntarily?

Little or no consideration has been given to this fundamental dilemma. Any comprehensive formulations of principle, and certainly any detailed rules or techniques for applying them, are not likely to be achieved in the immediate future. Nevertheless it is important to make a start.

The problems could be posed in at least three ways: the right of government to maintain a monopoly over a sector of the system by forbidding private ownership or operation of the medium; the right of private persons and groups to have access to a medium owned or operated by the government; and the obligation of the government, where it possesses a monopoly or near-monopoly of a medium of communication, to itself present a balance of viewpoints.

1. GOVERNMENT-ENFORCED MONOPOLY

The principle would certainly be accepted that the government may not maintain a monopoly of the means or institutions of communication in any significant sector of the system of expression the effect of which is to exclude private persons and groups from ownership or operation of similar facilities. Indeed this principle has been recognized by the Supreme Court in its decision in *Pierce v. Society of Sisters,* holding that the government cannot maintain a monopoly of educational institutions by forbidding other entries into the field. It can hardly be doubted that the same rule would apply to other media, such as printing presses, or to other institutions, such as voluntary associations. Again, such limitations upon government power are implicit in the Supreme Court's decisions on prior restraint and the right of association. Radio and television broadcasting is an exception only because of the limited physical facilities characteristic of the media. These rules preventing governmental monopoly of expression are clearcut and readily capable of judicial enforcement.[19]

19. *Pierce v. Society of Sisters,* 268 U.S. 510 (1925); see also *Meyer v.* *Nebraska,* 262 U.S. 390 (1923). Both cases are discussed in Chapter XVI. On

2. RIGHT OF ACCESS TO GOVERNMENT FACILITIES

Where, for whatever reason, the government does possess a monopoly of a medium of communication, distortion in the system can, at least partially, be avoided by giving private persons or groups access to the facilities. The obligation of government to do this has been accepted in the case of streets, parks and other open public places. We have argued in an earlier chapter that a similar obligation should be imposed on the government with respect to other government facilities, such as school buildings, if no other meeting places are available. It seems clear that if the government owned and managed all radio and television stations, it would be constitutionally bound to furnish a right of access to private expression on a nondiscriminatory basis. On the other hand the *Rutgers Law Review*, which is not part of a government monopoly of legal periodicals, would owe no right of access to all who might wish to use its columns.

Detailed rules for implementing a constitutional right of access would, of course, be difficult to devise. But the problem falls within the range of competence of a legislature, an executive tribunal, and the courts. Moreover, the reasons that make imposition of access requirements a delicate and dangerous operation when directed at privately owned media do not apply when the government is involved. There is no likelihood that the government's right of expression will be put in jeopardy, or that the amount of diversity within the system will decline. In the government's case, then, the right of access could be vigorously enforced without fear of impairing the system.

This principle of access to government facilities has limited application at present. But it could become a matter of far-reaching importance.

3. THE OBLIGATION OF BALANCED PRESENTATION

If private operation of the media of communication is not possible and private access to government facilities is not feasible or adequate, there remains only the alternative of forcing the government itself to present a balance of viewpoints. The obligation of the government to

prior restraint see Chapter XIII; and on right of association Chapter XII.

maintain vitality in the system through offering diversity in its own expression, when all other means of achieving openness in the system have failed, would seem to be clear in principle. But the principle is not readily translated into effective legal rules. The very statement of the doctrine is hard to formulate; obviously there are many different viewpoints and to say that all "responsible" positions should be aired does not carry very far toward the needed precision. Nor is administration of the rule easily achieved; compliance must depend upon the willingness of the executive to abide by the rules or the capacity of a court to compel adherence.

The most promising field for application of the principle at present appears to be in the system of public education—a near-monopoly of the government. Several factors make development of the principle more feasible here. In the first place there exists in the educational system a semi-autonomous group of teachers, scholars, and administrators which, while part of the government apparatus, forms a distinct institution of its own. Such a body generates diverse viewpoints, at variance with each other and with the official government viewpoint, and provides a base from which independent pressures for diversity of expression can be exerted. Secondly, in its application to the educational system the basic principle can be formulated in terms of requiring the government to present, or allow presentation of, all viewpoints held to be responsible in the scholarly or scientific community to which they are relevant. This endows the principle with a far more precise and established meaning than it has in other connections. Finally, the principles of academic freedom provide detailed substantive and procedural rules for implementing the fundamental concept that diverse positions should be given expression, despite the fact that the sole source of expression is the government itself.

Even in the system of public education, of course, there are serious difficulties to surmount in making the principle of balanced presentation effective. Under the *United Church of Christ* doctrine, a student, parent, or possibly a member of the general community might have standing to initiate litigation. But a court would probably act to force the government to present a suppressed or neglected position only in an extreme situation in which the issues were sharply delineated. An easier case is presented if the government has by statute specifically prohibited educational institutions or their members from expressing particular viewpoints. Such a situation arose in *Epperson v. Arkansas,* in which the State prohibited teaching the theory of evolution in the public school system. It is unfortunate that the Supreme Court did not take advantage of the opportunity to initiate development of the law in the *Epperson* decision. Only by making a beginning, on a case-by-case basis, is progress in implementing the principle of balanced presentation likely to be achieved.[20]

20. *Office of Communication of the United Church of Christ v. F.C.C.*, 359 F.2d 994 (D.C. Cir. 1966); *Epperson v. Arkansas*, 393 U.S. 97 (1968).

Conclusions

The principal aim of this book has been to formulate a legal structure for the system of freedom of expression that would be responsive to the needs of a modern democratic society. It is important in conclusion to review briefly the current state of legal theory and to stress the need for developing more adequate doctrine if we hope to maintain a viable system. Existing legal theory, as formulated by the Supreme Court over the past half century, is inadequate to support an effective system of freedom of expression for the following reasons:

(1) As pointed out in the first chapter, the Supreme Court has failed to develop a comprehensive, coherent theory of the First Amendment. It started with a bad tendency test and then moved to a clear and present danger test. When it reached the climactic *Dennis* case in 1951, it altered the clear and present danger test into a probable danger test. Thereafter it abandoned clear and present danger except for one isolated contempt of court case in 1961. Meanwhile, beginning with *Douds* in 1950, the Court turned primarily to the ad hoc balancing test. The balancing test was used extensively for a decade and a half, at first with the legislative judgment given special weight and later with the First Amendment interest gaining the preference. In the late nineteen-sixties the ad hoc balancing test apparently fell into disfavor, and was seemingly repudiated in a footnote in the *Robel* case in 1967. At about this time the incitement test came to the fore, at least in those situations in which the clear and present danger test would previously have been employed. Throughout the whole period occasional decisions seemed to be grounded on a full protection position, in some cases special rationales prevailed, and in many the theoretical basis remained obscure. There have been at all times, of course, innumerable variations among the individual justices.

(2) Insofar as the Supreme Court has developed any general theory of the First Amendment it is the ad hoc balancing formula. The

clear and present danger test and recently the incitement test have been employed in some cases in which the utterance might directly lead to a violation of law. Special rules have evolved in libel, privacy, and obscenity cases. But the Court's residual theory—its sole generalized formulation—has been ad hoc balancing. This test seems to be the only one acceptable to a majority for solving numerous First Amendment problems, such as those involved in denial of benefits or privileges, business regulations, legislative committees, free press-fair trial, and many other areas. The weaknesses of the ad hoc balancing test have been set forth at length in previous pages, and nothing further on that score need be said here. It should be reiterated, however, that a review of the decisions discloses that the courts in fact seldom apply the balancing test in a serious way. Even the leading experts on balancing, Justices Frankfurter and Harlan, have been unable to demonstrate convincingly that the balancing technique actually considers and evaluates all the relevant factors. In the hands of most judges the balancing test comes to be nothing more than a way of rationalizing preformed conclusions.

(3) The Supreme Court's efforts to deal with novel or complex problems of First Amendment law have often foundered for lack of a satisfactory theory. Thus, in dealing with newer issues of "symbolic speech," as in the draft card burning, flag burning, and armband cases, the Court has adopted such a narrow view of "expression" that important sectors of the system are removed from any First Amendment protection. The Court's "speech plus" analysis in picketing and demonstration cases is equally restrictive. Likewise, its approach to problems of the place in which First Amendment rights may be exercised, as evidenced in *Adderley,* is severely limited. Its failure to separate expression and action, in such cases as *Scales* and *Barenblatt,* further undermines the system.

(4) The Court's inability to develop a comprehensive theory of the First Amendment leaves it without satisfactory tools to deal with many new developments that are emerging in the system of freedom of expression. Thus the Court has never articulated the difference in the issues that arise when the government seeks to restrict expression in order to protect some other social interest, and issues involved when the government seeks to regulate traffic within the system or improve the operation of the system itself. It has never worked out any theory for dealing with many problems that would be presented if the government made more vigorous efforts to affirmatively promote freedom of

expression, or with problems concerned with the government's own participation in the system. It has not begun to think about doctrines necessary to support academic freedom in a way that would maintain our institutions of higher learning as a healthy, independent force in our society. It has not yet approached the crucial issues raised in conspiracy prosecutions or the whole area of inchoate crimes. It has never attempted to delineate the boundaries between the basic system of freedom of expression and other systems such as the commercial, the military, the children's and the foreign.

(5) The result of the Supreme Court's constant shifting of position without formulating a coherent theory has been to leave the lower courts, public officials, and private citizens in a state of confusion over the applicable rules. The lower Federal courts and the State courts usually apply the ad hoc balancing test. Yet as late as December 1967 the Attorney General of the United States, attempting to sum up current constitutional doctrine for the public, said: "Restrictions on freedom of speech are governed by the doctrine of 'clear and present danger.' Under this doctrine the Government can restrict speech only when it creates a clear and present danger to the public interest." [1]

Nor can it be said that the Black-Douglas "absolute" theory of the First Amendment provides a fully feasible alternative. Their theory undoubtedly has made an important contribution. It concentrates on the fundamental distinction between "expression" and "action," and it demands absolute protection for expression. But Justice Black, and to some extent Justice Douglas, have given a very narrow significance to "expression." Furthermore, Justice Black does not apply the theory to situations in which the government regulation is directed at control of action and has only an "indirect" effect upon expression. Both justices have applied the theory in overrigid ways in some areas such as obscenity, privacy, and libel. Neither justice has presented the full dimensions of a legal structure necessary to support the system of free expression.

As one reviews the course of Supreme Court decision, it must be acknowledged that the product in actual results is somewhat better than the product in doctrine. The Court has given protection to matters of belief. It has cut back the repressive effects of sedition laws, rendered the Internal Security Act ineffective, eliminated most State

1. Interview with Attorney General Ramsey Clark, *U.S. News and World Report,* Dec. 4, 1967, p. 52.

loyalty oaths, and partially curbed the excesses of legislative investigating committees. It has broadly upheld the right of peaceful demonstration, limited the obscenity laws, and narrowed the impact of libel and privacy laws. It has made a start in affording greater rights of expression to government employees and has established the basis for broader treatment of controversial issues on radio and television. These are no small accomplishments. Taken as a whole they definitely outweigh the failures.

Moreover the Court, from the time of Holmes and Brandeis, has understood and accepted the basic values and functions of freedom of expression and has often eloquently expounded on them to the country. To some degree the Court has come to appreciate the dynamics of the system of freedom of expression. This has been mainly the work of Justices Black and Douglas. But Justice Brennan in the *New York Times, Dombrowski,* and other cases has made significant contributions to a realistic understanding of the system in operation. Likewise, taken as a whole the Court has been willing to accept an active role in supporting the system of free expression.

Nevertheless the Court's performance has seriously suffered from its inability to develop the basic legal structure for the system. Much of the Court's achievement rests upon the use of doctrines such as vagueness, overbreadth, and alternative means, which do not come to grips with the basic issues. Furthermore its capacity to deal with coming issues of crucial importance seems unfortunately limited. One cannot doubt that the Court would have made a more effective and lasting contribution had it built a more solid foundation.

Such a foundation is afforded by the theory of free expression elaborated in the preceding chapters. That theory is based on the key concepts underlying the right to freedom of expression—the distinction between "expression" and "action" and the difference in the degree of social control allowed over each. It views the complex of principles, rules, customs, and institutions as a single system, designed for the purpose of assuring freedom of expression in the society. It distinguishes this system from other systems having other functions, and provides a framework of rational rules governing the operation of the system and its relation to other forms of social control. It has the advantage of relative simplicity for the courts, it facilitates application by the government, and it is understandable by the citizen. It supplies an instrument for meeting new problems as they develop in the system.

Finally the rules it provides are related to the functions of the system and to the realities of the society.

No system of freedom of expression can succeed in the end unless the ideas which underlie it become part of the life of the people. There must be a real understanding of the root concepts, a full acceptance of the guiding principles, and a deep resolve to make the system work. This state of affairs can be reached only if we succeed in building a comprehensible structure of doctrine and practice that is meaningful to all and meets the needs of a free society. The task remains largely unfulfilled.

Epilogue

This book has taken as its point of departure the traditional theory of freedom of expression, assuming the basic soundness of that theory and its workability in a modern democratic society. It has not undertaken to reexamine the premises upon which the theory rests or to question its general viability under present-day conditions. Nevertheless recent attacks upon the fundamentals of the system, which have mounted in the last few years, prompt me to add a few words about these broader issues.

It is interesting to note that current challenges to the system of freedom of expression in the United States have not proceeded, to any significant extent, along lines taken by some of the classical left in the past. There has been very little argument that modern society, with its need to plan and control on an extensive scale, cannot be organized on the principle that every member can say anything he likes at any time. The reason for this is undoubtedly that no strong movement of the old left presently exists in this country and no radical program of planning and control is now being seriously put forward. However that may be, in the absence of current controversy over this aspect of the problem, I shall confine my remarks to the challenges which have been produced by the particular period of strain which now exists.

The attack from the right proceeds on traditional grounds. It is urged that present-day society is filled with tensions, divisions and potential conflict; that opposition to existing policies and institutions is widespread and tends more and more to take the form of open disregard for laws; that, in short, the society faces an imminent breakdown of all law and order. In such a period, it is said, society cannot tolerate speech that stirs discontent, inflames passions, and moves people to violent action. Quite the contrary, the argument runs, additional laws are necessary, not only to curb disorder, but to prevent it from happening by eliminating conduct that might lead to it. Hence the Federal

Riot Control Act, the revival of the Subversive Activities Control Board, the withdrawal of Federal funds from universities which fail to punish student disruption, and similar measures are advocated. All such laws, as previously made clear, have a destructive impact on the system of freedom of expression.

There can be little doubt that concern over the widening conflict in our society is well founded. In recent years there has been a serious falling away of consensus, a polarization of viewpoints, an increasing inability to solve the problems of society without the compulsion of violence or other illegal action. Moreover, modern society is particularly vulnerable to disruption by small but determined groups, or even by angry individuals. Nevertheless the answer to the call for repressive measures remains, even in a time of acute tension, the orthodox one, reiterated many times in the preceding pages. Suppression of expression does not solve the underlying problems; on the contrary it frequently intensifies them. The rules supporting freedom of expression do not preclude the adoption of measures to control action. Nor, of course, do they preclude the taking of steps to remedy the basic ills that give rise to the conflict. Indeed the system of free expression facilitates efforts to proceed by orderly change. On the other hand repression has no stopping place. Once begun, it can quickly move all the way to a totalitarian system.

These are the premises upon which the system of freedom of expression is founded. They may prove unworkable if economic, political, and social conditions deteriorate to the point where our whole society collapses. If that occurs it is unlikely that firm adherence to the principles of free expression will be a material contributing cause. There is no reason, therefore, to abandon those principles beforehand. The choice is essentially between a system of freedom of expression and a police state.

The challenge from the left poses different issues. The charge from that quarter is not that the system of freedom of expression cripples society's efforts to defend itself from disruption but that it does not provide an adequate technique for effectuating urgent social change, and may indeed hamper it. The main exponent of this position has been Professor Herbert Marcuse. Other important figures in the New Left movement, both white and black, have expressed similar ideas. In the movement generally there seems to be a growing indifference to the theory or operation of the system of freedom of expression. This is not to say that the New Left is unanimous on these issues, or that there is majority support for the Marcuse position. But such attitudes are certainly widespread.[1]

The existence of these views in the New Left movement is a phenomenon of far-reaching consequence. In the past, proponents of social change in America have usually supported, though they may not have been the leading fighters for, the system of freedom of expression. Even radical political groups, with ties to totalitarian parties in other countries, have tended to accept most of the traditional theory. Were the incipient hostility of the New Left movement to progress, along with an increasing polarization of political forces, the future of the system of freedom of expression in the United States would indeed be dark.

To some extent, particularly in Professor Marcuse, the New Left opposition to the system of freedom of expression is based on the classic arguments regarding tolerance and the nature of government. Tolerance, at least to the degree embedded in the proposed system, is viewed as a lack of moral conviction, an absence of political direction, and an excuse for refusing to budge from the status quo. Government based on a balance of pluralistic forces is viewed with similar skepticism, and reliance is placed upon the ability of the state to represent the interests of all citizens fairly. These views are founded on philosophical premises quite different from those that underlie the system of freedom of expression, and will not be debated here. To some extent the New Left attitude, particularly in the young, may reflect a general distrust of all rational systems, or a lack of interest in them. This, again, is a philosophical position that will not be argued at this point. To some extent the hostility to freedom of expression may represent merely general disagreement with the main political, economic, and social institutions of our society. This is wide of the mark. The system of freedom of expression is not inevitably tied to existing institutions. It is applicable to any open society.

The more significant objections of the New Left movement, for our purposes, are those based upon the operation of the system of freedom of expression in our modern society, at this time of crisis. These objections raise more immediate issues, which are within the boundaries of this book. In essence the system of freedom of expression is seen as a wholly inadequate instrument for dealing with the urgent

---

1. See, *e.g.*, Robert P. Wolff, Barrington Moore, Jr., and Herbert Marcuse, *A Critique of Pure Tolerance* (Boston, Beacon Press, 1965); "Marcuse Defines His New Left Line," *The New York Times Magazine*, Oct. 27, 1968, p. 29.

problems of the day and, more than that, as a tool of repression used by the Establishment to maintain the status quo. Freedom of expression is viewed as part of the paraphernalia of liberal institutions which in practice operate to the detriment of submerged groups and against social change.

The position that significant change cannot be achieved in the present society through reliance upon the system of freedom of expression has, of course, ominous implications for the future of the country. If that view is carried to the point of violent revolution, then obviously the system of freedom of expression will have been destroyed. Short of this ultimate tragedy, however, the system would continue to perform its function, though perhaps on a reduced scale. The system is an instrument for facilitating orderly change and the degree to which it operates well depends upon how it is used and how it is supported. When any group makes the political judgment that it must pursue other tactics, outside the system, that is usually a sign that the system has not been put to proper use by those who participate in it, or that the dominant group in the society has failed to maintain the economic, political, and social conditions which permit the system to operate. But the occurrence of such events is not ground for either the dominant group, the challenging group, or any other part of society to abrogate the system. The system still provides the only method of avoiding resolution of the issues through force alone. Every effort must be made, despite previous failures, to continue use of the system as far as possible and to restore it to operating order. No one gains from scrapping it at the first sign of trouble.

The feeling on the part of the New Left that the system of freedom of expression operates actively against its interests, by enabling the Establishment to block change, rests on several grounds. The main contentions seem to be that (1) the system is actually a sham, in that really radical or deviant expression is not allowed, or if ostensibly allowed is punished by indirect methods including trumped-up criminal prosecutions; (2) the system is loaded in favor of the status quo, particularly through Establishment control of the mass media; and (3) the system is utilized to prolong discussion, focus on procedural complications, and assure delay, thereby allowing the Establishment to avoid the real issues and divert attention from the need for action. In all these ways, it is asserted, the system of freedom of expression is a meaningless sop, designed to siphon off protest and delude the populace into believing it has a participating voice. As the preceding pages have demonstrated, these contentions are not without some factual foundation. Nevertheless they do not add up to the position that the system should be ignored, opposed, or discarded.

It is true that the system of freedom of expression has never worked ideally and that expression which challenges the foundations of the society has often been suppressed or harassed. But the developments recounted in earlier chapters reveal that, as it operates today, the system affords even the most radical expression a substantial measure of protection. Significant progress has been made. It cannot be concluded that the gap between theory and reality which still exists justifies writing off the system. Even though the principle is not fully realized in practice, the existence and growth of the principle are significant. The alternative would be no legal protection whatever.

The control of the mass media by a small group representing the dominant element of our society is, as previously pointed out, a major weakness in the present system of freedom of expression. It is not a problem we show much sign of solving in the near future. Yet again this state of affairs is not fatal to the system. No society that ever existed has afforded equal access to the means of communication to all its members or groups. The dominant group, whether through power of government or the forces of laissez-faire, has always had the loudest voice, and probably always will. The validity of the system does not depend on exact equality. In fact the effort to achieve such equality by government allocation, without any reliance upon laissez-faire factors, might jeopardize rather than better the system. In any event the essential element in the system is the right of the minority to express its views through such methods as are available to it. The history of the civil-rights movement, the peace movement, the black movement, and others in recent years indicates that minorities have found ways to be heard and minority viewpoints have not been kept out of the marketplace altogether. The problem of equality is a crucial one, but the remedy is betterment of the system, not abandonment. Again, the alternative would be worse.

The charge that the system of freedom of expression is often used simply to prolong debate and avoid action likewise has considerable support in fact. Of course, any system of communication and persuasion necessarily involves delay. The more complex the system becomes the more entangled it gets in procedural niceties. However, if those in positions of power use the system merely to block action they can expect to reap the whirlwind. The problem here is similar to that with which we began. The system by itself does not produce any particular result. It is an instrument to be used by groups in society for conducting their affairs without resort to force. If the system is not properly used it will ultimately collapse. Short of that catastrophe, however, all groups are likely to benefit as long as it is maintained. Once more, the remedy is to force proper use of the system, not write it off.

What has been said up to this point concerns the immediate or short-term factors involved in the attitude of the New Left to the system of freedom of expression. There are also longer-range considerations that should be taken into account. Any society, no matter how organized, must face the question of the extent it will allow its members freedom of expression. No political movement looking to the future can forever ignore this problem. It would be unfortunate, therefore, if the shortcomings of the present system were to cloud the fact that in the long run the question must be resolved. Nor can the importance of the gains achieved in the last half century be ignored. The principles, traditions, institutions and attitudes that have been built up are not without their worth. If the system broke down, the road back would be long and hard.

Underlying these challenges to the system from both the right and the left are some hard, unresolved questions. Can the system of freedom of expression survive the shift from the liberal laissez-faire to the mass technological society? As one surveys the record, the older features of the system—protection of individual expression against government infringement—seem to present the more solvable problem. It is true that the growth in the functions and powers of government, the gradual disappearance of looseness in the structures of control, and the greater vulnerability of the society as a whole, all add to the complications. But the development of new doctrine, more sensitive institutions, and better understanding give hope that the problem can be mastered. The more difficult task will come with the need to call on government for removal of distortions from the system and for affirmative promotion of its operations. Here the laissez-faire approach must be replaced by new principles, new techniques, and new ways of thought. This is the great challenge and the open question.

Table of Cases

Index

About the Author

Thomas I. Emerson is Lines Professor of Law at the Yale School of Law, where he has been a member of the faculty since 1946. Admitted to the New York bar in 1932, Professor Emerson has served as counsel for a number of government agencies, including the National Recovery Administration, the National Labor Relations Board, the Social Security Board, and the Office of Price Administration. From 1937 to 1940 he served as associate general counsel to the NLRB. In 1940 he became special assistant to the Attorney General of the United States. During World War II he was deputy administrator for enforcement of the Office of Price Administration and general counsel to the Office of Economic Stabilization and the Office of War Mobilization and Reconversion. A Guggenheim fellow in 1953, Professor Emerson was also a visiting professor at the London School of Economics during that academic year and at the Brookings Institution in 1960 and 1961. A frequent contributor to legal periodicals on civil liberties and constitutional law, Professor Emerson is also the author of *Toward a General Theory of the First Amendment,* and (with David Haber and Norman Dorsen) *of Political and Civil Rights in the United States.* Professor Emerson makes his home in North Haven, Connecticut.